1000 YEARS OF IRISH POETRY

1000 YEARS OF IRISH POETRY

THE GAELIC AND ANGLO-IRISH
POETS FROM PAGAN TIMES
TO THE PRESENT

Edited

by .

KATHLEEN HOAGLAND

KONECKY&KONECKY

[1,000 Years of Irish Poetry]

Konecky & Konecky
150 Fifth Ave.
New York, NY 10011

This edition published by special arrangement
with The Devin-Adair Company.

ISBN: 1-56852-235-5

Manufactured in the United States of America

ACKNOWLEDGMENT

For counsel, advice, information, and aid of other kinds both publisher and editor are indebted to many different persons, but we would like especially to record our thanks to A. M. Sullivan, poet, essayist and executive of the Catholic Poetry Society, former president of the Poetry Society of America; James O'Beirne, folklorist and Gaelic scholar; Maurice Leahy, author, lecturer and formerly president of the Oxford Poetry Society; to Professors F. N. Robinson of Harvard, V. Hull of New York University, R. K. Alspach of the University of Pennsylvania and John E. Murphy, S.J. of Boston College; to Miss Maeve Brennan, of *Harper's Bazaar,* Miss Jean Lawlor of Brentano's and Mrs. Mary Slattery of the Irish Industries Depot; to Messrs. James McGurrin, President of the American Irish Historical Society, Denis Devlin, William Carlos Williams, Leslie Daiken, Seumas O'Sullivan and Oliver St. John Gogarty, the last five—poets all—for their help in particular in the period from 1900 to date.

I wish to acknowledge personally that this book would never have had being but for Coley B. Taylor, who, after a discussion and comparisons of various literatures, suggested, when I had finished talking, that I get busy and prove my thesis: that few were familiar with the great literary heritage of Ireland and that a general rather than a personal anthology of Irish and Anglo-Irish poetry from the earliest periods was imperative for the cultural background of Americans. I also wish to thank all those who loaned me rare books and manuscripts from their private collections; Devin A. Garrity my publisher for his enthusiasm and continuous help; my husband for time spent in bolstering my ambition and for careful checking and rechecking of the mss, my mother for her help in the ballads and folk songs.

Also a few words in appreciation of the libraries used; without the excellent and inclusive collection of Irish Literature housed in the New York Public Library and the Library of the American Irish Historical Society my task would have been much more difficult. I also wish to mention the continued

[v]

courtesy of the personnel of these libraries, particularly Mr. J. F. Cahill of the American Irish Historical Society, and Miss D. Burrows and her assistant Miss Colhoun of the Ruther- ford, New Jersey, Public Library for locating books and ma- terial so necessary for the biographies and history.

Permission to reprint material is hereby acknowledged to the following publishers: Contemporary Poetry for Oliver St. J. Gogarty; Coward-McCann for Francis Ledwidge; Dodd Mead & Co. for Monk Gibbon; Harcourt, Brace and Co. for W. R. Rodgers; The Macmillan Co. for AE, Austin Clarke, Padraic Colum, F. R. Higgins, James Stephens, W. B. Yeats; G. P. Putnam's Sons for Lord Dunsany; Random House for J. M. Synge, Louis MacNeice; Sheed & Ward for Robert Farren; The Viking Press for James Joyce and Thomas McGreevy.

K. H.

CONTENTS

CHRONOLOGICAL TABLE OF CONTENTS viii

PART I   ANCIENT IRISH POETRY 1

PART II   MODERN IRISH POETRY 139

PART III ANONYMOUS STREET BALLADS 245

PART IV   ANGLO-IRISH POETRY 305

CHRONOLOGICAL TABLE OF CONTENTS

Part I: Ancient Irish Poetry

POET	TITLE	TRANSLATOR	PAGE

[PRIOR TO 7TH CENTURY A.D.]

POET	TITLE	TRANSLATOR	PAGE
Amergin	The Mystery of Amergin	Douglas Hyde	3
"	Invocation of Amergin	Eoin MacNeill, & R. A. S. Macalister	4
"	Incantation	George Sigerson	5
Torna	Lament for Corc and Niall	Samuel Ferguson	6
Sedulius	From *Easter Song*	George Sigerson	8

[7TH OR 8TH CENTURY]

POET	TITLE	TRANSLATOR	PAGE
St. Patrick	Deer's Cry (Breastplate)	Whitley Stokes, John Strachan, & Kuno Meyer	12
St. Colman	Hymn Against Pestilence	Stokes, Strachan	15
Anonymous	The Holy Man	" "	16
Ninine	Prayer to St. Patrick	" "	17
Anonymous	My Little Lodge	F. N. Robinson	18
"	A Prayer	Eleanor Hull	18
St. Ita	Jesukin	George Sigerson	19
"	St. Ita's Fosterling	Robin Flower	20

[9TH CENTURY]

POET	TITLE	TRANSLATOR	PAGE
Cormac	The Heavenly Pilot	George Sigerson	21
Anonymous	From *The Triads of Ireland*	Kuno Meyer	22
"	Summer Is Gone	" "	24
St. Patrick	God's Blessing on Munster	Whitley Stokes	24
Anonymous	The Scribe	Stokes, Meyer	25
"	The Monk and His Pet Cat	Stokes, Strachan, & Meyer	26
"	Pangur Ban	Robin Flower	27
"	The Hermit's Song	Kuno Meyer	28
"	The Viking Terror	F. N. Robinson	30
"	Liadin and Curither	Kuno Meyer	30

[10TH CENTURY]

POET	TITLE	TRANSLATOR	PAGE
MacMore, Dallan	Song of Carroll's Sword	Kuno Meyer	32
Anonymous	Song of Crede	" "	35
"	Summer Has Come	" "	36
"	A Song of Winter	" "	37
"	The Old Woman of Beare	" "	39
"	Eve's Lament	" "	42
"	Prayer to the Virgin	Strachan, Meyer	43
"	On the Flightiness of Thought	Kuno Meyer	44

POET	TITLE	TRANSLATOR	PAGE
"	To Crinog	Kuno Meyer	46
"	The Feast of St. Brigid of Kildare	Eugene O'Curry	47
"	A Heavenly Banquet	Sean O'Faolain	48
"	Hospitality in Ancient Ireland	Kuno Meyer	49

[11TH CENTURY]

POET	TITLE	TRANSLATOR	PAGE
Anonymous	The Mothers' Lament	Kuno Meyer	50
Columcille	Columcille the Scribe	Kuno Meyer & others	51
MacColmain	Song of the Sea	"	52
Anonymous	The Ruined Nest	"	54
MacLiag	Kincora	James Clarence Mangan	55

[12TH CENTURY]

POET	TITLE	TRANSLATOR	PAGE
Anonymous	Prince Aldfrid's Itinerary	James Clarence Mangan	57
	Three Poems from *The Dinnshenchas*		
"	The Story of Macha	Samuel Ferguson	61
"	The Enchanted Fawn	E. Gwynn	63
"	Tara	"	67

[MYTHOLOGICAL CYCLE]

POET	TITLE	TRANSLATOR	PAGE
"	Sea God's Address to Bran	Kuno Meyer	71
	The Hosts of Faery	" "	73
	Song of the Fairies	A. H. Leahy	74

[RED BRANCH OR CUCHULAIN CYCLE]

POET	TITLE	TRANSLATOR	PAGE
"	Deirdre's Farewell to Alba	Samuel Ferguson	76
"	Deirdre's Farewell to Scotland	Whitley Stokes	77
"	Deirdre's Lament for the Sons of Usnagh	Samuel Ferguson	78
"	Deirdre's Lament	Whitley Stokes	81
"	The Combat of Ferdiad and Cuchulain	Joseph Dunn	82
"	The Testament of Cathaeir Mor	James Clarence Mangan	87
"	On the Defeat of Ragnall	Kuno Meyer	93
MacConglinne	A Vision That Appeared to Me	" "	93
"	Wheatlet Son of Milklet	" "	95
Anonymous	From *Sweeney The Mad*	J. G. O'Keefe	96
Columcille	Columcille's Greeting to Ireland	William Reeves	101
Anonymous	The Crucifixion	Howard Mumford Jones	104
"	The Blackbird	Kuno Meyer	104
"	The Church Bell at Night	Howard Mumford Jones	105
"	Lament of Maev Leith-Dherg	T. W. H. Rolleston	105

[ix]

POET	TITLE	TRANSLATOR	PAGE

[13TH TO 16TH CENTURY]

	Three poems from *The Life of Saint Cellach of Killala*		
Anonymous	He Who Forsakes the Clerkly Life	Standish Hayes O'Grady	108
"	Hail, Fair Morning	"	109
"	Dear Was He	"	111
"	Song of the Forest Trees	"	111
	From *The Battle of Magh Lena*		
"	I Hear The Wave	Eugene O'Curry	114
	From *The Death of King Dermot*		
"	An Evil World	Standish Hayes O'Grady	114
O'Gillan, Angus	The Dead at Clonmacnois	T. W. H. Rolleston	115
Donnchadh mor O'Dala	At St. Patrick's Purgatory	Sean O'Faolain	116
O'Daly, Carrol	Eivlin A Rúin	George Sigerson	117
" "	Lover and Echo	" "	118

[THE FENIAN OR OSSIANIC CYCLE: 9TH TO 16TH CENTURY]

Anonymous	Song of Finn	John O'Donovan	121
"	The Tryst After Death	Kuno Meyer	122
	From *Colloquy of the Ancients*		
"	Finn's Advice to MacLugach	Standish Hayes O'Grady	126
"	The Winter is Cold	O'Grady, Meyer	127
"	Arran	" "	128
"	Credhe's Lament	" "	129
	From *The Hunt of Sliabh Truim*		
"	A Description of the Hunt	Anonymous	131
"	Finn's Great Wolfdog Bran	"	132
	Three Poems from *The Duanaire Finn*		
"	Sleep Song of Diarmaid and Grainne	Eoin MacNeill	133
"	The Beagle's Cry	" "	136
"	The Wry Rowan	" "	137

Part II: Modern Irish Poetry

[16TH CENTURY]

POET	TITLE	TRANSLATOR	PAGE
O'Gnive, Fearflatha	The Downfall of the Gael	Samuel Ferguson	140
Anonymous	Dark Rosaleen	James Clarence Mangan	142

[x]

POET	TITLE	TRANSLATOR	PAGE
Anonymous	Roisin Dubh	Eleanor Hull	145
"	The Little Dark Rose	Padraic Pearse	146
Nugent, Gerald	A Farewell to Fál	" "	148

[17TH AND 18TH CENTURIES]

POET	TITLE	TRANSLATOR	PAGE
Anonymous	The Kiss	Earl of Longford	149
"	The Careful Husband	" "	150
O'Dugan, Maurice	The Coolun	Samuel Ferguson	151
Ferriter, Pierce	He Charges Her to Lay Aside Her Weapons	Earl of Longford	152
Keating, Geoffrey	O Woman Full of Wile	Padraic Pearse	154
" "	Keen Thyself, Poor Wight	" "	155
" "	From My Grief on Fal's Proud Plain	" "	156
Anonymous	Saint Brendan's Prophecy	T. C. Croker	158
O'Hussey, Eochadh	O'Hussey's Ode to the Maguire	James Clarence Mangan	160
Anonymous	The Woman of Three Cows	"	163
MacGawran, Hugh	Description of an Irish Feast	Jonathan Swift	165
Anonymous	Farewell, O Patrick Sarsfield	James Clarence Mangan	168
O'Ryan, Edmond	Ah, What Woes Are Mine	Charlotte Brooke	171
O'Rahilly, Egan	From On A Pair Of Shoes Presented to Him	P. S. Dinneen, & T. O'Donoghue	172
" "	The Storm	"	173
" "	More Power to Cromwell	"	173
" "	On a Cock Which Was Stolen From a Good Priest	"	174
" "	The Geraldine's Daughter	James Clarence Mangan	175
Carolan, Turlough	The Cup of O'Hara	Samuel Ferguson	177
"	Why, Liquor of Life	John D'Alton	177
"	Do You Remember That Night	Eugene O'Curry	179
Flavell, Thomas	The County of Mayo	George Fox	180
Anonymous	The White Cockade	J. J. Callanan	181
"	The Fair Hills of Ireland	Samuel Ferguson	182
"	O Say, My Brown Drimin	J. J. Callanan	183
"	The Roving Worker	George Sigerson	184
O'Tuomy, John	O'Tuomy's Drinking Song	James Clarence Mangan	186
Magrath, Andrew	Magrath's Reply to O'Tuomy	"	187
" "	The Boatman's Hymn	Samuel Ferguson	189
" "	Lament of the Mangaire Sugach	Edward Walsh	191
Anonymous	The Convict of Clonmel	J. J. Callanan	193
"	The Dawning of the Day	Edward Walsh	194
"	Pearl of the White Breast	George Petrie	195
"	The Outlaw of Loch Lene	J. J. Callanan	196
"	The Girl I Love	"	196

[xi]

POET	TITLE	TRANSLATOR	PAGE
Anonymous	Cashel of Munster	Samuel Ferguson	197
English, William	Youghall Harbor	" "	198
Healy, Patrick	Patrick Healy's Wishes	John D'Alton	199
O'Curnain, Diarmad	Love's Despair	George Sigerson	200
Anonymous	The Fair-Haired Girl	Samuel Ferguson	202
	Dear, Dark Head	"	203

[EARLY 18TH CENTURY TO THE PRESENT]

Merriman, Brian	The Midnight Court	Arland Ussher	204
Anonymous	The Little White Cat	Mrs. Costello of Tuam	228
"	Four Prayers	Eleanor Hull	229
Raftery, Anthony	I Am Raftery	Douglas Hyde	230
" " "	" " "	James Stephens	231
Anonymous	The Red Man's Wife	Douglas Hyde	232
"	My Grief on the Sea	" "	233
"	Ringleted Youth of My Love	" "	234
MacElgun, Cathal Buidhe	The Yellow Bittern	Thomas MacDonagh	235
Anonymous	Blessed Be The Holy Will of God	Douglas Hyde	237
"	How Happy the Little Birds	Padraic Pearse	237
"	Donall Oge: Grief of a Girl's Heart	Lady Gregory	238
Pearse, Padraic	Ideal	Thomas MacDonagh	240
" "	Lullaby of the Woman of the Mountain	"	241

Part III: Anonymous Street Ballads

TITLE	CENTURY	PAGE
Agricultural Irish Girl	19th	244
Bishop Butler of Kilcash	"	244
The Blackbird	18th	246
Bold Phelim Brady	Early 19th	248
The Boyne Water	17th	249
Brennan On the Moor	18th	250
Brian O'Linn	Early 19th	252
Castlehyde	18th	254
Cockles and Mussels	19th	256
Colleen Oge Asthore	16th	257
Colleen Rue	Early 19th	258
The Cruiskeen Lawn	17th	259
Doran's Ass	19th	260
Dumb, Dumb, Dumb	18th	262
Easter Week	20th	263
Garryowen	Late 18th	264
The Happy Beggarman	" "	265
The Humours of Donnybrook Fair	18th	265

TITLE	CENTURY	PAGE
I Know Where I'm Going	19th	267
I Want to Be Married and Cannot Tell How	Early 19th	268
I'll Never Get Drunk Any More	18th	268
An Irishman's Christening	"	270
Johnny, I Hardly Knew Ye	"	271
Killyburn Brae	19th	274
A Lay of the Famine	"	275
A Longford Legend	18th	277
Mackenna's Dream	"	279
The Maid That Sold Her Barley	"	281
The Maid of the Sweet Brown Knowe	"	282
Molly Bawn and Brian Oge	19th	284
Mrs. McGrath	"	285
The Native Irishman	"	287
Nell Flaherty's Drake	19th	289
The Night Before Larry Was Stretched	"	289
O'Duffy's Ironsides	20th	292
The Rakes of Mallow	Early 17th	294
Reynard the Fox	Late 18th	295
The Shan Van Vocht	18th	297
Tipperary Recruiting Song	19th	299
The Wearin' of the Green	18th	300
Willy Reilly	"	302
Young Molly Bawn	Early 19th	304

Part IV: Anglo-Irish Poetry

POET	LIVED	TITLE	PAGE
Anonymous	14th Century	Icham of Irlaunde	306
Friar Michael of Kildare	" "	Sweet Jesus	307
Anonymous	" "	The Land of Cokaygne	311
"	" "	"A Satire on the People of Kildare"	317
Tate, Nahum	1652-1715	While Shepherds Watched	322
Swift, Jonathan	1667-1745	Apples	323
		Onions	323
		Herrings	324
		A Riddle	324
		A Gentle Echo on Woman	324
		Mary the Cook Maid's Letter	325
		From On the Death of Dr. Swift	327
		The Progress of Poetry	328
		Description of a City Shower	329
Parnell, Thomas	1679-1718	The Small Silver-Coloured Bookworm	331
		From Night Piece on Death	332
Berkeley, George	1685-1753	On the Prospect of Planting Arts And Learning in America	333
Goldsmith, Oliver	1728-1774	The Deserted Village	334
		Stanzas on Woman	346

[xiii]

POET	LIVED	TITLE	PAGE
		Emma	346
		An Elegy on the Glory of Her Sex, Mrs. Mary Blaize	346
Bickerstaff, Isaac	c.1735-1812c.	Song from *Love in a Village*	347
		What are Outward Forms	347
O'Keeffe, John	1747-1833	The Friar of Orders Gray	348
O'Sullivan, Owen Roe	c.1748-1784	Rodney's Glory	349
Sheridan, Richard B.	1751-1816	By Coelia's Arbor	352
		Oh Yield, Fair Lids	352
		Let the Toast Pass	353
		Dry Be That Tear	354
O'Kelly, Patrick	1754- ?	The Curse of Doneraile	355
		Blessings on Doneraile	357
Drennan, William	1754-1820	The Wake of William Orr	359
		Eire	361
Millikin, Richard	1767-1815	The Groves of Blarney	362
Reynolds, George	1771-1802	Mary le More	366
Dermody, Thomas	1775-1802	A Decayed Monastery	367
		John Baynham's Epitaph	369
		An Ode to Myself	372
		The Shepherd's Despair	373
Moore, Thomas	1779-1852	The Time I've Lost in Wooing	374
		The Minstrel Boy	375
		Oh Blame Not the Bard	375
		The Song of O'Ruark	376
		Believe Me If All Those Endearing Young Charms	378
		The Last Rose of Summer	378
		The Song of Fionnuala	379
		Peace to the Slumberers	380
		Love Is a Hunter Boy	380
		The Harp that Once Through Tara's Halls	381
		Epistle of Condolence	381
		Paddy's Metamorphosis	382
		The Duke Is the Lad	383
Kenny, James	1780-1849	The Old Story Over Again	384
Barrett, Eaton	1786-1820	Woman	385
Anster, John	1789-1867	If I Might Choose	386
O'Leary, Joseph	1790-1850 (?)	Whisky, Drink Divine	386
Wolfe, Charles	1791-1823	The Burial of Sir John Moore	388
O'Flaherty, Charles	1794-1828	The Humours of Donnybrook Fair	390
Callanan, J. J.	1795-1829	Song	393
		Lines to the Blessed Sacrament	393
		Serenade	394
Darley, George	1795-1846	From *Errors of Ecstasie*	396
		Lay of the Forlorn	399
		The Call of the Morning	400
		Chorus of Spirits	400
		Serenade of a Loyal Martyr	401
		Runilda's Chant	401

[xiv]

POET	LIVED	TITLE	PAGE
		The Sea-Ritual	402
		Song from *Harvest Home*	403
		Robin's Cross	403
		Last Night	404
		From *Nepenthe*	404
Anonymous		The Fairies in New Ross	407
Lover, Samuel	1797-1868	What Will You Do, Love	407
		The Angel's Whisper	408
		Saint Kevin	409
		The Quaker's Meeting	411
		Barney O'Hea	413
Banim, John	1798-1844	He Said That He Was Not Our Brother	414
Griffin, Gerald	1803-1840	Aileen Aroon	415
		I Love My Love in the Morning	417
		Sleep That Like the Couchéd Dove	418
		Lines Addressed to a Seagull	419
		Gone! Gone! Forever Gone	420
		War Song of O'Driscol	420
		To the Blessed Virgin Mary	421
		Know Ye Not That Lovely River	422
Mangan, James Clarence	1803-1849	The Nameless One	423
		Gone in the Wind	425
		Cean-Salla	426
		Shapes and Signs	427
		To the Ingleezee Khafir	428
		Twenty Golden Years Ago	429
Mahony, Francis (Father Prout)	1804-1866	A Panegyric On Geese	431
		The Red Breast of Aquitania	432
		The Shandon Bells	437
Walsh, Edward	1805-1850	The Fairy Nurse	439
Lever, Charles	1806-1872	Bad Luck to This Marching	440
		The Man for Galway	441
		It's Little for Glory I Care	442
		Larry M'Hale	443
Ferguson, Samuel	1810-1886	Lament for the Death of Thomas Davis	444
		The Welshmen of Tirawley	446
		The Fairy Thorn	457
		The Burial of King Cormac	459
Geoghegan, Arthur G.	1810-1889	After Aughrim	464
Shanly, Charles Dawson	1811-1875	The Walker of the Snow	464
		Kitty of Coleraine	467
Davis, Thomas Osborne	1814-1845	The Fate of King Dathi	467
		My Grave	471
		The Girl I Left Behind Me	471
		The West's Asleep	472
		Lament for the Death of Owen Roe O'Neill	474
		The Irish Hurrah	475
		Fontenoy	476

[xv]

POET	LIVED	TITLE	PAGE
		The Battle Eve of the Brigade	478
		Clare's Dragoons	479
		Tone's Grave	481
Le Fanu, Sheridan	1814-1873	Hymn from *Beatrice*	483
		A Drunkard to His Bottle	484
		The Song of the Spirits	486
DeVere, Aubrey	1814-1902	Human Life	486
		Scene in a Madhouse	487
		The Little Black Rose	488
MacCarthy, Denis Florence	1817-1882	*From* The Foray of Con O'Donnell	489
Mulchinock, William Pembroke	1820 (?)-1864	The Rose of Tralee	493
Alexander, Cecil F.	1820 (?)-1895	Dreams	494
Wilde, Lady	1820 (?)-1896	The Famine Year	494
Williams, Richard D'Alton	1822-1862	The Dying Girl	497
		Extermination	499
Dowling, Bartholemew	1823-1863	The Revel	500
Irwin, Thomas Caulfield	1823-1892	The Faerie's Child	502
MacDermott, Martin	1823-1905	Girl of the Red Mouth	503
Ingram, John Kells	1823-1907	The Memory of the Dead	505
		The Social Future	506
		National Presage	507
McCann, Michael Joseph	1824-1883	O'Donnell Aboo	507
Allingham, William	1824-1889	The Fairies	509
		Abbey Asaroe	510
		Aeolian Harp	512
		The Lupracaun	513
		The Bubble	515
		Death Deposed	515
		The Maids of Elfin-Mere	517
McGee, Thomas D'Arcy	1825-1868	The Celts	518
		The Man of the North Countrie	520
		The Celtic Cross	520
Sullivan, Timothy	1827-1914	God Save Ireland	522
O'Brien, Fitz-James	1828-1862	Minot's Ledge	523
Kickham, Charles	1830-1882	Rory of the Hill	525
Joyce, Robert Dwyer	1830-1883	The Leprahaun	527
Stokes, Whitley	1830-1909	The Viking	528
Hogan, Michael	1832-1899	O'Neill's War Song	529
Brooke, Stopford A.	1832-1916	The Earth and Man	530
Sigerson, George	1836-1925	Smith's Song	531
Molloy, James Lyman	1837-1909	The Kerry Dance	532
		Bantry Bay	533

[xvi]

POET	LIVED	TITLE	PAGE
Lecky, Wm. E. Hartpole	1838-1903	Early Thoughts	534
Todhunter, John	1839-1916	The Banshee	535
		O Mighty Melancholy Wind	537
Dowden, Edward	1843-1913	Autumn Song	537
		Mona Lisa	538
O'Shaughnessy, Arthur	1844-1881	Ode	538
		The Line of Beauty	539
McBurney, William	1844 (?)-1890 (?)	The Croppy Boy	540
O'Reilly, John Boyle	1844-1890	Forever	541
		The Cry of the Dreamer	542
		A White Rose	543
		Disappointment	544
		Constancy	544
		A Message of Peace	544
		To-Day	545
		The Infinite	546
Lawless, Emily	1845-1913	The Stranger's Grave	547
		Dirge of the Munster Forest	547
Hickey, Emily H.	1845-1924	Beloved, It Is Morn	549
Casey, John Keegan	1846-1870	The Rising of the Moon	550
		Maire, My Girl	551
Clarke, J. I. C.	1846-1925	The Fighting Race	552
Graves, Alfred P.	1846-1931	Father O'Flynn	555
Crawford, Isabella V.	1850-1887	The Canoe	556
Larminie, William	1850-1900	The Sword of Tethra	559
		The Nameless Ruin	559
Gregory, Lady	1852-1932	The Old Woman Remembers	560
Parnell, Fanny	1854-1882	After Death	563
Wilde, Oscar	1854-1900	Requiescat	564
		Ballad of Reading Gaol	565
Rolleston, Thomas W. H.	1857-1920	The Grave of Rury	586
McCarthy, Denis A.	1871-1931	The Tailor That Came From Mayo	587
Hinkson, Katherine Tynan	1861-1931	Cuckoo Song	588
		The Witch	590
		Sheep and Lambs	591
		Aux Carmélites	592
		Larks	593
		A Girl's Song	593
Yeats, William Butler	1865-1939	The Stolen Child	594
		The Priest of Coloney	596
		Fairy Song	597
		Down by the Salley Gardens	598
		Lake Isle of Innisfree	598
		Ballad of Father Gilligan	599
		The Host of the Air	601
		Red Hanrahan's Song About Ireland	602

[xvii]

POET	LIVED	TITLE	PAGE
		The Wild Swans at Coole	603
		Byzantium	604
		"I am of Ireland"	605
		Tom the Lunatic	606
Carbery, Ethna	1866-1902	The Love-Talker	607
Shorter, Dora	1866-1918	The Piper on the Hill	608
Sigerson		Sixteen Dead Men	609
		The Kine of My Father	610
		Ballad of the Little Black Hound	611
Russell, George	1867-1935	The Lonely	616
Wm. (AE)		Salutation	616
		Refuge	618
		When	618
Weekes, Charles	1867-1946	Poppies	619
		Think	619
		Solstice	619
		In Brittany	620
Boyd, Thomas	1867-1927	To the Leanán Shee	621
		The Heath	622
Eglinton, John	1868-	The Winds	623
Gore-Booth, Eva	1870-1926	The Little Waves of Breffny	624
MacManus,	1870-	Shane O'Neill	624
Seumas			
Maguire, Tom	c.1870-	Bold Robert Emmet	626
Synge, John M.	1871-1909	Beg-Innish	627
		The Passing of the Shee	628
		Queens	628
MacDonough,	1871-	Bring Home the Poet	629
Patrick			
Doyle, Lynn	1873-	An Ulsterman	630
Cousins, J. H.	1873-	High and Low	631
		The Corn Crake	632
		Omens	632
MacDonagh,	1878-1916	John-John	633
Thomas		Of a Poet Patriot	634
		In Paris	635
Dunsany, Lord	1878-	A Call to the Wild	636
		A Heterodoxy	636
Gogarty, Oliver	1878-	Non Dolet	637
St. John		Leda and the Swan	638
		Between Brielle and Manasquan	642
		To a Friend in the Country	644
Corkery, Daniel	1878-	The Call	666
Pearse, Padraic	1879-1916	The Rebel	645
		The Mother	647
		The Fool	647
Campbell, Joseph	1879-1944	The Poet Loosed a Wingéd Song	649
		The Herb-Leech	650
		The Old Woman	651
		The Tinkers	651
		A Fighting Man	652
		The Besom-Man	653

[xviii]

POET	LIVED	TITLE	PAGE
		Three Colts Exercising	654
		The Unfrocked Priest	655
		O, Glorious Childbearer	656
		I Will Go With My Father	657
		I Am the Gilly of Christ	658
O'Sullivan, Seumas	1879-	The Twilight People	659
		Credo	659
		Rain (Donegal)	660
		Lullaby	661
O'Neill, Moira		Sea Wrack	662
Kettle, Thomas	1880-1916	To My Daughter, Betty	663
Milligan, Alice	1866-	When I Was a Little Girl	663
		A Song of Freedom	665
Colum, Padraic	1881-	Garadh	668
		The Plower	668
		A Cradle Song	669
Salkeld, Blanaid	1880-	Peggy	670
		That Corner	671
		Meditation	672
Figgis, Darrell	1882-1925	Inisgallun	673
Joyce, James	1882-1941	What Counsel Has the Hooded Moon	674
		Bid Adieu, Adieu, Adieu	674
		Strings in the Earth and Air	675
		All Day I Hear the Noise of Waters	675
Stephens, James	1882-	Chill of the Eve	676
		Fossils	677
		The Satyr	678
		Tanist	679
		On a Lonely Spray	679
Letts, Winifred	1882-	The Spires of Oxford	680
		A Soft Day	681
		Wishes For William	682
Ridge, Lola	1883-1941	The Edge	683
		Wind in the Alleys	684
Kearney, Peadar	1883-1942	The Soldier's Song	685
		The Tri-Colored Ribbon	686
		Whack Fol the Diddle	686
Leslie, Shane	1885-	The Four Winds	688
		Fleet Street	689
		Monaghan	689
Gregory, Padric	1886-	The Dream-Teller	690
Plunkett, Joseph Mary	1887-1916	Our Heritage	691
		See the Crocus' Golden Cup	692
		To G. K. Chesterton	692
		I See His Blood Upon the Rose	693
An Pilibin	1887-	Retrospect	693
MacGill, Patrick	1890-	The Conger Eel	694
		Dedication	695
Doak, H. L.	1890-	The Scarecrow	697
Ledwidge, Francis	1891-1917	The Herons	698
		A Little Boy in the Morning	698

[xix]

POET	LIVED	TITLE	PAGE
		To a Linnet in a Cage	699
		A Twilight in Middle March	699
		June	700
		Thomas MacDonagh	701
		The Death of Ailill	701
		Lament for the Poets: 1916	702
McGreevy, Thomas	1893-	Red Hugh	703
		Homage to Hieronymus Bosch	704
		Gioconda	706
Higgins, F. R.	1896-1941	The Gallows Tree	707
		Padraic O'Conaire, Gaelic Storyteller	709
		Song for the Clatter-Bones	710
Mitchell, Susan	1868-1930	Immortality	711
Clarke, Austin	1896-	The Fair at Windgap	711
Gibbon, Monk	1896-	The Bees	713
		The Discovery	715
		Dispossessed Poet	715
Shanahan, Eileen	1901-	Three Children Near Clonmel	716
Connell, Jim		New Words to O'Donnell Abu	717
MacDonogh, Patrick	1902-	She Walked Unaware	719
		Song for a Proud Relation	720
		The Widow of Drynam	720
Donaghy, Lyle	1902-1949	A Leitrim Woman	721
		Linota ·Rufescens	723
O'Connor, Frank	1903-	Three Old Brothers	724
Milne, Ewart	1903-	Tinker's Moon	725
Coghill, Rhoda	1903-	The Plough Horse	726
		Dead	727
Kavanagh, Patrick	1905-	A Glut on the Market	728
		Memory of Brother Michael	729
Fallon, Padraic	1906-	Wisdom	730
		Virgin	731
O'Sullivan, D. J.	1906-	Dawn in Inishtrahull	733
		Drinking Time	734
MacGowan, Liam		Connolly	734
MacMahon, Bryan		Corner Boys	737
Hewitt, John	1907-	Load	738
Lynch, Stanislaus	1907-	Blue Peter	738
MacNeice, Louis	1907-	Bagpipe Music	739
		Nostalgia	741
		Carrickfergus	742
		County Sligo	743
Devlin, Denis	1908-	Encounter	755
		The Statue and the Perturbed Burghers	756
Farren, Robert	1909-	The Mason	744
		To the Bellringer	745
		Immolation	746
Rodgers, W. R.	1909-	Beagles	747
		Spring	748
Stanford, W. B.	1910-	Undertone	749
Jennett, Sean	1910-	I Was a Labourer	749

POET	LIVED	TITLE	PAGE
ffrench Salkeld, Cecil	1910-	Water-Front	750
Ward, Terence	1910-	Kevin Barry	751
Wrafter, Denis	1910-	Braggart	752
MacDonagh, Donagh	1912-	The Invitation	753
		The Veterans	753
Sheridan, Niall	1912-	"As Rock to Sun or Storm"	754
Daiken, Leslie	1912-	Spring, St. Stephen's Green	757
		Bohernabreena	758
		Lines in a Country Parson's Orchard	759
		Larch Hill	760
Brennan, Eileen	1913-	Thoughts at the Museum	736
Brady, George M.	1916-	The Autumn House	761
		The Generations	762
Dooher, Muredach J.	1916-	Renascence	763
Laughton, Freda	1907-	Rain on a Cottage Roof	763
		The Woman With Child	764
Iremonger, Valentin	1918-	Spring Stops Me Suddenly	767
		Recollection in Autumn	768
		Icarus	769
Craig, Maurice	1919-	Winter	765
Greacen, Robert	1920-	Cycling to Dublin	765
		To a Faithless Lover	766
McFadden, Roy	1921-	The Orator	766

Note: Biographical data on Daniel Corkery, Denis Devlin, Eileen Brennan and Valentin Iremonger came too late to change their order of sequence in the text.

❧ *PART I* ❧

ANCIENT IRISH POETRY
From Early Pagan Times
Through The Fifteenth Century

TORNA

(Attributed)

Torna, was the last great bard of Pagan Ireland. He died some time in the 5th Century. Among the poems by him that have reached us is this lament over Corc and Niall of the Nine Hostages, to whom he was bound by the tie of fosterage. "The present version of this ancient relic is as nearly literal as possible, and expressly made in deprecation of the refining upon the original by which many of the poetical translations of the bards are characterized," Samuel Ferguson writes in his notes.

LAMENT FOR CORC AND NIALL OF THE NINE HOSTAGES

My FOSTER-CHILDREN were not slack;
Corc or Niall ne'er turned his back:
Niall, of Tara's palace hoar,
Worthy seed of Owen More;
Corc, of Cashel's pleasant rock,
Con-cead-caha's[1] honored stock.
Joint exploits made Erin theirs—
Joint exploits of high compeers;
Fierce they were, and stormy strong;
Niall, amid the reeling throng,
Stood terrific; nor was Corc
Hindmost in the heavy work.
Niall Mac Eochy Vivahain
Ravaged Albin, hill and plain;
While he fought from Tara far,
Corc disdained unequal war.
Never saw I man like Niall,
Making foreign foemen reel;
Never saw I man like Corc,
Swinging at the savage work;
Never saw I better twain,
Search all Erin round again—

[1] Con-cead-caha = Conn of the Hundred Battles.

[6]

Twain so stout in warlike deeds—
Twain so mild in peaceful weeds.

These the foster-children twain
Of Torna, I who sing the strain;
These they are, the pious ones,
My sons, my darling foster-sons!
Who duly every day would come
To glad the old man's lonely home.
Ah, happy days I've spent between
Old Tara's hall and Cashel-green!
From Tara down to Cashel ford,
From Cashel back to Tara's lord.
When with Niall, his regent, I
Dealt with princes royally.
If with Corc perchance I were,
I was his prime counsellor.

Therefore Niall I ever set
On my right hand—thus to get
Judgements grave, and weighty words,
For the right hand loyal lords;
But, ever on my left-hand side,
Gentle Corc, who knew not pride,
That none other so might part
His dear body from my heart.
Gone is generous Corc O'Yeon—woe is me!
Gone is valiant Niall O'Con—woe is me!
Gone the root of Tara's stock—woe is me!
Gone the head of Cashel rock—woe is me!
Broken is my witless brain—
Niall, the mighty king, is slain!
Broken is my bruised heart's core—
Corc, the Righ-More,[2] is no more!
Mourns Lea Con, in tribute's chain,
Lost Mac Eochy Vivahain,

[2] Righ-More = Great King.

[7]

And her lost Mac Lewy true—
Mourns Lea Mogha,[3] ruined too!

Translated by Samuel Ferguson

CAELIUS SEDULIUS

(5th century)

Sedulius was a fifth century bard who travelled to Rome and composed the first Christian epic there, *Carmen Paschale,* or Easter Song. Dante, Milton and others have borrowed from this epic. Four passages from *The Easter Song* follow:

INVOCATION

ETERNAL God omnipotent! The One
Sole Hope of worlds, Author and Guard alone
Of heaven and earth Thou art, whose high behest
Forbids the tempest's billow-bearing breast
The land to whelm—which fires the orb of noon,
And fills the crescent of the milder moon;
Who'st meted forth alternate day and night
And numbered all the stars—their places bright,
Their signs, times, courses only known to Thee—
Who hast to many forms, most wondrously,
The new earth shaped, and given to dead dust life:
Who hast lost Man restored, for fruit of strife
Forbid, bestown on him a higher food,
And healed the Serpent's sting by sacred blood:
  Who hast, when men (save those borne in the Ark)
Were tombed in floods of whelming waters dark
From one sole stock again the race renewed
(A sign that sin-slain man, through noble wood

---

[3] Lea Mogha: Leath Cuin or Con, and Leath Mogha were the names of the two great divisions of Ireland in ancient times. The princes Corc and Niall were the representatives. This territorial division was made in the reign of Conn of the Hundred Battles, circa. A.D. 180, and was marked by a great wall reaching from Galway to Dublin. See O'Curry's translation of "The Battle of Moylena."

[8]

Once more should be redeemed), and sent to save
One Fount baptismal all the world to lave!
  Ope me the way that to the City bright
Leads forth; let thy Word's lamp be light
To guide my footsteps through the narrow gate,
Where the Good Shepherd feeds His sheep elate:
There first the Virgin's white Lamb entered
And all His fair flock followed where He led!
  With Thee how smooth the way: for Nature all
Thine empire owns! Thou speak'st, her fetters fall
And all her wonted shows new forms assume:
The frozen fields will into verdure bloom
And winter gild with grain: if Thou but will
'Mid budding Spring the swelling grape shall fill,
And sudden labour tread the bursting vine.
All seasons answer to the call Divine!
So ancient Faith attests, so tell the hours—
No time can change, no age abate Thy powers!
  Whereof to sing, in little part, afraid
I seek, as entering a great forest-glade
One strives an over-arching bough to reach.
What were an hundred tongues, an iron speech,
Or what were man an hundredfold to show
Things more than all the lucid stars that glow,
And all the sands where all the oceans flow!

THE SLAUGHTER OF THE INNOCENTS
BY ORDER OF KING HEROD [1]

His hope undone, now raves the impious king
In raging wrath—if king we call that thing
Who justice lacks nor rules his passions right.
  So raves a lion, fierce from hunger's spite,
When from his jaws the tender lamb takes flight.
He rushes on the harmless flock amain

[1] *Cf.* Kuno Meyer's "Lament for the Innocents" from the Irish-Gaelic, p. 51.

[9]

To rend, to mangle:—O'er the bloody plain
The air is filled with bleating cries in vain.
    Thus ruthless Herod, when his prey he lost,
Let loose red Murder on the harmless host
Of Bethlem's babes.
                    Why die this multitude?
Their lips, scarce oped to breathe, are choked in blood!
Not reason, Fury rules the king, who slays
The first weak wail of Life—nor slaughter stays
Till guiltless thousands fall. One fearful cry—
A thousand Mothers' shriek!—assails the sky.
One tears the tresses from her head—one rends
Her cheeks—one smites her naked chest, one bends,—
    Ah, hapless Mother! 'tis no mother's breast
Upon the cold lips of thy child thou'st prest!

CHRIST QUIETS THE TEMPEST

    He sought the sea; His footsteps press the dry,
Shore-weed, and where an oaken skiff lay nigh,
He entered—His disciples followed fast
And raised the shiv'ring sail upon the mast;
The ship ploughed onward and with fav'ring breeze
Soon lost the land and crossed the middle seas.
But then a sudden storm the water smote
Which surged in fury and o'erleaped the boat.
Fear seized His people, deeming all was lost
They stretched their shipwrecked arms towards the coast.
    He peaceful mid the tempest slept, Who keeps
Eternal watch— (because He never sleeps
Who Israel guards), so when, tumultuous,
Their terrors cry: "Be merciful to us,
Lord, help, we perish"—naught delayed His will.
    The Lord arising bade the Winds be still,
The swelling Waves subsided at His word—
Not even Ocean when its deeps are stirred

[10]

With fellest rage resists; nor yet the course
Of storms careering all in furious force.
    The happy Sea to Christ in homage brings
Its lofty billows down, the Tempest springs
In joy away on softly wafting wings.

APOSTROPHE TO DEATH

    When now the end of Agony was come,
Himself His holy Spirit from its home
Corporeal sent, to be assumed again
And live for ever which had died for Men.
The body dying, God undying rives
Returning ways from Death and Hell, whose gyves
Lie broken:—rent the rocks, and of the Just
The Souls re-animate the buried dust,—
And they arose, and from their graves came forth!
    This Temple marvellous new-built on Earth
When th'elder Temple witnessed, sudden, prone
Its summit falls with noise as 'twere a groan.
Its Veil is rent in twain: its riven breast
Reveals the inner secrets, long represt,
To future man: so Moses' Veil shall fall
From off the Law, by Christ made free to all!
    Where now, O Grave, thy Victory? Where Death,
Thy dread sting irresistible, wherewith
Thy penal reign, insatiate of woe,
Was laid on suff'ring man? Thou didst not go
To Christ, but Christ to thee—thine Overthrow!
For He alone might deathless die, Whose grasp
Upholds the world. He made not thee—of Asp
And Disobedience born: lo, now at length
Thy reign is o'er, and stricken all thy strength!
    For when upon the Cross the Saviour died,
Wrath came and with a spear did pierce His side,
The Blood and Water from His Body flowed

Behold, three Gifts of Life on us bestowed:
That fount of water laves us with new birth,
These make us Temples of our God on earth,
Which rendered meet for that most high estate
He orders that we keep immaculate.

Translated from the Latin
by George Sigerson

Cf. St. Paul's Epistle, I Corinthians 15:55; Alexander Pope's *Dying Christian to His Soul.*

ST. PATRICK

(Attributed. 7th century)

"Patrick made this hymn. It was made in the time of Loeguire (Leary) son of Niall. The cause of its composition, however, was to protect him and his monks against deadly enemies that lay in wait for the clerics. And this is a corslet of faith for the protection of body and soul against devils and men and vices. Patrick sang this when the ambuscades were laid against his coming by Loeguire, that he might not go to Tara to sow the faith. And then it appeared before those lying in ambush (Loeguire's men) that they (Patrick and his monks) were wild deer with a fawn (Benen) following. And its name is 'Deer's Cry.'"

Modern scholars and translators say that the hymn as handed down in its present form is not earlier than the late 7th or early 8th century; that the language in which the poem is written is of that period. The hymn is also known as "Patrick's Breastplate."

DEER'S CRY

I ARISE to-day
    Through a mighty strength, the invocation of the Trinity,
    Through belief in the threeness,
    Through confession of the oneness
    Of the Creator of Creation.

I arise to-day
    Through the strength of Christ's birth with His baptism,
    Through the strength of His crucifixion with His burial,
    Through the strength of His resurrection with His ascension,

Through the strength of His descent for the Judgment of
    Doom.

I arise to-day
    Through the strength of the love of Cherubim,
    In obedience of angels,
    In the service of archangels,
    In hope of resurrection to meet with reward,
    In prayers of Patriarchs,
    In predictions of Prophets,
    In preachings of Apostles,
    In faiths of confessors,
    In innocence of holy Virgins,
    In deeds of righteous men.

I arise to-day
    Through the strength of heaven:
    Light of sun,
    Radiance of moon,
    Splendour of fire,
    Speed of lightning,
    Swiftness of wind,
    Depth of sea,
    Stability of earth,
    Firmness of rock.

I arise to-day
    Through God's strength to pilot me:
    God's might to uphold me,
    God's wisdom to guide me,
    God's eye to look before me,
    God's ear to hear me,
    God's word to speak for me,
    God's hand to guard me,
    God's way to lie before me,
    God's shield to protect me,
    God's host to save me
      From snares of devils,

From temptations of vices,
From every one who shall wish me ill,
Afar and anear,
Alone and in a multitude.

I summon to-day all these powers between me and those evils,
Against every cruel merciless power that may oppose my
body and my soul,
Against incantations of false prophets,
Against black laws of pagandom,
Against false laws of heretics,
Against craft of idolatry,
Against spells of women and smiths and wizards,
Against every knowledge that corrupts man's body and soul.

Christ to shield me to-day
Against poison, against burning,
Against drowning, against wounding,
So that there may come to me abundance of reward.
Christ with me, Christ before me, Christ behind me,
Christ in me, Christ beneath me, Christ above me,
Christ on my right, Christ on my left,
Christ when I lie down, Christ when I sit down, Christ when
I arise,
Christ in the heart of every man who thinks of me,
Christ in the mouth of every one who speaks of me,
Christ in every eye that sees me,
Christ in every ear that hears me.

I arise to-day
Through a mighty strength, the invocation of the Trinity,
Through belief in the threeness,
Through confession of the oneness
Of the Creator of Creation.

Domini est salus. Domini est Salus. Christi est salus,
Salus tua, Domine, sit semper nobiscum.

Amen.

Translations of Whitley Stokes,
John Strachan and Kuno Meyer

[14]

ST. COLMAN

(Attributed. 8th century)

"A great pestilence was sent on the men of Ireland, namely the *Buide Connaill* (the Yellow Plague), which ransacked all Ireland, and left only one man in every three alive. And it was to protect them and his school against that pestilence that Colman made this hymn. And it befell that he composed it when he began to make for a certain island of the sea of Ireland, outside, fleeing from this pestilence, so that there might be *nine waves between them and the land, for pestilence does not pass beyond that, ut ferunt periti.* And one of the school asked Colman what was the blessing wherein it had befallen them to take the road. So then has said Colman: "What blessing is it," said he, "but God's blessing?" For this is what they essayed, to go forth on islands of the sea, fleeing before the disease. *Dicunt alii* that Colman made all (the hymn). Others say that he made only two quatrains and that the school made the rest, half a quatrain by each of them. It was composed in Cork in the time of Blaithmac and Diarmait." Whitley Stokes. *Liber Hymnorum.*

It is a long prayer-poem or Lorica. The first eight quatrains follow:

HYMN AGAINST PESTILENCE

GOD's blessing lead us, help us!
May Mary's Son veil us!
May we be under His safeguard to-night!
Whither we go may He guard us well!

Whether in rest or motion,
Whether sitting or standing,
The Lord of Heaven against every strife,
This is the prayer that we will pray.

May the prayer of Abel son of Adam,
Enoch, Elias help us;
May they save us from swift disease
On whatever side, throughout the noisy world.

Noah and Abraham,
Isaac the wonderful son,
May they surround us against pestilence,
That famine may not come to us!

[15]

We entreat the father of three tetrads,
And Joseph their junior:
May their prayers save us
To the King many-angeled, noble!

May Moses the good leader protect us,
Who protected us through Rubrum Mare,
Joshua, Aaron Amre's son,
David the bold lad.

May Job with his trials
Protect us past the poisons!
May God's prophets defend us,
With Maccabee's seven sons!

John the Baptist we invoke,
May he be a safeguard to us, a protection!
May Jesus with His apostles
Be for our help against danger!

Translated by Whitley Stokes
and John Strachan

ANONYMOUS
(8th century)

The following fragment from "The Devil's Tribute to Moling" is found on the margin of *Codex S. Pauli* of the Monastery of Carinthia.

The Devil appears to St. Moling as he is at prayer, and asks him to bestow either a blessing or a curse on him, which the saint refuses to do. Then the Devil wonders how he can earn a blessing, and Moling tells him to fast. "I have been fasting since the beginning of the world, and not the better thereof am I," replies the Devil. "Make genuflexions," says Moling. "I cannot bend forward," says the Devil, "for backwards are my knees." "Go forth," says Moling; "I cannot teach thee, nor help thee." Then the Devil says, thoughtfully:

THE HOLY MAN

HE IS a bird round which a trap closes,
He is a leaky ship to which peril is dangerous,
He is an empty vessel, he is a withered tree,
Whoso doth not the will of the King above.
He is pure gold, he is the radiance round the sun,
He is a vessel of silver with wine,
He is happy, is beautiful, is holy,
Whoso doth the will of the King.

*Translated by Whitley Stokes
and John Strachan*

NININE
(8th century)

PRAYER TO ST. PATRICK

WE INVOKE holy Patrick, Ireland's chief apostle.
Glorious is his wondrous name, a flame that baptized heathen;
He warred against hard-hearted wizards.
He thrust down the proud with the help of our Lord of fair
    heaven.
He purified Ireland's meadow-lands, a mighty birth.
We pray to Patrick chief apostle; his judgment hath delivered
    us in Doom from the malevolence of dark devils.
God be with us, together with the prayer of Patrick, chief
    apostle.

*Translated by Whitley Stokes
and John Strachan*

ANONYMOUS .
(8th century)

MY LITTLE LODGE

On the margin of *Codex S. Pauli.*

MY LITTLE lodge in Tuaim Inbir,—
There's no great house of statelier timber;
With its stars at evening bright,
Sun by day and moon by night.

Gobban's was the hand that planned it—
Listen, would you understand it—
And God of heaven, my heart's beloved,
The roofer that built the roof above it.

A house in which the rain-storm falls not,
A spot where spear-point sharp appalls not;
A very garden, full of light,—
And no forbidding fence in sight!

Translated by F. N. Robinson

ANONYMOUS
(8th century?)

A PRAYER

BE THOU my vision, O Lord of my heart,
Naught is all else to me, save that Thou art.

Thou my best thought by day and by night,
Waking or sleeping, Thy presence my light.

Be Thou my wisdom, Thou my true word;
I ever with Thee, Thou with me, Lord.

Thou my great father, I Thy dear son;
Thou in me dwelling, I with Thee one.

Be Thou my battle-shield, sword for the fight,
Be Thou my dignity, Thou my delight.

Thou my soul's shelter, Thou my high tower;
Raise Thou me heavenward, power of my power.

Riches I heed not, nor man's empty praise,
Thou mine inheritance now and always.

Thou, and Thou only, first in my heart,
High king of heaven, my treasure Thou art.

King of the seven heavens, grant me for dole,
Thy love in my heart, Thy light in my soul.

Thy light from my soul, Thy love from my heart,
King of the seven heavens, may they never depart.

With the high king of heaven, after victory won,
May I reach heaven's joys, O bright heaven's sun!

Heart of my own heart, whatever befall,
Still be my vision, O Ruler of all.

Translated by Eleanor Hull

SAINT ITA
(Attributed. 8th century)

JESUKIN

JESUKIN
Lives my little cell within;
What were wealth of cleric high—
All is lie but Jesukin.

[19]

Nursling nurtured, as 'tis right—
Harbours here no servile sprite—
Jesu of the skies, who art
Next my heart thro' every night!

Jesukin, my good for aye,
Calling and will not have nay,
King of all things, ever true,
He shall rue who will away.

Jesu, more than angels aid,
Fosterling nor formed to fade,
Nursed by me in desert wild,
Jesu, child of Judah's Maid.

Son of Kings and kingly kin,
To my land may enter in;
Guest of none I hope to be,
Save of Thee, my Jesukin!

Unto heaven's High King confest
Sing a chorus, maidens blest!
He is o'er us, though within
Jesukin is on my breast!

Translated by George Sigerson

(Another Version)

SAINT ITA'S FOSTERLING

BABE Jesu lying
On my little pallet lonely,
Rich monks woo me to deny thee,
All things lie save Jesu only.

[20]

Tiny fosterling, I love thee,
Of no churlish house thou art;
Thou, with angels' wings above thee,
Nestlest night-long next my heart!

Tiny Jesu, baby lover,
Paying good and bad their due,
The whole world thou rulest over,
All must pray thee or they rue.

Jesu, thou angelic blossom,
No ill-minded monk art thou;
Child of Hebrew Mary's bosom,
In my cell thou slumberest now.

Though they come my friendship craving,
Sons of princes and of kings,
Not from them my soul finds saving,
But to tiny Jesu clings.

Virgins! sing your tuneful numbers,
Pay your little tribute so;
On my breast babe Jesu slumbers,
Yet in heaven his soft feet go.

Translated by Robin Flower

CORMAC

Cormac, King-Bishop of Cashel (837-903) wrote the "Psalter of Cashel."
According to O'Curry, he has always been considered "one of the most
distinguished scholars of Europe of his time. Besides the knowledge he is
recorded to have acquired of the Hebrew, Greek, and Latin, the British,
Saxon, Danish and other northern languages, he is regarded as having
been one of the greatest Gaedhelic scholars that ever lived." The piece
that follows is from the *Book of Leinster*.

THE HEAVENLY PILOT

Wilt Thou steer my frail black bark
O'er the dark broad ocean's foam?
Wilt Thou come, Lord, to my boat,
Where afloat, my will would roam?
Thine the mighty: Thine the small:
Thine to mark men fall, like rain;
God! wilt Thou grant aid to me
Who came o'er th' upheaving main?

Translated by George Sigerson

ANONYMOUS
(9th century)

FROM THE TRIADS OF IRELAND

THREE slender things that best support the world: the slender stream of milk from the cow's dug into the pail; the slender blade of green corn upon the ground; the slender thread over the hand of a skilled woman.

Three rude ones of the world: a youngster mocking an old man; a robust person mocking an invalid; a wise man mocking a fool.

Three fair things that hide ugliness: good manners in the ill-favoured; skill in a serf; wisdom in the misshapen.

Three glories of a gathering: a beautiful wife, a good horse, a swift hound.

Three signs of a fop: the track of his comb in his hair; the track of his teeth in his food; the track of his stick behind him.

[22]

Three idiots of a bad guest-house: an old hag with a chronic cough; a brainless tartar of a girl; a hobgoblin of a gilly.

Three things that constitute a physician: a complete cure; leaving no blemish behind; a painless examination.

Three nurses of theft: a wood, a cloak, night.

Three false sisters: "Perhaps," "Maybe," "I dare say."

Three timid brothers: "Hush!" "Stop!" "Listen!"

Three sounds of increase: the lowing of a cow in milk; the din of a smithy; the swish of a plough.

Three steadinesses of good womanhood: keeping a steady tongue, a steady chastity, a steady housewifery.

Three candles that illume every darkness: truth, nature, knowledge.

Three keys that unlock thoughts: drunkenness, trustfulness, love.

Three youthful sisters: desire, beauty, generosity.

Three aged sisters: groaning, chastity, ugliness.

Three services, the worst that a man can serve: serving a bad woman, a bad lord, and bad land.

Translated by Kuno Meyer

Cf. W. H. Auden *Poems* 1934, p. 129.

ANONYMOUS
(9th century)

SUMMER IS GONE

My TIDINGS for you: the stag bells,
Winter snows, summer is gone.

Wind high and cold, low the sun,
Short his course, sea running high.

Deep-red the bracken, its shape all gone—
The wild-goose has raised his wonted cry.

Cold has caught the wings of birds;
Season of ice—these are my tidings.

Translated by Kuno Meyer

ST. PATRICK
(Attributed. 9th century)

GOD'S BLESSING ON MUNSTER

From the *Book of Lismore* and *Tripartite Life of Patrick*. This is attributed to St. Patrick, but it is in the language of the 9th century.

God's blessing on Munster
Men, boys, women!
Blessing on the land
That gives them fruit!

Blessing on every treasure
That shall be produced on their plains,
Without anyone in want of help,
God's blessing on Munster!

Blessing on their peaks,
On their bare flagstones,
Blessing on their glens,
Blessing on their ridges.

Like sand of sea under ships,
Be the number of their hearths:
On slopes, on plains,
On mountains, or peaks.

Translated by Whitley Stokes

ANONYMOUS
(probably 9th century)

THE SCRIBE

Found on the margin of *St. Gall, Ms.* The Irish St. Gall, died 635 at the age of ninety-five, founded a monastery on Lake Constance, Switzerland.

A HEDGE of trees surrounds me:
A blackbird sings to me
Above my booklet, the lined one, ·
The thrilling birds sing to me

In a grey mantle, from the tops of bushes,
The cuckoo chants to me
May the Lord protect me from Doom!
I write well under the greenwood.

A new arrangement, by K. H.,
combining the Whitley Stokes and
John Strachan translations

ANONYMOUS
(8th or early 9th century)

THE MONK AND HIS PET CAT

A marginal poem on *Codex S. Pauli*, by a student of the Monastery of
Carinthia.

I AND my white Pangur
Each has his special art;
His mind is set on hunting mice
Mine on my special craft.

Better than fame I love to rest
With close study of my little book;
White Pangur does not envy me,
He loves to ply his childish art.

When we two are alone in our house
It is a tale without tedium;
Each of us has games never ending
Something to sharpen our wit upon.

At times by feats of valor
A mouse sticks in his net,
While into my net there drops
A loved law of obscure meaning.

His eye, this flashing full one,
He points against the fence wall
While against the fine edge of science
I point my clear but feeble eye.

He is joyous with swift jumping
When a mouse sticks in his sharp claw,
And I too am joyous when I have grasped
The elusive but well loved problem.

[26]

Though we thus play at all times
Neither hinders the other—
Each is happy with his own art,
Pursues it with delight.

He is master of the work
Which he does every day
While I am master of my work,
Bringing to obscure laws clarity.

Version based on translations by
Whitley Stokes, John Strachan,
and Kuno Meyer.

(*Another Version*)

PANGUR BAN

I AND Pangur Ban, my cat,
'Tis a like task we are at;
Hunting mice is his delight,
Hunting words I sit all night.

Better far than praise of men
'Tis to sit with book and pen;
Pangur bears me no ill will,
He too plies his simple skill.

'Tis a merry thing to see
At our tasks how glad are we,
When at home we sit and find
Entertainment to our mind.

Oftentimes a mouse will stray
In the hero Pangur's way;
Oftentimes my keen thought set
Takes a meaning in its net.

[27]

'Gainst the wall he sets his eye
Full and fierce and sharp and sly;
'Gainst the wall of knowledge I
All my little wisdom try.

When a mouse darts from its den,
O how glad is Pangur then!
O what gladness do I prove
When I solve the doubts I love!

So in peace our tasks we ply,
Pangur Ban, my cat, and I;
In our arts we find our bliss,
I have mine and he has his.

Practice every day has made
Pangur perfect in his trade;
I get wisdom day and night
Turning darkness into light.

Translated by Robin Flower

ANONYMOUS
(9th century)

The early Irish Church differed in many ways from the rest of the Christian world. The early religious poetry gives an interesting insight into many aspects of this religious life: The hermit in his cell; the monk at his devotion, or copying under the open sky; the ascetic, alone or with twelve chosen companions, living on an island, or in the solitude of the woods or mountains.

THE HERMIT'S SONG

I wish, O Son of the living God,
O ancient, eternal King,

[28]

For a hidden little hut in the wilderness
That it may be my dwelling.

An all-grey lithe little lark
To be by its side,
A clear pool to wash away sins
Through the grace of the Holy Spirit.

Quite near, a beautiful wood,
Around it on every side,
To nurse many-voiced birds,
Hiding it with its shelter.

And facing the south for warmth;
A little brook across its floor,
A choice land with many gracious gifts
Such as be good for every plant.

A few men of sense—
We will tell their number—
Humble and obedient,
To pray to the King:—

Four times three, three times four,
Fit for every need,
Twice six in the church,
Both north and south:—

Six pairs
Besides myself,
Praying forever to the King
Who makes the sun shine.

A pleasant church and with the linen altar-cloth,
A dwelling for God from Heaven;
Then, shining candles
Above the pure white Scriptures.

One house for all to go to
For the care of the body,
Without ribaldry, without boasting,
Without thought of evil.

This is the husbandry I would take,
I would choose, and will not hide it:
Fragrant leek,
Hens, salmon, trout, bees.

Raiment and food enough for me
From the King of fair fame,
And I to be sitting for a while
Praying God in every place.

Translated by Kuno Meyer

ANONYMOUS

(8th or 9th century)

THE VIKING TERROR

A marginal poem on the St. Gall Ms.

FIERCE is the wind tonight,
It ploughs up the white hair of the sea
I have no fear that the Viking hosts
Will come over the water to me.

Translated by F. N. Robinson

ANONYMOUS

(9th century)

Liadin, a poetess, went visiting in Connaught. There Curither, himself a
poet, made an ale-feast for her. "Why should not we two unite, Liadin?"
said Curither. "A son of us two would be famous." Liadin said: "Do not

[30]

let us do so now . . . but . . . if you will come for me again at my home, I shall go with you."

Curither did as she bade but when he arrived at her home he found that Liadin had made a vow of chastity. But faithful to her word she went with him. Then they proceeded to a monastery where they put themselves under the spiritual direction of St. Cummin the Tall. He imposed a probation upon them, allowing them to converse without seeing each other. Then, challenged by Liadin, Cummin permits them a perilous freedom. In the result he banishes Curither, who renounces love and becomes a pilgrim. When Liadin still seeks him he crosses the sea. She returns to the scene of their penance and dies. St. Cummin lovingly lays the stone where she had mourned her love, and upon which she died, over the grave of the unhappy maiden.

LIADIN AND CURITHER

CURITHER:

OF LATE
Since I parted from Liadin,
Long as a month is every day,
Long as a year each month.

LIADIN:

Joyless
The bargain I have made!
The heart of him I loved I wrung.

'Twas madness
Not to do his pleasure,
Were there not the fear of Heaven's King.

'Twas a trifle
That wrung Curither's heart against me:
To him great was my gentleness.

I am Liadin
That loved Curither:
It is true as they say.

A short while I was
In the company of Curither:
Sweet was my intimacy with him.

[31]

The music of the forest
Would sing to me when with Curither,
Together with the voice of the purple sea.

Would that
Nothing of all I have done
Had wrung his heart against me!

Conceal it not!
He was my heart's love,
Whatever else I might love.

A roaring flame
Has dissolved this heart of mine—
Without him for certain it cannot live.

Translated by Kuno Meyer

DALLAN MacMORE
(Attributed. Early 10th century)

Dallan mac More, to whom the poem is ascribed, was chief bard to King Carrol (Cerball) Mac Muiregan of Leinster, who reigned about 885-909 A.D.

THE SONG OF CARROLL'S SWORD

HAIL, sword of Carroll! Oft hast thou been in the great woof
    of war,
Oft giving battle, beheading high princes.

Oft has thou gone a-raiding in the hands of kings of great
    judgments
Oft hast thou divided the spoil with a good king worthy of
    thee.

[32]

Oft where men of Leinster were hast thou been in a white
    hand,
Oft hast thou been among kings, oft among great bands.

Many were the kings that wielded thee in fight,
Many a shield hast thou cleft in battle, many a head and chest,
    many a fair skin.

Forty years without sorrow Enna of the noble hosts had thee,
Never wast thou in a strait, but in the hands of a very fierce
    king.

Enna gave thee—'twas no niggardly gift—to his own son, to
    Dunling,
For thirty years in his possession, at last thou broughtest ruin
    on him.

Many a king upon a noble steed possessed thee unto Dermot
    the kingly, the fierce:
Sixteen years was the time Dermot had thee.

At the feast of Alenn, Dermot the hardy-born bestowed thee,
Dermot, the noble king, gave thee to the man of Mairg, to
    Murigan.

Forty years stoutly thou wast in the hand of Alenn's high-king,
With Murigan of mighty deeds thou never wast a year without
    battle.

In Wexford Murigan, the King of Vikings, gave thee to Car-
    roll:
While he was upon the yellow earth Carroll gave thee to none.

Thy bright point was a crimson point in the battle of Odva of
    the foreigners.
When thou leftest Aed Finnliath on his back in the battle of
    Odva of the noble routs.

[33]

Crimson was thy edge, it was seen; at Belach Moon thou wast
proved,
In the valorous battle of Alvy's Plain throughout which the
fighting raged.

Before thee the goodly host broke on a Thursday at Doon Och-
tair,
When Aed the fierce and brilliant fell upon the hillside above
Leafin.

Before thee the host broke on the day when Cealleadh was
slain,
Flannagan's son, with numbers of troops, in high lofty great
Tara.

Before thee they ebbed southwards in the battle of the Boyne
of the rough feats,
When Cnogva fell, the lance of valour, at seeing thee, for dread
of thee.

Thou wast furious, thou wast not weak, heroic was thy swift
force,
When Ailill Frosach of Fál fell in the front of the onset.

Thou never hadst a day of defeat with Carroll of the beautiful
garths,
He swore no lying oath, he went not against his word.

Thou never hadst a day of sorrow, many a night thou hadst
abroad;
Thou hadst awaiting thee many a king with many a battle.

O sword of the kings of mighty fires, do not fear to be astray!
Thou shalt find thy man of craft, a lord worthy of thee.

Who shall henceforth possess thee, or to whom wilt thou deal
ruin?
From the day that Carroll departed, with whom wilt thou be
bedded?

[34]

Thou shalt not be neglected until thou come to the house of
    glorious Naas:
Where Finn of the feasts is, they will hail thee with 'welcome.'

Translated by Kuno Meyer

ANONYMOUS

(10th century)

"In the battle of Aidne, Crede, the daughter of King Gooary of Aidne,
beheld Dinertach of the Hy Fidgenti, who had come to the help of Gooary,
with seventeen wounds upon his breast. Then she fell in love with him. He
died, and was buried in the cemetery of Colman's Church." Kuno Meyer.

THE SONG OF CREDE, DAUGHTER OF GOOARY

THESE are arrows that murder sleep
At every hour in the bitter-cold night:
Pangs of love throughout the day
For the company of the man from Roiny.

Great love of a man from another land
Has come to me beyond all else:
It has taken my bloom, no colour is left,
It does not let me rest.

Sweeter than songs was his speech,
Save holy adoration of Heaven's King;
He was a glorious flame, no boastful word fell from his lips,
A slender mate for a maid's side.

When I was a child I was bashful,
I was not given to going to trysts:
Since I have come to a wayward age,
My wantonness has beguiled me.

[35]

I have every good with Gooary,
The King of cold Aidne:
But my mind has fallen away from my people
To the meadow at Irluachair.

There is chanting in the meadow of glorious Aidne
Around the sides of Colman's Church:
Glorious flame, now sunk into the grave—
Dinertach was his name.

It wrings my pitiable heart, O chaste Christ,
What has fallen to my lot:
These are arrows that murder sleep
At every hour in the bitter-cold night.

Translated by Kuno Meyer

ANONYMOUS
(10th century)

SUMMER HAS COME

SUMMER has come, healthy and free,
Whence the brown wood is bent to the ground:
The slender nimble deer leap,
And the path of seals is smooth.

The cuckoo sings gentle music,
Whence there is smooth peaceful calm:
Gentle birds skip upon the hill,
And swift grey stags.

Heat has laid hold of the rest of the deer—
The lovely cry of curly packs!
The white extent of the strand smiles,
There the swift sea is roused.

[36]

A sound of playful breezes in the tops
Of a black oakwood is Drum Daill,
The noble hornless herd runs,
To whom Cuan-wood is a shelter.

Green bursts out on every herb,
The top of the green oakwood is bushy,
Summer has come, winter has gone,
Twisted hollies wound the hound.

The blackbird sings a loud strain,
To him the live wood is a heritage,
The sad angry sea is fallen asleep,
The speckled salmon leaps.

The sun smiles over every land,—
A parting for me from the brood of cares:
Hounds bark, stags tryst,
Ravens flourish, summer has come!

Translation by Kuno Meyer

ANONYMOUS

(10th century)

A SONG OF WINTER

COLD, cold!
Cold tonight is broad Moylurg.
Higher the snow than the mountain-range,
The deer cannot get at their food.

Cold till Doom!
The storm has spread over all:
A river is each furrow upon the slope,
Each ford a full pool.

[37]

A great tidal sea is each loch,
A full loch is each pool:
Horses cannot get over the ford of Ross,
No more can two feet get there.

The fish of Ireland are a-roaming,
There is no strand which the wave does not pound,
Not a town there is in the land,
Where a bell is heard, no crane talks.

The wolves of Cuan-wood get
Neither rest nor sleep in their lair,
The little wren cannot find
Shelter in her nest on the slope of Lon.

Keen wind and cold ice
Has burst upon the little company of birds,
The blackbird cannot get a lee to her liking,
Shelter for its side in Cuan-wood.

Cosy our pot on its hook,
Crazy the hut on the slope of Lon:
The snow has crushed the wood here,
Toilsome to climb up Ben-bo.

Glenn Rye's ancient bird
From the bitter wind gets grief;
Great her misery and her pain,
The ice will get into her mouth.

From flock and from down to rise—
Take it to heart!—were folly for thee:
Ice in heaps on every ford—
That is why I say 'cold' !

Translated by Kuno Meyer

[38]

ANONYMOUS

(10th century)

THE OLD WOMAN OF BEARE

Kuno Meyer suggests that this is so very ancient a poem that it might well have been known to Villon. Compare the similarities of this and Old Margaret, *Regrets de la Belle Heaulmière ja parvenue à viellesse,* of Villon. In this version from *Ancient Irish Poetry* Kuno Meyer has left out twelve quatrains. "The reason why she was called the Old Woman of Beare was that she had fifty foster-children in Beare. She had seven periods of youth one after the other, so that every man who had lived with her came to die of old age, and her grandsons and great-grandsons were tribes and races. For a hundred years she wore the veil which Cumine had blessed upon her head. Thereupon old age and infirmity came to her." A few minor changes have been made for clarification.

EBB TIDE to me as of the sea!
Old age causes me reproach.
Though I may grieve thereat—
Happiness comes out of fat.

I am the Old Woman of Beare,
An ever-new smock I used to wear:
Today—such is my mean estate—
I wear not even a cast-off shift.

It is riches
Ye love, it is not men:
In the time when *we* lived
It was men.

Swift chariots,
And steeds that carried off the prize,—
Their day of plenty has been,
A blessing on the King who lent them!

My body with bitterness has dropt
Towards the abode we know:

[39]

When the Son of God deems it time
Let Him come to deliver His behest.

My arms when they are seen
Now are bony and thin:
Once they would fondle and caress
The bodies of glorious kings.

When my arms are seen,
And they bony and thin,
They are not fit, I declare,
To be raised over comely men.

The maidens rejoice
When May-day comes to them:
For me, sorrow the share;
I am wretched, I am an old hag.

I hold no sweet converse.
No wethers are killed for my wedding-feast,
My hair is all but grey,
The mean veil over it is no pity.

I do not deem it ill
That a white veil be on my head;
Time was when cloths of every hue
Bedecked my head as we drank good ale.

The Stone of the Kings on Femen,
The Chair of Ronan in Bregon,
Long since storms have reached them:
The slabs of their tombs are old and decayed.

The wave of the great sea talks aloud,
Winter has arisen:
Fermuid the son of Mugh to-day
I do not expect on a visit.

I know what they are doing:
They row and row across
The reeds of the Ford of Alma—
Cold is the place where they sleep.

'Tis "O my God!"
To me today, whatever will come of it.
I must cover myself even in the sun:
The time is at hand that shall renew me.

Youth's summer in which we were
I have spent with its autumn:
Winter-age which overwhelms all men,
To me has come its beginning.

Amen! Woe is me!
Every acorn has to drop
After feasting by shining candles
To be in the gloom of a prayer-house!

I had my day with kings
Drinking mead and wine:
To-day I drink whey-water
Among shrivelled old hags.

I see upon my cloak the hair of old age,
My reason has beguiled me:
Grey is the hair that grows through my skin—
'Tis thus! I am an old woman.

The flood-wave
And the second ebb tide—
They have reached me,
I know them well.

The flood wave
Will not reach the silence of my kitchen:

[41]

Though many are my company in darkness,
A hand has been laid upon them all.

O happy the isle of the great sea
Which the flood reaches after the ebb!
As for me, I do not expect
Flood after ebb to come to me.

There is scarce a little place to-day
That I can recognise:
What was on flood
Is all on ebb.

Translated by Kuno Meyer

ANONYMOUS

(10th century)

EVE'S LAMENT

I AM Eve, great Adam's wife,
'Tis I that outraged Jesus of old;
'Tis I that robbed my children of Heaven,
By right 'tis I that should have gone upon the cross.

I had a kingly house to please me,
Grievous the evil choice that disgraced me,
Grievous the wicked advice that withered me!
Alas! my hand is not pure.

'Tis I that plucked the apple,
Which went across my gullet:
So long as they endure in the light of day,
So long women will not cease from folly.

There would be no ice in any place,
There would be no glistening windy winter,

[42]

There would be no hell, there would be no sorrow,
There would be no fear, if it were not for me.

Translated by Kuno Meyer

ANONYMOUS
(10th century)

PRAYER TO THE VIRGIN

GENTLE Mary, noble maiden, give us help!
Shrine of our Lord's body, casket of the mysteries!

Queen of queens, pure holy maiden,
Pray for us that our wretched transgression be forgiven for thy
    sake.

Merciful one, forgiving one, with the grace of the Holy Spirit,
Pray with us to the true-judging King of the goodly ambrosial
    clan.

Branch of Jesse's tree in the beauteous hazel-wood,
Pray for me until I obtain forgiveness of my foul sins.

Mary, splendid diadem, thou that hast saved our race,
Glorious noble torch, orchard of Kings!

Brilliant one, transplendent one, with the deed of pure chas-
    tity,
Fair golden illumined ark, holy daughter from Heaven!

Mother of righteousness, Thou that excellest all else,
Pray with me thy first-born to save me on the day of Doom.

Noble rare star, tree under blossom,
Powerful choice lamp, sun that warmeth every one.

[43]

Ladder of the great track by which every saint ascends,
Mayst thou be our safeguard towards the glorious Kingdom.

Fair fragrant seat chosen by the King,
The noble guest who was in thy womb three times three
months.

Glorious royal porch through which He was incarnated,
The splendid chosen sun, Jesus, Son of the living God.

For the sake of the fair babe that was conceived in thy womb,
For the sake of the holy child that is High-King in every place,

For the sake of His cross that is higher than any cross,
For the sake of His burial when He was buried in a stone-tomb,

For the sake of His resurrection when He arose before every
one,
For the sake of the holy household from every place to Doom,

Be thou our safeguard in the Kingdom of the good Lord,
That we may meet with dear Jesus—that is our prayer—hail!
Translations of John Strachan
and Kuno Meyer

ANONYMOUS
(10th century)

ON THE FLIGHTINESS OF THOUGHT

SHAME to my thoughts, how they stray from me!
I fear great danger from it on the day of eternal Doom.

During the psalms they wander on a path that is not right:
They fash, they fret, they misbehave before the eyes of great
God.

Through eager   crowds, through companies of wanton women,
Through woods, through cities—swifter they are than the
    wind.

Now through paths of loveliness, anon of riotous shame!

Without a ferry or ever missing a step they go across every sea:
Swiftly they leap in one bound from earth to heaven.

They run a race of folly anear and afar:
After a course of giddiness they return to their home.

Though one should try to bind them or put shackles on their
        feet,
They are neither constant nor mindful to take a spell of rest.

Neither sword-edge nor crack of whip will keep them down
        strongly:
As slippery as an eel's tail they glide out of my grasp.

Neither lock nor firm-vaulted dungeon nor any fetter on earth,
Stronghold nor sea nor bleak fastness restrains them from their
        course.

O beloved truly chaste Christ to whom every eye is clear,
May the grace of the seven-fold Spirit come to keep them, to
        check them!

Rule this heart of mine, O dread God of the elements,
That Thou mayst be my love, that I may do Thy will.

That I may reach Christ with His chosen companions, that we
        may be together!
They are neither fickle nor inconstant—not as *I* am.

                              Translated by Kuno Meyer

ANONYMOUS
(10th century)

TO CRINOG

Crinog belonged to that company of women known in the literature of the early Christian Church as *virgo subintroducta* or *conhospita*, i.e. a nun who lived with a priest, monk, or hermit like a sister or "spiritual wife" (uxor spiritualis). This practice, which was early suppressed and abandoned everywhere else, seems to have survived in the Irish Church until the tenth century.

CRINOG, melodious is your song.
Though young no more you are still bashful.
We two grew up together in Niall's northern land,
When we used to sleep together in tranquil slumber.

That was my age when you slept with me,
O peerless lady of pleasant wisdom:
A pure-hearted youth, lovely without a flaw,
A gentle boy of seven sweet years.

We lived in the great world of Banva
Without sullying soul or body,
My flashing eye full of love for you,
Like a poor innocent untempted by evil.

Your just counsel is ever ready,
Wherever we are we seek it:
To love your penetrating wisdom is better
Than glib discourse with a king.

Since then you have slept with four men after me,
Without folly or falling away:
I know, I hear it on all sides,
You are pure, without sin from man.

At last, after weary wondering,
You have come to me again,

Darkness of age has settled on your face:
Sinless your life draws near its end.

You are still dear to me, faultless one,
You shall have welcome from me without stint:
You will not let us be drowned in torment;
We will earnestly practise devotion with you.

The lasting world is full of your fame,
Far and wide you have wandered on every track:
If every day we followed your ways,
We should come safe into the presence of dread God.

You leave an example and a bequest
To every one in this world,
You have taught us by your life:
Earnest prayer to God is no fallacy.

Then may God grant us peace and happiness!
May the countenance of the King
Shine brightly upon us
When we leave behind us our withered bodies.

Translated by Kuno Meyer

ST. BRIGID
(Attributed. 10th century)

THE FEAST OF SAINT BRIGID OF KILDARE

I SHOULD like a great lake of ale
For the King of kings;
I should like the family of Heaven
To be drinking it through time eternal.
I should like the viands
Of belief and pure piety;

[47]

I should like the flails
Of penance at my house;
I should like the men of Heaven
In my own house; I should like kieves
Of peace to be at their disposal;
I should like the vessels
Of charity for distribution;
I should like caves
Of mercy for their company;
I should like cheerfulness
To be in their drinking;
I should like Jesus
Too to be here among them;
I should like the Three
Maries of illustrious renown;
I should like the people of Heaven
There from all parts;
I should like that I should be
A rent-payer to the Lord;
That, should I suffer distress,
He would bestow upon me a good blessing.

Translated by Eugene O'Curry

(*Another Version*)

THE HEAVENLY BANQUET

I WOULD like to have the men of Heaven
in my own house;
with vats of good cheer
laid out for them.

I would like to have the three Marys,
their fame is so great.
I would like people
from every corner of Heaven.

I would like them to be cheerful
in their drinking.
I would like to have Jesus, too,
here amongst them.

I would like a great lake of beer
for the King of Kings.
I would like to be watching Heaven's family
drinking it through all eternity.

Translated by Sean O'Faolain

ANONYMOUS
(13th century)

HOSPITALITY IN ANCIENT IRELAND

From the *Leabhar Breac,* or *Speckled Book.* A marginal note.

OH KING of stars!
Whether my house be dark or bright,
Never shall it be closed against any one,
Lest Christ close His house against me.

If there be a guest in your house
And you conceal aught from him,
'Tis not the guest that will be without it,
But Jesus, Mary's Son.

Translated by Kuno Meyer

ANONYMOUS

(11th century)

THE MOTHERS' LAMENT AT THE SLAUGHTER
OF THE INNOCENTS

Then as the executioner plucked her son from her breast one of the women said:

WHY do you tear from me my darling son,
The fruit of my womb?
It was I who bore him,
My breast he drank.
My womb carried him about,
My vitals he sucked,
My heart he filled.
He was my life,
'Tis death to have him taken from me.
My strength has ebbed,
My speech is silenced,
My eyes are blinded.

Then another woman said:

It is my son you take from me.
I did not do the evil,
But kill me—me!
Kill not my son!
My breasts are sapless,
My eyes are wet,
My hands shake,
My poor body totters.
My husband has no son,
And I no strength.
My life is like death.
O my own son, O God!
My youth without reward,
My birthless sicknesses

[50]

Without requital until Doom.
My breasts are silent,
My heart is wrung.

Then said another woman:

Ye are seeking to kill one,
Ye are killing many.
Infants ye slay,
The fathers ye wound,
The mothers ye kill.
Hell with your deed is full,
Heaven is shut,
Ye have spilt the blood of guiltless innocents.

And yet another woman said:

O Christ, come to me!
With my son take my soul quickly!
O great Mary, Mother of God's Son,
What shall I do without my son?
For Thy Son my spirit and sense are killed.
I am become a crazy woman for my son.
After the piteous slaughter
My heart is a clot of blood
From this day till Doom.

Translated by Kuno Meyer

Cf. Sedulius, p. 9.

COLUMCILLE
(Attributed. 11th century)

Columcille, famous Irish Saint, has had many poems ascribed to him, but authorities agree that the majority of poems said to be his are of later origin, probably belonging to the 11th and 12th centuries.

[51]

COLUMCILLE THE SCRIBE

My HAND is weary with writing,
My sharp quill is not steady.
My slender beaked pen pours forth
A black draught of shining dark-blue ink.

A stream of the wisdom of blessed God
Springs from my fair brown shapely hand:
On the page it squirts its draught
Of ink of the green skinned holly.

My little dripping pen travels
Across the plain of shining books,
Without ceasing for the wealth of the great—
Whence my hand is weary with writing.

Translated by Kuno Meyer

RUMANN MAC *COLMAIN*
(Attributed. 11th century)

The original of the following is ascribed to Rumann, who died in 707.

SONG OF THE SEA

A great tempest rages on the Plain of Ler, bold across its high
    borders,
Wind has arisen, fierce winter has slain us; it has come across
    the sea,
It has pierced us like a spear.

When the wind sets from the east, the spirit of the wave is
    roused,

It desires to rush past us westward to the land where sets the
     sun,
To the wild and broad green sea.

When the wind sets from the north, it urges the dark fierce
     waves
Towards the southern world, surging in strife against the wide
     sky,
Listening to the witching song.

When the wind sets from the west across the salt sea of swift
     currents,
It desires to go past us eastward towards the Sun-Tree,
Into the broad long-distant sea.

When the wind sets from the south across the land of Saxons
     of mighty shields,
The wave strikes the Isle of Scit, it surges up to the summit of
     Caladnet,
And pounds the grey-green mouth of the Shannon.

The ocean is in flood, the sea is full, delightful is the home of
     ships,
The wind whirls the sand around the estuary,
Swiftly the rudder cleaves the broad sea.

With mighty force the wave has tumbled across each broad
     river-mouth,
Wind has come, white winter has slain us, around Cantire,
     around the land of Alba,
Slieve-Dremon pours forth a full stream.

Son of the God the Father, with mighty hosts, save me from
     the horror of fierce tempests!
Righteous Lord of the Feast, only save me from the horrid
     blast,
From Hell with furious tempest!

Translated by Kuno Meyer

[53]

ANONYMOUS

(11th century)

THE RUINED NEST

SADLY talks the blackbird here.
Well I know the woe he found:
No matter who cut down his nest,
For its young it was destroyed.

I myself not long ago
Found the woe he now has found.
Well I read thy song, O bird,
For the ruin of thy home.

Thy heart, O blackbird, burnt within
At the deed of reckless man:
Thy nest bereft of young and egg
The cowherd deems a trifling tale.

At thy clear notes they used to come,
Thy new-fledged children, from afar;
No bird now comes from out thy house,
Across its edge the nettle grows.

They murdered them, the cowherd lads,
All thy children in one day:
One the fate to me and thee,
My own children live no more.

There was feeding by thy side
Thy mate, a bird from o'er the sea:
Then the snare entangled her,
At the cowherds' hands she died.

O Thou, the Shaper of the world!
Uneven hands Thou layst on us:

[54]

Our fellows at our side are spared,
Their wives and children are alive.

A fairy host came as a blast
To bring destruction to our house:
Though bloodless was their taking off,
Yet dire as slaughter by the sword.

Woe for our wife, woe for our young!
The sadness of our grief is great:
No trace of them within, without—
And therefore is my heart so sad.

Translated by Kuno Meyer

MAC LIAG

(Attributed. 11th century)

KINCORA

OH, WHERE, Kincora! is Brian the Great?
And where is the beauty that once was thine?
Oh, where are the princes and nobles that sate
At the feast in thy halls, and drank the red wine?
            Where, oh, Kincora?

Oh, where, Kincora! are thy valorous lords?
Oh, whither, thou Hospitable! are they gone?
Oh, where are the Dalcassians of the Golden Swords?
And where are the warriors Brian led on?
            Where, oh, Kincora?

And where is Murrough, the descendant of kings—
The defeater of a hundred—the daringly brave—
Who set but slight store by jewels and rings—
Who swam down the torrent and laughed at its wave?
            Where, oh, Kincora?

[55]

And where is Donogh, King Brian's worthy son?
And where is Conaing, the Beautiful Chief?
And Kian, and Corc? Alas! they are gone—
They have left me this night alone with my grief,
   Left me, Kincora!

And where are the chiefs with whom Brian went forth,
The ne'er vanquished son of Erin the Brave,
The great King of Onaght, renowned for his worth,
And the hosts of Baskinn, from the western wave?
    Where, oh, Kincora?

Oh, where is Duvlann of the swift-footed Steeds?
And where is Kian, who was son of Molloy?
And where is King Lonergan, the fame of whose deeds
In the red battle-field no time can destroy?
    Where, oh, Kincora?

And where is that youth of majestic height,
The faith-keeping Prince of the Scots?—Even he,
As wide as his fame was, as great as was his might,
Was tributary, oh, Kincora, to thee!
    Thee, oh, Kincora!

They are gone, those heroes of royal birth
Who plundered no churches, and broke no trust,
'Tis weary for me to be living on earth
When they, oh, Kincora, lie low in the dust!
    Low, oh, Kincora!

Oh, never again will Princes appear,
To rival the Dalcassians of the Cleaving Swords!
I can never dream of meeting afar or anear,
In the east or the west, such heroes and lords!
    Never, Kincora!

Oh, dear are the images my memory calls up
Of Brian Boru!—how he never would miss

To give me at the banquet the first bright cup!
Ah! why did he heap on me honour like this?
                    Why, oh, Kincora?

I am Mac Liag, and my home is on the Lake;
Thither often, to that palace whose beauty is fled
Came Brian to ask me, and I went for his sake.
Oh, my grief! that I should live, and Brian be dead!
                    Dead, oh, Kincora!
            Translated by James Clarence Mangan

FLANN FIONN
(Attributed. 12th century)

ALDFRID'S ITINERARY THROUGH IRELAND

Among the Anglo-Saxon students resorting to Ireland was Prince Aldfrid, afterwards King of the Northumbrian Saxons. His having been educated in Ireland about the year 684 is corroborated by Venerable Bede in his "Life of Saint Cuthbert." Mangan's translation is very close to the original. Four quatrains of John O'Donovan's literal translation follow for comparison. Prince Aldfrid was known as Flann Fionn while in Ireland.

I FOUND in Innisfail the fair,
In Ireland, while in exile there,
Women of worth, both grave and gay men,
Many clerics and many laymen.

I travelled its fruitful provinces round,
And in every one of the five I found,
Alike in church and in palace hall,
Abundant apparel, and food for all.

Gold and silver I found, and money,
Plenty of wheat and plenty of honey;
I found God's people rich in pity,
Found many a feast and many a city.

[57]

I also found in Armagh, the splendid,
Meekness, wisdom, and prudence blended,
Fasting, as Christ hath recommended,
And noble councillors untranscended.

I found in each great church moreo'er,
Whether on island or on shore,
Piety, learning, fond affection
Holy welcome and kind protection.

I found the good lay monks and brothers
Ever beseeching help for others,
And in their keeping the holy word
Pure as it came from Jesus the Lord.

I found in Munster unfettered of any,
Kings, and queens, and poets a many—
Poets well skilled in music and measure,
Prosperous doings, mirth and pleasure.

I found in Connaught the just, redundance
Of riches, milk in lavish abundance;
Hospitality, vigor, fame,
In Cruachan's land of heroic name.

I found in the country of Connall the glorious,
Bravest heroes, ever victorious;
Fair-complexioned men and warlike,
Ireland's lights, the high, the starlike!

I found in Ulster, from hill to glen,
Hardy warriors, resolute men;
Beauty that bloomed when youth was gone,
And strength transmitted from sire to son.

I found in the noble district of Boyle
    (Ms. here illegible.)

[58]

Brehon's, Erenachs, weapons bright,
And horsemen bold and sudden in fight.

I found in Leinster the smooth and sleek,
From Dublin to Slewmargy's peak;
Flourishing pastures, valor, health,
Long-living worthies, commerce, wealth.

I found, besides, from Ara to Glea,
In the broad rich country of Ossorie,
Sweet fruits, good laws for all and each,
Great chess-players, men of truthful speech.

I found in Meath's fair principality,
Virtue, vigor, and hospitality;
Candor, joyfulness, bravery, purity,
Ireland's bulwark and security.

I found strict morals in age and youth,
I found historians recording truth;
The things I sing of in verse unsmooth,
I found them all—I have written sooth.

Translated by James Clarence Mangan

Following are the first four quatrains of O'Donovan's literal translation from the original:

I found in the fair Inisfail,
In Ireland while in exile,
Many women, no silly crowd,
Many laics, many clerics.

I found in each province
Of the five provinces of Ireland,
Both in Church and State,
Much of food—much of raiment.

I found gold and silver,
I found honey and wheat,

[59]

I found affection with the people of God,
I found banquets, and cities.

I found in Armagh the splendid,
Meekness, wisdom, circumspection,
Fasting in obedience to the Son of God,
Noble, prosperous sages.

THREE POEMS FROM THE "DINNSHENCHAS"

The "Dinnshenchas" is a collection of legends, in Middle-Irish prose and verse, about the names of noteworthy places in Ireland—plains, mountains, ridges, cairns, lakes, rivers, rapids, fords, estuaries, islands and rocks. Several copies of this tract are in the great books of Ireland: *viz.,* The *Lebar Laignech,* or *Book of Leinster,* the *Book of Ballymote,* the *Book of Lecan.* There is a copy, incomplete, in the so-called "Bodleian Dinnshenchas"; another in the library of Trinity College, Dublin; an excellent and much older copy in the town library of Rennes, and there are some fragments of a copy in the Advocates' Library in Edinburgh.

Whitley Stokes says: "As to the date of the Dinnshenchas, O'Curry *Lectures,* p. 108, states that it 'was compiled at Tara about the year 550 A.D.' But this is one of his ludicrous exaggerations. The reference s.v. Laigin, to the 'King of Denmark and the Isles of the Foreigners,' i.e. the Hebrides, points to a period after the year 795 A.D. Dr. Petrie, in *Tara Hill,* p. 105, advised in the matter by the cool-headed O'Donovan, calls the collection 'a compilation of the 12th century,' and philological considerations prove that this is right, though some of the metrical materials may possibly be older. But whatever be their date, the documents as they stand are a storehouse of ancient Irish folklore, absolutely unaffected, so far as I can judge, by any foreign influence."

THE STORY OF MACHA

A story of the origin of the name of Armagh, Ard-Macha, in Ulster. The participants belong in the cycle of Tales of the Red Branch. This version appears in the "Dinnshenchas" of the *Book of Lecan.* The events occur some time in the 1st Century. It is a powerful example of the lore of the Pagan period.

ONE day there came with glowing soul,
    To the assembly of Conchobar,
    The gifted man from the eastern wave,
    Crunn of the flocks, son of Adnoman.

It was then were brought
    Two steeds to which I see no equals,
    Into the race-course, without concealment,
    At which the King of Uladh[1] then presided.

[1] Uladh = Ulster.

[61]

Although there were not the peers of these
  Upon the plain, of a yoke of steeds,
  Crunn, the rash hairy man, said
  That his wife was fleeter, though then pregnant.

Detain ye the truthful man,
  Said Conor, the chief of battles,
  Until his famous wife comes here,
  To nobly run with my great steeds.

Let one man go forth to bring her,
  Said the king of levelled stout spears,
  Till she comes from the wavy sea,
  To save the wise-spoken Crunn.

The woman reached, without delay,
  The assembly of the greatly wondering chiefs.
  Her two names in the west, without question,
  Were Bright Grian and Pure Macha.

Her father was not weak in his house,
  Midir of Bri Leith, son of Celtchar;
  In his mansion in the west,
  She was the sun of women-assemblies.

When she had come—in sobbing words,
  She begged immediately for respite
  From the host of assembled clans,
  Until the time of her delivery was past.

The Ultonians gave their plighted word,
  Should she not run—no idle boast—
  That *he* should not have a prosperous reign
  From the hosts of swords and spears.

Then stript the fleet and silent dame,
  And cast loose her hair around her head,

[62]

And started, without terror or fail,
To join in the race, but not its pleasure.

The steeds were brought to her eastern side,
To urge them past her in manner like;
To the Ultonians of accustomed victory,
The gallant riders were men of kin.

Although the monarch's steeds were swifter
At all times in the native race,
The woman was fleeter, with no great effort,
The monarch's steeds were then the slower.

As she reached the final goal,
And nobly won the ample pledge,
She brought forth twins without delay,
Before the hosts of the Red Branch fort,

A son and a daughter together.
 .   .   .   .
She left a long-abiding curse
On the chiefs of the Red Branch . . .

Translated by Samuel Ferguson

THE ENCHANTED FAWN

The Scribe is about to tell of the deed from which the place name Carn
Mail originated:

PLEASANT is the theme that falls to my care,
The lore not of one spot only,
While my spirit sheds light eastward
On the secret places of the world.

How is it that none of you demands,
If he seek to weave the web of knowledge,

[63]

When came at any time the name
Of Carn Mail in the eastern Plain of Ulaid?

Finally, after many quatrains, the scribe brings in Daire, a handsome and great warrior who had seven sons. This chieftain Daire possessed an enchanted fawn. One day four of Daire's sons loosed their hounds after the fawn. They sped from Tara to the northwest:

Swift fled the fawn before them
As far as the stream by Sinann:
The fawn fell a prey
To the four noble striplings.

The sons of Daire from Dun na n-Eicess
Cast lots gleefully,
That each might know his share
Of the enchanted fawn, without quarrel.

To Lugaid Corb, rough though he was,
There fell the carving of the fawn;
So from him is named the clan
Dal Mess Corb in the region of Cualu.

.   .   .   .

Three quatrains are omitted; they tell of the various tribes which the sons of Daire fathered. And now the princes have eaten of the fawn and are drowsing:

When the men were in the house
Sitting over by the fireside,
There entered a hag, a loathly offence;
She was hideous, unsightly.

Taller was she than a mast upright,
Bigger than a sleeping-hut her ear,
Blacker than any visage her form,
A weight on every heart was the hag.

Broader her row of teeth—what portends it?—
Than a board set with draughtsmen:

[64]

Her nose stood out far before her,
It was longer than a ploughshare.

Bigger than a basket full of sheaves
Was each fist of the mis-natured woman:
Bigger than rough-hewn stone in rampart
Each of her black bony knees.

A paunchy belly she bore, I trow,
Without rib to the armpits:
A scabby black crown with a crop of wens,
Like a furzy hillside, upon her.

She set upon them in the strong house
Where sat the King of Erin's sons;
Dire the dazzlement she cast upon them
From her eyes—alas the deed!

A change fell on the nature of the tender youths
Before that obese lustful horror:
Sooner than look upon her
They had chosen to be buried under earth alive.

Their spirit and senses turned,
With a throb sorer than stark combat:
The sons of Daire gave themselves
Over to a death of shame.

She addressed them with an evil saying:
"One of you must sleep with me to-night,
Or I will devour you all, unaided,
Hound and strong man alike."

When he saw the danger plain,
Lugaid Laigde spoke:
"I will sleep with her—unwelcome task:
Enough for you to lose me only."

[65]

As the firelight fell dim,
  She changed to another wondrous shape:
  She took on a radiant form, beyond praise:
  Rosy she grew, round-bosomed.

Such were her eyes
  (They were no tricks of cheating craft)—
  Three shafts of sunlight in each of them:
  Where her glance fell all was bright.

Down slid the crimson mantle fair
  From her breasts untouched by age,
  Till the flesh-worm might be crushed in the room
  By the light of her lovely body.

Then the young man asked her,
  "Fair maiden, whence comest thou?
  Name thy race, tell it now,
  Speak to me, hide it not from me!"

I will tell thee, gentle youth;
  With me sleep the High Kings:
  I, the tall slender maiden,
  Am the Kingship of Alba¹ and Erin.

"To thee have I revealed myself this night,
  Yet nothing more shall come of our meeting;
  The son thou shalt have, he it is
  That I shall sleep with—happier fate.". . .

                    Translated by Edward Gwynn

The poem ends with the woman foretelling the son's name and deeds.
Perhaps her appearance as a character in this episode is a manifestation of
the Old Woman of Beare?

¹ Alba = Scotland.

TARA

Tara, Temuri, Temair or Temrach was the palace of the monarchs of Ireland down to the reign of Diarmaid, son of Fergus Cerrbel, when it was deserted because it fell under the curses of two saints, one of whom had been compelled by the king to surrender a murderer to justice. The derivation of the name is described in the Bodleian "Dinnshenchas:" "Temuri, then, to wit, the *muir* 'rampart' of Tea, daughter of Lugaid, son of Ith, when she went with Geide the Loud-voiced. In his reign everyone in Erin deemed another's voice sweeter than strings of lutes would be, because of the greatness of the peace and quiet and the good will and friendship that each man had for the other in Ireland. Therefore, then, is Tea-mur more venerable than every rampart, and nobler than every heritor is its heritor, because the covenants of Tea, daughter of Lugaid, son of Ith, to Gede the Loud-voiced, were the first free covenants that were given in Erin." Or, according to another version, Tea, wife of Erimon, son of Mil of Spain, was buried therein." Whitley Stokes.

Praising Tara the Scribe begins:

TEMAIR noblest of hills,
    Under which is Erin of the forays,
    The lofty city of Cormac son of Art,
    Son of mighty Conn of the Hundred Fights.

Cormac, constant was his prosperity,
    He was sage, he was poet, he was prince;
    He was a true judge of the men of Fene.
    He was a friend, he was a comrade.

Cormac, who gained fifty fights,
    Disseminated the Psalter of Temair;
    In this Psalter there is
    All the best we have of history.

He describes the ancient site of the palace of the High Kings Of Ireland:

This world, transient its splendor!
    Perishable gathering of an hundred hosts;
    Deceitful to describe is the multitude of delights,
    Save only the adoration of the King of all things.

Perished is every law concerning high fortune,
    Crumbled to the clay is every ordinance;

[67]

Tara, though she be desolate to-day,
Once on a time was the habitation of heroes.

There was no exhaustion of her many-sided towers,
Where was the assembly of storied troops;
Many were the bands whose home was
The green-soiled grassy keep.

It was a stronghold of famous men and sages,
A castle like a trunk with warrior-scions,
A ridge conspicuous to view,
In the time of Cormac grandson of Conn.

Fair is the title that adorns it.

When Cormac was among the famous
Bright shone the fame of his career;
No keep like Temair could be found;
She was the secret place of the road of life.

He describes the various buildings, graves, etc.:

Let us consider too the Hall of the Heroes
Which is called the Palace of Vain Women;
The House of the Warriors, it was no mean hall,
With fourteen doors.

The Mound of the Women after their betrayal
Was hard by the upper structure;
South of it are Dall and Dorcha,
They were bowed down both alike.

Dall is south-west of sad Dorcha,
From them was called Duma Dall-Bodra;
Each of them killed the other
In fighting over their alms.

The dwarf came, to his sorrow,
To interpose between them,

[68]

So they killed the dwarf under their feet,
Through their dimness of sight.

Westward from the Grave of this dwarf
Are Mael Bloc, and Bluicne—foolish their wisdom!
Over them are the three stones
That the Prince of great Macha flung.

He explains the origin of the flour mill within the fortress:

Ciarnait, hand-maid of upright Cormac,
Used to feed from her quern many hundreds,
Ten measures a day she had to grind,
It was no task for an idler.

The noble king came upon her at her task
All alone in her house,
And got her with child privily;
Presently she was unable for heavy grinding.

Thereupon the grandson of Conn took pity on her,
He brought a mill-wright over the wide sea;
The first mill of Cormac mac Art
Was a help to Ciarnait.

He describes the great house of Tara. In treating of its law of hospitality
he tells how the portions of meat are allotted to the retainers, visitors, etc.
according to their stations in life:

The House of Temair, round which is the rath,
From it was given to each his due;
Honour still continues to such as them
At the courts of kings and princes.

King and Chief of the Poets,
Sage farmer, they received their due,
Couches that torches burn not,
The thighs and the chine-steaks.

[69]

Leech and spencer, stout smith,
  Steward, portly butler,
  The heads of the beasts to all of them
  In the house of the yellow-haired king.

Engraver, famed architect,
  Shield-maker, and keen soldier,
  In the king's house they drank a cup;
  This was the special right of their hands.

Jester, chess-player, sprawling buffoon,
  Piper, cheating juggler,
  The shank was their share of meat in truth,
  When they came into the king's house.

The shins were the share of the noble musician,
  Of the castle-builder and artificer, round the bowl,
  The cup-bearer, the lusty foot-servant,
  Both consumed the broken meats.

A charge on the prince of Meath,
  Were the cobblers and comb-makers,
  The due of the strong skilled folk
  Was the fat underside of the shoulder.

The backs, the chines in every dwelling
  Were given to druids and doorkeepers.
  There was protection for maidens with never an "ach"!
  After serving the house of Tara.

The scribe ends, recalling the ruin:

The faith of Christ who suffered in the flesh
  Has brought all strength to nought;
  Because of the sorrow of the people of God in its house
  He gave not protection to Temair.

                    Translated by Edward Gwynn

MYTHOLOGICAL CYCLE: THREE POEMS
(12th century)

THE SEA-GOD'S ADDRESS TO BRAN

The most important role Manannan fills in Irish legend is that of King of the Land of Promise, sometimes called Magh Mell, Tir na n-Og, etc. Both Bran and Manannan are connected in the Oversea Voyage Tales with this elysium. Bran and Manannan are Bendigeid Vran and Manawyddan in Welsh legend. Kuno Meyer writes: "The tale 'The Voyage of Bran Son of Febel to the Land of the Living,' was probably first written down early in the eighth, perhaps late in the seventh, century." It is one of the anonymous Imramba, or voyages in the *Book of Leinster.*

Bran went upon the sea. When he had been at sea two days and two nights, he saw a man in a chariot coming towards him over the sea. It was Manannan Mac Lir (the Ocean God), who sang these quatrains to Bran.

To BRAN in his coracle it seems
A marvellous beauty across the clear sea:
To me in my chariot from afar
It is a flowery plain on which he rides.

What is clear sea
For the prowed skiff in which Bran is,
That to me in my chariot of two wheels
Is a delightful plain with a wealth of flowers.

Bran sees
A mass of waves beating across the clear sea:
I see myself in the Plain of Sports,
Red-headed flowers that have no flaw.

Sea-horses glisten in summer
As far as Bran can stretch his glance:
Rivers pour forth a stream of honey
In the land of Manannan, son of Ler.

The sheen of the main on which thou art,
The dazzling white of the sea on which thou rowest about
Yellow and azure are spread out,
It is a light and airy land.

[71]

Speckled salmon leap from the womb
Out of the white sea on which thou lookest:
They are calves, they are lambs of fair hue,
With truce, without mutual slaughter.

Though thou seest but one chariot-rider
In the Pleasant Plain of many flowers,
There are many steeds on its surface,
Though thou dost not see them.

Large is the plain, numerous is the host,
Colours shine with pure glory:
A white stream of silver, stairs of gold
Afford a welcome with all abundance.

An enchanting game, most delicious,
They play over the luscious wine:
Men and gentle women under a bush
Without sin, without transgression.

Along the top of a wood
Thy coracle has swum across ridges:
There is a wood laden with beautiful fruit
Under the prow of thy little skiff.

A wood with blossom and with fruit
On which is the vine's veritable fragrance,
A wood without decay, without defect,
On which is foliage of golden hue.

From the beginning of creation we are
Without old age, without consummation of clay:
Hence we expect not there should be frailty—
The sin has not come to us.

An evil day when the serpent came
To the father into his citadel!

He has perverted the ages in this world,
So that there came decay which was not original.

By greed and lust he has slain us,
Whereby he has ruined his noble race:
The withered body has gone to the fold of torment,
An everlasting abode of torture.

It is a law of pride in this world
To believe in the creatures, to forget God:
Overthrow by diseases, and old age,
Destruction of the beguiled soul.

A noble salvation will come
From the King who has created us:
A white law will come over seas—
Besides being God, He will be man.

.   .   .

Steadily then let Bran row!
It is not far to the Land of Women:
Evna with manifold bounteousness
He will reach before the sun is set.

Translated by Kuno Meyer

THE HOSTS OF FAERY

Magh Mell—the invisible world, land of the unseen—was usually separated from human life by water, a lake or an ocean, which by some means had to be crossed. In Pagan days the Celt in Ireland visualized several fairy lands: Tir na n-Og, the Country of Youth; Tír Tairngiri, the Country of Promise; Magh Argatonél, the Silver Cloud Plain; and Magh Mell, the Plain of Honey, etc. Magh Mell is conceived either as existant on an island, or islands, or as a fair, flowery plain visible only to eyes opened under the waves of the sea. The following poem is from the tale "Laegaire mac Crimthainn's Visit to the Fairy Realm of Mag Mell."

WHITE shields they carry in their hands,
With emblems of pale silver;
With glittering blue swords,
With mighty stout horns.

[73]

In well-devised battle array,
Ahead of their fair chieftain
They march amid blue spears,
Pale-visaged, curly-headed bands.

They scatter the battalions of the foe,
They ravage every land they attack,
Splendidly they march to combat,
A swift, distinguished, avenging host!

No wonder though their strength be great:
Sons of queens and kings are one and all;
On their heads are
Beautiful golden-yellow manes.

With smooth comely bodies,
With bright blue-starred eyes,
With pure crystal teeth,
With thin red lips.

Good they are at man-slaying,
Melodious in the ale-house,
Masterly at making songs,
Skilled at playing chess.

Translated by Kuno Meyer

SONG OF THE FAIRIES

There are several stories connected with Etain the Goddess who married a mortal. The stories have become confused with repetition through centuries. The tales deal with the Dedanann personages though the style is that of the Cuchulain series. The composition is of about the same period. There is an extract of the tale in the *Book of the Dun Cow*.

Midir, the "Very Proud One," who dwelt at the fairy mound of Bri-Leith, is chiefly known as the husband of Etain the goddess, who became a mortal and was wedded to Eochaid, King of Ireland. In her human state, Midir still loves Etain and watches over her. Finally he wins her back. She is the stake in a game of chess played with Eochaid.

This song from *The Wooing of Etain*, is sung by the fairies when they are building a causeway across the bog of Lamrach. This task is one that Eochaid asks the fairy-king, Midir, to perform when he loses at chess.

[74]

PILE on the soil; thrust on the soil;
Red are the oxen around who toil:
Heavy the troops that my words obey;
Heavy they seem, and yet men are they
Strongly, as piles, are the tree-trunks placed:
Red are the wattles above them laced:
Tired are your hands, and your glances slant;
One woman's winning this toil may grant!

Oxen ye are, but revenge shall see;
Men who are white shall your servants be;
Rushes from Teffa are cleared away;
Grief is the price that the man shall pay:
Stones have been cleared from the rough Meath ground;
Where shall the gain or the harm be found?
Thrust it in hand! Force it in hand!
Nobles this night, as an ox-troop, stand;
Hard is the task that is asked, and who
From the bridging of Lamrach shall gain, or rue?

Translated by A. H. Leahy

THE RED BRANCH CYCLE: THREE POEMS
(12th century)

The cycle of tales relating the deeds of the Red Branch heroes forms the most interesting literary relic of Ireland. They are in prose, but interspersed are long poems and lyrics which date from a very early time. The stories deal with a group of heroes called "The Champions of the Red Branch," so named from one of their halls of assembly. The chief hero was Cuchulain, (pronounced—koo-hoo-lin) The Hound of Ulster, or The Hound, whose prowess showed itself in his early youth, and whose courage and powers were so extraordinary that, in the long and archaic tale which forms the center and pivot of the series, he is shown as holding at bay single-handed the allied forces of Ireland. He was at this time but a youth. The "Tain bo Cuailnge," or "The Cattle Raid of Cooley," the central tale, is the great epic of Ireland. It is far removed from the cattle drive of ancient life. The tale takes the form of a chronicle of mythological warfare in which gods and god-like heroes struggle for mastery.

The earliest written version of the "Tain bo Cuailnge" is said to be in part in the language of the 7th or 8th century, while the lengthy tales dealing with Finn and the Fianna, or Ossianic cycle, are of much later origin. The Tain versions are preserved in vellum books known as the *Leabhar na h-Uidhre,* or *The Book of the Dun Cow,* written or copied at Clonmacnois towards the end of the tenth century A.D.; the *Yellow Book of Lecan,* compiled late in the fourteenth century, and the *Book of Leinster,* compiled in the twelfth century. All of these books were compiled from older manuscripts.

The heroes were supposed to have been active during the reign of King Conor, or Conchobhar mac Nessa, reigned B.C. 30 to A.D. 30 or 33 (*Annals of Tigernach*), who is said to have died of grief and fury at the news that Christ had been crucified.

Conor, King of Ulster, was rival of Meave (pronounced Māve), warrior Queen of Connaught. Fergus mac Roy, Conor's stepfather, was the true King, but had submitted to his wife's blandishments and so allowed her son, Conor, to take his place. But Deirdre, a beautiful virgin, educated by Conor for his pleasure, eloped with a handsome youth Naoisi to Scotland, where later Fergus sought them, bringing with him Conor's pardon. But upon their return to Ireland Conor had Naoisi and his brothers murdered and seized Deirdre. Fergus took up arms, as well to regain his crown as to avenge the abuse of his safe-conduct, but Cuchulain and the principal chiefs, faithful to Conor, caused Fergus to take refuge with Meave of Connaught. In the story of Deirdre (that of "The Death of the Sons of Usnagh") she remains with Conor for a year, pining. Conor, tiring of Deirdre's sadness, gives her to one of his henchmen for his pleasure, but on the way to the man's house she throws herself from the chariot and is killed.

The poems which follow are from the middle Irish version of the tale of "The Sons of Usnagh."

DEIRDRE'S FAREWELL TO ALBA

FAREWELL to fair Alba, high house of the sun,
Farewell to the mountain, the cliff, and the dun;
Dun Sweeny, adieu! for my love cannot stay,
And tarry I may not when love cries away.

Glen Vashan! Glen Vashan! where roebucks run free,
Where my love used to feast on the red deer with me,
Where rocked on thy waters while stormy winds blew,
My love used to slumber—Glen Vashan, adieu!

Glendaro! Glendaro! where birchen boughs weep
Honey dew at high noon o'er the nightingale's sleep,
Where my love used to lead me to hear the cuckoo
'Mong the high hazel bushes—Glendaro, adieu!

[76]

Glen Urchy! Glen Urchy! where loudly and long
My love used to wake up the woods with his song,
While the son of the rock, from the depths of the dell,
Laughed sweetly in answer—Glen Urchy, farewell!

Glen Etive! Glen Etive! where dappled does roam,
Where I leave the green sheeling I first called a home;
Where with me and my true love delighted to dwell,
The sun made his mansion—Glen Etive, farewell!

Farewell to Inch Draynach, adieu to the roar
Of the blue billows bursting in light on the shore;
Dun Fiagh, farewell! for my love cannot stay,
And tarry I may not when love cries away.

Translated by Samuel Ferguson

(Another Version)

DEIRDRE'S FAREWELL TO SCOTLAND

A BELOVED land is yon land in the east,
Alba with its marvels.
I would not have come hither out of it,
Had I not come with Naoisi.[1]

Beloved are Dun Fidga and Dun Finn,
Beloved is the fortress above them,
Beloved is the Isle of the Thorn-Bush,
And beloved is Dun Sweeny.

Caill Cuan!
Unto which Ainnle would go, alas!
Short we thought the time there,
Naoisi and I in the land of Alba.

Glen Lay!
There I used to sleep under a shapely rock.

---

[1] Also spelled Noisi, Naisa and Neesa.

Fish and venison and badger's fat,
That was my portion in Glen Lay.

Glen Massan!
Tall is its wild garlic, white are its stalks:
We used to have a broken sleep
On the grassy river-mouth of Massan.

Glen Etive!
There I raised my first house.
Delightful its wood! when we rose in the morning
A sunny cattle-fold was Glen Etive.

Glen Urchain!
That was the straight, fair-ridged glen!
Never was man of his age prouder
Than Naoisi in Glen Urchain.

Glen da Ruadh!
Hail to him who hath it as an heritage!
Sweet is the cuckoo's voice on bending branch
On the peak above Glen Da Ruadh.

Beloved is Draighen over a firm beach!
Beloved its water in pure sand!
I would never have left it, from the east,
Had I not come with my beloved.

Translation by Whitley Stokes, with
minor corrections by Kuno Meyer

DEIRDRE'S LAMENT FOR THE SONS OF USNAGH

THE lions of the hill are gone,
And I am left alone—alone—
Dig the grave both wide and deep,
For I am sick, and fain would sleep!

The falcons of the wood are flown,
And I am left alone—alone—
Dig the grave both deep and wide,
And let us slumber side by side.

The dragons of the rock are sleeping,
Sleep that wakes not for our weeping:
Dig the grave, and make it ready;
Lay me on my true-love's body.

Lay their spears and bucklers bright
By the warriors' sides aright;
Many a day the three before me
On their linked bucklers bore me.

Lay upon the low grave floor,
'Neath each head, the blue claymore;
Many a time the noble three
Reddened these blue blades for me.

Lay the collars, as is meet,
Of their greyhounds at their feet;
Many a time for me have they
Brought the tall red deer to bay.

In the falcon's jesses throw
Hook and arrow, line and bow;
Never again by stream or plain
Shall the gentle woodsmen go.

Sweet companions ye were ever—
Harsh to me, your sister, never;
Woods and wilds and misty valleys
Were, with you, as good's a palace.

Oh! to hear my true love singing,
Sweet as sound of trumpets ringing:

Like the sway of ocean swelling
Rolled his deep voice round our dwelling.

Oh! to hear the echoes pealing
Round our green and fairy sheeling,
When the three, with soaring chorus,
Passed the silent skylark o'er us.

Echo, now sleep, morn and even—
Lark alone enchant the heaven!—
Ardan's lips are scant of breath,
Neesa's tongue is cold in death.

Stag, exult on glen and mountain—
Salmon, leap from loch to fountain—
Heron, in the free air warm ye—
Usnagh's sons no more will harm ye!

Erin's stay no more you are,
Rulers of the ridge of war;
Never more 'twill be your fate
To keep the beam of battle straight.

Woe is me! by fraud and wrong—
Traitors false and tyrants strong—
Fell Clan Usnagh, bought and sold,
For Barach's feast and Conor's gold!

Woe to Eman, roof and wall!—
Woe to Red Branch, hearth and hall!—
Tenfold woe and black dishonor
To the foul and false Clan Conor!

Dig the grave both wide and deep,
Sick I am, and fain would sleep!
Dig the grave and make it ready,
Lay me on my true love's body!

Translated by Samuel Ferguson

DEIRDRE'S LAMENT

LONG is the day without Usnagh's Children;
It was not mournful to be in their company.
A king's sons, by whom exiles were rewarded,
Three lions from the Hill of the Cave.

Three Dragons of Dun Monidh,
The three champions from the Red Branch:
After them I shall not live—
Three that used to break every onrush.

Three darlings of the women of Britain,
Three hawks of Slieve Gullion
Sons of a king whom valor served,
To whom soldiers used to give homage.

Three heroes who were not good at homage,
Their fall is cause of sorrow—
Three sons of Cathba's daughter,
Three props of the battle-host of Coolney.

Three vigorous bears,
Three lions out of Liss Una,
Three lions who loved their praise,
Three pet sons of Ulster.

That I should remain after Naoisi
Let no one in the world suppose!
After Ardan and Ainnle
My time would not be long.

Ulster's over-king, my first husband,
I forsook for Naoisi's love:
Short my life after them,
I will perform their funeral game.

[81]

After them I will not be alive—
Three that would go into every conflict,
Three who liked to endure hardships,
Three heroes who never refused combat.

O man that diggest the tomb,
And that puttest my darling from me,
Make not the grave too narrow,
I shall be beside the noble ones.

Translated by Whitley Stokes with some
minor corrections by Kuno Meyer

THE COMBAT OF FERDIAD AND CUCHULAIN

When the Tain begins we find Fergus, who has sought sanctuary in Connaught, being induced by Meave and her consort, Ailell, to take command of her army against his own people. Meave is jealous because the great bull of her herds has gone over to the herds of her husband, and therefore to be the better man, she wishes to gain possession of the most famous bull in the land, the Dond. She lays plans to get the Dond of Cuailnge by fair means or by foul, and thus the Great Cattle Spoil is conceived:

Cuchulain, the hero, and main actor in this drama, is possessed of human and superhuman powers. He is the offspring of Lugh, the Irish sun-god, and he inherits the capacities belonging to his divine origin. (He acquired his name at the age of six years in slaying the terrible watchdog of Culann the Smith.) Meave and the united hosts of Ireland, under the direction of Fergus, march into Eastern Ulster to gain possession of the Brown Bull of Cooley; they are stopped single-handed by Cuchulain. The unwillingness of Fergus to aid Meave against his country, his affection for his foster-son Cuchulain and his efforts to spare and aid him, form one of the subordinate but important themes of the tragedy.

In one of the most touching and tragic episodes in the Tain, Ferdiad (*pr.* Ferdia), former companion and schoolmate of Cuchulain, is pressed by Meave to give battle to Cuchulain. He finally agrees, and the heroes are to meet at the ford (later called Ferdiad's Ford). The morning of the combat arrives and Ferdiad is sleeping. He is wakened by his gilla, or servant, who touches him:

" 'Ferdiad, master,' said the youth, 'rise up! They are here to meet thee at the ford.' Then Ferdiad arose and girt his body in his war-dress of battle and combat. And the gilla spake these words:

'THE roll of a chariot,
Its fair yoke of silver;
A man great and stalwart
O'ertops the strong car!

[82]

O'er Bri Ross, o'er Brane
Their swift path they hasten;
Past Old-tree Town's tree-stump,
   Victorious they speed!

A sly Hound that driveth,
A fair chief that urgeth,
A free hawk that speedeth
   His steeds towards the south!
Gore-coloured, the Cua,[1]
'Tis sure he will take us;
We know—vain to hide it—
   He brings us defeat!

Woe him on the hillock,
The brave Hound before him;
Last year I foretold it,
   That sometime he'd come!
Hound from Emain Macha,
Hound formed of all colours,
The Border-hound, War-hound,
   I hear what I've heard!' "

In respite from their combat the heroes kiss, in memory of their earlier affection:

"Thereupon each of them went toward the other in the middle of the ford, and each of them put his hand on the other's neck and gave him three kisses in remembrance of his fellowship and friendship.

Finally Ferdiad is slain by Cuchulain and Cuchulain utters these words:

'All was play, all was sport,
Till came Ferdiad to the ford!
  One task for both of us,
    Equal our reward.
    Our kind, gentle nurse
    Chose him over all!

All was play, all was sport,
Till came Ferdiad to the ford!

[1] Nickname for Cuchulain.

[83]

One our life, one our fear,
　　One our skill in arms,
　　Shields gave Scatach twain
　　To Ferdiad and me!

All was play, all was sport,
Till came Ferdiad to the ford!
　　Dear the shaft of gold
　　I smote on the ford.
　　Bull-chief of the tribes,
　　Braver he than all!

Only games and only sport,
Till came Ferdiad to the ford!
Lion, furious, flaming, fierce;
Swollen wave that wrecks like doom!

Only games and only sport,
Till came Ferdiad to the ford!
Lovéd Ferdiad seemed to me
After me would live for aye!
Yesterday, a mountain's size—
He is but a shade to-day!

Three things countless on the Tain
Which have fallen by my hand:
Hosts of cattle, men and steeds,
I have slaughtered on all sides!

Though the hosts were e'er so great,
That came out of Cruachan wild,
More than third and less than half,
Slew I in my direful sport!

Never trod in battle's ring;
Banba nursed not on her breast:
Never sprang from sea or land,
King's son that had larger fame!'

"Thus far the Combat of Ferdiad with Cuchulain and the Tragical death of Ferdiad."

Towards the end of the epic in the part entitled "The Decision of the Battle," one of the strange and horrible Goddesses of war, the Morrigan, appears:

"It was on that night that the Morrigan, daughter of Ernmas, came, and she was engaged in fomenting strife and sowing dissension between the two camps on either side, and she spoke these words in the twilight between the two encampments:

'Ravens shall pick
The necks of men!
Blood shall gush
    In combat wild!
Skins shall be hacked;
Crazed with spoils!
    Men's sides pierced
In Battle brave,
Luibnech near!
Warriors' storm;
Mien of braves;
Cruachan's man!
    Upon them comes
Ruin complete!
Lines shall be strewn
Under foot;
Their race die out!
Then Ulster hail:
To Erna woe
To Ulster woe:
    Then Erna hail!' "

Night passed: "Then, when the sun arose, Cuchulain saw the kings from the east putting their crowns on their heads and relieving their men-at-arms. Cuchulain told his charioteer to awaken the men of Ulster. Laeg (Cuchulain's charioteer) came and roused the men of Ulster to battle:

'Arise, ye kings of Macha,
Valiant in your deeds!
Imbel's kine the Badb doth cover:
Blood of hearts pours out!
Goodly heroes' battle rushes in

[85]

With deeds of valour!
Hearts all red with gore:
Brows turned in flight.
Dismay of battle riseth.
For there was never found
One like unto Cuchulain,
Hound that Macha's weal doth work!
It is for Cualnge's kine,
Let them not arise!' "

The battle ends with Meave's forces put to rout. "Then when the battle
had been lost, Fergus began to view the host as it went westwards of Ath
Mor." . . . Fergus concludes his speech to Meave thus: " 'And even as a
brood-mare leads her foals into a land unknown, without a head to advise
or give counsel before them, such is the plight of this host today in the
train of a woman that hath ill counselled them.' "

The long and dramatic story is concluded by "The Battle of the Bulls,"
the Brown Bull tearing the White Bull to pieces which he strews over the
land; he then turns on the people of Cuailnge fiercely, finally his heart
bursts and he dies of sorrow. The death of both these terrible supernatural
beasts is told with extraordinary power.

At the end of the Irish text the scribe who had copied the *Tain* adds a
note in Irish. "A blessing be upon all such as shall faithfully keep the Tain
in memory as it stands here, and shall not add any other form to it." He
follows up with a note in Latin: "I, however, who have copied this history,
or more truly legend, give no credence to various incidents narrated in it.
For, some things herein are the feats of jugglery of demons, sundry others
poetic figments, a few are probable, others improbable, and even more in-
vented for the delectation of fools."

Translated by Joseph Dunn

ANONYMOUS

(12th century)

THE TESTAMENT OF CATHAEIR MOR

This is one of the most interesting relics connected with Irish literature. The poetical version was authorized by The Royal Irish Academy, and Mangan worked from the literal translation of John O'Donovan. It is from the *Book of Rights*, which O'Donovan translated. Of this "Will" O'Donovan wrote: "It was drawn up in its present form (verse etc.) some centuries after the death of Cathaeir Mor, when the race of his more illustrious sons had definite territories in Leinster." Cathaeir Mor was King of Ireland in the 2nd century. *The Book of Rights* was compiled about the end of the 11th century. See *Transactions of the Royal Irish Academy* for 1849.

HERE is the Will of Cathaeir Mor
     GOD REST HIM.
Among his heirs he divided his store,
    His treasures and lands,
    And, first, laying hands
On his son Ross Faly, he blessed him.

"My Sovereign Power, my nobleness,
My wealth, my strength to curse and bless,
My royal privilege of protection,
I leave to the son of my best affection,
Ross Faly, Ross of the Rings,
Worthy descendant of Ireland's Kings!
To serve as memorials of succession
For all who yet shall claim their possession
    In after-ages.
Clement and noble and bold
    Is Ross, my son.
Then, let him not hoard up silver and gold,
   But give unto all fair measure of wages.
Victorious in battle he ever hath been;
   He therefore shall yield the green
And glorious plains of Tara to none,
    No, not to his brothers!

[87]

Yet these shall he aid
When attacked or betrayed.
This blessing of mine shall outlast the tomb,
  And live till the Day of Doom,
    Telling and telling daily,
And a prosperous man beyond all others
    Shall prove Ross Faly!"

Then he gave him ten shields, and ten rings, and ten swords,
And ten drinking-horns; and he spake him those words.
    "Brightly shall shine the glory,
      O Ross, of thy sons and heirs,
    Never shall flourish in story
      Such heroes as they and theirs!"

Then, laying his royal hand on the head
Of his good son, Darry, he blessed him and said:—
    "My Valour, my daring, my martial courage,
    My skill in the field I leave to Darry,
    That he be a guiding Torch and·starry
Light and Lamp to the hosts of our age.
A hero to sway, to lead and command,
Shall be every son of his tribes in the land!
O Darry, with boldness and power
      Sit thou on the frontier of Tuath Laighean,[1]
    And ravage the lands of Deas Ghabhair.[2]
Accept no gifts for thy protection
      From woman or man.
    So shall Heaven assuredly bless
    Thy many daughters with fruitfulness,
      And none shall stand above thee,—
      For I, thy sire, who love thee
        With deep and warm affection,
      I prophesy unto thee all success
        Over the green battalions
        Of the redoubtable Galions." [3]

[1] Laighean = North Leinster.
[2] South Leinster.
[3] Leinstermen.

And he gave him, thereon, as memorials and meeds,
Eight bondsmen, eight handmaids, eight cups, and eight steeds.

The noble Monarch of Erin's men
Spake thus to the young Prince Brassal, then:—
"My Sea, with all its wealth of streams,
I leave to my sweetly-speaking Brassal,
To serve and to succour him as a vassal—
    And the lands whereon the bright sun beams
Around the waves of Amergin's Bay
As parcelled out in the ancient day:
By free men through a long, long time
    Shall this thy heritage be enjoyed—
    But the chieftaincy shall at last be destroyed,
Because of a Prince's crime.
And though others again shall regain it,
    Yet Heaven shall not bless it,
    For Power shall oppress it,
And Weakness and Baseness shall stain it!"

And he gave him six ships, and six steeds, and six shields,
    Six mantles and six coats of steel—
And six royal oxen that wrought in his fields,
    Those gave he to Brassal the Prince for his weal.

Then to Catach he spake:—
    "My border lands
Thou, Catach, shalt take,
    But ere long they shall pass from thy hands,
        And by thee shall none
        Be ever begotten, daughter or son!"

To Fearghus Luascan spake he thus:—
    "Thou Fearghus, also, art one of us,
But over-simple in all thy ways,
And babblest much of thy childish days.
For thee have I nought, but if lands may be bought

[89]

Or won hereafter by sword or lance,
     Of those, perchance,
I may leave thee a part,
All simple babbler and boy as thou art!"

Young Fearghus, therefore, was left bereaven,
And thus the Monarch spake to Creeven:—

  "To my boyish Hero, my gentle Creeven,
Who loveth in Summer, at morn and even,
  To snare the songful birds of the field,
  But shunneth to look on spear and shield,
I have little to give of all that I share.
His fame shall fail, his battles be rare.
And of all the Kings that shall wear his crown
But one alone shall win renown."

And he gave him six cloaks, and six cups, and seven steeds,
And six harnessed oxen, all fresh from the meads.

But on Aenghus Nic, a younger child,
  Begotten in crime and born in woe,
The father frowned, as on one defiled,
  And with louring brow he spake him so:—

  "To Nic, my son, that base-born youth,
  Shall nought be given of land or gold;
  He may be great and good and bold,
  But his birth is an agony all untold,
Which gnaweth him like a serpent's tooth.
      I am no donor
        To him or his race—
      His birth was dishonor;
       His life is disgrace!"

And thus he spake to Eochy Timin,
Deeming him fit but to herd with women:—

"Weak son of mine, thou shalt not gain
Waste or water, valley or plain.
From thee shall none descend save cravens,
    Sons of sluggish sires and mothers,
        Who shall live and die,
But give no corpses to the ravens!
        Mine ill thought and mine evil eye
    On thee beyond thy brothers
        Shall ever, ever lie!"

And to Oilioll Cadach his words were those:—
    "O Oilioll, great in coming years
Shall be thy fame among friends and foes
    As the first of Brughaidhs[4] and Hospitaliers!
        But neither noble nor warlike
            Shall show thy renownless dwelling;
                Nevertheless
                Thou shalt dazzle at chess,
            Therein supremely excelling
        And shining like somewhat starlike!"

And his chess-board, therefore, and chessmen eke,
He gave to Oilioll Cadach the Meek.

Now Fiacha,—youngest son was he,—
    Stood up by the bed . . . of his father, who said,
        The while, caressing
            Him tenderly:—
        "My son! I have only for thee my blessing,
            And nought beside—
            Hadst best abide
With thy brothers a time, as thine years are green."

Then Fiacha wept, with a sorrowful mien;
    So, Cathaeir spake, to encourage him, gaily,
        With cheerful speech—
        "Abide one month with thy brethren each,

4 Public victualers.

[91]

And seven years long with my son, Ross Faly.
    Do this, and thy sire, in sincerity,
    Prophesies unto thee fame and prosperity."

And further he spake, as one inspired:—
"A Chieftain flourishing, feared, and admired,
    Shall Fiacha prove!
The gifted Man from the boiling Berve[5]
Him shall his brothers' clansmen serve,
His forts shall be Aillin and proud Almain,
    He shall reign in Carman and Allen;
The highest renown shall his palaces gain
    When others have crumbled and fallen.
His power shall broaden and lengthen,
    And never know damage or loss;
The impregnable Naas he shall strengthen,
    And govern in Ailbhe and Arriged Ross.
Yes! O Fiacha, Foe of strangers,
    This shall be thy lot!
    And thou shalt pilot
Ladhrann[6] and Leeven with steady and even
Heart and arm through storm and dangers!
    Overthrown by the mighty hand
      Shall the Lords of Tara lie.
    And Taillte's fair, the first in the land,
      Thou, son, shalt magnify;
And many a country thou yet shalt bring
To own thy rule as Ceann and King.
    The blessing I give thee shall rest
      On thee and thy seed
        While Time shall endure,
    Thou grandson of Fiacha the Blest!
      It is barely thy meed,
        For thy soul is childlike and pure!

Here ends the Will of Cathaeir Mor, who was King of Ireland.
       Translated by James Clarence Mangan

[5] River Barrow.
[6] Forts on the eastern coast of Ireland.

ANONYMOUS

(12th century)

ON THE DEFEAT OF RAGNALL BY MURROUGH KING OF LEINSTER A.D. 994

YE people of great Murrough,
Against whom neither forest nor wild moor prevails,
Ye that before your Norse battle-standards of sunbright satin
Have routed the heathen hordes as far as the Boyne!
Blood breaks like snowflakes from their noses
As they flee across Aughty in the late evening.

Translated by Kuno Meyer

MacCONGLINNE

(12th century)

The "Vision of MacConglinne" is, as Professor Wollner shows in his introduction to Kuno Meyer's translation of the tale, the production of a twelfth-century Irish gleeman, who worked up a number of older folktales into a biting and rollicking satire against his natural enemies, the clergy. The folk tales are genuinely Irish, and owe nothing to the Continental versions of a Land of Cokaygne. These Irish tales were of a country of Guzzledom where lived a race of gluttonous giants, who have their homes by tanks of new milk, amid mountains of butter and lard. The hero of the "Vision," through his visit to the land of plenty, is enabled to outwit the demon of voracity, who had taken up his quarters inside the King of Munster, and who had already devoured three-fourths of the substance of Ireland. The author is considered a worthy predecessor of Rabelais.

A VISION THAT APPEARED TO ME

A VISION that appeared to me,
An apparition wonderful
        I tell to all:
There was a coracle all of lard
Within a port of New-milk Lake
        Upon the world's smooth sea.

[93]

We went into that man-of-war,
'Twas warrior-like to take the road
      O'er ocean's heaving waves.
Our oar-strokes then we pulled
Across the level of the main,
Throwing the sea's harvest up
      Like honey, the sea-soil.

The fort we reached was beautiful,
With works of custards thick,
      Beyond the lake.
Fresh butter was the bridge in front,
The rubble dyke was fair white wheat,
      Bacon the palisade.

Stately, pleasantly it sat,
A compact house and strong.
      Then I went in:
The door of it was hung beef,
The threshold was dry bread,
      Cheese-curds the walls.

Smooth pillars of old cheese
And sappy bacon props
      Alternate ranged;
Stately beams of mellow cream,
White posts of real curds
      Kept up the house.
Behind it was a well of wine,
Beer and bragget in streams,
      Each full pool to the taste.
Malt in smooth wavy sea
Over a lard-spring's brink
      Flowed through the floor.

A lake of juicy pottage
Under a cream of oozy lard
      Lay twixt it and the sea.

Hedges of butter fenced it round,
Under a crest of white-mantled lard
      Around the wall outside.

A row of fragrant apple-trees,
An orchard in its pink-tipped bloom,
      Between it and the hill.
A forest tall of real leeks,
Of onions and of carrots, stood
      Behind the house.

Within, a household generous,
A welcome of red, firm-fed men,
      Around the fire:
Seven bead-strings and necklets seven
Of cheeses and of bits of tripe
      Round each man's neck.

The Chief in cloak of beefy fat
Beside his noble wife and fair
      I then beheld.
Below the lofty caldron's spit
Then the Dispenser I beheld,
      His fleshfork on his back.

WHEATLET SON OF MILKLET

WHEATLET son of Milklet,
Son of juicy Bacon,
      Is mine own name.
Honeyed Butter-roll
Is the man's name
      That bears my bag.

Haunch of Mutton
Is my dog's name,
      Of lovely leaps.

[95]

Lard, my wife,
Sweetly smiles
　　　Across the brose.

Cheese-curds, my daughter,
Goes round the spit,
　　　Fair is her fame.
Corned Beef is my son,
Who beams over a cloak,
　　　Enormous, of fat.

Savour of Savours
Is the name of my wife's maid:
Morning-early
Across New-milk Lake she went.

Beef-lard, my steed,
An excellent stallion
　　　That increases studs;
A guard against toil
Is the saddle of cheese
　　　Upon his back.

A large necklace of delicious cheese-curds
　　　Around his back;
His halter and his traces all
　　　Of fresh butter.

Translated by Kuno Meyer

ANONYMOUS
(12th or 13th century)

From "SWEENEY THE MAD"

Sweeney, *Suibhne, surnamed Geilt,* was king of Dal Araidhe in Northern
Ireland, about 634 A.D. Saint Ronan Finn (the Fair), abbot of Drumiskin
County, Louth, marked out a site for a church in Dal Araidhe, but
Sweeney became angry over it and swore he would expel the cleric bodily.

[96]

He set out, in a storming rage, to do so, but Eorann his wife, in trying to prevent him, gripped his cloak and Sweeney, pulling away, was devested of his clothing. But he would not be stopped, and rushed, naked, to Ronan's abode. The saint was at prayers but Sweeney snatched the psalter and threw it into the lake. Now a messenger from Congal Cluin, King of Ulster, arrived bringing a summons for Sweeney to join him, Congal, at the battle of Magh Rath. An otter came carrying the psalter from the lake and Saint Ronan began to curse Sweeney:

> "HE came to me in his swift course
> on hearing my bell;
> He brought with him vast, awful wrath
> to drive me out, to banish me . . .
>
> Even as in an instant went
> the spear-shaft on high
> mayst thou go, O Sweeney
> in madness, without respite . . ."

He prays that Sweeney "Be ever wandering and flying stark-naked throughout the world."

The battle of Magh Rath follows; so dreadful is the din that Sweeney literally flies, a stark madman, from the battle-field. He wanders for seven years living in the trees with the wild birds, imagining himself flying from place to place and that feathers are growing on him. (It is an odd fact that the general belief in Ireland until recent times was that madmen were as light as feathers and could climb steeps and precipices.) Eventually a kinsman, Loingseachan, after three attempts, induces Sweeney to return to his kingdom. (Apparently the name Sweeney must have some association, at least to the poetic mind, with birds. See "Sweeney Among the Nightingales" by T. S. Eliot.)

"As he left the battlefield his feet seldom touched the ground because of the swiftness of his mania . . . and when he did touch it, he would not shake the dew from the tips of the grass. . . . For a long time he sought throughout Ireland until he reached the ever delightful Glen where the madmen of Ireland went when their year in madness was complete—the glen being ever a place of great delight for the crazy. He remained in the glen a long time until one night when he happened to be on the top of a tall ivyclad hawthorn tree . . . but he fell from the tree and was wounded and bloodied. So he remained, until at a certain time he raised himself into the air and came to Cluain Cille. Thereafter he went into the old tree of the church after a supper of watercress and water. That night came a great storm and Sweeney's misery was so great that he cried:

> The snow is cold tonight,
> my poverty now is lasting
> there is no strength in me for fight,
> famine has wounded me, madman as I am.

All men see that I am not shapely,
bare of thread is my tattered garment,
my name is Sweeney of Ros Earcain
the crazy madman am I.

I rest not when night comes,
my foot frequents no trodden way,
I bide not here for long,
the bonds of terror come upon me.

My goal lies beyond the teeming main,
voyaging the prow-abounding sea;
fear has laid hold of my poor strength
I am the crazy one of Glen Bolcain . . ."

It was now, when Sweeney had been hiding in the tree for some time that his people sent Loingseachan to bring him home. After many inducements Loingseachan decides to tell Sweeney that his son is dead:

"There is another famous story—
loath am I to tell it—
meetly are the men of the Arada
bewailing thy only son . . ."

SWEENEY: "That is the renowned drop
which brings a man to the ground,
that his little son who used to say "daddy"
should be without life.

It has called me to thee from the tree, . . ."

Sweeney returns, and the lies about his son's death have caused him to regain his sanity. One day he is alone in Loingseachan's bedroom with an old mill-woman or hag, who asked him to tell her of his adventures during his mad years. Afraid that his mania will return he rages at her:
" 'O hag, great are the hardships I have encountered; many a dreadful leap have I leaped from hill to hill, from fortress to fortress, from land to land, from valley to valley.' 'For God's sake,' said the hag, 'leap for us now one of the leaps you used to leap when you were mad.' Thereupon he bounded over the bedrail so that he reached the end of the bench. 'My conscience,' said the hag, 'I could leap that myself,' and in the same manner she did so. He took another leap out through the skylight of the hostel. 'I could leap that too,' said the hag, and straightway she leaped.

[98]

"Sweeney travelled through five cantreds of Dal Araidhe that day until he arrived at Glenn na nEachtach, and the hag followed him all that time. When Sweeney rested there on the summit of a tall ivy-branch, the hag rested on another tree beside him. It was then the end of harvest-time."

Sweeney heard a hunting-call. He heard the bellowing of the stag and he recited this lay: He began eulogizing the trees of Erin and recalling some of his own hardships:

"O little stag, thou bleating one,
O melodious little clamourer,
sweet to us is the music
thou makest in the glen . . .

O apple tree, little apple tree,
much thou art shaken;
O quicken, little berried one,
delightful is thy bosom . . .

O yew tree, little yew tree,
in churchyards thou art common;
O ivy, little ivy,
thou art familiar in the dark wood . . .

The aspen trembling:
I hear by turns
its leaves racing
meseems 'tis the foray! . . .

I flee before the skylarks,
a stern, great race;
I leap over the stumps
on the tops of the mountains.

When the proud turtle-dove
rises for us,
quickly I overtake it
since my feathers have grown.

The silly, foolish woodcock,
when it flushes for me,

methinks 'tis a bitter foe;
the blackbird, too, that gives the cry of alarm.

Every time I would bound
till I was on the ground
to see the little fox
below a-gnawing the bones . . .

Little foxes yelping
to me and from me,
wolves at their rending,
from their sound I flee.

They have striven to reach me,
coming in their swift course,
so that I fled before them
to the great mountain peaks.

There will come the starry frost
which will fall on every pool;
I am wretched, straying,
exposed to it on the mountain.

The herons a-calling
in chilly Glenn Aighle,
swift flocks of birds
coming and going. . . .

Though many are my wanderings,
my raiment today is scanty;
I myself keep my watch
on the top of the mountains.

O tall, russet fern,
thy mantle has been made red;
there is no bed for an outlaw
in the branches of thy crests.

The curse of Ronan Finn
has thrown me in thy company,
O little stag, little bleating one,
O melodious little clamourer."

After his lay, Sweeney travelled from place to place; but he found no
refuge from the hag until he arrived in Ulster where he leaped from a
cliff, the hag in his wake. She was broken to pieces and fell into the sea.
Sweeney wanders on to Britain and becomes friendly with another mad-
man. They travel together for a time and then Sweeney returns to Ireland.
He wanders wearily across the land and one day his woes crowd upon him:

"I am Sweeney alas!
my wretched body is utterly dead,
evermore without music, without sleep,
save the soughing of the rude gale . . .
A year have I been on the mountain
in this form in which I am,
without food going into my body
save crimson holly-berries.
The madman of Glen Balcain am I. . . .

He travels on and meets Saint Moling who gives him refuge. Sweeney dies
at peace in Moling's church in the Saint's arms.

Translated by J. G. O'Keefe

COLUMCILLE
(Attributed. 12th century)

COLUMCILLE'S GREETING TO IRELAND

DELIGHTFUL to be on the Hill of Howth
Before going over the white-haired sea:
The dashing of the wave against its face,
The bareness of its shores and of its border.

Delightful to be on the Hill of Howth
After coming over the white-bosomed sea;

[101]

To be rowing one's little coracle,
Ochone! on the wild-waved shore.

Great is the speed of my coracle,
And its stern turned upon Derry
Grievous is my errand over the main,
Travelling to Alba of the ravens.

My foot in my tuneful coracle,
My sad heart still bleeding;
A man without guidance is weak,
Blind are all the ignorant.

There is a grey eye
That will look back upon Erin:
It shall never see again
The men of Erin nor her women.

I stretch my glance across the brine
From the firm oaken planks:
Many are the tears of my soft grey eye
As I look back upon Erin.

My mind is upon Erin,
Upon Loch Lene, upon Linny,
Upon the land where Ulstermen are,
Upon gentle Munster and upon Meath.[1]

. . . . .

Gael! Gael! beloved name!
It gladdens the heart to invoke it:
Beloved is Cummin of the bright hair,
Beloved are Cainnech and Comgall.

Were all Alba mine
From its centre to its border,
I would rather have the site of a house
In the middle of fair Derry.

[1] Nine stanzas omitted.

It is for this I love Derry,
For its quietness, for its purity,
And for its crowds of white angels
From one end to another.

It is for this I love Derry,
For its quietness, for its purity;
All full of angels
Is every leaf on the oaks of Derry.

My Derry, my little oak-grove,
My dwelling and my little cell,
O eternal God in Heaven above,
Woe to him who violates it!

Beloved are Durrow and Derry,
Beloved is Raphoe in purity,
Beloved Drumhome of rich fruits;
Beloved are Swords and Kells.

Beloved also to my heart in the West
Drumcliff on Culcinne's strand:
To gaze upon fair Loch Foyle—
The shape of its shores is delightful.

Delightful is that, and delightful
The salt main where the sea-gulls cry,
On my coming from Derry afar,
It is quiet and it is delightful.
      Delightful.

*Translations of William Reeves
and Kuno Meyer*

ANONYMOUS
(12th century)

THE CRUCIFIXION

Found on a margin in the *Leabhar Breac,* or *Speckled Book.*

At the cry of the first bird
They began to crucify Thee, O Swan!
Never shall lament cease because of that.
It was like the parting of day from night.

Ah, sore was the suffering borne
By the body of Mary's Son,
But sorer still to Him was the grief
Which for His sake
Came upon His mother.
                Translated by Howard Mumford Jones

ANONYMOUS
(12th century)

THE BLACKBIRD

Found on a margin in the *Leabhar Breac,* or *Speckled Book.*

Ah, blackbird, thou art satisfied
Where thy nest is in the bush:
Hermit that clinkest no bell,
Sweet, soft, peaceful is thy note.
                Translated by Kuno Meyer

[104]

ANONYMOUS

(Probably 12th century)

THE CHURCH BELL AT NIGHT

Sweet little bell, struck on a windy night,
I would liefer keep tryst with thee
Than be
With a woman foolish and light.

Translated by Howard Mumford Jones

ANONYMOUS

THE LAMENT OF MAEV LEITH-DHERG

From an extremely ancient Irish poem in the BOOK OF LEINSTER, fol. 24.
See O'Curry's *Manuscript Materials of Irish History*, p. 480. This Maev is
not the warrior-goddess of Connacht, but a Queen of Ireland in times
approaching the historic, about A.D. 20. Cucorb ("Chariot Hound") was
slain on Mount Leinster on the borders of Wexford. (*Translator's note.*)

RAISE the Cromlech high!
    MacMoghcorb is slain,
And other men's renown
    Has leave to live again.

Cold at last he lies
    Neath the burial-stone;
All the blood he shed
    Could not save his own.

Stately-strong he went,
    Through his nobles all
When we paced together
    Up the banquet-hall.

[105]

Dazzling white as lime
  Was his body fair,
Cherry-red his cheeks,
  Raven-black his hair.

Razor-sharp his spear,
  And the shield he bore,
High as champion's head—
  His arm was like an oar.

Never aught but truth
  Spake my noble king;
Valour all his trust
  In all his warfaring.

As the forkéd pole
  Holds the roof-tree's weight,
So my hero's arm
  Held the battle straight.

Terror went before him,
  Death behind his back;
Well the wolves of Erinn
  Knew his chariot's track.

Seven bloody battles
  He broke upon his foes;
In each a hundred heroes
  Fell beneath his blows.

Once he fought at Fossud
  Thrice at Ath-finn-Fail
'Twas my king that conquered
  At bloody Ath-an-Scail.

At the boundary Stream
  Fought the Royal Hound,

And for Bernas battle
Stands his name renowned.

Here he fought with Leinster—
Last of all his frays—
On the Hill of Cucorb's Fate
High his Cromlech raise.

Translated by T. W. Rolleston

THREE POEMS FROM THE "LIFE OF ST. CELLACH OF KILLALA"

"The Life of St. Cellach" is one of the most interesting and beautiful pieces contained in the *Book of Lismore*, which was compiled about 1411 A.D. and has been translated by various scholars. The following poems are from Standish Hayes O'Grady's *Silva Gadhelica*. There have been few changes made; only those which eliminate redundancies and clarify the image.

HE WHO FORSAKES THE CLERKLY LIFE

ALAS for him that for any of the vile rude world's estates
forsakes the clerkly life
Woe to him that for a transient world's royalty
gives up a faithful God's great love!

Alas for him that in this life takes arms,
unless that for the same he shall do penance;
Better for one are the white-paged books with which
canonical psalmody is chanted.

Grand as may be the art of arms,
'tis yet of slender profit and fraught with heavy toil;
Of it one shall have but a most brief life,
which in the end must be exchanged for Hell.

But of all callings stealth is the worst:
sneaking, perjured, nimble thieving—he that commits it
though at one time he had been weak
thenceforward is but as a wicked one.

Of all which evil things a large portion is fallen
to Cellach son of Eoghan now:
From table to table as he wanders with a gang of villains
let him beware of death.

[108]

Alas for him who to have black murk servitude of Hell
abandons Heaven, blest abode of saints;
O Christ, O Ruler of Battles,
woe to him that deserts his mighty Lord!

Cellach, prince and poet, had retired from the world. He was seized by
his enemies the day before his murder and was carried into the depths of
the forest where he was imprisoned in the hollow trunk of a tree to await
his death. His murderers, fellow-pupils and former friends, had been
induced by bribes to desert and slay him.

After a night of foreboding, as day breaks, the Saint sees his murderers
approaching. He hears the noises of the forest's awakening; and in the
various sounds he imagines ominous warnings. But as the sun bursts forth,
Cellach, even in his extremity, forgets his misery in the glory of morning
and breaks into this magnificent hymn of farewell:

HAIL, FAIR MORNING

Hail, fair morning
That as flame falls on the ground
Hail to Him that sends her
Morning many-virtued ever new!

O fair Morning so full of pride
O sister of the brilliant Sun
Hail to thee, lovely Morning,
That lightest my little book for me!

Thou seest the guest in every dwelling
Shinest on every tribe and kin
Hail O thou white-necked, beautiful,
Here with us now, O golden-fair and wonderful!

My little book with chequered page
Tells me my life hath not been right;
Maelcroin—'tis he whom I do well to fear:
He it is that comes to smite me at the last.

O scallcrow, scallcrow,
Grey-coated, sharp-beaked, paltry fowl!

[109]

The intent of thy desire is apparent to me,
No friend art thou to Cellach.

O raven, thou that makest croaking!
If hungry thou be now, O bird!
From this same rath depart not
Until thou have a surfeit of my flesh.

Fiercely the kite of Cluain-éo's yew tree
Will take part in the scramble;
His horn-hued talons full he'll carry off,
He will not part from me in kindness.

To the blow that fells me the fox
That's in the darkling wood will make response at speed
He too in cold and trackless confines
Shall devour a portion of my flesh and blood.

The wolf that's in the rath
Upon the eastern side of Druim mic **Dair:**
He on a passing visit comes to me,
That he may rank as chieftain of the meaner pack.

On Wednesday's night last past I saw a dream:
As one the wild dogs dragged me
Eastwards and westwards
Through the russet ferns.

I saw a dream:
That into a green glen men took me;
Four they were that bore me thither,
But ne'er brought me back again.

I saw a dream:
That to their house my co-disciples led me;
For me they poured out a drink,
A draught too they quaffed off to me.

O tiny wren most scant of tail!
Dolefully thou hast piped prophetic lay;
Surely thou art come to betray me,
And to curtail my gift of life . . .

(Seven stanzas follow)

The saint is then set upon by the young men and killed. Later Cellach's brother, Muiredach, finds the body of the Saint "part eaten by the creatures." He laments:

DEAR WAS HE

Dear was he whose body this is:
To mine own death his death I liken:
The corpse of Eoghen Bel's son Cellach
I see drenched in its own blood.
Sister for me there is none, alas!
In Ireland nor in Scotland;
My father is dead and my mother is dead,
And now God has left me brotherless.
Thy bands of kerne thou, Cellach,
Didst renounce to follow psalmody with light;
Valour's deeds thou gavest up
For books full of all purity.
The feastinghouse thou didst desert
For attendance of the altar;
Tributes thou didst forego, O man!
In Jesus the Beloved thou didst place thy love.

Translated by Standish Hayes O'Grady

ANONYMOUS

A "Man of Smoke," or fire-servant while gathering wood for a fire in the open air, accidentally threw upon the fire a limb around which woodbine had twined. The onlookers protested declaring that the burning of woodbine would bring ill luck. The incident led one to sing this lay. The poem contains folk-lore concerning trees: It belongs to the 13th century.

SONG OF THE FOREST TREES

O man that for Fergus of the feasts dost kindle fir,
Whether afloat or ashore burn not the king of woods.

Monarch of Innisfail's forests the woodbine is, whom none may
    hold captive;
No feeble sovereign's effort is it to hug all tough trees in his
    embrace.

The pliant woodbine if thou burn, wailings for misfortune
    will abound,
Dire extremity at weapons' points or drowning in great waves
    will follow.

Burn not the precious apple-tree of spreading and lowsweeping
    bough;
Tree ever decked in bloom of white, against whose fair head
    all men put forth the hand.

The surly blackthorn is a wanderer, a wood that the artificer
    burns not;
Throughout his body, though it be scanty, birds in their flocks
    warble.

The noble willow burn not, a tree sacred to poems;
Within his bloom bees are a-sucking, all love the little cage.

The graceful tree with the berries, the wizard's tree, the rowan,
    burn;
But spare the limber tree; burn not the slender hazel.

Dark is the colour of the ash; timber that makes the wheels
    to go;
Rods he furnishes for horsemen's hands, his form turns battle
    into flight.

Tenterhook among woods the spiteful briar is, burn him that
     is so keen and green;
He cuts, he flays the foot, him that would advance he forcibly
     drags backward.

Fiercest heat-giver of all timber is green oak, from him none
     may escape unhurt;
By partiality for him the head is set on aching, and by his
     acrid embers the eye is made sore.
Alder, very battle-witch of all woods, tree that is hottest in the
     fight—
Undoubtedly burn at thy discretion both the alder and white-
     thorn.

Holly, burn it green; holly, burn it dry;
Of all trees whatsoever the critically best is holly.

Elder that hath tough bark, tree that in truth hurts sore;
Him that furnishes horses to the armies from the *sidh* burn so
     that he be charred.

The birch as well, if he be laid low, promises abiding fortune;
Burn up most sure and certainly the stalks that bear the con-
     stant pods.

Suffer, if it so please thee, the russet aspen to come headlong
     down;
Burn, be it late or early, the tree with the palsied branch.

Patriarch of long-lasting woods is the yew, sacred to feasts, as
     is well-known;
Of him now build ye dark-red vats of goodly size.

Ferdedh, thou faithful one, wouldst thou but do my behest:
To thy soul as to thy body, O man, 'twould work advantage.
             Translated by Standish Hayes O'Grady

ANONYMOUS
(13th century)

I HEAR THE WAVE

The Druid of the court of the King of Spain recites the following lay upon the coming of Eoghan Mor to sue for the King of Spain's daughter, Momera (or Beara). Eoghan Mor, King of Munster in the 2nd century, was a rival of Conn of The Hundred Battles.

I HEAR the wave clamour from the shore,
   The sound is an omen,—the harbinger of a king,
   This king who comes across the green sea,
   Shall by his valour take Erinn to himself.

Eoghan is the man, great shall be his triumph,
   He shall hold sway over noble Erinn,
A chief of chiefs is the scion who comes over the waters;
   You shall be the wife of Eoghan the strong.
   This strand below is Eibhear's cold strand,
   I understand the shore when I hear its sound.

Translated by Eugene O'Curry

ANONYMOUS
(12th century)

AN EVIL WORLD

Dermot, upon his defeat by the partisans of Saint Columcille, asks the Seer, Beg mac Dé, what he sees in the future for him. Beg answers in these verses:

AN EVIL world is now at hand:
In which men shall be in bondage, women free;

[114]

Mast wanting, woods smooth, blossom bad;
Winds many, wet summer, green corn;
Much cattle, scant milk;
Dependants burdensome in every country!
Hogs lean, chiefs wicked;
Bad faith, chronic killings:
A world withered, graves in number.

Translated by Standish Hayes O'Grady

ANGUS O'GILLAN
(14th century)

THE DEAD AT CLONMACNOIS

In a quiet water'd land, a land of roses,
    Stands Saint Kieran's city fair:
And the warriors of Erin in their famous generations
    Slumber there.

There beneath the dewy hillside sleep the noblest
    Of the clan of Conn,
Each below his stone with name in branching Ogham[1]
    And the sacred knot thereon.

There they laid to rest the seven Kings of Tara,
    There the sons of Cairbré sleep—
Battle-banners of the Gael, that in Kieran's plain of crosses
    Now their final hosting keep.

And in Clonmacnois they laid the men of Teffia,
    And right many a lord of Breagh;
Deep the sod above Clan Creidé and Clan Conaill,
    Kind in hall and fierce in fray.

[1] Ogham—a mode of inscription used by the ancient Irish.

Many and many a son of Conn, the Hundred-Fighter,
  In the red earth lies at rest;
Many a blue eye of Clan Colman the turf covers,
  Many a swan-white breast.

Translated by T. W. Rolleston

DONNCHADH MOR O'DALA

(Attributed. 13th century)

AT SAINT PATRICK'S PURGATORY

Loch Derg (Red Lake) in Co. Donegal has been a place of pilgrimage from very early times. Some think Dante may have received inspiration from its legends.

PITY me on my pilgrimage to Loch Derg!
O King of the churches and the bells—
bewailing your sores and your wounds,
but not a tear can I squeeze from my eyes!

Not moisten an eye
after so much sin!
Pity me, O King! What shall I do
with a heart that seeks only its own ease?

Without sorrow or softening in my heart,
bewailing my faults without repenting them!
Patrick the high priest never thought
that he would reach God in this way.

O lone son of Calpurn—since I name him—
O Virgin Mary, how sad is my lot!—
he was never seen as long as he was in this life
without the track of tears from his eyes.

In a narrow, hard, stone-wall cell
I lie after all my sinful pride—

[116]

O woe, why cannot I weep a tear!—
and I buried alive in the grave.

On the day of Doom we shall weep heavily,
both clergy and laity;
the tear that is not dropped in time,
none heeds in the world beyond.

I shall have you go naked, go unfed,
body of mine, father of sin,
for if you are turned Hellwards
little shall I reck your agony tonight.

O only begotten Son by whom all men were made,
who shunned not the death by three wounds,
pity me on my pilgrimage to Loch Derg
and I with a heart not softer than a stone!

Translated by Sean O'Faolain

CARROL O'DALY
(14th century)

EILEEN AROON

"The story of this song anticipates and possibly suggested that of Young
Lochinvar. The youthful poet-chief, O'Daly, had been plighted to Eivlin
Kavanagh, of the princely house of Leinster, who loved him. In his absence,
her parents forced another suitor on her. Carrol O'Daly, however, disguised
as a harper, appeared at the feast and won her to fly with him." The oldest
version of this famous poem follows: (*Cf. p. 415*)

FAIN would I ride with thee,
     Eivlin a rúin;
Fain would I ride with thee,
     Eivlin a rúin!
Fain would I ride with thee,

To Tirawley's tide with thee,
In hope to abide with thee,
    Eivlin a rúin!

I'd spend kine with thee,
    Eivlin a rúin!
Kine upon kine with thee,
    Eivlin a rúin!
I'd walk the world so wide,
To win thee for my bride,
Never to leave thy side
    Eivlin a rúin!

"Wilt thou come,—wilt thou stay?
    Eivlin a rúin!
Wilt thou come,—wilt thou stay?
    Earth's only boon!"
"I'll come, I will not stay!
I'll come, I will not stay!
I'll come, I will not stay!
    But flee with thee soon!"

Cead mile fáilte, here!
    Eivlin a rúin!
Cead mile fáilte, here!
    Eivlin a rúin!
A hundred thousand welcomes dear,
Nine hundred thousand welcomes here,
O welcomes forever here!
    Eivlin a rúin!

Translated by George Sigerson

LOVER AND ECHO

This is one of the first—possibly the very first—echo-poems in European literature. *cf.* Swift's "Gentle Echo on Woman" p. 324.

Tell me, Echo fair!
From the air above
Since thou knowest, why
I to sorrow clove?
Echo: Love

Love!—O no, of course,
That source ceased to flow;
That I knew of yore
Now no more I know.
Echo: No?

Lo, if Fortune hard
Will thy bard oppress,
Is there—tell me sure
Cure for my distress?
Echo: Yes.

Sage and witty Sprite
Rightly now reply,
Since there's healing calm
Choose what balm should I?
Echo: Die.

Die!—if so 'tis so,
Death puts woe away;
Since 'twill cure my ail
Then all hail I say.
Echo: Icy.

[119]

I say thrice all hail
  None will wail my fate;
But tell none my tale,
  This I supplicate.
      Echo: Like Kate.

Kate! the devil flee
  With thee, mocking Sprite!
Kate's unkind, and care
  Beareth no respite.
      Echo: Spite!

If Narcissus such
  Jealous touch did wake,
'Tis not strange that he
  Left thee for a lake.
      Echo: Ache!

Aching sobbing sighs
  Still I daily hear;
What can cause thy cries,
  Is not comfort near.
      Echo: Ne'er.

Shall Narcissus hold
  Old Love against the new?
Other fate may fall—
  Always needst not rue.
      Echo: True!

Blessings on thy Voice,
  I rejoice anew!
Since thou far wilt fare,
  Farewell and adieu.
      Echo: Adieu!

Translated by George Sigerson

THE OSSIANIC CYCLE
(9th-16th century)

The production of tales dealing with the Red Branch or Cuchulain of Ulster stopped about the 12th century, while the invention of tales dealing with Finn and the Fianna of Munster began to increase. The great bulk of Fenian or Ossianic literature comes to us from the fifteenth century onward. The name Finn was not derived from the Fianna nor the Fianna from Finn.

While the Cuchulian tales, which told of single combats, chariot riding, great feasts and great deeds of chivalry, were pagan and aristocratic in their content and conception, the tales of Finn and the Fianna appealed more to the popular taste. The leaders of the Fianna were not, like those of the Cuchulain stories, princes of a tribe or sept; they were officers of men who were professional soldiers. Of the heroes of the Fianna the most famous is Finn mac Cumhaill, Finn Mac Cool. There are more hunting tales than those of battles in the Fenian Cycle, and it was in those tales that the wolf-dog rather than the chariot horse came into his own. And, instead of the awful quality of the supernatural in the Cuchulian Cycle, we find in this later series a fairy element more akin to the modern conception of the supernatural.

The Fenian Cycle with its love of hunting, war, song, delight in nature; its love of the humorous, of the grotesque and of the bombastic; its democratic humors, is a creation for the people by the people. And while the saga of Finn Mac Cool flourishes among the Gaelic speakers of Ireland and Scotland, that of Cuchulian has died out.

The mingling of the two sagas is attributed to James Macpherson, the eighteenth century Scotsman who raised a storm of approval and disapproval with his so-called discovery of the poems of Ossian. More good than ill came of his work; it aroused the nationals of both Scotland and Ireland and brought to the attention of the public the great literary heritage of the Gaelic speaking peoples.

THE SONG OF FINN

"The Song of Finn MacCool, composed after his eating of the Salmon of Knowledge." One of the earliest fragments of Irish poetry, and composed before the great cycle of tales.

MAY-DAY, delightful time! How beautiful the color!
The blackbirds sing their full lay. Would that Laeg were here!
The cuckoos sing in constant strains. How welcome is the
      noble
Brilliance of the seasons ever! On the margin of the branching
      woods

[121]

The summer swallows skim the stream: the swift horses seek
  the pool:
The heather spreads out her long hair: the weak fair bog-down
  grows.
Sudden consternation attacks the signs; the planets, in their
  courses running, exert an influence:
The sea is lulled to rest, flowers cover the earth.

Translated by John O'Donovan

THE TRYST AFTER DEATH

This is included in the stories of the Fianna, but is very early, probably
ninth century. The saga had not as yet replaced the Cuchulain cycle in
importance.

Fothad Canann, the leader of a Connaught warrior-band, had carried
off the wife of Alill of Munster with her consent. The outraged husband
pursued them and a fierce battle was fought, in which Fothad and Alill
fell by each other's hand. The lovers had arranged to meet on the evening
after the battle. Faithful to his word, the spirit of the slain warrior kept the
tryst and addressed the following to his beloved:

HUSH, woman, do not speak to me!
  my thoughts are not with thee.
  My thoughts are still
  in the encounter at Feic.

My bloody corpse lies by the side
  of the Slope of two Brinks;
  my head all unwashed is among warrior-bands
  in fierce slaughter.

From afar I have come to my tryst—
  my noble mate is horror-stricken—
  had we known it would be thus,
  it had not been hard to desist!

It is blindness for any one making a tryst
  to set aside the tryst with Death:
  the tryst that we made at Claragh
  had been kept by me in pale death.

[122]

It was destined for me,—unhappy journey!
    at Feic my grave had been marked out;
    it was ordained for me—O sorrowful fight!
    to fall by warriors of another land.

'Tis not I alone who in the fulness of desires
    has gone astray to meet a woman—
    no reproach to thee, though it was for thy sake—
    wretched is our last meeting!

My men, the noble-faced, grey-horsed warrior-band
    have not betrayed me.
    Alas! for the wonderful yew-forest,
    that they should have gone into the abode of clay.

        .   .   .   .

To their very end they were brave;
    they ever strove for victory over their foes;
    they would still sing a stave—a deep-toned shout—
    they sprang from the race of a noble lord.

That was a joyous, lithe-limbed band
    to the very hour when they were slain:
    the green-leaved forest has received them—
    it was an all-fierce slaughter.

Well-armed Donall, he of the red draught,
    he was the Lugh of the well-accoutred hosts:
    by him in the ford—it was doom of death—
    fell Congal the Slender.

The three Eogans, the three Flanns,
    they were renowned outlaws;
    by each of them four men fell,
    it was not a coward's portion.

Swiftly Cu-Domna reached us,
    making for his namesake:
    on the hill of the encounter will be found
    the body of Flann the Little.

[123]

With him where his bloody bed is
  thou wilt find eight men:
  though we thought them feeble,
  the leavings of the weapon of Mughirne's son.

Not feebly fights Falvey the Red;
  the play of his spear-strings withers the host;
  Ferchorb of radiant body leapt upon the field
  and dealt seven murderous blows.

Front to front twelve warriors
  stood against me in mutual fight:
  not one remains of them all
  that I did not leave in slaughter.

Then we two exchanged spears,
  I and Alill, Eogan's son:
  We both perished—
  O the fierceness of those stout thrusts!

We fell by each other,—though it was senseless,
  It was the encounter of two heroes.

Do not await the terror of night upon the battlefield
  among the slain warriors:
  One should not hold converse with ghosts!
  betake thee home, carry my spoils with thee!

Fourteen quatrains consisting of minute descriptions of the spoils are omitted.
  .   .   .   .

There are around us here and there
  many spoils of famous luck:
  Horrible are the huge entrails
  which the Morrigan¹ washes.

From the edge of a spear she came to us,
  'tis she that egged us on.
  Many are the spoils she washes,
  terrible the hateful laugh she laughs.

¹ Morrigan, a war goddess.

[124]

She has flung her mane over her back—
    it is a stout heart that will not quail at her:
    though she is so near to us,
    do not let fear overcome thee!

In the morning I shall part from all that is human,
    I shall follow the warrior-band;
    Go to thy house, stay not here,
    the end of the night is at hand.[2]

  .   .   .   .

My riddled body must now part from thee awhile,
    my soul to be tortured by the black Demon.
    Save for the worship of Heaven's King,
    love of this world is folly.

I hear the dusky ousel
    that sends a joyous greeting to all the faithful:
    My speech, my shape are spectral—
    Hush, woman, do not speak to me!

Translated by Kuno Meyer

FROM THE "COLLOQUY OF THE ANCIENTS"

"The Colloquy of the Ancients," *Agallamh na Senorach,* is the longest and most important of the prose pieces belonging to the Fenian cycle. It is a collection of tales strung together in the form of a geographical guide or Dinnshenchas. The stories are related by Caeilte mac Ronan to St. Patrick as they travel through Ireland with their followers. Each place at which they stop suggests to Caeilte some event or circumstance of the olden days when the Fianna and Finn were in their glory. Caeilte and Oisín, with eighteen companions, are supposed to have survived 150 years after the destruction of their comrades at the Battle of Gaura.

One day as St. Patrick is ending his prayers, he sees approaching a company of huge men followed by great wolf dogs. Both men and dogs are obviously from another age. Caeilte, one of the great heroes and poets of the Fianna, answers the amazement and fear of the priests; and he and Patrick discuss the various merits of paganism and Christianity. This Pagan and Patrick have a number of gossipy times together. It is delightful when Patrick the Christian nods sympathetically and nostalgically at Caeilte's tales; catching himself suddenly, the Saint protests the glories of Christianity. Throughout, Caeilte and Patrick have perfect appreciation and

[2] Two quatrains are omitted here.

respect and courtesy for and toward each other. Towards the close of the sequence Caeilte and Oisín meet again at Tara; they have been baptized; they and the remnant of the Fianna who followed them "lay their lips to the earth and die." All Ireland mourns silently for them.

Four passages follow:

MacLugach was apparently the great hero Finn's grandson. The youth had been a year in the Fianna, but had shown little prowess. A young man of many faults, he would beat his hounds and his servants. The Fianna complained to their chief, Finn, who called MacLugach to him and gave him counsel, as follows:

MacLugach! says Finn,
  If armed service be thy design,
  In a great man's household be quiet,
  Be surly in the rugged pass.
  Without a fault of his
  Beat not thy hound;
  Until thou ascertain her guilt
  Bring not a charge against thy wife;
  In battle meddle not with a buffoon,
  For, O MacLugach, he is but a fool.
  Censure not any if he be of grave repute;
  Stand not up to take part in a brawl;
  Neither have anything to do with
  either a mad man or a wicked one.
  Two-thirds of thy gentleness be shewn
  to women and to creepers on the floor,
  Likewise to men of art that make the duans;
  And be not violent to the common people.
  With thy familiars, with them that are of thy counsel,
  Hasten not to be the first into bed;
  Perverse alliance shun, and all that is prohibited;
  Yield not thy reverence to all.
  Utter not swaggering speech,
  Nor say that thou wilt not render the thing that is right;
  For a shameful thing it is to speak too stiffly
  Unless that it be possible[1] to carry out thy words.
  So long as in the universe thou shalt exist,
  Thy lord forsake not;

---

[1] Except for some minor changes this stands as translated by O'Grady. For example I have changed feasible to possible.

[126]

Neither for gold nor for other earthly valuables
Abandon thou thy guarantee.
To a chief utter not harsh criticism of his people;
For it is not a 'good man's' occupation
To abuse a great lord's people to their chief.
Be not a frequenter of the drinking-house,
Nor given to carping at an ancient man;
The conduct thou hearest recommended, that is the right:
Meddle not with a man of mean estate.
Deal not in refusing of thy meat,
And any that is penurious have not for a familiar;
Force not thyself upon a chief,
Nor give a chief lord occasion to speak ill of thee.
Stick to thy raiment,
Hold fast to thine armature,
Until the stern fight with its weapon-glitter be well ended;
Never renounce to back thy luck,
Yet follow after gentleness, MacLugach.

Caeilte with St. Patrick and followers are travelling through heavy winter weather "Upon the whole province now distress of cold settled and heavy snow came down so that it reached men's shoulders and chariots' axel-trees, and of the russet forest's branches made a twisting together as it had been of withes, so that men might not progress there." Caeilte thinks of the past in the days of the Fianna when he was a great hero and he says "a fitting time it is now for wild stags and for does to seek the topmost points of hills and rocks; a timely season for salmons to betake them into cavities of the banks." He composes a poem on the spot:

THE winter is cold, the wind is risen,
The brave stag is on foot.
The whole mountainside is cold tonight
But the bold stag is belling.

The deer of Slievecarn is restless
He sleeps not tonight on the ground,
And the stag of cold Echtage's peak is wary
He too hears the chorus of the wolves.

I, Caeilte, with brown Dermot,
And light-footed Oscar,

[127]

On a cold night's pale waning
Oft would listen to the wailing of the pack.

But well the red deer sleeps
With his hide to the crevice wall—
Hidden as though he were buried—
The cold night touches him not.

Today I am an old man,
And but few men I know;
Once though on an ice-bound morning
I would hurl a javelin boldly.

To Heaven's King I offer thanks,
To the Virgin Mary's Son as well;
Many times I have daunted a host of men
Whose sleep to-night is very cold.

Recalling happy days on Arran Island off Scotland, Caeilte describes it
for Patrick:

ARRAN of the many stags,
The sea strikes against her shoulder
Island where great companies are fed
And blue spears reddened.

Skittish deer on her peaks,
Lush blackberries on her waving heather
Cool water flows in all her rivers
And mast clusters upon her bronze oaks.

There are greyhounds and beagles there
Blueberries and the dark sloes of the blackthorn
Her dwellings set close against her woods
And scattered deer feed by her oak thickets.

On her rocks grows a red-purple crop
And on all her slopes a faultless grass

Over her shapely crags and shady refuge
Leaping goes on, dappled fawns a-skipping.

Smooth her level ground, and fat the wild swine
Cheerful too, her bright fields
And nuts hang high on her forest hazel boughs;
The long galleys go rowing past her.

When the fair weather comes—the warm season—
Trout lie under her rivers' brinks
Seagulls wheel, screaming each to each (about the tall cliff)
Oh, Arran! is delightful at all times.

Cael drowned during the battle of Ventry. Credhe laments her lover's
death. Caeilte chants this for Patrick:

> THE haven roars
> Over the swirling waters of Ventry
> Cael the great warrior is drowned
> It is for him the beating wave laments.
>
> Melodious is the crane
> In the marshlands of Druim du thren
> She cannot save her nestlings
> The red fox has torn them.
>
> A woeful note
> Is the cry of the thrush in Drumqueen
> And the blackbird in Letterlee
> Cries not more cheerfully.
>
> A sad sound
> Is the call of the deer in Drumlast
> The doe of Drumsilon lies dead
> The great stag bells after her.
>
> Sore suffering to me
> Is the hero's death—

[129]

He that lay with me
That he should now lie dead

Sore suffering to me
That he lies dead beside me
That the wave took him—Woe! Woe!—
So great was my delight in his white body.

O dismal roar
The shore's surf makes on the strand
That it has drowned the comely man—
Why did he encounter it?

O boom of woe
That the wave sounds on the northward beach,
Beating against the polished rock
It laments for Cael who is dead.

O woeful fight
Is that of the wave against the southern shore
My day is over now
My beauty is fading.

O woeful melody
Is that of the heavy surf of Tullachlash
This calamity has shattered me
For me there is no more life

Now since Cael is drowned
There is none whom I would love
Many a chieftain has fallen by his hand
In battle his shield never cried out.

Based on Standish Hayes O'Grady
and Kuno Meyer translations.

FROM "THE HUNT OF SLIABH TRUIM"

A description of what a Fenian hunt was supposed to be in the days of
Finn and his Fianna and his Irish Wolf dogs. Probably fifteenth century.

"ONE day that we mustered on Sliabh Truim,
The Fianna of Finn full of valor,
Many a brave hero and hound were there
Which on the turf were matchless.

No hero was without a shield,
And two hounds upon the hill,
And a pair of dogs in the glen,
Around the valorous Finn.

We were spread over every glen,
Great was our might facing hills,
We were held by no sorrow,
Our force was lucky without fail.

We roused from the top of the hills
The game of the glens and brakes,
On each side of us on the plain
Was many a doe and badger.

Many a hero and hound
Were coming forth early on the plain;
To hunt every glen
Finn, lord of tribes, came forth.

In every man's hand two hounds
Of the Fianna that mustered there,
It is I that know it
Though bereft of sense, alas, to-day.

.   .   .   .

Many hundreds were in pursuit of the deer
Around us on the southern hill,
The battalions were on the watch for them—
Fierce was the onset.

Many were the cries of deer and boar
On the hill where the hunt took place;
When the hounds came on the prey,
Loud were the moans of boar and deer

[131]

A deer did not escape east or west,
Or a wild boar on the hill left alive;
All of them were slain
By the hounds in rough uproar.

    We killed ten hundred deer upon the hill
And ten hundred wild boars;
Our hounds on account of their fury
Made red every field.
Neither the hinds nor the badgers were counted
Nor the hares which fell on the plain;
Though they were not counted by Finn
Great was the number that fell to our share.

    A day's hunt by which more were slain,
In the kingdom of Banba at any time,
And the best that was in my day—
Was the chase made then by Finn.

    As we divided the chase,
We sat upon a hill to divide;
The faultless hosts collected
From every hill around Finn."

    .   .   .   .

    A Description of Finn's Great Wolfdog, Bran, considered the greatest dog ever bred in Ancient Ireland. In size and shape these dogs were tall, straight, slender and handsome and wonderfully powerful.

YELLOW legs had Bran,
Both sides black and her belly white,
Above her loins a speckled back,
And two crimson ears very red.

    Of the strength of a hound this is a good example. The pigs mentioned were warriors turned into that form by a Tuatha Dé Danann wizard for the purpose of killing Finn's hounds. This is an excerpt from the "Lay of the Enchanted Pigs."

Finn of the Fianna was amazed
At seeing each pig as tall as a deer;
One pig before them of boisterous mien,
Blacker was she than smith's coals;

[132]

Longer than an erect mast
Were the bristles of her face and ears;
Like that of a brake was the colour
Of the hair of her eyelids and old brow."

Bran tackled her at once

Bran broke forth from her leash
And left the hands of the king.

. . . .

She takes the pig by the neck
And assumes the difficult task.
She takes the pig by the neck,
That hold was the hold of a foe;
She did not suffer the pig to escape,
And never became breathless."

Translator anonymous

The "Book of the Lays of Fionn" was compiled at Louvain in 1626-1627 by three different scribes from earlier manuscripts. The work was undertaken at the direction of Captain Somhairle, or Sorley, MacDonnell, who was probably serving in the Netherlands at that time. The manuscript is preserved in the Franciscan Library, Dublin. Three poems from this collection (*Duanaire Finn*) follow; they date from the 16th century.

THE SLEEP SONG OF DIARMAID AND GRAINNE

One of the most famous love stories of Irish literature is that of Diarmaid and Grainne. No mss. copy is earlier than the 15th century though the incidents on which the story is founded may have been known in the 10th century. The story tells of Finn's intention to marry in his old age after the death of his wife. His friends advise him to marry Grainne, the young and beautiful daughter of Cormac mac Art, King of Tara. Finn and Cormac agree to the marriage but Grainne has never seen Finn; when she realizes he is older than her father, she flees with Diarmaid, who is unwilling, but whom she has put under a spell. They are followed by Finn and the tale describes their wanderings and Diarmaid's death.

Grainne's character is unusual in Irish literature. She is selfish, frivolous and light-minded. Although she obliges Diarmaid to sacrifice his honor and renown for her she reneges on her promises to him and consents to marry Finn who has compassed Diarmaid's death.

There is a close parallel between portions of this story and that of *Tristan and Isolde.*

[133]

Grainne sings a sleep-song for Diarmaid. Though she wishes him to sleep soundly, she notes that all the animals of the wilds are awake and restless (for the place is surrounded by the pursuers of Diarmaid).

SLEEP a little, a little little,
    for thou needst not fear the least,
    lad to whom I have given love,
    son of O Duibhne, Diarmaid.

Sleep thou soundly here,
    offspring of Duibhne, noble Diarmaid:
    I will watch over thee the while,
    son of shapely O Duibhne.

Sleep a little, a blessing on thee!
    above the water of the spring of Trénghart,
    little lamb of the land above the lake,
    from the womb of the country of strong torrents.

Be it even as the sleep in the south
    of Dedidach of the high poets
    when he took the daughter of ancient Morann
    in spite of Conall from the Red Branch.

Be it even as the sleep in the north
    of fair comely Finnchadh of Assaroe,
    when he took stately Sláine
    in spite of Failbhe Hardhead.

Be it even as the sleep in the west
    Of Aine Daughter of Gailian,
    that time she fared by torchlight
    with Dubhthach from Doirinis.

Be it even as the sleep in the east
    of Degha gallant and proud,
    when he took Coinchenn daughter of Binn
    in spite of fierce Dechell of Duibhreann.

O fold of valor of the world west from Greece,
   over whom I stay watching,
   my heart will well-nigh burst
   if I see thee not at any time.

The parting of us twain
   is the parting of children of one home,
   is the parting of body with soul,
   hero of bright Loch Carmain.

Caoinche will be loosed on thy track:
   Caoilte's running will not be amiss:
   never may death or dishonor reach thee,
   never leave thee in lasting sleep.

This stag eastward sleepeth not,
   ceaseth not from bellowing:
   though he be in the groves of the blackbirds,
   it is not in his mind to sleep.

The hornless doe sleepeth not,
   bellowing for her spotted calf:
   she runs over the tops of bushes,
   she does not sleep in her lair.

The lively linnet sleepeth not
   in the tops of the fair-curved trees:
   it is a noisy time there,
   even the thrush does not sleep.

The duck of numerous brood sleepeth not,
   she is well prepared for good swimming:
   she maketh neither rest nor slumber there,
   in her lair she does not sleep.

Tonight the grouse sleepeth not
   up in the stormy heaths of the height:

[135]

sweet is the sound of her clear cry:
between the streamlets she does not sleep.
Sleep a little.

Translated by Eoin MacNeill

THE BEAGLE'S CRY

The aged Oisin rejoices in memories of the great days of the Fianna,
aroused by the baying of a hound.

OISIN recalls:

A beagle's cry on the hill of kings!
    the mound it circles is dear to me:
    we often had a fians' hunting feast
    between the moorland and the sea.

Here were the followers of Fionn[1]
    to whom the sounds of strings were sweet:
    dear to me the active band
    that went on hostings of many hundreds.

Fair to see was their chase, methinks:
    many red stags fell by their prowess:
    many a speckled speedy hound
    coming to meet them on the moor.

Bran and beautiful Sceolang,
    his own hounds, in the king's hand:
    dearly Fionn loved the hounds,
    good was their courage and their achievement.

Crú Dheireoil in the king's bosom,
    good son of Lugh of comely form:
    he kept playing a harp for Fionn,
    the fair-haired man of strong voice . . .

[1] Fionn, a variant spelling of Finn.

Fifty many-antlered stags
   fell by my own hand, O king,
   and boars likewise,
   though to-night there is nothing mine . . .

I have heard a red beagle's cry
   on the slope beside the stream:
   it has raised the waves of my head,
   the sweet-voiced beagle's bay.

I am Oisin the king's son:
   it is long since my form has withered:
   although my heart is sore,
   nevertheless the cry is musical to me.

A beagle's cry.
Translated by Eoin MacNeill

THE WRY ROWAN

Oisin, old and blind, and compelled to fast, asks a swineherd to guide him to a certain rowan tree, that he may feast on its berries.

OISIN says:

Swineherd, let us make for the moorland:
   I am without food for three days:
   lead before me to Gleann Da Ghealt:
   Come, my son, and take my hand.

There is on the north side of the glen,
   if we were both brought thither,
   a tree whose berries are good to taste,
   which is named the Wry Rowan.

If thou wert nine days without food—
   I tell thee, it is no foolish thought,
   it would relieve thy dryness and thy thirst,
   when thou shouldst see the color of the berries.

We were two thousand in the hunting
  on the slope beside the hill:
we brought in no prey to Fionn
but the berries of the tree and two swine.
                              Swineherd.
                    Translated by Eoin MacNeill

❧ *PART II* ❧

MODERN IRISH POETRY
From the Sixteenth Century to the Present

FEARFLATHA O'GNIVE
(fl. 1562)

THE DOWNFALL OF THE GAEL

My heart is in woe,
And my soul deep in trouble,—
    For the mighty are low,
And abased are the noble:

    The Sons of the Gael
Are in exile and mourning,
    Worn, weary, and pale,
As spent pilgrims returning,

    Or men who, in flight
From the field of disaster,
    Beseech the black night
On their flight to fall faster;

    Or seamen aghast
When their planks gape asunder,
    And the waves fierce and fast
Tumble through in hoarse thunder;

    Or men whom we see
That have got their death-omen—
    Such wretches are we
In the chains of our foemen!

    Our course is fear,
Our nobility vileness,
    Our hope is despair,
And our comeliness foulness.

    There is mist on our heads,
And a cloud chill and hoary

Of black sorrow, sheds
An eclipse on our glory.

From Boyne to the Linn
Has the mandate been given,
   That the children of Finn
From their country be driven.

   That the sons of the king—
Oh, the treason and malice!—
   Shall no more ride the ring
In their own native valleys;

   No more shall repair
Where the hill foxes tarry,
   Nor forth to the air
Fling the hawk at her quarry;

   For the plain shall be broke
By the share of the stranger,
   And the stone-mason's stroke
Tell the woods of their danger;

   The green hills and shore
Be with white keeps disfigured,
   And the Mote of Rathmore
Be the Saxon churl's haggard!

   The land of the lakes
Shall no more know the prospect
   Of valleys and brakes—
So transformed is her aspect!

   The Gael cannot tell,
In the uprooted wildwood
   And red ridgy dell,
The old nurse of his childhood:

[141]

The nurse of his youth
Is in doubt as she views him,
If the wan wretch, in truth,
Be the child of her bosom.

We starve by the board,
And we thirst amid wassail—
For the guest is the lord,
And the host is the vassal!

Through the woods let us roam,
Through the wastes wild and barren;
We are strangers at home!
We are exiles in Erin!

And Erin's a bark
O'er the wide waters driven!
And the tempest howls dark,
And her side planks are riven!

And in billows of might
Swell the Saxon before her,—
Unite, oh, unite!
Or the billows burst o'er her!

Translated by Samuel Ferguson

OWEN ROE MAC WARD
(Attributed. 16th century)

THREE VERSIONS OF "DARK ROSALEEN"

There were several versions in Irish of "Roisin Dubh." In O'Daly's *Poets and Poetry of Munster* two are given, and it is probable Mangan combined these for his lyric. The Irish poem, composed in the reign of Elizabeth of England, is an address to Ireland.

[142]

O, MY Dark Rosaleen,
  Do not sigh, do not weep!
The priests are on the ocean green,
  They march along the Deep.
There's wine . . . from the royal Pope,
  Upon the ocean green;
And spanish ale shall give you hope,
  My Dark Rosaleen!
  My own Rosaleen!
Shall glad your heart, shall give you hope,
Shall give you health, and help, and hope,
  My Dark Rosaleen!

Over hills, and through dales,
  Have I roamed for your sake;
All yesterday I sailed with sails
  On river and on lake.
The Erne, . . . at its highest flood,
  I dashed across unseen,
For there was lightning in my blood,
  My Dark Rosaleen!
  My own Rosaleen!
Oh! there was lightning in my blood,
Red lightning lightened through my blood,
  My Dark Rosaleen!

All day long, in unrest,
  To and fro, do I move.
The very soul within my breast
  Is wasted for you, love!
The heart . . . in my bosom faints
  To think of you, my Queen,
My life of life, my saint of saints,
  My dark Rosaleen!
  My own Rosaleen!
To hear your sweet and sad complaints,
My life, my love, my saint of saints,
  My Dark Rosaleen!

Woe and pain, pain and woe,
  Are my lot, night and noon,
To see your bright face clouded so,
  Like to the mournful moon.
But yet . . . will I rear your throne
  Again in golden sheen;
'Tis you shall reign, shall reign alone,
  My Dark Rosaleen!
  My own Rosaleen!
'Tis you shall have the golden throne,
'Tis you shall reign, and reign alone,
  My Dark Rosaleen!

Over dews, over sands,
  Will I fly, for your weal:
Your holy delicate white hands
  Shall girdle me with steel
At home . . . in your emerald bowers,
  From morning's dawn till e'en,
You'll pray for me, my flower of flowers,
  My Dark Rosaleen!
  My fond Rosaleen!
You'll think of me through Daylight's hours,
My virgin flower, my flower of flowers,
  My Dark Rosaleen!

I could scale the blue air,
  I could plough the high hills,
Oh, I could kneel all night in prayer,
  To heal your many ills!
And one . . . beamy smile from you
  Would float like light between
My toils and me, my own, my true,
  My Dark Rosaleen!
  My fond Rosaleen!
Would give me life and soul anew,
A second life, a soul anew,
  My dark Rosaleen!

[144]

O! the Erne shall run red
  With redundance of blood,
The earth shall rock beneath our tread,
  And flames wrap hill and wood,
And gun-peal, and slogan cry,
  Wake many a glen serene.
Ere you shall fade, ere you shall die,
  My Dark Rosaleen!
  My own Rosaleen!
The Judgment Hour must first be nigh,
Ere you can fade, ere you can die,
  My Dark Rosaleen!

                    Translated by James Clarence Mangan

(*Another version*)

ROISIN DUBH

THERE's black grief on the plains, and a mist on the hills;
There is fury on the mountains, and that is no wonder;
I would empty the wild ocean with the shell of an egg,
If I could be at peace with thee, my Ros geal dubh.

Long is the course I travelled from yesterday to-day,
Without, on the edge of the hill, lightly bounding, as I know,
I leapt Loch Erne to find her, though wide was the flood
With no light of the sun to guide my path, but the Ros geal
    dubh.

If thou shouldst go to the Aonach to sell thy kine and stock,
If you go, see that you stay not out in the darkness of the night;
Put bolts upon your doors, and a heavy reliable lock,
Or, in faith, the priest will be down on you, on my Ros geal
    dubh!

[145]

O little Rose, sorrow not, nor be lamenting now,
There is pardon from the Pope for thee, sent straight home
    from Rome,
The friars are coming overseas, across the heaving wave,
And Spanish wine will then be thine, my Ros geal dubh.

There is true love in my heart for thee for the passing of a year,
Love tormenting, love lamenting, heavy love that wearies me,
Love that left me without health, without a path, gone all
    astray,
And for ever, ever, I did not get my Ros geal dubh!

I would walk Munster with thee and the winding ways of the
    hills,
In hope I would get your secret and a share of your love;
O fragrant Branch, I have known it, that thou hast love for me,
The flower-blossom of wise women is my Ros geal dubh.

The sea will be red floods, and the skies like blood,
Blood-red in war the world will show on the ridges of the hills;
The mountain glens through Erinn and the brown bog will be
    quaking
Before the day she sinks in death, my Ros geal dubh!
Translated by Eleanor Hull

(*Another version*)

THE LITTLE DARK ROSE

LITTLE Rose, be not sad for all that hath
    behapped thee:
The friars are coming across the sea, they
    march on the main,
From the Pope shall come thy pardon,
    and from Rome, from the East—

And stint not Spanish wine to my Little
Dark Rose.

Long the journey that I made with her
from yesterday till to-day,
Over mountains did I go with her, under
the sails upon the sea,
The Erne I passed by leaping, though
wide the flood,
And there was string music on each side
of me and my Little Dark Rose!

Thou hast slain me, O my bride, and
may it serve thee no whit,
For the soul within me loveth thee, not
since yesterday nor to-day,
Thou hast left me weak and broken in
mien and in shape,
Betray me not who love thee, my Little
Dark Rose!

I would walk the dew with thee and the
meadowy wastes,
In hope of getting love from thee, or
part of my will,
Fragrant branch, thou didst promise me
that thou hadst for me love—
And sure the flower of all Munster is my
Little Dark Rose!

Soft modest Little Rose of the round
white breasts,
'Tis thou hast left a thousand pains in the
centre of my heart:
Fly with me, my hundred loves, and leave
the land,
And if I could would I not make a Queen
of thee, my Little Dark Rose!

Had I a yoke of horses I would plough
    against the hills,
In middle-Mass I'd make a gospel of my
    Little Dark Rose,
I'd give a kiss to the young girl that
    would give her mouth to me,
And behind the liss would lie embracing
    my Little Dark Rose!

The Erne shall rise in rude torrents, hills
    shall be rent,
The sea shall roll in red waves, and blood
    be poured out,
Every mountain glen in Ireland, and the
    bogs shall quake
Some day ere shall perish my Little Dark
    Rose!

Translated by Padraic Pearse

GERALD NUGENT
(c. 1573)

A FAREWELL TO FÁL

SAD to fare from the hills of Fál,
Sad to leave the land of Ireland!
The sweet land of the bee-haunted bens,
Isle of the hoof-prints of young horses!

Ableit my faring is over the eastward ocean,
And my back is turned to the land of Fionntain,
All heart for the road hath left me:
No sod shall I love but the sod of Ireland.

Sod that is heaviest with fruit of trees,
Sod that is greenest with grassy meadows,

[148]

Old plain of Ir, dewy, crop-abounding,
The branchy, wheat bearing-country!
. . . .
If God were to grant me back again
To come to my native world,
From the Galls I would not take it to go
Among the crafty clans of England.

Were there even no peril of the sea
In leaving the lios of Laoghaire,
I shall not deny that my courage would droop—
To fare from Delvin is hard!

Good-bye to the band I leave behind,
The lads of Dundargveis,
The songs and minstrelsy of the plain of Meath,
Plain of the noblest companies!

Translated by Padraic Pearse

ANONYMOUS
(16th century)

THE KISS

OH, KEEP your kisses, young provoking girl!
    I find no taste in any maiden's kiss.
Altho' your teeth be whiter than the pearl,
    I will not drink at fountains such as this.

I know a man whose wife did kiss my mouth
    With kiss more honeyed than the honeycomb.
And never another's kiss can slake my drought
    After that kiss, till judgment hour shall come.

Till I do gaze on her for whom I long,
    If ever God afford such grace to men,

I would not love a woman old or young,
   Till she do kiss me as she kissed me then.
Translated by the Earl of Longford

ANONYMOUS
(17th century)

THE CAREFUL HUSBAND

I am told, sir, you're keeping an eye on your wife,
But I can't see the reason for that, on my life.
For if you go out, O most careful of men,
It is clear that you can't keep an eye on her then.

Even when you're at home and take every care,
It is only a waste of your trouble, I swear.
For if you for one instant away from her look,
She'll be off into some inaccessible nook.

If you sit close beside her and don't let her move,
By the flick of an eyelid she'll signal her love.
If you keep her in front of you under your eye,
She will do what she likes and your caution defy.

When she goes out to mass, as she'd have you suppose,
You must not stay a minute, but go where she goes.
You must not walk in front nor yet too far behind her.
But she's got such a start that I doubt if you'll find her.
Translated by the Earl of Longford

MAURICE O'DUGAN
(c.1641)

THE COOLUN

O HAD you seen the Coolun,
  Walking down by the cuckoo's street,
With the dew of the meadow shining
  On her milk-white twinkling feet!
My love she is, and my coleen oge,
  And she dwells in Bal'nagar;
And she bears the palm of beauty bright,
  From the fairest that in Erin are.

In Bal'nagar is the Coolun,
  Like the berry on the bough her cheek;
Bright beauty dwells for ever
  On her fair neck and ringlets sleek;
Oh, sweeter is her mouth's soft music
  Than the lark or thrush at dawn,
Or the blackbird in the greenwood singing
  Farewell to the setting sun.

Rise up, my boy! make ready
  My horse, for I forth would ride,
To follow the modest damsel,
  Where she walks on the green hillside:
For ever since our youth were we plighted,
  In faith, troth, and wedlock true—
She is sweeter to me nine times over,
  Than organ or cuckoo!

For, ever since my childhood
  I loved the fair and darling child;
But our people came between us,
  And with lucre our pure love defiled:
Ah, my woe it is, and my bitter pain,

And I weep it night and day,
That the coleen bawn of my early love
   Is torn from my heart away.

Sweetheart and faithful treasure,
   Be constant still, and true;
Nor for want of herds and houses
   Leave one who would ne'er leave you.
I'll pledge you the blessèd Bible,
   Without and eke within,
That the faithful God will provide for us,
   Without thanks to kith or kin.

Oh, love, do you remember
   When we lay all night alone,
Beneath the ash in the winter storm,
   When the oak wood round did groan?
No shelter then from the blast had we,
   The bitter blast or sleet,
But your gown to wrap about our heads,
   And my coat around our feet.

Translated by Samuel Ferguson

PIERCE FERRITER
(Died 1653)

HE CHARGES HER TO LAY ASIDE HER WEAPONS

I CHARGE you, lady young and fair,
   Straightway to lay your arms aside.
Lay by your armour, would you dare
   To spread the slaughter far and wide?

O lady, lay your armour by,
   Conceal your curling hair also,

[152]

For never was a man could fly
    The coils that o'er your bosom flow.

And if you answer, lady fair,
    That north or south you ne'er took life,
Your very eyes, your glance, your air
    Can murder without axe or knife.

And oh! If you but bare your knee,
    If you your soft hand's palm advance,
You'll slaughter many a company.
    What more is done with shield and lance?

Oh, hide your bosom limey white,
    Your naked side conceal from me.
Ah, show them not in all men's sight,
    Your breasts more bright than flowering tree.

And if in you there's shame or fear
    For all the murders you have done,
Let those bright eyes no more appear,
    Those shining teeth be seen of none.

Lady, we tremble far and near!
    Be with these conquests satisfied,
And lest I perish, lady dear,
    Oh, lay those arms of yours aside.

Translated by the Earl of Longford

[153]

GEOFFREY KEATING
(1570?-1646?)

O WOMAN FULL OF WILE

This poem is generally attributed to Keating, with O'Curry dissenting;
compare with the preceding.

O WOMAN full of wile,
Keep from me thy hand:
I am not a man of the flesh,
Tho' thou be sick for my love.

See how my hair is grey!
See how my body is powerless!
See how my blood hath ebbed!
For what is thy desire?

Do not think me besotted:
Bend not again thy head,
Let our love be without act
Forever, O slender witch.

Take thy mouth from my mouth,
Graver the matter so;
Let us not be skin to skin:
From heat cometh will.

'Tis thy curling ringleted hair,
Thy grey eye bright as dew,
Thy lovely round white breast,
That draw the desire of eyes.

Every deed but the deed of the flesh
And to lie in thy bed of sleep
Would I do for thy love,
O woman full of wile!

Translated by Padraic Pearse

[154]

KEEN THYSELF, POOR WIGHT

KEEN thyself, poor wight:
From weeping others restrain thine eyes;
Keen not daughter, keen not son
That hath been shrouded in clay.

Keen first thine own sin
Ere thy body goeth into dust;
Keen, since thou must pay for it,
The passion Christ suffered for thy sake.

Keen the sufferings on thy behalf
of Christ, Who redeemed all upon a tree,
Keen His two hands and His two feet,
And His heart which the blind man clave.

Every single one shall go:
Yet keen none that shall pass from thee,—
Beyond all that have ever been laid in earth,
Thine own case, poor wretch, toucheth thee most nearly.

Of all that the Creator's right hand hath made,
Of boys, of women, and of men,
There is none, weak or mighty,
But shall pass unto his death.

Couldst thou see all that have gone from thee,
As these hosts beneath us are,
Before all that have ever gone into earth,
Thou wouldst keen thyself first.

On Sion hill, on the day of the hosts,
Thy face shall be blacker than a coal,
Though fair thy aspect now,—
Unless thou keen thyself while here.

Since death is the messenger of God,
Shouldst thou repine at his doings,

[155]

Thou wouldst achieve thine own misfortune
And the misfortune of him that hath gone.

Alas, poor witless wight,
Didst thou understand thyself as thou art,
Thou wouldst cease to keen for others
And yet wouldst be weeping forever!
Translated by Padraic Pearse

From "MY GRIEF ON FÁL'S PROUD PLAIN"

FROM my grief on Fál's proud plain I sleep
    no night,
And till doom the plight of her native folk
    hath crushed me:
Tho' long they stand a fence against a
    rabble of foes,
At last there hath grown full much of the
    wild tare through them.

Ah, faithless Fódla, 'tis shame that thou
    see'st not clearly
That 'twere meeter to give thy milk to the
    clustering clan of Mileadh,—
No drop hath been left in the expanse of
    thy smooth white breast
That the litter of every foreign sow hath
    not sucked!

Every common crew that hath chosen to
    come across the sea
To the olden golden comely race of
    Cobhthach Caol mBreagh,
Theirs without challenge of battle are our
    stricken palaces,
Every field most fruitful of our pleasant-
    bordered places.

[156]

There are many waxing strong in this plain
    of Lugh the smooth,
Who ought to be weak, though high their roll
    extends;
Eoghan's seed hath no honour, the Dalcas-
    sian blood dumb-stricken,
And the heroes from Strabane scattered in
    foreign countries.

The famous chiefs of Naas make no manly
    movement,
Though once those fiery bands were fierce
    in fight;
In the State's despite they waged their war
    in squadrons—
Not theirs the shame, but of those who
    fulfilled not justice.

If the high chief lived of Aine and Druim
    Daoile
And the strong lions of Maigue who granted
    gifts,
There surely were no place for this rabble
    where Bride meets Blackwater,
But shouts and outcries on high announcing
    their ruin and rout.

Unless the artisan of the high heavens help
    the folk of Corc's territories
Against the violence of bold, ever-ready,
    vengeful enemies,
'Twere almost better that they were straight-
    way winnowed and gleaned,
And sent safe into exile over the waves of
    Clíodhna!

Translated by Padraic Pearse

ANONYMOUS

(Early 17th century)

SAINT BRENDAN'S PROPHECY

The following dialogue between Saint Senan and Saint Brendan, the founder of the Ancient Cathedral of Ardfert, and after whom a very high hill in County Kerry has been named, is translated from the Irish. It is probably a composition of the 16th or 17th century, and is a good example of the prophetic verses in which the Irish, in all periods, seem to have placed wonderful faith. (From T. Crofton Croker, in *The Amulet*, 1828).

SAINT SENAN BRENDAN, holy Brendan of the blessed beard;
I have heard it said among pious men,
that thy guardian angel comes to visit thee.
That angel to be thy guardian
must belong to the highest choir
to whom is given the gift of revelation.

Brendan, holy Brendan of the blessed beard!
Therefore ceases my wonder at thy power of
      prophecy,
Tell me, for I doubt not to thee it is known,
what weight of evils hang over this land?

SAINT BRENDAN Changes sad and alteration
Will befall this sinful nation.
Alas! I weep that my prediction
Is a true one, and no fiction!

SAINT SENAN Brendan, holy Brendan of the blessed beard,
I ask thee to enlighten
the darkness of my mind
by thy heavenly wisdom?—

SAINT BRENDAN Senan, know the consolation
Of an Angel's conversation,
To my midnight vigils given,
Is the precious gift of Heaven.

[158]

SAINT SENAN   Brendan, holy Brendan of the blessed beard,
I ask of thee to reveal the future to my sight.

SAINT BRENDAN   Senan, pious Senan, dear,
The end of ages is drawing near;
As the world grows withered and old,
Charity will grow icy cold,
Love and friendship will be strangers.
Between clansmen strife and danger;
Judges will from Justice falter,
Bishops careless of their altar;
Barley-cakes and water-cresses
Our food, will change for gross excesses,
And, while ponderous dishes carving,
Leave the poor and aged starving.
Pious men must pray on mountains,
Or beside secluded fountains;
Pale-faced abstinence and watches
Will be changed for paint and patches;
Abbots from their vows defaulting,
Monks in darkness blindly halting:
Priests, like grease-pots flat and burly,
Will preach errors loud and surly;
Laymen, pulpits will ascend,
And there false novelties defend;
Theft, they'll say, pride and sedition,
Are less sins than superstition;
Heaven they will grant to all,
Who in their new readings fall!—
Three Peers of the Dalcassan line
Will usurp this glebe of mine;
Then, alas! comes my undoing,
Then my houses sink to ruin.
For the reign of twenty kings
Error soars on eagle wings;
In the course of this confusion,
Truth they'll call a vain illusion,
'Til a prince of Brian's race

[159]

Shall set justice in her place;
When that prince ascends the throne,
Then my monks shall have their own.
A Dalcassian, and no other,
Both by father and by mother,
Then shall rule for forty winters,
From the time that first he enters;
Lands and tythes, impropriation,
He will change throughout the nation;
And religion's pristine form
Shall give peace and calm the storm.

Translated by T. Crofton Croker

EOCHADH O'HUSSEY

(c. 1630)

ODE TO THE MAGUIRE

WHERE is my Chief, my Master, this bleak night, *mavrone!*
O, cold, cold, miserably cold is this bleak night for Hugh,
Its showery, arrowy, speary sleet pierceth one through and
     through
Pierceth one to the very bone!

Rolls real thunder? Or, was that red, livid light
Only a meteor? I scarce know; but through the midnight dim
The pitiless ice-wind streams. Except the hate that persecutes
     him
Nothing hath crueler venomy might.

An awful, a tremendous night is this, meseems!
The flood-gates of the rivers of heaven, I think, have been
     burst wide—
Down from the overcharged clouds, like unto headlong ocean's
     tide,
Descends grey rain in roaring streams.

[160]

Though he were even a wolf ranging the round green woods,
Though he were even a pleasant salmon in the unchainable
　　sea,
Though he were a wild mountain eagle, he could scarce bear,
　　he,
This sharp, sore sleet, these howling floods.

O, mournful is my soul this night for Hugh Maguire!
Darkly, as in a dream he strays! Before him and behind
Triumphs the tyrannous anger of the wounding wind,
The wounding wind, that burns as fire!

It is my bitter grief—it cuts me to the heart—
That in the country of Clan Darry this should be his fate!
O, woe is me, where is he? Wandering, houseless, desolate,
Alone, without a guide or chart!

Medreams I see just now his face, the strawberry-bright,
Uplifted to the blackened heavens, while the tempestuous
　　winds
Blow fiercely over and round him, and the smiting sleet-
　　shower blinds
The hero of Galang to-night!

Large, large affliction unto me and mine it is,
That one of his majestic bearing, his fair, stately form,
Should thus be tortured and o'erborne—that this unsparing
　　storm
Should wreck its wrath on head like his!

That his great hand, so oft the avenger of the oppressed,
Should this chill, churlish night, perchance, be paralyzed by
　　frost—
While through some icicle-hung thicket—as one lorn and
　　lost—
He walks and wanders without rest.

The tempest-driven torrent deluges the mead,
It overflows the low banks of the rivulets and ponds—

The lawns and pasture-grounds lie locked in icy bond,
So that the cattle cannot feed.

The pale bright margins of the streams are seen by none,
Rushes and sweeps along the untamable flood on every side—
It penetrates and fills the cottagers' dwellings far and wide—
Water and land are blent in one.

Through some dark woods, 'mid bones of monsters, Hugh now
     strays,
As he confronts the storm with anguished heart, but manly
     brow—
O! what a sword-wound to the tender heart of his were now
A backward glance at peaceful days!

But other thoughts are his—thoughts that can still inspire
With joy and an onward-bounding hope the bosom of Mac-
     Nee—
Thoughts of his warriors charging like bright billows of the
     sea,
Borne on the wind's wings, flashing fire!

And though frost glaze to-night the clear dew of his eyes,
And white ice-gauntlets glove his noble fine fair fingers o'er,
A warm dress is to him that lightning-garb he ever wore,
The lightning of the soul, not skies.

Avran[1]

Hugh marched forth to the fight—I grieved to see him so
     depart;
And lo! to-night he wanders frozen, rain-drenched, sad, be-
     trayed—
But the memory of the limewhite mansions his right hand hath
     laid
In ashes, warms the hero's heart!
Translated by James Clarence Mangan

[1] Avran: A concluding stanza, usually intended as a recapitulation of the poem;
cf. *L'envoi.*

ANONYMOUS
(17th century)

THE WOMAN OF THREE COWS

O WOMAN of Three Cows, *agra!* don't let your tongue thus
    rattle!
Oh, don't be saucy, don't be stiff, because you may have cattle.
I have seen—and, here's my hand to you, I only say what's
    true—
A many a one with twice your stock not half so proud as you.

Good luck to you, don't scorn the poor, and don't be their
    despiser;
For worldly wealth soon melts away, and cheats the very miser;
And death soon strips the proudest wreath from haughty
    human brows—
Then don't be stiff, and don't be proud, good Woman of Three
    Cows!

See where Mononia's heroes lie, proud Owen Mór's descend-
    ants.
'Tis they that won the glorious name, and had the grand
    attendants;
If *they* were forced to bow to Fate, as every mortal bows,
Can *you* be proud, can *you* be stiff, my Woman of Three Cows?

The brave sons of the Lord of Clare, they left the land to
    mourning;
Mavrone! for they were banished, with no hope of their return-
    ing.
Who knows in what abodes of want those youths were driven
    to house?
Yet *you* can give yourself these airs, O Woman of Three Cows.

Oh, think of Donnell of the Ships, the Chief whom nothing
    daunted,

[163]

See how he fell in distant Spain unchronicled, unchanted!
He sleeps, the great O'Sullivan, where thunder cannot rouse—
Then ask yourself, should *you* be proud, good Woman of
  Three Cows?

O'Ruark, Maguire, those souls of fire, whose names are shrined
  in story:
Think how their high achievements once made Erin's greatest
  glory.
Yet now their bones lie mouldering under weeds and cypress
  boughs—
And so, for all your pride, will yours, O Woman of Three
  Cows.

Th' O'Carrols, also, famed when fame was only for the boldest,
Rest in forgotten sepulchres with Erin's best and oldest;
Yet who so great as they of yore in battle or carouse?
Just think of that, and hide your head, good Woman of Three
  Cows.

Your neighbour's poor; and you, it seems, are big with vain
  ideas,
Because, forsooth, you've got three cows—one more, I see, than
  she has;
That tongue of yours wags more at times than charity allows;
But if you're strong, be merciful—great Woman of Three
  Cows.

                    Avran

Now, there you go; you still, of course, keep up your scornful
  bearing,
And I'm too poor to hinder you; but, by the cloak I'm wearing,
If I had but four cows myself, even though you were my spouse,
I'd thwack you well, to cure your pride, my Woman of Three
  Cows.

                Translated by James Clarence Mangan

HUGH MAC GOWRAN

(c. 1700)

THE DESCRIPTION OF AN IRISH FEAST, or
O'ROURK'S FROLIC

Translated almost literally from the original Irish, 1720.

O'ROURK's noble fare
  Will ne'er be forgot,
By those who were there
  Or those who were not.

His revels to keep,
  We sup and we dine
On seven score sheep,
  Fat bullocks and swine.

Usquebaugh[1] to our feast
  In pails was brought up,
A hundred at least,
  And a madder[2] our cup.

O there is the sport!
  We rise with the light
In disorderly sort,
  From snoring all night.

O how was I trick'd!
  My pipe it was broke,
My pocket was pick'd
  I lost my new cloak.

I'm rifled, quoth Nell.
  Of mantle and kercher:
Why then fare them well,
  The de'el take the searcher.

[1] Whisky.
[2] A wooden vessel.

Come harper, strike up;
  But, first, by your favor,
Boy, give us a cup:
  Ah! this hath some savour.

O'Rourk's jolly boys
  Ne'er dreamt of the matter,
'Till rous'd by the noise,
  And musical clatter.

They bounce from their nest,
  No longer will tarry,
They rise ready dress'd
  Without one Ave-Mary.

They dance in a round,
  Cutting capers and ramping;
A mercy the ground
  Did not burst with their stamping.

The floor is all wet
  With leaps and with jumps,
While the water and sweat
  Splish-splash in their pumps.

Bless you late and early,
  Laughlin O'Enagin!
By my hand, you dance rarely,
  Margery Grinagin.

Bring straw for our bed,
  Shake it down to the feet,
Then over us spread
  The winnowing sheet.

To show I don't flinch,
  Fill the bowl up again;

Then give us a pinch
   Of your sneezing, a Yean.

Good Lord! what a sight,
   After all their good cheer,
For people to fight
   In the midst of their beer!

They rise from their feast,
   And hot are their brains,
A cubit at least
   The length of their skeans.[1]

What stabs and what cuts,
   What clattering of sticks;
What strokes on the guts,
   What bastings and kicks!

With cudgels of oak,
   Well harden'd in flame,
A hundred heads broke,
   A hundred struck lame.

You churl, I'll maintain
   My father built Lusk,
The castle of Slane,
   And Carrick Drumrusk:

The Earl of Kildare,
   And Moynalta his brother,
As great as they are,
   I was nursed by their mother.[2]

Ask that of old madam;
   She'll tell you who's who,
As far up as Adam,
   She knows it is true.

[1] Daggers or short swords.
[2] The same foster mother.

[167]

Come down with that beam,
    If cudgels are scarce,
A blow on the weam,
    Or a kick on the arse.

Translated by Jonathan Swift

ANONYMOUS

(late 17th century)

FAREWELL, O PATRICK SARSFIELD

Patrick Sarsfield, Titular Earl of Lucan, was an Irish Jacobite and
soldier, descendant of an Anglo-Norman family; served against Monmouth
at Sedgemoor in 1685; assisted in James II's re-organization of Irish forces
into a Roman Catholic army; fled with James II to France, and returned
with him to Ireland in 1689. He caused William III to raise the Siege of
Limerick in 1690; after the capitulation of Limerick, he joined the French
service with the remnants of his troops. He was mortally wounded on
July 29, 1693, at Landen, "heading his countrymen in the van of victory,
King William flying. He could not have died better. His last thoughts were
for his country. As he lay on the field unhelmed and dying, he put his
hand to his breast. When he took it away it was bloody. Looking at it sadly,
he said faintly, 'Oh! that this were for Ireland.'"
    The Catholic people of Ireland had espoused the cause of the Stuarts.
But the Irish believed they were fighting to free Ireland and to free Irish
Catholics from the severe laws enacted against them by the English Parlia-
ment. An excellent life of Sarsfield and history of his times has been
written by Alice Curtayne, and published by the Talbot Press, Dublin in
1935.
    The "Lament" which follows, translated by Mangan is one of many
composed about the beloved hero of Ireland. The refrain, *och! ochone!* is
omitted at the end of each stanza.

FAREWELL, O Patrick Sarsfield! May luck be on your path!
    Your camp is broken up—your work is marred for years—
But you go to kindle into flame the King of France's wrath,
    Though you leave sick Eire in tears.

May the white sun and moon rain glory on your head,
    All hero as you are, and holy Man of God!
To you the Saxons owe a many an hour of dread
    In the land you have often trod.

[168]

The Son of Mary guard you, and bless you to the end!
  'Tis altered is the time since your legions were astir,
When at Cullen you were hailed as the Conqueror and Friend,
  And you crossed narrow water near Birr.

I'll journey to the North, over mount, moor, and wave.
  'Twas there I first beheld, drawn up in file and line,
The brilliant Irish hosts—they were bravest of the Brave,
  But, alas! they scorned to combine!

I saw the royal Boyne, when its billows flashed with blood.
  I fought at Grána Oge, where a thousand horsemen fell.
On the dark empurpled field of Aughrim, too, I stood,
  On the plain by Tubberdonny's Well.

To the heroes of Limerick, the City of the Fights,
  Be my best blessing borne on the wings of the air!
We had card-playing there o'er our camp-fires at night,
  And the Word of Life, too, and prayer.

But, for you, Londonderry, may Plague smite and slay
  Your people! May ruin desolate you stone by stone!
Through you a many a gallant youth lies coffinless today,
  With the winds for mourners alone!

I clomb the high hill on a fair summer noon,
  And saw the Saxon Muster, clad in armour blinding
    bright,
Oh, rage withheld my hand, or gunsman and dragoon
  Should have supped with Satan that night!

How many a noble soldier, how many a cavalier,
  Careered along this road seven fleeting weeks ago,
With silver-hilted sword, with matchlock and with spear,
  Who now, *movrone*, lieth low!

All hail to thee Ben Hedir—But ah, on thy brow
  I see a limping soldier, who battled and who bled

[169]

Last year in the cause of the Stuart, though now
   The worthy is begging his bread!

And Diarmuid! oh Diarmuid! he perished in the strife—
   His head it was spiked on a halbert so high;
His colours they were trampled; he had no chance of life,
   If the Lord God himself stood by.

But most, oh, my woe! I lament and lament
   For the ten valiant heroes who dwelt nigh the Nore,
And my three blessed brothers! They left me, and they went
   To the wars—and returned no more!

On the Bridge of the Boyne was our first overthrow;
   By Slaney the next, for we battled without rest:
The third was at Aughrim. Oh, Eire thy woe
   Is a sword in my bleeding breast!

O! the roof above our heads it was barbarously fired,
   While the black Orange guns blazed and bellowed around.
And as volley followed volley, Colonel Mitchel enquired
   Whether Lucan[1] still stood his ground.

But O'Kelly still remains, to defy and to toil;
   He has memories that Hell won't permit him to forget,
And a sword that will make the blue blood flow like oil
   Upon many an Aughrim yet!

And I never shall believe that my Fatherland can fall
   With the Burkes, and the Decies, and the son of Royal
      James,
And Talbot the Captain, and *Sarsfield* above all,
   The beloved of damsels and dames.
                  Translated by James Clarence Mangan

[1] Sarsfield was Earl of Lucan.

EDMOND O'RYAN

(17th century)

AH! WHAT WOES ARE MINE

Supposedly written when the poet's mistress forsook him on the loss of his fortune. He had cast his lot with the last king of the Stuarts and his property was confiscated after the battle of the Boyne. He was one of the Rapparees.

AH! WHAT woes are mine to bear,
   Life's fair morn with clouds o'ercasting!
Doomed the victim of despair!
   Youth's gay bloom, pale sorrow blasting!

Sad the bird that sings alone,
   Flies to wilds, unseen to languish,
Pours, unheard, the ceaseless moan,
   And wastes on desert air its anguish!

Mine, O hapless bird! thy fate—
   The plundered nest,—the lonely sorrow!—
The lost—loved—harmonious mate!—
   The wailing night,—the cheerless morrow!

O thou dear hoard of treasured love!
   Though these fond arms should ne'er possess thee,
Still—still my heart its faith shall prove,
   And its last sighs shall breathe to bless thee!

Translated by Charlotte Brooke

[171]

EGAN O'RAHILLY
(c.1700)

From ON A PAIR OF SHOES PRESENTED TO HIM

There are twenty-three stanzas in praise of the shoes; each stanza is more extravagant than the preceding. The nine stanzas which follow are from the first part.

I HAVE received jewels of conspicuous beauty:
A pair of shoes, fair, smooth, handsome,
Of leather that was in white Barbary in the south,
And which the fleet of King Philip brought over the sea;

A pair of shoes, neat, decorated, well-trimmed;
A pair of shoes, durable, in stamping on great hills;
A pair of well finished shoes, beautifully trimmed:
A pair of shoes that are a protection from the roughness of the
        meads.

A pair of shoes, of light gear;
A pair of shoes, steady, in encounters with a foe;
A pair of shoes, slender, without fold, or wrinkle;
A pair of shoes, nimble, without seam, or gap;

A pair of shoes, valiant, splendid in public places:
A pair of shoes, made of the hide torn from the white cow,
The cow that was guarded in a desert place,
And watched over by a giant most carefully.

Phoebus for a season was in love with her,
So that he put Cadmus into black melancholy after her,
Until a bailiff stole her by night,
From the hundred-eyed head, the poor, ugly monster.

Shoes of this hide, they do not soften by the rain,
Nor do hot seasons harden their tops, or their soles;
Winds do not consume their beauty, or their lustre;
They do not shrink, or shrivel, through excessive heat.

[172]

The bristle that bound their edges, and their heels,
Was a most beautiful feather bristle which belonged to Tuis,
Which the children of Tuireann brought in their bark across
      sea
To Lughaidh, who was vigorous and strong.

      .   .   .   .

The awl that pierced this hide I tell you of,
Was made of steel the best tempered that could be procured;
Seven hundred years were the demons
Fashioning the point with the guile of Vulcan.

On the brink of Acheron grew the black hemp,
Spun by the hags of the band of Atropos,
By which the borders of the beauteous shoes were sewn,
Through the magical power of the three powerful Fates.

Translated by P. S. Dinneen
and T. O'Donoghue

THE STORM

A fragment from a longer poem of the same title.

Pitiful the playing of the flood with dire destruction!
Great the bulk of the waves, through the fury of the whirl-
      winds!
The ship's side and her crew were rocked mightily,
Screaming as they sank to the bottom without obtaining relief.

Translated by P. S. Dinneen
and T. O'Donoghue

MORE POWER TO CROMWELL

(A satiric salute)

MORE power to thee, O Cromwell,
   O king who hast established each rustic,

[173]

It is with thy coming we obtained peace,
 Honey, cream, and honour.

We ask that not Kavanagh,
 Nor Nolan, nor Kinsella,
Nor Burke, nor Rice, nor Roche,
 Ever get a sod of their ancestor's portion.

We ask that Cromwell be supreme,
 The noble king of Clan Lobus,
Who gave plenty to the man of the flail,
 And left the heir of the land without "nothing,"

We ask that all in this house,
 In goodness and in wealth,
Be better a year from today,
 And everyone whom we like.

Translated by P. S. Dinneen
and T. O'Donoghue

ON A COCK WHICH WAS STOLEN FROM
A GOOD PRIEST

WHEREAS Aongus, the philosophic,
 A pious, religious priest,
Came today into our presence,
 Making his complaint, and avouching:

That he bought a cock of high pedigree
 For his town and manor hens;
Whose crow and whose bloom of beauty were of the rarest,
 And whose neck was bright with every full color;

He gave fifty fair shillings
 For this bird of comeliest comb:
But a sprite, of druidical power,
 Stole it from the fair of the country town.

One like him (the priest), indeed, much requires
    A cock that crows and wakens,
To watch and keep him from soft slumber
    In the time of vesper devotions.

For this reason I command you,
    Ye state bailiffs of my court
Search ye the highways,
    And do it with zeal and earnestness:

Do not leave a *lios* or a fairy hillock,
    In which you hear noise or cackling,
Without searching for the fairy urchin,
    Who did the deed through plunder.

Wheresoever, in whatever hiding place,
    Ye find the little crab,
Bring him to me by a slender hair,
    That I may hand him as a silly oaf.

For your so doing, as is due,
    We hereby give you authority;
Given under our hand with a quillet
    This day of our era.

Translated by P. S. Dinneen
and T. O'Donoghue

THE GERALDINE'S DAUGHTER

A Beauty all stainless, a pearl of a maiden,
    Has plunged me in trouble, and wounded my heart:
With sorrow and gloom are my soul overladen;
    An anguish is there, that will never depart.
I could voyage to Egypt across the deep water,
    Nor care about bidding dear Eire farewell,
So I only might gaze on the Geraldine's Daughter,
    And sit by her side in some pleasant green dell.

[175]

Her curling locks wave round her figure of lightness,
    All dazzling and long, like the purest of gold;
Her blue eyes resemble twin stars in their brightness,
    And her brow is like marble or wax to behold!
The radiance of Heaven illumines her features,
    Where the Snows and the Rose have erected their throne;
It would seem that the sun had forgotten all creatures
    To shine on the Geraldine's Daughter alone!

Her bosom is swan-white, her waist smooth and slender,
    Her speech is like music, so sweet and so free;
The feelings that glow in her noble heart lend her
    A mien and a majesty lovely to see.
Her lips, red as berries, but riper than any,
    Would kiss away even a sorrow like mine.
No wonder such heroes and noblemen many
    Should cross the blue ocean to kneel at her shrine!

She is sprung from the Geraldine race—the great Grecians,
    Niece of Mileadh's sons of the Valorous Bands,
Those heroes, the sons of the olden Phenicians,
    Though now trodden down, without fame, without lands!
Of her ancestors flourished the Barrys and Powers,
    To the Lords of Bunratty she too is allied;
And not a proud noble near Cashel's high towers
    But is kin to this maiden—the Geraldine's Pride!

Of Saxon or Gael there are none to excel in
    Her wisdom, her features, her figure, this fair;
In all she surpasses the far-famed Helen,
    Whose beauty drove thousands to death and despair.
Whoe'er could but gaze on her aspect so noble
    Would feel from thenceforward all anguish depart,
Yet for me 'tis, alas! my worst woe and my trouble,
    That her image will always abide in my heart!

                Translated by James Clarence Mangan

TURLOUGH CAROLAN
(1670-1738)

THE CUP OF O'HARA

WERE I west in green Arran,
    Or south in Glanmore,
Where the long ships come laden
    With claret in store;
Yet I'd rather than shiploads
    Of claret, and ships,
Have your white cup, O'Hara,
    Up full at my lips.

But why seek in numbers
    Its virtues to tell,
When O'Hara's own chaplain
    Has said, saying well,—
"Turlough, bold son of Brian,
    Sit ye down, boy again,
Till we drain the great cupaun
    In another health to Keane." [1]
        Translated by Samuel Ferguson

WHY, LIQUOR OF LIFE?

THE BARD addresses whisky—
    Why, liquor of life! do I love you so;
    When in all our encounters you lay me low?
    More stupid and senseless I every day grow,
        What a hint—if I'd mend by the warning!
    Tattered and torn you've left my coat,
    I've not a cravat—to save my throat,
    Yet I pardon you all, my sparkling doat,
        If you'd cheer me again in the morning!

[1] Keane O'Hara, the patron of Carolan.

[177]

WHISKY replies—
        When you've heard prayers on Sunday next,
        With a sermon beside, or at least—the text,
        Come down to the alehouse—however you're vexed,
            And though thousands of cares assault you,
        You'll find tippling there—till morals mend,
        A cock shall be placed in the barrel's end,
        The jar shall be near you, and I'll be your friend,
            And give you a *Céad Mile Fáilte.*

THE BARD resumes his address—
        You're my soul and my treasure, without and within,
        My sister and cousin and all my kin;
        'Tis unlucky to wed such a prodigal sin,—
            But all other enjoyment is vain, love!
        My barley ricks all turn to you—
        My tillage—my plow—and my horses too—
        My cows and my sheep they have—bid me adieu,
            I care not while you remain, love!

        Come, vein of my heart! then come in haste,
        You're like Ambrosia, my liquor and feast,
        My forefathers all had the very same taste—
            For the genuine dew of the mountain.
        Oh! Usquebaugh! I love its kiss!—
        My guardian spirit, I think it is.
        Had my christening bowl been filled with this,
            I'd have swallowed it—were it a fountain.

        Many's the quarrel and fight we've had,
        And many a time you made me mad,
        But while I've a heart—it can never be sad,
            When you smile at me full on the table;
        Surely you are my wife and brother—
        My only child—my father and mother—
            My outside coat—I have no other!
            Oh! I'll stand by you—while I am able.

[178]

If family pride can aught avail,
I've the sprightliest kin of all the Gael—
Brandy and Usquebaugh, and Ale!
    But Claret untasted may pass us;
To clash with the clergy were sore amiss,
So, for righteousness' sake, I leave them this,
For Claret the gownsman's comfort is,
    When they've saved us with matins and masses.

Translated by John D'Alton

ANONYMOUS
(17th century)

DO YOU REMEMBER THAT NIGHT?

Do YOU remember that night
When you were at the window,
With neither hat nor gloves
Nor coat to shelter you?
I reached out my hand to you,
And you ardently grasped it,
I remained to converse with you
Until the lark began to sing.

Do you remember that night
That you and I were
At the foot of the rowan-tree,
And the night drifting snow?
Your head on my breast,
And your pipe sweetly playing?
Little thought I that night
That our love ties would loosen!

Beloved of my inmost heart,
Come some night, and soon,

[179]

When my people are at rest,
That we may talk together.
My arms shall encircle you
While I relate my sad tale,
That your soft, pleasant converse
Hath deprived me of heaven.

The fire is unraked,
The light is unextinguished,
The key under the door,
Do you softly draw it.
My mother is asleep,
But I am wide awake;
My fortune in my hand,
I am ready to go with you.

Translated by Eugene O'Curry

THOMAS FLAVELL
(Attributed. Late 17th century)

THE COUNTY OF MAYO

ON THE deck of Patrick Lynch's boat I sat in woeful plight,
Through my sighing all the weary day and weeping all the
    night.
Were it not that full of sorrow from my people forth I go,
By the blessed sun, 'tis royally I'd sing thy praise, Mayo.

When I dwelt at home in plenty, and my gold did much
    abound,
In the company of fair young maids the Spanish ale went
    round.
'Tis a bitter change from those gay days that now I'm forced
    to go,
And must leave my bones in Santa Cruz, far from my own
    Mayo.

[180]

They're altered girls in Irrul now; 'tis proud they're grown
    and high,
With their hair-bags and their top-knots—for I pass their
    buckles by.
But it's little now I heed their airs, for God will have it so,
That I must depart for foreign lands, and leave my sweet Mayo.

'Tis my grief that Patrick Loughlin is not Earl in Irrul still,
And that Brian Duff no longer rules as Lord upon the Hill;
And that Colonel Hugh MacGrady should be lying dead and
    low,
And I sailing, sailing swiftly from the county of Mayo.

Translated by George Fox

ANONYMOUS
(18th century)

THE WHITE COCKADE

KING CHARLES he is King James's son,
And from a royal line is sprung;
Then up with shout, and out with blade,
And we'll raise once more the white cockade.
Oh! my dear, my fair-haired youth,
Thou yet hast hearts of fire and truth;
Then up with shout, and out with blade—
We'll raise once more the white cockade.

My young men's hearts are dark with woe,
On my virgins' cheeks the grief-drops flow;
The sun scarce lights the sorrowing day,
Since our rightful prince went far away.
He's gone, the stranger holds his throne,
The royal bird far off is flown;
But up with shout, and out with blade—
We'll stand or fall with the white cockade.

[181]

No more the cuckoo hails the spring,
The woods no more with the staunch-hounds ring;
The song from the glen, so sweet before,
Is hushed since our Charles has left our shore.
The Prince is gone; but he soon will come,
With trumpet sound and with beat of drum:
Then up with shout, and out with blade;
Huzza for the right and the white cockade!

Translated by J. J. Callanan

ANONYMOUS
(18th century)

THE FAIR HILLS OF IRELAND

Attributed to an Irish student in one of the French Colleges.

A PLENTEOUS place is Ireland for hospitable cheer,
             Uileacán dubh O! [1]
Where the wholesome fruit is bursting from the yellow barley
       ear;
             Uileacán dubh O!
There is honey in the trees where her misty vales expand,
And her forest paths, in summer, are by falling waters fanned,
There is dew at high noontide there, and springs i' the yellow
       sand
On the fair hills of holy Ireland.

Curled he is and ringleted, and plaited to the knee,
             Uileacán dubh O!
Each captain who comes sailing across the Irish sea;
             Uileacán dubh O!
And I will make my journey, if life and health but stand,
Unto that pleasant country, that fresh and fragrant strand,

[1] O sad lament.

[182]

And leave your boasted braveries, your wealth and high com-
    mand,
For the fair hills of holy Ireland.

Large and profitable are the stacks upon the ground,
        Uileacán dubh O!
The butter and the cream do wondrously abound,
        Uileacán dubh O!
The cresses on the water and the sorrels are at hand,
And the cuckoo's calling daily his note of music bland,
And the bold thrush sings so bravely his song i' the forests
    grand,
On the fair hills of holy Ireland.

Translated by Samuel Ferguson

ANONYMOUS
(18th century)

O SAY, MY BROWN DRIMIN

O SAY, my brown Drimin, thou silk of the kine,
Where, where are thy strong ones, last hope of thy line?
Too deep and too long is the slumber they take;
At the loud call of Freedom why don't they awake?

My strong ones have fallen—from the bright eye of day,
All darkly they sleep in their dwelling of clay;
The cold turf is o'er them—they hear not my cries,
And since Louis no aid gives, I cannot arise.

Oh! where art thou, Louis? our eyes are on thee;
Are thy lofty ships walking in strength o'er the sea?
In Freedom's last strife if you linger or quail,
No morn e'er shall break on the night of the Gael.

[183]

But should the king's son, now bereft of his right,
Come proud in his strength for his country to fight;
Like leaves on the trees will new people arise,
And deep from their mountains shout back to my cries.

When the Prince, now an exile, shall come for his own,
The isles of his father, his rights and his throne,
My people in battle the Saxons will meet,
And kick them before, like old shoes from their feet.

O'er mountains and valleys they'll press on their route,
The five ends of Erin[1] shall ring to their shout:
My sons all united, shall bless the glad day
When the flint-hearted Saxons they've chased far away.

Translated by J. J. Callanan

ANONYMOUS
(18th century)

THE ROVING WORKER

This country ballad was popular in Ireland during the 18th century. It is known as the *Spailpiin Faanach* (The Roving Worker). The tune is that generally used in "The Girl I Left Behind Me." The Gaelic words date from the Fall of Limerick in 1694, when the Irish Brigade was formed.

No MORE—no more in Cashel town
I'll sell my health a-raking,
Nor on days of fairs rove up and down,
Nor join the merry making.
There, mounted farmers came in throngs
To seek and hire me over,
But now I'm hired, my journey's long,
The journey of the Rover!

[1] Five ends of Erin—The five kingdoms: Ulster, Munster, Leinster Connaught and Meath; as divided by the Milesian dynasty.

I've found what Rovers often do,
I trod my health down fairly;
And that wand'ring out in morning dew
Will gather fevers early.
No more shall flail swing o'er my head,
Nor my hand a spade-shaft cover,
But the Banner of France will float instead,
And the Pike stand by the Rover!

When to Callan once, with hook in hand,
I'd go for early shearing,
Or to Dublin town—the news was grand
That the "Rover gay" was nearing.
And soon with good gold home I'd go,
And my mother's field dig over,
But no more—no more this land shall know
My name as the "Merry Rover!"

Five hundred farewells to Fatherland!
To my loved and lovely island!
And to Culach boys—they'd better stand
Her guards by glen and highland.
But now that I am poor and lone,
A wand'rer—not in clover—
My heart it sinks with bitter moan
To have ever lived a Rover.

In pleasant Kerry lives a girl,
A girl whom I love dearly;
Her cheek's a rose, her brow's a pearl,
And her blue eyes shine so clearly!
Her long fair locks fall curling down
O'er breasts untouched by lover—
More dear than dames with a hundred poun'
Is she unto the Rover!

Ah, well I mind, my own men drove
My cattle in a small way;

With cows, with sheep, with calves, they'd move,
With steeds, too, west to Galway.
Heaven willed I'd loose each horse and cow,
And my health but half recover—
It breaks my heart, for *her* sake, now
That I'm only a sorry Rover.

But when once the French come o'er the main,
With stout camps in each valley,
With Buck O'Grady back again,
And poor brave Tadhg O'Dalaigh—
Oh, the Royal Barracks in dust shall lie,
The yeomen we'll chase over;
And the English clan be forced to fly—
'Tis the sole hope of the Rover!

Translated by George Sigerson

JOHN O'TUOMY
(1706-1775)

O'TUOMY'S DRINKING SONG

(Air: "The Growling Old Woman")

I SELL the best brandy and sherry,
To make my good customers merry;
  But at times their finances
  Run short, as it chances
And then I feel very sad, very!

Here's brandy! Come, fill up your tumbler;
Or ale, if your liking be humbler;
  And while you've a shilling,
  Keep filling and swilling—
A fig for the growls of the grumbler!

[186]

I like, when I'm quite at my leisure,
Mirth, music and all sorts of pleasure;
    When Margery's bringing
    The glass, I like singing
With bards—if they drink within measure.

Libation I pour on libation,
I sing the past fame of our nation
    For valour-won glory,
    For song and for story,
This, this is my grand recreation!

*Version by James Clarence Mangan
from the literal English of John O'Daly*

ANDREW MAGRATH
(1723?-179?)

ANDREW MAGRATH'S REPLY TO JOHN O'TUOMY

"Andrew Magrath and John O'Tuomy, two of the celebrated 18th century
Munster Bards, were friends and contemporaries. O'Tuomy, known as
O'Tuomy "the gay," ran an ale house which, despite the accusations of
Magrath in the lines below, did not prosper due to the spendthrift ways of
its proprietor; over his door was a large sign with this welcome:
        Should one of the stock of the noble Gael
        A brother bard who is fond of good cheer,
        Be short of the price of a tankard of ale,
        He is welcome to O'Tuomy a thousand times here!
This spirit of hospitality eventually led to bankruptcy and O'Tuomy died
in poverty, August 31, 1775. The drinking song and Magrath's reply were
written during the heyday of his hostel."
The "Boatman's Hymn" following has been attributed to Magrath.

O, TUOMY! you boast yourself handy
At selling good ale and bright brandy,
    But the fact is your liquor
    Makes every one sicker,
I tell you that, I, your friend Andy.

[187]

Again, you affect to be witty,
And your customers—more is the pity—
　　　　Give in to your folly,
　　　　While you, when you're jolly,
Troll forth some ridiculous ditty.

But your poems and pints, by your favour,
Are alike wholly wanting in flavour,
　　　　Because it's your pleasure,
　　　　You give us short measure,
And your ale has a ditch-water savour!

Vile swash do you sell us for porter,
And you draw the cask shorter and shorter;
　　　　Your guests then disdaining
　　　　To think of complaining,
Go tipple in some other quarter.

Very oft in your scant over-frothing
Tin quarts we found little or nothing;
　　　　They could very ill follow
　　　　The road, who would swallow
Such stuff for the inner man's clothing!

You sit gaily enough at the table,
But in spite of your mirth you are able
　　　　To chalk down each tankard,
　　　　And if a man drank hard
On tick—oh! we'd have such a Babel!

You bow to the floor's very level
When customers enter to revel,
　　　　But if one in shy raiment
　　　　Takes a drink without payment,
You score it against the poor devil.

When quitting your house rather heady,
They'll get nought without more of "the ready".

You leave them to stumble
And stagger and tumble
Into dykes, as folks will when unsteady.

Two vintners late went about killing
Men's fame by their vile Jack-and-Gilling;
Now, Tuomy, I tell you
I know very well you
Would, too, sell us all for a shilling.

The Old Bards never vainly shall woo me,
But your tricks and your capers, O'Tuomy,
Have nought in them winning—
You jest and keep grinning,
But your thoughts are all guileful and gloomy!

*Version by James Clarence Mangan
from the literal English of John O'Daly*

BOATMAN'S HYMN

BARK that bare me through foam and squall,
You in the storm are my castle wall:
Though the sea should redden from bottom to top,
From tiller to mast she takes no drop;
On the tide-top, the tide-top,
Wherry *aroon,* my land and store!
On the tide-top, the tide-top,
She is the boat can sail *go leor.*[1]

She dresses herself, and goes gliding on,
Like a dame in her robes of the Indian lawn;
For God has blessed her, gunnel and whale,
And oh! if you saw her stretch out to the gale,
On the tide-top, the tide-top,
Wherry *aroon,* my land and store!

[1] This word has come over into English as *galore.*

[189]

On the tide-top, the tide-top,
　　She is the boat can sail *go leor*.

Whillan,[2] ahoy! old heart of stone,
Stooping so black o'er the beach alone,
Answer me well—on the bursting brine
Saw you ever a bark like mine?
　　On the tide-top, the tide-top,
　　　　Wherry *aroon*, my land and store!
　　On the tide-top, the tide-top,
　　　　She is the boat can sail *go leor*.

Says Whillan: "Since first I was made of stone,
I have looked abroad o'er the beach alone—
But till to-day, on the bursting brine,
Saw I never a bark like thine,"
　　On the tide-top, the tide-top,
　　　　Wherry *aroon*, my land and store!
　　On the tide-top, the tide-top,
　　　　She is the boat can sail *go leor*.

"God of the air!" the seamen shout,
When they see us tossing the brine about;
"Give us shelter of strand or rock,
Or through and through us she goes with a shock!"
　　On the tide-top, the tide-top,
　　　　Wherry *aroon*, my land and store!
　　On the tide-top, the tide-top,
　　　　She is the boat can sail *go leor!*
　　　　　　　Translation by Samuel Ferguson

A literal translation of the third and fourth stanzas of "The Boatman's Hymn" follows. These are quoted by Ferguson and are presumably his.

O Whillan, rough, bold-faced rock, that stoopst o'er the bay,
Look forth at the new back beneath me cleaving her way;
Saw ye ever, on sea or river, 'mid the mounting of spray,

[2] Name of a rock in Blacksod Harbor, County Mayo.

Boat made of a tree that urges through the surges like mine
    to-day,
          On the tide-top, the tide-top?

"I remember," says Whillan, "a rock I have ever been;
And constant my watch, each day, o'er the sea-wave green;
But of all that I ever of barks and of galleys have seen,
This that urges through the surges beneath you to-day is
    queen
          On the tide-top, the tide-top."

LAMENT OF THE MANGAIRE SUGACH

"Andrew Magrath, commonly called the *Mangaire Sugaeh* (or "Jolly Merchant"), having been expelled from the Catholic Church for his licentious life, offered himself as a convert to the doctrines of Protestantism; but the Protestant clergyman having also refused to accept him, the unfortunate *Mangaire* gave vent to his feelings in this lament." *Translator's note.*

BELOVED, do you pity not my doleful case,
Pursued by priest and minister in dire disgrace?
The churchmen brand the vagabond upon my brow—
Oh! they'll take me not as Protestant or Papist now!

The parson calls me wanderer and homeless knave;
And though I boast the Saxon creed with aspect grave,
He says that claim my Popish face must disallow,
Although I'm neither Protestant nor Papist now!

He swears (and oh, he'll keep his oath) he's firmly bent
To hunt me down by penal Acts of Parliament;
Before the law's coercive might to make me bow,
And choose between the Protestant and Papist now!

The priest me deems a satirist of luckless lay,
Whose merchant-craft hath often led fair maids astray,
And, worse than hunted fugitive all disavow,
He'll take me not a Protestant or Papist now!

[191]

That, further, I'm a foreigner devoid of shame,
Of hateful, vile, licentious life and evil name;
A ranting, rhyming wanderer, without a cow,
Who now is deemed a Protestant—a Papist now!

Alas! it was not charity or Christian grace
That urged to drag my deeds before the Scotic race.
What boots it him to write reproach upon my brow,
Whether they deem me Protestant or Papist now?

Lo! David, Israel's poet-king, and Magdalene,
And Paul, who of the Christian creed the foe had been—
Did Heaven, when sorrow filled their heart, reject their vow
Though they were neither Protestant nor Papist now?

Oh! since I weep my wretched heart to evil prone,
A wanderer in the paths of sin, all lost and lone,
At other shrines with other flocks I fain must bow.
Who'll take me, whether Protestant or Papist, now?

Beloved, whither can I flee for peace at last,
When thus beyond the Church's pale I'm rudely cast?
The Arian creed, or Calvinist, I must avow,
When severed from the Protestant and Papist now!

Avran

Lo Peter the Apostle, whose lapses from grace were three,
Denying the Saviour, was granted a pardon free;
O God! though the *Mangaire* from him Thy mild laws cast,
Receive him, like Peter, to dwell in THY HOUSE at last!

Translated by Edward Walsh

[192]

ANONYMOUS
(18th century)

THE CONVICT OF CLONMEL

How hard is my fortune,
  And vain my repining!
The strong rope of fate
  For this young neck is twining!
My strength is departed,
  My cheeks sunk and sallow,
While I languish in chains
  In the jail of Clonmala.

No boy of the village
  Was ever yet milder;
I'd play with a child
  And my sport would be wilder;
I'd dance without tiring
  From morning till even,
And the goal-ball I'd strike
  To the lightning of heaven.

At my bed-foot decaying,
  My hurl-bat is lying;
Through the boys of the village
  My goal-ball is flying;
My horse 'mong the neighbors
  Neglected may fallow,
While I pine in my chains
  In the jail of Clonmala.

Next Sunday the patron
  At home will be keeping,
And the young active hurlers
  The field will be sweeping;
With the dance of fair maidens
  The evening they'll hallow,

[193]

While this heart once so gay
Shall be cold in Clonmala.

Translated by J. J. Callanan

ANONYMOUS

(18th century)

THE DAWNING OF THE DAY

At early dawn I once had been
  Where Lene's blue waters flow,
When summer bid the groves be green,
  The lamp of light to glow.
As on by bower, and town, and tower,
  And widespread fields I stray,
I met a maid in the greenwood shade
  At the dawning of the day.

Her feet and beauteous head were bare,
  No mantle fair she wore;
But down her waist fell golden hair,
  That swept the tall grass o'er.
With milking-pail she sought the vale,
  And bright her charms' display;
Outshining far the morning star
  At the dawning of the day.

Beside me sat that maid divine
  Where grassy banks outspread.
'Oh, let me call thee ever mine,
  Dear maid,' I sportive said.
'False man, for shame, why bring me blame?'
  She cried, and burst away—
The sun's first light pursued her flight
  At the dawning of the day.

Translated by Edward Walsh

[194]

ANONYMOUS
(18th century)

PEARL OF THE WHITE BREAST

THERE'S a colleen fair as May,
For a year and for a day
I've sought by every way—Her heart to gain.
There's no art of tongue or eye,
Fond youths with maidens try,
But I've tried with ceaseless sigh—Yet tried in vain.

If to France or far-off Spain,
She'd cross the watery main,
To see her face again—The sea I'd brave.
And if 't is Heaven's decree,
That mine she may not be,
May the Son of Mary me—In mercy save!

O thou blooming milk-white dove,
To whom I've given true love,
Do not ever thus reprove—My constancy.
There are maidens would be mine,
With wealth in hand and kine,
If my heart would but incline—To turn from thee.
But a kiss, with welcome bland,
And a touch of thy dear hand,
Are all that I demand,—Wouldst thou not spurn;
For if not mine, dear girl,
O Snowy-breasted Pearl!
May I never from the Fair—With life return!

Translated by George Petrie

[195]

ANONYMOUS
(18th century)

THE OUTLAW OF LOCH LENE

OH, MANY a day have I made good ale in the glen.
That came not of stream, or malt, like the brewing of men;
My bed was the ground; my roof the greenwood above,
And the wealth that I sought—one far kind glance from my
    love.

Alas! on the night when the horses I drove from the field,
That I was not near, from terror my angel to shield!
She stretched forth her arms—her mantle she flung to the wind,
And swam o'er Loch Lene, her outlawed lover to find.

Oh, would that a freezing, sleet-winged tempest did sweep,
And I and my love were alone far off on the deep!
I'd ask not a ship, or a bark, or pinnace to save—
With her hand round my waist, I'd fear not the wind or the
    wave.

'Tis down by the lake where the wild tree fringes its sides,
The maid of my heart, the fair one of heaven resides:
I think, as at eve she wanders its mazes along,
The birds go to sleep by the sweet wild twist of her song.

Translated by J. J. Callanan

ANONYMOUS
(18th century)

THE GIRL I LOVE

THE girl I love is comely, straight, and tall,
Down her white neck her auburn tresses fall;

[196]

Her dress is neat, her carriage light and free—
Here's a health to that charming maid, who e'er she be!

The rose's blush but fades beside her cheek,
Her eyes are blue, her forehead pale and meek,
Her lips like cherries on a summer tree—
Here's a health to the charming maid, who e'er she be!

When I go to the field no youth can lighter bound,
And I freely pay when the cheerful jug goes round;
The barrel is full, but its heart we soon shall see—
Come, here's to that charming maid, who e'er she be!

Had I the wealth that props the Saxon's reign,
Or the diamond crown that decks the King of Spain,
I'd yield them all if she kindly smiled on me—
Here's a health to the maid I love, who e'er she be!

Five pounds of gold for each lock of her hair I'd pay,
And five times five for my love one hour each day;
Her voice is more sweet than the thrush on its own green tree—
Then, my dear, may I drink a fond deep health to thee!

Translated by J. J. Callanan

WILLIAM ENGLISH
(died 1778)

CASHEL OF MUNSTER

I'D WED you without herds, without money, or rich array,
And I'd wed you on a dewy morning at day-dawn gray;
My bitter woe it is, love, that we are not far away
In Cashel town, though the bare deal board were our marriage
    bed this day!

[197]

Oh, fair maid, remember the green hill side,
Remember how I hunted about the valleys wide;
Time now has worn me; my locks are turned to gray,
The year is scarce and I am poor, but send me not, love, away!

Oh, deem not my blood is of base strain, my girl,
Oh, deem not my birth was as the birth of the churl;
Marry me, and prove me, and say soon you will,
That noble blood is written on my right side still!

My purse holds no red gold, no coin of the silver white,
No herds are mine to drive through the long twilight!
But the pretty girl that would take me, all bare though I be and
    lone,
Oh, I'd take her with me kindly to the county Tyrone.

Oh, my girl, I can see 'tis in trouble you are,
And, oh, my girl, I see 'tis your people's reproach you bear:
"I am a girl in trouble for his sake with whom I fly,
And, oh, may no other maiden know such reproach as I!"

Translated by Samuel Ferguson

ANONYMOUS
(18th century)

YOUGHALL HARBOR

One Sunday morning, into Youghall walking,
    I met a maiden upon the way;
Her little mouth sweet as fairy music,
    Her soft cheeks blushing like dawn of day!
I laid a bold hand upon her bosom,
    And asked a kiss: but she answered, "No:
Fair sir, be gentle; do not tear my mantle;
    'Tis none in Erin my grief can know.

[198]

" 'Tis but a little hour since I left Youghall,
   And my love forbade me to return;
And now my weary way I wander
   Into Cappoquin, a poor girl forlorn:
Then do not tempt me; for, alas! I dread them
   Who with tempting proffers teach girls to roam,
Who'd first deceive us, then faithless leave us,
   And send us shame-faced and barefoot home."

"My heart and hand here! I mean you marriage!
   I have loved like you and known love's pain;
And if you turn back now to Youghall Harbor,
   You ne'er shall want house or home again:
You shall have a lace cap like any lady,
   Cloak and capuchin, too, to keep you warm,
And if God please, maybe, a little baby,
   By and by to nestle within your arm."

Translated by Samuel Ferguson

PATRICK HEALY
(18th century)

MY WISHES

OH! COULD I acquire my fullest desire.
   To mould my own life, were it given;
I would be like the sage, who in happy old age.
   Disowns every link—but with heaven.

An acre or two, as my wants would be few,
   Could supply quite enough for my welfare;
In that scope I would deem my power supreme,
   And acknowledge no king but—myself there.

The soil of this spot, the best to be got,
   Should furnish me fruit—and a choice store;

[199]

Be sheltered and warm from rain and from storm,
    And favoured with sunshine and moisture.

My home should abound, and my table be crowned
    With comfort, but not ostentation;
The music of mirth should hum round my hearth,
    And books be my night's recreation:

Delightful retreat, in simplicity sweet!
    A wood and a streamlet should bound it;
And the birds when I wake, from each bower and brake,
    Should pour their wild melodies round it.

This streamlet midst flowers, and murmuring bowers,
    In the shade of rich fruits should meander;
While the brisk finny race, o'er its sunshiny face,
    Should leap—flit—and sportively wander.

These joys—yet one more might enliven my store,
    Redouble each comfort and pleasure;
A wife, of such truth, such virtue and youth,
    That her smiles would be more than a treasure.

Let nineteen, and no more, to my twenty-four,
    Be the scale of her years to a letter;
Then a babe every Easter, I think won't molest her,
    No—I warrant she'll like me the better.

                              Translated by John D'Alton.

DIARMAD O'CURNAIN
(1740-182-?)

LOVE'S DESPAIR

    I AM desolate,
    Bereft by bitter fate;

No cure beneath the skies can save me,
  No cure on sea or strand,
  Nor in any human hand—
But hers, this paining wound who gave me.

  I know not night from day,
  Nor thrush from cuckoo gray,
Nor cloud from the sun that shines above thee—
  Nor freezing cold from heat,
  Nor friend—if friend I meet;
I but know—heart's love!—I love thee.

  Love that my life began,
  Love that will close life's span,
Love that grows ever by love-giving;
  Love from the first to last,
  Love till all life be passed,
Love that loves on after living!

  This love I gave to thee,
  For pain love has given me,
Love that can fail or falter never—
  But, spite of earth above,
  Guards thee, my Flower of love,
Thou Marvel-maid of·life, for ever.

  Bear all things evidence,
  Thou art my very sense,
My past, my present, and my morrow!
  All else on earth is crossed,
  All in the world is lost—
Lost all, but the great love-gift of sorrow.

  My life not life, but death:
  My voice not voice—a breath;
No sleep, no quiet—thinking ever
  On thy fair phantom face,

Queen eyes and royal grace,
Lost loveliness that leaves me never.

I pray thee grant but this:
From thy dear mouth one kiss,
That the pang of death-despair pass over:
Or bid make ready nigh
The place where I shall lie,
For aye, thy leal and silent lover.

Translated by George Sigerson

ANONYMOUS
(18th century)

THE FAIR-HAIRED GIRL

THE sun has set, the stars are still,
The red moon hides behind the hill;
The tide has left the brown beach bare,
The birds have fled the upper air;
Upon her branch the lone cuckoo
Is chanting still her sad adieu;
And you, my fair-haired girl, must go
Across the salt sea under woe!

I through love have learned three things,
Sorrow, sin, and death it brings;
Yet day by day my heart within
Dares shame and sorrow, death and sin:
Maiden, you have aimed the dart
Rankling in my ruined heart:
Maiden, may the God above
Grant you grace to grant me love!

Sweeter than the viol's string,
And the notes that blackbirds sing;

Brighter than the dewdrops rare
Is the maiden wondrous fair:
Like the silver swans at play
Is her neck, as bright as day!
Woe is me, that e'er my sight
Dwelt on charms so deadly bright!

Translated by Samuel Ferguson

ANONYMOUS
(18th century)

DEAR DARK HEAD

Put your head, darling, darling, darling,
  Your darling black head my heart above;
Oh, mouth of honey, with the thyme for fragrance,
  Who, with heart in breast, could deny you love?
Oh, many and many a young girl for me is pining,
  Letting her locks of gold to the cold wind free,
For me, the foremost of our gay young fellows;
  But I'd leave a hundred, pure love, for thee!
Then put your head, darling, darling, darling,
  Your darling black head my heart above;
Oh, mouth of honey, with the thyme for fragrance,
  Who, with heart in breast, could deny you love?

Translated by Samuel Ferguson

BRIAN MERRIMAN

(c.1780)

THE MIDNIGHT COURT

One of the greatest late Gaelic poems, this witty and broad satire is
written in the usual Irish form of a vision or *Aisling*. The issues up for
debate at the court of the Fairy Queen Eevell are the misfortunes of Ireland.

Part One

'TWAS my wont to wander beside the stream
On the soft greensward in the morning beam,
Where the woods stand thick on the mountain-side
Without trouble or care what might betide.
My heart would leap at the lake's near blue,
The horizon and the far-off view,
The hills that rear their heads on high
Over each other's backs to spy.
'Twould gladden the soul with dole oppressed,
With sorrows seared and with cares obsessed
Of the outcast Gael without gold or goods
To watch for a while o'er the tops of the woods
The ducks in their flocks on the tide, the swan
Gliding with stately gait along,
The fish that leap on the air with glee
And the speckled perch with gambols free,
The labouring waves laving the shore
With glistening spray and rumbling roar,
The sea-gulls shrieking and reeling wide,
And the red deer romping in woodland ride,
The bugle's blare and the huntsman's yell
And the hue and cry of the pack pell-mell.
Yesterday morn the sky was clear
In the dog-days' heat of the mad mid-year,
And the sun was scouring the slumb'rous air
With his burning beams and gleaming glare,
And the leaves lay dense on the bending trees
And the lush grass waved in the scented breeze.

Blossom and spray and spreading leaf
Lightened my load and laid my grief,
Weary and spent with aching brain
I sank and lay on the murmuring plain,
In the shade of a tree with feet outspread
With my hot brow bared and shoe-gear shed.
When I closed the lids on my languid eyes
And covered my face from teasing flies
In slumber deep and in sleep's delusion
The scene was changed in strange confusion,
My frame was heaved and my head turned round
Without sense or sight in sleep profound.
I fancied there as I dare avouch
That the land was quaking beneath my couch,
And a hurricane blew with fury o'er me
And tongues of fire flared forth before me.
I threw a glance with beglamoured eyes
And beheld a hag of hideous guise,
Her shape with age and ague shook,
The plain she scoured with glowering look,
Her girth was huge, her height was quite
Seven yards or more if I reckoned it right,
Her cloak's tail trailed a perch's length,
She gripped a staff with manful strength,
Her aspect stark with angry stare,
Her features tanned by wind and air,
Her rheumy eyes were red and blear,
Her mouth was stretched from ear to ear,
A plate of brass held fast her bonnet
With bailiff's powers inscribed upon it.
She grimly gazed and gruffly spake:—
'You lazy laggard, arise! awake!
Is this the way for you, wretch, to be,
When the court is seated for all to see?
No court of robbers and spoilers strong
To maintain the bane of fraud and wrong,
But the court of the poor and lowly-born,
The court of women and folk forlorn.

[205]

It's joyful hearing for Erin that
The Good Folk's Host have in Council sat
On the mountain's summit for three days' space
In Brean Moy Graney's meeting-place.
His Highness grieves and his noble throng
That Erin lingers in thraldom long,
Wasted by woe without respite,
To misery's hand abandoned quite,
Her land purloined, her laws decayed,
Her wealth destroyed and her trust betrayed,
Her fields and pastures with weeds o'ergrown,
Her ground untilled and her crops unsown,
Her chieftains banished and an upstart band
Of hirelings holding the upper hand,
Who'd skin the widow and orphan child
And grind the weak and the meek and mild.
Shame 'tis, sure, that the poor oppressed
By lawless might, in plight distressed,
Get nought for aught but extortion vile,
The judge's fraud and the lawyer's wile,
The tyrant's frown and the sycophant's sneer
Bribing with fee and with fawning leer.
'Twas among the plaints that there were pleaded—
For every wrong was heard and heeded—
A charge in which you'll be implicated,
That the men and youths remain unmated,
And your maids in spinsterhood repining
And their bloom and beauty in age declining,
And the human race apace decreasing
With wars and famines and plagues unceasing,
The pride of kings and princes feeding,
Since your lads and lasses have left off breeding.
Your scanty brood 'tis sad to see
With women in bands on land and sea,
Buxom maids that fade obscure
And tender slips with lips that lure,
Damsels shy by shame retarded
And willing wenches unregarded.

[206]

'Tis sad no noble seed should rise
From lads of lusty thews and thighs,
'Twere well could all know what maids' woes are,
Prepared to fall on the first proposer.
To consider the case with due precision
The council came to a new decision,
To find the fittest among the throng
To learn the right and requite the wrong.
They appointed straight a maid serene,
Eevell of Craglee, Munster's queen,
To hold her court and preside there o'er it
And invite the plaintiffs to plead before it.
The gentle lady swore to elicit
Of falsehood purged the truth explicit,
To hear the plea of the unbefriended
And see the state of the hapless mended.
This court is seated in Feakle now,
Arise and trudge, for you thither must go,
Arise and trudge without more delay,
Arise at once for I'll take no nay!'
She clapped her claw on my cape behind
And whisked me away like a wisp on the wind
O'er mud and mire, mountain and valley,
To Moinmoy Hill at the churchyard alley.
'Tis sure I saw with torches flaring
A lofty hall with trumpets blaring,
With glare of light and brightly burnished,
With fleeces draped and great doors furnished,
And the portly queen with a courtly gesture
On the judge's bench in a splendid vesture,
And a troop of toughs with gruff demeanour
To clear the court and escort and screen her,
And people in throngs along the benches
Both women and men and boys and wenches,
And a weeping nymph in the witness-box
Of comely mould and golden locks,
With heaving breast and face aflame
And tears that gushed with grief and shame,

[207]

With flowing hair and staring eyes
And moans and groans and sobs and sighs.
Her passion's blast at last abated,
Weary of woe, with sorrow sated,
She dried her eyes, her sighs surmounted,
And in these words her woes recounted:—
'We give you greeting, Eevell fair,
Gracious queen, your people's care,
Who pity the poor and relieve their plight
And save the brave and retrieve the right.
'Tis the cause of my anguish and grief of heart,
The source of my sorrow and inward smart,
My wounding rending pain unending,
The way our women thro' life are wending,
Gray gloomy nuns with the grave pursuing,
Since our men and maidens have left off wooing;
Myself among them condemned to wait
Without hope and mope in the maiden state,
Without husband heaping the golden store
Or children creeping on hearth and floor,
In dread and fear—a drear subsistence—
Of finding nought to support existence,
By troubles pressed and by rest forsaken,
By cares consumed and by sorrows shaken.
Chaste Eevell, hasten to the relief
Of the women of Erin in their grief,
Wasting their pains in vain endeavour
To meet with mates who elude them ever,
Till in the ages is such disparity
We would not touch them except from charity,
With bleary eyes and wry grimaces
To scare a maiden from their embraces.
And if in manhood's warm pulsation
A youth is tempted to change his station,
He chooses a dour and sour-faced scold
Who's wasted her days in raising gold;
No lively lass of sweet seventeen
Of figure neat and features clean,

[208]

But blear-eyed hag or harridan brown
With toothless jaws and hairless crown
And snotty nose and dun complexion
And offering constant shrill correction.
My heart is torn and worn with grieving,
And my breast distressed with restless heaving,
With torture dull and with desperation
At the thought of my dismal situation,
When I see a bonny and bold young blade
With comely features and frame displayed,
A sturdy swearer or spanking buck,
A sprightly strapper with spunk and pluck,
A goodly wopper well made and planned,
A gamey walloper gay and grand,
Nimble and brave and bland and blithe,
Eager and active and brisk and lithe,
Of noted parts and of proved precocity,
Sold to a scold or old hidiosity,
Withered and worn and blear and brown,
A mumbling, grumbling, garrulous clown,
A surly, sluttish and graceless gawk
Knotted and gnarled like a cabbage's stalk,
A sleepy, sluggish decayed old stump,
A useless, juiceless and faded frump.
Ah, woe is me! there's a crumpled crone
Being buckled to-night while I'm left lone,
She's a surly scold and a bold-faced jade
And this moment she's merry—and me a maid!
Why wouldn't they have myself in marriage?
I'm comely and shapely, of stately carriage,
I've a mouth and a smile to make men dream
And a forehead that's fair with ne'er a seam,
My teeth are pearls in a peerless row,
Cherries to vie with my lips pray show,
I've a dancing, glancing, entrancing eye,
Roguish and rakish and takish and sly,
Gold lacks lustre beside my hair,
And every curl might a saint ensnare,

[209]

My cheeks are smooth without stain or spot,
Dimpled and fresh without blemish or blot,
My throat, my hands, my neck, my face,
Rival each other in dainty grace,
I've hips and ankles and lips and breast
And limbs to offer as good as the best.
Look at my waist tight-laced and slim,
I'm not coarse or ragged or rank of limb,
Not stringy or scraggy or lanky or lean
But as fair a female as e'er was seen
A pleasing, teasing and tempting tart
That might coax and entice the coldest heart.
If I were a tasteless, graceless, baggage,
A slummocky scut of cumbrous carriage,
A sloven or slut or frump or fright,
Or maid morose and impolite,
An awkward gawk of ungainly make,
A stark and crooked and stiff old stake,
A senseless, sightless, bent old crone,
I wouldn't complain if they left me alone.
I've never been present that I'm aware
At wedding or wake or fete or fair,
At the racing-ring or the hurling-ground
Or wherever the menfolk may be found,
But I've managed to make some shape and show
And been bedizened from top to toe
With stylish hood and starched coiffure
And powder-sprinkled chevelure,
My speckled gown with ribbons tied
And ruffles with the richest vied,
With cardinal of scarlet hue
And facings pleasing to the view,
And cambric apron gaily sown
With blowsy flowers of kind unknown,
And rigid hoops and buckled shoes
With smooth high heels attached by screws
And silken gloves and costly lace
And flounces, fringes, frills and stays.

Mind, do not think I'm an artless gull,
A stupid, unsocial or bashful trull,
Timid, a prey to wayward fancies,
Or shy or ashamed of a man's advances.
I'm ever on view to the crowds that pass
At market or meeting or Sunday Mass,
At supper or social or raffle or race
Or wherever the gayest are going the pace,
At party or pattern or picnic or fete
In hopes that I'd click with some lad soon or late;
But all my pursuit is a futile endeavour,
They've baulked me and bilked me and slipped from me ever,
They've baffled my schemes and my best-conceived art,
They've spurned me and turned from me and tattered my
     heart;
After all my advances, my ogling and sighing,
My most killing glances, my coaxing and eyeing,
After all I have spent upon readers of palms
And tellers of tea-leaves and sellers of charms.
There isn't a plan you can conceive
For Christmas or Easter or All Saints' Eve,
At the moon's eclipse or the New Year's chime
That I haven't attempted time on time.
I never would sleep a night in bed
Without fruit-stuffed stocking beneath my head,
I would steep my shift in the millstream deep
And await the vows of my spouse in sleep,
With broom I brushed the barn as bid,
My nails and hair in ashpit hid,
Beneath the hearth the flail I laid,
Below my pillow placed the spade,
My distaff in the graveyard's bed,
In lime-kiln low my ball of thread,
The flax I strewed amid the dust,
A cabbage-head in bed-straw thrust,
At every stage, by rage distraught,
The deuce and his dam aloud besought.
'Tis why I'm laying my case before ye

[211]

That I'm single still at the end of the story,
And age draws near with outrageous pace
To rob my form of its former grace.
O matchless maid, have mercy, pray,
E'er my freshness fade and my charms decay
And you see me left in plight forlorn
My beauty's prime and pride to mourn,
With bleaching hairs, by cares oppressed,
On unfriendly hearths an unwelcome guest.
By blood and wounds, fire, thunder, air,
Of shame and scorn I've borne my share,
My plans and plots foiled and frustrated
Whilst I view my nearest kindred mated.
Jane has a fine and fair-faced spouse
And Kate is waiting to take the vows,
Helen has hooked a handsome buck
And with jeers and gibes derides my luck,
My neighbour Nan is spliced with a spanker
While I'm left on the shelf to cark and canker,
Consider my case and face my plight,
And say if you dare that it's fair and right.
Too long I wait and waste my pains,
One hope untried as yet remains,
A potent charm as I have heard
Is putrid herbs well stewed and stirred,
I know the sort and will proceed
To make it aid me in my need.
A subtle spell that succour brings
Is orchid's leaves and dungfly's wings
And roots of figwort powdered well
With more besides I may not tell.
'Twas wondered everywhere of late
How yonder maid secured a mate,
At Shrove her secret she confessed
And Hallow E'en has seen her braced,
For water-spiders soaked in beer
And withered grass formed all her fare.

[212]

So, pity, queen, my lonely plight
Or troth! I'll try the plan to-night.'

Part Two

Scarce ended was the maid's harangue
When a gruff old warrior upsprang
Of rugged build and rude attire
And trembling less with age than ire,
A ragged, tattered, battered figure,
And up he stood and spoke with vigour:—
'The devil snatch you, snotty bitch,
You dowdy daughter of a witch,
Our sun's eclipse, sure, is no wonder
And all the ills we labour under,
That still our numbers, wealth and worth
Decay and dwindle from the earth,
For artful women are our ruin
And all we suffer is their doing.
You shameless drab, where is the man
That knows not you and all your clan
Who begging of your betters pass
A streeling, straying, cadging class?
Who is there doesn't know your dad
A brutal, brawling, crawling cad,
A spalpeen without friends or fame
Whom no one speaks of but to blame,
A withe around his waist, his back
Unclad but for a clout of sack?
Believe my words, if he and his
Were all sold up, from what there is
The proceeds would not quench your thirst
When every debt had been disbursed.
Is't not a joke uncommon how
A beggar without sheep or cow
Parades in satin, silk and lace
With handkerchief to fan her face?
Your ruffles and your cambric sleeve

[213]

And bonnet cleverly deceive
Altho' beneath your coat, alack,
No shred nor tatter clothes your back.
But who could your make-up discover
Or guess unless he were your lover
That canvas bands your hips encased
And they're not stays that press your waist,
Or that beneath the gloves you wore
Your hands were chapped and cracked and sore?
But tell the court or else must I
How long you've ate your dinner dry
And griped your stomach as with hooks
By eating sour unsalted Bucks.
I've seen the place in which you sleep,
Nor quilt nor cover there you keep,
Nought but a dirty mat outspread
Where not a dog would lay his head,
With neither blanket, rag nor sheet
In your poor frame to keep the heat,
Within a reeking, leaking shack
With sprouting weeds in every crack,
With water springing thro' the floor
And trail of hens from door to door
And crazy roof and couples bending
And rain in fearful floods descending.
By all the saints, to see her pass
You'd say she was a likely lass,
With flaunting gown and fine array,
Where did she raise it, who can say?
Come tell us where you got the gown,
Whence have the frills and flounces flown,
Whence came the shoes, whence came the coat,
Whence did the rings and ribbons float?
Just Eevell, grant me too a hearing
And help the hapless men of Erin
By scheming females bought and bound
And like stray bullocks put in pound.
Come hear a case, my own next neighbour

[214]

Who makes a living off his labour,
A simple, sober, honest boy
Has taken a jilt to kill his joy.
It makes my heart to smart with passion
To see her flounced out in the fashion,
With corn in barn and scores of cattle
And land and cash in hand to rattle.
I saw her lately at the fair
With lofty look and nose in air
Compelling every passer-by
To doff before her queenly eye.
So proud her air and her address,
So grave her carriage, who would guess
What light repute, what evil fame,
The country gave her whence she came,
Or that the name of that wild wench
Made every matron blush and blench?
The world will talk, as well it may,
Of all her deeds for many a day,
And what at Ibrickane was seen
Or Tiermaclane of meadows green;
Her name and fame will never fade
In Craglee where the rope is made,
At Ennis, Quin and Killaloe,
And up and down the county thro'.
Oh fie, alas for female fame!
I might forgive her former shame,
But lately far from her abode
I spied her on the Doora Road,
Stretched out as naked as a nigger
Beneath each rude and rough turf-digger.
What grace in rite of clergy dwells!
Or who can read the riddle else?
That she was slender all her life
Until she was a wedded wife,
Tho' every gallant in the land
'Tis known enjoyed her favours bland,
And from the day the priest did read

The Ego Vos that Christ decreed
Till she was running at the paps
Not less than nine months did elapse.
What man alive, if warned before
The wedding service shut the door
And barred escape, would mar his life
And kill contentment with a wife?
Alas! the theme affects me nearly,
And for my knowledge I've paid dearly;
The world knows well how once I held
My head up high, my heart unquelled,
My house with meat and drink replete
Where squires and justices might meet,
My fields in flocks and herds abounding
And rich and poor my praises sounding,
With friends and fame among the great,
A man of substance, worth and weight,
With peace and plenty as my portion—
With Kate I lost both fame and fortune.
She was a damsel plump and fair,
A curl in her comely auburn hair,
A light in her lewd insidious eyes,
And each lure that the daughters of Eve devise,
Shapely and smooth in frame and face,
With a ravishing charm in her air and grace,
My sense and my reason the rogue did steal
And I shook with desire from head to heel.
Lord! for my folly I've paid in full
In taking for wife that trolloping trull,
Day and night I am treading on needles and pins
Since I buckled that bride to my side—for my sins!
We were joined by the glue of the joiner for ever
In the splice we might split not till death should dissever,
With my own purse I paid without stint or evasion
Every debt that was due for that day's dissipation,
The town I regaled with a fabulous feast
And paid a fat fee to the clerk and the priest,
The neighbours were gathered from far and from wide

To carouse at the cost of the bridegroom and bride,
The torches were lit and the tables spread thick
With drink till each guest was stretched speechless and sick,
There was music and singing and sets of quadrilles
With the men in their frocks and the ladies in frills.
Ah, would they had crammed me with meat and with wine
Till I choked and I never had lived to repine
With the wretch who has wrested my comfort away
And driven me senseless and friendless and gray!
Not long was I married before I was told
By neighbours and strangers, by young and by old,
She was gadding to revels and reckless carouses
With lovers in legions, both single and spouses.
I believed not a word that I heard of her fame
Nor would suffer one speck to besmirch her good name
And set down to malice or idle invention
Whatever the gossips against her might mention,
Whilst like a fond fool I believed all the lies
Which her false lips affirmed with sobs and with sighs.
No idle reports or vain rumours were they
That came to my ears both by night and by day,
For no further the painful account to pursue—
Young master appeared long before he was due.
Picture at waking my wonder and fright—
A family warming me after the night!
The mother in bed and the midwife attending,
For posset and sugar and fresh fuel sending.
Not a sight nor a peep could I get of the pup,
The women to hoodwink me covered him up,
' 'Twere wrong to expose him, so young and so frail,
The wind would destroy if a breath should assail.'
They argued and pleaded and weeping implored,
I threatened with fury and swore by the Lord,
I stamped and I ramped and I raged and reviled
Until weary of strife they surrendered the child.
'Lift him up gently, have care how you take him,
Mind not to bruise him or squeeze him or shake him,
A fall she had forced him before the date surely,

[217]

It's ten chances to one that he'll die prematurely,
If he lives till the morning in time for the priest
To be called for the christening he's better deceased.'
I cut the knot from the swathing wrap
And laid the baby across my lap—
By heaven, the child was a powerful brat,
Sturdy and strong and bonny and fat,
Without flaw in flesh, in blood or in bone,
With nostrils wide and with nails full-grown,
Broad and brawny in thighs and chest
And with face and figure as good as the best!
I laughed aloud at the vain delusion
And the women were covered with fright and confusion.
This bond of the prelates I pray you revoke
For the sake of the necks not yet under the yoke,
'Tis the cause of the dearth and decrease of our nation
And the source of our sickly and sad generation,
But a brave breed of heroes would spring in its place,
If this bar were removed, to replenish the race,
For why call a priest in to bind and to bless
Before candid nature can give one caress?
Why lay the banquet and why pay the band
To blow their bassoons and their cheeks to expand?
Since Mary the Mother of God did conceive
Without calling the clergy or begging their leave,
The love-gotten children are famed as the flower
Of man's procreation and nature's power;
For love is a lustier sire than law
And has made them sound without fault or flaw,
And better and braver in heart and head
Than the puny breed of the bridal bed,
In body and brains and gifts and grace
The palm is borne by the bastard race.
'Tis easy to prove the thing I say
For I've one of my own, mavrone, this day,
Look at him on his nurse's knee,
Let him be brought that the court may see.
Say when did you see so fine a creature?

Where is his flaw in form or feature?
'Tis easily known when grown a man
Passers will pause his shape to scan.
He's not feeble or frail or pale or thin
Nor a shapeless bundle of bone and skin,
Not lean or lanky or sickly or sad
But an eager and active and lusty lad.
Never an aged sire begat
In a cold embrace that comely brat,
A weary, wasted and worn old man,
Wrinkled and shrunk and weak and wan,
But some sturdy stripling, brisk and brave,
Tingling and taut with nature's crave.
Then, O peerless maid, impose no more
To sully our stock this senseless law,
But let simple nature and noble blood
Mix and make a godlike brood;
Let high and low in love unite
Like the birds and beasts by nature's right,
And tell the tidings of this decree
In the cot and the castle from sea to sea.
'Twill restore to Erin the spirit of old
And rear a race of heroic mould
With back and sinews and thighs and chest
Such as Gaull MacMorna of yore possessed;
The seas will be filled with more fish than now
And the mountains yield to the tooth of the plough
And your name will be lauded far and wide
And your fame in the land for ever abide."

Part Three

Meanwhile the maid could scarce restrain
The angry tears which sprang amain,
With shaking voice and eyes inflamed
Rose she in wrath and thus exclaimed:—
'O wretch, by Craglee's crown I swear
But that you're old and crazed with care
And but for the ceremony that's due

[219]

To this court 'twould be short till I'd do for you!
I'd knock your noddle 'gainst the table
And break your bones and your limbs disable,
And wring your stringy windpipe well
And pitch your soul to the pit of hell.
I wonder breathless at your brass
But I'll not let the libel pass,
The story straightway I'll relate
Of that unhappy fair one's fate.
She was poor and in sad plight
Without shelter from wind and rain at night,
Homeless and driven for no sin
From fence to ditch without friends or kin.
The old stick offered her silver and gold,
A roof and turf from the rain and cold,
Flax and wool to weave and wear,
And cattle and sheep and goods and gear.
The world and this worm himself well knew
She cared not for him nor ever could do,
But worn by want and her abject state
Chose the lesser ill of an unloved mate.
Woeful work was his weak embrace
And the old goat's rough mouth on her face,
His limbs of lead and his legs of ice
And his lifeless load on her breast and thighs,
His blue-blotched shins so bleak and cold
And the bleached skin hanging in fold on fold.
Was there ever a fine girl fresh and fair
Who would not grow gray with grief and care
To bed with a bundle of skin and bone
As cold and stiff as a stick or stone,
Who would scarcely lift the lid from the dish
To know was it flesh or fowl or fish?
Ah say, I pray, had she not the right
To one caress in the course of a night?
Did she fail thro' her fault d'you think?
'Tis sure from her share she ne'er would shrink;
The brunt of the battle she would not burke

[220]

Or blench if the livelong night were work.
If he got the horns he deserved the same
And the luckless lady was not to blame;
Where's the fox that prowls or the owl that preys
Or the fish that swims or the stag that strays
That would starve or stint for a single day
With booty there to be borne away?
Is there bird or beast in the whole wide earth
That would droop and die from drouth or dearth
And peck the pavement or bite the ground
Where pastures fat and fruits abound?
Come answer me this, you cur, confess,
Is the table poorer, the banquet less,
Does the dish disgust which pleased before,
Does the pang of hunger plague the more,
Is the rapture fainter, the flavour fled,
If a score of others before have fed?
Do you dread, you dotard, of drouth to die,
Can you drain the Shannon or drink it dry,
Can you draw the sea from its base of sand,
Or hold its waters within your hand?
Learn your folly, you mangy hound,
Go bind your eyes with a bandage round,
Don't fume or fret or resentment chew,
If the fair has favours for more than you,
If she saw her lovers the livelong day
Is the night not enough for your purpose, pray?
The blame, I own, would be not so great
In a young and limber and lusty mate,
A frisky flaker in manhood's noon,
A sly heart-breaker or gay gossoon,
A roguish coaxer or sprightly spark,
A tasty trickster nate and smart,
Bonny and brisk and blithe and bold
With features and form of comely mould;
But see what he is, a stunted stick
Lifeless and limp with scarce a kick.
It's often I've asked and sought in vain

[221]

What is the use of the rule insane
That marriage has closed to the clerical clan
In the church of our fathers since first it began.
It's a melancholy sight to a needy maid
Their comely faces and forms displayed,
Their hips and thighs so broad and round,
Their buttocks and breasts that in flesh abound,
Their lustrous looks and their lusty limbs,
Their fair fresh features, their smooth soft skins,
Their strength and stature, their force and fire,
Their craving curbed and uncooled desire.
They eat and drink of the fat of the land,
They've wealth and comfort at their command,
They sleep on beds of the softest down,
They've ease and leisure their lot to crown,
They commence in manhood's prime and flood,
And well we know that they're flesh and blood!
If I thought that sexless saints they were
Or holy angels, I would not care,
But they're lusty lads with a crave unsated
In slothful sleep, and the maids unmated.
We know it is true there are few but hate
The lonely life and the celibate state;
Is it fair to condemn them to mope and moan,
Is it fair to force them to lie alone,
To bereave of issue a sturdy band
The fruit of whose loins might free the land?
Tho' some of them ever were grim and gruff,
Intractable, sullen and stern and tough,
Crabbed and cross, unkind and cold,
Surly and wont to scowl and scold,
Many are made of warmer clay,
Affectionate, ardent, kind and gay;
It's often a woman got land or wealth,
Store or stock from a priest by stealth,
Many's the case I call to mind
Of clergymen who were slyly kind,
I could show you women who were their flames,

[222]

And their children reared beneath false names;
And often I must lament in vain
How they waste their strength on the old and plain
While marriageable maids their plight deplore
Waiting unwooed thro' this senseless law;
'Tis a baleful ban to our hapless race
And beneath its sway we decay apace.
O fount of wisdom, I leave to you
To declare and reveal the reason true;
Deceived and undone they sleep I deem,
Illumine my mind with the gospel's gleam,
What did the prophets preach, I pray,
Or Saint Paul whose words were weighty say?
The scripture, if I remember, ran
The taint of the flesh is the fruit of this ban,
Paul the Apostle said to none
To abandon marriage, but lust to shun,
Your closest kindred to leave and go
To cleave to your wife for weal or woe;
God did not wish the mother forsaken
And the part of the women the prophets have taken.
'Tis a senseless thing for the like of me
Your instructor in sacred writ to be,
You yourself, O sovran bright,
Remember the holy words aright,
The sense of every saying is plain
To you, and each act that the saints ordain.
Then, O daughter of kings, revoke this law,
Let it stand to mar our stock no more,
Release the clergy to mate and breed
That the land may teem with their sturdy seed,
Do not deny the women redress
Nor leave them to languish in this distress,
See how the ground in crowds they cumber
And by three to one they the men outnumber;
The smallest shoots that you pass to-day
Springing unseen from the fertile clay
To-morrow will yield a crop mature

[223]

To rot on the stem and drop obscure.
Ah woe is me! my words are vain
And to what end do I thus complain?
What are my tears and entreaties worth
Or how can I hope in the face of this dearth?
With this land of the best of its men bereft
And none but weaklings and wastrels left,
With our comely girls growing old and gray
Waiting for someone the word to say,
And so desperate and desolate grown that they'll
Take anything that can be called a male.
Take the men, harness them by our side
And there obedient bid them bide.'

Part Four

Soon as the maid had told her woes
The gentle lady radiant rose,
Her face the fairest eye has scanned,
Her voice the sweetest in the land.
She rose with mien and manner grave
And thus considered sentence gave,
The whole court hearkening in suspense
With eager expectation tense:—
'Oh sorrow-stricken maid, your tear
And prayer fall not unheeded here;
We see, and the sad sight deplore,
The seed of Orla, Maive and Mor
A dwindling, dying, shrinking breed
Unsought by suitors in their need,
Unwooed, unwed and gone to waste,
By waxing offspring unreplaced.
Hence we decree that from this date
The adult male without a mate
Be taken up and tightly tied
Against this tree the tomb beside,
Of coat and shirt be naked stript
And with a stout cord soundly whipt.
But those who well in years have gone

[224]

And still have basely hid the horn,
Who've wasted manhood's force and fire
Without delight from their desire,
Who've spent their strength and past their prime
And not made hay in summertime,
Ye spinsters sad, I leave to you
To wreak revenge upon the crew;
Go wrack and wrench and rend and flay
Or with slow fire consume their clay,
With wracking pangs your wrongs requite
And straightway strive to sate your spite,
With female art their fate devise
And heed ye not their craven cries.
There came a whisper to my ears—
Speak soft and low, who knows who hears?
With hand on mouth, by me be taught,
It is not safe to say your thought—
Beware the while the powers that be,
They'll have to marry yet, you'll see,
Tho' long deferred the day will come
With licence from the Pope at Rome;
They'll sit in council on your case
And straight release the priestly race
In east and west and south and north
To woo and wed and wax thenceforth.
Good folk, farewell, I cannot stay,
The hour is late and long the way,
Delay won't suit, my calls won't bide,
The guilt is proved, the case is tried.
'Twill not be long till I return—
The men unmarried 'twill concern,
And heartless gallants who aspire
To rouse and not requite desire,
Who love to lightly kiss and tell
And boast what fortune them befell,
Who woo with false and feigning smiles
And ruin maids with wanton wiles;
They do not act from am'rous fire,

[225]

From youth's hot blood and bland desire,
But as bold rogues and rakes to pose
And puff their breasts and boast as beaus.
I'll deal with these without delay,
But first I hence must haste away,
I'll bind them with the nuptial vow
When I return, a month from now.'
She ceased and I was seized with dread,
My heart sank sick and swam my head,
My blood ran cold, my sight grew blear,
My knees knocked fit to fail with fear;
Her sentence did my sense dumbfound
And still there dinned its dismal sound.
The bailiff on the bench beheld
My fainting fit by fright compelled,
She dragged me by the ear and drew
And dropped me in the public view.
The maid leapt up on vengeance bent
To vent her venom and torment,
With vigorous spite and vexéd spleen
She rose and yelled with oaths obscene:—
' 'Tis long I've marked you, lousy lout,
A lazy lump your life throughout,
How oft you were pursued and sought
By needy maids, responding nought!
What sons you as their sire proclaim?
What woman thanks you for the same?
What favour can you hope to find
Or how escape the scourge assigned?
To whose protection can you trust
Or how evade our vengeance just?
O queen, your justice now begin,
There's no excuse can save his skin
Tho' bent his back and rude his build
When blooms are rare a weed is culled,
Whate'er is male for mating's meet,
Mis-shapen cows give milk that's sweet,
'Twixt homely swain and handsome spark

[226]

We see no difference in the dark.
I shake with zeal to testify,
'Tis vain to shuffle or deny,
Your guilt is graven on your brow—
Two score without the nuptial vow!
O peerless maid, my wrongs I pray
Upon this wretch I may repay,
Come friends and catch and bind him fast,
Let's make the rogue repent at last!
Go, Una, fetch a knotted rope,
Be busy, Anne, and cease to mope,
Go, Mary, bring a cord and bind
The prisoner's hands his back behind,
Come, Maureen, Jane and Kate and Maive,
And sate your spite upon the slave,
Lay on the lash with might and main
And pierce him with the sharpest pain!
Regard not cries or screams or groans
But flay the flesh from off his bones,
And let the blood in rivers flow
From back and sides at every blow!
Strain arms and raise the scourge on high,
With tireless zeal the torment ply,
And let the rumour run and make
The hearts of the unmarried quake!
To-day a new reign is begun
Of peace since women's rights are won;
Our waiting and our weeping past,
Our tears and prayers prevail at last.
I beg you take five score and ten,
Subtract it from a thousand then,
And double the remainder pray,
And date the year One from that day!'
I heard with reeling head my fate,
When as she paused to pen the date
I broke from sleep, forgot my pain,
And woke to light and life again.

Translated by Arland Ussher

[227]

ANONYMOUS
(18th century)

THE LITTLE WHITE CAT

(Folk song from the Gaelic)

THE little gray cat was walking prettily,
When she found her little son stretched dead
And 'twas only a year since her family
Were cast out and drowned in a trench.
    The little white cat, white, white, white,
    The little white cat, Breed's cat.
    The little white cat, snowy white
    That was drowned in a trench.

The little mother stood upright,
When she found her little son dead;
She brought him in and made a bed for him,
And then began to lament him.
    The little white cat, white, white, white,
    The little white cat, Breed's cat.
    The little white cat, snowy white
    That was drowned in a trench.

Andrew, the blind, had some of her family,
And they came together to lament him,
I am sure if Barry hears it,
He will regret the death of Breed's cat.
    The little white cat, white, white, etc.

He broke no chest, nor lock of the neighbors,
Nor did he destroy the cows' butter.
And you never heard such discourse,
As the mice had in telling it.
    The little white cat, white, white, etc.

His eye was grey, his walk was pretty,
His step was light and active:

[228]

And I'd rather far be going to the clay
Than that the povince of Munster should hear of it.
      The little white cat, white, white, etc.

The little white cat would hump his back
As big as a three pint jug.
Wasn't he a fine show for the gentry to see,
Poll, Breed's pretty little cat?
      The little white cat, white, white, etc.

Walter's Martin will put a wooden coffin on him,
And it's he that is able.
And were it not for the time at which he died
We should have every cause for lamenting.
      The little white cat, white, white, white,
      The little white cat, Breed's cat.
      The little white cat, snowy white
      That was drowned in a trench.
          Translated by Mrs. Costello of Tuam

ANONYMOUS
(Traditional)

FOUR PRAYERS

I REST with Thee, O Jesus,
And do Thou rest with me.
The oil of Christ on my poor soul,
The creed of the Twelve to make me whole,
Above my head I see.
O Father, who created me,
O Son, who purchased me,
O Spirit Blest, who blessest me,
Rest ye with me.

Great Giver of the open hand,
We stand to thank Thee for our meat,

[229]

A hundred praises, Christ, 'tis meet,
For all we drink, for all we eat.

I lie down with God, and may God lie down with me;
The right hand of God under my head,
The two hands of Mary round about me,
The cross of the nine white angels
From the back of my head
To the sole of my feet.
May I not lie with evil,
And may evil not lie with me.

.   .   .   .   .   .

Three folds of the cloth, yet one only napkin is there,
Three joints in the finger, but still only one finger fair;
Three leaves of the shamrock, yet no more than one shamrock
     to wear.
Frost, snow-flakes and ice, all in water their origin share,
Three Persons in God; to one God alone we make prayer.

Translated by Eleanor Hull

ANTHONY RAFTERY
(c 1784-1835)

I AM RAFTERY

This is Raftery's reply to the man who did not recognize him as he
fiddled to a crowd, and asked "who is the musician?"

I AM Raftery the poet,
Full of hope and love,
With eyes that have no light,
With gentleness that has no misery.

Going west upon my pilgrimage
By the light of my heart,

[230]

Feeble and tired
To the end of my road.

Behold me now,
And my face to a wall,
A-playing music
Unto empty pockets.

Translated by Douglas Hyde

(*Another version*)

I AM RAFTERY

I AM Raftery the poet,
Full of hope and love,
My eyes without sight,
My mind without torment,

Going west on my journey
By the light of my heart,
Tired and weary
. To the end of the road.

Behold me now
With my back to a wall,
Playing music
To empty pockets.

Translated by James Stephens

ANONYMOUS
(early 19th century)

THE RED MAN'S WIFE

'Tis what they say,
  Thy little heel fits in a shoe,
'Tis what they say,
  Thy little mouth kisses well, too.
'Tis what they say,
  Thousand loves that you leave me to rue;
That the tailor went the way
  That the wife of the Red man knew.

Nine months did I spend
  In a prison closed tightly and bound;
Bolts on my smalls[1]
  And a thousand locks frowning around;
But o'er the tide
  I would leap with the leap of a swan,
Could I once set my side
  By the bride of the Red-haired man.

I thought, O my life,
  That one house between us love would be;
And I thought I would find
  You once coaxing my child on your knee;
But now the curse of the High One
  On him let it be,
And on all of the band of the liars
  Who put silence between you and me.

There grows a tree in the garden
  With blossoms that tremble and shake,
I lay my hand on its bark
  And I feel that my heart must break.

[1] Smalls = wrists and ankles.

[232]

On one wish alone
    My soul through the long months ran,
One little kiss
    From the wife of the Red-haired man.

But the day of doom shall come,
    And hills and harbors be rent;
A mist shall fall on the sun
    From the dark clouds heavily sent;
The sea shall be dry,
    And earth under mourning and ban;
Then loud shall he cry
    For the wife of the Red-haired man.

Translated by Douglas Hyde

ANONYMOUS
(19th century)

MY GRIEF ON THE SEA

MY GRIEF on the sea,
    How the waves of it roll!
For they heave between me
    And the love of my soul!

Abandoned, forsaken,
    To grief and to care,
Will the sea ever waken
    Relief from despair?

My grief and my trouble!
    Would he and I were
In the province of Leinster
    Or the county of Clare.

[233]

Were I and my darling—
    Oh, heart-bitter wound!—
On board of the ship
    For America bound.

On a green bed of rushes
    All last night I lay,
And I flung it abroad
    With the heat of the day.

And my love came behind me—
    He came from the South;
His breast to my bosom.
    His mouth to my mouth.
                    Translated by Douglas Hyde

ANONYMOUS

(19th century)

RINGLETED YOUTH OF MY LOVE

Ringleted youth of my love,
    With thy locks bound loosely behind thee,
You passed by the road above,
    But you never came in to find me;
Where were the harm for you
    If you came for a little to see me;
Your kiss is a wakening dew
    Were I ever so ill or so dreamy.

If I had golden store
    I would make a nice little boreen
To lead straight up to his door,
    The door of the house of my storeen;
Hoping to God not to miss
    The sound of his footfall in it,

I have waited so long for his kiss
    That for days I have slept not a minute.

I thought, O my love! you were so—
    As the moon is, or sun on a fountain,
And I thought after that you were snow,
    The cold snow on top of the mountain;
And I thought after that you were more
    Like God's lamp shining to find me,
Or the bright star of knowledge before,
    And the star of knowledge behind me.

You promised me high-heeled shoes,
    And satin and silk, my storeen,
And to follow me, never to lose,
    Though the ocean were round us roaring;
Like a bush in a gap in a wall
    I am now left lonely without thee,
And this house, I grow dead of, is all
    That I see around or about me.

Translated by Douglas Hyde

CATHAL BUIDHE MacELGUN
(c. 1750)

THE YELLOW BITTERN

THE yellow bittern that never broke out
    In a drinking-bout, might well have drunk;
His bones are thrown on a naked stone
    Where he lived alone like a hermit monk.
O yellow bittern! I pity your lot,
    Though they say that a sot like myself is curst—
I was sober a while, but I'll drink and be wise
    For fear I should die in the end of thirst.

[235]

It's not for the common birds that I'd mourn,
  The blackbird, the corncrake or the crane,
But for the bittern that's shy and apart
  And drinks in the marsh from the lone bog-drain.
Oh! if I had known you were near your death,
  While my breath held out I'd have run to you,
Till a splash from the Lake of the Son of the Bird
  Your soul would have stirred and waked anew.

My darling told me to drink no more
  Or my life would be o'er in a little short while;
But I told her 'tis drink gives me health and strength,
  And will lengthen my road by many a mile.
You see how the bird of the long smooth neck,
  Could get his death from the thirst at last—
Come, son of my soul, and drain your cup,
  You'll get no sup when your life is past.

In a wintering island by Constantine's halls,
  A bittern calls from a wineless place,
And tells me that hither he cannot come
  Till the summer is here and the sunny days.
When he crosses the stream there and wings o'er the sea,
  Then a fear comes to me he may fail in his flight—
Well, the milk and the ale are drunk every drop,
  And a dram won't stop our thirst this night.

                    Translated by Thomas MacDonagh

ANONYMOUS
(19th century)

BLESSED BE THE HOLY WILL OF GOD

A morning prayer which they have in Connemara; it has been heard in
many places in Galway, and Dr. Hyde heard it in Roscommon.

THE will of God be done by us.
The law of God be kept by us,
Our evil will controlled by us,
Our tongue in check be held by us,
Repentance timely made by us,
Christ's passion understood by us,
Each sinful crime be shunned by us,
Much on the *End* be mused by us,
And Death be blessed found by us,
With Angels' music heard by us,
And God's high praise sung to us,
For ever and for aye.

Translated by Douglas Hyde

ANONYMOUS
(19th century)

HOW HAPPY THE LITTLE BIRDS

How happy the little birds
That rise up on high
And make music together
On a single bough!
Not so with me
And my hundred thousand loves:
Far apart on us
Rises every day.

Whiter she than the lily,
Than beauty more fair,
Sweeter voiced than the violin,
More lightsome than the sun;
Yet beyond all that
Her nobleness, her mind,—
And O God Who art in Heaven,
Relieve my pain!

Translated by Padraic Pearse

ANONYMOUS

(19th century)

DONALL OGE: GRIEF OF A GIRL'S HEART

According to various authorities there exist two long folk songs quite similar: "Donall Oge" and "The Grief of a Girl's Heart." Through some generations of singing these ballads various stanzas have become intermingled. Following are the original fourteen stanzas of Lady Gregory's translation:

O DONALL OGE, if you go across the sea,
Bring myself with you and do not forget it;
And you will have a sweetheart for fair days and market days,
And the daughter of the King of Greece beside you at night.

It is late last night the dog was speaking of you;
The snipe was speaking of you in her deep marsh.
It is you are the lonely bird through the woods;
And that you may be without a mate until you find me.

You promised me, and you said a lie to me,
That you would be before me where the sheep are flocked;
I gave a whistle and three hundred cries to you,
And I found nothing there but a bleating lamb.

You promised me a thing that was hard for you,
A ship of gold under a silver mast;

[238]

Twelve towns with a market in all of them,
And a fine white court by the side of the sea.

You promised me a thing that is not possible,
That you would give me gloves of the skin of a fish;
That you would give me shoes of the skin of a bird;
And a suit of the dearest silk in Ireland.

O Donall oge, it is I would be better to you
Than a high, proud, spendthrift lady:
I would milk the cow; I would bring help to you;
And if you were hard pressed, I would strike a blow for you.

O, ochone, and it's not with hunger
Or with wanting food, or drink, or sleep,
That I am growing thin, and my life is shortened;
But it is the love of a young man has withered me away.

It is early in the morning that I saw him coming,
Going along the road on the back of a horse;
He did not come to me; he made nothing of me;
And it is on my way home that I cried my fill.

When I go by myself to the Well of Loneliness,
I sit down and I go through my trouble;
When I see the world and do not see my boy,
He that has an amber shade in his hair.

It was on that Sunday I gave my love to you;
The Sunday that is last before Easter Sunday.
And myself on my knees reading the Passion;
And my two eyes giving love to you for ever.

O, aya! my mother, give myself to him;
And give him all that you have in the world;
Get out yourself to ask for alms,
And do not come back and forward looking for me.

My mother said to me not to be talking with you to-day,
Or tomorrow, or on Sunday;
It was a bad time she took for telling me that;
It was shutting the door after the house was robbed.

My heart is as black as the blackness of the sloe,
Or as the black coal that is on the smith's forge;
Or as the sole of a shoe left in white halls;
It was you put that darkness over my life.

You have taken the east from me; You have taken the west
    from me
You have taken what is before me and what is behind me;
You have taken the moon, you have taken the sun from me,
And my fear is great that you have taken God from me!

Translated by Lady Gregory

PADRAIC PEARSE
(1879-1916)

IDEAL

NAKED I saw thee,
O beauty of beauty!
And I blinded my eyes
For fear I should flinch.

I heard thy music,
O sweetness of sweetness!
And I shut my ears
For fear I should fail.

I kissed thy lips
O sweetness of sweetness!
And I hardened my heart
For fear of my ruin.

[240]

I blinded my eyes
And my ears I shut,
I hardened my heart,
And my love I quenched.

I turned my back
On the dream I had shaped,
And to this road before me
My face I turned.

I set my face
To the road here before me,
To the work that I see,
To the death that I shall meet.

Translated by Thomas MacDonagh

LULLABY OF THE WOMAN OF THE MOUNTAIN

O LITTLE head of gold! O candle of my house!
Thou wilt guide all who travel this country.

Be quiet, O house! And O little grey mice,
Stay at home to-night in your hidden lairs!

O moths on the window, fold your wings!
Stay at home to-night, O little black chafers!

O plover and O curlew, over my house do not travel!
Speak not, O barnacle-goose, going over the mountain here!

O creatures of the mountain, that wake so early
Stir not to-night till the sun whitens over you.

Translated by Thomas MacDonagh

✣ PART III ✤

ANONYMOUS STREET BALLADS
From the Seventeenth Century to the Present

Note: Wherever authorship has been determined, ballads properly belonging in this section have been placed in chronological order in Part IV. See index of titles.

THE AGRICULTURAL IRISH GIRL

If all the women in the town were bundled up together,
I know a girl could beat them all, in any kind of weather;
The rain can't wash the powder off, because she does not wear
 it,
Her face and figure's all her own: it's true, for I declare it!

Chorus

For she's a big stout, strong lump of an agricultural Irish
 girl
She neither paints nor powders and her figure is all her
 own.
And she can strike that hard that you'd think that you'd
 been struck by the kick of a mule,
It's "The full of the house" of Irish love is Mary Ann
 Malone.

She was only seventeen last grass, and still improving greatly;
I wonder what she'll be at when her bones are set completely,
You'd think your hand was in a vice the moment that she
 shakes it,
And if there's any cake around, it's Mary Ann that takes it!

For she's a big stout, strong lump, etc.

BISHOP BUTLER OF KILCASH

Over a hundred years ago, Bishop Butler of Kilcash, the Catholic
Bishop of Cork, conformed to the Protestant religion. He had originally
belonged to this faith but his return caused a sensation all over Ireland.
Many popular songs and ballads were composed to commemorate the
event.

LET the Catholic Church be now arrayed
 In deep disconsolation;
Let her banners sad be now displayed
 Throughout each Christian Nation:

[244]

At the Isle of Saints a bishop there
   Has lost his consecration,
And a pillar great has fell of late
   By Satan's operation.

In Cork of late for a small estate
   A spiritual lord revolted
From that noble ecclesiastic state
   To which the Pope exalted.
Not born a member of the Church of Rome,
   To Luther he did adhere,
From darkness to our Church he came,
   And to darkness did retire.

Our Church was built upon a rock
   And founded by our Saviour;
The powers of hell, that region dark,
   Shall ne'er prevail against her:
She is a ship that can't be wrecked,
   Nor ever drown a sailor;
But such as plunge down from her deck
   Are sunk and lost for ever.

From our bright faith you did retreat
   And joined the court of Venus;
Profligate, void of every hope,
   You threw off the robes of Jesus;
Your power was greater than St. John's
   Who did baptise our Saviour;
For you could take Him in your hands,
   Then why did you forsake Him!

From our bright faith you did retreat
   When you its light extinguished,
Excluded far from heaven's bright gates,
   All graces you relinquished;
At the imperial throne your guilt was shown
   When first you changed your station;

⌈245⌉

Justice divine at that same time
    Pronounced your condemnation.

I'm sure you're worse than Henry the Eighth
    Who put away his consort;
Your virtuous spouse you did forsake,
    When the holy Church you abandoned.
As the shepherd now is gone astray,
    God keep the flock from random,
That on the great accounting day
    His blood may prove our ransom.

Now sure you know there is but one God
    By whom we are all created;
And sure you know there is but one Faith
    By which we are consecrated:
And sure you know there is but one Ark
    To keep us from desolation;
And sure you know there is but one Church
    Can ever expect salvation.

THE BLACKBIRD

The Blackbird meant the Young Pretender, Charles Edward Stuart.
The custom of using allegorical names for the Pretender and more often
for Ireland was common in the 18th and early 19th centuries so that people
could sing Jacobite and political songs without danger during the period
of the Penal Laws.

ON A FAIR summer's morning of soft recreation,
    I heard a fair lady amaking great moan;
With sighing and sobbing and sad lamentation,
    A-saying, "My Blackbird most royal is flown.
        My thoughts they deceive me,
        Reflections do grieve me,
And I am over burden'd with sad misery;
        Yet if death it should blind me
        As true love inclines me,
My Blackbird I'd seek out wherever he be."

[246]

"Once in fair England my Blackbird did flourish,
   He was the chief flower that in it did spring;
Prime ladies of honor his person did nourish,
   Because that he was the true son of a king.
      But this false fortune,
      Which still is uncertain,
Has caused this parting between him and me.
      His name I'll advance
      In Spain and in France;
And I'll seek out my Blackbird wherever he be.

"The birds of the forest they all met together—
   The Turtle was chosen to dwell with the Dove:
And I am resolved in fair or foul weather,
   In winter or in spring, for to seek out my love.
      He is all my heart's treasure,
      My joy and my pleasure,
And justly my love my heart shall follow thee;
      He is constant and kind,
      And courageous of mind;
All bliss to my Blackbird wherever he be.

"In England my Blackbird and I were together,
   Where he was still noble and generous of heart;
And woe to the time that he first went from hither,
   Alas, he was forced from thence to depart;
      In Scotland he is deemed
      And highly esteemed;
In England he seemed a stranger to be;
      Yet his name shall remain
      In France and in Spain;
All bliss to my Blackbird wherever he be.

"It is not the ocean can fright me with danger;
   For though like a pilgrim I wander forlorn,
I may still meet with friendship from one that's a stranger
   Much more than from one that in England was born.
      Oh, Heaven so spacious,
      To Britain be gracious,

Tho' some there be odious both to him and to me;
  Yet joy and renown
  And laurel shall crown
My Blackbird with honor wherever he be."

BOLD PHELIM BRADY, THE BARD OF ARMAGH

OH! LIST to the lay of a poor Irish harper,
And scorn not the strains of his old withered hand,
But remember those fingers they could once move sharper
To raise the merry strains of his dear native land;
It was long before the shamrock our green isle's loved emblem
Was crushed in its beauty 'neath the Saxon lion's paw
I was called by the colleens of the village and valley
Bold Phelim Brady, the Bard of Armagh.

How I long for to muse on the days of my boyhood,
Though four score and three years have flitted since then,
Still it gives sweet reflections, as every young joy should,
That merry-hearted boys make the best of old men.
At a pattern[1] or fair I could twist my shillela
Or trip through a jig with my brogues bound with straw,
Whilst all the pretty maidens around me assembled
Loved bold Phelim Brady, the Bard of Armagh.

Although I have travelled this wide world over,
Yet Erin's my home and a parent to me,
Then oh, let the ground that my old bones shall cover
Be cut from the soil that is trod by the free.
And when sergeant death in his cold arms shall embrace me,
O lull me to sleep with sweet Erin go bragh,
By the side of my Kathleen, my young wife, O place me,
Then forget Phelim Brady, the Bard of Armagh.

[1] Pattern—a gathering at a saint's shrine or well, a festival for a patron saint. Pattern is derived from patron.

THE BOYNE WATER

This is the oldest version of the most famous Orange Song.

JULY the First, of a morning clear, one thousand six hundred
  and ninety,
King William did his men prepare, of thousands he had thirty;
To fight King James and all his foes, encamped near the Boyne
  Water,
He little fear'd, though two to one, their multitudes to scatter.

King William call'd his officers, saying: "Gentlemen, mind
  your station,
And let your valour here be shown before this Irish nation;
My brazen walls let no man break, and your subtle foes you'll
  scatter,
Be sure you show them good English play as you go over the
  water."

. . . .

Both foot and horse they marched on, intending them to
  batter,
But the brave Duke Schomberg he was shot as he cross'd over
  the water.
When that King William did observe the brave Duke Schom-
  berg falling,
He rein'd his horse with a heavy heart, on the Enniskilleners
  calling:

"What will you do for me, brave boys—see yonder men re-
  treating?
Our enemies encourag'd are and English drums are beating;"
He says, "My boys, feel no dismay at the losing of one com-
  mander,
For God shall be our king this day, and I'll be general under."

. . . .

Within four yards of our fore-front, before a shot was fired,
A sudden snuff they got that day, which little they desired;

For horse and man fell to the ground, and some hung in their
saddle:
Others turn'd up their forked ends, which we call 'coup de
ladle.'

Prince Eugene's regiment was the next, on our right hand
advanced,
Into a field of standing wheat, where Irish horses pranced—
But the brandy ran so in their heads, their senses all did scatter,
They little thought to leave their bones that day at the Boyne
Water.

Both men and horse lay on the ground, and many there lay
bleeding:
I saw no sickles there that day—but, sure, there was sharp
shearing.

Now, praise God, all true Protestants, and heaven's and earth's
Creator,
For the deliverance that He sent our enemies to scatter.
The Church's foes will pine away, like churlish-hearted Nabal,
For our deliverer came this day like the great Zorobabel.

So praise God, all true Protestants, and I will say no further,
But had the Papists gain'd the day there would have been open
murder.
Although King James and many more were ne'er that way
inclined,
It was not in their power to stop what the rabble they designed.

BRENNAN ON THE MOOR

It's of a famous highway-man a story I will tell;
His name was Willie Brennan, and in Ireland he did dwell;
And on the Kilworth mountains he commenced his wild career,
Where many a wealthy gentleman before him shook with fear.

[250]

Brennan on the Moor, Brennan on the Moor,
A brave undaunted robber was bold Brennan on the Moor.

A brace of loaded pistols he carried night and day;
He never robbed a poor man upon the king's highway;
But what he'd taken from the rich, like Turpin and Black Bess,
He always did divide it with the widow in distress.

Brennan on the Moor &c.

One night he robbed a packman by name of Pedlar Bawn;
They travelled on together till the day began to dawn;
The pedlar seeing his money gone, likewise his watch and
    chain,
He at once encountered Brennan and he robbed him back
    again.

Brennan on the Moor &c.

One day upon the highway, as Willie he went down,
He met the Mayor of Cashel a mile outside the town:
The Mayor he knew his features; "I think, young man," said
    he,
"Your name is Willie Brennan; you must come along with me."

Brennan on the Moor &c.

As Brennan's wife had gone to town, provisions for to buy,
And when she saw her Willie, she began to weep and cry;
He says, "Give me that tenpenny;" as soon as Willie spoke,
She handed him a blunderbuss from underneath her cloak.

Brennan on the Moor &c.

Then with his loaded blunderbuss, the truth I will unfold,
He made the Mayor to tremble, and robbed him of his gold;
One hundred pounds was offered for his apprehension there,
So he with horse and saddle to the mountains did repair.

Brennan on the Moor &c.

Then Brennan being an outlaw upon the mountains high,
When cavalry and infantry to take him they did try;

[251]

He laughed at them with scorn, until at length, 'tis said,
By a false-hearted young man he basely was betrayed.

Brennan on the Moor &c.

In the county of Tipperary, in a place they call Clonmore,
Willie Brennan and his comrade that day did suffer sore;
He lay amongst the fern, which was thick upon the field,
And nine deep wounds he did receive before that he did yield.

Brennan on the Moor &c.

So they were taken prisoners, in irons they were bound,
And both conveyed to Clonmel jail, strong walls did them
    surround;
They were tried and there found guilty, the judge made this
    reply:
"For robbing on the king's highway you're both condemned
    to die."
Brennan on the Moor &c.

Farewell unto my dear wife and to my children three,
Likewise my aged father, he may shed tears for me;
And to my loving mother, who tore her locks and cried,
Saying, "I wish, my Willie Brennan, in your cradle you had
    died!"

Brennan on the Moor, Brennan on the Moor,
A brave undaunted robber was bold Brennan on the Moor.

BRIAN O'LINN

The last stanza figures in most collections of 'Mother Goose.'

BRIAN O'LINN was a gentleman born,
His hair it was long and his beard unshorn,
His teeth were out and his eyes far in—
"I'm a wonderful beauty," says Brian O'Linn!

Brian O'Linn was hard up for a coat,
He borrowed the skin of a neighboring goat,
He buckled the horns right under his chin—
"They'll answer for pistols," says Brian O'Linn!

Brian O'Linn had no breeches to wear,
He got him a sheepskin to make him a pair,
With the fleshy side out and the woolly side in—
"They are pleasant and cool," says Brian O'Linn!

Brian O'Linn had no hat to his head,
He stuck on a pot that was under the shed,
He murdered a cod for the sake of his fin—
" 'T will pass for a feather," says Brian O'Linn!

Brian O'Linn had no shirt to his back,
He went to a neighbor and borrowed a sack,
He puckered a meal-bag under his chin—
"They'll take it for ruffles," said Brian O'Linn!

Brian O'Linn had no shoes at all,
He bought an old pair at a cobbler's stall,
The uppers were broke and the soles were thin—
"They'll do me for dancing," says Brian O'Linn!

Brian O'Linn had no watch for to wear,
He bought a fine turnip and scooped it out fair,
He slipped a live cricket right under the skin—
"They'll think it is ticking," says Brian O'Linn!

Brian O'Linn was in want of a brooch,
He stuck a brass pin in a big cockroach,
The breast of his shirt he fixed it straight in—
"They'll think it's a diamond," says Brian O'Linn!

Brian O'Linn went a-courting one night,
He set both the mother and daughter to fight—

"Stop, stop," he exclaimed, "if you have but the tin,
I'll marry you both," says Brian O'Linn!

Brian O'Linn went to bring his wife home,
He had but one horse, that was all skin and bone—
"I'll put her behind me, as nate as a pin,
And her mother before me," says Brian O'Linn!

Brian O'Linn and his wife and wife's mother,
They all crossed over the bridge together,
The bridge broke down and they all tumbled in—
"We'll go home by water," says Brian O'Linn!

CASTLEHYDE

This song is commonly regarded as a type of the absurd English songs composed by some of the Irish peasant bards who knew English only imperfectly. . . . In burlesque imitation of this song, Richard Alfred Milliken of Cork composed the famous "Groves of Blarney"; this song— working as a sort of microbe—gave origin to a number of imitations of the same general character.

(Air: "The Last Rose of Summer")

As I ROVED out on a summer's morning down by the banks of
    Blackwater side,
To view the groves and the meadows charming, the pleasant
    gardens of Castlehyde;
'Tis there I heard the thrushes warbling, the dove and par-
    tridge I now describe;
The lambkins sporting on ev'ry morning, all to adorn sweet
    Castlehyde.

The richest groves throughout this nation and fine plantations
    you will see there;
The rose, the tulip, and sweet carnation, all vying with the lily
    fair.
The buck, the doe, the fox, the eagle, they skip and play by
    the river side;

[254]

The trout and salmon are always sporting in the clear streams of sweet Castlehyde.

There are fine walks in these pleasant gardens, and seats most charming in shady bowers.
The gladiaathors both bold and darling each night and morning to watch the flowers.
There's a church for service in this fine arbour where nobles often in coaches ride
To view the groves and the meadow charming, the pleasant gardens of Castlehyde.

There are fine horses and stall-fed *oxes,* and dens for foxes to play and hide;
Fine mares for breeding and foreign sheep there with snowy fleeces in Castlehyde.
The grand improvements they would amuse you, the trees are drooping with fruit all kind;
The bees perfuming the fields with music, which yields more beauty to Castlehyde.

If noble princes from foreign nations should chance to sail to this Irish shore,
'Tis in this valley they would be feasted as often heroes have been before.
The wholesome air of this habitation would recreate your heart with pride;
There is no valley throughout this nation in beauty equal to Castlehyde.

I rode from Blarney to Castlebarnet, to Thomastown, and sweet Doneraile,
To Kilshannick that joins Rathcormack, besides Killarney and Abbeyfeale;
The flowing Nore and the rapid Boyne, the river Shannon and pleasant Clyde;
In all my ranging and serenading I met no equal to Castlehyde.

COCKLES AND MUSSELS

In Dublin's fair city,
Where the girls are so pretty,
   I first set my eyes on sweet Mollie Malone.
She wheeled her wheel-barrow
Through streets broad and narrow,
   Crying, "Cockles and mussels, alive, alive, oh!

        "Alive, alive, oh!
        Alive, alive, oh!"
   Crying, "Cockles and mussels, alive, alive, oh!"

She was a fishmonger,
But sure 'twas no wonder,
   For so were her father and mother before.
And they both wheeled their barrow
Through streets broad and narrow,
   Crying, "Cockles and mussels, alive, alive, oh!

        "Alive, alive, oh! &c.

She died of a fever,
And none could relieve her,
   And that was the end of sweet Mollie Malone.
But her ghost wheels her barrow
Through streets broad and narrow,
   Crying, "Cockles and mussels, alive, alive, oh!"

        "Alive, alive, oh! &c.

COLLEEN OGE ASTHORE

The air to "Colleen Oge Asthore" is one of the most ancient Irish airs. It was popular in England during the reign of Elizabeth and it is included in her Virginal. Shakespeare makes use of the title in King Henry V, Act 4, Scene 4. (See notes to Israel Gollancz's Temple Shakespeare). The air is that to which words of "The Croppy Boy" are sung.

WHEN I marched away to war,
How you kissed me o'er and o'er;
Weeping, pressed me, sobbing, blessed me,
Colleen, Colleen Oge asthore.

Ah! but when you dreamed me dead,
Sad was your heart my lonely maid;
Ever grieving, ever weaving
Willow, willow for your head.

"Nay! he lives"—your mother said,
But you only shook your head;
"Why deceive me, ah! believe me,
Mother, mother, he is dead."

So you pined and pined away,
Till, when in the winter grey,
Home I hasted—wan and wasted
Colleen, Colleen Oge, you lay.

Then your cheek so pale before,
With the rose of hope once more
Softly blooming, flower-like perfuming
Blossomed, Colleen Oge asthore.

Till upon the chapel floor,
Side by side we knelt and swore,
Duty dearest, love sincerest,
Colleen, Colleen Oge, asthore.

COLLEEN RUE

As I ROVED out one summer's morning, speculating most curi-
    ously,
To my surprise, I soon espied a charming fair one approaching
    me;
I stood awhile in deep meditation, contemplating what should
    I do,
But recruiting all my sensations, I thus accosted the *Colleen
    Rue:*—

"Are you Aurora, or the beauteous Flora, Euterpasia, or Venus
    bright?
Or Helen fair, beyond compare, that Paris stole from her
    Grecian's sight?
Thou fairest creature, you have enslaved me, I am intoxicated
    by Cupid's clue,
Whose golden notes and infatuation deranged my ideas for
    you, *Colleen Rue.*"

"Kind sir, be easy, and do not tease me, with your false praise
    so jestingly,
Your dissimulations and invitations, your fantastic praises,
    seducing me.
I am not Aurora, or the beauteous Flora, but a rural maiden
    to all men's view,
That 's here condoling my situation, and my appellation is the
    Colleen Rue."

"Was I Hector, that noble victor, who died a victim of Grecian
    skill,
Or was I Paris, whose deeds were various, as an arbitrator on
    Ida's hill,
I would roam through Asia, likewise Arabia, through Penn-
    sylvania seeking you,
The burning regions, like famed Vesuvius, for one embrace of
    the *Colleen Rue.*"

"Sir, I am surprised and dissatisfied at your tantalizing inso-
lence,
I am not so stupid, or enslaved by Cupid, as to be dupèd by
your eloquence,
Therefore desist from your solicitations, I am engaged, I de-
clare it's true,
To a lad I love beyond all earthly treasures, and he'll soon em-
brace his *Colleen Rue*."

THE CRUISKEEN LAWN

Literally "My full little jug." This famous drinking song has many
versions.

LET the farmer praise his grounds,
Let the huntsman praise his hounds,
    The shepherd his dew-scented lawn;
But I, more blest than they,
Spend each happy night and day
    With my charming little cruiskeen lawn, lawn, lawn,
    My charming little cruiskeen lawn.
        Gra ma chree ma cruiskeen,
        Slainté geal mavourneen,
        Gra machree a coolin bawn.

        Gra machree ma cruiskeen,
        Slainté geal mavourneen,
        Gra machree a coolin bawn, bawn, bawn,
        Gra machree a coolin bawn.

Immortal and divine,
Great Bacchus, god of wine,
    Create me by adoption your son:
In hope that you'll comply
My glass shall ne'er run dry,
    Nor my smiling little cruiskeen lawn. &c.

And when grim death appears,
In a few but pleasant years,
    To tell me that my glass has run;
I'll say, Begone, you knave,
For bold Bacchus gave me leave,
    To take another cruiskeen lawn. &c.

Then fill your glasses high,
Let's not part with lips a-dry,
    Though the lark now proclaims it is dawn;
And since we can't remain,
May we shortly meet again,
    To fill another cruiskeen lawn, lawn, lawn
    To fill another cruiskeen lawn.
        Gra ma chree ma cruiskeen,
        Slainté geal mavourneen,
        Gra machree a coolin bawn.

        Gra ma chree ma cruiskeen,
        Slainté geal mavourneen,
        Gra machree a coolin bawn, bawn, bawn,
        Gra machree a coolin bawn.

DORAN'S ASS

One Paddy Doyle lived near Killarney,
    And loved a maid called Betty Toole;
His tongue, I own, was tipped with blarney,
    Which seemed to him a golden rule.
From day to dawn he watched his colleen,
    And often to himself would say,
What need I care? sure here's my darling,
    Advancing to meet me on the way.
        Whack fol de darral ido.
        Whack fol de darral lal do.

One heavenly night in last November,
　　The moon shone gently from above,
What night it was I don't remember,
　　But Paddy went to meet his love.
That day Paddy took some liquor,
　　Which made his spirits light and gay,
Says he, where's the use in me walking quicker?
　　Don't I know she'll meet me on the way.
　　　　　　Whack fol de darral, etc.

So he tuned his pipes and fell a-humming,
　　As slowly onward he did creep,
But fatigue and whiskey soon over came him
　　And down he lay and fell asleep.
But he wasn't long without a comrade,
　　And one that could kick up the hay,
For a big jack-ass soon smelled out Pat,
　　And lay down beside him on the way.
　　　　　　Whack fol de darral, etc.

Pat stretched his arms on the grass,
　　Thinking of his little dear.
He dreamt of comforts without number,
　　Coming on in the ensuing year.
He stretched his arms on the grass,
　　His spirits felt so light and gay,
But instead of Bet—he gripped the ass,
　　And he roared—I have her, any way.
　　　　　　Whack fol de darral, etc.

He hugged and smugged his hairy messer,
　　And flung his hat to heavenly care.
Says Pat, she's mine, and may heaven bless her,
　　But, oh, be my soul, she's like a bear.
He put his hands on the donkey's nose,
　　With that the ass began to bray;
Pat jumped up and roared out,

Who sarved me in such a way?
    Whack fol de darral, etc.

Like blazes then away he cut
    At railway speed, or as fast I'm sure,
But he never stopt a leg or foot,
    Until he came to Betty's door,
By this time now 'twas dawning morning,
    So down on his knees he fell to pray,
Saying—Let me in, och Betty darlin',
    For I'm kilt--I'm murdered on the way.
    Whack fol de darral, etc.

So up and told her all quite civil
    While she prepared a burned glass,
How he had hugged and smugged the devil,
    Says she—sure that was Doran's ass.
And so I believe it was, says Pat.
    They both got wed on the ensuing day,
But he never got back that new straw hat,
    That the jack-ass ate up on the way.
    Whack fol de darral, etc.

DUMB, DUMB, DUMB

(Air: a variant of the "Cruiskeen Lawn")

THERE was a jolly blade that married a country maid,
    And soon he conducted her home, home, home;
In ev'ry household art she was comfort to his heart:
    But alas, and alas, she was dumb, dumb, dumb.

She could brew and she could bake, she could wring, wash, and
    shake,
    And keep the house clean with her broom, broom, broom;
She could knit, card, and spin, and do ev'ry thing;
    But what good was all that—she was dumb, dumb, dumb.

[262]

To the doctor then he went with mournful discontent,
  Saying, "Doctor, dear doctor, I'm come, come, come;
I'll pay you fifty pounds—and that in pure gold—
  If you make my wife speak that is dumb, dumb, dumb."

To the doctor then she went and he cut some little strings,
  And gave her tongue liberty to run, run, run:—
O, 'twas like a silly brute then her husband she abused,
  Saying, "You dog, I'll let you know I'm not dumb, dumb,
    dumb."

To the doctor then he went with mournful discontent,
  Saying, "Doctor, dear doctor, I'm come, come, come;
My wife is turned scold and with her I cannot hold:
  I'd give anything at all to have her dumb, dumb, dumb!"

"I could freely undertake for to make your wife speak,
  Though that was not easily done, done, done:—
It's not in the power of man, let him do whate'er he can,
  To make a scolding wife hold her tongue, tongue, tongue."

EASTER WEEK

(The Song of 1916)

WHO fears to speak of Easter Week,
    Who dares its fate deplore?
The red-gold flame of Erin's name
    Confronts the world once more.

So Irishmen remember them
    And raise your heads with pride,
That great men, and straight men,
    Have fought for you and died.

The storied page of this, our age,
    Will save our land from shame;

[263]

The ancient foe had boasted low
    That Irishmen were tame.

They'd bought their souls with paltry doles,
    They told the world of slaves,
That lie, men, will die, men,
    In Pearse and Plunkett's graves.

GOD SAVE IRELAND

GARRYOWEN

LET Bacchus's sons be not dismayed,
But join with me, each jovial blade;
Come, drink and sing and lend your aid
    To help me with the chorus.

Chorus
    Instead of spa, we'll drink brown ale,
    And pay the reck'ning on the nail,
    No man for debt shall go to jail
    From Garryowen in glory.

We are the boys that take delight in
Smashing the Limerick lamps when lighting,
Through the streets like sporters fighting,
    And tearing all before us.

We'll beat the bailiffs out of fun,
We'll make the mayor and sheriffs run,
We are the boys no man dares dun,
    If he regards a whole skin.

Our hearts so stout have got no fame,
For soon 'tis known from whence we came,
Where'er we go they dread the name
    Of Garryowen in glory.

[264]

THE HAPPY BEGGARMAN

This song gives a picture of the professional beggar who flourished before the famine of 1846.

OF ALL trades agoing, begging it is my delight;
My rent it is paid and I lay down my bags ev'ry night:
I'll throw away care and take a long staff in my hand,
And I'll flourish each day courageously looking for chance.

With my belt round my shoulder and down my bags they do
    hang;
With a push and a joult it's quickly I'll have them yoked on;
With my horn by my side, likewise my skiver and can;
With my staff and long pike to fight the dogs as I gang.

To patterns and fairs I'll go round for collection along,
I'll seem to be lame and quite useless of one of my hands;
Like a pilgrim I'll pray each day with my hat in my hand,
And at night in the alehouse I'll stay and pay like a man.

THE HUMOURS OF DONNYBROOK FAIR

D'Alton in *History of the County of Dublin* (1838), writing of Donnybrook, says, "This place was long celebrated for its annual August fair—the 'Bartholomew' of Dublin; but which, in consequence of several riotous and disgraceful results, it has been found necessary to suppress."

To DONNYBROOK steer, all you sons of Parnassus—
    Poor painters, poor poets, poor newsmen, and knaves,
To see what the fun is, that all fun surpasses—
    The sorrow and sadness of green Erin's slaves.
Oh, Donnybrook, jewel! full of mirth is your quiver,
    Where all flock from Dublin to gape and to stare
At two elegant bridges, without e'er a river:
    So, success to the humours of Donnybrook Fair!

O you lads that are witty, from famed Dublin city,
    And you that in pastime take any delight,

To Donnybrook fly, for the time's drawing nigh
   When fat pigs are hunted, and lean cobblers fight;
When maidens, so swift, run for a new shift;
   Men, muffled in sacks, for a shirt they race there;
There jockeys well booted, and horses sure-footed,
   All keep up the humours of Donnybrook Fair.

The mason does come, with his line and his plumb;
   The sawyer and carpenter, brothers in chips;
There are carvers and gilders, and all sort of builders,
   With soldiers from barracks and sailors from ships.
There confectioners, cooks, and printers of books,
   There stampers of linen, and weavers, repair;
There widows and maids, and all sort of trades,
   Go join in the humours of Donnybrook Fair.

There tinkers and nailers, and beggars and tailors,
   And singers of ballads, and girls of the sieve;
With Barrack Street rangers, the known ones and strangers,
   And many that no one can tell how they live:
There horsemen and walkers, and likewise fruit-hawkers,
   And swindlers, the devil himself that would dare,
With pipers and fiddlers, and dandies and diddlers,—
   All meet in the humours of Donnybrook Fair.

'Tis there are dogs dancing, and wild beasts a-prancing,
   With neat bits of painting in red, yellow, and gold;
Toss-players and scramblers, and showmen and gamblers,
   Pickpockets in plenty, both of young and of old.
There are brewers, and bakers, and jolly shoemakers,
   With butchers, and porters, and men that cut hair;
There are mountebanks grinning, while others are sinning,
   To keep up the humours of Donnybrook Fair.

Brisk lads and young lasses can there fill their glasses
   With whisky, and send a full bumper around;
Jig it off in a tent till their money's all spent,
   And spin like a top till they rest on the ground.

[266]

Oh, Donnybrook capers, to sweet catgut-scrapers,
  They bother the vapours, and drive away care;
And what is more glorious—there's naught more uproarious—
  Huzza for the humours of Donnybrook Fair!

I KNOW WHERE I'M GOING

I KNOW where I'm going,
I know who's going with me,
I know who I love,
But the dear knows who I'll marry.

I'll have stockings of silk,
Shoes of fine green leather,
Combs to buckle my hair
And a ring for every finger.

Feather beds are soft,
Painted rooms are bonny;
But I'd leave them all
To go with my love Johnny.

Some say he's dark,
I say he's bonny,
He's the flower of them all
My handsome, coaxing Johnny.

I know where I'm going,
I know who's going with me,
I know who I love,
But the dear knows who I'll marry.

I WANT TO BE MARRIED AND CANNOT TELL HOW

To THE field I carried my milking pail
  On a May day morning early,
And there I met with a smart young man,
  Who said that he lov'd me dearly.
I made him a curtsey, he made me a bow,
  He kissed me, and promised to marry, I vow,
Oh! I wish that young fellow was with me just now,
  On a May day morning early.

I try to forget him, but all in vain,
  On every day morning early,
And if I never should see him again,
  It will break my heart—or nearly,
I can't bear the sight of a sheep or cow
  I want to be married and cannot tell how,
Oh! I wish that young fellow was with me now,
  On a May day morning early.

I'LL NEVER GET DRUNK ANY MORE

(A Temperance Song)

Thomas Crofton Croker says of this "it was sung with much effect by a man named Eagan at the early meetings of a temperance society in the south of Ireland, upon which occasions the lines referring to the suicidal proceeding of hard drinking were always received with marked approbation."

Tune—"Mall Brook."

ONE night when I got frisky
Over some poteen whisky,
Like waves in the Bay of Biscay,
  I began to tumble and roar.
My face was red as a lobster,
I fell and I broke my nob, sir,
My watch was picked from my fob, sir—
  Oh, I'll never get drunk any more!

Now I'm resolved to try it,
I'll live upon moderate diet;
I'll not drink, but will deny it,
    And shun each alehouse-door;
For that's the place, they tell us,
We meet with all jovial good fellows;
But I swear by the poker and bellows
    I'll never get drunk any more.

The landlady is unwilling
To credit you for a shilling;
She straightway sends her bill in,
    And asks you to pay your score.
And if with money you're stocked,
She'll not stop till she's emptied your pocket;
Then the cellar-door is locked,
    And you cannot get drunk any more.

So by me now take caution,
Put drinking out of fashion,
For your own brains out you're dashing:
    Don't you feel your head quite sore?
For when all night you've tarried
Drinking of punch and claret,
In the morning home you're carried,
    (Saying) "I'll never get drunk any more."

A man that's fond of boozing,
His cash goes daily oozing;
His character he's losing,
    And its loss he will deplore.
His wife is unprotected,
His business is neglected,
Himself is *dis*-respected,
    So, do not get drunk any more.

AN IRISHMAN'S CHRISTENING

OF MYSELF, my dear joy, if you wish to be told
The first day I was born, I was not a night old,
                    Hillaloo!

The parson was sent for to christen the child;
He looked at the water, he grinned and he smiled,
                    Hillaloo!

He looked at the water, he grinned and he smiled;
Says he, " 'Tis with whisky I've christened the child;
            Oh, what a blunder, dear joy!"
So the day I was christened, I've never forgot
My first taste of whisky, it made me a sot;
            And could that be a wonder, my boy?

So, you see, I loved whisky while yet but a boy,
And I loved it still better, a hobbledehoy,
                    Hillaloo!

When I went to be married, they asked for the ring;
Says I, "Wait a minute, I'll give you that thing,"
                    Hillaloo!

Says I, "Wait a minute, I'll give you that thing,"
But I pulled out the whisky instead of the ring;
            Oh, what a blunder, dear joy!
"So," says I, "as it's here, we'll just taste it, I think,
To the bride's happy wedding we'll all of us drink;"
            And could that be a wonder, my boy?

I drank to her health, and drank on to her death,
For Kitty, sweet soul, soon gave up her breath,
                    Hillaloo!

One day I must follow her to the cold ground,
Where, to moisten the throat, no whisky is found,
                    Hillaloo!

[270]

Where, to moisten the throat, no whisky is found,
Though the nights are so long, and so cold is the ground;
Oh, what a blunder, dear joy!
Then should a dead man of his christening dream,
And call out from his grave to be christened again;
Oh! could that be a wonder, my boy?

JOHNNY, I HARDLY KNEW YE

WHILE going the road to sweet Athy,
Hurroo! hurroo!
While going the road to sweet Athy,
Hurroo! hurroo!
While going the road to sweet Athy,
A stick in my hand and a drop in my eye,
A doleful damsel I heard cry:
"Och Johnny, I hardly knew ye!
With drums and guns, and guns and drums
The enemy nearly slew ye;
My darling dear, you look so queer,
Och, Johnny, I hardly knew ye!

"Where are your eyes that looked so mild?
Hurroo! hurroo!
Where are your eyes that looked so mild?
Hurroo! hurroo!
Where are your eyes that looked so mild,
When my poor heart you first beguiled?
Why did you run from me and the child?
Och, Johnny, I hardly knew ye!
With drums, etc.

"Where are the legs with which you run?
Hurroo! hurroo!
Where are the legs with which you run?
Hurroo! hurroo!

[271]

Where are the legs with which you run
When you went to carry a gun?
Indeed, your dancing days are done!
   Och, Johnny, I hardly knew ye!
            With drums, etc.

"It grieved my heart to see you sail,
    Hurroo! hurroo!
It grieved my heart to see you sail,
    Hurroo! hurroo!
It grieved my heart to see you sail,
Though from my heart you took leg-bail;
Like a cod you're doubled up head and tail.
   Och, Johnny, I hardly knew ye!
            With drums, etc.

"You haven't an arm and you haven't a leg,
    Hurroo! hurroo!
You haven't an arm and you haven't a leg,
    Hurroo! hurroo!
You haven't an arm and you haven't a leg,
You're an eyeless, noseless, chickenless egg;
You'll have to be put with a bowl to beg:
   Och, Johnny, I hardly knew ye!
            With drums, etc.

"I'm happy for to see you home,
    Hurroo! hurroo!
I'm happy for to see you home,
    Hurroo! hurroo!
I'm happy for to see you home,
All from the island of Sulloon,
So low in flesh, so high in bone;
   Och, Johnny, I hardly knew ye!
            With drums, etc.

"But sad as it is to see you so,
    Hurroo! hurroo!

But sad as it is to see you so,
        Hurroo! hurroo!
But sad as it is to see you so,
And to think of you now as an object of woe,
Your Peggy'll still keep ye on as her beau;
    Och, Johnny, I hardly knew ye!
        With drums and guns, and guns and drums
            The enemy nearly slew ye;
        My darling dear, you look so queer,
        Och, Johnny, I hardly knew ye!"

(Parodied versions)

In Dublinese

WHERE are those legs with which you run
When you went to shoulder the gun?
Indeed your dancing days are done.
        Oh Johnny, I hardly knew you!

Where are those eyes that were so mild,
When of my love you me beguiled?
Why did you skedaddle from me and the child?
        Oh Johnny, I hardly knew you!
                        (*Anonymous*)

In Swinburnese

Alas! for the going of swiftness, for the feet of the running of
    thee,
    When thou wentest among the swords and the shoutings of
        captains made shrill.
Woe is me for the pleasant places! Yea, one shall say of thy glee
    "It is not," and as for delight, the feet of thy dancing are
        still.

Also thine eyes were mild as a lowlit flame of fire,
    When thou wovest the web whereof wiles were the woof, and
        the warp was my heart!

[273]

Why left'st thou the fertile field whence thou reaped'st the
    fruit of desire?
For the change of the face of thy colour I know thee not who
    thou art.

                           (*Robert Yelverton Tyrrell*)

In Miltonese

Johnny, though clear mine eyes, to speculate
No more than thine that smoke of battle fogs
By Him permitted are who grants to frogs
The usage of blunt orbs: to remonstrate
Be loth. Forgive me when I hesitate
To hail thee, darkling. Rather with the hogs
Would I consort than summon back to clogs
Limbs overplied in service of the State.
Thou in that service zealous wast, and we
Can proudly answer to detractors rude:
We loved our Saints espoused: but Liberty
Loved more. Thou sharest in the glorious mood
Of him whom his much-tried Penelope
Met, reaching to great fame by Fortitude.

                         (*Oliver St. John Gogarty*)

KILLYBURN BRAE

The eleven stanzas are all arranged in the manner of the first two.

THERE was an ould man down by Killyburn brae,
   Right fol, right fol, titty fol lay.
There was an ould man down by Killyburn brae,
Had a scolding ould wife for the most of his day,
   With a right fol da dol, titty fol lol,
     Fol da-da dol, da dol da-da day.

One day as this man he walk'd out in the glen,
   Right fol, right fol, titty fol lay.
One day as this man he walk'd out in the glen,

Sure he met with the divil, says "How are you then?"
  With a right fol da dol, titty fol lol,
    Fol da-da dol, da dol da-da day.

Says he, me ould man I have come for yer wife,
For I hear she's the plague an' torment of yer life,

So the divil he hoisted her up on his back,
An' hot-fut for hell with her then he did pack,

An' when at the finish they got to hell's gate,
Sure he threw her right down with a thump on her pate,

There were two little divils there playing at ball,
Whilst the one he was wee sure the other was small,

There were two other divils there tied up in chains,
An' she lifted her stick an' she scattered their brains,

So the divil he hoisted her up on his back,
They were seven years goin'—nine *days* comin' back,

Says he, me ould man here's yer wife safe an' well,
For the likes of herself we would not have in hell,

Now I've been a divil the most of me life,
But I ne'er was in hell till I met with yer wife,

So it's true that the women is worse than the men,
When they go down to hell they are thrown out again.

A LAY OF THE FAMINE

Hush! hear you how the night wind keens around the craggy
    reek?
Its voice peals high above the waves that thunder in the creek.

[275]

"Aroon! aroon! arouse thee, and hie thee o'er the moor!
Ten miles away there's bread, they say, to feed the starving
    poor.

"God save thee, Eileen *bawn astor,* and guide thy naked feet,
And keep the fainting life in us till thou come back with meat.

"God send the moon to show thee light upon the way so drear,
And mind thou well the rocky dell, and heed the rushy mere."

She kissed her father's palsied hand, her mother's pallid cheek,
And whirled out on the driving storm beyond the craggy reek.

All night she tracks, with bleeding feet, the rugged mountain
        way,
And townsfolks meet her in the street at flushing of the day.

But God is kinder on the moor than man is in the town,
And Eileen quails before the stranger's harsh rebuke and
    frown.

Night's gloom enwraps the hills once more and hides a slender
        form
That shudders o'er the moor again before the driving storm.

No bread is in her wallet stored, but on the lonesome heath
She lifts her empty hands to God, and prays for speedy death.

Yet struggles onward, faint and blind, and numb to hope or
        fear,
Unmindful of the rocky dell or of the rushy mere.

But, ululu! what sight is this?—what forms come by the reek?
As white and thin as evening mist upon the mountain's peak.

Mist-like they glide across the heath—a weird and ghostly
        band;
The foremost crosses Eileen's path, and grasps her by the hand.

"Dear daughter, thou has suffered sore, but we are well and
    free;
For God has ta'en our life from us, nor wills it long to thee.

"So hie thee to our cabin lone, and dig a grave so deep,
And underneath the golden gorse our corpses lay to sleep—

"Else they will come and smash the walls upon our moldering
    bones,
And screaming mountain birds will tear our flesh from out the
    stones.

"And, daughter, haste to do thy work, so thou mayest quickly
    come,
And take with us our grateful rest, and share our peaceful
    home."

        .   .   .

The sun behind the distant hills far-sinking down to sleep;
A maiden on the lonesome moor, digging a grave so deep;

The moon above the craggy reek, silvering moor and wave,
And the pale corpse of a maiden young stretched on a new-
    made grave.

A LONGFORD LEGEND

OH! 'TIS of a bold major a tale I'll relate,
Who possessed a fine house and a charming estate,
Who, when possible, always his pleasure would take
From morning till night in a boat on his lake.
So a steam-launch he bought from a neighbouring peer,
And learnt how to start her, to stroke, and to steer;
But part of the craft he omitted to learn—
How to ease her, and to stop her, and back her astern.

Well, one lovely spring morn from their moorings they cast,
The furnace alight and the steam in full blast.

[277]

As they cruised through the lake, oh! what pleasure was theirs!
What congratulations! what swagger! what airs!
"Evening's come," says the major; "let's home for the night.
I'll pick up the mooring and make her all right;
Whilst you, my gay stoker, your wages to earn,
Just ease her, and stop her, and back her astern."

"Do what?" asked the stoker. "Why, stop her, of course!"
"Faith! it's aisier stopping a runaway horse!
Just try it yourself!" The field officer swore!
But that was no use,—they were nearly on shore!
He swore at himself, at the boat, and the crew;
He cursed at the funnel, the boiler, and screw,—
But in vain! He was forced from his mooring to turn,
Shouting, "Ease her, and stop her, and back her astern!"

It was clear that on shore they that night would not dine,
So they drank up the brandy, the whisky and wine;
They finished the stew and demolished the cake
As they steamed at full speed all the night round the lake.
Weeks passed; and with terror and famine oppressed,
One by one of that ill-fated crew sank to rest;
And grim death seized the major before he could learn
How to ease her, and stop her, and back her astern.

And still round the lake their wild course they pursue,
While the ghost of the major still swears at the crew,
And the ghosts of the crew still reply in this mode,
"Just ease her, and stop her yourself—and be blowed!"
Here's the moral: Imprimis, whene'er you're afloat,
Don't use haughty words to your crew on your boat;
And ere starting, oh! make this your deepest concern—
Learn to ease her, and stop her, and back her astern.

MACKENNA'S DREAM

(Air: Captain Rock)

ONE evening late I chanced to stray,
All in the pleasant month of May,
When all the land in slumber lay,
The moon on the deep.
The soft breeze was rustling round,
The murmur of the ocean huzhoed me to sleep.
I dreamt I saw brave Brian Boru,
Who did the Danish race subdue,
The mighty man his sword he drew,
These words he spoke to me:—
"The harp melodiously shall sound,
When Erin's sons shall be unbound
And they shall gather safe around the green laurel tree."

I thought brave Sarsfield drew up nigh,
And to my question made reply:—
"For Erin's cause I'll live and die
As thousands did of yore.
My sword again on Aughrim's plain
Old Erin's rights shall well maintain,
Though thousands lie in battle slain,
And hundreds in their gore."
I thought St. Ruth stood on the ground
And said, "I will your monarch crown;"
Encompassed by the French around
All ready for the field.
He raised a cross and thus did say:—
"Brave boys, we'll shew them gallant play;
Let no man dare to run away,
But die ere they yield."

Then Billy Byrne he came there
From Ballymanus, I declare,
Brought Wicklow, Carlow, and Kildare
That day at his command.

[279]

Westmeath and Cavan also join;
The County Louth men crossed the Boyne;
Slane, Trim, and Navan fell in line,
      And Dublin to a man.
O'Reilly on the Hill of Skreen
He drew his sword both bright and keen,
And swore by all his eyes had seen
      He would avenge the fall
Of Erin's sons and daughters brave,
Who nobly filled a martyr's grave,
They died before they'd live enslaved,
      For vengeance they call!

Then Father Murphy he did say,
"Behold, my lord, I'm here to-day,
With eighteen thousand pikemen gay
      From Wexford so brave.
Our country's fate it does depend
On you and on our gallant friends;
And Heaven will our cause defend,
      We'll die ere we be slaves."
Methought each band played Patrick's Day
To marshal all in proud array,
With caps and feathers white and gay,
      A grand and warlike show;
With drums and trumpets loud and shrill,
And cannons placed on ev'ry hill,
The pikemen did the valley fill
      To strike the fatal blow.

Then all at once appeared in sight
An army clad in armour bright;
Both front and rear and left and right
      March on to the fore:
The chieftains pitched their camp with skill,
Determined tyrants' blood to spill
Beneath us ran a mountain rill
      As rapid as the Nore;

Along the line they raised a shout,
Crying "Quick March, right about!"
With bayonets fixed they all marched out
        To face the deadly foe;
The enemy were no ways shy,
With thundering cannon planted nigh;
Now thousands in death's struggle lie,
        The streams redly flow.

The enemy they made a square
And drove our cavalry to despair,
They were nearly routed, rank and rear,
        But yet did not yield,
For up came Wexford—never slack—
With brave Tipperary at their back,
And Longford next, who in a crack
        Straight swept them off the field.
They gave three cheers for liberty,
As the enemy all routed flee;
Methought I looked but could not see
        One foeman on the plain.
Then I awoke—'twas break of day:
No wounded on the ground there lay,
No warriors there, no fierce affray:—
        So ended my dream.

THE MAID THAT SOLD HER BARLEY

It's COLD and raw the north winds blow
    Black in the morning early,
When all the hills were covered with snow,
    Oh when it was winter fairly,
As I was riding over the moor,
    I met a farmer's daughter,
Her cherry cheeks and sloe black eyes,
    They caused my heart to falter.

I bowed my bonnet very low
  To let her know my meaning.
She answered with a courteous smile,
  Her looks they were engaging.
"Where are you bound my pretty maid,
  It's now in the morning early?"
The answer that she made to me,
  "Kind Sir, to sell my barley."

"Now twenty guineas I've in my purse,
  And twenty more that's yearly,
You need not go to the market town,
  For I'll buy all your barley.
If twenty guineas would gain the heart,
  Of the maid that I love so dearly,
All for to tarry with me one night,
  And go home in the morning early."

As I was riding o'er the moor,
  The very evening after,
It was my fortune for to meet
  The farmer's only daughter.
Although the weather being cold and raw
  With her I thought to parley,
This answer then she made to me,
  "Kind sir, I've sold my barley."

THE MAID OF THE SWEET BROWN KNOWE

COME all ye lads and lassies and listen to me a while,
And I'll sing for you a verse or two will cause you all to smile;
It's all about a young man, and I'm going to tell you now,
How he lately came a-courting of the Maid of the Sweet Brown
    Knowe.

Said he, "My pretty fair maid, will you come along with me,
We'll both go off together, and married we will be;

We'll join our hands in wedlock bands, I'm speaking to you
    now,
And I'll do my best endeavour for the Maid of the Sweet
    Brown Knowe."

This fair and fickle young thing, she knew not what to say,
Her eyes did shine like silver bright, and merrily did play;
She said, "Young man, your love subdue, for I am not ready
    now,
And I'll spend another season at the foot of the Sweet Brown
    Knowe.

Said he, "My pretty fair maid, how can you say so,
Look down in yonder valley where my crops do gently grow,
Look down in yonder valley where my horses and my plough
Are at their daily labour for the Maid of the Sweet Brown
    Knowe."

"If they're at their daily labour, kind sir, it's not for me,
For I've heard of your behaviour, I have indeed," said she;
"There is an Inn where you call in, I have heard the people
    say,
Where you rap and call and pay for all, and go home at the
    break of day."

"If I rap and call and pay for all, the money is all my own,
And I'll never spend your fortune, for I hear you have got
    none.
You thought you had my poor heart broke in talking with me
    now,
But I'll leave you where I found you, at the foot of the Sweet
    Brown Knowe."

MOLLY BAWN AND BRIAN OGE

COME listen to my story, Molly Bawn;
I'm bound for death or glory Molly Bawn,
For I've listed in the army
Where no more your eyes will harm me;
Faith, they kill me whilst they charm me, Molly Bawn.

Musha, Brian you're drinking now you rogue;
I know it by your winking, Brian Oge;
But would you be the villain
For to take the Saxon shilling
And do their dirty killing, Brian Oge?
And what would all the boys say, Brian Oge,
If you turned a redcoat haythen, Brian Oge?
Go list then if it please ye,
You villain do not tease me,
Sure you'd drive a colleen crazy, Brian Oge.

It was you that drove me to it, Molly Bawn,
When you read my death you'll rue it, Molly Bawn;
When I die mid foemen wrestling,
Where the balls like hail are whistling
And bloody bayonets bristling, Molly Bawn;
And the last words I'll be speaking, Molly Bawn,
When my soul its leave is taking, Molly Bawn,
Are *gra ma chree asthoreen,*
Your sweetheart Brian Oireen
And for you my blood is pouring, Molly Bawn.

Oh, sure I did it just to prove you, Brian Oge;
I hate you! No, I love you, Brian Oge.
But keep your heart, *a chara,*
For I'll buy you out to-morrow
Or I'll die of shame and sorrow, Brian Oge.
And to think that you should doubt me, Brian Oge,
And myself so wild about you, Brian Oge;
Would you let that thief, Phil Dorman

Come and wed me in the morning?
Faith, you might have give me warning, Brian Oge.

I am strong and hale and hearty, Molly Bawn;
I war like Bonaparty, Molly Bawn.
Sure the devil a list I listed,
The sergeant tried and missed it—
You are mine, I have confessed it, Molly Bawn.
So I'll buy for you a bonnet, Molly Bawn,
There'll be lots of ribbons on it, Molly Bawn,
And it's you that will look shining,
With your golden hair entwining;
We'll get wed and cease repining, Molly Bawn.

Oh, I'm sick and tired of scheming, Brian Oge,
'Tis yourself that thinks it's shaming, Brian Oge;
But as you did not take that shilling,
Just to save your life I'm willing—
We'll get wed—behave you villain—Brian Oge.

MRS. MC GRATH

"Oh Mrs. McGrath!" the sergeant said,
"Would you like to make a soldier out of your son, Ted,
With a scarlet coat and a gib cocked hat,
Now Mrs. McGrath, wouldn't you like that?"

Chorus
Wid yer too-ri-aa, fol-the-diddle-aa,
Too-ri-oo-ri-oo-ri-aa,
Wid yer too-ri-aa, fol-the-diddle-aa,
Too-ri-oo-ri-oo-ri-aa,
Lav beg, the Cracker, O.

So Mrs. McGrath lived on the sea-shore
For the space of seven long years or more
Till she saw a big ship sailing into the bay

[285]

"Here's my son Ted, wisha, clear the way."
        Wid yer too-ri-aa, etc.

"Oh, Captain dear, where have you been
Have you been sailing on the Mediterreen
Or have ye any tidings of my son Ted
Is the poor boy living or is he dead?"
        Wid yer too-ri-aa, etc.

Then up comes Ted without any legs
And in their place he has two wooden pegs
She kissed him a dozen times or two
Saying "Holy Moses 'tisn't you."
        Wid yer too-ri-aa, etc.

"Oh then were ye drunk or were ye blind
That ye left yer two fine legs behind
Or was it walking upon the sea
Wore yer two fine legs from the knees away?"
        Wid yer too-ri-aa, etc.

"Oh I wasn't drunk and I wasn't blind
But I left my two fine legs behind
For a cannon ball on the fifth of May
Took my two fine legs from the knees away."
        Wid yer too-ri-aa, etc.

"Oh then Teddy me boy," the widow cried,
"Yer two fine legs were yer mammy's pride
Them stumps of a tree wouldn't do at all
Why didn't ye run from the big cannon ball?
        Wid yer too-ri-aa, etc.

All foreign wars I do proclaim
Between Don John and the King of Spain
And by herrins I'll make them rue the time
That they swept the legs from a child of mine.
        Wid yer too-ri-aa, etc.

[286]

Oh then, if I had you back again
I'd never let ye go to fight the King of Spain
For I'd rather my Ted as he used to be
Than the King of France and his whole Navee.
      Wid yer too-ri-aa, etc.

THE NATIVE IRISHMAN

(By a Converted Saxon)

BEFORE I came across the sea
  To this delightful place,
I thought the native Irish were
  A funny sort of race;

I thought they bore shillelagh-sprigs,
  And that they always said:
"Och hone, acushla, tare-an-ouns,"
  "Begorra," and "bedad!"

I thought they sported crownless hats
  With dhudeens in the rim;
I thought they wore long trailing coats
  And knickerbockers trim;
I thought they went about the place
  As tight as they could get;
And that they always had a fight
  With every one they met.

I thought their noses all turned up
  Just like a crooked pin;
I thought their mouths six inches wide
  And always on the grin;
I thought their heads were made of stuff
  As hard as any nails;
I half suspected that they were
  Possessed of little tails.

[287]

But when I came unto the land
    Of which I heard so much,
I found that the inhabitants
    Were not entirely such;
I found their features were not all
    Exactly like baboons';
I found that some wore billycocks,
    And some had pantaloons.

I found their teeth were quite as small
    As Europeans' are,
And that their ears, in point of size,
    Were not pecul-iar.
I even saw a face or two
    Which might be handsome called;
And by their very largest feet
    I was not much appalled.

I found them sober, now and then;
    And even in the street,
It seems they do not have a fight
    With every boy they meet.
I even found some honest men
    Among the very poor;
And I have heard some sentences
    Which did not end with "shure."

It seems that praties in their skins
    Are not their only food,
And that they have a house or two
    Which is not built of mud.
In fact, they're not all brutes or fools,
    And I suspect that when
They rule themselves they'll be as good,
    Almost, as Englishmen!

NELL FLAHERTY'S DRAKE

My name it is Nell, quite candid I tell,
    That I live near Coote hill, I will never deny;
I had a fine drake, the truth for to spake,
    That my grandmother left me and she going to die;
He was wholesome and sound, he would weigh twenty pound,
    The universe round I would rove for his sake—
Bad wind to the robber—be he drunk or sober—
    That murdered Nell Flaherty's beautiful drake.

His neck it was green—most rare to be seen,
    He was fit for a queen of the highest degree;
His body was white—and would you delight—
    He was plump, fat and heavy, and brisk as a bee.
The dear little fellow, his legs they were yellow,
    He would fly like a swallow and dive like a hake,
But some wicked savage, to grease his white cabbage,
    Has murdered Nell Flaherty's beautiful drake.

May his pig never grunt, may his cat never hunt,
    May a ghost ever haunt him at dead of the night;
May his hen never lay, may his ass never bray,
    May his goat fly away like an old paper kite.
That the flies and the fleas may the wretch ever tease,
    And the piercing north breeze make him shiver and shake,
May a lump of a stick raise bumps fast and thick
    On the monster that murdered Nell Flaherty's drake.

THE NIGHT BEFORE LARRY WAS STRETCHED

The authorship of this extraordinary piece of poetic ribaldry has been
much discussed, but has never been discovered. It is written in Dublin
slang of the end of the eighteenth century.

The night before Larry was stretched,
    The boys they all paid him a visit;

[289]

A bait in their sacks, too, they fetched;
  They sweated their duds till they riz it:
For Larry was ever the lad,
  When a boy was condemned to the squeezer,
Would fence all the duds that he had
  To help a poor friend to a sneezer,
    And warm his gob 'fore he died.

The boys they came crowding in fast,
  They drew all their stools round about him,
Six glims round his trap-case were placed,
  He couldn't be well waked without 'em.
When one of us asked could he die
  Without having duly repented,
Says Larry, "That's all in my eye;
  And first by the clargy invented,
    To get a fat bit for themselves."

"I'm sorry, dear Larry," says I,
  "To see you in this situation;
And, blister my limbs if I lie,
  I'd as lieve it had been my own station."
"Ochone! it's all over," says he,
  "For the neckcloth I'll be forced to put on
And by this time to-morrow you'll see
  Your poor Larry as dead as a mutton,"
    Because, why, his courage was good.

"And I'll be cut up like a pie,
  And my nob from my body be parted."
"You're in the wrong box, then," says I,
  "For blast me if they're so hard-hearted:
A chalk on the back of your neck
  Is all that Jack Ketch dares to give you;
Then mind not such trifles a feck,
  For why should the likes of them grieve you?
    And now, boys, come tip us the deck."

[290]

The cards being called for, they played,
   Till Larry found one of them cheated;
A dart at his napper he made
   (The boy being easily heated):
"Oh, by the hokey, you thief,
   I'll scuttle your nob with my daddle!
You cheat me because I'm in grief,
   But soon I'll demolish your noddle,
      And leave you your claret to drink."

Then the clergy came in with his book,
   He spoke him so smooth and so civil;
Larry tipped him a Kilmainham look,
   And pitched his big wig to the devil;
Then sighing, he threw back his head
   To get a sweet drop of the bottle,
And pitiful sighing, he said:
   "Oh, the hemp will be soon round my throttle
      And choke my poor windpipe to death.

"Though sure it's the best way to die,
   Oh, the devil a betther a-livin'!
For, sure, when the gallows is high
   Your journey is shorter to Heaven:
But what harasses Larry the most,
   And makes his poor soul melancholy,
Is to think of the time when his ghost
   Will come in a sheet to sweet Molly—
      Oh, sure it will kill her alive!"

So moving these last words he spoke,
   We all vented our tears in a shower;
For my part, I thought my heart broke,
   To see him cut down like a flower,
On his travels we watched him next day;
   Oh, the throttler! I thought I could kill him;
But Larry not one word did say,

Nor changed till he come to "King William"—
Then, *musha!* his color grew white.

When he came to the nubbling chit,
    He was tucked up so neat and so pretty,
The rumbler jogged off from his feet,
    And he died with his face to the city;
He kicked, too—but that was all pride,
    For soon you might see 'twas all over;
Soon after the noose was untied,
    And at darky we waked him in clover,
        And sent him to take a ground sweat.

"TOM MOORE, JR."

O'DUFFY'S IRONSIDES

"If only two men go to Spain, I will be one of them"—O'Duffy.
General Eoin O'Duffy was Chief of Police under the Cosgravite Government. Later he organized a company to fight in Spain against the Loyalists. This is a typical Dublin street ballad in all its irony.

You've heard of Slattery's light dragoons,
Who fought at Waterloo,
And those who ran at Bunker's Hill
Or bunked at Timbuctoo.
There is still a page of history
Which may never be uncut
To tell the glorious story of
O'Duffy's mounted foot.

"In old Dublin town my name is tarred
On pavement and slum wall.
In thousands on its Christian Front
The starving children call,
But with my gallant Ironsides
They call to us in vain,

For we're off to slaughter workers
In the sunny land of Spain.

"Let loose my fierce Crusaders,"
O'Duffy wildly cries,
"My grim and bold moss-troopers
That poached by Shannon sides.
Their shirts are green, their backs are strong,
They've cobwebs on the brain.
If Franco's Moors are beaten down
My Irish troops remain!

"Fall in, fall in," O'Duffy cries,
"There's work in Spain to do,
A martyr's crown we all will gain,
And shoot the toilers through.
In paradise an Irish Harp,
A Moor to dance a jig,
A traitor's hope, a hangman's rope
An Irish peeler's pig."

On Badajoz' red ramparts,
The Spanish workers died,
And Duffy's bellowing Animal Gang
Sang hymns of hate with pride.
The sleuths who called for Connolly's blood,
And Sean MacDiarmid's too,
Are panting still for workers' gore,
From Spain to far Peru.

"Bring forth my war horse Rosinant,"
The bold O'Duffy cries,
"My squire Patsy Panza,
The man who never lies;
My peeler's baton in my hand
A gay knight-errant I,
Oh, Allah guide our gallant band,
And Hitler, guard the sky.

[293]

"Put on my suit of *'Daily Mail'*,
A crescent on my back,
And hoist the 'Independent' flag,
The Freeman's Castle-hack;
My name is tarred in Dublin town,
On pavement and slum wall,
But far away in distant Spain
Grandee and landlord call.
With Foreign Legion, Riff and Moor,
We'll fight for Al-fon-so
And the fame of Duffy's Ironsides
Will down the ages go."

.   .   .

On the village pump in Skibbereen
An eagle screams[1] its woe,
As it hears the tramp of armèd men
From the bogs of Timahoe,
The war drums roll in Dublin town
And from each lusty throat,
The Fascists sing the ancient hymn,
"The Peeler and the Goat."

[1] A punning reference to "The Skibbereen Eagle", a Co. Cork newspaper.

THE RAKES OF MALLOW

BEAUING, belle-ing, dancing, drinking,
Breaking windows, damning, sinking,[1]
Ever raking, never thinking,
        Live the rakes of Mallow.

Spending faster than it comes,
Beating waiters, bailiffs, duns,
Bacchus's true-begotten sons,
        Live the rakes of Mallow.

[1] *Sinking*, cursing extravagantly—*i.e.* damning you to hell and *sinking* you lower.

One time nought but claret drinking,
Then like politicians thinking
To raise the sinking funds when sinking,
    Live the rakes of **Mallow.**

When at home with dadda dying,
Still for Mallow water crying;
But where there's good claret plying,
    Live the rakes of **Mallow.**

Living short but merry lives;
Going where the devil drives;
Having sweethearts, but no wives,
    Live the rakes of **Mallow.**

Racking tenants, stewards teasing,
Swiftly spending, slowly raising,
Wishing to spend all their days in
    Raking as at **Mallow.**

Then to end this raking life
They get sober, take a wife,
Ever after live in strife,
    And wish again for **Mallow.**

REYNARD THE FOX

(A Song Celebrating the Great Hunt of 1793)

This hunting song was very popular in the midland counties of Ireland
in the middle part of the nineteenth century. See also "The Hunting of
the Hare, with Her Last Will and Testament." Chappell, *Popular Music
of the Olden Time.*

THE first day of spring in the year ninety-three,
The first recreation was in this counterie:
The King's County gentlemen o'er hills, dales and rocks,
They rode out so jovially in search of a fox.

[295]

Tally-ho hark-away, Tally-ho hark-away, Tally-ho hark-
away
    My boys, away, hark-away!

When Reynard was started he faced Tullamore,
Arklow and Wicklow along the sea-shore;
We kept his brush in view ev'ry yard of the way,
And it's straight he took his course through the street of
    Roscrea!
    Tally-ho hark-away, etc.

But Reynard, sly Reynard, lay hid there that night,
And they swore they would watch him until the day-light;
Early next morning the woods they did resound
With the echo of horns and the sweet cry of hounds.
    Tally-ho etc.

When Reynard was started he faced to the hollow,
Where none but the hounds and footmen could follow;
The gentlemen cried, "Watch him, watch him, what shall we
    do?
If the rocks do not stop him he will cross Killaloe!"
    Tally-ho etc.

When Reynard was taken, his wishes to fulfil,
He called for ink and paper and pen to write his will:
And what he made mention of, they found it no blank,
For he gave them a cheque on the National Bank.
    Tally-ho etc.

"To you, Mr. Casey, I give my whole estate;
And to you, young O'Brien, my money and my plate;
And I give to you, Sir Francis, my whip, spurs and cap,
For you crossed walls and ditches and ne'er looked for a gap.
    Tally-ho etc.

THE SHAN VAN VOCHT

This song was written when the French fleet sailed for Ireland in 1796; but like the Spanish Armada, the fleet was scattered by a storm and but few ships entered Bantry Bay. *Shan Van Vocht* means "poor old woman," *i.e.* Ireland.

Many parodies have been composed, one of the more sprightly by Susan Mitchell; the first two stanzas of this are appended.

OH! THE French are on the sea,
   Says the Shan Van Vocht;
The French are on the sea,
   Says the Shan Van Vocht:
Oh! the French are in the Bay,
They'll be here without delay,
And the Orange will decay,
   Says the Shan Van Vocht.
     Oh! the French are in the Bay,
     They'll be here by break of day,
     And the Orange will decay,
       Says the Shan Van Vocht.

And where will they have their camp?
   Says the Shan Van Vocht;
Where will they have their camp?
   Says the Shan Van Vocht;
On the Curragh of Kildare,
The boys they will be there,
With their pikes in good repair,
   Says the Shan Van Vocht.
     To the Curragh of Kildare
     The boys they will repair,
     And Lord Edward will be there,
       Says the Shan Van Vocht.

Then what will the yeomen do?
   Says the Shan Van Vocht;
What will the yeomen do?
   Says the Shan Van Vocht;
What should the yeomen do

[297]

But throw off the Red and Blue,
And swear that they'll be true
  To the Shan Van Vocht?
    What should the yeomen do
    But throw off the red and blue,
    And swear that they'll be true
      To the Shan Van Vocht?

And what colour will they wear?
  Says the Shan Van Vocht;
What colour will they wear?
  Says the Shan Van Vocht;
What colour should be seen
Where our fathers' homes have been,
But our own immortal Green?
  Says the Shan Van Vocht.
    What colour should be seen
    Where our fathers' homes have been.
    But our own immortal Green?
      Says the Shan Van Vocht.

And will Ireland then be free?
  Says the Shan Van Vocht;
Will Ireland then be free?
  Says the Shan Van Vocht;
Yes! Ireland shall be free,
From the centre to the sea;
Then hurrah for Liberty!
  Says the Shan Van Vocht.
    Yes! Ireland shall be free,
    From the centre to the sea:
    Then hurrah for Liberty!
      Says the Shan Van Vocht.

THE IRISH COUNCIL BILL, 1907

Is it this you call Home Rule?
  Says the Shan Van Vocht.
Do you take me for a fool?
  Says the Shan Van Vocht.
To be sending round the hat.
Five-and-twenty years for that
Isn't good enough for Pat,
  Says the Shan Van Vocht.

And the Lord-Lieutenant too,
  Says the Shan Van Vocht,
Is he still to be on view?
  Says the Shan Van Vocht.
And all them big police,
Monumentally obese,
Must I go on feeding these?
  Says the Shan Van Vocht?

.   .   .   .   .   .

(Susan Mitchell)

TIPPERARY RECRUITING SONG

'T is now we'd want to be wary, boys,
The recruiters are out in Tipperary, boys;
If they offer a glass, we'll wink as they pass—
We're old birds for chaff in Tipperary, boys.

Then, hurrah for the gallant Tipperary boys,
Although we're "cross and contrary," boys;
The never a one will handle a gun,
Except for the Green and Tipperary, boys,

Now mind what John Bull did here, my boys,
In the days of our famine and fear, my boys;

[299]

He burned and sacked, he plundered and racked,
Old Ireland of Irish to clear, my boys.

Now Bull wants to pillage and rob, my boys,
And put the proceeds in his fob, my boys;
But let each Irish blade just stick to his trade,
And let Bull do his own dirty job, my boys.

So never to 'list be in haste, my boys,
Or a glass of drugged whisky to taste, my boys;
If to India you go, it's to grief and to woe,
And to rot and to die like a beast, my boys.

But now he is beat for men, my boys,
His army is getting so thin, my boys,
With the fever and ague, the sword and the plague,
O, the devil a fear that he'll win, my boys.

Then mind not the nobblin' old schemer, boys,
Though he says that he's richer than Damer, boys;
Though he bully and roar, his power is o'er,
And his black heart will shortly be tamer, boys.

Now, isn't Bull peaceful and civil, boys,
In his mortal distress and his evil, boys?
But we'll cock each caubeen when his sergeants are seen,
And we'll tell them to go to the devil, boys.

Then hurrah for the gallant Tipperary boys!
Although "we're cross and contrary," boys;
The never a one will handle a gun,
Except for the Green and Tipperary, boys.

THE WEARIN' OF THE GREEN

O Paddy dear, an' did ye hear the news that's goin' round?
The shamrock is by law forbid to grow on Irish ground!

No more Saint Patrick's Day we'll keep, his colour can't be
   seen,
For there's a cruel law agin the wearin' o' the Green!
I met wid Napper Tandy, and he took me by the hand,
And he said, 'How's poor ould Ireland, and how does she
   stand?"
She's the most disthressful country that iver yet was seen,
For they're hangin' men an' women there for the wearin' o' the
   Green.

And if the colour we must wear is England's cruel Red,
Let it remind us of the blood that Ireland has shed;
Then pull the shamrock from your hat, and throw it on the
   sod,
And never fear, 'twill take root there, tho' under foot 'tis trod!
When law can stop the blades of grass from growin' as they
   grow,
And when the leaves in summer-time their colour dare not
   show,
Then I will change the colour, too, I wear in my caubeen,
But till that day, plase God, I'll stick to wearin' o' the Green.

   The above represents the anonymous, street version of the song dating
from 1798. It was slightly altered by Dion Boucicault (1822-1890) who
added a third stanza in his published version:

But if at last our colour should be torn from Ireland's heart,
Her sons with shame and sorrow from the dear old isle will
   part;
I've heard a whisper of a country that lies beyond the sea,
Where rich and poor stand equal in the light of freedom's day.
O Erin, must we leave you, driven by a tyrant's hand?
Must we ask a mother's blessing from a strange and distant
   land?
Where the cruel cross of England shall nevermore be seen
And where, please God, we'll live and die still wearin' o' the
   Green.

[301]

WILLY REILLY

"OH! RISE UP, Willy Reilly, and come along with me,
I mean for to go with you and leave this counterie,
To leave my father's dwelling, his houses and free land;"
And away goes Willy Reilly and his dear *Coolen Ban.*

They go by hills and mountains, and by yon lonesome plain,
Through shady groves and valleys, all dangers to refrain;
But her father followed after with a well-armed band,
And taken was poor Reilly and his dear *Coolen Ban.*

It's home then she was taken, and in her closet bound;
Poor Reilly all in Sligo jail lay on the stony ground,
Till at the bar of justice, before the Judge he'd stand,
For nothing but the stealing of his dear *Coolen Ban.*

"Now in the cold, cold iron my hands and feet are bound,
I'm handcuffed like a murderer, and tied unto the ground.
But all the toil and slavery I'm willing for to stand,
Still hoping to be succored by my dear *Coolen Ban.*"

The jailor's son to Reilly goes, and thus to him did say:
"Oh! get up, Willy Reilly, you must appear this day,
For great Squire Foillard's anger you never can withstand,
I'm afeered you'll suffer sorely for your dear *Coolen Ban.*

"This is the news, young Reilly, last night that I did hear:
The lady's oath will hang you or else will set you clear."
"If that be so," says Reilly, "her pleasure I will stand,
Still hoping to be succored by my dear *Coolen Ban.*"

Now Willy's drest from top to toe all in a suit of green,
His hair hangs o'er his shoulders most glorious to be seen;
He's tall and straight, and comely as any could be found;
He's fit for Foillard's daughter, was she heiress to a crown.

The Judge he said: "This lady being in her tender youth,
If Reilly has deluded her she will declare the truth."
Then, like a moving beauty bright before him she did stand,
"You're welcome there, my heart's delight and dear *Coolen
Ban*."

"Oh, gentlemen," Squire Foillard said, "with pity look on me,
This villain came amongst us to disgrace our family,
And by his base contrivances this villainy was planned;
If I don't get satisfaction I'll quit this Irish land."

The lady with a tear began, and thus replied she:
"The fault is none of Reilly's, the blame lies all on me;
I forced him for to leave this place and come along with me;
I loved him out of measure, which wrought our destiny."

Out bespoke the noble Fox, at the table he stood by:
"Oh gentlemen, consider on this extremity;
To hang a man for love is a murder, you may see:
So spare the life of Reilly, let him leave this counterie."

"Good my lord, he stole from her her diamonds and her rings,
Gold watch and silver buckles, and many precious things,
Which cost me in bright guineas more than five hundred
          pounds,
I'll have the life of Reilly should I lose ten thousand pounds."

"Good my lord, I gave them him as tokens of true love,
And when we are a-parting I will them all remove;
If you have got them, Reilly, pray send them home to me."
"I will, my loving lady, with many thanks to thee."

"There is a ring among them I allow yourself to wear,
With thirty locket diamonds well set in silver fair,
And as a true-love token wear it on your right hand,
That you'll think on my poor broken heart when you're in
          a foreign land."

[303]

Then out spoke noble Fox: "You may let the prisoner go;
The lady's oath has cleared him, as the Jury all may know.
She has released her own true love, she has renewed his name;
May her honor bright gain high estate, and her offspring rise
    to fame!"

YOUNG MOLLY BAWN

COME, all you young gallants that follow the gun,
Beware of late shooting at the setting of the sun;
For it's little you know of what happened of late
To young Molly *asthoreen,* whose beauty was great.

It happened one evening in a shower of hail,
This maid in a bower herself did conceal;
Her love being a-shooting, took her for a fawn;
He levelled his gun and he shot Molly Bawn.

And when he came to her and found it was she,
His limbs they grew feeble and his eyes could not see;
His heart it was broken with sorrow and grief;
And with eyes up to heaven he implored for relief.

He ran to his uncle with the gun in his hand,
Saying, "Uncle, dear uncle, I'm not able to stand;
I shot my own true lover—alas! I'm undone
While she was in the shade by the setting of the sun.

"I rubbed her fair temples and found she was dead,
And a fountain of tears for my darling I shed;
And now I'll be forced by the laws of the land
For the killing of my darling my trial to stand."

PART IV

ANGLO-IRISH POETRY
Irish Poetry Written in English; from the Fourteenth
Century to the Present

ANONYMOUS

(c. 1300-1350)

I AM OF IRELAND

A one-stanza song in ms. Rawlinson D. 913. Although of doubtful origin, Seymour and others ascribe it to an Anglo-Irish minstrel of the fourteenth century. Yeats used it in a poem of the same name. (See p. 605.)

> ICHAM of Irlaunde
> Ant of the holy londe of irlande
> Gode sir pray ich ye
> for of saynte charite,
> come ant daunce wyt me,
> in irlaunde.

The three poems that follow appear in a manuscript which survives from the early part of the 14th century, known as ms. #913 of the Harley Collection in the British Museum. It is partly in Middle English and partly in Latin and was written at the Franciscan, or Grey Friar's Monastery at Kildare, an Abbey founded between 1260 and 1277.

Friar Michael, author of *Sweet Jesus*, was one of the monks of this monastery. His authorship is assumed from the last stanza of the poem.

The Land of Cokaygne given here in its entirety also appears in this ms., and its Irish authorship is pretty generally conceded by scholars. Dr. Sigerson and others ascribe it to Friar Michael.

A Satire on the People of Kildare is a third original poem from the Harley ms. Some authorities attribute it to the same hand as *Cokaygne*.

The similarity between *The Vision of MacConglinne* and *The Land of Cokaygne* has been noted and commented on, especially by Prof. Kuno Meyer and Dr. George Sigerson. (See p. 93).

Sweet Jesus and *The Land of Cokaygne* have been rendered into modern English by Professor Russell K. Alspach of the University of Pennsylvania, who has endeavoured to preserve as much of the flavor of the originals as possible. *A Satire on the People of Kildare* is given in the St. John D. Seymour version. Professor Seymour has retained even more of the original wording. Several stanzas of the original of each poem are given for comparison.

FRIAR MICHAEL OF KILDARE

(early 14th century)

SWEET JESUS

SWEETEST Jesus, gracious, free,
That was stretched upon the tree,
Now and ever with us be,
And us shield from sin;
Let Thou not to hell land draw
They that be herein.
So bright of face, Thou hearest me,
Hope of all mankind.
Grant us sight of Trinity
And heaven's land to see.

[1] This world, its love is gone away,
Like dew on grass in summer's day,
Few there be-eth, wellaway,
That loveth God His lore.
All we be-eth shrunk as clay,
We should rue that sore;
Prince and ruler, what think they,
To live evermore?
Leave thy play and crieth aye:
"Jesus Christ, thy grace!"

Alas, alas, ye wealthy men,
Why will ye fill with muck your den?
Thinketh ye to bear it hence?
Nay, as I may thrive!
Ye shall see that all is dross,
The chattel of this life.
To Christ ye run and to Him kneel—

[1] first four lines, second stanza, in the original:
This world is loue is gon awai
So dew on grasse in somer is dai,
Few ther beth, weilawai,
That louith goddis lore.

[307]

Who suffered woundings five;
For ye are trees that should be burned
In hell's deep fiery pit.

God you here to earth hath sent,
Little time to you hath lent,
He shall know how it is spent,
I counsel you, take heed.
If it be hid, thou be-est ruined,
And hell shall be your end.
The bow is bent, the fire intent
For you, if ye be mean.
Except ye change, ye sure shall wend
To ever-burning fire.

2 Poor was thine own incoming
So shall be thine outgoing
Thou shalt not of all thy thing
A penny bear to mould.
O that is a rueful tiding
Hear it whoso would.
Lord, our King, to horrid dung
What causeth man to hold?
In hell no charity he'll give
Even though he would.

O rich man, bethinketh thee,
Take good heed what thou shalt be!
Thou art but a worthless tree
Of only seven foot,
Clothed without with gold and gilt—
The axe is at the root;
The fiend so base takes all delight
This tree adown to root.

2 and this from the fifth stanza of the original:
                   Pouir was thin incomming,
                   So ssal be thin outegoing,
                   Thou ne ssalt of al thi thing
                   A peni ber to molde.

So as I live I tell thee: "Flee,"
And give thy soul its help.

O now thou art in ease and rest,
Of all the land thou art the best,
Thou givest no strength to God's behest;
Of death thou dost not think.
When thou thinkest to live best
Thy body death shall quench.
A wooden box shall be thy nest,
That sittest bold on bench;
East and west shall be thy quest,
And thou wilt nothing shrink.

Be thou baron or great knight,
Thou shalt be a sorry wight,
When, arrayed, thou liest in bier
In full and ample weed;
Thou hast neither main nor might,
And thou no man will dread;
With sorrowful sight—and that is right—
To earth men shall thee lead;
Then shall thy light turn into night—
Bethink, man, this I warn.

The poor man beggeth every day
Good of thee, thou sayest aye:
"Begger, to the devil away!
Thou deafenest mine ear."
Hunger-sore he goeth his way
With many woeful tears.
A wellaway! thou clod of clay!
When thou liest on bier,
Of cloth or fur of red or grey
Hast thou but a hair.

Christ telleth it in holy writ
That a man of evil wit

[309]

Buried was in hell land pit,
Who in life was rich;
He shall never rise and flit
From that direful pit.
He shall sit in hell in strife
Without wine and bread,
The fiend shall sit his knot to knit;
Though he screecheth sore.

The poor man goeth up to thee,
All idried up as a tree,
He shall cry, "Lord, help thou me,
Hunger me hath bound.
Let me die *pour charité*
I am brought to ground."
As I may prosper Christ to see:
If he die that cries
His death shall be iblamed on thee
Though thou give him no wound.

I thee warneth: rise and wake
From the horrid sinners' lake.
If thou be therein to take,
Thou shalt go to hell,
To dwell with all the fiends so black
In that horrid well.
Go make thy way, thou know the charge,
To priest thy sins to tell;
So woe and guilt shall from thee go
With fiends so grim and fell.

If in sin thy life is led,
To do penance be not sad;
Whoso doeth, is not mad,
Holy Church so teacheth;
Therefore be thou not afraid,
Christ shall be thy leech,
Thus Christ us told, who died on cross,

With a blissful speech.
When He so bade, thou mayest be glad,
For loveth He no wretch.

Jesus, King of Heaven free,
Ever blessed may'st Thou be!
Lord, I do beseecheth Thee,
To me Thou take heed.
From deadly sin O keepeth me
While I live with men!
The maid so free that bareth thee
So sweetly under weed,
Grant us sight of Trinity—
All we have the need.

This song wrought a friar
Jesus Christ be his succour,
Lord, bring him to the tower,
Friar Michael Kildare;
Shield him from the hell land bower
When from hence he fare!
Lady, flower of all honor,
Cast away his care:
From the scourge of pain so sure
Shield him here and there.

                        Amen.

                                Modern version by
                                Russell K. Alspach

ANONYMOUS
(early 14th century)

THE LAND OF COKAYGNE

FAR at sea and west of Spain
Is a land that's called Cokaygne,

No land under heaven's blue
Has its wealth or goodness, too.
Though Paradise be fair and bright,
Cokaygne is of fairer sight,
In Paradise what can you see
But flowers, grass, and greenest tree?
Though joy and pleasure there are good
Ripe fruit's the only kind of food;
There is no hall nor bower nor bench
But water man his thirst to quench.
No men be there but only two,
Enoch and Elijah too;
Sadly there do people go,
Where dwelleth other men no mo.

Meat and drink are in Cokaygne
Without care or thought or pain;
Meat is choice, and drink is clear
At noon and supper always near.
I say it's truth, no doubt I fear,
There is no land on earth its peer,
No land is under heaven, I wis
That is of so great joy and bliss.
There is many a pleasant sight,
All is day, there is no night.
There is neither feud nor strife,
Nor is death but only life,
Nor is lack of meat nor cloth,
Nor is man or woman wroth,
Nor is serpent, wolf, nor fox,
Nor is horse nor cow nor ox,
Nor is sheep, nor swine, nor goat,
Nor is dirt, lo! God it wot.
Nor is any horses' stud,
Full the land of every good.
Nor is fly, nor flea, nor louse
In cloth or farm or bed or house;
Nor is thunder, sleet, nor hail

[312]

Nor vilest worm nor creeping snail,
Nor storm nor rain nor blowing wind;
Nor man nor woman that is blind.
But all is sport and joy and glee,
Well is he who there may be.
There are rivers great and fine
Of milk and honey, oil and wine,
Water there hath only use
For boiling, washing, its excuse;
There is every kind of fruit,
All is fashioned man to suit.

Here there is a right fair abbey
Both of white monks and of grey.
Here are bowers and high halls,
And of pasties are the walls,
Of flesh and fish and of rich meat,
All the best that men may eat.
Flour-cakes, the shingles all
Of church and cloister, bower and hall,
Pins there are of puddings rich,
Meat that princes can bewitch.
Men may sit and eat it long,
All with right and not with wrong.
All belongs to young and old,
Stout and stern, and meek and bold.
There's a cloister fair and bright,
Broad and long, a seemly sight.
And that cloister's pillars tall
Are enscrolled in pure crystal,
With their base and capital
Of jasper green and red coral.

On the lawn there is a tree
Very pleasant for to see.
Ginger, galingal its roots,
Zedoary are its shoots,
Maces choice make up the flower,

Rind is canel, sweetest odour,
Fruit is gillyflower good;
Cubebs too are in the food;
Roses red as they can be
Lilies pleasant for to see.
Never fade they day nor night—
This is all a lovely sight.
Four wells in the abbey stand
Of treacle and of balsam grand,
Of balm and also honey wine,
Ever flowing by design.
[1] For the beds of all the streams
Precious stones and gold make gleams.
Sapphire, pearl—called uniune,
Carbuncle and astiune,
Emerald, jacynth, chrysopraze,
Beryl, onyx, and topaz,
Amethyst and chrysolite,
Chalcedony and epetite.

Many birds fill hill and dale:
Throstle, thrush, and nightingale.
Woodlark, finch with yellow wing,
Many other birds I sing,
Never cease they with their might
Singing ever day and night.
Yet I tell you more, to wit:
The geese a-roasted on the spit
To that abbey flee, God wot,
And crieth "Geese, all hot, all hot."
Out they come with garlic plenty,
Best prepared that man may see.
Larks well-trained and very couth

[1] The last eight lines of the fourth stanza in the original:
Of thai stremis al the molde:
Stonis preciuse and golde.
Ther is saphir and vniune,
Carbuncle and astiune,
Smaragde, lugre and prassiune,
Beril, onix, topasiune,
Ametist and crisolite,
Calcedun and epetite.

Cometh down to man his mouth,
Fixed in stew-pan very well,
Stuffed with gillyflowers, canel.
No one speaks of lack of drink,
But takes enough nor does he shrink.

When the monks go in to mass,
All the windows made of glass
Turn themselves to crystal bright
Thus to give the monks more light.
When the masses have been said
And the books have been uplaid,
The crystal turneth back to glass
In the state before it was.

And the young monks every day
After meat go out to play.
There's not hawk nor fowl so fast
Better flying in the blast
Than the monks when high of mood
In their sleeves and in their hood.
When the abbot sees them flee,
That he holds for so much glee,
But ne'ertheless all there among
He bids them light to evensong.
But the monks they disobey
Fleeing further in their play.
When the abbot thus doth see
That the monks from him will flee,
He takes a maiden of the route
And turneth up her small white toute
And beats the tabors with his hand,
To make his monks alight on land.
When his monks that sight i-seeth,
To the maiden down they fleeth
And gather they the wench about
And thwacketh all her small white toute.
After all this pleasant play

[315]

Go they home at close of day,
To collation then attend;
A fair procession as they wend.

Another abbey is thereby,
Forsooth a great fair nunnery,
Up a river of sweet milk,
Where is plenty great of silk.
When the summer day is hot,
All the young nuns take a boat
And goeth on the river clear,
Row with oars, with rudder steer.
When far enought from all the abbey,
They make them naked for to play
And leapeth down into the brim
And starteth timidly to swim.
The young monks when the nuns they see
Get them up and forth they flee
And cometh to the nuns anon,
And every monk he taketh one,
And slyly beareth forth their prey
Unto the abbey great and grey,
And teach the nuns an orison
With an ambling up and down.
The monk who is a worker good
And can set a-right his hood,
He shall have, no danger near,
Twelve good wives in every year,
All through right and not through grace
For to do himself solace.
And the monk that sleepeth best
And liketh most of all to rest,
Of him is hope, O God it wot,
That he some day will be abbot.

Whoso will that land come to,
Full great penance he must do:

[316]

Seven years in dirt of swine
He must wade, although he pine,
All anon up to the chin
So he to that land shall win.

Lordlings all, ye here below,
May ye from the world ne'er go
Till each have his rightful chance
To fulfill that good penance,
That ye might that land to see
And ne'er return, ye will agree.
Pray we God, so may it be,
Amen, *pour saint charité.*

Modern version by
Russell K. Alspach

ANONYMOUS
(early 14th century)

A SATIRE ON THE PEOPLE OF KILDARE

HAIL, St Michael with the long spear!
Fair be thy wings upon thy shoulder.
Thou hast a red kirtle anon to thy feet,
Thou art the best angel that God ever made.
    This verse is full well iwrought,
    'Tis from very far ibrought.

Hail, St Christopher with thy long stake!
Thou bearest our Lord Jesus Christ over the broad lake.
Many great congers swim about thy feet.
How many herrings for a penny at Westcheap in London?
    This verse is of holy writ,
    It comes of noble wit.

[317]

Saint Mary's bastard, the Magdalen's son,
To be well clothëd indeed was thy wone[1].
Thou bearest a box in thy hand ipainted all of gold.
Thou wert wont to be gracious, give us some of thy spices.
    This verse is imakëd well
    Of consonants and of vowel.

Hail, St Dominic with thy long staff!
It is at the top end crooked like a gaff;
Thou bearest a book on thy back, I think it is a Bible.
Though thou be a good clerk, be thou not too high[2].
    Trie rime la! God it wot [3];
    Such another on earth is not.

Hail, St Francis, with thy many fowls,
Kites and crows, ravens and owls,
Four and twenty wildges[4], and a peacock!
Many a bold beggar followeth thy route[5].
    This verse is full well iset,
    From right far it was ifet [6].

Hail be ye friars with the white copes!
Ye have a house at Drogheda, where men make ropes.
Ever ye be roving the land all about;
Of the water-dashers[7] ye rob the churches.
    Master he was very good [8]
    That this sentence understood.

Hail be ye gilmins with your black gowns!
Ye leave the wilderness and fill the towns.
Minor without, and preacher within:
Your habit is of gadering[9], that is muckle shame.
    Slyly is this verse isaid,
    It were harm adown ilaid [10].

---

[1] Custom. [2] Do not be too proud. [3] Lo, a choice rhyme, God knows it! [4] Wild geese. [5] Company. [6] Fetched. [7] Apparently holy-water sprinklers. [8] He was a very good master who, etc. [9] Gathering together. [10] It would be a pity if it were laid aside, neglected. [11] Pot, can. [12] Cunningly made. [13] Tread awry. [14] Misfortune, ill luck to the cobbler. [15] Laymen. [16] Give but a hood. [17] Assuredly. [18] Skilful. [19] Merchandise sold by weight. [20] A coin of the value of 13s. 4d.

Hail, ye holy monks with your corrin[11]
Late and early filled with ale and wine!
Deep can ye booze, that is all your care,
With St Benedict's scourge oft ye are disciplined.
        Take ye heed all to me!
        That this is sly[12] ye may well see.

Hail be ye nuns of St Mary's house,
God's bower-maidens, and His own spouse!
Often mistread [13] ye your shoes, your feet be full tender;
Datheit the sotter[14] that tans your leather!
        Very well he understood
        That made this ditty so good.

Hail be ye priests with your broad books!
Though your crowns be shaven, fair be your crooks.
Ye and other lewidmen[15] deal but a houve[16]
When ye deal holy bread, give me but a little.
        Sikirlich[17] he was a clerk
        That wrought this crafty[18] work.

Hail be ye merchants with your great packs
Of drapery, avoirdupois[19], and your wool-sacks,
Gold, silver, stones, rich marks[20], and eke pounds!
Little give ye thereof to the wretched poor.
        Sly he was, and full of wit,
        That this lore put in writ.

Hail be ye tailors with your sharp shears!
To make wrong hoods ye cut many gores.
Against midwinter hot be your needles;
Though your seams seem fair, they last a short while.
        The clerk that this baston wrought,
        Well he woke, and slept right nought.

Hail be ye cobblers with your many lasts,
With your dried hides of various beasts,

[319]

And trobles, and treisuses, bochevamp¹, and awls!
Black and filthy be your teeth, dirty was that route².
    Is not this baston well ipight? ³
    Each word him sit aright.

Hail be ye skinners with your drench kive! ⁴
Whoso smelleth thereto, woe is him alive!
When that it thundereth, ye might therein—
Datheit ⁵ your courtesy, ye stink all the street.
    Worthy it were, that he were king
    That dited ⁶ this choice thing.

Hail be ye potters⁷ with your pole-axe!
Fair be your apron, yellow be your fax⁸.
Ye stand at the schamil ⁹, broad ferlich bernes¹⁰;
Flies you follow, ye swallow enow¹¹.
    The best clerk of all this town
    Craftfully made this baston.

Hail be ye bakers with your loaves small
Of white bread and black, full many and fale! ¹²
Ye pinch on the right weight ¹³ against God's law,
To the fair pillory, I rede, ye take heed.
    This verse is iwrought so well
    That no tongue iwis may tell.

Hail be ye brewers¹⁴ with your gallons,
Pottles, and quarts over all the towns¹⁵.
Your thumbs bear much away¹⁶, shame have the guile¹⁷:
Beware of the cucking-stool ¹⁸, the lake is deep and filthy.
    Sikerlich¹⁹ he was a clerk
    That so slyly wrought this work.

¹ *Trobles* = waste leather. *Treisuses* = worn pieces of leather. *Bochevamp* =
botched vamps or fronts of shoes. ² Company. ³ Set. ⁴ Drenching-vat in which skins
are steeped. ⁵ Misfortune to. ⁶ Prepared. ⁷ A scribal error for *bochers* = butchers.
⁸ Hair. ⁹ Meat-block. ¹⁰ Great strong fellows. ¹¹ You swallow enough of them. ¹² Nu-
merous. ¹³ You give short weight. ¹⁴ *Brewers* and *hucksters* (next verse) are feminine
forms, so the reference appears to be to *women*, not men. ¹⁵ I.e. everywhere. ¹⁶ This
alludes to the custom of the seller of liquor sticking his thumb into the vessel, so as
to avoid filling it to the brim, and in this way cheating the customer. ¹⁷ May the
deceit bring shame! ¹⁸ The instrument used for ducking evildoers in a pond or river.
¹⁹ Assuredly.

Hail be ye hucksters down by the lake,
With candles, and golokes[1], and the pots black,
Tripe, and cows' feet, and sheeps' heads!
With this foul trumpery filthy is your inn.
    He is sorry of his life
    That is fast to such a wife.

Fi a debles, kaites[2], that comb the wool!
All the schindes of the tronn on high upon your skull! [3]
Ye made me such a goshorne[4] over all the wowes[5];
Therefore I made one of you sit upon a heckle[6].
    He was noble clerk and good,
    That this deep lore understood.

Make glad, my friends, ye sit too long still,
Speak now, and be glad, and drink all your fill!
Ye have heard of men's life that dwell in the land;
Drink deep, and make glad, for have ye no other need.
    This song is isaid of me,
    Ever iblessed mote ye be.

Modern version by
St. John Seymour

The second stanza as it reads in the original. Compare p. 317.
    Hail seint Christofre with thi lang stake!
    Thou ber ur louerd Iesus Crist ouer the brod lake,
    Mani grete kunger swimmeth abute thi fete.
    Hou mani hering to peni at West Chep in London?
        This uers is of holi writte,
        Hit com of noble witte.
    Hail be ye brewesters with yur galuns,
    Potels and quartes ouer al the tounes.
    Yur thowmes berrith moch awai, schame hab the gyle;
    Beth iwar of the coking-stole, the lak is dep and hori.
        Sikerlich he was a clerk
        That so sleilich wroughte this werk.

[1] Tubs. [2] Fie in the devil's name, caitiffs. [3] This line may mean: All the fragments of wool be on your heads. [4] Such a fool (?). [5] Walls, buildings, i.e. everywhere. [6] An instrument for carding wool.

NAHUM TATE
(1652-1715)

WHILE SHEPHERDS WATCHED THEIR FLOCKS
BY NIGHT

WHILE shepherds watched their flocks by night,
  All seated on the ground,
The angel of the Lord came down,
  And glory shone around.

"Fear not," said he, for mighty dread
  Had seized their troubled mind;
"Glad tidings of great joy I bring
  To you and all mankind.

"To you, in David's town, this day
  Is born of David's line,
The Saviour, who is Christ the Lord,
  And this shall be the sign:

"The heavenly babe you there shall find
  To human view displayed,
All meanly wrapped in swaddling bands,
  And in a manger laid."

Thus spake the seraph; and forthwith
  Appeared a shining throng
Of angels, praising God, who thus
  Addressed their joyful song:

"All glory be to God on high,
  And to the earth be peace;
Good will henceforth from Heaven to men
  Begin and never cease."

JONATHAN SWIFT
(1667-1745)

APPLES[1]

COME buy my fine wares,
Plums, apples, and pears.
A hundred a penny,
In conscience too many:
Come, will you have any?
My children are seven,
I wish them in Heaven;
My husband a sot,
With his pipe and his pot,
Not a farthing will gain them,
And I must maintain them.

ONIONS

COME, follow me by the smell,
Here are delicate onions to sell;
I promise to use you well.
They make the blood warmer,
You'll feed like a farmer;
For this is every cook's opinion,
No savoury dish without an onion;
But, lest your kissing should be spoiled,
Your onions must be thoroughly boiled:
Or else you may spare
Your mistress a share,
The secret will never be known:
She cannot discover
The breath of her lover,
But think it as sweet as her own.

[1] "Apples," "Onions," and "Herrings" are only a few of the "Verses for Fruit-
women, etc." from Swift's Collected Works, Dublin, 1795.

HERRINGS

Be not sparing,
Leave off swearing.
Buy my herring
Fresh from Malahide,
Better never was tried.
Come, eat them with pure fresh butter and mustard,
Their bellies are soft, and as white as a custard.
Come, sixpence a dozen, to get me some bread,
Or, like my own herrings, I soon shall be dead.

A RIDDLE

The Vowels

We are little airy creatures,
All of different voice and features;
One of us in glass is set,
One of us you'll find in jet.
T'other you may see in tin,
And the fourth a box within.
If the fifth you should pursue,
It can never fly from you.

A GENTLE ECHO ON WOMAN

(In the Doric Manner)

SHEPHERD Echo, I ween, will in the woods reply,
          And quaintly answer questions: shall I try?
ECHO   Try.
SHEPHERD What must we do our passion to express?
ECHO   Press.

          .   .   .   .   .   .

SHEPHERD What most moves women when we them address?
ECHO   A dress.

[324]

SHEPHERD	Say, what can keep her chaste whom I adore?
ECHO	A door.
SHEPHERD	If music softens rocks, love tunes my lyre.
ECHO	Liar.
SHEPHERD	Then teach me, Echo, how shall I come by her?
ECHO	Buy her.
SHEPHERD	But what can glad me when she's laid on bier?
ECHO	Beer.
SHEPHERD	What must I do when women will be kind?
ECHO	Be kind.
SHEPHERD	What must I do when women will be cross?
ECHO	Be cross.
SHEPHERD	Lord, what is she that can so turn and wind?
ECHO	Wind.
SHEPHERD	If she be wind, what stills her when she blows.
ECHO	Blows.

.   .   .   .   .   .

SHEPHERD	Is there no way to moderate her anger?
ECHO	Hang her.
SHEPHERD	Thanks, gentle Echo! right thy answers tell
	What woman is and how to guard her well.
ECHO	Guard her well.

MARY THE COOK MAID'S LETTER TO
DR. SHERIDAN

WELL, if ever I saw such another man since my mother bound
    my head!
You a gentleman! marry come up! I wonder where you were
    bred.
I'm sure such words do not become a man of your cloth;
I would not give such language to a dog, faith and troth.
Yes, you call'd my master a knave: fie, Mr. Sheridan! 'tis a
    shame
For a parson, who should know better things, to come out with
    such a name.

[325]

Knave in your teeth, Mr. Sheridan! 'tis both a shame and a sin;
And the Dean my master is an honester man than you and all
your kin:
He has more goodness in his little finger than you have in your
whole body:
My master is a parsonable man, and not a spindle-shanked
hoddy doddy.
And now, whereby I find you would fain make an excuse,
Because my master one day, in anger, call'd you goose:
Which, and I am sure I have been his servant four years since
October,
And he never call'd me worse than sweetheart, drunk or sober:
Not that I know his reverence was ever concern'd to my knowl-
edge,
Though you and your come-rogues keep him out so late in
your college.
You say you will eat grass on his grave: a Christian eat grass!
Whereby you now confess yourself to be a goose or an ass:
But that's as much as to say, that my master should die before
ye;
Well, well, that's as God pleases; and I don't believe that's a
true story:
And so say I told you so, and you may go tell my master; what
care I?
And I don't care who knows it; 'tis all one to Mary.
Everybody knows that I love to tell truth, and shame the devil;
I am but a poor servant; but I think gentlefolks should be civil.
Besides, you found fault with our victuals one day that you
was here;
I remember it was on a Tuesday of all days in the year.
And Saunders the man says you are always jesting and mock-
ing:
Mary, said he, (one day as I was mending my master's stock-
ing;)
My master is so fond of that minister that keeps the school—
I thought my master a wise man, but that man makes him a
fool.

[326]

Saunders, said I, I would rather than a quart of ale
He would come into our kitchen, and I would pin a dishclout
    to his tail.
And now I must go, and get Saunders to direct this letter;
For I write but a bad scrawl; but my sister Marget, she writes
    better.
Well, but I must run and make the bed, before my master
    comes from prayers;
And see now, it strikes ten, and I hear him coming up stairs;
Whereof I could say more to your verses, if I could write
    written hand:
And so I remain, in a civil way, your servant to command,
                                                    Mary

From ON THE DEATH OF DR. SWIFT

    "Perhaps I may allow the dean
    Had too much satire in his vein,
    And seemed determined not to starve it,
    Because no age could more deserve it.
    Yet malice never was his aim;
    He lashed the vice, but spared the name;
    No individual could resent
    Where thousands equally were meant;
    His satire points at no defect
    But what all mortals may correct;
    For he abhorred that senseless tribe
    Who call it humor when they gibe;
    He spared a hump or crooked nose,
    Whose owners set not up for beaux.
    True genuine dullness moved his pity,
    Unless it offered to be witty.
    Those who their ignorance confessed
    He ne'er offended with a jest;
    But laughed to hear an idiot quote

[327]

A verse from Horace learned by rote.

"He knew a hundred pleasing stories,
With all the turns of Whigs and Tories;
Was cheerful to his dying day,
And friends would let him have his way.

"He gave the little wealth he had
To build a house for fools and mad;
And showed by one satiric touch
No nation wanted it so much.
That kingdom he had left his debtor,
I wish it soon may have a better."

THE PROGRESS OF POETRY

THE farmer's goose, who in the stubble
Has fed without restraint or trouble,
Grown fat with corn and sitting still,
Can scarce get o'er the barndoor sill;
And hardly waddles forth to cool
Her belly in the neighbouring pool!
Nor loudly cackles at the door;
For cackling shows the goose is poor.

But, when she must be turn'd to graze,
And round the barren common strays,
Hard exercise and harder fare,
Soon make my dame grow lank and spare:
Her body light, she tries her wings,
And scorns the ground, and upward springs;
While all the parish, as she flies,
Hear sounds harmonious from the skies.

Such is the poet fresh in pay,
The third night's profits of his play;
His morning draughts till noon can swill,
Among his brethren of the quill:
With good roast beef his belly full,
Grown lazy, foggy, fat, and dull,

[328]

Deep sunk in plenty and delight,
What poet e'er could take his flight?
Or, stuff'd with phlegm up to the throat,
What poet e'er could sing a note?
Nor Pegasus could bear the load
Along the high celestial road;
The steed, oppress'd, would break his girth,
To raise the lumber from the earth.
    But view him in another scene,
When all his drink is Hippocrene,
His money spent, his patrons fail,
His credit out for cheese and ale;
His two-years coat so smooth and bare,
Through every thread it lets in air;
With hungry meals his body pined,
His guts and belly full of wind;
And like a jockey for a race,
His flesh brought down to flying case;
Now his exalted spirit loathes
Encumbrances of food and clothes;
And up he rises, like a vapour,
Supported high on wings of paper;
He singing flies, and flying sings,
While from below all Grub-street rings.

A DESCRIPTION OF A CITY SHOWER

CAREFUL observers may foretell the hour.
(By sure prognostics) when to dread a shower.
While rain depends, the pensive cat gives o'er
Her frolics, and pursues her tail no more.
Returning home at night, you'll find the sink
Strike your offended sense with double stink.
If you be wise, then go not far to dine;
You'll spend in coach-hire more than save in wine.
A coming shower your shooting corns presage,

Old aches will throb, your hollow tooth will rage;
Sauntering in coffeehouse is Dulman seen;
He damns the climate, and complains of spleen.
  Meanwhile the South, rising with dabbled wings,
A sable cloud athwart the welkin flings,
That swill'd more liquor than it could contain,
And, like a drunkard, gives it up again.
Brisk Susan whips her linen from the rope,
While the first drizzling shower is borne aslope:
Such is that sprinkling which some careless quean
Flirts on you from her mop, but not so clean:
You fly, invoke the gods; then, turning, stop
To rail; she, singing, still whirls on her mop.
Not yet the dust had shunn'd th' unequal strife,
But, aided by the wind, fought still for life,
And, wafted with its foe by violent gust,
'Twas doubtful which was rain, and which was dust.
Ah! where must needy poet seek for aid,
When dust and rain at once his coat invade?
Sole coat! where dust, cemented by the rain,
Erects the nap, and leaves a cloudy stain!
  Now in contiguous drops the flood comes down,
Threatening with deluge this *devoted* town.
To shops in crowds the daggled females fly,
Pretend to cheapen goods, but nothing buy.
The Templar spruce, while every spout's abroach,
Stays till 'tis fair, yet seems to call a coach.
The tuck'd-up seamstress walks with hasty strides,
While streams run down her oil'd umbrella's sides.
Here various kinds, by various fortunes led,
Commence acquaintance underneath a shed.
Triumphant tories, and desponding whigs,
Forget their feuds, and join to save their wigs.
Box'd in a chair, the Beau impatient sits,
While spouts run clattering o'er the roof by fits,
And ever and anon with frightful din
The leather sounds; he trembles from within.
So when Troy chairmen bore the wooden steed,

[330]

Pregnant with Greeks impatient to be freed,
(Those bully Greeks, who, as the moderns do,
Instead of paying chairmen, ran them through)
Laocoon struck the outside with his spear,
And each imprison'd hero quak'd for fear.
　　Now from all parts the swelling kennels flow,
And bear their trophies with them as they go:
Filths of all hues and odour, seem to tell
What street they sail'd from, by their sight and smell.
They, as each torrent drives, with rapid force,
From Smithfield to St. 'Pulchre's shape their course,
And in huge confluence join'd at Snowhill ridge,
Fall from the conduit prone to Holborn bridge.
Sweepings from butchers' stalls, dung, guts, and blood,
Drown'd puppies, stinking sprats, all drench'd in mud,
Dead cats, and turnip-tops come tumbling down the flood.

THOMAS PARNELL
(1679-1718)

THE SMALL SILVER-COLOURED BOOKWORM

　　"INSATIATE brute, whose teeth abuse
　　The sweetest servants of the muse!
　　His roses nipt in every page,
　　My poor Anacreon mourns thy rage;
　　By thee my Ovid wounded lies;
　　By thee my Lesbia's sparrow dies;
　　Thy rabid teeth have half destroy'd
　　The work of love in Biddy Floyd;
　　They rent Belinda's locks away,
　　And spoil'd the Blouzelind of Gay;
　　For all, for every single deed,
　　Relentless justice bids thee bleed.
　　Then fall a victim to the Nine,
　　Myself the priest, my desk the shrine."

From NIGHT PIECE ON DEATH

DEATH speaks:
  When men my scythe and darts supply,
  How great a King of Fears am I!
  They view me like the last of things;
  They make, and then they dread my stings.
  Fools! If you less provoked your fears,
  No more my spectre-form appears.
  Death's but a pass that must be trod,
  If man would ever pass to God:
  A port of calms, a state of ease
  From the rough rage of swelling seas.
  Why then thy flowing sable stoles,
  Deep pendent cypress, mourning poles,
  Loose scarfs to fall athwart thy weeds,
  Long palls, drawn hearses, covered steeds,
  And plumes of black, that as they tread,
  Nod o'er the escutcheons of the dead?
  Nor can the parted body know,
  Nor wants the soul, these forms of woe:
  As men who long in prison dwell,
  With lamps that glimmer round the cell,
  Whene'er their suffering years are run,
  Spring forth to greet the glittering sun;
  Such joy, though far transcending sense,
  Have pious souls at parting hence.
  On earth, and in the body placed,
  A few and evil years they waste;
  But when their chains are cast aside,
  See the glad scene unfolding wide,
  Clap the glad wing, and tower away,
  And mingle with the blaze of day.

GEORGE BERKELEY
(1684-1753)

ON THE PROSPECT OF PLANTING ARTS AND LEARNING IN AMERICA

THE Muse, disgusted at an age and clime
    Barren of every glorious theme,
In distant lands now waits a better time
    Producing subjects worthy fame:

In happy climes, where from the genial sun
    And virgin earth such scenes ensue,
The force of art by nature seems outdone,
    And fancied beauties by the true.

In happy climes, the seat of innocence,
    Where nature guides and virtue rules;
Where men shall not impose for truth and sense
    The pedantry of courts and schools;

There shall be sung another golden age,
    The rise of empire and of arts,
The good and great inspiring epic rage.
    The wisest heads and noblest hearts—

Not such as Europe breeds in her decay—
    Such as she bred when fresh and young,
When heavenly flame did animate her clay,
    By future poets shall be sung.

Westward the course of empire takes its way,
    The four first acts already past;
A fifth shall close the drama with the day—
    Time's noblest offspring is the last.

[333]

OLIVER GOLDSMITH
(1728-1774)

THE DESERTED VILLAGE

SWEET Auburn! loveliest village of the plain;
Where health and plenty cheered the laboring swain,
Where smiling spring its earliest visit paid,
And parting summer's lingering blooms delayed:
Dear lovely bowers of innocence and ease,
Seats of my youth, when every sport could please,
How often have I loitered o'er thy green,
Where humble happiness endeared each scene!
How often have I paused on every charm,
The sheltered cot, the cultivated farm,
The never-failing brook, the busy mill,
The decent church that topped the neighboring hill,
The hawthorn bush, with seats beneath the shade,
For talking age and whispering lovers made!
How often have I blest the coming day,
When toil remitting lent its turn to play,
And all the village train, from labor free,
Led up their sports beneath the spreading tree,
While many a pastime circled in the shade,
The young contending as the old surveyed;
And many a gambol frolicked o'er the ground,
And sleights of art and feats of strength went round.
And still, as each repeated pleasure tired,
Succeeding sports the mirthful band inspired;
The dancing pair that simply sought renown,
By holding out to tire each other down;
The swain mistrustless of his smutted face,
While secret laughter tittered round the place;
The bashful virgin's side-long looks of love,
The matron's glance that would those looks reprove:
These were thy charms, sweet village! sports like these,
With sweet succession, taught even toil to please:

These round thy bowers their cheerful influence shed:
These were thy charms—but all these charms are fled.
  Sweet smiling village, loveliest of the lawn,
Thy sports are fled, and all thy charms withdrawn:
Amidst thy bowers the tyrant's hand is seen,
And desolation saddens all thy green:
One only master grasps the whole domain,
And half a tillage stints thy smiling plain.
No more thy glassy brook reflects the day,
But, choked with sedges, works its weedy way;
Along thy glades, a solitary guest,
The hollow sounding bittern guards its nest;
Amidst thy desert walks the lapwing flies,
And tires their echoes with unvaried cries;
Sunk are thy bowers in shapeless ruin all,
And the long grass o'er-tops the moldering wall;
And trembling, shrinking from the spoiler's hand,
Far, far away thy children leave the land.

  Ill fares the land, to hastening ills a prey,
Where wealth accumulates, and men decay:
Princes and lords may flourish, or may fade;
A breath can make them, as a breath has made;
But a bold peasantry, their country's pride,
When once destroyed, can never be supplied.

  A time there was, ere England's griefs began,
When every rood of ground maintained its man;
For him light labor spread her wholesome store,
Just gave what life required, but gave no more:
His best companions, innocence and health;
And his best riches, ignorance of wealth.

  But times are altered; trade's unfeeling train
Usurp the land and dispossess the swain;
Along the lawn, where scattered hamlets rose,
Unwieldy wealth and cumbrous pomp repose,
And every want to opulence allied,

And every pang that folly pays to pride.
Those gentle hours that plenty bade to bloom,
Those calm desires that asked but little room,
Those healthful sports that graced the peaceful scene,
Lived in each look, and brightened all the green;
These, far departing, seek a kinder shore,
And rural mirth and manners are no more.

Sweet Auburn! parent of the blissful hour,
Thy glades forlorn confess the tyrant's power.
Here, as I take my solitary rounds
Amidst thy tangling walks and ruined grounds,
And, many a year elapsed, return to view
Where once the cottage stood, the hawthorn grew,
Remembrance wakes with all her busy train,
Swells at my breast, and turns the past to pain,

In all my wanderings round this world of care,
In all my griefs—and God has given my share—
I still had hopes, my latest hours to crown,
Amidst these humble bowers to lay me down;
To husband out life's taper at the close,
And keep the flame from wasting by repose:
I still had hopes, for pride attends us still,
Amidst the swains to show my book-learned skill,
Around my fire an evening group to draw,
And tell of all I felt, and all I saw;
And, as an hare whom hounds and horns pursue,
Pants to the place from whence at first she flew,
I still had hopes, my long vexations past,
Here to return—and die at home at last.
O' blest retirement, friend to life's decline,
Retreats from care, that never must be mine,
How happy he who crowns in shades like these,
A youth of labor with an age of ease;
Who quits a world where strong temptations try,
And, since 'tis hard to combat, learns to fly!
For him no wretches, born to work and weep,

Explore the mine, or tempt the dangerous deep;
No surly porter stands in guilty state,
To spurn the imploring famine from the gate;
But on he moves to meet his latter end,
Angels around befriending Virtue's friend;
Bends to the grave with unperceived decay,
While resignation gently slopes the way;
And, all his prospects brightening to the last,
His heaven commences ere the world be past!

Sweet was the sound, when oft at evening's close
Up yonder hill the village murmur rose.
There, as I passed with careless steps and slow,
The mingling notes came softened from below;
The swain responsive as the milk-maid sung,
The sober herd that lowed to meet their young,
The noisy geese that gabbled o'er the pool,
The playful children just let loose from school,
The watch-dog's voice that bayed the whispering wind,
And the loud laugh that spoke the vacant mind;—
These all in sweet confusion sought the shade,
And filled each pause the nightingale had made.
But now the sounds of population fail,
No cheerful murmurs fluctuate in the gale,
No busy steps the grass-grown foot-way tread,
For all the bloomy flush of life is fled.
All but yon widowed, solitary thing,
That feebly bends beside the plashy spring:
She, wretched matron, forced in age, for bread,
To strip the brook with mantling cresses spread,
To pick her wintry faggot from the thorn,
To seek her nightly shed, and weep 'til morn;
She only left of all the harmless train,
The sad historian of the pensive plain.

Near yonder copse, where once the garden smiled,
And still where many a garden flower grows wild;
There, where a few torn shrubs the place disclose,

The village preacher's modest mansion rose.
A man he was to all the country dear,
And passing rich with forty pounds a year;
Remote from towns he ran his godly race,
Nor e'er had changed, nor wished to change his place;
Unpracticed he to fawn, or seek for power,
By doctrines fashioned to the varying hour;
Far other aims his heart had learned to prize,
More skilled to raise the wretched than to rise.
His house was known to all the vagrant train;
He chid their wanderings but relieved their pain:
The long-remembered beggar was his guest,
Whose beard descending swept his aged breast;
The ruined spendthrift, now no longer proud,
Claimed kindred there, and had his claims allowed;
The broken soldier, kindly bade to stay,
Sat by the fire, and talked the night away,
Wept o'er his wounds or, tales of sorrow done,
Shouldered his crutch and showed how fields were won.
Pleased with his guests, the good man learned to glow,
And quite forgot their vices in their woe;
Careless their merits or their faults to scan
His pity gave ere charity began.

   Thus to relieve the wretched was his pride,
And e'en his failings leaned to Virtue's side;
But in his duty prompt at every call,
He watched and wept, he prayed and felt for all;
And, as a bird each fond endearment tries
To tempt its new-fledged offspring to the skies,
He tried each art, reproved each dull delay,
Allured to brighter worlds, and led the way.

   Beside the bed where parting life was laid,
And sorrow, guilt, and pain by turns dismayed,
The reverend champion stood. At his control
Despair and anguish fled the struggling soul;

Comfort came down the trembling wretch to raise,
And his last faltering accents whispered praise.

At church, with meek and unaffected grace,
His looks adorned the venerable place;
Truth from his lips prevailed with double sway,
And fools, who came to scoff, remained to pray.
The service past, around the pious man,
With steady zeal, each honest rustic ran;
Even children followed with endearing wile,
And plucked his gown to share the good man's smile.
His ready smile a parent's warmth exprest;
Their welfare pleased him, and their cares distrest:
To them his heart, his love, his griefs were given,
But all his serious thoughts had rest in heaven.
As some tall cliff that lifts its awful form,
Swells from the vale, and midway leaves the storm,
Though round its breast the rolling clouds are spread,
Eternal sunshine settles on its head.

Beside yon straggling fence that skirts the way,
With blossomed furze unprofitably gay,
There, in his noisy mansion, skilled to rule,
The village master taught his little school.
A man severe he was, and stern to view;
I knew him well, and every truant knew;
Well had the boding tremblers learned to trace
The day's disasters in his morning face;
Full well they laughed with counterfeited glee
At all his jokes, for many a joke had he;
Full well the busy whisper circling round
Conveyed the dismal tidings when he frowned.
Yet he was kind, or, if severe in aught,
The love he bore to learning was in fault;
The village all declared how much he knew:
'Twas certain he could write, and cipher too;
Lands he could measure, terms and tides presage,

And even the story ran that he could gauge;
In arguing, too, the parson owned his skill,
For, even though vanquished, he could argue still;
While words of learned length and thundering sound
Amazed the gazing rustics ranged around;
And still they gazed, and still the wonder grew,
That one small head could carry all he knew.

But past is all his fame. The very spot
Where many a time he triumphed, is forgot.
Near yonder thorn, that lifts its head on high,
Where once the sign-post caught the passing eye,
Low lies that house where nut-brown draughts inspired,
Where graybeard mirth and smiling toil retired,
Where village statesmen talked with looks profound,
And news much older than their ale went round.
Imagination fondly stoops to trace
The parlor splendors of that festive place:
The white-washed wall, the nicely sanded floor,
The varnished clock that clicked behind the door;
The chest contrived a double debt to pay,
A bed by night, a chest of drawers by day;
The pictures placed for ornament and use,
The twelve good rules, the royal game of goose;
The hearth, except when winter chilled the day,
With aspen boughs and flowers and fennel gay;
While broken tea-cups, wisely kept for show,
Ranged o'er the chimney, glistened in a row.

Vain transitory splendours! could not all
Reprieve the tottering mansion from its fall?
Obscure it sinks, nor shall it more impart
An hour's importance to the poor man's heart.
Thither no more the peasant shall repair
To sweet oblivion of his daily care;
No more the farmer's news, the barber's tale,
No more the woodman's ballad shall prevail;
No more the smith his dusky brow shall clear,

Relax his ponderous strength, and lean to hear;
The host himself no longer shall be found
Careful to see the mantling bliss go round;
Nor the coy maid, half willing to be prest,
Shall kiss the cup to pass it to the rest.

    Yes! let the rich deride, the proud disdain,
These simple blessings of the lowly train;
To me more dear, congenial to my heart,
One native charm, than all the gloss of art.
Spontaneous joys, where Nature has its play,
The soul adopts, and owns their first born sway;
Lightly they frolic o'er the vacant mind,
Unenvied, unmolested, unconfined.
But the long pomp, the midnight masquerade,
With all the freaks of wanton wealth arrayed—
In these, ere triflers half their wish obtain,
The toiling pleasure sickens into pain;
And, even while fashion's brightest arts decoy,
The heart distrusting asks if this be joy.

    Ye friends to truth, ye statesmen, who survey
The rich man's joy increase, the poor's decay,
'Tis yours to judge, how wide the limits stand
Between a splendid and an happy land.
Proud swells the tide with loads of freighted ore,
And shouting Folly hails them from her shore;
Hoards even beyond the miser's wish abound,
And rich men flock from all the world around.
Yet count our gains! This wealth is but a name
That leaves our useful products still the same.
Not so the loss. The man of wealth and pride
Takes up a space that many poor supplied;
Space for his lake, his park's extended bounds,
Space for his horses, equipage, and hounds:
The robe that wraps his limbs in silken sloth
Has robbed the neighboring fields of half their growth;
His seat, where solitary sports are seen,

[341]

Indignant spurns the cottage from the green:
Around the world each needful product flies,
For all the luxuries the world supplies;
While thus the land adorned for pleasure all
In barren splendor feebly waits the fall.
As some fair female unadorned and plain,
Secure to please while youth confirms her reign,
Slights every borrowed charm that dress supplies,
Nor shares with art the triumph of her eyes;
But when those charms are past, for charms are frail,
When time advances, and when lovers fail,
She then shines forth, solicitous to bless,
In all the glaring impotence of dress.
Thus fares the land by luxury betrayed:
In nature's simplest charms at first arrayed,
But verging to decline, its splendors rise,
Its vistas strike, its palaces surprise;
While, scourged by famine from the smiling land
The mournful peasant leads his humble band,
And while he sinks, without one arm to save,
The country blooms—a garden and a grave.

   Where then, ah! where shall poverty reside,
To 'scape the pressure of contiguous pride?
If to some common's fenceless limits strayed,
He drives his flock to pick the scanty blade,
Those fenceless fields the sons of wealth divide,
And even the bare-worn common is denied.

   If to the city sped—what waits him there?
To see profusion that he must not share;
To see ten thousand baneful arts combined
To pamper luxury, and thin mankind;
To see those joys the sons of pleasure know
Extorted from his fellow-creature's woe.
Here while the courtier glitters in brocade,
There the pale artist plies the sickly trade;
Here while the proud their long-drawn pomps display,

There the black gibbet glooms beside the way.
The dome where Pleasure holds her midnight reign,
Here, richly decked, admits the gorgeous train:
Tumultuous grandeur crowds the blazing square,
The rattling chariots clash, the torches glare.
Sure scenes like these no troubles e'er annoy!
Sure these denote one universal joy!
Are these thy serious thoughts?—Ah, turn thine eyes
Where the poor houseless shivering female lies.
She once, perhaps, in village plenty blest,
Has wept at tales of innocence distrest;
Her modest looks the cottage might adorn,
Sweet as the primrose peeps beneath the thorn;
Now lost to all; her friends, her virtue fled,
Near her betrayer's door she lays her head,
And, pinched with cold, and shrinking from the shower,
With heavy heart deplores that luckless hour,
When idly first, ambitious of the town,
She left her wheel and robes of country brown.

Do thine, sweet Auburn, thine, the loveliest train,
Do thy fair tribes participate her pain?
Even now, perhaps, by cold and hunger led,
At proud men's doors they ask a little bread!
Ah, no! To distant climes, a dreary scene,
Where half the convex world intrudes between,
Through torrid tracts with fainting steps they go,
Where wild Altama murmurs to their woe.
Far different there from all that charmed before
The various terrors of that horrid shore;
Those blazing suns that dart a downward ray,
And fiercely shed intolerable day;
Those matted woods, where birds forget to sing,
But silent bats in drowsy clusters cling;
Those poisonous fields with rank luxuriance crowned,
Where the dark scorpion gathers death around;
Where at each step the stranger fears to wake
The rattling terrors of the vengeful snake;

Where crouching tigers wait their hapless prey,
And savage men more murderous still than they;
While oft in whirls the mad tornado flies,
Mingling the ravaged landscape with the skies.
Far different these from every former scene,
The cooling brook, the grassy vested green,
The breezy covert of the warbling grove,
That only sheltered thefts of harmless love.

    Good Heaven! what sorrows gloomed that parting day,
That called them from their native walks away:
When the poor exiles, every pleasure past,
Hung round the bowers, and fondly looked their last,
And took a long farewell, and wished in vain
For seats like these beyond the western main,
And shuddering still to face the distant deep,
Returned and wept, and still returned to weep.
The good old sire, the first prepared to go
To new found worlds, and wept for others' woe;
But for himself, in conscious virtue brave,
He only wished for worlds beyond the grave.
His lovely daughter, lovelier in her tears,
The fond companion of his helpless years,
Silent went next, neglectful of her charms,
And left a lover's for a father's arms.
With louder plaints the mother spoke her woes,
And blest the cot where every pleasure rose,
And kist her thoughtless babes with many a tear
And claspt them close, in sorrow doubly dear,
Whilst her fond husband strove to lend relief,
In all the silent manliness of grief.

    O Luxury! thou curst by Heaven's decree,
How ill exchanged are things like these for thee!
How do thy potions, with insidious joy,
Diffuse their pleasure only to destroy!
Kingdoms by thee, to sickly greatness grown,
Boast of a florid vigor not their own.

At every draught more large and large they grow,
A bloated mass of rank, unwieldy woe;
Till sapped their strength, and every part unsound,
Down, down, they sink, and spread a ruin round.

   Even now the devastation is begun,
And half the business of destruction done;
Even now, methinks, as pondering here I stand,
I see the rural virtues leave the land.
Down where yon anchoring vessel spreads the sail
That idly waiting flaps with every gale,
Downward they move, a melancholy band,
Pass from the shore, and darken all the strand.
Contented toil, and hospitable care,
And kind connubial tenderness, are there;
And piety with wishes placed above,
And steady loyalty, and faithful love.
And thou, sweet Poetry, thou loveliest maid,
Still first to fly where sensual joys invade;
Unfit in these degenerate times of shame
To catch the heart, or strike for honest fame;
Dear charming nymph, neglected and decried,
My shame in crowds, my solitary pride;
Thou source of all my bliss, and all my woe,
That found'st me poor at first, and keep'st me so;
Thou guide by which the nobler arts excel,
Thou nurse of every virtue fare thee well!
Farewell, and oh! where'er thy voice be tried,
On Torno's cliff or Pambamarca's side,
Whether where equinoctial fervors glow,
Or winter wraps the polar world in snow,
Still let thy voice, prevailing over time,
Redress the rigors of the inclement clime;
Aid slighted truth with thy persuasive strain;
Teach erring man to spurn the rage of gain:
Teach him, that states of native strength possest,
Though very poor, may still be very blest;
That trade's proud empire hastes to swift decay,

[345]

As ocean sweeps the labored mole away;
While self-dependent power can time defy,
As rocks resist the billows and the sky.

STANZAS ON WOMAN

(from: *The Vicar of Wakefield*)

WHEN lovely woman stoops to folly,
   And finds too late that men betray,
What charm can soothe her melancholy,
   What art can wash her guilt away?

The only art her guilt to cover,
   To hide her shame from every eye,
To give repentance to her lover,
   And wring his bosom, is—to die.

EMMA

IN ALL my Emma's beauties blest,
   Amidst profusion still I pine;
For though she gives me up her breast,
   Its panting tenant is not mine.

AN ELEGY ON THE GLORY OF HER SEX,
MRS. MARY BLAIZE

GOOD people all, with one accord,
   Lament for Madam Blaize,
Who never wanted a good word—
   From those who spoke her praise

The needy seldom passed her door,
   And always found her kind;

[346]

She freely lent to all the poor—
   Who left a pledge behind.

She strove the neighborhood to please,
   With manners wondrous winning;
And never followed wicked ways—
   Unless when she was sinning.

At church, in silks and satins new,
   With hoop of monstrous size,
She never slumbered in her pew—
   But when she shut her eyes.

Her love was sought, I do aver,
   By twenty beaux and more;
The king himself has followed her—
   When she has walked before.

But now her wealth and finery fled,
   Her hangers-on cut short all;
The doctors found, when she was dead—
   Her last disorder mortal.

Let us lament, in sorrow sore,
   For Kent-street well may say,
That had she lived a twelvemonth more—
   She had not died today.

ISAAC BICKERSTAFF
(1735?-1812?)

SONG

(from *Love in a Village*)

THERE was a jolly miller once,
   Lived on the River Dee;

[347]

He worked and sang, from morn to night;
  No lark so blithe as he.
And this the burden of his song,
  Forever used to be,—
"I care for nobody, not I,
  If no one cares for me."

WHAT ARE OUTWARD FORMS?

WHAT are outward forms and shows,
  To an honest heart compared?
Oft the rustic, wanting those,
  Has the nobler portion shared.

Oft we see the homely flower,
  Bearing, at the hedge's side,
Virtues of more sovereign power
  Than the garden's gayest pride.

JOHN O'KEEFFE
(1747-1833)

THE FRIAR OF ORDERS GRAY

I AM a friar of orders gray:
As down the valley I take my way,
  I pull not blackberry, haw, or hip,
  Good store of venison does fill my scrip:
  My long bead-roll I merrily chaunt,
  Where'er I walk, no money I want;
And why I'm so plump the reason I'll tell—
Who leads a good life is sure to live well.
    What baron or squire
    Or knight of the shire
  Lives half so well as a holy friar!

[348]

After supper, of heaven I dream,
But that is fat pullet and clouted cream.
　　Myself, by denial, I mortify
　　With a dainty bit of a warden pie:
I'm clothed in sackcloth for my sin:
With old sack wine I'm lined within:
A chirping cup is my matin song,
And the vesper bell is my bowl's ding dong.
　　　What baron or squire
　　　Or knight of the shire
Lives half so well as a holy friar!

OWEN ROE O'SULLIVAN
(1748?-1784)

RODNEY'S GLORY

This ballad, one of the few written by O'Sullivan in English, was composed shortly after the famous sea-battle off San Domingo. The poet was one of many Irish (mostly impressed) who took part.

GIVE ear, ye British hearts of gold,
That e'er disdain to be controlled,
Good news to you I will unfold,
　'Tis of brave Rodney's glory,
Who always bore a noble heart,
And from his colours ne'er would start,
But always took his country's part
Against each foe who dared t' oppose
Or blast the bloom of England's Rose,
　So now observe my story.

'Twas in the year of Eighty Two,
The Frenchmen know full well 'tis true,
Brave Rodney did their fleet subdue,
　Not far from old Fort Royal.

[349]

Full early by the morning's light,
The proud De Grasse appeared in sight,
And thought brave Rodney to affright,
With colours spread at each mast-head,
Long pendants, too, both white and red,
    A signal for engagement.

Our Admiral then he gave command,
That each should at his station stand,
"Now, for the sake of Old England,
    We'll show them British valour."
Then we the British Flag displayed,
No tortures could our hearts invade,
Both sides began to cannonade,
Their mighty shot we valued not,
We plied our "Irish pills" so hot,
    Which put them in confusion.

This made the Frenchmen to combine,
And draw their shipping in a line,
To sink our fleet was their design,
    But they were far mistaken;
Broadside for broadside we let fly,
Till they in hundreds bleeding lie,
The seas were all of crimson dye,
Full deep we stood in human blood,
Surrounded by a scarlet flood,
    But still we fought courageous.

So loud our cannons that the roar
Re-echoed round the Indian shore,
Both ships and rigging suffered sore,
    We kept such constant firing;
Our guns did roar and smoke did rise,
And clouds of sulphur veiled the skies,
Which filled De Grasse with wild surprise;
Both Rodney's guns and Paddy's sons

Make echo shake where'er they come,
  They fear no French or Spaniards.

From morning's dawn to fall of night,
We did maintain this bloody fight,
Being still regardless of their might,
  We fought like Irish heroes.
Though on the deck did bleeding lie
Many of our men in agony,
We resolved to conquer or die,
To gain the glorious victory,
And would rather suffer to sink or die
  Than offer to surrender.

So well our quarters we maintained,
Five captured ships we have obtained,
And thousands of their men were slain,
  During this hot engagement;
Our British metal flew like hail,
Until at length the French turned tail,
Drew in their colours and made sail
In deep distress, as you may guess,
And when they got in readiness
  They sailed down to Fort Royal.

Now may prosperity attend
Brave Rodney and his Irishmen,
And may he never want a friend
  While he shall reign commander;
Success to our Irish officers,
Seamen bold and jolly tars,
Who like darling sons of Mars
Take delight in the fight
And vindicate bold England's right
  And die for Erin's glory.

[351]

RICHARD BRINSLEY SHERIDAN
(1751-1816)

BY COELIA'S ARBOR

By Coelia's arbor, all the night,
    Hang, humid wreath—the lover's vow;
And haply, at the morning's light,
    My love will twine thee round her brow.

And if upon her bosom bright
    Some drops of dew should fall from thee;
Tell her they are not drops of night,
    But tears of sorrow shed by me.

OH YIELD, FAIR LIDS

(from an unfinished ms. drama, *The Foresters*)

Oh yield, fair lids, the treasures of my heart,
    Release those beams, that make this mansion bright;
From her sweet sense, Slumber! though sweet thou art,
    Begone, and give the air she breathes-in light.

Or while, O Sleep, thou dost those glances hide,
    Let rosy Slumbers still around her play,
Sweet as the cherub Innocence enjoyed,
    When in thy lap, new-born, in smiles he lay.

And thou, O Dream, that com'st her sleep to cheer,
    Oh take my shape, and play a lover's part;
Kiss her from me, and whisper in her ear,
    Till her eyes shine, 'tis night within my heart.

LET THE TOAST PASS

(from *The School for Scandal*)

HERE's to the maiden of bashful fifteen,
  Here's to the widow of fifty;
Here's to the flaunting extravagant queen,
  And here's to the housewife that's thrifty.

Chorus
Let the toast pass,
Drink to the lass,
I'll warrant she'll prove an excuse for the glass.

Here's to the charmer whose dimples we prize,
  Now to the maid who has none, sir,
Here's to the girl with a pair of blue eyes,
  And here's to the nymph with but one, sir!
    Let the toast pass, *etc.*

Here's to the maid with a bosom of snow,
  And to her that's as brown as a berry;
Here's to the wife, with a face full of woe,
  And now to the damsel that's merry:
    Let the toast pass, *etc.*

For let 'em be clumsy, or let 'em be slim,
  Young or ancient, I care not a feather;
So fill the pint bumper quite up to the brim,
  And let us e'en toast them together:

Chorus
Let the toast pass,
Drink to the lass,
I'll warrant she'll prove an excuse for the glass.

[353]

DRY BE THAT TEAR

DRY be that tear, my gentlest love,
  Be hushed that struggling sigh:
Nor seasons, day, nor fate shall prove
  More fixed, more true, than I:
Hushed be that sigh, be dry that tear,
Cease boding doubt, cease anxious fear—
            Dry be that tear.

Ask'st thou how long my love shall stay,
  When all that's new is past?
How long? ah! Delia, can I say
  How long my life shall last?
Dry be that tear, be hushed that sigh,
At least I'll love thee till I die—
            Hushed be that sigh.

And does that thought affect thee too,
  The thought of Sylvio's death,
That he who only breath'd for you,
  Must yield that faithful breath?
Hushed be that sigh, be dry that tear,
Nor let us lose our heaven here—
            Dry be that tear.

PATRICK O'KELLY
(c.1754)

  Widely circulated through Ireland, this poem caused a great deal of
amusement. To appease O'Kelly Lady Doneraile presented him with a
"watch and seal," in place of the one he "lost," upon receipt of which he
wrote "Blessings on Doneraile."

THE CURSE OF DONERAILE

ALAS! how dismal is my tale,
I lost my watch in Doneraile.
My Dublin watch, my chain and seal,
Pilfered at once in Doneraile.
May Fire and Brimstone never fail,
To fall in showers on Doneraile.
May all the leading fiends assail,
The thieving town of Doneraile,
As lightnings flash across the vale,
So down to Hell with Doneraile.
The fate of Pompey at Pharsale,
Be that the curse of Doneraile.
May Beef, or Mutton, Lamb or Veal
Be never found in Doneraile.
But Garlic Soup and scurvy Kale,
Be still the food for Doneraile.
And forward as the creeping snail,
Th' industry be, of Doneraile.
May Heaven a chosen curse entail,
On rigid, rotten Doneraile.
May Sun and Moon forever fail,
To beam their lights on Doneraile.
May every pestilential gale,
Blast that cursed spot called Doneraile.
May not a Cuckoo, Thrush, or Quail,
Be ever heard in Doneraile.
May Patriots, Kings and Commonweal,
Despise and harass Doneraile.
May ev'ry Post, Gazette, and Mail,
Sad tidings bring of Doneraile.
May loudest thunders ring a peal,
To blind and deafen Doneraile.
May vengeance fall at head and tail,
From North to South at Doneraile.
May profit light and tardy sale,
Still damp the trade of Doneraile.

[355]

May Fame resound a dismal tale,
Whene'er she lights on Doneraile.
May Egypt's plagues at once prevail,
To thin the knaves of Doneraile.
May frost and snow, and sleet and hail
Benumb each joint in Doneraile.
May wolves and bloodhounds trace and trail,
The cursèd crew of Doneraile.
May Oscar with his fiery flail,
To Atoms thrash all Doneraile.
May every mischief fresh and stale,
Abide henceforth in Doneraile.
May all from Belfast to Kinsale,
Scoff, curse, and damn you, Doneraile.
May neither Flow'r nor Oatenmeal,
Be found or known in Doneraile.
May want and woe each joy curtail,
That e'er was known in Doneraile.
May no one coffin want a nail,
That wraps a rogue in Doneraile.
May all the thieves that rob and steal,
The gallows meet in Doneraile.
May all the sons of Granuale,
Blush at the thieves of Doneraile.
May mischief big as Norway whale,
O'erwhelm the knaves of Doneraile.
May curses wholesale and retail,
Pour with full force on Doneraile.
May ev'ry transport wont to sail,
A convict bring from Doneraile.
May ev'ry churn and milking pail,
Fall dry to staves in Doneraile.
May cold and hunger still congeal,
The stagnant blood of Doneraile.
May ev'ry hour new woes reveal,
That Hell reserves for Doneraile.
May ev'ry chosen ill prevail,
O'er all the Imps of Doneraile.

May no one wish or prayer avail,
To soothe the woes of Doneraile.
May th' Inquisition straight impale,
The rapparees of Doneraile.
May curse of Sodom now prevail,
And sink to ashes Doneraile.
May Charon's Boat triumphant sail,
Completely manned from Doneraile.
Oh! may my Couplets never fail,
To find new curse for Doneraile.
And may Grim Pluto's inner jail,
For ever groan with Doneraile.

BLESSINGS ON DONERAILE

How vastly pleasing is my tale
I found my watch in Doneraile.
My Dublin watch, my chain and seal
Were all restored at Doneraile.
May fire and brimstone ever fail
To hurt or injure Doneraile.
May neither friend nor foe assail
The splendid town of Doneraile.
May lightning never singe the vale
That leads to generous Doneraile.
May Pompey's fate and old Pharsale
Be still reversed at Doneraile.
May beef and mutton, lamb and veal
Plentyful be in Doneraile.
May garlic soup and scurvy kale
No palate spoil in Doneraile.
May neither frog nor creeping snail
Subtract the crops of Doneraile.
May Heaven each chosen bliss entail
On honest, friendly Doneraile.
May Sol and Luna never fail

To shed their light on Doneraile.
May every soft ambrosial gale
Waft heavenly bliss to Doneraile.
May every cuckoo, thrush and quail
A concert sing in Doneraile.
May every post, gazette and mail
Glad tidings bring to Doneraile.
May no harsh thunder sound a peal
To incommode sweet Doneraile.
May profit high and speedy sale
Enlarge the trade of Doneraile.
May fame resound a pleasant tale
Of all the joys in Doneraile.
May Egypt's plagues forever fail
To hurt or injure Doneraile.
May frost and snow, and rain and hail
No mischief do at Doneraile.
May Oscar with his fiery flail
Thrash all the foes of Doneraile.
May all from Belfast to Kinsale
Respect the town of Doneraile.
May choisest flour and oatenmeal
Be still to spare in Doneraile.
May want and woe no joy curtail
That's always known in Doneraile.
No coffin that grim death can nail
May wrap a rogue in Doneraile.
There are no thieves to rob and steal
Within two leagues of Doneraile.
And all the sons of Granuale
Can well be proud of Doneraile.
May no dire monster, shark or whale
Annoy or torture Doneraile.
May no disaster e'er assail
The bliss and peace of Doneraile.
May every transport wont to sail
Increase the wealth of Doneraile.
May every churn and milking pail

O'erflow with cream at Donerail.
May cold and hunger ne'er congeal
The good rich blood of Doneraile.
May every day new joys reveal
To crown the bliss of Doneraile.
May every soft ambrosial gale
Sweet odours waft to Doneraile.
May no corroding ill prevail
To damp the joys of Doneraile.
May the Inquisition ne'er impale
Or hurt a limb from Doneraile.
May Sodom's curse forever fail
To hurt and injure Doneraile
But may each wish and prayer prevail
To crown with peace sweet Doneraile.

WILLIAM DRENNAN
(1754-1820)

THE WAKE OF WILLIAM ORR

THERE our murdered brother lies;
Wake him not with woman's cries;
Mourn the way that manhood ought—
Sit in silent trance of thought.

Write his merits on your mind;
Morals pure and manners kind;
In his head, as on a hill,
Virtue placed her citadel.

Why cut off in palmy youth?
Truth he spoke, and acted truth.
"Countrymen, UNITE," he cried,
And died for what our Saviour died.

[359]

God of peace and God of love!
Let it not Thy vengeance move—
Let it not Thy lightnings draw—
A nation guillotined by law.

Hapless Nation, rent and torn,
Thou wert early taught to mourn;
Warfare for six hundred years!
Epoch marked with blood and tears!

Hunted thro' thy native grounds,
Or flung reward to human hounds,
Each one pulled and tore his share,
Heedless of thy deep despair.

Hapless Nation! hapless Land!
Heap of uncementing sand!
Crumbled by a foreign weight:
And by worse, domestic hate.

God of mercy! God of peace!
Make this mad confusion cease;
O'er the mental chaos move,
Through it SPEAK the light of love.

Monstrous and unhappy sight!
Brothers' blood will not unite;
Holy oil and holy water
Mix, and fill the world with slaughter.

Who is she with aspect wild?
The widowed mother with her child—
Child new stirring in the womb
Husband waiting for the tomb!

Angel of this sacred place,
Calm her soul and whisper peace—
Cord, or axe, or guillotine,
Make the sentence—not the sin.

[360]

Here we watch our brother's sleep:
Watch with us, but do not weep:
Watch with us thro' dead of night—
But expect the morning light.

EIRE

WHEN Eire first rose from the dark-swelling flood,
God blessed the green island, and saw it was good;
The emerald of Europe, it sparkled and shone,
In the ring of the world, the most precious stone.
In her sun, in her soil, in her station thrice blest,
With her back towards Britain, her face to the west,
Eire stands proudly insular, on her steep shore,
And strikes her high harp 'mid the ocean's deep roar.

But when its soft tones seem to mourn and to weep,
A dark chain of silence is thrown o'er the deep;
At the thought of the past the tears gush from her eyes,
And the pulse of her heart makes her white bosom rise.
O! sons of green Eire, lament o'er the time
When religion was war, and our country a crime;
When man in God's image inverted His plan,
And moulded his God in the image of man.

When the interest of state wrought the general woe,
The stranger a friend, and the native a foe;
While the mother rejoiced o'er her children oppressed,
And clasped the invader more close to her breast;
When, with Pale for the body and Pale for the soul,
Church and State joined in compact to conquer the whole;
And, as Shannon was stained with Milesian blood,
Eyed each other askance and pronounced it was good.

By the groans that ascend from your forefathers' grave,
For their country thus left to the brute and the slave,

Drive the demon of Bigotry home to his den,
And where Britain made brutes now let Eire make men.
Let my sons like the leaves of the shamrock unite,
A partition of sects from one footstalk of right,
Give each his full share of the earth and the sky,
Nor fatten the slave where the serpent would die.

Alas! for poor Eire, that some are still seen
Who would dye the grass red from their hatred to Green;
Yet, O! when you're up and they're down, let them live,
Then yield them that mercy which they would not give.
Arm of Eire, be strong! but be gentle as brave!
And, uplifted to strike, be still ready to save!
Let no feeling of vengeance presume to defile
The cause of, or men of, the Emerald Isle.

The cause it is good, and the men they are true,
And the Green shall outlive both the Orange and Blue!
And the triumphs of Eire her daughters shall share,
With the full swelling chest, and the fair flowing hair.
Their bosom heaves high for the worthy and brave,
But no coward shall rest on that soft-swelling wave;
Men of Eire! awake, and make haste to be blest,
Rise—Arch of the Ocean, and Queen of the West!

RICHARD ALFRED MILLIKIN
(1767-1815)

THE GROVES OF BLARNEY

(Air: "Castle—Hyde")

Millikin at a party declared he could write a piece of absurdity that
would surpass "Castle Hyde" *q.v.* p. 254. The Groves of Blarney was the
result and Millikin became famous for it.

THE Groves of Blarney
They look so charming,

[362]

Down by the purling
   Of sweet silent streams,
Being banked with posies,
That spontaneous grow there,
Planted in order
   By the sweet rock close.
'Tis there's the daisy
And the sweet carnation,
The blooming pink,
   And the rose so fair;
The daffodowndilly—
Likewise the lily,
All flowers that scent
   The sweet fragrant air.

'Tis Lady Jeffers
That owns this station;
Like Alexander,
   Or Queen Helen fair;
There's no commander
In all the nation,
For emulation,
   Can with her compare.
Such walls surround her,
That no nine-pounder
Could dare to plunder
   Her place of strength;
But Oliver Cromwell,
Her he did pommel,
And made a breach
   In her battlement.

There's gravel walks there,
For speculation,
And conversation
   In sweet solitude.
'Tis there the lover
May hear the dove, or

The gentle plover
   In the afternoon;
And if a lady
Would be so engaging
As to walk alone in
   Those shady bowers,
'Tis there the courtier
He may transport her
Into some fort, or
   All under ground.

For 'tis there's a cave where
No daylight enters,
But cats and badgers
   Are for ever bred;
Being mossed by nature,
That makes it sweeter
Than a coach-and-six,
   Or a feather-bed.
'Tis there the lake is,
Well stored with perches,
And comely eels in
   The verdant mud;
Besides the leeches,
And groves of beeches,
Standing in order
   For to guard the flood.

There's statues gracing
This noble place in—
All heathen gods
   And nymphs so fair:
Bold Neptune, Plutarch,
And Nicodemus,
All standing naked
   In the open air!
So now to finish
This brave narration,

Which my poor geni'
    Could not entwine;
But were I Homer,
Or Nebuchadnezzar,
'Tis in every feature
    I would make it shine.

Francis Sylvester Mahony (Father Prout) composed an additional verse to this song. Samuel Lover said that any editor who omitted it deserved to be "hung up to dry on Lis own lines".

There is a boat on
The lake to float on,
And lots of beauties
    Which I can't entwine;
But were I a preacher,
Or a classic teacher,
In every feature
    I'd make 'em shine!
There is a stone there,
That whoever kisses,
Oh! he never misses
To grow eloquent;
'Tis he may clamber
To a lady's chamber,
Or become a member
    Of parliament.
A clever spouter
He'll soon turn out, or
An out-and-outer,
    To be let alone.
Don't hope to hinder him,
Or to bewilder him,
Sure he's a pilgrim
    From the Blarney Stone!

GEORGE NUGENT REYNOLDS
(1771-1802)

MARY LE MORE

As I STRAY'D o'er the common on Cork's rugged border,
  While the dew-drops of morn the sweet primrose array'd
I saw a poor maiden whose mental disorder,
  Her quick-glancing eye and wild aspect betray'd.
On the sward she reclined, by the green fern surrounded,
At her side speckled daisies and wild flow's abounded:
To its utmost recesses her heart had been wounded;
  Her sighs were unceasing—'twas Mary le More.

Her charms by the keen blasts of sorrow were faded,
  Yet the soft tinge of beauty still play'd on her cheek;
Her tresses a wreath of pale primroses braided,
  And strings of fresh daisies hung loose on her neck.
While with pity I gazed, she exclaim'd, "O my Mother!
See the blood on that lash, 'tis the blood of my brother;
They have torn his poor flesh, and they now strip another—
  'Tis Connor, the friend of poor Mary le More.

"Though his locks were as white as the foam of the ocean,
  Those wretches shall find that my father is brave;
My father!" she cried, with the wildest emotion,
  "Ah! no, my poor father now sleeps in the grave!
They have toll'd his death-bell, they've laid the turf o'er him
His white locks were bloody! no aid could restore him;
He is gone! he is gone! and the good will deplore him,
  When the blue waves of Erin hide Mary le More."

A lark, from the gold blossom'd furze that grew near her,
  Now rose, and with energy caroll'd his lay;
"Hush! hush!" she continued, "the trumpet sounds clearer;
  The horsemen approach! Erin's daughters away!
Ah! soldiers, 'twas foul, while the cabin was burning,

And o'er a pale father a wretch had been mourning—
Go, hide with the sea-mew, ye maids, and take warning,
 Those ruffians have ruin'd poor Mary le More.

"Away, bring the ointment—O God! see those gashes!
 Alas! my poor brother, come dry the big tear;
Anon we'll have vengeance for these dreadful lashes;
 Already the screech-owl and raven appear.
By day the green grave, that lies under the willow,
With wild flow'rs I'll strew, and by night make my pillow,
Till the ooze and dark sea-weed, beneath the curl'd billow,
Shall furnish a death-bed for Mary le More."

Thus raved the poor maniac, in tones more heartrending
 Than sanity's voice ever pour'd on my ear,
When, lo! on the waste, and their march tow'rd her bending,
 A troop of fierce cavalry chanced to appear;
"O ye fiends!" she exclaim'd, and with wild horror started,
Then through the tall fern, loudly screaming, she darted!
With an overcharged bosom I slowly departed,
And sigh'd for the wrongs of poor Mary le More.

THOMAS DERMODY
(1775-1802)

A DECAYED MONASTERY

HERE, where the pale grass struggles with each wind,
Pregnant with form the turf unheeded lies;
Here the fat abbot sleeps, in ease reclined,
And here the meek monk folds his modest eyes.
 The nun, more chaste than bolted snow,
 Mingles with the dust below,
 Nor capricious turns away.
 Lo! to the taper's tremulous ray

White veiled shades their frames disclose,
Vests of lily, cheeks of rose;
In dim fancy's vision seen,
Alive, awake, they rush between.

Ah! who so cruel, in eternal gloom
To close the sweetest workmanship of God;
In cloistered aisles to waste their heav'nly bloom,
And dull their bright eyes in the drear abode?
  Not real penance claimed them here;
  Nor lowliness, with melting tear:
  But superstition, fiend deform,
  Sent forth the persecuting storm,
  And in a charnel's baleful arms
  Enclosed the virgin's with'ring charms;
  Despotic ruled the fearful band,
  Prayer and despondence in his hand,—
  His own right hand, that seemed to wield
  Heav'n's lightning, and oppression's shield.

  Poor tremblers! all your griefs are o'er:
  Beads deep-murmured tire no more;
  Pageants dressed in pious guise,
  Lank fasts, and pity-pouring eyes,
  All, all eclipsed and sunk! Those stones,
  'Scutcheon'd with rude gigantic bones,
  Shew the tyrant zealot's end,
  And where his schemes of power tend.

  Near pebbled beds, where riv'lets play,
  And linger in the beams of day;
  'Mid sods by kneeling martyrs worn,
  Embrowned with many a horrid thorn,
  On whose branches off'rings fade,
  (Proof of vows devoutly paid;)
  Where the owlet shrieking hides,
  Cov'ring with leaves his ragged sides;
  Wont the solemn bell to flow

[368]

In silver notes, prolonging slow
Tides of matchless melody,
Rousing the friar to secret glee;
While the vot'ries creep along,
And, half-unwilling, join the throng,
Their fates depending on his word,
Own'd of their breasts almighty lord:—
Yes, let them slumber here at last,
Their tyrannies, *their* suff'rings past;
And lend a venerable dread
To the lone abbey's rocking head.

JOHN BAYNHAM'S EPITAPH

John Baynham was parish-clerk of Killeigh, and merry friend and
sociable companion of Thomas Dermody.

HERE lieth Hercules the Second,
A penman fine by critics reckon'd;
With back so huge, and brawny neck on't,
                    And shrewdish head,
Which oft to smoking hotpot beckon'd:
                    John Baynham's dead.

Woe's me! no more shall younkers crowd
About thy hearth, and gabble loud;
Where thou, in magistracy proud,
                    Nought humbly said:
Alas! we never thought thee good
                    Till thou wast dead.

Though, by my soul! still sober, mellow,
I ken'd thee aye a special fellow,
Catches or psalm-staves prompt to bellow,
                    O pious breed!
I ween thou'rt fixt 'tween heav'n and hell: oh!
                    Our comfort's dead.

[369]

But for that plaguy profligate,
We early might enjoy and late
The knowledge of thy teeming pate
             From board to bed:
But now thou'rt 'neath a puny slate:
             Droll Johnny's dead.

Full many a hard bout hast thou weather'd:
By merry Bob severely tether'd;
More sadly than if tarr'd and feather'd,
             Like bull-dog led:
Now all my tools are fairly gather'd;
             Blythe Baynham's dead.

Heav'n lend thy soul its surest port,
And introduce thee to the court;
Revive again thy earthly sport,
             And melt thy lead!
Alas! we mourn; for, by the mort!
             John Baynham's dead.

No curate now can work thy throat,
And alter clean thy jocund note;
Charon has plump'd thee in his boat,
             And run a-head:
My curse on death, the meddling sot!
             Gay Johnny's dead.

With gills of noblest usquebaugh
Will we anoint thy epitaph;
While thou at the full bowl shalt laugh,
             A precious meed:
At last thou liest in harbour safe;
             Sage Johnny's dead.

News shall no more thy mornings muzzle,
Or schemes good spirit-punch to guzzle;

Wounds! thou art past this mortal bustle,
                    With manna fed;
Satan and thou hadst a long tussel;
                    At last thou'rt dead.

May blessings light upon thy gloom,
And geese grow fat upon thy tomb!
While no rash scribbler's impious thumb
                    Shall maul thy head;
But greet thee soft 'in kingdom come,'
                    Though thou art dead.

Postscript

After inditing these sad stories,
I happed to hear some brother tories
Ranting and roaring loud at Lory's[1],
                    Not quite well bred;
I enter'd, and exclaim'd, "Ye glories,
                    John Baynham's dead."

Scarce had I spoke, when 'neath the table
Something sigh'd out most lamentable:
Anon, to make my song a fable,
                    Starts out brave John;
Sitting, by Jove above! most stable
                    On wicked throne.

They press'd my sitting: marv'lous dull,
I gap'd at Banquo like a fool,
And cried "Good Sirs, the table's full,
                    And there's a spirit,"
"Come reach," quote sprite, "an easy stool:"
                    And lent a wherret.

"You rogue," said he, "how dare you write
Such stuff on me, as dead outright;

. . . .

[1] Another friend who kept a public house where the tradesmen of the village gathered with Baynham and Dermody as their oracle.

[371]

AN ODE TO MYSELF

THRICE hail, thou prince of jovial fellows,
Tuning so blithe thy lyric bellows,
Of no one's brighter genius jealous;
    Whose little span
Is spent 'twixt poetry and alehouse,
    'Twixt quill and cann!

Reckless howe'er the world may fadge,
Variety thy only badge:
Now courting Susan, Kate, or Madge,
    Or black-eyed Molly;
For living in one sullen lodge
    Is downright folly.

Thy classics sleeping on the shelf,
Thou'rt muse and patron to thyself:
Aye frolic when profuse of pelf;
    Grim as the gallows
When dunned by that obstreperous elf,
    False-scoring Alice.

Long may'st thou punch ambrosial swill,
Drinking no water from that hill
By temperate bards recorded still
    In tasteless rhime;
For noble punch shall sweetly fill
    The thought sublime.

By many wrong'd, gay bloom of song,
Thou yet art innocent of wrong,
Virtue and truth to thee belong,
    Virtue and truth;
Though Pleasure led thy step along,
    And trapp'd thy youth.

With Baynham, social spring of wit,
Thou hadst full many a merry fit;

[372]

And whether haply thou shalt sit
                    With clown or peer,
Never shall lingering honour quit
                    Thy heart sincere.

THE SHEPHERD'S DESPAIR

MY LUCY was charming and fair,
Love shot all his shafts from her eyes:
So sweet, so commanding her air,
It could soften at once and surprise.
Such pity, such tenderness, played
Serene in her face and her mind!
But the vision of hope is decayed,
Though the shadows still linger behind.

My flute was melodious and soft,
The joy of the pastoral throng;
The linnet would join from aloft,
And Lucy embolden the song:
My cheeks which pale sorrow will fade,
Were the red rose and lily combined.
But the vision of hope is decayed,
Though its shadows still linger behind.

As, fair as the blossoms of spring,
Ah! how could that bosom be cold?
More love lay in Corydon's ring,
More wealth than in Floridel's gold.
The dotard now woos my dear maid,
Now feels every rapture refined:—
Yes: the vision of hope's quite decayed,
Though the shadows still linger behind.

No more to my flocks will I sing,
No more tend the calls of the fold,

[373]

No more shall the glad valleys ring,
Since affection is barter'd for gold.
I will fly with Despair to the shade,
I will die on some rude rock reclined;
For the vision of hope is decayed,
Though the shadows still linger behind.

THOMAS MOORE
(1779-1852)

THE TIME I'VE LOST IN WOOING

THE time I've lost in wooing,
In watching and pursuing
        The light that lies
        In woman's eyes,
Has been my heart's undoing.
Though wisdom oft has taught me
I scorn the lore that bought me,
        My only books
        Were woman's looks,
And folly's all they've taught me.

Her smile when beauty granted,
I hung with gaze enchanted,
        Like him, the sprite,
        Whom maids by night
Oft meet in glen that's haunted.
Like him, too, beauty won me,
But while her eyes were on me,
        If once their ray
        Was turned away,
Oh! winds could not outrun me.

Are those follies going!
And is my proud heart growing

Too cold or wise
For brilliant eyes
Again to set it glowing?
No—vain, alas! the endeavor
From bonds so sweet to sever;—
Poor wisdom's chance
Against a glance
Is now as weak as ever!

THE MINSTREL BOY

THE minstrel boy to the war is gone,
    In the ranks of death you'll find him,
His father's sword he has girded on,
    And his wild harp slung behind him.
"Land of song!" said the warrior bard,
    "Though all the world betrays thee,
One sword, at least, thy rights shall guard,
    One faithful harp shall praise thee!"

The minstrel fell!—but the foeman's chain
    Could not bring his proud soul under;
The harp he loved ne'er spoke again,
    For he tore its chords asunder;
And said, "No chains shall sully thee,
    Thou soul of love and bravery!
Thy songs were made for the pure and free,
    They shall never sound in slavery!"

OH BLAME NOT THE BARD

OH BLAME not the bard if he flies to the bowers
    Where pleasure lies carelessly smiling at fame;
He was born for much more, and in happier hours
    His soul might have burned with a holier flame.

[375]

The string that now languishes loose o'er the lyre,
  Might have bent a bright bow to the warrior's dart,
And the lip which now breathes but the song of desire,
  Might have poured the full tide of a patriot's heart!

But, alas for his country!—her pride is gone by,
  And that spirit is broken which never would bend.
O'er the ruin her children in secret must sigh,
  For 'tis treason to love her, and death to defend.
Unprized are her sons, till they've learned to betray;
  Undistinguished they live, if they shame not their sires;
And the torch that would light them through dignity's way
  Must be caught from the pile where their country expires!

Then blame not the bard, if, in pleasure's soft dream,
  He should try to forget what he never can heal;
Oh! give but a hope—let a vista but gleam
  Through the gloom of his country, and mark how he'll feel!
That instant his heart at her shrine would lay down
  Every passion it nursed, every bliss it adored,
While the myrtle, now idly entwined with his crown,
  Like the wreath of Harmodius, should cover his sword.

But though glory be gone, and though hope fade away,
  Thy name, loved Erin! shall live in his songs;
Not even in the hour when his heart is most gay
  Will he lose the remembrance of thee and thy wrongs!
The stranger shall hear thy lament on his plains;
  The sigh of thy harp shall be sent o'er the deep,
Till thy masters themselves, as they rivet thy chains,
  Shall pause at the song of their captive and weep!

THE SONG OF O'RUARK, PRINCE OF BREFFNI

THE valley lay smiling before me,
  Where lately I left her behind,

Yet I trembled, and something hung o'er me,
    That saddened the joy of my mind.
I looked for the lamp which, she told me,
    Should shine when her pilgrim returned,
But though darkness began to enfold me,
    No lamp from the battlements burned!

I flew to her chamber—'twas lonely
    As if the loved tenant lay dead!—
Ah, would it were death, and death only!
    But no—the young false one had fled.
And there hung the lute that could soften
    My very worst pains into bliss,
While the hand that had waked it so often,
    Now throbbed to my proud rival's kiss.

There *was* a time, falsest of women!
    When Breffni's good sword would have sought
That man, through a million of foemen,
    Who dared but to doubt thee *in thought!*
While now—O degenerate daughter
    Of Erin, how fallen is thy fame!
And, through ages of bondage and slaughter,
    Thy country shall bleed for thy shame.

Already the curse is upon her.
    And strangers her valleys profane;
They come to divide—to dishonor,
    And tyrants they long will remain!
But, onward!—the green banner rearing,
    Go, flesh every sword to the hilt;
On *our* side is Virtue and Erin!
    On *theirs* is the Saxon and Guilt.

[377]

BELIEVE ME, IF ALL THOSE ENDEARING
YOUNG CHARMS

BELIEVE me, if all those endearing young charms,
  Which I gaze on so fondly to-day,
Were to change by tomorrow, and fleet in my arms,
  Like fairy gifts fading away!
Thou wouldst still be adored, as this moment thou art,
  Let thy loveliness fade as it will,
And around the dear ruin each wish of my heart
  Would entwine itself verdantly still.

It is not while beauty and youth are thine own,
  And thy cheeks unprofaned by a tear,
That the fervor and faith of a soul may be known,
  To which time will but make thee more dear!
Oh the heart that has truly loved never forgets,
  But as truly loves on to the close,
As the sunflower turns to her god when he sets
  The same look which she turned when he rose!

THE LAST ROSE OF SUMMER

'TIS the last rose of summer,
  Left blooming alone;
All her lovely companions
  Are faded and gone;
No flower of her kindred,
  No rose bud is nigh
To reflect back her blushes,
  Or give sigh for sigh!

I'll not leave thee, thou lone one!
  To pine on the stem;
Since the lovely are sleeping,
  Go, sleep thou with them;

Thus kindly I scatter
 Thy leaves o'er the bed,
Where thy mates of the garden
 Lie scentless and dead.

So soon may I follow,
 When friendships decay,
And from love's shining circle
 Thy gems drop away!
When true hearts lie withered,
 And fond ones are flown,
Oh! who would inhabit
 This bleak world alone?

THE SONG OF FIONNUALA

SILENT, O Moyle! be the roar of thy water,
 Break not, ye breezes, your chain of repose,
While, murmuring mournfully, Lir's lonely daughter
 Tells to the night-star her tale of woes.
When shall the swan, her death-note singing,
 Sleep, with wings in darkness furled?
When will heaven, its sweet bell ringing,
 Call my spirit from this stormy world?

Sadly, O Moyle! to thy winter wave weeping,
 Fate bids me languish long ages away!
Yet still in her darkness doth Erin lie sleeping,
 Still doth the pure light its dawning delay!
When will that day-star, mildly springing,
 Warm our isle with peace and love?
When will heaven, its sweet bell ringing,
 Call my spirit to the fields above?

PEACE TO THE SLUMBERERS!

Peace to the slumberers!
  They lie on the battle plain
With no shroud to cover them
  The dew and the summer rain
Are all that weep over them.
            Peace to the slumberers!

Vain was their bravery!—
  The fallen oak lies where it lay
Across the wintry river;
  But brave hearts, once swept away
Are gone, alas! forever.
            Vain was their bravery!

Woe to the conqueror!
  Our limbs shall lie as cold as theirs
Of whom his sword bereft us,
  Ere we forget the deep arrears
Of vengeance they have left us!
            Woe to the conqueror!

LOVE IS A HUNTER BOY

Love is a hunter boy,
  Who makes young hearts his prey
And, in his nets of joy,
  Ensnares them night and day.
In vain concealed they lie—
  Love tracks them everywhere;
In vain aloft they fly—
  Love shoots them flying there.

But 'tis his joy most sweet,
  At early dawn to trace

[380]

The print of Beauty's feet,
    And give the trembler chase.
And if, through virgin snow,
    He tracks her footsteps fair,
How sweet for Love to know
    None went before him there.

THE HARP THAT ONCE THROUGH TARA'S HALLS

THE harp that once through Tara's halls
    The soul of music shed,
Now hangs as mute on Tara's walls
    As if that soul were fled.
So sleeps the pride of former days,
    So glory's thrill is o'er,
And hearts that once beat high for praise,
    Now feel that pulse no more!

No more to chiefs and ladies bright
    The harp of Tara swells;
The chord alone that breaks at night,
    Its tale of ruin tells.
Thus Freedom now so seldom wakes,
    The only throb she gives
Is when some heart indignant breaks,
    To show that still she lives.

EPISTLE OF CONDOLENCE

(From a Slave-Lord to a Cotton-Lord)

ALAS! my dear friend, what a state of affairs!
    How unjustly we both are despoiled of our rights!
Not a pound of black flesh shall I leave to my heirs,
    Nor must *you* any more work to death little whites.

Both forced to submit to that general controller
  Of Kings, Lords, and cotton mills, Public Opinion,
No more shall *you* beat with a big-billy-roller,
  Nor *I* with the cart-whip assert my dominion.

Whereas, were we suffered to do as we please
  With our Blacks and our Whites, as of yore we were let,
We might range them alternate, like harpsichord keys,
  And between us thump out a good piebald duet.

But this fun is all over;—farewell to the zest
  Which Slavery now lends to each tea-cup we sip;
Which makes still the cruellest coffee the best,
  And that sugar the sweetest which smacks of the whip.

Farewell, too, the Factory's white picaninnies—
  Small, living machines, which, it flogged to their tasks,
Mix so well with their namesakes, the "Billies" and "Jennies,"
  That *which* have got souls in 'em nobody asks;—

Little Maids of the Mill, who, themselves but ill-fed,
  Are obliged, 'mong their other benevolent cares
To "keep feeding the scribblers,"—and better, 'tis said,
  Than old Blackwood or Frazer have ever fed theirs.

All this is now o'er, and so dismal *my* loss is,
  So hard 'tis to part from the smack of the thong,
That I mean (from pure love for the old whipping process)
  To take to whipped syllabub all my life long.

PADDY'S METAMORPHOSIS

1833

ABOUT fifty years since, in the days of our daddies,
  That plan was commenced which the wise now applaud,
Of shipping off Ireland's most turbulent Paddies,
  As good raw materials for *settlers*, abroad.

Some West-Indian island, whose name I forget,
　　Was the region then chosen for this scheme so romantic;
And such the success the first colony met,
　　That a second, soon after, set sail o'er th' Atlantic.

Behold them now safe at the long looked-for shore,
　　Sailing in between banks that the Shannon might greet,
And thinking of friends whom, but two years before,
　　They had sorrowed to lose, but would soon again meet.

And, hark! from the shore a glad welcome there came—
　　"Arrah, Paddy from Cork, is it you, my sweet boy?"
While Pat stood astounded, to hear his own name
　　Thus hailed by black devils, who capered for joy!

Can it possibly be?—half amazement—half doubt,
　　Pat listens again—rubs his eyes and looks steady;
Then heaves a deep sigh, and in horror yells out,
　　"Good Lord! only think—black and curly already!"

Deceived by that well-mimicked brogue in his ears,
　　Pat read his own doom in these wool-headed figures,
And thought, what a climate, in less than two years,
　　To turn a whole cargo of Pats into niggers!

Moral

'Tis thus,—but alas!—by a marvel more true
　　Than is told in this rival of Ovid's best stories,—
Your Whigs, when in office a short year or two,
　　By a *lusus naturae*, all turn into Tories,

And thus, when I hear them "strong measures" advise,
　　Ere the seats that they sit on have time to get steady,
I say, while I listen, with tears in my eyes,
　　"Good Lord! only think,—black and curly already!"

[383]

THE DUKE IS THE LAD

THE Duke is the lad to frighten a lass,
 Galloping, dreary duke;
The Duke is the lad to frighten a lass,
He's an ogre to meet, and the devil to pass,
  With his charger prancing,
  Grim eye glancing,
  Chin, like a Mufti,
  Grizzled and tufty,
 Galloping, dreary Duke.

Ye misses, beware of the neighborhood
 Of this galloping, dreary Duke;
Avoid him, all who see no good
In being run o'er by a Prince of the Blood.
  For, surely, no nymph is
  Fond of a grim phiz,
  And of the married,
  Whole crowds have miscarried
 At sight of this dreary Duke.

JAMES KENNEY
(1780-1849)

THE OLD STORY OVER AGAIN

WHEN I was a maid,
 Nor of lovers afraid,
My mother cried, "Girl, never listen to men."
 Her lectures were long,
 But I thought her quite wrong,
And I said, "Mother, whom should I listen to, then?"

Now teaching, in turn,
What I never could learn,

I find, like my mother, my lessons all vain;
    Men ever deceive,—
    Silly maidens believe,
And still 'tis the old story over again.

    So humbly they woo,
    What can poor maidens do
But keep them alive when they swear they must die?
    Ah! who can forbear,
    As they weep in despair,
The crocodile tears in compassion to dry?

    Yet, wedded at last,
    When the honeymoon's past,
The lovers forsake us, the husbands remain;
    Our vanity's checked,
    And we ne'er can expect
They will tell us the old story over again.

EATON STANNARD BARRETT
(1786-1820)

WOMAN

Not she with traitorous kiss her Saviour stung,
Not she denied Him with unholy tongue;
She, while apostles shrank, could dangers brave,
Last at the cross and earliest at the grave.

JOHN ANSTER
(1789-1867)

IF I MIGHT CHOOSE

IF I might choose where my tired limbs shall lie
When my task here is done, the oak's green crest
  Shall rise above my grave—a little mound,
Raised in some cheerful village cemetery.
  And I could wish, that, with unceasing sound,
A lonely mountain rill was murmuring by—
  In music—through the long soft twilight hours.
And let the hand of her, whom I love best,
  Plant round the bright green grave those fragrant flowers
In whose deep bells the wild-bee loves to rest;
  And should the robin from some neighboring tree
Pour his enchanted song—oh! softly tread,
For sure, if aught of earth can soothe the dead,
  He still must love that pensive melody!

JOSEPH O'LEARY
(1790-1850)

WHISKY, DRINK DIVINE

WHISKY, drink divine!
  Why should drivelers bore us
With the praise of wine
  While we've thee before us?
Were it not a shame,
  Whilst we gayly fling thee
To our lips of flame,
  If we could not sing thee?

[386]

Chorus

Whisky, drink divine!
  Why should drivelers bore us
With the praise of wine
  While we've thee before us?

Greek and Roman sung
  Chian and Falernian—
Shall no harp be strung
  To thy praise, Hibernian?
Yes! let Erin's sons—
  Generous, brave, and frisky—
Tell the world at once
  They owe it to their whisky—

    Whisky, drink divine! *etc.*

If Anacreon—who
  Was the grape's best poet—
Drank our *mountain-dew,*
  How his verse would show it!
As the best then known,
  He to wine was civil;
Had he *Inishowen,*
  He'd pitch wine to the devil—

    Whisky, drink divine! *etc.*

Bright as beauty's eye,
  When no sorrow veils it:
Sweet as beauty's sigh,
  When young love inhales it:
Come, then, to my lips—
  Come, thou rich in blisses!
Every drop I sip
  Seems a shower of kisses—

[387]

Whisky, drink divine! *etc.*

Could my feeble lays
    Half thy virtues number,
A whole *grove* of bays
    Should my brows encumber.
Be his name adored,
    Who summed up thy merits
In one little word,
    When we call thee *spirits*—

Whisky, drink divine! *etc.*

Send it gayly round—
    Life would be no pleasure,
If we had not found
    This enchanting treasure:
And when tyrant death's
    Arrow shall transfix ye,
Let your latest breaths
    Be whisky! whisky! whisky!

Whisky, drink divine! *etc.*

CHARLES WOLFE
(1791-1823)

THE BURIAL OF SIR JOHN MOORE

Not a drum was heard, not a funeral note,
    As his corse to the rampart we hurried;
Not a soldier discharged his farewell shot
O'er the grave where our hero we buried.

We buried him darkly at dead of night,
    The sods with our bayonets turning,

[388]

By the struggling moonbeam's misty light,
  And the lantern dimly burning.

No useless coffin enclosed his breast,
  Not in sheet or in shroud we wound him;
But he lay like a warrior taking his rest,
  With his martial cloak around him.

Few and short were the prayers we said,
  And we spoke not a word of sorrow;
But we steadfastly gazed on the face that was dead,
  And we bitterly thought of the morrow.

We thought, as we hollowed his narrow bed,
  And smoothed down his lonely pillow,
That the foe and stranger would tread o'er his head,
  And we far away on the billow!

Lightly they'll talk of the spirit that's gone,
  And o'er his cold ashes upbraid him,—
But little he'll reck, if they let him sleep on
  In the grave where a Briton has laid him.

But half of our heavy task was done,
  When the clock struck the hour for retiring;
And we heard the distant and random gun
  That the foe was sullenly firing.

Slowly and sadly we laid him down,
  From the field of his fame, fresh and gory;
We carved not a line, we raised not a stone—
But we left him alone in his glory!

CHARLES O'FLAHERTY
(1794-1828)

THE HUMOURS OF DONNYBROOK FAIR

OH! 'T WAS Dermot O'Nowlan McFigg,
That could properly handle a twig.
   He went to the Fair,
   And kicked up a dust there,
In dancing the Donnybrook Jig,
   With his twig.
Oh! my blessing to Dermot McFigg!

When he came to the midst of the Fair,
He was all in a paugh for fresh air,
   For the Fair very soon
   Was as full as the moon,
Such mobs upon mobs as were there,
   Oh! rare.
So more luck to sweet Donnybrook Fair.

The souls they came crowding in fast,
To dance while the leather would last,
   For the Thomas Street brogue
   Was there much in vogue,
And oft with a brogue the joke passed,
   Quite fast,
While the Cash and the Whisky did last!

But Dermot, his mind on love bent,
In search of his sweetheart he went;
   Peeped in here and there,
   As he walked thro' the Fair,
And took a small taste in each tent,
   As he went.
Och! on Whisky and Love he was bent.

[390]

And who should he spy in a jig,
With a Meal-man so tall and so big,
 But his own darling Kate
 So gay and so neat;
Faith, her partner he hit him a dig,
 The pig,
He beat the meal out of his wig!

Then Dermot, with conquest elate,
Drew a stool near his beautiful Kate;
 "Arragh! Katty," says he,
 "My own Cushlamachree,
Sure the world for Beauty you beat,
 Complete,
So we'll just take a dance while we wait!"

The Piper, to keep him in tune,
Struck up a gay lilt very soon,
 Until an arch wag
 Cut a hole in his bag,
And at once put an end to the tune
 Too soon.
Oh! the music flew up to the moon!

To the Fiddler says Dermot McFigg,
"If you'll please to play 'Sheela na gig,'
 We'll shake a loose toe
 While you humor the bow.
To be sure you must warm the wig
 Of McFigg,
While he's dancing a neat Irish jig!"

But says Katty, the darling, says she,
"If you'll only just listen to me,
 It's myself that will show
 Billy can't be your foe,

Tho' he fought for his Cousin, that's me,"
    Says she,
"For sure Billy's related to me!

"For my own cousin-german, Ann Wilde,
Stood for Biddy Mulrooney's first child,
    And Biddy's step-son,
    Sure he married Bess Dunn,
Who was gossip to Jenny, as mild
    A child
As ever at mother's breast smiled.

"And maybe you don't know Jane Brown,
Who served goat's whey in sweet Dundrum town.
    'T was her uncle's half-brother
    That married my mother,
And bought me this new yellow gown,
    To go down,
When the marriage was held in Miltown!"

"By the Powers, then," says Dermot, " 't is plain,
Like a son of that rapscallion Cail,
    My best friend I've kilt,
    Tho' no blood it is spilt,
And the devil a harm did I mean,
    That's plain,
But by me he'll be ne'er kilt again!"

Then the Meal-man forgave him the blow,
That laid him a-sprawling so low,
    And being quite gay,
    Asked them both to the play,
But Katty, being bashful, said "No,"
    "No!" "No!"
Yet he treated them all to the show!

J. J. CALLANAN
(1795-1828)

SONG

AWAKE thee, my Bessy, the morning is fair,
The breath of young roses is fresh on the air,
The sun has long glanced over mountain and lake—
Then awake from thy slumbers, my Bessy, awake.

Oh, come whilst the flowers are still wet with the dew—
I'll gather the fairest, my Bessy, for you;
The lark poureth forth his sweet strain for thy sake—
Then awake from thy slumbers, my Bessy, awake.

The hare from her soft bed of heather hath gone,
The coot to the water already hath flown;
There is life on the mountain and joy on the lake—
Then awake from thy slumbers, my Bessy, awake.

LINES TO THE BLESSED SACRAMENT

THOU dear and mystic semblance,
    Before whose form I kneel,
I tremble as I think upon
    The glory thou dost veil,
And ask myself, can he who late
    The ways of darkness trod,
Meet face to face, and heart to heart,
    His sin-avenging God?

My Judge and my Creator,
    If I presume to stand
Amid thy pure and holy ones,
    It is at thy command,

[393]

To lay before thy mercy's seat
  My sorrows and my fears,
To wail my life and kiss thy feet
  In silence and in tears.

O God! that dreadful moment,
  In sickness and in strife,
When death and hell seem'd watching
  For the last weak pulse of life,
When on the waves of sin and pain
  My drowning soul was toss'd,
Thy hand of mercy saved me then,
  When hope itself was lost.

I hear thy voice, my Saviour,
  It speaks within my breast,
"Oh, come to me, thou weary one,
  I'll hush thy cares to rest;"
Then from the parch'd and burning waste
  Of sin, where long I trod,
I come to thee, thou stream of life,
  My Saviour and my God!

SERENADE

THE blue waves are sleeping;
  The breezes are still;
The light dews are weeping
  Soft tears on the hill;
The moon in mild beauty
  Looks bright from above;
Then come to the casement,
  O Mary, my love.

Not a sound or a motion
  Is over the lake,

But the whisper of ripples,
    As shoreward they break;
My skiff wakes no ruffle
    The waters among;
Then listen, dear maid,
    To thy true lover's song.

No form from the lattice
    Did ever recline
Over Italy's waters,
    More lovely than thine;
Then come to thy window,
    And shed from above
One glance of thy dark eye,
    One smile of thy love.

Oh! the soul of that eye,
    When it breaks from its shroud,
Shines beauteously out,
    Like the moon from a cloud;
And thy whisper of love,
    Breathed thus from afar,
Is sweeter to me
    Than the sweetest guitar.

From the storms of this world
    How gladly I'd fly
To the calm of that breast,
    To the heaven of that eye!
How deeply I love thee
    'Twere useless to tell;
Farewell, then, my dear one—
    My Mary, farewell.

GEORGE DARLEY
(1795-1846)

From ERRORS OF ECSTASIE

(A dialogue between a Mystic and the Moon)

THE MOON: ECSTASIE, rash production of the thoughts
To that right sanity would never lead,
Doth spread a dark confusion o'er the brain
Of false creations, wild and fabulous,
Vain dreams, perplexities inexplicable,
Misty conceits, and phantom imagery;
From one poor thought, conjures a host of
  forms,
Irrelevancies sur-exaggerates,
And lost in such fantastic combinations,
Differs from madness scarcely by a line.

MYSTIC: Fair monitress! is Genius nothing more?
Yet Genius is exalted feeling—

MOON: Yes,
Exalted, but not sightless.
Builds not presumptuous Babels, out of size,
Till reason topple down. Seeks not, to climb
The unraught heav'n of infinite Conception
Intangible, like Titan's phrenetic son,
Piled mountain tottering on unstable hill,
The site of eminent Jove; the fable's pat
For those who will to profit, and apply
Its moral to the brain.
       There is a scale
Of intellectual feeling, graduate
Through indivisible and invisible parts,
Each different yet partaking of the next,
From apathetic dulness to insanity;

[396]

The common-sense o' th' world poaches i' th'
    former,
But Ecstasie's near neighbour to the last;
Genius, or Fancy its more passionate name,
Lies equally between. Here, thou 'st trans-
    gress'd;
And, here transgressing, thou dost pay the pen-
    alty:
Dulness itself is happier than thou.

MYSTIC: Why then I'll pray the Heavens to strike me
    surd!
To paralyze the techy nerves of the brain,
Dry up the tubes and organs of sensation,
And turn my heart to preferable stone!
I'll rob the ditch-roots of their lazy pith,
The green ores of their nocuous potency,
Mix the narcotic juices for a drink,
To kill the fine vibrations of the brain,
And dull the vigilant sense to lethargy;
I'll rid their keen perceptions from each nerve,
Choke up their pores with unctuous pharmacies,
Grow fat and fatuate, heartless and heart-free!
Since to be dull is surely to be happy.

MOON: Still in extremes!

MYSTIC: Hear me, sweet Spirit!
                  Though I stand
A pensive, poor, and visionary boy,
With bloodless cheek, in shuddering attitude,
The bitter salutation of the night,
Thus; like a rigid statue—or more like
A living representative in stone,
A wretched mockery of the human form,
Wishing for some impetuous thunderbolt
To scatter me beyond the ken of God,
Beyond the hope or power of resurrection,

[397]

The chance of future bliss appropriate,
I would not change the temper of my blood
For that which stagnates in an idiot's veins,
To gain the sad salvation of a fool.

　　　·　　　·　　　·　　　·　　　·　　　·

Moon:　　　Is there no mean, no golden mean of action,
Which kept, leads on to happiness and joy?
Are you not made with Passions and with
　　　　Reason,
One to incite, the other to restrain,
And both necessitous to ordinate Liberty?
If Man was nought but mortal mechanism,
Turned at the will and pleasure of the artist,
Where lies his liberty? If he was left
To the rough domination of his passions,
What would the emblem of its spirit be?

Go, stand upon the turbid water's edge,
And view the hideous figure in the stream
Made by its quivering mirror, obvious starts
A horrid face, in shadowy channels torn;
Its flickering features, varying types of fiends,
Work through the several fashions of deform;
The hair flies tortuous, like a knot of snakes
In restless agitation of their kind;
Whilst the drawn optice, darting oblique flames,
Fright the abused spectator from the scene.
O! how unlike, the beauteous image smiles,
In yon pure, motionless, and peaceful lake!
This is the model of a healthful mind;
That, the less terrible spectre of the insane.

But wherefore seek for parables abroad,
When the reality is found at home?
Look at thyself, the plaything of thy Will,
Mad in thy ecstasies, a fool in tenderness,
Fantastical beyond all reach of rule,

Romantic even to very girlishness,
And impious too, in spite of "Meditation";
Giving to Passion such imperial sway,
As turns thy Reason's sceptre to a straw,
And makes him the dishonored satellite of
    Fancy.
Hence come thy misery. Answer, if you can.

LAY OF THE FORLORN

FAREWELL to Sliev Morna,
  The hills of the winds!
Where the hunters of Ullin
  Pursue the brown hinds!
Farewell to Lock Ern where the wild eagles dwell!
Farewell to Shan-avon, Shan-avon farewell!

Farewell to bright tresses
  Farewell to bright eyes,
To the snow-covered bosoms
  That heave with their sighs!
Long, long for their heroes in vain may they swell,
Farewell to fair maidens, fair maidens, farewell

Farewell to our castles,
  Our oak-blazing halls,
Where the red fox is prowling
  Alone in the walls!
Farewell to the joys of the harp and the shell,
Farewell to Ierné! Ierné, farewell.

THE CALL OF THE MORNING

VALE of the waterfalls!
  Glen of the streams!

Wake from your slumbering!
  Wake from your dreams!

Wild sings the mountain-lark,
  Bird of the air!
Calling the valley-birds
  Up to him there!

Sweet ring the mountain-bells
  High o'er the dale,
Waking the little bells
  Down in the vale.

Fresh breathes the morning-wind,
  Bright looks the day,—
Up to the heather hills,
  Lilian, away!

CHORUS OF SPIRITS

GENTLY!—gently!—down!—down!
  From the starry courts on high,
Gently step adown, down
  The ladder of the sky.

Sunbeam steps are strong enough
  For such airy feet:
Spirits, blow your trumpets rough,
  So as they be sweet!

Breathe them loud, the Queen descending,
  Yet a lowly welcome breathe,
Like so many flowerets bending
  Zephyr's breezy foot beneath.

[400]

SERENADE OF A LOYAL MARTYR

Sweet in her green cell the Flower of Beauty slumbers,
　Lulled by the faint breezes sighing through her hair;
Sleeps she, and hears not the melancholy numbers
　Breathed to my sad lute amid the lonely air?

Down from the high cliffs the rivulet is teeming,
　To wind round the willow banks that lure him from above:
Oh that in tears from my rocky prison streaming,
　I, too, could glide to the bower of my love!

Ah! where the woodbines with sleepy arms have wound her,
　Opes she her eyelids at the dream of my lay,
Listening, like the dove, while the fountains echo round her,
　To her lost mate's call in the forests far away?

Come, then, my Bird!—for the peace thou ever bearest,
　Still heaven's messenger of comfort to me,
Come!—this fond bosom, my faithfullest, my fairest!
　Bleeds with its death-wound, but deeper yet for thee.

RUNILDA'S CHANT

O'er the wild gannet's bath
Come the Norse coursers!
O'er the whale's heritance
Gloriously steering!
With beaked heads peering,
Deep-plunging, high-rearing,
Tossing their foam abroad,
Shaking white manes aloft,
Creamy-necked, pitchy ribbed,
Steeds of the Ocean!

O'er the Sun's mirror green
Come the Norse coursers!

[401]

Trampling its glassy breadth
Into bright fragments!
Hollow-backed, huge-bosomed,
Fraught with mailed riders,
Clanging with hauberks,
Shield, spear, and battleaxe.
Canvas-winged, cable-reined,
Steeds of the Ocean!

O'er the Wind's ploughing-field
Come the Norse coursers!
By a hundred each ridden,
To the bloody feast bidden,
They rush in their fierceness
And ravine all round them!
Their shoulders enriching
With fleecy-light plunder,
Fire-spreading, foe-spurning,
Steeds of the Ocean!

THE SEA RITUAL

PRAYER unsaid, and mass unsung,
Deadman's dirge must still be rung:
  Dingle-dong, the dead-bells sound!
  Mermen chant his dirge around!

Wash him bloodless, smooth his fair,
Stretch his limbs, and sleek his hair:
  Dingle-dong, the dead-bells go!
  Mermen swing them to and fro!

In the wormless sand shall he
Feast for no foul glutton be:
  Dingle-dong, the dead-bells chime!
  Mermen keep the tone and time!

We must with a tombstone brave
Shut the shark out from his grave:
  Dingle-dong, the dead-bells toll!
  Mermen dirgers ring his knoll!

Such a slab will we lay o'er him
All the dead shall rise before him!
  Dingle-dong, the dead-bells boom!
  Mermen lay him in his tomb!

SONG

Down the dimpled green-sward dancing
  Bursts a flaxen headed bevy,
Bud-lipt boys and girls advancing
  Love's irregular little levy.

Rows of liquid eyes in laughter,
  How they glimmer, how they quiver!
Sparkling one another after,
  Like the ripples on a river.

Tipsy band of rubious faces,
  Flushed with joys ethereal spirit,
Make your mocks and sly grimaces
  At Love's self, and do not fear it.

ROBIN'S CROSS

A little cross,
To tell my loss;
A little bed
To rest my head;

[403]

A little tear is all I crave
Under my very little grave.

I strew thy bed
Who loved thy lays
The tear I shed,
The cross I raise,
With nothing more upon it than—
Here lies the little Friend of Man!

LAST NIGHT

I SAT with one I love last night,
She sang to me an olden strain;
In former times it woke delight,
Last night—but pain.

Last night we saw the stars arise,
But clouds soon dimmed the ether blue;
And when we sought each other's eyes
Tears dimmed them too!

We paced along our favorite walk,
But paced in silence broken-hearted:
Of old we used to smile and talk;
Last night—we parted.

from NEPENTHE

. . . As FROM the moist and gelid sleep
Of Death we rise on shuddering bones,
The waste of that long night to weep,
We pined us down to skeletons;
So shuddering, weeping, weltering, worn,
Gleaming with spectral eyes forlorn,

[404]

Upon my bleak estate and bare
Greyly I rose; like wan Despair
Slow roused from Dissolution's lair.
But in what dread dominion? Air
Hung like a hell-blue vapour there,
Steaming from some thick ooze, that cold
Over my foot like reptiles rolled
Sluggish, with many a slimy fold;
Lethe's foul self, perchance, or flood
Made slab with gouts of gall and blood
Wept by the woe that wades the mud,
Cocytus, bubbling with drowned sighs.
But lo! what shadowy forms arise,
Far off, to these ferruginous skies?
Mountains, as sharp as squally clouds
When fell winds whistle in the shrouds,
Upcall to Fury, above, before,
My vision by this ominous shore,
Where each a burning pyramid seems,
O'er flown with liquorous fire, that teems
Down the slope edges in four streams.
Most sure the abysmal fen I tread
Shelves to the River of the Dead
That bears unto the eternal sea
Millions of ghastly things like me.
Hark! from slow-floating bier and bier
Murmurs and rueful sobs I hear,
The while from these sepulchring hills
A yewtree wind the valley fills
That whispers with fast-fleeting breath,
"This is the dolorous Valley of Death!
Valley of Dolour—and of Death!"

Oh sorrow of Sinfulness! the gate
To pain, kept wide by watchful Hate!
Sloping aloft with cliffy sides,
Thro' the burnt air the porchway rides;
Demoniac shapes, devices grim,

Trenching the storied panels dim.
And mystic signs, dark oracles
Of Destiny, and Hell's decrees!
Alas! what scalding sand-wind rolls
Me to the sulphury rack of souls
Fierce on, and scarfs my victim eyes
With careless wreaths for sacrifice?
Thus weep I, whirlwind-rapt amain:
Save me! O save, ye mighty Twain,
Arbiters here twixt Sin and Pain!
Tho' Angels still of Judgment, be
Angels of Mercy now to me!
Bend down your level looks, or raise
One iron finger from the knee,
So Cherubin Pities sing your praise!
Thus to a Twain that reared their forms
Like promontories o'er the storms,
Methought, dread Umpires of my doom,
Sitting impalled within the gloom
As ebon Seraphim by Night's throne,
Low at their feet I made my moan.
They stirred not at my prayer; but dumb,
Sate like the symbols of the world to come
Immutable, inscrutable!
     I lay
Drowned in my heart-blood, wept away
Fruitlessly at those feet, long time
Like the dust-clung outcast corse of Crime.

ANONYMOUS
(early 19th century)

THE FAIRIES IN NEW ROSS
(County Wexford)

"When moonlight
Near midnight
Tips the rock and waving wood;
When moonlight
Near midnight
Silvers o'er the sleeping flood;
When yew-tops
With dew-drops
Sparkle o'er deserted graves;
'Tis then we fly
Through welkin high,
Then we sail o'er yellow waves."

SAMUEL LOVER
(1797-1868)

WHAT WILL YOU DO, LOVE?

"What will you do, love, when I am going,
With white sail flowing,
    The seas beyond?—
What will you do, love, when waves divide us,
And friends may chide us
    For being fond?"
"Though waves divide us, and friends be chiding,
In faith abiding,
    I'll still be true!
And I'll pray for thee on the stormy ocean,

[407]

In deep devotion—
  That's what I'll do!"

"What would you do, love, if distant tidings
Thy fond confidings
  Should undermine?—
And I, abiding 'neath sultry skies,
Should think other eyes
  Were as bright as thine?"
"Oh, name it not!—though guilt and shame
Were on thy name,
  I'd still be true:
But that heart of thine—should another share it—
I could not bear it!
  What would I do?"

"What would you do, love, when home returning,
With hopes high-burning,
  With wealth for you,
If my bark, which bounded o'er foreign foam,
Should be lost near home—
  Ah! what would you do?"
"So thou wert spared—I'd bless the morrow
In want and sorrow,
  That left me you;
And I'd welcome thee from the wasting billow,
This heart thy pillow—
  That's what I'd do!"

THE ANGEL'S WHISPER

A superstition of great beauty prevails in Ireland, that when a child
smiles in its sleep, it is "talking with angels."

A BABY was sleeping,
  Its mother was weeping,
For her husband was far on the wild raging sea;

[408]

And the tempest was swelling
  Round the fisherman's dwelling,
And she cried, "Dermot, darling, oh! come back to me."

  Her beads while she number'd,
  The baby still slumber'd,
And smiled in her face as she bended her knee;
  "Oh blest be that warning,
  My child's sleep adorning,
For I know that the angels are whispering with thee.

  "And while they are keeping
  Bright watch o'er thy sleeping,
Oh, pray to them softly, my baby, with me
  And say thou wouldst rather
  They'd watch o'er thy father!—
For I know that the angels are whispering with thee."

  The dawn of the morning
  Saw Dermot returning,
And the wife wept with joy her babe's father to see;
  And closely caressing
  Her child, with a blessing,
Said, "I knew that the angels were whispering with thee."

ST. KEVIN

A legend of Glendalough

AT GLENDALOUGH lived a young saint,
  In odor of sanctity dwelling,
An old-fashioned odor, which now
  We seldom or never are smelling;
A book or a hook were to him
  The utmost extent of his wishes;
Now, a snatch at the "Lives of the Saints;"
  Then a catch at the lives of the fishes.

[409]

There was a young woman one day,
    Stravagin[1] along by the lake, sir;
She look'd hard at St. Kevin, they say,
    But St. Kevin no notice did take, sir.
When she found looking hard wouldn't do,
    She look'd soft—in the old sheep's eye fashion;
But, with all her sheep's eyes, she could not
    In St. Kevin see signs of soft passion.

"You're a great hand at fishing," says Kate;
    " 'Tis yourself that knows how, faith, to hook them;
But, when you have caught them, *agra,*
    Don't you want a young woman to cook them?"
Says the saint, "I am 'sayrious inclined,'
    I intend taking orders for life, dear."
"Only marry," says Kate, "and you'll find
    You'll get orders enough from your wife, dear."

"You shall never be flesh of my flesh,"
    Says the saint, with an anchorite groan, sir;
"I see that myself," answer'd Kate,
    "I can only be 'bone of your bone,' sir.
And even your bones are so scarce,"
    Said Miss Kate, at her answers so glib, sir,
"That I think you would not be the worse
    Of a little additional rib, sir."

The saint, in a rage, seized the lass,—
    He gave her one twirl round his head, sir,
And, before Doctor Arnott's invention,
    Prescribed her a watery bed, sir.
Oh!—cruel St. Kevin!—for shame!
    When a lady her heart came to barter,
You should not have been Knight of the Bath,
    But have bowed to the order of Garter.

¹ Sauntering.

[410]

THE QUAKER'S MEETING

A TRAVELLER wended the wilds among,
With a purse of gold and a silver tongue;
His hat it was broad and all drab were his clothes,
For he hated high colors—except on his nose,
And he met with a lady, the story goes.
Heigho! yea thee and nay thee.

The damsel she cast him a beamy blink,
And the traveller nothing was loth, I think;
Her merry black eye beamed her bonnet beneath,
And the Quaker he grinned—for he'd very good teeth.
And he asked, "Art thee going to ride on the heath?"
Heigho! yea thee and nay thee.

"I hope you'll protect me, kind sir," said the maid,
"As to ride this heath over I'm sadly afraid;
For robbers, they say, here in numbers abound,
And I shouldn't 'for anything' I should be found,
For—between you and me—I have five hundred pound."
Heigho! yea thee and nay thee.

"If that is thee own, dear," the Quaker he said,
"I ne'er saw a maiden I sooner would wed;
And I have another five hundred just now,
In the padding that's under my saddle-bow,
And I'll settle it all upon thee, I vow!"
Heigho! yea thee and nay thee.

The maiden she smiled, and her rein she drew,
"Your offer I'll take—though I'll not take you."
A pistol she held at the Quaker's head—
"Now give me your gold—or I'll give you my lead—
'Tis under the saddle I think you said."
Heigho! yea thee and nay thee.

The damsel she ripp'd up the saddle-bow,
And the Quaker was never a Quaker till now,

[411]

And he saw, by the fair one he wished for a bride,
His purse borne away with a swaggering stride,
And the eye that shammed tender, now only defied.
     Heigho! *yea* thee and *nay* thee.

"The spirit doth move me, friend Broadbrim," quoth she,
"To take all this filthy temptation from thee,
For Mammon deceiveth—and beauty is fleeting;
Accept from thy maid'n a right loving greeting,
For much doth she profit by this Quaker's meeting."
     Heigho! *yea* thee and *nay* thee.

"And hark! jolly Quaker, so rosy and sly,
Have righteousness, more than a wench, in thine eye,
Don't go again peeping girls' bonnets beneath,
Remember the one that you met on the heath,—
Her name's *Jimmy* Barlow—I tell to your teeth!"
     Heigho! *yea* thee and *nay* thee.

"*Friend* James," quoth the Quaker, "pray listen to me,
For thou canst confer a great favor, d'ye see;
The gold thou hast taken is not mine, my friend,
But my master's—and truly on thee I depend,
To make it appear I my trust did defend."
     Heigho! *yea* thee and *nay* thee.

"So fire a few shots through my clothes, here and there,
To make it appear 'twas a desp'rate affair."—
So Jim he popped first through the skirt of his coat,
And then through his collar—quite close to his throat;
"Now one through my broadbrim," quoth Ephraim, "I vote."
     Heigho! *yea* thee and *nay* thee.

"I have but a brace," said bold Jim, "and they're spent,
And I won't load again for a make-believe rent."—
"Then"—said Ephraim, producing his pistols—"just give
My five hundred pounds back—or as sure as you live
I'll make of your body a riddle or sieve."
     Heigho! *yea* thee and *nay* thee.

Jim Barlow was diddled—and, though he was game,
He saw Ephraim's pistol so deadly in aim,
That he gave up the gold, and he took to his scrapers;
And when the whole story got into the papers,
They said that *"the thieves were no match for the Quakers."*
                    Heigho! *yea* thee and *nay* thee.

BARNEY O'HEA

Now let me alone, though I know you won't,
        Impudent Barney O'Hea!
        It makes me outrageous
        When you're so contagious,
And you'd better look out for the stout Corney Creagh;
        For he is the boy
        That believes I'm his joy,
So you'd better behave yourself, Barney O'Hea!
        Impudent Barney,
        None of your blarney,
        Impudent Barney O'Hea!

I hope you're not going to Bandon Fair,
For indeed I'm not wanting to meet you there,
        Impudent Barney O'Hea!
        For Corney's at Cork,
        And my brother's at work,
And my mother sits spinning at home all the day,
        So no one will be there
        Of poor me to take care,
So I hope you won't follow me, Barney O'Hea!
        Impudent Barney,
        None of your blarney,
        Impudent Barney O'Hea!

But as I was walking up Bandon Street,
Just who do you think that myself should meet,
        But impudent Barney O'Hea!

[413]

He said I looked killin',
I called him a villain,
And bid him that minute get out of the way;
He said I was joking
And grinned so provoking,
I couldn't help laughing at Barney O'Hea!
Impudent Barney,
None of your blarney,
Impudent Barney O'Hea!

He knew 'twas all right when he saw me smile,
For he was the rogue up to ev'ry wile,
Impudent Barney O'Hea!
He coaxed me to choose him,
For if I'd refuse him
He swore he'd kill Corney the very next day;
So, for fear 'twould go further,
And just to save murther,
I think I must marry that madcap, O'Hea!
Bothering Barney,
'Tis he has the blarney
To make a girl Mistress O'Hea.

JOHN BANIM

(1798-1844)

HE SAID THAT HE WAS NOT OUR BROTHER

(Induced by some utterances of the Duke of Wellington)

HE SAID that he was not our brother—
The mongrel! he said what we knew.
No, Eire! our dear Island-mother,
He ne'er had his black blood from you!
And what though the milk of your bosom
Gave vigour and health to his veins?

[414]

He was but a foul foreign blossom,
　Blown hither to poison our plains!

He said that the sword had enslaved us—
　That still at its point we must kneel.
The liar!—though often it braved us,
　We cross'd it with hardier steel!
This witness his Richard—our vassal!
　His Essex—whose plumes we trod down!
His Willy—whose peerless sword-tassel
　We tarnish'd at Limerick town!

No! falsehood and feud were our evils,
　While force not a fetter could twine.
Come Northmen—come Normans—come Devils!
　We give them our *Sparth* to the chine!
And if once again he would try us,
　To the music of trumpet and drum,
And no traitor among us or nigh us—
　Let him come, the Brigand! let him come!

GERALD GRIFFIN
(1803-1840)

AILEEN AROON

WHEN, like the early rose,
　　　Aileen aroon!
Beauty in childhood blows,
　　　Aileen aroon!
When, like a diadem,
Buds blush around the stem,
Which is the fairest gem?
　　　Aileen aroon!

Is it the laughing eye?
　　　Aileen aroon!

[415]

Is it the timid sigh?
       Aileen aroon!
Is it the tender tone,
Soft as the stringed harp's moan?
Oh, it is truth alone,
       Aileen aroon!

When, like the rising day,
       Aileen aroon!
Love sends his early ray,
       Aileen aroon!
What makes his dawning glow
Changeless through joy or woe?
Only the constant know,
       Aileen aroon!

I know a valley fair,
       Aileen aroon!
I knew a cottage there,
       Aileen aroon!
Far in that valley's shade
I knew a gentle maid,
Flower of the hazel glade,
       Aileen aroon!

Who in the song so sweet,
       Aileen aroon!
Who in the dance so sweet,
       Aileen aroon!
Dear were her charms to me,
Dearer her laughter free,
Dearest her constancy,
       Aileen aroon!

Were she no longer true,
       Aileen aroon!
What should her lover do?
       Aileen aroon!

[416]

Fly with his broken chain
Far o'er the sounding main,
Never to love again,
     Aileen aroon!

Youth must with time decay,
     Aileen aroon!
Beauty must fade away,
     Aileen aroon!
Castles are sacked in war,
Chieftains are scattered far,
Truth is a fixed star,
     Aileen aroon!

(*Cf. p. 117*)

I LOVE MY LOVE IN THE MORNING

I LOVE my love in the morning,
  For she like morn is fair—
Her blushing cheek, its crimson streak,
  It clouds her golden hair.
Her glance, its beam, so soft and kind;
  Her tears, its dewy showers;
And her voice, the tender whispering wind
  That stirs the early bowers.

I love my love in the morning,
  I love my love at noon,
For she is bright as the lord of light,
  Yet mild as autumn's moon:
Her beauty is my bosom's sun,
  Her faith my fostering shade,
And I will love my darling one,
  Till even the sun shall fade.

I love my love in the morning,
  I love my love at even;

Her smile's soft play is like the ray
That lights the western heaven:
I loved her when the sun was high,
I loved her when he rose;
But best of all when evening's sigh
Was murmuring at its close.

SLEEP THAT LIKE THE COUCHÉD DOVE

SLEEP, that like the couchéd dove,
Broods o'er the weary eye,
Dreams that with soft heavings move
The heart of memory—
Labor's guerdon, golden rest,
Wrap thee in its downy vest;
Fall like comfort on thy brain,
And sing the hush-song to thy pain!

Far from thee be startling fears,
And dreams the guilty dream;
No banshee scare thy drowsy ears
With her ill-omened scream.
But tones of fairy minstrelsy
Float like the ghosts of sound o'er thee,
Soft as the chapel's distant bell,
And lull thee to a sweet farewell.

Ye, for whom the ashy hearth
The fearful housewife clears—
Ye, whose tiny sounds of mirth
The nighted carman hears—
Ye, whose pigmy hammers make
The wonderers of the cottage wake—
Noiseless be your airy flight,
Silent as the still moonlight.

Silent go and harmless come,
  Fairies of the stream—
Ye, who love the winter gloom,
  Or the gay moonbeam—
Hither bring your drowsy store,
Gathered from the bright lusmore,[1]
Shake o'er temples—soft and deep—
The comfort of the poor man's sleep.

LINES ADDRESSED TO A SEAGULL

WHITE bird of the tempest! oh, beautiful thing,
With the bosom of snow, and the motionless wing;
Now sweeping the billow, now floating on high,
Now bathing thy plumes in the light of the sky;
Now poising o'er ocean thy delicate form,
Now breasting the surge with thy bosom so warm;
Now darting aloft, with a heavenly scorn,
Now shooting along, like a ray of the morn;
Now lost in the folds of the cloud-curtained dome,
Now floating abroad like a flake of the foam;
Now silently poised o'er the war of the main,
Like the spirit of charity brooding o'er pain;
Now gliding with pinion, all silently furled,
Like an angel descending to comfort the world!
Thou seem'st to my spirit—as upward I gaze,
And see thee, now clothed in mellowest rays,
Now lost in the storm-driven vapors that fly
Like hosts that are routed across the broad sky—
Like a pure spirit, true to its virtue and faith
'Mid the tempests of nature, of passion, and death!

Rise! beautiful emblem of purity! rise
On the sweet winds of heaven, to thine own brilliant skies,
Still higher! still higher! till lost to our sight,

[1] Fairy finger plant.

[419]

Thou hidest thy wings in a mantle of light;
And I think how a pure spirit gazing on thee
Must long for the moment—the joyous and free—
When the soul, disembodied from nature, shall spring,
Unfettered, at once to her Maker and King;
When the bright day of service and suffering past,
Shapes fairer than thine shall shine round her at last,
While the standard of battle triumphantly furled,
She smiles like a victor, serene on the world!

GONE! GONE! FOREVER GONE

GONE, gone, forever gone
   Are the hopes I cherished,
Changed like the sunny dawn,
   In sudden showers perished.

Withered is the early flower,
   Like a bright lake broken,
Faded like a happy hour,
   Or Love's secret spoken.

Life! what a cheat art thou!
   On youthful fancy stealing,
A prodigal in promise now;
   A miser in fulfilling!

WAR SONG OF O'DRISCOL

FROM the shieling that stands by the lone mountain river,
Hurry, hurry down with the axe and the quiver;
From the deep-seated Coom, from the storm-beaten highland,
Hurry, hurry down to the shores of your island.
     Hurry down, hurry down!
     Hurry, hurry down to the shores of your island.

Galloglach and Kern, hurry down to the sea—
There the hungry Raven's beak is gaping for a prey;
Farrah! to the onset! Farrah! to the shore!
Feast him with the pirate's flesh, the bird of gloom and gore!
       Hurry down, hurry down!
       Hurry, etc.

Hurry, for the slaves of Bel are mustering to meet ye;
Hurry by the beaten cliff, the Nordman longs to greet ye;
Hurry from the mountain! hurry, hurry from the plain!
Welcome him, and never let him leave our land again!
       Hurry down, hurry down!
       Hurry, etc.

On the land a sulky wolf, and in the sea a shark,
Hew the ruffian spoiler down, and burn his gory bark!
Slayer of the unresisting! ravager profane!
Leave the White sea-tyrant's limbs to moulder on the plain.
       Hurry down, hurry down!
       Hurry, hurry down to the shores of your island.

TO THE BLESSED VIRGIN MARY

As THE mute nightingale in closest groves
   Lies hid at noon, but when day's piercing eye
   Is locked in night, with full heart beating high,
Poureth her plain song o'er the light she loves,
So, Virgin, ever pure and ever blest,
   Moon of religion, from whose radiant face,
   Reflected, streams the light of heavenly grace
On broken hearts, by contrite thoughts oppressed—
So, Mary, they who justly feel the weight
   Of Heaven's offended majesty, implore
   Thy reconciling aid, with suppliant knee.
Of sinful man, O sinless Advocate!
   To thee they turn, nor him the less adore;
   'Tis still *his* light they love, less dreadful seen in thee.

[421]

KNOW YE NOT THAT LOVELY RIVER

(Air: "Roy's Wife of Aldivallask")

Know ye not that lovely river?
Know ye not that smiling river?
    Whose gentle flood,
    By cliff and wood,
With wildering sound goes winding ever.
    Oh! often yet with feeling strong,
On that dear stream my memory ponders,
    And still I prize its murmuring song,
For by my childhood's home it wanders.
                    Know ye not that lovely river?

There's music in each wind that flows
    Within our native woodland breathing;
There's beauty in each flower that blows
    Around our native woodland wreathing.
The memory of the brightest joys
    In childhood's happy morn that found us,
Is dearer than the richest toys
    The present vainly sheds around us.
                    Know ye not that lovely river?

Oh, sister! when 'mid doubts and fears,
    That haunt life's onward journey ever,
I turn to those departed years,
    And that beloved and lonely river;
With sinking mind and bosom riven,
    And heart with lonely anguish aching;
It needs my long-taught hope in heaven
    To keep this weary heart from breaking!
                    Know ye not that lovely river?

JAMES CLARENCE MANGAN
(1803-1849)

THE NAMELESS ONE

Roll forth, my song, like the rushing river
  That sweeps along to the mighty sea;
God will inspire me while I deliver
      My soul of thee!

Tell thou the world, when my bones lie whitening
  Amid the lost homes of youth and eld,
That there was once one whose veins ran lightning
      No eye beheld.

Tell how his boyhood was one drear night-hour,
  How shone for *him*, through his griefs and gloom,
No star of all Heaven sends to light our
      Path to the tomb.

Roll on, my song, and to after ages
  Tell how, disdaining all earth can give,
He would have taught men, from Wisdom's pages,
      The way to live.

And tell how trampled, derided, hated,
  And worn by weakness, disease, and wrong,
He fled for shelter to God, who mated
      His soul with song—

With song which alway, sublime or vapid,
  Flowed like a rill in the morning-beam,
Perchance not deep, but intense and rapid—
      A mountain stream.

Tell how this Nameless, condemned for years long
  To herd with demons from Hell beneath,

Saw things that made him, with groans and tears, long
        For even death.

Go on to tell how, with genius wasted,
    Betrayed in friendship, befooled in love,
With spirit shipwrecked, and young hopes blasted,
        He still, still strove.

Till, spent with toil, dreeing death for others,
    And some whose hands should have wrought for *him;*
(If children live not for sires and mothers),
        His mind grew dim.

And he fell far through that pit abysmal,
    The gulf and grave of Maginn and Burns,
And pawned his soul for the devil's dismal
        Stock of returns.

But yet redeemed it in days of darkness,
    And shapes and signs of the final wrath,
When death, in hideous and ghastly starkness,
        Stood on his path.

And tell how now, amid wreck and sorrow,
    And want, and sickness, and houseless nights,
He bides in calmness the silent morrow,
        That no ray lights.

And lives he still, then? Yes! Old and hoary
    At thirty-nine, from despair and woe,
He lives, enduring what future story
        Will never know.

Him grant a grave to, ye pitying noble,
    Deep in your bosoms! There let him dwell!
He, too, had tears for all souls in trouble,
        Here and in Hell.

GONE IN THE WIND

Mangan claimed this to be a translation from the German poet Friedrich
Ruckert. It is mostly Mangan—as are very many of his translations.

SOLOMON! where is thy throne? It is gone in the wind.
Babylon! where is thy might? It is gone in the wind.
Like the swift shadows of Noon, like the dreams of the Blind,
Vanish the glories and pomps of the earth in the wind.

Man! canst thou build upon aught in the pride of thy mind?
Wisdom will teach thee that nothing can tarry behind;
Though there be thousand bright actions embalmed and en-
        shrined,
Myriads and millions of brighter are snow in the wind.

Solomon! where is thy throne? It is gone in the wind.
Babylon! where is thy might? It is gone in the wind.
All that the genius of man hath achieved or designed
Waits but its hour to be dealt with as dust by the wind.

Say, what is Pleasure? A phantom, a mask undefined.
Science? An almond, whereof we can pierce but the rind.
Honor and Affluence? Firmans that Fortune hath signed
Only to glitter and pass on the wings of the wind.

Solomon! where is thy throne? It is gone in the wind.
Babylon! where is thy might? It is gone in the wind.
Who is the Fortunate? He who in anguish hath pined!
He shall rejoice when his relics are dust in the wind!

Mortal! be careful with what thy best hopes are entwined;
Woe to the miners for Truth—where the Lampless have mined!
Woe to the seekers on earth for—what none ever find!
They and their trust shall be scattered like leaves on the wind.

Solomon! where is thy throne? It is gone in the wind.
Babylon! where is thy might? It is gone in the wind.
Happy in death are they only whose hearts have consigned
All Earth's affections and longings and cares to the wind.

[425]

Pity, thou, reader! the madness of poor Humankind,
Raving of Knowledge,—and Satan so busy to blind!
Raving of Glory,—like me,—for the garlands I bind
(Garlands of song) are but gathered, and—strewn in the wind!

Solomon! where is thy throne? It is gone in the wind.
Babylon! where is thy might? It is gone in the wind.
I, Abul-Namez, must rest; for my fire hath declined,
And I hear voices from Hades like bells on the wind!

CEAN-SALLA

WEEP not the Brave Dead!
  Weep rather the Living—
    On them lies the curse
Of a Doom unforgiving!
Each dark hour that rolls,
    Shall the memories they nurse,
Like molten hot lead,
Burn into their souls
  A remorse long and sore!
    They have helped to enthral a
Great land evermore,
    They who fled from Cean-Salla!

Alas, for thee, slayer
  Of the kings of the Norsemen!
    Thou land of sharp swords,
And strong korns and swift horsemen!
  Land ringing with song!
    Land, whose abbots and lords,
Whose Heroic and Fair,
    Through centuries long,
Made each palace of thine
  A new western Walhalla—
Thus to die without sign
    On the field of Cean-Salla;

My ship cleaves the wave—
    I depart for Iberia—
        But, oh! with what grief,
        With how heavy and dreary a
        Sensation of ill!
I could welcome a grave:
    My career has been brief,
    But I bow to God's will!
Not if now all forlorn,
    In my green years, I fall, a
Lone exile, I mourn—
    But I mourn for Cean-Salla!

SHAPES AND SIGNS

I SEE black dragons mount the sky,
    I see earth yawn beneath my feet—
    I feel within the asp, the worm
That will not sleep and cannot die,
    Fair though may show the winding-sheet!
        I hear all night as through a storm
        Hoarse voices calling, calling
            My name upon the wind—
    All omens monstrous and appalling
        Affright my guilty mind.

I exult alone in one wild hour—
    That hour in which the red cup drowns
    The memories it anon renews
In ghastlier guise, in fiercer power—
    Then Fancy brings me golden crowns,
        And visions of all brilliant hues
        Lap my lost soul in gladness,
            Until I wake again,
        And the dark lava-fires of madness
            Once more sweep through my brain.

[427]

TO THE INGLEEZEE KHAFIR, CALLING HIMSELF
DJANN BOOL DJENKINZUN

(From the Persian)

Thus writeth Meer Djafrit—
   I hate thee, Djann Bool,
Worse than Marid or Afrit,
   Or corpse-eating Ghool
I hate thee like Sin,
   For thy mop-head of hair,
Thy snub nose and bald chin,
   And thy turkeycock air.
Thou vile Ferindjee!
   That thou thus shouldst disturb an
Old Moslim like me,
   With my Khizzilbash turban!
Old fogy like me,
   With my Khizzilbash turban!

I spit on thy clothing,
   That garb for baboons!
I eye with deep loathing
   Thy tight pantaloons!
I curse the cravat
   That encircles thy throat,
And thy cooking-pot hat,
   And thy swallow-tailed coat!
Go, hide thy thick sconce
   In some hovel suburban;
Or else don at once
   The red Moosleman turban.
Thou dog, don at once
   The grand Khizzilbash turban!

TWENTY GOLDEN YEARS AGO

O, THE rain, the weary, dreary rain,
  How it plashes on the window-sill!
Night, I guess too, must be on the wane,
  Strass and Gass around are grown so still.
Here I sit, with coffee in my cup—
  Ah! t'was rarely I beheld it flow
In the tavern where I loved to sup
  Twenty golden years ago!

Twenty years ago, alas!—but stay—
  On my life, 'tis half-past twelve o'clock!
After all, the hours *do* slip away—
  Come, here goes to burn another block!
For the night, or morn, is wet and cold;
  And my fire is dwindling rather low:—
I had fire enough, when young and bold
  Twenty golden years ago.

Dear! I don't feel well at all, somehow:
  Few in Weimar dream how bad I am;
Floods of tears grow common with me now,
  High-Dutch floods, that Reason cannot dam.
Doctors think I'll neither live nor thrive
  If I mope at home so—I don't know—
Am I living *now?* I *was* alive
  Twenty golden years ago.

Wifeless, friendless, flaggonless, alone,
  Not quite bookless, though, unless I choose,
Left with nought to do, except to groan,
  Not a soul to woo, except the muse—
O! this is hard for *me* to bear,
  Me, who whilome lived so much *en haut,*
Me, who broke all hearts like china-ware,
  Twenty golden years ago!

[429]

Perhaps 'tis better;—time's defacing waves,
    Long have quenched the radiance of my brow—
They who curse me nightly from their graves,
    Scarce could love me were they living now;
But my loneliness hath darker ills—
    Such dun duns as Conscience, Thought & Co.,
Awful Gorgons! worse than tailors' bills
    Twenty golden years ago!

Did I paint a fifth of what I feel,
    O, how plaintive you would ween I was!
But I won't, albeit I have a deal
    More to wail about than Kerner has!
Kerner's tears are wept for withered flowers,
    Mine for withered hopes, my scroll of woe
Dates, alas! from youth's deserted bowers,
    Twenty golden years ago!

Yet, may Deutschland's bardlings flourish long,
    Me, I tweak no beak among them;—hawks
Must not pounce on hawks: besides, in song
    I could once beat all of them by chalks.
Though you find me as I near my goal,
    Sentimentalizing like Rousseau,
O! I had a grand Byronian soul
    Twenty golden years ago!

Tick-tick, tick-tick!—not a sound save Time's,
    And the windgust as it drives the rain—
Tortured torturer of reluctant rhymes,
    Go to bed, and rest thine aching brain!
Sleep!—no more the dupe of hopes or schemes;
    Soon thou sleepest where the thistles blow—
Curious anticlimax to thy dreams
    Twenty golden years ago!

FRANCIS S. MAHONY (FATHER PROUT)
(1804-1866)

A PANEGYRIC ON GEESE

I HATE to sing your hackneyed birds—
  So, doves and swans, a truce!
Your nests have been too often stirred;
My hero shall be—in a word—
        A goose.

The nightingale, or else "bulbul,"
  By Tommy Moore let loose,
Is grown intolerably dull—
I from the feathered nation cull
        A goose.

Can roasted Philomel a liver
  Fit for a pie produce?
Fat pies that on the Rhine's sweet river
Fair Strasburg bakes. Pray who's the giver?
        A goose!

An ortolan is good to eat,
  A partridge is of use;
But they are scarce—whereas you meet
At Paris, ay, in every street,
        A goose!

When tired of war the Greeks became,
  They pitched Troy to the deuce;
Ulysses, then, was not to blame
For teaching them the noble "game
        Of goose."

May Jupiter and Bonaparte,
  Of thunder less profuse,

Suffer their eagles to depart,
Encourage peace, and take to heart
                            A goose.

THE RED-BREAST OF AQUITANIA

(A Humble Ballad)

"Are not two sparrows sold for a farthing? yet not one of them shall fall
to the ground without your Father." St. Matthew, x. 29.
"Gallos ab Aquitanis Garumna flumen." Julius Caesar.
"Sermons in stones, and good in every thing." Shakespeare
"Genius, left to shiver
On the bank, 'tis said,
Died of that cold river." Tom Moore

River trip
from Tou-
louse to
Bordeaux.
Thermome-
ter at 0.
Snow 1 foot
and a half
deep. Use
of wooden
shoes.

OH, 'TWAS bitter cold
As our steamboat rolled
Down the pathway old
    Of the deep Garonne,—
And the peasant lank,
While his *sabot* sank
In the snow-clad bank,
    Saw it roll on, on.

Ye Gascon
farmer hieth
to his cot-
tage, and
drinketh a
flaggonne.

And he hied him home
To his *toit de chaume;*
And for those who roam
    On the broad bleak flood
Cared he? Not a thought;
For his beldame brought
His wine-flask fraught
    With the grape's red blood.

He warmeth
his cold
shins at a
wooden fire.
Good b'ye to
him.

And the wood-block blaze
Fed his vacant gaze
As we trod the maze
    Of the river down.
Soon we left behind

[432]

On the frozen wind
All farther mind
Of that vacant clown.

But there came anon,
As we journeyed on
Down the deep Garonne,
An acquaintancy,
Which we deemed, I count,
Of more high amount,
For it oped the fount
Of sweet sympathy.

'Twas a stranger dressed
In a downy vest,
'Twas a wee Red-breast
(Not an "Albatross"),
But a wanderer meek,
Who fain would seek
O'er the bosom bleak
Of that flood to cross.

And we watched him oft
As he soared aloft
On his pinions soft,
Poor wee weak thing,
And we soon could mark
That he sought our bark,
As a resting ark
For his weary wing.

But the bark, fire-fed,
On her pathway sped,
And shot far ahead
Of the tiny bird,
And quicker in the van
Her swift wheels ran,

[433]

As the quickening fan
  Of his winglets stirred.

Ye byrde is led a wilde goose chace adown ye river.

Vain, vain pursuit!
Toil without fruit!
For his forkéd foot
  Shall not anchor there,
Though the boat meanwhile
Down the stream beguile
For a bootless mile
  The poor child of air!

Symptomes of fatigue. 'Tis melancholie to fall between 2 stools.

And 'twas plain at last
He was flagging fast,
That his hour had past
  In that effort vain;
Far from either bank,
Sans a saving plank,
Slow, slow he sank,
  Nor uprose again.

Mort of ye birde.

And the cheerless wave
Just one ripple gave
As it oped him a grave
  In its bosom cold,
And he sank alone,
With a feeble moan,
In that deep Garonne,
  And then all was told.

Ye old man at ye helm weepeth for a soune lost in ye bay of Biscaye.

But our pilot gray
Wiped a tear away—
In the broad Biscaye
  He had lost his boy!
That sight brought back
On its furrowed track
The remembered wreck
  Of long-perished joy.

[434]

Condole-
ance of ye
ladyes; eke
of le chasseur
d'infanterie
légére.

And the tear half hid
In soft Beauty's lid
Stole forth unbid
    For that red-breast bird;—
And the feeling crept,—
For a Warrior wept;
And the silence kept
    Found no fitting word.

Olde Father
Proutte
sadly mo-
ralizeth
anent ye
birde.

But *I* mused alone,
For I thought of one
Whom I well had known
    In my earlier days,
Of a gentle mind,
Of a soul refined,
Of deserts designed
    For the Palm of Praise.

And well would it seem
That o'er Life's dark stream,
Easy task for him
    In his flight of Fame,
Was the Skyward Path
O'er the billow's wrath,
That for Genius hath
    Ever been the same.

And I saw him soar
From the morning shore,
While his fresh wings bore
    Him athwart the tide,
Soon with powers unspent
As he forward went,
His wings he had bent
    On the sought-for side.

A newe ob-
ject calleth
his eye from

But while thus he flew,
Lo! a vision new

[435]

Caught his wayward view
  With a semblance fair,
And that new-found wooer
Could, alas! allure
From his pathway sure
  The bright child of air.

For he turned aside,
And adown the tide
For a brief hour plied
  His yet unspent force.
And to gain that goal
Gave the powers of soul
Which, unwasted, whole,
  Had achieved his course.

A bright Spirit, young,
Unwept, unsung,
Sank thus among
  The drifts of the stream;
Not a record left,—
Of renown bereft,
By thy cruel theft,
  O DELUSIVE DREAM!

L'ENVOY TO W. L. H. AINSWORTH, ESQ.

Whilome, author of the Admirable "Crichton," subsequent chronicler of
"Jack Sheppard"

Thus sadly I thought
As that bird unsought
The remembrance brought
  Of thy bright day;
And I penned full soon
This Dirge, while the moon
On the broad Garonne
  Shed a wintry ray.

[436]

THE SHANDON BELLS

Sabbata pango
Funera plango
Solemnia clango

Inscription on an old bell.

WITH deep affection
And recollection
I often think of
  Those Shandon bells,
Whose sounds so wild would,
In the days of childhood,
Fling round my cradle
  Their magic spells.
On this I ponder
Where'er I wander,
And thus grow fonder,
  Sweet Cork, of thee,
With thy bells of Shandon,
That sound so grand on
The pleasant waters
  Of the river Lee.

I've heard bells chiming
Full many a clime in,
Tolling sublime in
  Cathedral shrine,
While at a glib rate
Brass tongues would vibrate—
But all their music
  Spoke naught like thine;
For memory dwelling
On each proud swelling
Of the belfry knelling
  Its bold notes free,
Made the bells of Shandon
Sound far more grand on

[437]

The pleasant waters
    Of the river Lee.

I've heard bells tolling
Old "Adrian's Mole" in
Their thunder rolling
    From the Vatican,
And cymbals glorious
Swinging uproarious
In the gorgeous turrets
    Of Notre Dame;
But thy sounds were sweeter
Than the dome of Peter
Flings o'er the Tiber
    Pealing solemnly;—
Oh! the bells of Shandon
Sound far more grand on
The pleasant waters
    Of the river Lee.

There's a bell in Moscow,
While a tower and kiosk o!
In Saint Sophia
    The Turkman gets,
And loud in air
Calls men to prayer
From the tapering summit
    Of tall minarets.
Such empty phantom
I freely grant them;
But there is an anthem
    More dear to me,—
'Tis the bells of Shandon
That sound so grand on
The pleasant waters
    Of the river Lee.

EDWARD WALSH
(1805-1850)

THE FAIRY NURSE

Sweet babe! a golden cradle holds thee,
And soft the snow-white fleece enfolds thee;
In airy bower I'll watch thy sleeping,
Where branchy trees to the breeze are sweeping.
    Shuheen, sho, lulo lo!

When mothers languish broken-hearted,
When young wives are from husbands parted,
Ah! little think the keeners lonely,
They weep some time-worn fairy only.
    Shuheen, sho, lulo lo!

Within our magic halls of brightness,
Trips many a foot of snowy whiteness;
Stolen maidens, queens of fairy—
And kings and chiefs a slaugh-shee airy.
    Shuheen, sho, lulo lo!

Rest thee, babe! I love thee dearly,
And as thy mortal mother nearly;
Ours is the swiftest steed and proudest,
That moves where the tramp of the host is loudest.
    Shuheen, sho, lulo lo!

Rest thee, babe! for soon thy slumbers
Shall flee at the magic koelshie's numbers;
In airy bower I'll watch thy sleeping,
Where branchy trees to the breeze are sweeping.
    Shuheen, sho, lulo lo!

[439]

CHARLES JAMES LEVER
(1806-1872)

BAD LUCK TO THIS MARCHING

BAD luck to this marching,
Pipeclaying and starching;
How neat one must be to be killed by the French!
I'm sick of parading,
Through wet and cold wading,
Or standing all night to be shot in a trench.
To the tune of a fife
They dispose of your life,
You surrender your soul to some illigant lilt;
Now I like "Garryowen"
When I hear it at home,
But it's not half so sweet when you're going to be kilt.

Then, though up late and early
Our pay comes so rarely,
The devil a farthing we've ever to spare;
They say some disaster
Befell the paymaster;
On my conscience I think that the money's not there.
And, just think, what a blunder,
They won't let us plunder,
While the convents invite us to rob them, 'tis clear;
Though there isn't a village
But cries, "Come and pillage!"
Yet we leave all the mutton behind for Mounseer.

Like a sailor that's nigh land,
I long for that Island
Where even the kisses we steal if we please;
Where it is no disgrace
If you don't wash your face,

And you've nothing to do but to stand at your ease.
With no sergeant to abuse us,
We fight to amuse us,
Sure it's better beat Christians than kick a baboon;
How I'd dance like a fairy
To see ould Dunleary,
And think twice ere I'd leave it to be a dragoon!

THE MAN FOR GALWAY

To DRINK a toast,
A proctor roast,
    Or bailiff, as the case is;
To kiss your wife,
Or take your life
    At ten or fifteen paces;
To keep game cocks, to hunt the fox,
    To drink in punch the Solway,
With debts galore, but fun far more;
    Oh, that's "the man for Galway."

Chorus:
    With debts galore, but fun far more;
        Oh, that's "the man for Galway."

The King of Oude
Is mighty proud,
    And so were onest the Caysars;
But ould Giles Eyre
Would make them stare,
    Av he had them with the Blazers.
To the divil I fling Ould Runjeet Sing,
    He's only a prince in a small way,
And knows nothing at all of a six-foot wall;
    Oh, he'd never "do for Galway."
        With debts galore, *etc.*

[441]

Ye think the Blakes
Are no "great shakes;"
 They're all his blood relations;
And the Bodkins sneeze
At the grim Chinese,
 For they come from the Phenaycians.
So fill to the brim, and here's to him
 Who'd drink in punch the Solway;
With debts galore, but fun far more;
 Oh! that's "the man for Galway."

   Chorus:
  With debts galore, but fun far more;
  Oh, that's "the man for Galway."

IT'S LITTLE FOR GLORY I CARE

IT's little for glory I care;
 Sure ambition is only a fable;
I'd as soon be myself as Lord Mayor,
 With lashins of drink on the table.
I like to lie down in the sun,
 And drame when my faytures is scorchin',
That when I'm too ould for more fun,
 Why, I'll marry a wife with a fortune.

And in winter, with bacon and eggs,
 And a place at the turf-fire basking,
Sip my punch as I roasted my legs,
 Oh! the devil a more I'd be asking.
For I haven't a jaynius for work,—
 It was never the gift of the Bradies,—
But I'd make a most illigant Turk,
 For I'm fond of tobacco and ladies.

[442]

LARRY M'HALE

OH! LARRY M'HALE he had little to fear,
  And never could want when the crops didn't fail;
He'd a house and demesne and eight hundred a year,
  And the heart for to spend it, had Larry M'Hale!

The soul of a party,—the life of a feast,
  And an illigant song he could sing, I'll be bail;
He would ride with the rector, and drink with the priest,
  Oh! the broth of a boy was old Larry M'Hale.

It's little he cared for the judge or recorder,
  His house was as big and as strong as a jail;
With a cruel four-pounder, he kept all in great order,
  He'd murder the country, would Larry M'Hale.

He'd a blunderbuss too; of horse-pistols a pair;
  But his favorite weapon was always a flail:
I wish you could see how he'd empty a fair,
  For he handled it nately, did Larry M'Hale.

His ancéstors were kings before Moses was born;
  His mother descended from great Grana Uaile;
He laughed all the Blakes and the Frenches to scorn:
  They were mushrooms compared to old Larry M'Hale.

He sat down every day to a beautiful dinner,
  With cousins and uncles enough for a tail;
And, though loaded with debt, oh! the devil a thinner
  Could law or the sheriff make Larry M'Hale.

With a larder supplied, and a cellar well-stored,
  None lived half so well, from Fair-Head to Kinsale,
And he piously said, "I've a plentiful board,
  And the Lord he is good to old Larry M'Hale."

[443]

So fill up your glass, and a high bumper give him,
It's little we'd care for the tithes or repale;
For ould Erin would be a fine country to live in,
If we only had plenty, like Larry M'Hale.

SAMUEL FERGUSON
(1810-1886)

LAMENT FOR THE DEATH OF THOMAS DAVIS

I WALKED through Ballinderry in the springtime,
When the bud was on the tree,
And I said, in every fresh-ploughed field beholding
The sowers striding free,
Scattering broadcast for the corn in golden plenty,
On the quick, seed-clasping soil,
"Even such this day among the fresh-stirred hearts of Erin,
Thomas Davis, is thy toil!"

I sat by Ballyshannon in the summer,
And saw the salmon leap,
And I said, as I beheld the gallant creatures
Spring glittering from the deep,
"Through the spray and through the prone heaps striving on-
ward
To the calm clear streams above,
So seekest thou thy native founts of freedom, Thomas Davis,
In thy brightness of strength and love!"

I stood on Derrybawn in the autumn,
I heard the eagle call,
With a clangorous cry of wrath and lamentation
That filled the wide mountain hall,
O'er the bare, deserted place of his plundered eyrie,
And I said, as he screamed and soared,

"So callest thou, thou wrathful-soaring Thomas Davis,
  For a nation's rights restored."

And alas! to think but now that thou art lying,
  Dear Davis, dead at thy mother's knee,
And I, no mother near, on my own sick-bed,
  That face on earth shall never see.
I may lie and try to feel that I am not dreaming,
  I may lie and try to say, "Thy Will be done"—
But a hundred such as I will never comfort Erin
  For the loss of that noble son.

Young husbandman of Erin's fruitful seed-time,
  In the fresh track of danger's plough!
Who will walk the heavy, toilsome, perilous furrow,
  Girt with freedom's seed-sheets now?
Who will vanish with the wholesome crop of knowledge,
  The flaunting weed and the bitter thorn,
Now that thou thyself art but a seed for hopeful planting
  Against the resurrection morn?

Young salmon of the flood-time of freedom
  That swells round Erin's shore,
Thou wilt leap against their loud, oppressive torrents
  Of bigotry and hate no more!
Drawn downward by their prone material instinct,
  Let them thunder on their rocks, and foam;
Thou hast leaped, aspiring soul, to founts beyond their raging,
  Where troubled waters never come.

But I grieve not, eagle of the empty eyrie,
  That thy wrathful cry is still,
And that the songs alone of peaceful mourners
  Are heard to-day on Erin's hill.
Better far if brothers' war be destined for us—
  God avert that horrid day, I pray!—
That ere our hands be stained with slaughter fratricidal,
  Thy warm heart should be cold in clay.

[445]

But my trust is strong in God who made us brothers,
   That He will not suffer these right hands,
Which thou hast joined in holier rites than wedlock,
   To draw opposing brands.
O many a tuneful tongue that thou madest vocal,
   Would lie cold and silent then,
And songless long once more should often-widowed Erin,
   Mourn the loss of her brave young men.

O brave young men, my love, my pride, my promise,
   'Tis on you my hopes are set,
In manliness, in kindliness, in justice,
   To make Erin a nation yet;
Self-respecting, self-relying, self-advancing,
   In union or in severance, free and strong,
And if God grant this, then, under God, to Thomas Davis,
   Let the greater praise belong!

THE WELSHMEN OF TIRAWLEY

Tirawley, an ancient Barony in County Mayo, Ireland. Several Welsh families, associates in the invasion of Strongbow, settled in the west of Ireland. Of these the principal, whose names have been preserved, were the Walshes, Joyces, Heils (now MacHale), Lawlesses, Tomlyns, Lynotts, and Barretts.

SCORNA BOY, the Barretts' bailiff, lewd and lame,
To lift the Lynotts' taxes when he came,
Rudely drew a young maid to him;
Then the Lynotts rose and slew him,
And in Tubber-na-Scorney threw him—
         Small your blame,
         Sons of Lynott!
Sing the vengeance of the Welshmen of Tirawley.

Then the Barretts to the Lynotts gave a choice,
Saying, "Hear, ye murderous brood, men and boys,

For this deed to-day ye lose
Sight or manhood: say and choose
Which ye keep and which refuse;
        And rejoice
        That our mercy
Leaves you living for a warning to Tirawley."

Then the little boys of the Lynotts, weeping, said,
"Only leave us our eyesight in our head."
But the bearded Lynotts then
Made answer back again—
"Take our eyes, but leave us men,
        Alive or dead,
        Sons of Wattin!"
Sing the vengeance of the Welshmen of Tirawley.

So the Barretts, with sewing-needles sharp and smooth,
Let the light out of the eyes of every youth,
And of every bearded man
Of the broken Lynott clan;
Then their darken'd faces wan
        Turning south
        To the river—
Sing the vengeance of the Welshmen of Tirawley.

O'er the slippery stepping-stones of Clochan-na-n'all
They drove them, laughing loud at every fall,
As their wandering footsteps dark
Failed to reach the slippery mark,
And the swift stream swallowed, stark,
        One and all,
        As they stumbled—
From the vengeance of the Welshmen of Tirawley.

Of all the blinded Lynotts one alone
Walked erect from stepping-stone to stone:
So back again they brought you,
And a second time they wrought you

[447]

With their needles; but never got you
          Once to groan,
          Emon Lynott,
For the vengeance of the Welshmen of Tirawley.

But with prompt-projected footsteps sure as ever,
Emon Lynott again crossed the river,
Though Duvowen was rising fast,
And the shaking stones o'ercast
By cold floods boiling past;
          Yet you never,
          Emon Lynott,
Faltered once before your foemen of Tirawley!

But, turning on Ballintubber bank, you stood,
And the Barretts thus bespoke o'er the flood—
"Oh, ye foolish sons of Wattin,
Small amends are these you've gotten,
For, while Scorna Boy lies rotten,
          I am good
          For vengeance!"
Sing the vengeance of the Welshmen of Tirawley.

"For 'tis neither in eye nor eyesight that a man
Bears the fortunes of himself or of his clan,
But in the manly mind,
And in loins with vengeance lined,
That your needles could never find,
          Though they ran
          Through my heart-strings!"
Sing the vengeance of the Welshmen of Tirawley.

"But, little your women's needles do I reck:
For the night from heaven never fell so black,
But Tirawley, and abroad
From the Moy to Cuan-an-fod,[1]

[1] Moy River to Blacksod Haven.

I could walk it, every sod,
                Path and track,
                Ford and togher,
Seeking vengeance on you, Barretts of Tirawley.

"The night when Dathy O'Dowda broke your camp,
What Barrett among you was it held the lamp—
Showed the way to those two feet,
When, through wintry wind and sleet,
I guided your blind retreat,
                In the swamp
                Of Beäl-an-asa?
O ye vengeance-destined ingrates of Tirawley!"

So, leaving loud-shriek-echoing Garranard,
The Lynott, like a red dog hunted hard,
With his wife and children seven,
'Mong the beasts and fowls of heaven,
In the hollows of Glen Nephin,
                Light-debarred,
                Made his dwelling,
Planning vengeance on the Barretts of Tirawley.

And ere the bright-orbed year its course had run,
On his brown round-knotted knee he nursed a son,
A child of light, with eyes
As clear as are the skies
In summer, when sunrise
                Has begun;
                So the Lynott
Nursed his vengeance on the Barretts of Tirawley.

And, as ever the bright boy grew in strength and size,
Made him perfect in each manly exercise,
The salmon in the flood,
The dun deer in the wood,

[449]

The eagle in the cloud
                To surprise
                On Ben Nephin,
Far above the foggy fields of Tirawley.

With the yellow-knotted spear-shaft, with the bow,
With the steel, prompt to deal shot and blow,
He taught him from year to year,
And trained him, without a peer,
For a perfect cavalier,
                Hoping so—
                Far his forethought—
For vengeance on the Barretts of Tirawley.

And, when mounted on his proud-bounding steed,
Emon Oge[1] sat a cavalier indeed;
Like the ear upon the wheat,
When winds in autumn beat
On the bending stems, his seat;
                And the speed
                Of his courser
Was the wind from Barna-na-gee[2] o'er Tirawley!

Now when fifteen sunny summers thus were spent
(He perfected in all accomplishment),
The Lynott said: "My child,
We are over-long exiled
From mankind in this wild—
                Time we went
                Through the mountain
To the countries lying over-against Tirawley."

So, out over mountain-moors, and mosses brown,
And green stream-gathering vales, they journeyed down;
Till, shining like a star,
Through the dusky gleams afar,

[1] Oge = son of.
[2] Gap of the Winds, a pass on the southern side of Mt. Nephin, on the road to Castlebar.

[450]

The bailey of Castlebar
     And the town
     Of Mac William
Rose bright before the wanderers of Tirawley.

"Look southward, my boy, and tell me, as we go,
What seest thou by the lock-head below."
"Oh, a stone-house, strong and great,
And a horse-host at the gate,
And their captain in armor of plate—
     Grand the show
     Great the glancing!
High the heroes of this land below Tirawley!

"And a beautiful woman-chief by his side,
Yellow gold on all her gown-sleeves wide;
And in her hand a pearl
Of a young, little, fair-haired girl."
Said the Lynott, "It is the Earl!
     Let us ride
     To his presence!"
And before him came the exiles of Tirawley.

"God save thee, Mac William," the Lynott thus began;
"God save all here besides of this clan;
For gossips dear to me
Are all in company—
For in these four bones ye see
     A kindly man
     Of the Britons—
Emon Lynott of Garranard of Tirawley.

"And hither, as kindly gossip-law allows,
I come to claim a scion of thy house
To foster; for thy race
Since William Conquer's[1] days,

[1] I.e., William Fitz Adelm de Burgho, who conquered Connaught.

[451]

Have ever been wont to place,
        With some spouse
        Of a Briton,
A Mac William Oge, to foster in Tirawley.

"And to show thee in what sort our youth are taught,
I have hither to thy home of valor brought
This one son of my age,
For a sample and a pledge
For equal tutelage,
        In right thought,
        Word, and action,
Of whatever son ye give into Tirawley."

When Mac William beheld the brave boy ride and run,
Saw the spear-shaft from his white shoulder spun—
With a sigh, and with a smile,
He said; "I would give the spoil
Of a county, that Tibbot Moyle,
        My own son,
        Were accomplished
Like this branch of the kindly Britons of Tirawley."

When the Lady Mac William she heard him speak,
And saw the ruddy roses on his cheek,
She said; "I would give a purse
Of red gold to the nurse
That would rear my Tibbot no worse;
        But I seek
        Hitherto vainly—
Heaven grant that I now have found her in Tirawley!"

So they said to the Lynott; "Here, take our bird!
And as pledge for the keeping of thy word,
Let this scion here remain
Till thou comest back again:
Meanwhile the fitting train
        Of a lord

[452]

Shall attend thee
With the lordly heir of Connaught into Tirawley."

So back to strong-throng-gathering Garranard,
Like a lord of the country with his guard,
Came the Lynott, before them all.
Once again over Clochan-na-n'all,
Steady-striding, erect, and tall,
      And his ward
      On his shoulders;
To the wonder of the Welshmen of Tirawley.

Then a diligent foster-father you would deem
The Lynott, teaching Tibbot, by mead and stream,
To cast the spear, to ride,
To stem the rushing tide,
With what feats of body beside
      Might beseem
      A Mac William,
Fostered free among the Welshmen of Tirawley.

But the lesson of hell he taught him in heart and mind;
For to what desire soever he inclined,
Of anger, lust, or pride,
He had it gratified,
Till he ranged the circle wide
      Of a blind
      Self-indulgence,
Ere he came to youthful manhood in Tirawley.

Then, even as when a hunter slips a hound,
Lynott loosed him—God's leashes all unbound—
In the pride of power and station,
And the strength of youthful passion,
On the daughters of thy nation,
      All around,
      Wattin Barrett!
Oh, the vengeance of the Welshmen of Tirawley!

[453]

Bitter grief and burning anger, rage and shame,
Filled the houses of the Barretts where'er he came;
Till the young men of the Bac
Drew by night upon his track,
And slew him at Cornassack—
        Small your blame,
        Sons of Wattin!
Sing the vengeance of the Welshmen of Tirawley.

Said the Lynott: "The day of my vengeance is drawing near,
The day for which, through many a long dark year,
I have toiled through grief and sin—
Call ye now the Brehons in,
And let the plea begin
        Over the bier
        Of Mac William,
For an eric[1] upon the Barretts of Tirawley.

Then the Brehons of Mac William Burke decreed
An eric upon Clan Barrett for the deed;
And the Lynott's share of the fine,
As foster-father, was nine
Ploughlands and nine score kine;
        But no need
        Had the Lynott,
Neither care, for land or cattle in Tirawley.

But rising, while all sat silent on the spot,
He said: "The law says—doth it not?—
If the foster-sire elect
His portion to reject,
He may then the right exact
        To applot
        The short eric."
"Tis the law," replied the Brehons of Tirawley.

[1] *The Eric* was the fine for maimings and homicides. In the old Brehon code if a
criminal were put to death for some unlawful act his family did not suffer materially
—they were given compensation in full.

[454]

Said the Lynott: "I once before had a choice
Proposed me, wherein law had little voice;
But now I choose, and say,
As lawfully I may,
I applot the mulct to-day;
        So rejoice
        In your ploughlands
And your cattle which I renounce throughout Tirawley.

"And thus I applot the mulct: I divide
The land throughout Clan Barrett on every side
Equally, that no place
May be without the face
Of a foe of Wattin's race—
        That the pride
        Of the Barretts
May be humbled hence forever throughout Tirawley.

"I adjudge a seat in every Barrett's hall
To Mac William: in every stable I give a stall
To Mac William: and, beside,
Whenever a Burke shall ride
Through Tirawley, I provide
        At his call
        Needful grooming,
Without charge from any hostler of Tirawley.

"Thus lawfully I avenge me for the throes
Ye lawlessly caused me and caused those
Unhappy shamefaced ones,
Who, their mothers expected once,
Would have been the sires of sons—
        O'er whose woes
        Often weeping,
I have groaned in my exile from Tirawley.

"I demand not of you your manhood; but I take—
For the Burkes will take it—your Freedom! for the sake

[455]

Of which all manhood's given,
And all good under heaven,
And, without which, better even
　　　Ye should make
　　　Yourselves barren,
Than see your children slaves throughout Tirawley!

"Neither take I your eyesight from you; as you took
Mine and ours: I would have you daily look
On one another's eyes,
When the strangers tyrannize
By your hearths, and blushes arise,
　　　That ye brook,
　　　Without vengeance,
The insults of troops of Tibbots throughout Tirawley!

"The vengeance I designed, now is done,
And the days of me and mine nearly run—
For, for this, I have broken faith,
Teaching him who lies beneath
This pall, to merit death:
　　　And my son
　　　To his father
Stands pledged for other teaching in Tirawley."

Said Mac William, "Father and son, hang them high!"
And the Lynott they hanged speedily;
But across the salt sea water,
To Scotland, with the daughter
Of Mac William—well you got her!—
　　　Did you fly,
　　　Edmund Lindsay,
The gentlest of all the Welshmen of Tirawley!

'Tis thus the ancient Ollaves of Erin tell
How, through lewdness and revenge, it befell
That the sons of William Conquer
Came over the sons of Wattin,

[456]

Throughout all the bounds and borders
Of the land of Auley Mac Fiachra;
Till the Saxon Oliver Cromwell,
And his valiant, Bible-guided,
Free heretics of Clan London
Coming in, in their succession,
Rooted out both Burke and Barrett,
And in their empty places
New stems of freedom planted,
With many a goodly sapling
Of manliness and virtue;
Which while their children cherish,
Kindly Irish of the Irish,
Neither Saxons nor Italians,
May the mighty God of Freedom
       Speed them well,
       Never taking
Further vengeance on his people of Tirawley.

THE FAIRY THORN

"GET up, our Anna dear, from the weary spinning-wheel;
  For your father's on the hill, and your mother is asleep:
Come up above the crags, and we'll dance a highland reel
  Around the fairy thorn on the steep."

At Anna Grace's door 'twas thus the maidens cried,
  Three merry maidens fair in kirtles of the green;
And Anna laid the rock and the weary wheel aside,
  The fairest of the four, I ween.

They're glancing through the glimmer of the quiet eve,
  Away in milky wavings of neck and ankle bare;
The heavy-sliding stream in its sleepy song they leave,
  And the crags in the ghostly air:

[457]

And linking hand and hand, and singing as they go,
   The maids along the hill-side have ta'en their fearless way,
Till they come to where the rowan-trees in lonely beauty grow
   Beside the Fairy Hawthorn gray.

The Hawthorn stands between the ashes tall and slim,
   Like matron with her twin grand-daughters at her knee;
The rowan-berries cluster o'er her low head gray and dim,
   In ruddy kisses sweet to see.

The merry maidens four have ranged them in a row,
   Between each lovely couple a stately rowan stem,
And away in mazes wavy, like skimming birds they go:
   Oh, never carolled bird like them!

But solemn is the silence of the silvery haze
   That drinks away their voices in echoless repose,
And dreamily the evening has stilled the haunted braes,
   And dreamier the gloaming grows.

And sinking one by one, like lark-notes from the sky
   When the falcon's shadow saileth across the open shaw,
Are hushed the maidens' voices, as cowering down they lie
   In the flutter of their sudden awe.

For, from the air above, and the grassy ground beneath,
   And from the mountain-ashes and the old white-thorn between,
A Power of faint enchantment doth through their beings breathe,
   And they sink down together on the green.

They sink together silent, and stealing side to side,
   They fling their lovely arms o'er their drooping necks so fair,
Then vainly strive again their naked arms to hide,
   For their shrinking necks again are bare.

Thus clasped and prostrate all, with their heads together
      bowed,
   Soft o'er their bosom's beating—the only human sound—
They hear the silky footsteps of the silent fairy crowd,
   Like a river in the air, gliding round.

No scream can any raise, nor prayer can any say,
   But wild, wild, the terror of the speechless three—
For they feel fair Anna Grace drawn silently away,
   By whom they dare not look to see.

They feel their tresses twine with her parting locks of gold,
   And the curls elastic falling, as her head withdraws;
They feel her sliding arms from their trancèd arms unfold,
   But they may not look to see the cause:

For heavy on their senses the faint enchantment lies
   Through all that night of anguish and perilous amaze;
And neither fear nor wonder can ope their quivering eyes,
   Or their limbs from the cold ground raise,

Till out of night the earth has rolled her dewy side,
   With every haunted mountain and streamy vale below;
When, as the mist dissolves in the yellow morning tide,
   The maidens' trance dissolveth so.

Then fly the ghastly three as swiftly as they may,
   And tell their tale of sorrow to anxious friends in vain—
They pined away and died within the year and day,
   And ne'er was Anna Grace seen again.

THE BURIAL OF KING CORMAC

"Cormac, son of Art, son of Con Cead-Catha, enjoyed the sovereignty of
Ireland for forty years, commencing A.D. 213. During the latter part of his
reign, he resided at Sletty on the Boyne, being, it is said, disqualified for
the occupation of Tara by the personal blemish he had sustained in the

[459]

loss of an eye. It was in the time of Cormac and his son Carbre, if we are to credit the Irish annals, that Finn, son of Comhal, and the Fenian heroes, celebrated by Ossian, flourished. Cormac has obtained the reputation of wisdom and learning, and appears justly entitled to the honour of having provoked the enmity of the Pagan priesthood, by declaring his faith in a God not made by hands of men."

"CROM CRUACH and his sub-gods twelve,"
    Said Cormac, "are but carven treene;
The axe that made them, haft or helve,
    Had worthier of our worship been.

"But He who made the tree to grow,
    And hid in earth the iron-stone,
And made the man with mind to know
    The axe's use, is God alone."

Anon to priests of Crom was brought—
    Where, girded in their service dread,
They minister'd on red Moy Slaught—
    Word of the words King Cormac said.

They loosed their curse against the king;
    They cursed him in his flesh and bones;
And daily in their mystic ring
    They turn'd the maledictive stones,

Till, where at meat the monarch sate,
    Amid the revel and the wine,
He choked upon the food he ate,
    At Sletty, southward of the Boyne.

High vaunted then the priestly throng,
    And far and wide they noised abroad
With trump and loud liturgic song
    The praise of their avenging God.

But ere the voice was wholly spent
    That priest and prince should still obey,

To awed attendants o'er him bent
 Great Cormac gather'd breath to say,—

"Spread not the beds of Brugh for me
 When restless death-bed's use is done:
But bury me at Rossnaree
 And face me to the rising sun.

"For all the kings who lie in Brugh
 Put trust in gods of wood and stone;
And 'twas at Ross that first I knew
 One, Unseen, who is God alone.

"His glory lightens from the east;
 His message soon shall reach our shore;
And idol-god, and cursing priest
 Shall plague us from Moy Slaught no more."

Dead Cormac on his bier they laid:—
 "He reign'd a king for forty years,
And shame it were," his captains said,
 "He lay not with his royal peers.

"His grandsire, Hundred-Battle, sleeps
 Serene in Brugh: and, all around,
Dead kings in stone sepulchral keeps
 Protect the sacred burial ground.

"What though a dying man should rave
 Of changes o'er the eastern sea?
In Brugh of Boyne shall be his grave,
 And not in noteless Rossnaree."

Then northward forth they bore the bier,
 And down from Sletty side they drew,
With horsemen and with charioteer,
 To cross the fords of Boyne to Brugh.

[461]

There came a breath of finer air
   That touch'd the Boyne with ruffling wings,
It stirr'd him in his sedgy lair
   And in his mossy moorland springs.

And as the burial train came down
   With dirge and savage dolorous shows,
Across their pathway, broad and brown
   The deep, full-hearted river rose;

From bank to bank through all his fords,
   'Neath blackening squalls he swell'd and boil'd;
And thrice the wondering gentile lords
   Essay'd to cross, and thrice recoil'd.

Then forth stepp'd grey-hair'd warriors four:
   They said, "Through angrier floods than these,
On link'd shields once our king we bore
   From Dread-Spear and the hosts of Deece.

"And long as loyal will holds good,
   And limbs respond with helpful thews,
Nor flood, nor fiend within the flood,
   Shall bar him of his burial dues."

With slanted necks they stoop'd to lift;
   They heaved him up to neck and chin;
And, pair and pair, with footsteps swift,
   Lock'd arm and shoulder, bore him in.

'Twas brave to see them leave the shore;
   To mark the deep'ning surges rise,
And fall subdued in foam before
   The tension of their striding thighs.

'Twas brave, when now a spear-cast out,
   Breast-high the battling surges ran;

For weight was great, and limbs were stout,
  And loyal man put trust in man.

But ere they reach'd the middle deep,
  Nor steadying weight of clay they bore,
Nor strain of sinewy limbs could keep
  Their feet beneath the swerving four.

And now they slide, and now they swim,
  And now, amid the blackening squall,
Grey locks afloat, with clutching grim,
  They plunge around the floating pall.

While, as a youth with practised spear
  Through justling crowds bears off the ring,
Boyne from their shoulders caught the bier
  And proudly bore away the king.

At morning, on the grassy marge
  Of Rossnaree, the corpse was found,
And shepherds at their early charge
  Entomb'd it in the peaceful ground.

A tranquil spot: a hopeful sound
  Comes from the ever youthful stream,
And still on daisied mead and mound
  The dawn delays with tenderer beam.

Round Cormac Spring renews her buds:
  In march perpetual by his side,
Down come the earth-fresh April floods,
  And up the sea-fresh salmon glide:

And life and time rejoicing run
  From age to age their wonted way;
But still he waits the risen Sun,
  For still 'tis only dawning Day.

ARTHUR GERALD GEOGHEGAN
(1810-1889)

AFTER AUGHRIM

Do you remember, long ago,
    Kathaleen?
When your lover whispered low,
"Shall I stay or shall I go,
    Kathaleen?"
And you answered proudly, "Go!
And join King James and strike a blow
    For the Green!"

Mavrone, your hair is white as snow,
    Kathaleen;
Your heart is sad and full of woe.
Do you repent you made him go,
    Kathaleen?
And quick you answer proudly, "No!
For better die with Sarsfield so
Than live a slave without a blow
    For the Green!"

CHARLES DAWSON SHANLY
(1811-1875)

THE WALKER OF THE SNOW

Speed on, speed on, good master!
  The camp lies far away;
We must cross the haunted valley
  Before the close of day.

[464]

How the snow-blight came upon me
   I will tell you as we go,—
The blight of the Shadow-hunter,
   Who walks the midnight snow.

To the cold December heaven
   Came the pale moon and the stars,
As the yellow sun was sinking
   Behind the purple bars.

The snow was deeply drifted
   Upon the ridges drear,
That lay for miles around me
   And the camp for which we steer.

'T was silent on the hillside,
   And by the solemn wood
No sound of life or motion
   To break the solitude,

Save the wailing of the moose-bird
   With a plaintive note and low,
And the skating of the red leaf
   Upon the frozen snow.

And said I,—"Though dark is falling,
   And far the camp must be,
Yet my heart it would be lightsome,
   If I had but company."

And then I sang and shouted,
   Keeping measure, as I sped,
To the harp-twang of the snow-shoe
   As it sprang beneath my tread;

Nor far into the valley
   Had I dipped upon my way,

When a dusky figure joined me,
 In a capuchon of gray,

Bending upon the snow-shoes,
 With a long and limber stride;
And I hailed the dusky stranger,
 As we travelled side by side.

But no token of communion
 Gave he by word or look,
And the fear-chill fell upon me
 At the crossing of the brook.

For I saw by the sickly moonlight,
 As I followed, bending low,
That the walking of the stranger
 Left no footmarks on the snow.

Then the fear-chill gathered o'er me,
 Like a shroud around me cast,
As I sank upon the snow-drift
 Where the Shadow-hunter passed.

And the otter-trappers found me,
 Before the break of day,
With my dark hair blanched and whitened
 As the snow in which I lay.

But they spoke not as they raised me;
 For they knew that in the night
I had seen the Shadow-hunter,
 And had withered in his blight.

Sancta Maria speed us!
 The sun is falling low,—
Before us lies the valley
 Of the Walker of the Snow!

[466]

KITTY OF COLERAINE

Justin McCarthy is authority for Shanly's authorship of this poem, usually attributed to others, or called anonymous. There is still some doubt.

As BEAUTIFUL Kitty one morning was tripping
    With a pitcher of milk for the fair of Coleraine,
When she saw me she stumbled, the pitcher down tumbled,
    And all the sweet buttermilk watered the plain.
"Oh, what shall I do now? 'Twas looking at you now!
    I'm sure such a pitcher I'll ne'er see again.
'Twas the pride of my dairy. Oh, Barney McCleary,
    You're sent as a plague to the girls of Coleraine."

I sat down beside her, and gently did chide her
    That such a misfortune should give her such pain;
A kiss then I gave her, and before I did leave her
    She vowed for such pleasure she'd break it again.
'Twas the haymaking season—I can't tell the reason—
    Misfortunes will never come single, 'tis plain!
For very soon after poor Kitty's disaster
    The devil a pitcher was whole in Coleraine.

THOMAS OSBORNE DAVIS
(1814-1845)

THE FATE OF KING DATHI

Dathi was the last pagan monarch of Ireland, and also the last who extended his conquests to the continent of Europe, invading the decaying Roman empire. He was killed by lightning in the Alps and his body carried home and buried in Roscommon. See John O'Donovan's *Tribes and Customs of the UiFiachrach.*

Compare this poem with Tennyson's "Charge of The Light Brigade at Balaklava," which was privately published in 1855, ten years after the death of Thomas Davis.

    DARKLY their glibs[1] o'erhang,
    Sharp is their wolf-dog's fang,

[1] Glibs = long locks of hair.

[467]

Bronze spear and falchion clang—
    Brave men might shun them
Heavy the spoil they bear—
Jewels and gold are there—
Hostage and maiden fair—
    How have they won them?

From the soft sons of Gaul,
Roman, and Frank, and thrall,
Borough, and hut, and hall,—
    These have been torn.
Over Britannia wide,
Over fair Gaul they hied,
Often in battle tried,—
    Enemies mourn!

Fiercely their harpers sing,—
Led by their gallant king,
They will to Eiré bring
    Beauty and treasure.
Britain shall bend the knee—
Rich shall their households be—
When their long ships the sea
    Homeward shall measure.

Barrow and Rath shall rise,
Towers, too, of wondrous size,
Táiltin[2] they'll solemnize,
    Feis-Teamhrach[3] assemble.
Samhain and Béal[4] shall smile
On the rich holy isle—
Nay! in a little while
    Œtius[5] shall tremble!

Up on the glacier's snow,
Down on the vales below,

---

[2] *Tailtin*, games held at Tailtin, Co. Meath.
[3] *Feis-Teamhrach*, the Parliament of Tara.
[4] *Samhain and Beal*, the Moon and Sun, which pagan Ireland worshipped.
[5] *Œtius*, consul, the "shield of Italy, terror of the barbarian," contemporary of King Dathi.

Monarch and clansmen go—
    Bright is the morning.
Never their march they slack,
Jura is at their back,
When falls the evening black,
    Hideous, and warning.

Eagles scream loud on high;
Far off the chamois fly;
Hoarse comes the torrent's cry,
    On the rocks whitening.
Strong are the storm's wings;
Down the tall pine it flings;
Hailstone and sleet it brings—
    Thunder and lightning.

Little these veterans mind
Thundering, hail, or wind;
Closer their ranks they bind—
    Matching the storm.
While, a spear-cast or more,
On, the front ranks before,
Dathi the sunburst bore—
    Haughty his form.

Forth from the thunder-cloud
Leaps out a foe as proud—
Sudden the monarch bowed—
    On rush the vanguard;
Wildly the king they raise—
Struck by the lightning's blaze—
Ghastly his dying gaze,
    Clutching his standard!

Mild is the morning beam,
Gently the rivers stream,
Happy the valleys seem;
    But the lone Islanders—

[469]

Mark how they guard their king!
Hark to the wail they sing!
Dark is their counselling—
    Helvetia's highlanders.

Gather, like ravens, near—
Shall Dathi's soldiers fear!
Soon their home-path they clear—
    Rapid and daring;
On through the pass and plain,
Until the shore they gain,
And, with their spoil, again,
    Landed in Eirinn.

Little does Eire care
For gold or maiden fair—
"Where is King Dathi?—where,
    Where is my bravest?"
On the rich deck he lies,
O'er him his sunburst flies—
Solemn the obsequies,
    Eire! thou gavest.

See ye that countless train
Crossing Ros-Comain's plain,
Crying, like hurricane,
    Uile liú ai?—
Broad is his *carn's* base
Nigh the "King's burial-place,"
Last of the Pagan race,
    Lieth king Dathi.

MY GRAVE

SHALL they bury me in the deep,
Where wind-forgetting waters sleep?
Shall they dig a grave for me,

[470]

Under the green-wood tree?
Or on the wild heath,
Where the wilder breath
Of the storm doth blow?
Oh, no! oh, no!

Shall they bury me in the Palace Tombs,
Or under the shade of Cathedral domes?
Sweet 't were to lie on Italy's shore;
Yet not there—nor in Greece, though I love it more.
In the wolf or the vulture my grave shall I find?
Shall my ashes career on the world-seeing wind?
Shall they fling my corpse in the battle mound,
Where coffinless thousands lie under the ground?
Just as they fall they are buried so—
Oh, no! oh, no!

No! on an Irish green hill-side,
On an opening lawn—but not too wide;
For I love the drip of the wetted trees—
I love not the gales, but a gentle breeze,
To freshen the turf—put no tombstone there,
But green sods decked with daisies fair;
Nor sods too deep, but so that the dew,
The matted grass-roots may trickle through.
Be my epitaph writ on my country's mind,
"He served his country, and loved his kind."

Oh! 't were merry unto the grave to go,
If one were sure to be buried so.

THE GIRL I LEFT BEHIND ME

THE dames of France are fond and free,
    And Flemish lips are willing,
And soft the maids of Italy,
    And Spanish eyes are thrilling;

Still, though I bask beneath their smile,
    Their charms fail to bind me,
And my heart flies back to Erin's isle,
    To the girl I left behind me.

For she's as fair as Shannon's side,
    And purer than its water,
But she refused to be my bride
    Though many a year I sought her;
Yet, since to France I sailed away,
    Her letters oft remind me
That I promised never to gainsay
    The girl I left behind me.

She says—"My own dear love, come home,
    My friends are rich and many,
Or else abroad with you I'll roam
    A soldier stout as any;
If you'll not come, nor let me go,
    I'll think you have resigned me."
My heart nigh broke when I answered—No!
    To the girl I left behind me.

For never shall my true love brave
    A life of war and toiling;
And never as a skulking slave
    I'll tread my native soil on;
But, were it free, or to be freed,
    The battle's close would find me
To Ireland bound—nor message need
    From the girl I left behind me.

THE WEST'S ASLEEP

(Air: "The Brink of the White Rocks")

WHEN all besides a vigil keep,
The West's asleep, the West's asleep—

Alas! and well may Erin weep,
When Connaught lies in slumber deep.
There lake and plain smile fair and free,
'Mid rocks—their guardian chivalry—
Sing oh! let man learn liberty
From crashing wind and lashing sea.

That chainless wave and lovely land
Freedom and Nationhood demand—
Be sure, the great God never planned,
For slumbering slaves, a home so grand.
And, long, a brave and haughty race
Honoured and sentinelled the place—
Sing oh! not even their sons' disgrace
Can quite destroy their glory's trace.

For often, in O'Connor's van,
To triumph dashed each Connaught clan—
And fleet as deer the Normans ran
Through Corlieu's Pass and Ardrahan.
And later times saw deeds as brave;
And glory guards Clanricard's[1] grave—
Sing oh! they died their land to save,
At Aughrim's slopes and Shannon's wave.

And if, when all a vigil keep,
The West's asleep, the West's asleep—
Alas! and well may Erin weep,
That Connaught lies in slumber deep.
But—hark!—some voice like thunder spake,
"The West's awake, the West's awake"—
"Sing oh! hurrah! let England quake,
We'll watch till death for Erin's sake!"

[1] Clanricard, Earls and marquises of. Titles held by members of the de Burgh family of Galway in Connaught. Ulick, the "great earl," fifth earl and 1st marquis was the sole member of the Irish Catholic nobility on the side of King Charles I. He served with Charles against the Scots; and in Ireland was, in 1652, forced to submit to the Parliamentary force. Also John, the ninth earl, by supporting James II, forfeited his estates which were not recovered until 1702.

LAMENT FOR THE DEATH OF OWEN ROE O'NEILL

Time—10th November, 1649. Scene—Ormond's Camp, Co. Waterford. Speakers—a Veteran of Eoghan O'Neill's clan, and one of the horsemen just arrived with an account of his death.

"DID they dare, did they dare, to slay Eoghan Ruadh O'Neill?"
"Yes, they slew with poison him they feared to meet with steel."
"May God wither up their hearts! May their blood cease to
    flow!
May they walk in living death, who poisoned Eoghan Ruadh!

"Though it break my heart to hear, say again the bitter words."
"From Derry, against Cromwell, he marched to measure
    swords;
But the weapon of the Sacsanach met him on his way,
And he died at Cloch Uachtar,[1] upon Saint Leonard's day."

"Wail, wail ye for the Mighty One! Wail, wail ye for the Dead;
Quench the hearth, and hold the breath—with ashes strew the
    head.
How tenderly we loved him! How deeply we deplore!
Holy Saviour! but to think we shall never see him more!

"Sagest in the council was he, kindest in the Hall:
Sure we never won a battle—'twas Eoghan won them all.
Had he lived—had he lived—our dear country had been free;
But he's dead, but he's dead, and 'tis slaves we'll ever be.

"O'Farrell and Clanricard, Preston and Red Hugh,
Audley and MacMahon—ye are valiant, wise, and true;
But—what, what are ye all to our darling who is gone?
The Rudder of our ship was he, our Castle's corner-stone!

"Wail, wail him through the Island! Weep, weep for our pride!
Would that on the battle-field our gallant chief had died!
Weep the Victor of Benburb—weep him, young man and old;
Weep for him, ye women—your Beautiful lies cold!

[1] Clough Aughter.

[474]

"We thought you would not die—we were sure you would not
   go,
And leave us in our utmost need to Cromwell's cruel blow—
Sheep without a shepherd, when the snow shuts out the sky—
Oh! why did you leave us, Eoghan? Why did you die?

"Soft as woman's was your voice, O'Neill! bright was your eye,
Oh! why did you leave us, Eoghan? why did you die?
Your troubles are all over, you're at rest with God on high;
But we're slaves, and we're orphans, Eoghan!—why did you
   die?"

THE IRISH HURRAH

HAVE you hearkened the eagle scream over the sea?
Have you hearkened the breaker beat under your lee?
A something between the wild waves, in their play,
And the kingly bird's scream, is The Irish Hurrah!

How it rings on the rampart when Saxons assail,
How it leaps on the level, and crosses the vale,
Till the talk of the cataract faints on its way,
And the echo's voice cracks with The Irish Hurrah!

How it sweeps o'er the mountain when hounds are on scent,
How it presses the billows when rigging is rent,
Till the enemy's broadside sinks low in dismay,
As our boarders go in with The Irish Hurrah!

Oh! there's hope in the trumpet and glee in the fife,
But never such music broke into a strife,
As when at its bursting the war-clouds give way,
And there's cold steel along with The Irish Hurrah!

What joy for a death-bed, your banner above,
And round you the pressure of patriot love,
As you're lifted to gaze on the breaking array
Of the Saxon reserve at The Irish Hurrah!

[475]

FONTENOY

The battle of Fontenoy, fought in Flanders in 1745 between the French and the Allies—English, Dutch, and Austrians—in which the Allies were worsted. The Irish Brigade fought by the side of the French, and won great renown by their splendid conduct in the field.

THRICE at the huts of Fontenoy the English column failed,
And twice the lines of Saint Antoine the Dutch in vain assailed;
For town and slope were filled with fort and flanking battery,
And well they swept the English ranks and Dutch auxiliary.
As vainly, through De Barri's wood, the British soldiers burst,
The French artillery drove them back, diminished and dis-
  persed.
The bloody Duke of Cumberland beheld with anxious eye,
And ordered up his last reserve, his latest chance to try.
On Fontenoy, on Fontenoy, how fast his generals ride!
And mustering come his chosen troops, like clouds at eventide.

Six thousand English veterans in stately column tread,
Their cannon blaze in front and flank, Lord Hay is at their
  head;
Steady they step a-down the slope—steady they climb the hill;
Steady they load—steady they fire, moving right onward still,
Betwixt the wood and Fontenoy, as through a furnace blast,
Through rampart, trench, and palisade, and bullets showering
  fast;
And on the open plain above they rose, and kept their course,
With ready fire and grim resolve, that mocked at hostile force:
Past Fontenoy, past Fontenoy, while thinner grow their ranks—
They break, as broke the Zuyder Zee through Holland's ocean
  banks.

More idly than the summer flies, French tirailleurs rush round;
As stubble to the lava tide, French squadrons strew the ground;
Bomb-shell, and grape, and round-shot tore, still on they
  marched and fired—
Fast, from each volley, grenadier and voltigeur retired.
"Push on my household cavalry!" King Louis madly cried:

[476]

To death they rush, but rude their shock—not unavenged they
    died.
On through the camp the column trod—King Louis turns his
    rein:
"Not yet, my liege," Saxe interposed, "the Irish troops remain;"
And Fontenoy, famed Fontenoy, had been a Waterloo,
Were not these exiles ready then, fresh, vehement, and true.

"Lord Clare," he said, "you have your wish, there are your
    Saxon foes!"
The marshal almost smiles to see, so furiously he goes!
How fierce the look these exiles wear, who 're wont to be so gay,
The treasured wrongs of fifty years are in their hearts today—
The treaty broken, ere the ink wherewith 't was writ could dry,
Their plundered homes, their ruined shrines, their women's
    parting cry,
Their priesthood hunted down like wolves, their country over-
    thrown,—
Each looks as if revenge for all were staked on him alone.
On Fontenoy, on Fontenoy, nor ever yet elsewhere,
Rushed on to fight a nobler band than these proud exiles were.

O'Brien's voice is hoarse with joy, as, halting, he commands,
"Fix bay'nets"—"charge,"—Like mountain storm, rush on
    these fiery bands!
Thin is the English column now, and faint their volleys grow,
Yet, must'ring all the strength they have, they make a gallant
    show.
They dress their ranks upon the hill to face that battle-wind—
Their bayonets the breakers' foam; like rocks, the men be-
    hind!
One volley crashes from their line, when, through the surging
    smoke,
With empty guns clutched in their hands, the headlong Irish
    broke.
On Fontenoy, on Fontenoy, hark to that fierce huzza!
"Revenge! remember Limerick! dash down the Sacsanach!"

[477]

Like lions leaping at a fold, when mad with hunger's pang,
Right up against the English line the Irish exiles sprang:
Bright was their steel, 't is bloody now, their guns are filled
    with gore;
Through shattered ranks, and severed files, and trampled flags
    they tore;
The English strove with desperate strength, paused, rallied,
    staggered, fled—
The green hillside is matted close with dying and with dead.
Across the plain and far away passed on that hideous wrack,
While cavalier and fantassin dash in upon their track.
On Fontenoy, on Fontenoy, like eagles in the sun,
With bloody plumes the Irish stand—the field is fought and
    won!

THE BATTLE EVE OF THE BRIGADE

After the flight of the Earls, O'Neill and O'Donnell in 1607, numbers of Irish crowded into all the Continental services (Spain, France, Austria, and Italy). Many of the Irish who had had their fortunes taken by Cromwell served in the foreign armies. Throughout the years the number of Irishmen in foreign service increased particularly at the time of the Jacobite wars. Sarsfield and the remnants of his army went to France—one of the most dramatic scenes in Irish history. The heroic deeds of the officers and men of the various Irish battalions have been a fertile source of inspiration for the poets of Ireland. The recruiting for the Brigade was carried on in the French ships which smuggled brandies, wines, silks, etc., to the western and southwestern coasts. Their return cargoes were recruits for the Brigade, and were entered in their books as *Wild Geese*. Hence this became the common name in Ireland for the Irish serving in the Brigade. The recruiting was chiefly in Clare, Limerick, Cork, Kerry, and Galway.

THE mess-tent is full, and the glasses are set,
And the gallant Count Thomond is president yet;
The vet'ran arose, like an uplifted lance,
Crying—"Comrades, a health to the monarch of France!"
With bumpers and cheers they have done as he bade,
For King Louis is loved by The Irish Brigade.

"A health to King James," and they bent as they quaffed;
"Here's to George the *Elector*," and fiercely they laughed;

[478]

"Good luck to the girls we wooed long ago,
Where Shannon, and Barrow, and Blackwater flow;"
"God prosper Old Ireland,"—you'd think them afraid,
So pale grew the chiefs of The Irish Brigade.

"But, surely, that light cannot come from our lamp?
And the noise—are they *all* getting drunk in the camp?"
"Hurrah! boys, the morning of battle is come,
And the *generale's* beating on many a drum."
So they rush from the revel to join the parade;
For the van is the right of The Irish Brigade.

They fought as they revelled, fast, fiery, and true,
And, though victors, they left on the field not a few;
And they, who survived, fought and drank as of yore,
But the land of their heart's hope they never saw more;
For in far foreign fields, from Dunkirk to Belgrade,
Lie the soldiers and chiefs of The Irish Brigade.

CLARE'S DRAGOONS

WHEN, on Ramillies' bloody field,
The baffled French were forced to yield,
The victor Saxon backward reeled
　　Before the charge of Clare's Dragoons.
The Flags, we conquered in that fray,
Look lone in Ypres' choir, they say;
We'll win them company to-day.
　　Or bravely die like Clare's Dragoons.
　　　　Chorus
　　Viva la, for Ireland's wrong!
　　　Viva la, for Ireland's right!
　　Viva la, in battle throng,
　　　　For a Spanish steed, and sabre bright!

The brave old lord died near the fight,
But, for each drop he lost that night,

A Saxon cavalier shall bite
  The dust before Lord Clare's Dragoons.
For never, when our spurs were set,
And never, when our sabres met,
Could we the Saxon soldiers get
  To stand the shock of Clare's Dragoons.
      Chorus
  Viva la, the New Brigade!
    Viva la, the Old One, too!
  Viva la, the rose shall fade,
    And the Shamrock shine forever new!

Another Clare is here to lead,
The worthy son of such a breed;
The French expect some famous deed,
  When Clare leads on his bold Dragoons.
Our Colonel comes from Brian's race,
His wounds are in his breast and face,
The *bearna baoghail* [1] is still his place,
  The foremost of his bold Dragoons.
      Chorus
  Viva la, the New Brigade!
    Viva la, the Old One, too!
  Viva la, the rose shall fade,
    And the Shamrock shine forever new!

There's not a man in squadron here
Was ever known to flinch or fear;
Though first in charge and last in rere,
  Have ever been Lord Clare's Dragoons;
But, see! we'll soon have work to do,
To shame our boasts, or prove them true,
For hither comes the English crew,
  To sweep away Lord Clare's Dragoons.
      Chorus
  Viva la, for Ireland's wrong!
    Viva la, for Ireland's right!

[1] Bearna baoghail = gap of danger.

[480]

Viva la, in battle throng,
   For a Spanish steed and sabre bright!

Oh! comrades! think how Ireland pines
Her exiled lords, her rifled shrines,
Her dearest hope, the ordered lines,
   And bursting charge of Clare's Dragoons.
Then bring your Green Flag to the sky,
Be Limerick your battle-cry,
And charge, till blood floats fetlock-high,
   Around the track of Clare's Dragoons!
            Chorus
   Viva la, the New Brigade!
    Viva la, the Old One, too!
   Viva la, the rose shall fade,
    And the Shamrock shine forever new!

TONE'S GRAVE

Theobald Wolfe Tone, one of the founders of the United Irishmen, promoted the political union of dissenters with Catholics against the British government. Came to America, because of his activities, in 1795; then to France where he sought to promote the landing of a French force for the invasion of Ireland. He was adjutant general of this expedition under Hoche. The force consisted of 43 sail and 15,000 men, but a storm dispersed the expedition. Later, 1798, with a smaller force of French he was captured by the British off Lough Swilly. He was imprisoned, and being refused a soldier's death, he committed suicide. He is one of the great modern heroes of Ireland.

IN BODENSTOWN Churchyard there is a green grave,
And wildly along it the winter winds rave;
Small shelter, I ween, are the ruined walls there,
When the storm sweeps down on the plains of Kildare,

Once I lay on that sod—it lies over Wolfe Tone—
And I thought how he perished in prison alone,
His friends unavenged, and his country unfreed—
"Oh, bitter," I said, "is the patriot's meed;

[481]

For in him the heart of a woman combined
With a heroic life, and a governing mind—
A martyr for Ireland—his grave has no stone—
His name seldom named, and his virtues unknown."

I was woke from my dream by the voices and tread
Of a band, who came into the home of the dead;
They carried no corpse, and they carried no stone,
And they stopped when they came to the grave of Wolfe
    Tone

There were students and peasants, the wise and the brave,
And an old man who knew him from cradle to grave,
And children who thought me hard-hearted; for they,
On the sanctified sod were forbidden to play.

But the old man, who saw I was mourning there, said:
"We come, sir, to weep where young Wolfe Tone is laid;
And we're going to raise him a monument, too—
A plain one, yet fit for the simple and true."

My heart overflowed, and I clasped his old hand,
And I blessed him, and blessed every one of his band;
"Sweet! sweet! 'tis to find that such faith can remain
To the cause, and the man so long vanquished and slain."

In Bodenstown Churchyard there is a green grave,
And freely around it let winter winds rave—
Far better they suit him—the ruin and gloom,—
Till Ireland, a Nation, can build him a tomb.

JOSEPH SHERIDAN LEFANU
(1814-1873)

HYMN

(from *Beatrice*)

Hush! oh ye billows,
    Hush! oh thou wind,
Watch o'er us, angels,
    Mary, be kind!

Fishermen followed
    The steps of the Lord;
Oft in their fishing boats
    Preached He the Word.

Pray for us, Pietro,
    Pray for us, John,
Pray for us, Giacomo,
    Zebedee's son.

If it be stormy,
    Fear not the sea;
Jesus upon it
    Is walking by thee.

Billows, be gentle,
    Soft blow the wind,
Watch o'er us, angels,
    Mary, be kind!

Soft be the billows,
    Gentle the wind,
Angels watch over thee,
    Mary, be kind!

A DRUNKARD TO HIS BOTTLE

From what dripping cell, through what fairy glen,
  Where 'mid old rocks and ruins the fox makes his den;
Over what lonesome mountain,
        Acushla machree!
    Where gauger never has trod,
    Sweet as the flowery sod,
    Wild as the breath
    Of the breeze on the heath,
And sparkling all o'er like the moon-lighted fountain,
        Are you come to me—
        Sorrowful me?

    Dancing—inspiring—
    My wild blood firin';
    Oh! terrible glory—
        Oh! beautiful siren—
    Come, tell the old story—
        Come light up my fancy, and open my heart.

    Oh, beautiful ruin—
    My life—my undoin'—
    Soft and fierce as a pantheress,
        Dream of my longing, and wreck of my soul,
I never knew love till I loved you, enchantress!

At first, when I knew you, 'twas only flirtation,
  The touch of a lip and the flash of an eye;
But 'tis different now—'tis desperation!
        I worship before you,
        I curse and adore you,
        And without you I'd die.

    Wirrasthrue!
    I wish 'twas again
    The happy time when
    I cared little about you,

[484]

Could do well without you,
But would just laugh and view you;
'Tis little I knew you!

Oh! terrible darling,
How have you sought me,
Enchanted, and caught me?
See, now, where you've brought me—
To sleep by the road-side, and dress out in rags.
Think how you found me;
Dreams come around me—
The dew of my childhood, and life's morning beam;
Now I sleep by the road-side, a wretch all in rags.
My heart that sang merrily when I was young,
Swells up like a billow and bursts in despair;
And the wreck of my hopes on sweet memory flung,
And cries on the air,
Are all that is left of the dream.

Wirrasthrue!
My father and mother,
The priest, and my brother—
Not a one has a good word for you.
But I can't part you, darling, their preaching's all vain;
You'll burn in my heart till these thin pulses stop;
And the wild cup of life in your fragrance I'll drain
To the last brilliant drop.
Then oblivion will cover
The shame that is over,
The brain that was mad, and the heart that was sore;
Then, beautiful witch,
I'll be found—in a ditch,
With your kiss on my cold lips, and never rise more.

THE SONG OF THE SPIRITS

(from *The Legend of the Glaive*)

FAR behind him crept blackness and flickering glimmer,
To the northward, slow mounting, the tempest was rising,
While luridly glaring all earth lay expecting,
Voiceless and breathless, the yell of the tyrant.

Thus he entered the high, vacant halls of the forest:
No bird in its branches, no antler beneath them,
Nor boom of the beetle, nor bay of the wild dog.
Only, Priestess of Mystery, glides a White Shadow,
On her lip her forefinger—and faithful he followed,
Well knowing his fate led him on to the combat,
Well knowing a mandate of silence upon him.

The trunks of the great trees like time-furrowed castles,
Gray glimmered through darkness impassive and awful,
Broad at base and at battlement broader the oak boles,
And a canopy dusky, snake-twisted, of branches,
Like crypts of cathedrals, low-groined and broad-pillared,
Stretched mazily this way and that in perspective.

AUBREY DE VERE
(1814-1902)

HUMAN LIFE

SAD is our youth, for it is ever going,
Crumbling away beneath our very feet;
Sad is our life, for onward it is flowing,
In current unperceived because so fleet;
Sad are our hopes, for they were sweet in sowing,
But tares, self-sown, have overtopped the wheat;
Sad are our joys, for they were sweet in blowing;
And still, O still, their dying breath is sweet:

[486]

And sweet is youth, although it hath bereft us
Of that which made our childhood sweeter still:
And sweet our life's decline, for it hath left us
A nearer Good to cure an older Ill:
And sweet are all things, when we learn to prize them
Not for their sake, but His who grants them or denies them.

SCENE IN A MADHOUSE

She sings her wild dirges, and smiles 'mid the strain;
   Then turns to remember her sorrow.
Men gaze on that smile till their tears fall like rain,
   And she from their weeping doth borrow.
She forgets her own story: and none, she complains,
   Of the cause for her grief will remind her:
She fancies but one of her kindred remains—
   She is certain he never can find her.
Whence caught you, sweet mourner, the swell of that song?
   "From the arch of yon wind-laden billow."
Whence learned you, sweet lady, your sadness?—"From
    Wrong."
   Your meekness who taught you?—"The Willow."

She boasts that her tresses have never grown grey;
   Yet murmurs—"How long I am dying!
My sorrows but make me more lovely, men say;
   But I soon in my grave shall be lying!
My grave will embrace me all round and all round,
   More warmly than thou, my false lover:—
No rival will steal to my couch without sound;
   No sister will come to discover!"
Whence caught you, sweet mourner, the swell of that song?
   "From the arch of the wind-laden billow."
Whence learned you, sweet lady, your sadness?—"From
    Wrong."
   Your meekness who taught you?—"The Willow."

[487]

She courts the cold wind when the tempests blow hard,
   And at first she exults in their raving.
She clasps with her fingers the lattice close-barred—
   Like the billows her bosom is waving:—
And ere long with strange pity her spirit is crossed,
   And she sighs for poor mariners drowning:
And—"thus in my passion of old I was tossed"—
   And—"thus stood my grey father frowning!"
Whence caught you, sweet mourner, the swell of that song?
   "From the arch of the wind-laden billow."
Whence learned you, sweet lady, your sadness?—"From
     Wrong."
   Your meekness who taught you?—"The Willow."

On the wall the rough water chafes ever its breast;
   'Mid the willows my bark was awaiting;
Passing by, on her cold hand a sad kiss I prest,
   And slowly moved on to the grating.
"For my lips, not my fingers, your bounty I crave!"
   She cried with a laugh and light shiver:
"You drift o'er the ocean, and I to the grave;
   Henceforward we meet not for ever!"
Where found you, sweet mourner, the swell of that song?
   "In the arch of yon wind-laden billow."
Whence caught you, sweet lady, your sadness?—"From
     Wrong."
   Your meekness who taught you?—"The Willow."

THE LITTLE BLACK ROSE

Little Black Rose, and Silk of the Kine are mystical names for Ireland.

THE Little Black Rose shall be red at last;
   What made it black but the March wind dry,
And the tear of the widow that fell on it fast?
   It shall redden the hills when June is nigh.

The Silk of the Kine shall rest at last;
  What drove her forth but the dragon-fly?
In the golden vale she shall feed full fast,
  With her mild gold horn and slow, dark eye.

The wounded wood-dove lies dead at last!
  The pine long bleeding, it shall not die!
This song is secret. Mine ear it passed
  In a wind o'er the plains at Athenry.

DENIS FLORENCE MacCARTHY
(1817-1882)

A long ballad based on an episode recorded in the *Annals of the Four Masters:* Con, son of Red Hugh O'Donnell, goaded on by his bard's rapturous descriptions of a neighboring chieftain's wife, steed and wolfhound decides to take them for himself. With his "small powerful force" he succeeds after a surprise night raid. On the way home he relents and frees them just before arriving at his own castle in the "valleys of Tirhugh" (Tir-Hugh=Land of Hugh). In causing O'Donnell to relent MacCarthy departs sharply from the recorded version. Portions of the O'Donnell castle built in the twelfth century still stand.

From THE FORAY OF CON O'DONNELL A.D. 1495

    .   .   .   .

  "Now, by Columba!" Con exclaimed,
  "Methinks this Scot should be ashamed
  To snatch at once, in sateless greed,
  The fairest maid and finest steed;
  My realm is dwindled in mine eyes,
  I know not what to praise or prize,
  And even my noble dog, O Bard,
  Now seems unworthy my regard!"

  "When comes the raven of the sea
    To nestle on an alien strand,

Oh! ever, ever will he be
　　The master of the subject land.
The fairest dame, he holdeth her—
　　For him the noblest steed doth bound;
Your dog is but a household cur,
　　Compared to John MacDonnell's hound!

"As fly the shadows o'er the grass,
　　He flies with step as light and sure,
He hunts the wolf through Trosstan pass,
　　And starts the deer by Lisànoure!
The music of the Sabbath bells,
　　O Con, has not a sweeter sound
Than when along the valley swells
　　The cry of John MacDonnell's hound.

"His stature tall, his body long,
　　His back like night, his breast like snow,
His fore-leg pillar-like and strong,
　　His hind-leg like a bended bow;
Rough, curling hair, head long and thin,
　　His ear a leaf so small and round:
Not Bran, the favourite hound of Fin,
　　Could rival John MacDonnell's hound.

　　.　　.　　.　　.　　.　　.　　.　　.

Their lances in the red dawn flash,
As down by Easky's side they dash;
Their quilted jackets shine the more,
From gilded leather broidered o'er;
With silver spurs, and silken rein,
And costly riding-shoes from Spain;
Ah! much thou hast to fear, MacJohn,
The strong, small-powerful force of Con!

As borne upon autumnal gales,
Wild whirring gannets pierce the sails
Of barks that sweep by Arran's shore,
Thus swept the train through Barnesmore.

[490]

Through many a varied scene they ran,
By Castle Fin, and fair Strabane,
By many a hill, and many a clan,
Across the Foyle and o'er the Bann:—

. . . .

They leave the castle stripped and bare,
Each has his labour, each his share;
For some have cups, and some have plate,
And some have scarlet cloaks of state,
And some have wine, and some have ale,
And some have coats of iron mail,
And some have helms, and some have spears,
And all have lowing cows and steers!

. . . .

The chieftain on a raven steed,
Himself the peerless dame doth lead,
Now like a pallid, icy corse,
And lifts her on her husband's horse;
His left hand holds his captive's rein,
His right is on his black steed's mane,
And from the bridle to the ground
Hangs the long leash that binds the hound.

. . . .

By this time, on Ben Bradagh's height,
Brave Con had rested in his flight,
Beneath him, in the horizon's blue,
Lay his own valleys of Tirhugh.
It may have been the thought of home,
While resting on that mossy dome,
It may have been his native trees
That woke his mind to thoughts like these.

. . . .

"If thus I madly teach my clan,
What can I hope from beast or man?
Fidelity a crime is found,
Or else why chain this faithful hound?
Obedience, too, a crime must be,

Or else this steed were roaming free;
And woman's love the worst of sins,
Or Anne were queen of Antrim's glynnes!

.   .   .   .

He turned and loosed MacDonnell's hand,
And led him where his steed doth stand;
He placed the bride of peerless charms
Within his longing, outstretched arms;
He freed the hound from chain and band,
Which, leaping, licked his master's hand;
And thus, while wonder held the crowd,
The generous chieftain spoke aloud:—

"MacJohn, I heard in wrathful hour
    That thou in Antrim's glynnes possessed
The fairest pearl, the sweetest flower
    That ever bloomed on Erin's breast.
I burned to think such prize should fall
    To any Scotch or Saxon man,
But find that Nature makes us all
    The children of one world-spread clan.

"Within thy arms thou now doest hold
    A treasure of more worth and cost
Than all the thrones and crowns of gold
    That valour ever won or lost;
Thine is that outward perfect form,
    Thine, too, the subtler inner life,
The love that doth that bright shape warm:
    Take back, MacJohn, thy peerless wife!

"They praised thy steed. With wrath and grief
    I felt my heart within me bleed,
That any but an Irish chief
    Should press the back of such a steed;
I might to yonder smiling land
    The noble beast reluctant lead;

[492]

But, no!—he'd miss thy guiding hand—
    Take back, MacJohn, thy noble steed.

"The praises of thy matchless hound,
    Burned in my breast like acrid wine;
I swore no chief on Irish ground
    Should own a nobler hound than mine;
'Twas rashly sworn, and must not be,
    He'd pine to hear the well-known sound,
With which thou call'st him to thy knee,
    Take back, MacJohn, thy matchless hound.

.   .   .   .

WILLIAM PEMBROKE MULCHINOCK
(1820?-1864)

THE ROSE OF TRALEE

THE pale moon was rising above the green mountain,
    The sun was declining beneath the blue sea,
When I stray'd with my love to the pure crystal fountain
    That stands in the beautiful vale of Tralee.

She was lovely and fair as the rose of the summer,
    Yet 'twas not her beauty alone that won me,
Oh, no, 'twas the truth in her eyes ever beaming
    That made me love Mary, the Rose of Tralee.

The cool shades of evening their mantle were spreading,
    And Mary, all smiling, was list'ning to me,
The moon through the valley her pale rays was shedding
    When I won the heart of the Rose of Tralee.

Tho' lovely and fair as the rose of the summer,
    Yet 'twas not her beauty alone that won me,
Oh, no, 'twas the truth in her eyes ever beaming
    That made me love Mary, the Rose of Tralee.

[493]

CECIL FRANCES ALEXANDER
(1820?-1895)

DREAMS

BEYOND, beyond the mountain line,
　The grey-stone and the boulder,
Beyond the growth of dark green pine,
　That crowns its western shoulder,
There lies that fairy-land of mine,
　Unseen of a beholder.

Its fruits are all like rubies rare;
　Its streams are clear as glasses;
There golden castles hang in air,
　And purple grapes in masses,
And noble knights and ladies fair
　Come riding down the passes.

Ah me! they say if I could stand
　Upon those mountain ledges,
I should but see on either hand
　Plain fields and dusty hedges;
And yet I know my fairy-land
　Lies somewhere o'er their edges.

LADY WILDE (SPERANZA)
(c.1820-1896)

THE FAMINE YEAR

WEARY men, what reap ye?—"Golden corn for the stranger."
What sow ye?—"Human corses that wait for the avenger."

[494]

Fainting forms, hunger-stricken, what see ye in the offing?
"Stately ships to bear our food away amid the stranger's scoff-
    ing."
There's a proud array of soldiers—what do they round your
    door?
"They guard our master's granaries from the thin hands of the
    poor."
Pale mothers, wherefore weeping? "Would to God that we
    were dead—
Our children swoon before us, and we cannot give them
    bread!"

Little children, tears are strange upon your infant faces,
God meant you but to smile within your mother's soft em-
    braces.
"Oh! we know not what is smiling, and we know not what is
    dying;
But we're hungry, very hungry, and we cannot stop our crying.
And some of us grow cold and white—we know not what it
    means;
But as they lie beside us we tremble in our dreams."
There's a gaunt crowd on the highway—are you come to pray
    to man,
With hollow eyes that cannot weep, and for words your faces
    wan?

"No; the blood is dead within our veins—we care not now for
    life;
Let us die hid in the ditches, far from children and from wife!
We cannot stay to listen to their raving famished cries—
Bread! Bread! Bread! and none to still their agonies.
We left an infant playing with her dead mother's hand:
We left a maiden maddened by the fever's scorching brand:"
Better, maiden, thou wert strangled in thy own dark-twisted
    tresses!
Better, infant, thou wert smothered in thy mother's first ca-
    resses.

[495]

"We are fainting in our misery, but God will hear our groan;
Yet, if fellow-men desert us, will He hearken from His throne?
Accursed are we in our own land, yet toil we still and toil;
But the stranger reaps our harvest—the alien owns our soil.
O Christ! how have we sinned, that on our native plains
We perish homeless, naked, starved, with branded brow like
     Cain's?
Dying, dying wearily, with a torture sure and slow—
Dying as a dog would die, by the wayside as we go.

"One by one they're falling round us, their pale faces to the
     sky;
We've no strength left to dig them graves—there let them lie.
The wild bird, if he's stricken, is mourned by the others,
But we—we die in Christian land,—we die amid our brothers,
In the land which God has given, like a wild beast in his cave,
Without a tear, a prayer, a shroud, a coffin, or a grave.
Ha! but think ye the contortions on each livid face ye see,
Will not be read on Judgement-day by eyes of Deity?

"We are wretches, famished, scorned, human tools to build
     your pride,
But God will yet take vengeance for the souls for whom Christ
     died.
Now is your hour of pleasure—bask ye in the world's caress;
But our whitening bones against ye will rise as witnesses,
From the cabins and the ditches in their charred, uncoffined
     masses,
For the Angel of the Trumpet will know them as he passes.
A ghastly spectral army, before great God we'll stand,
And arraign ye as our murderers, O spoilers of our land!"

RICHARD D'ALTON WILLIAMS
(1822-1862)

THE DYING GIRL

FROM a Munster vale they brought her,
  From the pure and balmy air;
An Ormond peasant's daughter,
  With blue eyes and golden hair.
They brought her to the city
  And she faded slowly there—
Consumption has no pity
  For blue eyes and golden hair.

When I saw her first reclining
  Her lips were mov'd in prayer,
And the setting sun was shining
  On her loosen'd golden hair.
When our kindly glances met her,
  Deadly brilliant was her eye;
And she said that she was better,
  While we knew that she must die.

She speaks of Munster valleys,
  The pattern, dance, and fair,
And her thin hand feebly dallies
  With her scattered golden hair.
When silently we listen'd
  To her breath with quiet care,
Her eyes with wonder glisten'd,
  And she asked us, "What was there?"

The poor thing smiled to ask it,
  And her pretty mouth laid bare,
Like gems within a casket,
  A string of pearlets rare.

[497]

We said that we were trying
    By the gushing of her blood
And the time she took in sighing
    To know if she were good.

Well, she smil'd and chatted gaily,
    Though we saw in mute despair
The hectic brighter daily,
    And the death-dew on her hair.
And oft her wasted fingers
    Beating time upon the bed:
O'er some old tune she lingers,
    And she bows her golden head.

At length the harp is broken;
    And the spirit in its strings,
As the last decree is spoken,
    To its source exulting springs.
Descending swiftly from the skies
    Her guardian angel came,
He struck God's lightning from her eyes,
    And bore Him back the flame.

Before the sun had risen
    Through the lark-loved morning air,
Her young soul left its prison,
    Undefiled by sin or care.
I stood beside the couch in tears
    Where pale and calm she slept,
And though I've gazed on death for years,
    I blush not that I wept.

I check'd with effort pity's sighs
    And left the matron there,
To close the curtains of her eyes
    And bind her golden hair.

EXTERMINATION

WHEN tyranny's pampered and purple-clad minions
   Drive forth the lone widow and orphan to die,
Shall no angel of vengeance unfurl his red pinions,
   And grasping sharp thunderbolts, rush from on high?

"Pity! oh, Pity!—A little while spare me,
   My baby is sick—I am feeble and poor;
In the cold winter blast, from the hut if you tear me,
   My lord, we must die on the desolate moor!"

'Tis vain—for the despot replies with much laughter,
   While rudely his serfs thrust her forth on the wold;
Her cabin is blazing, from threshold to rafter,
   And she crawls o'er the mountain, sick, weeping and cold.

Her thinly clad child on the stormy hill shivers—
   The thunders are pealing dread anthems around—
Loud roar in their anger the tempest lashed rivers—
   And the loosened rocks down with the wild torrent bound.

Vainly she tries in her bosom to cherish
   Her sick infant boy, 'mid the horrors around,
Till, faint and despairing, she sees her babe perish—
   Then lifeless she sinks on the snow covered ground.

Tho' the children of Ammon, with trumpets and psalters,
   To Devils poured torrents of innocents' gore,
Let them blush from deep hell at the far redder altars
   Where the death dealing tyrants of Ireland adore!

But for Erin's life-current, thro' long ages flowing
   Dark demons that pierce her, you shall yet atone;
Even *now* the volcano beneath you is glowing,
   And the Molock of tyranny reels on his throne.

[499]

BARTHOLOMEW DOWLING
(1823-1863)

THE REVEL

The scene is East India at the time of the pestilence. This poem has
often, erroneously, been attributed to Alfred Dommett.

WE MEET 'neath the sounding rafter,
  And the walls around are bare;
As they shout back our peals of laughter
  It seems that the dead are there.
Then stand to your glasses, steady!
  We drink in our comrades' eyes:
One cup to the dead already—
  Hurrah for the next that dies!

Not here are the goblets glowing,
  Not here is the vintage sweet;
'Tis cold, as our hearts are growing,
  And dark as the doom we meet.
But stand to your glasses, steady!
  And soon shall our pulses rise:
A cup to the dead already—
  Hurrah for the next that dies!

There's many a hand that's shaking,
  And many a cheek that's sunk;
But soon, though our hearts are breaking,
  They'll burn with the wine we've drunk.
Then stand to your glasses, steady!
  'Tis here the revival lies:
Quaff a cup to the dead already—
  Hurrah for the next that dies!

[500]

Time was when we laughed at others;
  We thought we were wiser then;
Ha! ha! let them think of their mothers,
  Who hope to see them again.
No! stand to your glasses, steady!
  The thoughtless is here the wise:
A cup to the dead already—
  Hurrah for the next that dies!

Not a sigh for the lot that darkles,
  Not a tear for the friends that sink;
We'll fall, 'mid the wine-cup's sparkles,
  As mute as the wine we drink.
Come! Stand to your glasses, steady!
  'Tis this that the respite buys:
One cup to the dead already—
  Hurrah for the next that dies!

There's a mist on the glass congealing,
  'Tis the hurricane's sultry breath;
And thus does the warmth of feeling
  Turn ice in the grasp of Death.
But stand to your glasses, steady!
  For a moment the vapor flies:
Quaff a cup to the dead already—
  Hurrah for the next that dies!

Who dreads to the dust returning?
  Who shrinks from the sable shore,
Where the high and haughty yearning
  Of the soul can sting no more?
No, stand to your glasses, steady!
  The world is a world of lies:
A cup to the dead already—
  And hurrah for the next that dies!

Cut off from the land that bore us,
  Betrayed by the land we find,

When the brightest have gone before us,
  And the dullest are most behind—
Stand, stand to your glasses, steady!
  'Tis all we have left to prize:
One cup to the dead already—
  Hurrah for the next that dies!

THOMAS CAULFIELD IRWIN
(1823-1892)

THE FAERIE'S CHILD

AMID the nut grove, still and brown,
  The Faerie's Child is walking.
List, list, as the leaves come down,
  To the sprites around her talking.
    Along the windy, waving grass
      Their evening whispers breathe and pass:
    From yon aged bending bough
      Their leafy language floats below:
And now o'erhead in the air 'tis streaming.
    Oh! who can tell what things she hears—
    What secrets of the faery spheres,
      That fill her eyes with silent tears!
Sweet wandering fancy-charmed child,
With cheek so pale, and eyes so wild.
Oh! what shall come of this lonely dreaming!

Down by the sun-dry harvest road,
  Through quiet evening's hours,
She paces with her scented load
  Of late-year moss and flowers.
    Blooms from the wood of every hue,
    Moon pale, purple, jet, and blue;
      Woven in bunches, and lightly press'd
      Upon her simple, snowy breast,

[502]

And through the brown locks wildly tressed
Nodding in crownlets o'er her.
And, lo! as the cloud on ocean's brim
With moonlight has enriched its rim,
A quaint wild shape, with kindly eyes,
And a smile like a star of the distant skies,
Goes tripping along the path before her.

Now by her pillow, small and white,
    'Mid faded leaflets lying,
An eager star, like a taper light,
    O'er the curtain's edge is spying.
        The scent of the broom-buds fills the room;
        The window is full of the bare blue gloom,
        And by the low hearth ashily sinking,
        Half asleep is the faery winking.
        Out in the air there comes a sound
        Of music eddying round and round
        The ivied chimneys—swooning near
        The glassy pane, and streaming clear
        As moonlight into the little ear,
    Like a shell in brown weed gleaming;
        And, just as the first bird, mounted high
        On the sycamore's tinkling canopy,
        Sings to the first red streak of day,
        Her soul with the faeries speeds away,
        O'er field, and stream, and hamlet grey,
    Where the weary folk are dreaming.

MARTIN MacDERMOTT
(1823-1905)

GIRL OF THE RED MOUTH

GIRL of the red mouth,
    Love me! Love me!

[503]

Girl of the red mouth,
                Love me!
'Tis by its curve, I know,
Love fashioneth his bow,
And bends it—ah, even so!
    Oh, girl of the red mouth, love me!

Girl of the blue eye,
        Love me! Love me!
Girl of the dew eye,
            Love me!
Worlds hang for lamps on high;
And thought's world lives in thy
Lustrous and tender eye—
    Oh, girl of the blue eye, love me!

Girl of the swan's neck,
        Love me! Love me!
Girl of the swan's neck,
            Love me!
As a marble Greek doth grow
To his steed's back of snow,
Thy white neck sits thy shoulder so—
    Oh, girl of the swan's neck, love me!

Girl of the low voice,
        Love me! Love me!
Girl of the sweet voice,
            Love me!
Like the echo of a bell—
Like the bubbling of a well—
Sweeter! Love within doth dwell—
    Oh, girl of the low voice, love me!

JOHN KELLS INGRAM
(1823-1907)

THE MEMORY OF THE DEAD (1798)

WHO fears to speak of Ninety-Eight?
  Who blushes at the name?
When cowards mock the patriot's fate,
  Who hangs his head for shame?
He's all a knave, or half a slave,
  Who slights his country thus;
But a true man, like you, man,
  Will fill your glass with us.

We drink the memory of the brave,
  The faithful and the few:
Some lie far off beyond the wave,
  Some sleep in Ireland, too;
All, all are gone; but still lives on
  The fame of those who died;
All true men, like you, men,
  Remember them with pride.

Some on the shores of distant lands
  Their weary hearts have laid,
And by the stranger's heedless hands
  Their lonely graves were made;
But, though their clay be far away
  Beyond the Atlantic foam,
In true men, like you, men,
  Their spirit's still at home.

The dust of some is Irish earth,
  Among their own they rest,
And the same land that gave them birth
  Has caught them to her breast;
And we will pray that from their clay
  Full many a race may start

[505]

Of true men, like you, men,
   To act as brave a part.

They rose in dark and evil days
   To right their native land;
They kindled here a living blaze
   That nothing shall withstand.
Alas! that Might can vanquish Right—
   They fell and passed away;
But true men, like you, men,
   Are plenty here to-day.

Then here's their memory—may it be
   For us a guiding light,
To cheer our strife for liberty,
   And teach us to unite—
Through good and ill, be Ireland's still,
   Though sad as theirs your fate,
And true men be you, men,
   Like those of Ninety-Eight.

THE SOCIAL FUTURE

As, WITH enforced yet unreluctant pace
We downward move along life's westward slope,
Slow fades the once bright gleam of personal hope,
And larger looms the future of the race;
Our wistful eyes the goodly prospect trace,
Seen through a haze of forecast; there outspread
Lie the fair fields our children's feet shall tread
When we have passed to our abiding place.
Oh! sons and daughters of the coming age,
Give worthy meed of gratitude and praise
To those true souls who, in less happy days,
Have lived for others—most of all for you—
Have stored the wealth which is your heritage,
And planned the work it will be yours to do.

NATIONAL PRESAGE

UNHAPPY Erin, what a lot was thine!
Half-conquered by a greedy robber band;
Ill governed with now lax, now ruthless hand;
Misled by zealots, wresting laws divine
To sanction every dark or mad design;
Lured by false lights of pseudo-patriot league
Through crooked paths of faction and intrigue;
And drugged with selfish flattery's poisoned wine.
Yet, reading all thy mournful history,
Thy children, with a mystic faith sublime,
Turn to the future, confident that Fate,
Become at last thy friend, reserves for thee,
To be thy portion in the coming time,
They know not what—but surely something great.

MICHAEL JOSEPH McCANN
(1824-1883)

O'DONNELL ABOO

PROUDLY the note of the trumpet is sounding,
Loudly the war-cries arise on the gale;
Fleetly the steed by Lough Swilly is bounding,
To join the thick squadrons in Saimear's green vale.
    On, ev'ry mountaineer,
    Strangers to flight and fear!
Rush to the standard of dauntless Red Hugh!
    Bonnaught and gallowglass,
    Throng from each mountain pass;
On for old Erin, "O'Donnell Aboo!"

Princely O'Neill to our aid is advancing
With many a chieftain and warrior clan,
A thousand proud steeds in his vanguard are prancing

'Neath the borderers brave from the banks of the Bann;
    Many a heart shall quail
    Under its coat of mail;
Deeply the merciless foeman shall rue,
    When on his ear shall ring,
    Borne on the breezes' wing,
Tir Connell's dread war-cry, "O'Donnell Aboo!"

Wildly o'er Desmond the war-wolf is howling,
Fearless the eagle sweeps over the plain,
    The fox in the streets of the city is prowling;
    All, all who would scare them are banished or slain.
      Grasp every stalwart hand
      Hackbut and battle brand,
Pay them all back the debt so long due;
    Norris and Clifford well
    Can of Tir Connell tell;
Onward to glory, "O'Donnell Aboo!"

Sacred the cause of Clan Connaill's defending,
The altars we kneel at, the homes of our sires;
Ruthless the ruin the foe is extending,
Midnight is red with the plunderers' fires.
    On with O'Donnell, then,
    Fight the old fight again,
Sons of Tir Connell, all valiant and true.
    Make the false Saxon feel
    Erin's avenging steel!
Strike for your country, "O'Donnell Aboo!"

WILLIAM ALLINGHAM
(1824-1889)

THE FAIRIES

(A Child's Song)

Up the airy mountain,
    Down the rushy glen,
We daren't go a-hunting
    For fear of little men;
Wee folk, good folk,
    Trooping all together;
Green jacket, red cap,
    And white owl's feather!

Down along the rocky shore
    Some make their home—
They live on crispy pancakes
    Of yellow tide-foam;
Some in the reeds
    Of the black mountain lake,
With frogs for their watch-dogs,
    All night awake.

High on the hill-top
    The old King sits;
He is now so old and gray
    He's nigh lost his wits.
With a bridge of white mist,
    Columbkill he crosses,
On his stately journeys
    From Slieveleague to Rosses;
Or going up with music
    On cold starry nights,
To sup with the Queen
    Of the gay Northern Lights.

[509]

They stole little Bridget
    For seven years long;
When she came down again
    Her friends were all gone.
They took her lightly back,
    Between the night and morrow;
They thought that she was fast asleep,
    But she was dead with sorrow.
They have kept her ever since
    Deep within the lakes,
On a bed of flag-leaves,
    Watching till she wakes.

By the craggy hill-side,
    Through the mosses bare,
They have planted thorn-trees
    For pleasure here and there.
Is any man so daring
    As dig one up in spite,
He shall find their sharpest thorns
    In his bed at night.

Up the airy mountain,
    Down the rushy glen,
We daren't go a-hunting
    For fear of little men;
Wee folk, good folk,
    Trooping all together;
Green jacket, red cap,
    And white owl's feather!

ABBEY ASAROE

GRAY, gray is Abbey Asaroe, by Ballyshanny town,
It has neither door nor window, the walls are broken down;
The carven-stones lie scatter'd in briar and nettle-bed;
The only feet are those that come at burial of the dead.

A little rocky rivulet runs murmuring to the tide,
Singing a song of ancient days, in sorrow, not in pride;
The elder-tree and lightsome ash across the portal grow,
And heaven itself is now the roof of Abbey Asaroe.

It looks beyond the harbour-stream to Gulban mountain blue;
It hears the voice of Erna's fall,—Atlantic breakers too;
High ships go sailing past it; the sturdy clank of oars
Brings in the salmon-boat to haul a net upon the shores;
And this way to his home-creek, when the summer day is done,
Slow sculls the weary fisherman across the setting sun;
While green with corn is Sheegus Hill, his cottage white below;
But gray at every season is Abbey Asaroe.

There stood one day a poor old man above its broken bridge;
He heard no running rivulet, he saw no mountain-ridge;
He turn'd his back on Sheegus Hill, and view'd with misty sight
The abbey walls, the burial-ground with crosses ghostly white;
Under a weary weight of years he bow'd upon his staff,
Perusing in the present time the former's epitaph;
For, gray and wasted like the walls, a figure full of woe,
This man was of the blood of them who founded Asaroe.

From Derry to Bundrowas Tower, Tirconnell broad was theirs;
Spearmen and plunder, bards and wine, and holy abbot's
        prayers;
With chanting always in the house which they had builded
        high
To God and to Saint Bernard,—whereto they came to die.
At worst, no workhouse grave for him! the ruins of his race
Shall rest among the ruin'd stones of this their saintly place.
The fond old man was weeping; and tremulous and slow
Along the rough and crooked lane he crept from Asaroe.

AEOLIAN HARP

WHAT saith the river to the rushes grey,
  Rushes sadly bending,
  River slowly wending?
Who can tell the whispered things they say?
  Youth, and prime, and life, and time,
  For ever, ever fled away!

Drop your withered garlands in the stream,
  Low autumnal branches,
  Round the skiff that launches
Wavering downward through the lands of dream.
  Ever, ever fled away!
  This the burden, this the theme.

What saith the river to the rushes grey,
  Rushes sadly bending,
  River slowly wending?
It is near the closing of the day.
  Near the night. Life and light
  For ever, ever fled away!

Draw him tideward down; but not in haste.
  Mouldering daylight lingers;
  Night with her cold fingers
Sprinkles moonbeams on the dim sea-waste.
  Ever, ever fled away!
  Vainly cherished! vainly chased!

What saith the river to the rushes grey,
  Rushes sadly bending,
  River slowly wending?
Where in darkest glooms his bed we lay,
  Up the cave moans the wave,
  For ever, ever, ever fled away!

THE LUPRACAUN, OR FAIRY SHOEMAKER

(A Rhyme for Children)

LITTLE cowboy, what have you heard,
  Up on the lonely rath's green mound?
Only the plaintive yellow-bird
  Sighing in sultry fields around
Chary, Chary, Chary, chee-e!
Only the grasshopper and the bee?
  "Tip-tap, rip-rap,
  Tick-a-tack-too!
Scarlet leather sewn together,
  This will make a shoe.
Left, right, pull it tight;
  Summer days are warm;
Underground in winter,
  Laughing at the storm!"
Lay your ear close to the hill:
  Do you not catch the tiny clamour,
  Busy click of an elfin hammer,
Voice of the Lupracaun singing shrill
  As he merrily plies his trade?
    He's a span
  And a quarter in height.
Get him in sight, hold him tight,
  And you're a made
    Man!

You watch your cattle the summer day,
  Sup on potatoes, sleep in the hay;
How would you like to roll in your carriage,
Look for a duchess's daughter in marriage?
  Seize the shoemaker—then you may!
    "Big boots a-hunting,
    Sandals in the hall,
  White for a wedding-feast,
    Pink for a ball:
  This way, that way,

[513]

So we make a shoe,
   Getting rich every stitch,
      Tick-tack-too!"
Nine-and-ninety treasure-crocks,
   This keen miser-fairy hath,
Hid in mountains, woods, and rocks,
Ruin and round-tower, cave and rath,
   And where the cormorants build;
      From times of old
         Guarded by him;
      Each of them filled
         Full to the brim
            With gold!

I caught him at work one day, myself,
   In the castle-ditch where foxglove grows,—
A wrinkled, wizened, and bearded Elf,
   Spectacles stuck on his pointed nose,
   Silver buckles to his hose,
   Leather apron, shoe in his lap—
      "Rip-rap, tip-tap,
      Tick-tack-too!
   (A grig skipped upon my cap,
      Away the moth flew!)
   Buskins for a fairy prince,
      Brogues for his son,
   Pay me well, pay me well,
      When the job is done!"
The rogue was mine, beyond a doubt.
   I stared at him; he stared at me!
   "Servant, Sir!" "Humph!" says he,
And pulled a snuff-box out.
   He took a long pinch, looked better pleased,
      The queer little Lupracaun;
   Offered the box with a whimsical grace—
   Pouf! he flung the dust in my face—
      And, while I sneezed,
         Was gone!

[514]

THE BUBBLE

SEE, the pretty Planet!
  Floating sphere!
Faintest breeze will fan it
  Far or near;

World as light as feather;
  Moonshine rays,
Rainbow tints together,
  As it plays;

Drooping, sinking, failing,
  Nigh to earth,
Mounting, whirling, sailing,
  Full of mirth;

Life there, welling, flowing,
  Waving round;
Pictures coming, going,
  Without sound.

Quick now, be this airy
  Globe repelled!
Never can the fairy
  Star be held.

Touched—it in a twinkle
  Disappears!
Leaving but a sprinkle,
  As of tears.

DEATH DEPOSED

DEATH stately came to a young man, and said,
        "If thou wert dead,
What matter?" The young man replied,
        "See my young bride,

Whose life were all one blackness if I died.
My land requires me; and the world's self, too,
Methinks, would miss some things that I can do."

Then Death in scorn this only said,
      "Be dead."
And so he was. And soon another's hand
      Made rich his land.
The sun, too, of three summers had the might
To bleach the widow's hue, light and more light,
      Again to bridal white.
And nothing seem'd to miss beneath that sun
      His work undone.

But Death soon met another man, whose eye
      Was Nature's spy;
Who said, "Forbear thy too triumphant scorn.
      The weakest born
Of all the sons of men, is by his birth
Heir of the Might Eternal; and this Earth
Is subject to him in his place.
      Thou leav'st no trace.

"Thou—the mock Tyrant that men fear and hate,
      Grim fleshless Fate,
Cold, dark, and wormy thing of loss and tears!
      Not in the sepulchres
Thou dwellest, but in my own crimson'd heart;
Where while it beats we call thee Life. Depart!
A name, a shadow, into any gulf,
Out of this world, which is not thine,
      But mine:
      Or stay!—because thou art
      Only Myself."

THE MAIDS OF ELFIN-MERE

WHEN the spinning-room was here,
Came three Damsels, clothed in white,
With their spindles every night;
One and two and three fair Maidens,
Spinning to a pulsing cadence,
Singing songs of Elfin-Mere;
Till the eleventh hour was toll'd,
Then departed through the wold,
   Years ago, and years ago;
   And the tall reeds sigh as the wind doth blow.

Three white Lilies, calm and clear,
And they were loved by every one;
Most of all, the Pastor's Son,
Listening to their gentle singing,
Felt his heart go from him, clinging
To these Maids of Elfin-Mere;
Sued each night to make them stay,
Sadden'd when they went away.
   Years ago, and years ago;
   And the tall reeds sigh as the wind doth blow.

Hands that shook with love and fear
Dared put back the village clock—
Flew the spindle, turn'd the rock,
Flow'd the song with subtle rounding,
Then these Maids of Elfin-Mere
Swiftly, softly left the room,
Like three doves on snowy plume.
   Years ago, and years ago;
   And the tall reeds sigh as the wind doth blow.

One that night who wander'd near
Heard lamentings by the shore,
Saw at dawn three stains of gore
In the waters fade and dwindle.

[517]

Never more with song and spindle
Saw we Maids of Elfin-Mere.
The Pastor's Son did pine and die;
Because true love should never lie.
Years ago, and years ago;
And the tall reeds sigh as the wind doth blow.

THOMAS D'ARCY McGEE

(1825-1868)

THE CELTS

Long, long ago, beyond the misty space
        Of twice a thousand years,
In Erin old there dwelt a mighty race,
        Taller than Roman spears;
Like oaks and towers they had a giant grace,
        Were fleet as deers,
With wind and waves they made their 'biding place,
        These western shepherd seers.

Their Ocean-God was Manannan MacLir,
        Whose angry lips,
In their white foam, full often would inter
        Whole fleets of ships;
Cromah their Day-God, and their Thunderer
        Made morning and eclipse;
Bride was their Queen of Song, and unto her
        They prayed with fire-touched lips.

Great were their deeds, their passions and their sports;
        With clay and stone
They piled on strath and shore those mystic forts,
        Not yet o'erthrown;
On cairn-crowned hills they held their council-courts;
        While youths alone,

[518]

With giant dogs, explored the elk resorts,
     And brought them down.

Of these was Finn, the father of the Bard
     Whose ancient song
Over the clamour of all change is heard,
     Sweet-voiced and strong.
Finn once o'ertook Grania, the golden-haired,
     The fleet and young;
From her the lovely, and from him the feared,
     The primal poet sprung.

Ossian! two thousand years of mist and change
     Surround thy name—
Thy Fenian heroes now no longer range
     The hills of fame.
The very names of Finn and Gaul sound strange—
     Yet thine the same—
By miscalled lake and desecrated grange—
     Remains, and shall remain!

The Druid's altar and the Druid's creed
     We scarce can trace,
There is not left an undisputed deed
     Of all your race,
Save your majestic song, which hath their speed,
     And strength and grace;
In that sole song, they live and love, and bleed—
     It bears them on through space.

O, inspired giant! shall we e'er behold,
     In our own time,
One fit to speak your spirit on the wold,
     Or seize your rhyme?
One pupil of the past, as mighty-souled
     As in the prime,
Were the fond, fair, and beautiful, and bold—
     They of your song sublime!

THE MAN OF THE NORTH COUNTRIE

HE CAME from the North, and his words were few,
But his voice was kind and his heart was true;
And I knew by his eyes no guile had he,
So I married the man of the North Countrie.

Oh! Garryowen may be more gay,
Than this quiet street of Ballibay;
And I know the sun shines softly down
On the river that passes my native town.

But there's not—I say it with joy and pride—
Better man than mine in Munster wide;
And Limerick town has no happier hearth
Than mine has been with my man of the North.

I wish that in Munster they only knew
The kind, kind neighbours I came unto:
Small hate or scorn would ever be
Between the South and the North Countrie.

THE CELTIC CROSS

THROUGH storm and fire and gloom, I see it stand
    Firm, broad, and tall,
The Celtic Cross that marks our Fatherland,
    Amid them all!
Druids and Danes and Saxons vainly rage
    Around its base;
It standeth shock on shock, and age on age,
    Star of our scatter'd race.

O Holy Cross! dear symbol of the dread
    Death of our Lord,
Around thee long have slept our martyr dead
    Sward over sward.

[520]

An hundred bishops I myself can count
  Among the slain:
Chiefs, captains, rank and file, a shining mount
  Of God's ripe grain.

The monarch's mace, the Puritan's claymore,
  Smote thee not down;
On headland steep, on mountain summit hoar,
  In mart and town,
In Glendalough, in Ara, in Tyrone,
  We find thee still,
Thy open arms still stretching to thine own,
  O'er town and lough and hill.

And would they tear thee out of Irish soil,
  The guilty fools!
How time must mock their antiquated toil
  And broken tools!
Cranmer and Cromwell from thy grasp retired,
  Baffled and thrown;
William and Anne to sap thy site conspir'd—
  The rest is known.

Holy Saint Patrick, father of our faith,
  Beloved of God!
Shield thy dear Church from the impending scaith,
  Or, if the rod
Must scourge it yet again, inspire and raise
  To emprise high
Men like the heroic race of other days,
  Who joyed to die.

Fear! wherefore should the Celtic people fear
  Their Church's fate?
The day is not—the day was never near—
  Could desolate
The Destined Island, all whose clay
  Is holy ground:

Its Cross shall stand till that predestin'd day
When Erin's self is drowned.

TIMOTHY DANIEL SULLIVAN
(1827-1914)

GOD SAVE IRELAND

(Air: "Tramp, Tramp, The Boys Are Marching")

High upon the gallows tree swung the noble-hearted three,
  By the vengeful tyrant stricken in their bloom;
But they met him face to face, with the courage of their race,
  And they went with souls undaunted to their doom.
"God save Ireland," said the heroes; "God save Ireland," said
      they all:
"Whether on the scaffold high, or the battle-field we die,
"O what matter, when for Erin dear we fall!"

Girt around with cruel foes, still their spirit proudly rose,
  For they thought of hearts that loved them, far and near,
Of the millions true and brave, o'er the ocean's swelling wave,
  And the friends in holy Ireland, ever dear.
"God save Ireland," said they proudly; "God save Ireland,"
      said they all:
"Whether on the scaffold high, or the battle-field we die,
"O what matter, when for Erin dear we fall!"

Climbed they up the rugged stair; rung their voices out in
      prayer;
  Then, with England's fatal cord around them cast,
Close beneath the gallows tree, kissed like brothers lovingly,
  True to home and faith and freedom to the last.
"God save Ireland," prayed they loudly; "God save Ireland,"
      said they all:
"Whether on the scaffold high, or the battle-field we die,
"O what matter, when for Erin dear we fall!"

[522]

Never till the latest day shall the memory pass away
  Of the gallant lives thus given for our land;
But on the cause must go, amidst joy, or weal or woe,
  Till we've made our isle a nation free and grand.
"God save Ireland," say we proudly; "God save Ireland," say
    we all:
"Whether on the scaffold high, or the battle-field we die,
"O what matter, when for Erin dear we fall!"

FITZ-JAMES O'BRIEN
(1828-1862)

MINOT'S LEDGE

    LIKE spectral hounds across the sky,
    The white clouds scud before the storm;
    And naked in the howling night
    The red-eyed lighthouse lifts its form.
    The waves with slippery fingers clutch
    The massive tower, and climb and fall,
    And, muttering, growl with baffled rage
    Their curses on the sturdy wall.

    Up in the lonely tower he sits,
    The keeper of the crimson light:
    Silent and awestruck does he hear
    The imprecations of the night.
    The white spray beats against the panes
    Like some wet ghost that down the air
    Is hunted by a troop of fiends,
    And seeks a shelter anywhere.

    He prays aloud, the lonely man,
    For every soul that night at sea,
    But more than all for that brave boy
    Who used to gayly climb his knee,—

Young Charlie, with his chestnut hair
And hazel eyes and laughing lip.
"May Heaven look down," the old man cries,
"Upon my son, and on his ship!"

While thus with pious heart he prays,
Far in the distance sounds a boom:
He pauses; and again there rings
That sullen thunder through the room.
A ship upon the shoals to-night!
She cannot hold for one half-hour;
But clear the ropes and grappling-hooks,
And trust in the Almighty Power!

On the drenched gallery he stands,
Striving to pierce the solid night:
Across the sea the red eye throws
A steady crimson wake of light;
And, where it falls upon the waves,
He sees a human head float by,
With long drenched curls of chestnut hair,
And wild but fearless hazel eye.

Out with the hooks! One mighty fling!
Adown the wind the long rope curls.
Oh, will it catch? Ah, dread suspense!
While the wild ocean wilder whirls.
A steady pull; it tightens now:
Oh! his old heart will burst with joy,
As on the slippery rocks he pulls
The breathing body of his boy.

Still sweep the spectres through the sky;
Still scud the clouds before the storm;
Still naked in the howling night
The red-eyed lighthouse lifts its form.
Without, the world is wild with rage;
Unkennelled demons are abroad:

But with the father and the son
Within, there is the peace of God.

CHARLES JOSEPH KICKHAM
(1830-1882)

RORY OF THE HILL

'THAT rake up near the rafters, why leave it there so long?
The handle, of the best of ash, is smooth, and straight, and
    strong;
And, mother, will you tell me, why did my father frown,
When to make the hay, in summer-time, I climbed to take it
    down?'
She looked into her husband's eyes, while her own with light
    did fill,
'You'll shortly know the reason, boy!' said Rory of the Hill.

The midnight moon is lighting up the slopes of Sliav-na-man,—
Whose foot affrights the startled hares so long before the dawn?
He stopped just where the Anner's stream winds up the woods
    anear,
Then whistled low and looked around to see the coast was
    clear.
A sheeling door flew open—in he stepped with right good
    will—
'God save all here, and bless your work,' said Rory of the Hill.

Right hearty was the welcome that greeted him, I ween,
For years gone by he fully proved how well he loved the Green;
And there was one among them who grasped him by the
    hand—
One who through all that weary time roamed on a foreign
    strand;
He brought them news from gallant friends that made their
    heart-strings thrill—
'My sowl! I never doubted them!' said Rory of the Hill.

[525]

They sat around the humble board till dawning of the day,
And yet not song nor shout I heard—no revellers were they:
Some brows flushed red with gladness, while some were grimly
    pale;
But pale or red, from out those eyes flashed souls that never
    quail!
'And sing us now about the vow, they swore for to fulfil'—
'You'll read it yet in History,' said Rory of the Hill.

Next day the ashen handle, he took down from where it hung,
The toothed rake, full scornfully, into the fire he flung;
And in its stead a shining blade is gleaming once again—
Oh! for a hundred thousand of such weapons and such men!
Right soldierly he wielded it, and, going through his drill,
'Attention!'—'Charge!'—'Front, point!'—'Advance!' cried Rory
    of the Hill.

She looked at him with woman's pride, with pride and woman's
    fears;
She flew to him, she clung to him, and dried away her tears;
He feels her pulse beat truly, while her arms around him
    twine—
'Now God be praised for your stout heart, brave little wife of
    mine.'
He swung his first-born in the air, while joy his heart did fill—
'You'll be a Freeman yet, my boy,' said Rory of the Hill.

Oh! knowledge is a wondrous power, and stronger than the
    wind;
And thrones shall fall, and despots bow before the might of
    mind;
The poet and the orator, the heart of man can sway,
And would to the kind heavens that Wolfe Tone were here
    to-day!
Yet trust me, friends, dear Ireland's strength, her truest
    strength, is still
The rough and ready roving boys, like Rory of the Hill.

[526]

ROBERT DWYER JOYCE
(1830-1883)

THE LEPRAHAUN

IN A shady nook one moonlit night,
  A leprahaun I spied
In scarlet coat and cap of green,
  A cruiskeen by his side.
'Twas tick, tack, tick, his hammer went,
  Upon a weeny shoe,
And I laughed to think of a purse of gold,
  But the fairy was laughing too.

With tip-toe step and beating heart,
  Quite softly I drew nigh.
There was mischief in his merry face,
  A twinkle in his eye;
He hammered and sang with tiny voice,
  And sipped the mountain dew;
Oh! I laughed to think he was caught at last,
  But the fairy was laughing, too.

As quick as thought I grasped the elf,
  "Your fairy purse," I cried,
"My purse?" said he, " 'tis in her hand,
  That lady by your side."
I turned to look, the elf was off,
  And what was I to do?
Oh! I laughed to think what a fool I'd been,
  And, the fairy was laughing too.

WHITLEY STOKES
(1830-1909)

THE VIKING

Time—Nightfall in the middle of the ninth century. Place—at sea, on the poop of a Norse Viking's galley. Author—A Gaelic bard captured by the Viking. Cause of Making—Orders to praise the Viking and his gods.

"BITTER in sooth is the wind to-night,
   Rousing the wrath of the white-haired sea;
But smooth-sea-sailing is no delight
   To Norroway's heroes fierce and free.

"Strong and swift are the waves to-night,
   Roaring over the reefs a-lee:
Stronger, swifter thy ranks in fight,
   Charging thy foes till they break and flee.

"Bright and keen are the stars to-night,
   Sending their shafts to pierce the sea:
Brighter thy swords when they flash and smite,
   Keener thy darts when they drench the lea.

"Glad are the hearts of thy gods to-night:
   Odin, the Father, is fain to see
Eyeballs of fire and arms of might,
   Sea-kings sailing in warriors' glee.

"Why do I launch this lay to-night,
   I, a singer from Christentie?
Thor is stronger than Christ the White:
   Therefore I praise thy gods and thee.

"Little but song have I to-night:
   Guerdon of gold give thou to me:
Laud the singer who sings aright:
   Give him his sword, and set him free!"

[528]

MICHAEL HOGAN
(1832-1899)

O'NEILL'S WAR SONG

FIERCE is the flame of the vengeance of Erin
  When roused by the blast of the battle to shine;
Fierce is the flash of her broad sword uprearing
  To strike for her rights and her altars divine.
       Haste, snatch the spear and shield,
       Rush to the battlefield,
The Saxon is come from the towers of the Pale!
       Sons of the vale and glen!
       Children of mighty men!
Swell the dread war-note of conq'ring O'Neill.

Lightly the Red Hand of terror is streaming,
  Like a fire-cloud of death on the hills of Tyrone,
Brightly the spears of Clan Conaill are gleaming,
  Like Swilly's blue waves in the beams of the sun.
       Hark, the wild battle-cry
       Rings through the sounding sky!
Valley and mountain are blazing with steel!
       Eagles and forest deer
       Flee from the heights with fear,
Scared at the war-shout of conq'ring O'Neill.

O'Donnell descends from his father's dark mountains,
  He comes, noble prince, to the strife of the Gael;
He comes like the rush of his own stormy fountains,
  Sweeping, impetuous, o'er moorland and vale.
       On to the Yellow Ford
       Chiefs of the flashing sword!
Drive the proud Sassenach back to the Pale!
       Fierce to the scene of blood
       Wild as a mountain flood,
Charge the stout warriors of conq'ring O'Neill.

[529]

Our war-shouts shall ring and our musket peals rattle,
   Our swords shall not rest from the hot, weary toil.
Our plains shall be drenched with the red show'rs of battle,
   Till the Godless invaders are swept from our soil!
            Pikemen and musketeer!
            Kern and cavalier—
The wolves and the ravens are scenting their meal!
            Carve to them, red and fresh,
            Plenty of Saxon flesh!
Follow your princely chief—conq'ring O'Neill.

Onward, O'Neill, with thy Red Hand of glory!
   Thy sword lighteth thousands to conquests and fame;
The annals of Eire are emblazed with thy story,
   Her valleys are fill'd with the praise of thy name!
            On with the Bloody Hand!
            Shake the dread battle brand—
Woe to the spoilers of green Inisfail!
            Lo! their red ranks appear—
            Up, every gun and spear—
Charge—charge, O'Donnell and conq'ring O'Neill!

STOPFORD A. BROOKE
(1832-1916)

THE EARTH AND MAN

A LITTLE sun, a little rain,
   A soft wind blowing from the west,
And woods and fields are sweet again,
   And warmth within the mountain's breast.

So simple is the earth we tread,
   So quick with love and life her frame,
Ten thousand years have dawned and fled,
   And still her magic is the same.

A little love, a little trust,
    A soft impulse, a sudden dream,
And life as dry as desert dust
    Is fresher than a mountain stream.

So simple is the heart of man,
    So ready for new hope and joy;
Ten thousand years since it began
    Have left it younger than a boy.

GEORGE SIGERSON
(1835-1925)

SMITH'S SONG [1]

(Adapted from the Irish)

DING dong didero,
    Blow big bellows,
Ding dong didero,
    Black coal yellows,
Ding dong didero,
    Blue steel mellows
Ding dong didero,
    Strike!—good fellows.

Up with the hammers,
    Down with the sledges,
Hark to the clamours,
    Pound now the edges,
Work it and watch it,
    Round, flat, or square O,
Spade, hook, or hatchet—
    Sword for a hero.

[1] " 'The Smith's Song,' " Petrie remarks, "has very evidently been suggested—like Handel's 'Harmonious Blacksmith'—by the measured time and varied notes of his hammers striking upon the anvil; and its melody is therefore one of much interest as an ancient example of imitative music."

Ding dong didero,
    Ding dong didero,
Spade for a labourer,
    Sword for a hero,
Hammer it, stout smith,
    Rightly, lightly,
Hammer it, hammer it,
    Hammer at it brightly.

JAMES LYMAN MOLLOY
(1837-1909)

THE KERRY DANCE

O, THE days of the Kerry dancing, O, the ring of the piper's
    tune!
O, for one of those hours of gladness, gone, alas! like our youth
    too soon;
When the boys began to gather in the glen of a summer night,
And the Kerry piper's tuning made us long with wild delight,
O, to think of it, O, to dream of it, fills my heart with tears.

O, the days of the Kerry dancing, O, the ring of the piper's
    tune!
O, for one of those hours of gladness, gone, alas! like our youth
    too soon.

Was there ever a sweeter colleen in the dance than Eily Moore?
Or a prouder lad than Thady, as he boldly took the floor?
"Lads and lasses to your places; up the middle and down
    again."
Ah! the merry hearted laughter ringing through the happy
    glen!
O, to think of it, O, to dream of it, fills my heart with tears!
    O, the days, etc.

[532]

Time goes on and the happy years are dead,
And one by one the merry hearts are fled;
Silent now is the wild and lonely glen,
Where the bright glad laugh will echo ne'er again,
Only dreaming of days gone by, fills my heart with tears!
      O, the days, etc.

Loving voices of old companions, stealing out of the past once
      more,
And the sound of the dear old music, soft and sweet as in days
      of yore,
When the boys began to gather in the glen of a summer night,
And the Kerry piper's tuning made us long with wild delight,
O, to think of it, O, to dream of it, fills my heart with tears!
      O, the days, etc.

BANTRY BAY

As I'm sitting all alone in the gloaming,
It might have been but yesterday,
That I watched the fisher sails all homing,
Till the little herring fleet at anchor lay;
Then the fisher girls with baskets swinging,
Came running down the old stone way,
Every lassie to her sailor lad was singing
A welcome back to Bantry Bay.

Then we heard the piper's sweet note tuning,
And all the lassies turned to hear,
Till it mingled with a soft voice crooning,
Till the music floated down the wooden pier;
"Save ye kindly, colleens all"—said the piper,
"Hands across and trip it while I play."—
And a tender sound of song and merry dancing,
Stole softly over Bantry Bay.

[533]

As I'm sitting all alone in the gloaming,
The shadows of the past draw near,
And I see the loving faces round me,
That used to glad the old brown pier;
Some are gone upon their last long homing,
Some are left, but they are old and grey,
And we're waiting for the tide in the gloaming,
To sail upon the Great Highway,
To the Land of Rest Unending—
All peacefully from Bantry Bay.

WILLIAM EDWARD HARTPOLE LECKY

(1838-1903)

EARLY THOUGHTS

OH GATHER the thoughts of your early years,
    Gather them as they flow,
For all unmarked in those thoughts appears
    The path where you soon must go.

Full many a dream will wither away,
    And Springtide hues are brief,
But the lines are there of the autumn day,
    Like the skeleton in the leaf.

The husbandman knows not the worth of his seed
    Until the flower be sprung,
And only in age can we rightly read
    The thoughts that we thought when young.

JOHN TODHUNTER
(1839-1916)

THE BANSHEE

GREEN, in the wizard arms
Of the foam-bearded Atlantic,
An isle of old enchantment,
A melancholy isle,
Enchanted and dreaming lies;
And there, by Shannon's flowing,
In the moonlight, spectre-thin,
The spectre Erin sits.

An aged desolation,
She sits by old Shannon's flowing,
A mother of many children,
Of children exiled and dead,
In her home, with bent head, homeless,
Clasping her knees she sits,
Keening, keening!

And at her keen the fairy-grass
Trembles on dun and barrow;
Around the foot of her ancient crosses
The grave-grass shakes and the nettle swings;
In haunted glens the meadow-sweet
Flings to the night wind
Her mystic mournful perfume;
The sad spearmint by holy wells
Breathes melancholy balm.
Sometimes she lifts her head,
With blue eyes tearless,
And gazes athwart the reek of night
Upon things long past,
Upon things to come.

[535]

And sometimes, when the moon
Brings tempest upon the deep,
And roused Atlantic thunders from his caverns in the west,
The wolfhound at her feet
Springs up with a mighty bay,
And chords of mystery sound from the wild harp at her side,
Strung from the heart of poets;
And she flies on the wings of tempest
With grey hair streaming:
A meteor of evil omen,
The spectre of hope forlorn,
Keening, keening!

She keens, and the strings of her wild harp shiver
On the gusts of night:
O'er the four waters she keens—over Moyle she keens,
O'er the Sea of Milith, and the Strait of Strongbow,
And the Ocean of Columbus.

And the Fianna hear, and the ghosts of her cloudy hovering
        heroes;
And the swan, Fianoula, wails o'er the waters of Inisfail,
Chanting her song of destiny,
The rune of the weaving Fates.
And the nations hear in the void and quaking time of night,
Sad unto dawning, dirges,
Solemn dirges,
And snatches of bardic song;
Their souls quake in the void and quaking time of night,
And they dream of the weird of kings,
And tyrannies moulting, sick
In the dreadful wind of change.

Wail no more, lonely one, mother of exiles, wail no more,
Banshee of the world—no more!
Thy sorrows are the world's, thou art no more alone;
Thy wrongs, the world's.

O MIGHTY, MELANCHOLY WIND

BRING from the craggy haunts of birch and pine,
  Thou wild wind, bring
Keen forest odours from that realm of thine,
  Upon thy wing!

O wind, O mighty, melancholy wind,
  Blow through me, blow!
Thou blowest forgotten things into my mind,
  From long ago.

EDWARD DOWDEN
(1843-1913)

AUTUMN SONG

          LONG Autumn rain;
White mists which choke the vale, and blot the sides
Of the bewildered hills; in all the plain
No field agleam where the gold pageant was,
And silent o'er a tangle of drenched grass
          The blackbird glides.

          In the heart,—fire,
Fire and clear air and cries of water-springs,
And large, pure winds; all April's quick desire,
All June's possession; a most fearless Earth
Drinking great ardours; and the rapturous birth
          Of wingéd things.

MONA LISA

MAKE thyself known, Sibyl, or let despair
Of knowing thee be absolute: I wait
Hour-long and waste a soul. What word of fate
Hides 'twixt the lips which smile and still forbear?
Secret perfection! Mystery too fair!
Tangle the sense no more, lest I should hate
The delicate tyranny, the inviolate
Poise of thy folded hands, the fallen hair.
Nay, nay—I wrong thee with rough words; still be
Serene, victorious, inaccessible;
Still smile but speak not; lightest irony
Lurk ever 'neath thy eyelids' shadow; still
O'ertop our knowledge; Sphinx of Italy,
Allure us and reject us at thy will!

ARTHUR O'SHAUGHNESSY
(1844-1881)

ODE

WE ARE the music-makers,
    And we are the dreamers of dreams,
Wandering by lone sea-breakers,
    And sitting by desolate streams;—

World-losers and world-forsakers,
    On whom the pale moon gleams:
Yet we are the movers and shakers
    Of the world for ever, it seems.

With wonderful deathless ditties
We build up the world's great cities,
    And out of a fabulous story
    We fashion an empire's glory:

One man with a dream, at pleasure,
   Shall go forth and conquer a crown;
And three with a new song's measure
   Can trample an empire down.

We, in the ages lying
   In the buried past of the earth,
Built Nineveh with our sighing,
   And Babel itself with our mirth;
And o'erthrew them with prophesying
   To the old of the new world's worth;
For each age is a dream that is dying,
   Or one that is coming to birth.

THE LINE OF BEAUTY

When mountains crumble and rivers all run dry,
   When every flower has fallen and summer fails
   To come again, when the sun's splendour pales,
And earth with lagging footsteps seems well-nigh
Spent in her annual circuit through the sky;
   When love is a quenched flame, and nought avails
   To save decrepit man, who feebly wails
And lies down lost in the great grave to die;
What is eternal? What escapes decay?
   A certain faultless, matchless, deathless line,
   Curving consummate. Death, Eternity,
And nought to it, from it take nought away:
   'Twas all God's gift and all man's mastery,
   God become human and man grown divine.

WILLIAM B. McBURNEY (CARROLL MALONE)
(c.1855-d.1892?)

THE CROPPY BOY [1]

(A Ballad of 1798)

'GOOD men and true! in this house who dwell,
To a stranger bouchal, I pray you tell
Is the Priest at home? or may he be seen?
I would speak a word with Father Green.'

'The Priest's at home, boy, and may be seen;
'Tis easy speaking with Father Green;
But you must wait, till I go and see
If the holy father alone may be.'

The youth has entered an empty hall—
What a lonely sound has his light foot-fall!
And the gloomy chamber's chill and bare,
With a vested Priest in a lonely chair.

The youth has knelt to tell his sins;
'Nomine Dei,' the youth begins:
At 'mea culpa' he beats his breast,
And in broken murmurs he speaks the rest.

'At the siege of Ross did my father fall,
And at Gorey my loving brothers all,
I alone am left of my name and race,
I will go to Wexford and take their place.

'I cursed three times since last Easter day—
At mass-time once I went to play:
I passed the churchyard one day in haste,
And forgot to pray for my mother's rest.

[1] Nickname given to the Wexford rebels because of their close-cropped hair.

[540]

'I bear no hate against living thing;
But I love my country above my King.
Now, Father! bless me, and let me go
To die, if God has ordained it so.'

The Priest said nought, but a rustling noise
Made the youth look above in wild surprise;
The robes were off, and in scarlet there
Sat a yeoman captain with fiery glare.

With fiery glare and with fury hoarse,
Instead of blessing, he breathed a curse:—
' 'Twas a good thought, boy, to come here and shrive,
For one short hour is your time to live.

'Upon yon river three tenders float,
The Priest's in one, if he isn't shot—
We hold his house for our Lord the King,
And, Amen, say I, may all traitors swing!'

At Geneva Barrack that young man died,
And at Passage they have his body laid.
Good people who live in peace and joy,
Breathe a prayer and a tear for the Croppy boy.

JOHN BOYLE O'REILLY
(1844-1890)

FOREVER

THOSE we love truly never die,
Though year by year the sad memorial wreath,
A ring and flowers, types of life and death,
Are laid upon their graves.

[541]

For death the pure life saves,
And life all pure is love; and love can reach
From heaven to earth, and nobler lessons teach
Than those by mortals read.

Well blest is he who has a dear one dead:
A friend he has whose face will never change—
A dear communion that will not grow strange;
The anchor of a love is death.

The blessed sweetness of a loving breath
Will reach our cheek all fresh through weary years.
For her who died long since, ah! waste not tears,
She's thine unto the end.

Thank God for one dear friend,
With face still radiant with the light of truth,
Whose love comes laden with the scent of youth,
Through twenty years of death.

THE CRY OF THE DREAMER

I AM tired of planning and toiling
In the crowded hives of men;
Heart-weary of building and spoiling
And spoiling and building again.
And I long for the dear old river,
Where I dreamed my youth away;
For a dreamer lives forever,
And a toiler dies in a day.

I am sick of the showy seeming
Of a life that is half a lie;
Of the faces lined with scheming
In the throng that hurries by.
From the sleepless thoughts' endeavour,

I would go where the children play;
For a dreamer lives forever,
And a thinker dies in a day.

I can feel no pride but pity
For the burdens the rich endure;
There is nothing sweet in the city
But the patient lives of the poor.
Ah, the little hands too skillful,
And the child-mind choked with weeds!
The daughter's heart grown willful,
And the father's heart that bleeds!

No, No! from the street's rude bustle,
From trophies of mart and stage,
I would fly to the woods' low rustle
And the meadows' kindly page.
Let me dream as of old by the river,
And be loved for the dream alway;
For a dreamer lives forever,
And a toiler dies in a day.

A WHITE ROSE

THE red rose whispers of passion,
    And the white rose breathes of love;
Oh, the red rose is a falcon,
    And the white rose is a dove.

But I send you a cream-white rosebud
    With a flush on its petal tips;
For the love that is purest and sweetest
    Has a kiss of desire on the lips.

DISAPPOINTMENT

HER hair was a waving bronze and her eyes
Deep wells that might cover a brooding soul;
And who, till he weighed it, could ever surmise
That her heart was a cinder instead of a coal?

CONSTANCY

"You gave me the key of your heart, my love;
    Then why do you make me knock?"
"Oh, that was yesterday, Saints above!
    And last night—I changed the lock!"

A MESSAGE OF PEACE

THERE was once a pirate, greedy and bold,
    Who ravaged for gain, and saved the spoils;
Till his coffers were bursting with blood-stained gold,
    And millions of captives bore his toils.

Then fear took hold of him, and he cried:
    "I have gathered enough; now, war should cease!"
And he sent out messengers far and wide
    (To the strong ones only) to ask for peace.

"We are Christian brethren!" thus he spake;
    "Let us seal a contract—never to fight!
Except against rebels who dare to break
    The bonds we have made by the victor's right."

And the strong ones listen; and some applaud
    The kindly offer and righteous word;
With never a dream of deceit or fraud,
    They would spike the cannon and break the sword.

[544]

But others, their elders, listen and smile
At the sudden convert's unctuous style.
They watch for the peacemaker's change of way;
Even now, while his godly messengers speak,
His guns are aflame on his enemies weak.
He has stolen the blade from the hand of his foe,
And he strikes the unarmed a merciless blow.

To the ends of the earth his oppression runs,
The rebels are blown from the mouths of his guns.
His war-tax devours his subject's food;
He taxes their evil and taxes their good;
He taxes their salt till he rots their blood.
He leaps on the friendless as on a prey,
And slinks, tail-down, from the strong one's way.
The pharisee's cant goes up for peace,
But the cries of his victims never cease;
The stifled voices of brave men rise
From a thousand cells; while his rascal spies
Are spending their blood-money fast and free.

And this is the Christian to oversee
A world of evil! a saint to preach!
A holy well-doer come to teach!
A prophet to tell us war should cease!
A pious example of Christian peace!

TO-DAY

ONLY from day to day
    The life of a wise man runs;
What matter if seasons far away
    Have gloom or have double suns?

To climb the unreal path,
    We stray from the roadway here;

[545]

We swim the rivers of wrath
    And tunnel the hills of fear.

Our feet on the torrent's brink,
    Our eyes on the cloud afar,
We fear the things we think,
    Instead of the things that are.

Like a tide our work should rise,
    Each later wave the best;
"To-day is a king in disguise,"
    To-day is the special test.

Like a sawyer's work is life—
    The present makes the flaw,
And the only field for strife
    Is the inch before the saw.

THE INFINITE

THE Infinite always is silent:
It is only the Finite speaks.
Our words are the idle wave-caps
On the deep that never breaks.
We may question with wand of science,
Explain, decide and discuss;
But only in meditation
The Mystery speaks to us.

EMILY LAWLESS
(1845-1913)

THE STRANGER'S GRAVE

LITTLE feet too young and soft to walk,
Little lips too young and pure to talk,
Little faded grass-tufts, root and stalk.

I lie alone here, utterly alone,
Amid pure ashes my wild ashes mingle;
A drownéd man, with a name, unknown,
A drifting waif, flung by the drifting shingle.
Oh, plotting brain, and restless heart of mine,
What strange fate brought you to so strange a shrine?

Sometimes a woman comes across the grass,
Bare-footed, with pit-patterings scarcely heard,
Sometimes the grazing cattle slowly pass,
Or on my turf sings loud some mating bird.
Oh, plotting brain, and restless heart of mine,
What strange fate brought you to so strange a shrine?

Little feet too young and soft to walk,
Little lips too young and pure to talk,
Little faded grass-tufts, root and stalk.

DIRGE OF THE MUNSTER FOREST

(1591)

BRING out the hemlock! bring the funeral yew!
The faithful ivy that doth all enfold;
Heap high the rocks, the patient brown earth strew,
And cover them against the numbing cold.
Marshal my retinue of bird and beast,

[547]

Wren, titmouse, robin, birds of every hue;
Let none keep back, no, not the very least,
Nor fox, nor deer, nor tiny nibbling crew,
Only bid one of all my forest clan
Keep far from us on this our funeral day.
On the grey wolf I lay my sovereign ban,
The great grey wolf who scrapes the earth away;
Lest, with hooked claw and furious hunger, he
Lay bare my dead for gloating foes to see—
Lay bare my dead, who died, and died for me.

For I must surely die as they have died,
And lo! my doom stands yoked and linked with theirs;
The axe is sharpened to cut down my pride:
I pass, I die, and leave no natural heirs,
Soon shall my sylvan coronals be cast;
My hidden sanctuaries, my secret ways,
Naked must stand to the rebellious blast;
No Spring shall quicken what this Autumn slays.
Therefore, while still I keep my russet crown,
I summon all my lieges to the feast.
Hither, ye flutterers! black, or pied, or brown;
Hither, ye furred ones! Hither every beast!
Only to one of all my forest clan
I cry, "Avaunt! Our mourning revels flee!"
On the grey wolf I lay my sovereign ban,
The great grey wolf with scraping claws, lest he
Lay bare my dead for gloating foes to see—
Lay bare my dead, who died, and died for me.

EMILY HENRIETTA HICKEY
(1845-1924)

BELOVED, IT IS MORN

BELOVED, it is morn!
  A redder berry on the thorn,
  A deeper yellow on the corn,
For this good day new-born.
    Pray, Sweet, for me
    That I may be
    Faithful to God and thee.

Beloved, it is day!
  And lovers work, as children play,
  With heart and brain untired alway:
Dear love, look up and pray.
    Pray, Sweet, for me
    That I may be
    Faithful to God and thee.

Beloved, it is night!
  Thy heart and mine are full of light,
  Thy spirit shineth clear and white,
God keep thee in His sight!
    Pray, Sweet, for me
    That I may be
    Faithful to God and thee.

JOHN KEEGAN CASEY
(1846-1870)

THE RISING OF THE MOON A.D. 1798

(Air: "The Wearing of the Green")

"Oh, THEN, tell me, Shawn O'Ferrall,
  Tell me why you hurry so?"
"Hush! *ma bouchal,* hush, and listen;"
  And his cheeks were all a-glow:
"I bear orders from the Captain—
  Get you ready quick and soon;
For the pikes must be together
  At the risin' of the moon."

"Oh, then, tell me, Shawn O'Ferrall,
  Where the gath'rin' is to be?"
"In the ould spot by the river,
  Right well known to you and me;
One word more—for signal token
  Whistle up the marchin' tune,
With your pike upon your shoulder,
  By the risin' of the moon."

Out from many a mud-wall cabin
  Eyes were watching thro' that night;
Many a manly chest was throbbing
  For the blessed warning light.
Murmurs passed along the valleys,
  Like the banshee's lonely croon,
And a thousand blades were flashing
  At the risin' of the moon.

There, beside the singing river,
  That dark mass of men was seen—
Far above the shining weapons
  Hung their own beloved "Green;"

[550]

"Death to ev'ry foe and traitor!
   Forward! strike the marchin' tune,
And hurrah, my boys, for freedom!
   'T is the risin' of the moon."

Well they fought for poor Old Ireland,
   And full bitter was their fate;
(Oh! what glorious pride and sorrow
   Fill the name of 'Ninety-Eight!)
Yet, thank God, e'en still are beating
   Hearts in manhood's burning noon,
Who would follow in their footsteps
   At the risin' of the moon!

MAIRE, MY GIRL

OVER the dim blue hills
   Strays a wild river,
Over the dim blue hills
   Rests my heart ever.
Dearer and brighter than
   Jewels and pearl,
Dwells she in beauty there,
   Maire, my girl.

Down upon Claris heath
   Shines the soft berry,
On the brown harvest tree
   Droops the red cherry.
Sweeter thy honey lips,
   Softer the curl
Straying adown thy cheeks,
   Maire, my girl.

'Twas on an April eve
   That I first met her;

[551]

Many an eve shall pass
    Ere I forget her.
Since, my young heart has been
    Wrapped in a whirl,
Thinking and dreaming of
    Maire, my girl.

She is too kind and fond
    Ever to grieve me,
She has too pure a heart
    E'er to deceive me.
Were I Tryconnell's chief
    Or Desmond's earl,
Life would be dark, wanting
    Maire, my girl!

Over the dim blue hills
    Strays a wild river,
Over the dim blue hills
    Rests my heart ever.
Dearer and brighter than
    Jewels or pearl,
Dwells she in beauty there,
    Maire, my girl.

JOSEPH IGNATIUS CONSTANTINE CLARKE
(1846-1925)

THE FIGHTING RACE

"READ out the names!" and Burke sat back,
    And Kelly drooped his head.
While Shea—they call him Scholar Jack—
    Went down the list of the dead.
Officers, seamen, gunners, marines,
    The crews of the gig and yawl,

The bearded man and the lad in his teens,
  Carpenters, coal passers—all.
Then, knocking the ashes from out his pipe,
  Said Burke in an offhand way:
"We're all in that dead man's list, by Cripe!
  Kelly and Burke and Shea."
"Well, here's to the Maine, and I'm sorry for Spain,"
  Said Kelly and Burke and Shea.

"Wherever there's Kellys there's trouble," said Burke.
  "Wherever fighting's the game,
Or a spice of danger in grown man's work,"
  Said Kelly, "you'll find my name."
"And do we fall short," said Burke, getting mad,
  "When it's touch and go for life?"
Said Shea, "It's thirty-odd years, bedad,
  Since I charged to drum and fife
Up Marye's Heights, and my old canteen
  Stopped a rebel ball on its way.
There were blossoms of blood on our sprigs of green—
  Kelly and Burke and Shea—
And the dead didn't brag." "Well, here's to the flag!"
  Said Kelly and Burke and Shea.

"I wish't was in Ireland, for there's the place,"
  Said Burke, "that we'd die by right,
In the cradle of our soldier race,
  After one good stand-up fight.
My grandfather fell on Vinegar Hill,
  And fighting was not his trade;
But his rusty pike's in the cabin still,
  With Hessian blood on the blade."
"Aye, aye," said Kelly, "the pikes were great
  When the word was 'clear the way!'
We were thick on the roll in ninety-eight—
  Kelly and Burke and Shea."
"Well, here's to the pike and the sword and the like!"
  Said Kelly and Burke and Shea.

And Shea, the scholar, with rising joy,
 Said, "We were at Ramillies;
We left our bones at Fontenoy
 And up in the Pyrenees;
Before Dunkirk, on Landen's plain,
 Cremona, Lille, and Ghent,
We're all over Austria, France, and Spain,
 Wherever they pitched a tent.
We've died for England from Waterloo
 To Egypt and Dargai;
And still there's enough for a corps or crew,
 Kelly and Burke and Shea."
"Well, here is to good honest fighting blood!"
 Said Kelly and Burke and Shea.

"Oh, the fighting races don't die out,
 If they seldom die in bed,
For love is first in their hearts, no doubt,"
 Said Burke; then Kelly said:
"When Michael, the Irish Archangel, stands,
 The angel with the sword,
And the battle-dead from a hundred lands
 Are ranged in one big horde,
Our line, that for Gabriel's trumpet waits,
 Will stretch three deep that day,
From Jehoshaphat to the Golden Gates—
 Kelly and Burke and Shea."
"Well, here's thank God for the race and the sod!"
 Said Kelly and Burke and Shea.

ALFRED PERCEVAL GRAVES
(1846-1931)

FATHER O'FLYNN

OF PRIESTS we can offer a charmin' variety,
Far renowned for larnin' and piety;
Still, I'd advance ye widout impropriety,
  Father O'Flynn as the flower of them all.

Chorus
  Here's a health to you, Father O'Flynn,
  Slainte, and *slainte,* and *slainte* agin;
      Powerfullest preacher, and
      Tinderest teacher, and
  Kindliest creature in ould Donegal.

Don't talk of your Provost and Fellows of Trinity,
Famous for ever at Greek and Latinity,
Dad and the divels and all at Divinity,
  Father O'Flynn 'd make hares of them all.
    Come, I vinture to give you my word,
    Never the likes of his logic was heard,
        Down from Mythology
        Into Thayology,
    Troth! and Conchology if he'd the call

      Here's a health to you, etc.

Och! Father O'Flynn you've the wonderful way wid you,
All ould sinners are wishful to pray wid you,
All the young childer are wild for to play wid you,
  You've such a way wid you, Father avick!
    Still for all you've so gentle a soul,
    Gad, you've your flock in the grandest control;
        Checking the crazy ones,
        Coaxin' onaisy ones,
    Liftin' the lazy ones on wid the stick.

      Here's a health to you, etc.

[555]

And though quite avoidin' all foolish frivolity,
Still at all seasons of innocent jollity,
Where was the play-boy could claim an equality
    At comicality, Father, wid you?
        Once the Bishop looked grave at your jest,
        Till this remark set him off wid the rest:
            "Is it lave gaiety
            All to the laity?
    Cannot the clargy be Irishmen too?"

        Here's a health to you, etc.

ISABELLA VALANCY CRAWFORD
(1850-1887)

THE CANOE

My MASTERS twain made me a bed
Of pine-boughs resinous, and cedar;
Of moss, a soft and gentle breeder
Of dreams of rest; and me they spread
With furry skins, and, laughing, said—
"Now she shall lay her polished sides
As queens do rest, or dainty brides,
Our slender lady of the tides!"

My masters twain their camp-soul lit,
Streamed incense from the hissing cones;
Large crimson flashes grew and whirled,
Thin golden nerves of sly light curled,
Round the dun camp, and rose faint zones
Half-way about each grim bole knit,
Like a shy child that would bedeck
With its soft clasp a Brave's red neck,
Yet sees the rough shield on his breast,
The awful plumes shake on his crest,

And fearful drops his timid face,
Nor dares complete the sweet embrace.

Into the hollow hearts of brakes
Yet warm from sides of does and stags,
Passed to the crisp dark river flags,
Sinous, red as copper, snakes—
Sharp-headed serpents, made of light,
Glided and hid themselves in night.

My masters twain the slaughtered deer
Hung on forked boughs, with thongs of leather.
Bound were his stiff, slim feet together,
His eyes like dead stars cold and drear;
The wandering firelight drew near
And laid its wide palm, red and anxious,
On the sharp splendor of his branches;
On the white foam grown hard and sere
   On flank and shoulder.
Death, hard as breast of granite boulder,
   And under his lashes,
Peered through his eyes at his life's gray ashes.

My masters twain sang songs that wove
(As they burnished hunting blade and rifle)
A golden thread with a cobweb trifle,
Loud of the chase, and low of love.

"O Love! art thou a silver fish,
Shy of the line and shy of gaffing,
Which we do follow, fierce, yet laughing,
Casting at thee the light-winged wish?
And at the last shall we bring thee up
From the crystal darkness under the cup
   Of lily folden,
   On broad leaves golden?

"O Love! art thou a silver deer?
Swift thy starred feet as wing of swallow,

[557]

While we with rushing arrows follow:
And at the last shall we draw near,
And over thy velvet neck cast thongs,
Woven of roses, of stars, of songs,
New chains all moulden
Of rare gems olden?"

They hung the slaughtered fish like swords
On saplings slender; like scimitars
Bright, and ruddied from new-dead wars,
Blazed in the light the scaly hordes.

They piled up boughs beneath the trees,
Of cedar-web and green fir tassel;
Low did the pointed pine tops rustle,
The camp fire blushed to the tender breeze.

The hounds laid dew-laps on the ground,
With needles of pine sweet, soft and rusty,
Dreamed of the dead stag stout and lusty;
A bat by the red flames wove its round.

The darkness built its wigwam walls
Close round the camp, and at its curtain
Pressed shapes, thin woven and uncertain,
As white locks of tall waterfalls.

WILLIAM LARMINIE
(1850-1900)

THE SWORD OF TETHRA

The sword of Tethra, one of the Kings of the Fohmors, is captured by the sun-god Lu. This sword is Death.

(from *Moytura*)

Do YOU seek to bind me, ye gods,
And the deeds of me only beginning?
Shall I gloat over triumphs achieved
When the greatest remains for the winning?
Ye boast of this world ye have made,
This corpse-built world?
Show me an atom thereof
That hath not suffered and struggled,
And yielded its life to Tethra?
The rocks they are built of the mold,
And the mold of the herb that was green,
And the beast from the herb,
And man from the beast,
And downward in hurried confusion,
Through shapes that are loathsome,
Beast, man, worm, pellmell,
What does it matter to me?
All that have lived go back to the mold,
To stiffen through ages of pain
In the rock-rigid realms of death.

THE NAMELESS RUIN

WHO were the builders? Question not the silence
That settles on the lake for evermore,
Save when the sea-bird screams and to the islands
The echo answers from the steep-cliffed shore.

[559]

O half-remaining ruin, in the lore
Of human life a gap shall all deplore
Beholding thee; since thou art like the dead
Found slain, no token to reveal the why,
The name, the story. Some one murder'd
We know, we guess; and gazing upon thee,
And, filled by thy long silence of reply,
We guess some garnered sheaf of tragedy;—
Of tribe or nation slain so utterly
That even their ghosts are dead, and on their grave
Springeth no bloom of legend in its wildness;
And age by age weak washing round the islands
No faintest sigh of story lisps the wave.

LADY GREGORY
(1852?-1932)

THE OLD WOMAN REMEMBERS

An old woman is sitting in an almost dark room. She has placed seven
candlesticks on the table. At the end of the first verse she lights a candle
and puts it in a candlestick, and after that lights each one from the candle
last lighted. She sits by the table and speaks as to herself:

SEVEN hundred and a half of years
Are gone since Strongbow took the sway,
Put Ireland under grief and tears,
A ball struck here and there at play.
When the white cities turned to flames
Who lived to hear the Masses said?
Now on the beads I'll tell out names,
And light a candle for the dead.

When John mocked in his jibing youth
Men had big names e'er he was born;
Laid on hard burdens, breaking truth,
Donald O'Brien blew the horn.

It's Munster held the flail that day;
The scattered scoffers ran for life;
They found that no great year for play,
Eleven hundred eighty-five.

(She lights a candle.)

Rebel and King, a Connacht lad
Stood in the gap at Athenry;
Phelim O'Connor, proud and glad
To shout the Connacht battle cry;
But in the losing fight he went
The hard high way that rebels go;
And so his score of years was spent
Five and six hundred years ago.

(She lights the second candle.)

When Art MacMurrough joined the rout
And faced the King of England's sword
The cards were shuffled and showed out
The trumps upon the Leinster board;
For Richard's credit ran to naught,
His fortune's fatness turned to lean;
But Art MacMurrough reigned and fought
Till fourteen hundred seventeen.

(She lights the third candle.)

O'Neill took Ulster in his hand
In fifteen hundred fifty-one;
He'd have no meddlers on his land
He kept their armies on the run;
Beat Sussex on the open plain—
It's little but the Gael were free—
It was no man that put down Shane
But Scottish treachery and the sea.

(She lights the fourth candle.)

[561]

Five hundred blessings on your head
And blessings on the earth you trod,
It's well you earned the prayers are said,
Sarsfield, that was a man with God.
When King and broken Treaty lied
You brought your Wild Geese through the sea,
And out in foreign, conquering, died
In sixteen hundred ninety-three.

(She lights the fifth candle.)

With five and five score years gone by
Tone and Lord Edward struck the ball—
My grief such hurlers had to die
And leave the goal to the Gall!
So each new age breaks each new hope,
And so in eighteen-hundred-three,
Another twisting of the rope
Set Robert Emmet's spirit free.

(She lights the sixth candle.)

In Easter Week the wisp was lit
Waked Dublin from her drowsy years;
I moan the battle-anger, yet
What did we ever win by tears?
The ballad singers long have cried
The shining names of far-away;
Now let them rhyme out those that died
With the three colours, yesterday.

And later yet. That quick quenched flame,
Thin rushlight in the dipper's hand,
Burnt out before his fulness came,
His name[1] a Saint's, with Saints to stand.
Or him the skillet and the mould

---

[1] Kevin Barry, aged 18, led an attack on an armoured force in Dublin in 1920. He was hanged in Mountjoy Jail.

Had rounded right to Nature's plan;
Teherence,[2] who waned, while moons grown old
Thrice gazed on an unconquered man.

(Having lighted the seventh candle she stands up.)

This is our rosary of praise
For some whose names are sung or said
Through seven hundred years of days
The silver beads upon the thread.
When near the Company of Heaven
The wondering shadow-armies stand,
The barren shadow-weapons fall
The bitter battle-angers cease;
So may God give to them and all
The blessing of His lasting peace!

FANNY PARNELL
(1854-1882)

AFTER DEATH

SHALL mine eyes behold thy glory, O my country?
  Shall mine eyes behold thy glory?
Or shall the darkness close around them, ere the sunblaze
  Break at last upon thy story?

When the nations ope for thee their queenly circle,
  As a sweet new sister hail thee,
Shall these lips be sealed in callous death and silence,
  That have known but to bewail thee?

Shall the car be deaf that only loved thy praises,
  When all men their tribute bring thee?

[2] Terence MacSwiney, Lord Mayor of Cork, who died on hunger strike in England.

Shall the mouth be clay that sang thee in thy squalor,
    When all poets' mouths shall sing thee?

Ah! the harpings and the salvos and the shoutings
    Of thy exiled sons returning!
I should hear, tho' dead and mouldered, and the grave-damps
    Should not chill my bosom's burning.

Ah! the tramp of feet victorious! I should hear them
    'Mid the shamrocks and the mosses,
And my heart should toss within the shroud and quiver,
    As a captive dreamer tosses.

I should turn and rend the cere-clothes round me,
    Giant sinews I should borrow—
Crying, "O, my brothers, I have also loved her
    In her loneliness and sorrow!

"Let me join with you the jubilant procession;
    Let me chant with you her story;
Then contented I shall go back to the shamrocks,
    Now mine eyes have seen her glory!"

OSCAR WILDE
(1854-1900)

REQUIESCAT

Tread lightly, she is near
    Under the snow,
Speak gently, she can hear
    The daisies grow.

All her bright golden hair
    Tarnished with rust,
She that was young and fair
    Fallen to dust.

[564]

Lily-like, white as snow,
  She hardly knew
She was a woman, so
  Sweetly she grew.

Coffin-board, heavy stone,
  Lie on her breast,
I vex my heart alone,
  She is at rest.

Peace, Peace, she cannot hear
  Lyre or sonnet,
All my life's buried here,
  Heap earth upon it.

THE BALLAD OF READING GAOL

HE DID not wear his scarlet coat,
  For blood and wine are red,
And blood and wine were on his hands
  When they found him with the dead,
The poor dead woman whom he loved,
  And murdered in her bed.

He walked amongst the Trial Men
  In a suit of shabby gray;
A cricket cap was on his head,
  And his step seemed light and gay;
But I never saw a man who looked
  So wistfully at the day.

I never saw a man who looked
  With such a wistful eye
Upon that little tent of blue
  Which prisoners call the sky,
And at every drifting cloud that went
  With sails of silver by.

[565]

I walked, with other souls in pain,
    Within another ring,
And was wondering if the man had done
    A great or little thing,
When a voice behind me whispered low,
    "That fellow's got to swing."

Dear Christ! the very prison walls
    Suddenly seemed to reel,
And the sky above my head became
    Like a casque of scorching steel;
And, though I was a soul in pain,
    My pain I could not feel.

I only knew what hunted thought
    Quickened his step, and why
He looked upon the garish day
    With such a wistful eye;
The man had killed the thing he loved,
    And so he had to die.

Yet each man kills the thing he loves,
    By each let this be heard,
Some do it with a bitter look,
    Some with a flattering word,
The coward does it with a kiss,
    The brave man with a sword!

Some kill their love when they are young,
    And some when they are old;
Some strangle with the hands of Lust,
    Some with the hands of Gold:
The kindest use a knife, because
    The dead so soon grow cold.

Some love too little, some too long,
    Some sell, and others buy;

[566]

Some do the deed with many tears,
    And some without a sigh:
For each man kills the thing he loves,
    Yet each man does not die.

He does not die a death of shame
    On a day of dark disgrace,
Nor have a noose about his neck,
    Nor a cloth upon his face,
Nor drop feet foremost through the floor
    Into an empty space.

He does not sit with silent men
    Who watch him night and day;
Who watch him when he tries to weep,
    And when he tries to pray;
Who watch him lest himself should rob
    The prison of its prey.

He does not wake at dawn to see
    Dread figures throng his room,
The shivering Chaplain robed in white,
    The Sheriff stern with gloom,
And the Governor all in shiny black,
    With the yellow face of Doom.

He does not rise in piteous haste
    To put on convict-clothes,
While some coarse-mouthed Doctor gloats, and notes
    Each new and nerve-twitched pose,
Fingering a watch whose little ticks
    Are like horrible hammer-blows.

He does not know that sickening thirst
    That sands one's throat, before
The hangman with his gardener's gloves
    Slips through the padded door,

[567]

And binds one with three leathern thongs
  That the throat may thirst no more.

He does not bend his head to hear
  The Burial Office read,
Nor, while the terror of his soul
  Tells him he is not dead,
Cross his own coffin, as he moves
  Into the hideous shed.

He does not stare upon the air
  Through a little roof of glass:
He does not pray with lips of clay
  For his agony to pass;
Nor feel upon his shuddering cheek
  The kiss of Caiaphas.

II

Six weeks our guardsman walked the yard
  In the suit of shabby gray:
His cricket cap was on his head,
  And his step seemed light and gay,
But I never saw a man who looked
  So wistfully at the day.

I never saw a man who looked
  With such a wistful eye
Upon that little tent of blue
  Which prisoners call the sky.
And at every wandering cloud that trailed
  Its ravelled fleeces by.

He did not wring his hands, as do
  Those witless men who dare
To try to rear the changeling Hope
  In the cave of black Despair:
He only looked upon the sun,
  And drank the morning air.

[568]

He did not wring his hands nor weep,
    Nor did he peek or pine,
But he drank the air as though it held
    Some healthful anodyne;
With open mouth he drank the sun
    As though it had been wine!

And I and all the souls in pain,
    Who tramped the other ring,
Forgot if we ourselves had done
    A great or little thing,
And watched with gaze of dull amaze
    The man who had to swing.

And strange it was to see him pass
    With step so light and gay,
And strange it was to see him look
    So wistfully at the day,
And strange it was to think that he
    Had such a debt to pay.

For oak and elm have pleasant leaves
    That in the spring-time shoot:
But grim to see is the gallows-tree,
    With its adder-bitten root,
And, green or dry, a man must die
    Before it bears its fruit.

The loftiest place is that seat of grace
    For which all worldlings try:
But who would stand in hempen band
    Upon a scaffold high,
And through a murderer's collar take
    His last look at the sky?

It is sweet to dance to violins
    When Love and Life are fair:

[569]

To dance to flutes, to dance to lutes
   Is delicate and rare:
But it is not sweet with nimble feet
   To dance upon the air!

So with curious eyes and sick surmise
   We watched him day by day,
And wondered if each one of us
   Would end the self-same way,
For none can tell to what red Hell
   His sightless soul may stray.

At last the dead man walked no more
   Amongst the Trial Men,
And I knew that he was standing up
   In the black dock's dreadful pen,
And that never would I see his face
   In God's sweet world again.

Like two doomed ships that pass in storm
   We had crossed each other's way:
But we made no sign, we said no word,
   We had no word to say;
For we did not meet in the holy night,
   But in the shameful day.

A prison wall was round us both,
   Two outcast men we were:
The world had thrust us from its heart,
   And God from out His care:
And the iron gin that waits for Sin
   Had caught us in its snare.

III

In Debtors' Yard the stones are hard,
   And the dripping wall is high,
So it was there he took the air
   Beneath the leaden sky.

And by each side a Warder walked,
  For fear the man might die.

Or else he sat with those who watched
  His anguish night and day;
Who watched him when he rose to weep,
  And when he crouched to pray;
Who watched him lest himself should rob
  Their scaffold of its prey.

The Governor was strong upon
  The Regulations Act:
The Doctor said that Death was but
  A scientific fact:
And twice a day the Chaplain called,
  And left a little tract.

And twice a day he smoked his pipe,
  And drank his quart of beer:
His soul was resolute, and held
  No hiding-place for fear;
He often said that he was glad
  The hangman's hands were near.

But why he said so strange a thing
  No warder dared to ask:
For he to whom a watcher's doom
  Is given as his task,
Must set a lock upon his lips,
  And make his face a mask.

Or else he might be moved, and try
  To comfort or console:
And what should Human Pity do
  Pent up in Murderers' Hole?
What word of grace in such a place
  Could help a brother's soul?

[571]

With slouch and swing around the ring
 We trod the Fools' Parade!
We did not care: we knew we were
 The Devil's Own Brigade:
And shaven head and feet of lead
 Make a merry masquerade.

We tore the tarry rope to shreds
 With blunt and bleeding nails:
We rubbed the doors, and scrubbed the floors,
 And cleaned the shining rails:
And, rank by rank, we soaped the plank,
 And clattered with the pails.

We sewed the sacks, we broke the stones.
 We turned the dusty drill:
We banged the tins, and bawled the hymns,
 And sweated on the mill:
But in the heart of every man
 Terror was lying still.

So still it lay that every day
 Crawled like a weed-clogged wave:
And we forgot the bitter lot
 That waits for fool and knave,
Till once, as we tramped in from work,
 We passed an open grave.

With yawning mouth the yellow hole
 Gaped for a living thing;
The very mud cried out for blood
 To the thirsty asphalt ring:
And we knew that ere one dawn grew fair
 Some prisoner had to swing.

Right in we went, with soul intent
 On Death and Dread and Doom:

The hangman, with his little bag,
　Went shuffling through the gloom:
And each man trembled as he crept
　Into his numbered tomb.

That night the empty corridors
　Were full of forms of Fear,
And up and down the iron town
　Stole feet we could not hear,
And through the bars that hide the stars
　White faces seemed to peer.

He lay as one who lies and dreams
　In a pleasant meadow-land,
And watchers watched him as he slept,
　And could not understand
How one could sleep so sweet a sleep
　With a hangman close at hand.

But there is no sleep when men must weep
　Who never yet have wept:
So we—the fool, the fraud, the knave—
　That endless vigil kept,
And through each brain on hands of pain
　Another's terror crept.

Alas! it is a fearful thing
　To feel another's guilt!
For, right within, the sword of Sin
　Pierced to its poisoned hilt,
And as molten lead were the tears we shed
　For the blood we had not spilt.

The Warders with their shoes of felt
　Crept by each padlocked door,
And peeped and saw, with eyes of awe,
　Gray figures on the floor,

And wondered why men knelt to pray
  Who never prayed before.

All through the night we knelt and prayed,
  Mad mourners of a corse!
The troubled plumes of midnight were
  The plumes upon a hearse:
And bitter wine upon a sponge
  Was the savor of Remorse.

The gray cock crew, the red cock crew,
  But never came the day:
And crooked shapes of Terror crouched,
  In the corners where we lay:
And each evil sprite that walks by night
  Before us seemed to play.

They glided past, they glided fast,
  Like travelers through a mist:
They mocked the moon in a rigadoon
  Of delicate turn and twist,
And with formal pace and loathsome grace
  The phantoms kept their tryst.

With mop and mow, we saw them go,
  Slim shadows hand in hand:
About, about, in ghostly rout
  They trod a saraband:
And the damned grotesques made arabesques,
  Like the wind upon the sand!

With the pirouettes of marionettes,
  They tripped on pointed tread:
But with flutes of Fear they filled the ear,
  As their grisly masque they led,
And loud they sang, and long they sang,
  For they sang to wake the dead.

[574]

"Oho!" they cried, "The World is wide,
  But fettered limbs go lame!
And once, or twice, to throw the dice
  Is a gentlemanly game;
But he does not win who plays with Sin
  In the secret House of Shame."

No things of air these antics were,
  That frolicked with such glee:
To men whose lives were held in gyves,
  And whose feet might not go free,
Ah! wounds of Christ! they were living things,
  Most terrible to see.

Around, around, they waltzed and wound;
  Some wheeled in smirking pairs;
With the mincing step of a demirep
  Some sidled up the stairs:
And with subtle sneer, and fawning leer,
  Each helped us at our prayers.

The morning wind began to moan,
  But still the night went on:
Through its giant loom the web of gloom
  Crept till each thread was spun:
And, as we prayed, we grew afraid
  Of the Justice of the Sun.

The moaning wind! went wandering round
  The weeping prison-wall:
Till like a wheel of turning steel
  We felt the minutes crawl:
O moaning wind! what had we done
  To have such a seneschal?

At last I saw the shadowed bars,
  Like a lattice wrought in lead,

Move right across the whitewashed wall
  That faced my three-plank bed,
And I knew that somewhere in the world
  God's dreadful dawn was red.

At six o'clock we cleaned our cells,
  At seven all was still,
But the sough and swing of a mighty wing
  The prison seemed to fill,
For the Lord of Death with icy breath
  Had entered in to kill.

He did not pass in purple pomp,
  Nor ride a moon-white steed.
Three yards of cord and a sliding board
  Are all the gallows' need:
So with rope of shame the Herald came
  To do the secret deed.

We were as men who through a fen
  Of filthy darkness grope:
We did not dare to breathe a prayer,
  Or to give our anguish scope:
Something was dead in each of us,
  And what was dead was Hope.

For Man's grim Justice goes its way,
  And will not swerve aside:
It slays the weak, it slays the strong,
  It has a deadly stride:
With iron heel it slays the strong,
  The monstrous parricide!

We waited for the stroke of eight:
  Each tongue was thick with thirst:
For the stroke of eight is the stroke of Fate
  That makes a man accursed,
And Fate will use a running noose
  For the best man and the worst.

[576]

We had no other thing to do,
    Save to wait for the sign to come:
So, like things of stone in a valley lone,
    Quiet we sat and dumb:
But each man's heart beat thick and quick,
    Like a madman on a drum!

With sudden shock the prison clock
    Smote on the shivering air,
And from all the gaol rose up a wail
    Of impotent despair,
Like the sound that frightened marshes hear
    From some leper in his lair.

And as one sees most fearful things
    In the crystal of a dream,
We saw the greasy hempen rope
    Hooked to the blackened beam,
And heard the prayer the hangman's snare
    Strangled into a scream.

And all the woe that moved him so
    That he gave that bitter cry,
And the wild regrets, and the bloody sweats,
    None knew so well as I:
For he who lives more lives than one
    More deaths than one must die.

IV

There is no chapel on the day
    On which they hang a man:
The Chaplain's heart is far too sick,
    Or his face is far too wan,
Or there is that written in his eyes
    Which none should look upon.

So they kept us close till nigh on noon,
    And then they rang the bell,

And the Warders with their jingling keys
  Opened each listening cell,
And down the iron stair we tramped,
  Each from his separate Hell.

Out into God's sweet air we went,
  But not in wonted way,
For this man's face was white with fear,
  And that man's face was gray,
And I never saw sad men who looked
  So wistfully at the day.

I never saw sad men who looked
  With such a wistful eye
Upon that little tent of blue
  We prisoners called the sky,
And at every careless cloud that passed
  In happy freedom by.

But there were those amongst us all
  Who walked with downcast head,
And knew that, had each got his due,
  They should have died instead:
He had but killed a thing that lived,
  Whilst they had killed the dead.

For he who sins a second time
  Wakes a dead soul to pain,
And draws it from its spotted shroud,
  And makes it bleed again,
And makes it bleed great gouts of blood,
  And makes it bleed in vain!

Like ape or clown, in monstrous garb
  With crooked arrows starred,
Silently we went round and round
  The slippery asphalt yard;

Silently we went round and round,
  And no man spoke a word.

Silently we went round and round,
  And through each hollow mind
The Memory of dreadful things
  Rushed like a dreadful wind,
And Horror stalked before each man,
  And Terror crept behind.

The Warders strutted up and down,
  And kept their herd of brutes,
Their uniforms were spick and span,
  And they wore their Sunday suits,
But we knew the work they had been at,
  By the quicklime on their boots.

For where a grave had opened wide,
  There was no grave at all:
Only a stretch of mud and sand
  By the hideous prison-wall,
And a little heap of burning lime,
  That the man should have his pall.

For he has a pall, this wretched man,
  Such as few men can claim:
Deep down below a prison-yard,
  Naked for greater shame,
He lies, with fetters on each foot,
  Wrapt in a sheet of flame!

And all the while the burning lime
  Eats flesh and bone away;
It eats the brittle bone by night,
  And the soft flesh by day,
It eats the flesh and bone by turns,
  But it eats the heart away.

[579]

For three long years they will not sow
  Or root or seedling there:
For three long years the unblessed spot
  Will sterile be and bare,
And look upon the wondering sky
  With unreproachful stare.

They think a murderer's heart would taint
  Each simple seed they sow.
It is not true! God's kindly earth
  Is kindlier than men know,
And the red rose would but blow more red,
  The white rose whiter blow.

Out of his mouth a red, red rose!
  Out of his heart a white!
For who can say by what strange way,
  Christ brings His will to light,
Since the barren staff the pilgrim bore
  Bloomed in the great Pope's sight?

But neither milk-white rose nor red
  May bloom in prison air;
The shard, the pebble, and the flint,
  Are what they give us there:
For flowers have been known to heal
  A common man's despair.

So never will wine-red rose or white,
  Petal by petal, fall
On that stretch of mud and sand that lies
  By the hideous prison-wall,
To tell the men who tramp the yard
  That God's Son died for all.

Yet though the hideous prison-wall
  Still hems him round and round,

And a spirit may not walk by night
  That is with fetters bound,
And a spirit may but weep that lies
  In such unholy ground.

He is at peace—this wretched man—
  At peace, or will be soon:
There is no thing to make him mad,
  Nor does Terror walk at noon,
For the lampless Earth in which he lies
  Has neither Sun nor Moon.

They hanged him as a beast is hanged:
  They did not even toll
A requiem that might have brought
  Rest to his startled soul,
But hurriedly they took him out,
  And hid him in a hole.

They stripped him of his canvas clothes,
  And gave him to the flies;
They mocked the swollen purple throat,
  And the stark and staring eyes;
And with laughter loud they heaped the shroud
  In which their convict lies.

The Chaplain would not kneel to pray
  By his dishonored grave:
Nor mark it with that blessed Cross
  That Christ for sinners gave,
Because the man was one of those
  Whom Christ came down to save.

Yet all is well; he has but passed
  To Life's appointed bourne:
And alien tears will fill for him
  Pity's long-broken urn,

For his mourners will be outcast men,
And outcasts always mourn.

V

I know not whether Laws be right,
Or whether Laws be wrong;
All that we know who lie in gaol
Is that the wall is strong;
And that each day is like a year,
A year whose days are long.

But this I know, that every Law
That men have made for Man,
Since first Man took his brother's life,
And the sad world began,
But straws the wheat and saves the chaff
With a most evil fan.

This too I know—and wise it were
If each could know the same—
That every prison that men build
Is built with bricks of shame,
And bound with bars lest Christ should see
How men their brothers maim.

With bars they blur the gracious moon,
And blind the goodly sun:
And they do well to hide their Hell,
For in it things are done
That Son of God nor Son of Man
Ever should look upon!

The vilest deeds like poison weeds
Bloom well in prison-air:
It is only what is good in Man
That wastes and withers there:
Pale Anguish keeps the heavy gate,
And the Warder is Despair.

[582]

For they starve the little frightened child
    Till it weeps both night and day:
And they scourge the weak, and flog the fool,
    And gibe the old and gray,
And some grow mad, and all grow bad,
    And none a word may say.

Each narrow cell in which we dwell
    Is a foul and dark latrine.
And the fetid breath of living Death
    Chokes up each grated screen,
And all, but Lust, is turned to dust
    In Humanity's machine.

The brackish water that we drink
    Creeps with a loathsome slime,
And the bitter bread they weigh in scales
    Is full of chalk and lime,
And Sleep will not lie down, but walks
    Wild-eyed, and dries to Time.

But though lean Hunger and green Thirst
    Like asp with adder fight,
We have little care of prison fare,
    For what chills and kills outright
Is that every stone one lifts by day
    Becomes one's heart by night.

With midnight always in one's heart,
    And twilight in one's cell,
We turn the crank, or tear the rope,
    Each in his separate Hell,
And the silence is more awful far
    Than the sound of a brazen bell.

And never a human voice comes near
    To speak a gentle word:

[583]

And the eye that watches through the door
  Is pitiless and hard:
And by all forgot, we rot and rot,
  With soul and body marred.

And thus we rust Life's iron chain
  Degraded and alone:
And some men curse, and some men weep,
  And some men make no moan:
But God's eternal Laws are kind
  And break the heart of stone.

And every human heart that breaks,
  In prison-cell or yard,
Is as that broken box that gave
  Its treasure to the Lord,
And filled the unclean leper's house
  With the scent of costliest nard.

Ah! happy they whose hearts can break
  And peace of pardon win!
How else may man make straight his plan
  And cleanse his soul from Sin?
How else but through a broken heart
  May Lord Christ enter in?

And he of the swollen purple throat,
  And the stark and staring eyes
Waits for the holy hands that took
  The Thief to Paradise;
And a broken and a contrite heart
  The Lord will not despise.

The man in red who reads the Law
  Gave him three weeks of life,
Three little weeks in which to heal
  His soul of his soul's strife,

And cleanse from every blot of blood
  The hand that held the knife.

And with tears of blood he cleansed the hand,
  The hand that held the steel:
For only blood can wipe out blood,
  And only tears can heal:
And the crimson stain that was of Cain
  Became Christ's snow-white seal.

VI

In Reading gaol by Reading town
  There is a pit of shame,
And in it lies a wretched man
  Eaten by teeth of flame,
In a burning winding-sheet he lies,
  And his grave has got no name.

And there, till Christ call forth the dead,
  In silence let him lie:
No need to waste the foolish tear,
  Or heave the windy sigh:
The man had killed the thing he loved,
  And so he had to die.

And all men kill the thing they love,
  By all let this be heard,
Some do it with a bitter look,
  Some with a flattering word,
The coward does it with a kiss,
  The brave man with a sword!

THOMAS W. H. ROLLESTON
(1857-1920)

THE GRAVE OF RURY

CLEAR as air, the western waters
Evermore their sweet, unchanging song
Murmur in their stony channels
Round O'Conor's sepulchre in Cong.

Crownless, hopeless, here he lingered;
Year on year went by him like a dream,
While the far-off roar of conquest
Murmured faintly like the singing stream.

Here he died, and here they tombed him,
Men of Fechin, chanting round his grave.
Did they know, ah! did they know it,
What they buried by the babbling wave?

Now above the sleep of Rury
Holy things and great have passed away;
Stone by stone the stately Abbey
Falls and fades in passionless decay.

Darkly grows the quiet ivy,
Pale the broken arches glimmer through;
Dark upon the cloister-garden
Dreams the shadow of the ancient yew.

Through the roofless aisles the verdure
Flows, the meadow-sweet and fox-glove bloom.
Earth, the mother and consoler,
Winds soft arms about the lonely tomb.

Peace and holy gloom possess him,
Last of Gaelic monarchs of the Gael,
Slumbering by the young, eternal
River-voices of the western vale.

DENIS A. McCARTHY
(1871-1931)

THE TAILOR THAT CAME FROM MAYO

THE little old tailor that came from Mayo—
God be good to him! Dead he is, ages ago.
But I'll never forget him—himself and his brogue,
And the comical gleam in his eye, the old rogue!
For 'twas he that could talk, in those days, with the best;
And you'd laugh at his jokes till you'd fear for your vest.
And you'd never grow tired of the wonderful flow
Of the language that came from the man from Mayo.

In the long winter nights by the light of the lamp,
When the weather outside would be dreary and damp,
Now, I tell you, 'twas grand to his place to drop in
For a pull at the pipe with the rest of the men.
For a pull at the pipe, and a bit of a chat,
And an argument, too, about this thing or that;
But the best of the argument always would go
To the little old tailor that came from Mayo.

For he'd listen awhile, as he basted away,
And when every one else in the house had his say,
And when all who were there had exhausted the store
Of the knowledge they had, and were groping for more,
He would bite off the end of his thread with a jerk,
And he'd lift up his face for a while from his work,
And he'd give his opinion, and no one said no
To the little old tailor that came from Mayo.

Was it battles we talked of? He ended the talk;
For he'd mark out the lines on his board with the chalk;
And he'd point out, perhaps, just where Bonaparte stood
When his empire, at Waterloo, ended in blood.
Or he'd show the grand charge which, before that, was made

[587]

Back at famed Fontenoy by the Irish Brigade,
Till the heart of myself would be all in a glow
At the words of the tailor that came from Mayo.

The story of Ireland—he knew it by heart,
And 'tis often he'd speak about Cormac MacArt,
Or of Brian Boru and his battles of old,
Or of Malachi wearing the collar of gold.
And of Daniel O'Connell—I almost would split
At the samples he gave of the Counsellor's wit.
But 'twas Emmet he loved and how grave he would grow
When that martyr was mentioned—the man from Mayo.

Well, he's gone and God rest him, his life is long past;
He went back to Mayo, and he died there at last.
But I'll never forget him, cross-legged as he sat
While he gave out his verdict on this thing and that.
And the jokes that he made! And the scorn that he poured
On the foes and false friends of the land he adored!
For the faithfullest soul that I ever shall know
Was the soul of the tailor that came from Mayo.

KATHERINE TYNAN HINKSON
(1861-1931)

CUCKOO SONG

Cuckoo, cuckoo!
In April skies were blue
As every hedgerow knew;
And there was you.
In April
The cuckoo shows his bill,
With windflowers on vale and hill
O. Love!
Sweet was April, sweet was April!

[588]

Cuckoo, cuckoo!
In May his song was true,
And the world was new
For me and you.
In May
He sings all day,
All the long night that's sweet with hay.
        O, Love!
Blithe was the May, blithe was the May!

Cuckoo, cuckoo!
Last June the roses grew
In many a place we knew,
I and you.
In June
He changes his tune.
A young man's fancy changes soon.
        O, Love!
Fleet was June, fleet was June!

Cuckoo, cuckoo!
His notes are faint and few,
The lily is dying too,
For the rose there is rue.
In July
Away will he fly,
His notes blown back from an empty sky.
        O, Love!
Sad was July, sad was July!

Cuckoo, cuckoo!
No more we listen to
The merry song we knew,
I and you.
In August
Go he must,
Love and lovers will turn to dust.
        O, Love!
Cold is August, cold is August!

THE WITCH

Margaret Grady—I fear she will burn—
Charmed the butter off my churn;
'Tis I would know it the wide world over,
Yellow as saffron, scented with clover.

At Omagh market the witch displayed it:
Ill she had gathered, ill she had made it.
Hid in my cloak's hood, one glance I threw it,
Passed on smiling; my troth! I knew it!

Sheila, the kindest cow in the parish,
Mild and silken, and good to cherish,
Shame her own gold butter should leave her
To enrich the milk of a low-bred heifer!

I said not Yea or Nay to the mocker,
But called the fairy-man over from Augher;
Like a russet he is that's withered,
Bent in two with his wisdom gathered.

He touched the butter, he peered and pondered,
And crooned strange rhymes while I watched and wondered:
Then he drew me out through the gloaming
O'er the fields where the mist was coming.

He bewitched me so that I know not
Where they may grow, where they may grow not;
Those witch-hazels he plucked and plaited,
Crooning on while the twigs he mated.

There's the wreath on the churn-dash yonder.
All the neighbours view it with wonder;
And 'spite of Father Tom I avow it
The yield is doubled since that came to it.

[590]

I bless the fairy-man though he be evil;
Yet fairy-spells come not from the Devil;
And Margaret Grady—I fear she will burn—
I do forgive her, with hate and scorn.

SHEEP AND LAMBS

ALL in the April evening,
  April airs were abroad,
The sheep with their little lambs
  Passed me by on the road.

The sheep with their little lambs
  Passed me by on the road;
All in the April evening
  I thought on the Lamb of God.

The lambs were weary, and crying
  With a weak, human cry.
I thought on the Lamb of God
  Going meekly to die.

Up in the blue, blue mountains
  Dewy pastures are sweet;
Rest for the little bodies,
  Rest for the little feet,

But for the Lamb of God,
  Up on the hill-top green,
Only a cross of shame
  Two stark crosses between.

All in the April evening,
  April airs were abroad,
I saw the sheep with their lambs,
  And thought on the Lamb of God.

[591]

AUX CARMÉLITES

MADAME LOUISE sleeps well o' nights,
Night is still at the Carmelites:
      Down at Versailles
The dancers dance, and the violins play.

There's a crucifix on the wall at her head,
And a rush chair set by her pallet bed,
      Stony and hard,
Sweeter than balm or the spikenard.

Daughter of France and the King's daughter,
She hath one poor serge gown to her wear:
      And her little feet
Shall naked go in the wind and sleet.

From things that stabbed her cheek to red
She hath taken her milk-white soul and fled.
      Down at Versailles
The revels go till the break of day.

Sweetly singeth the nightingale
In his screen of boughs while the moon is pale,
      Sweet and so sweet,
That the night-world is faint with it.

The roses dream and the lilies wake,
While the bird of love with his wild heart-break
      Pierceth her dream;
Soft she sighs in the faint moon-beam.

And all night long in the dark by her
An angel sits with its wings astir,
      And his hidden eyes
Keeping the secrets of Paradise.

Madame Louise sleeps well o' nights,
Night is still at the Carmelites:
      Down at Versailles
The dancers dance while the dawn is grey.

LARKS

ALL day in exquisite air
The song clomb an invisible stair,
Flight on flight, story on story,
Into the dazzling glory.

There was no bird, only a singing,
Up in the glory, climbing and ringing,
Like a small golden cloud at even,
Trembling 'twixt earth and heaven.

I saw no staircase winding, winding,
Up in the dazzle, sapphire and blinding,
Yet round by round, in exquisite air,
The song went up the stair.

A GIRL'S SONG

THE Meuse and Marne have little waves;
   The slender poplars o'er them lean.
One day they will forget the graves
   That give the grass its living green.

Some brown French girl the rose will wear
   That springs above his comely head;
Will twine it in her russet hair,
   Nor wonder why it is so red.

His blood is in the rose's veins,
   His hair is in the yellow corn.
My grief is in the weeping rains
   And in the keening wind forlorn.

Flow softly, softly, Marne and Meuse;
   Tread lightly all ye browsing sheep;
Fall tenderly, O silver dews,
   For here my dear Love lies asleep.

The earth is on his sealèd eyes,
   The beauty marred that was my pride;
Would I were lying where he lies,
   And sleeping sweetly by his side!

The Spring will come by Meuse and Marne,
   The birds be blithesome in the tree.
I heap the stones to make his cairn
   Where many sleep as sound as he.

WILLIAM BUTLER YEATS
(1865-1939)

THE STOLEN CHILD

WHERE dips the rocky highland
Of Sleuth Wood in the lake,
There lies a leafy island
Where flapping herons wake
The drowsy water rats;
There we've hid our faery vats,
Full of berries,
And of reddest stolen cherries.
Come away, O human child!

[594]

To the waters and the wild
With a faery, hand in hand,
For the world's more full of weeping than you can
  understand.

Where the wave of moonlight glosses
The dim gray sands with light,
Far off by furthest Rosses
We foot it all the night,
Weaving olden dances,
Mingling hands and mingling glances
Till the moon has taken flight;
To and fro we leap
And chase the frothy bubbles,
While the world is full of troubles
And is anxious in its sleep.
Come away, O human child!
To the waters and the wild
With a faery, hand in hand,
For the world's more full of weeping than you can
  understand.

Where the wandering water gushes
From the hills above Glen-Car,
In pools among the rushes
That scarce could bathe a star,
We seek for slumbering trout
And whispering in their ears
Give them unquiet dreams;
Leaning softly out
From ferns that drop their tears
Over the young streams,
Come away, O human child!
To the waters and the wild
With a faery, hand in hand,
For the world's more full of weeping than you can
  understand.

Away with us he's going,
The solemn-eyed:
He'll hear no more the lowing
Of the calves on the warm hillside
Or the kettle on the hob
Sing peace into his breast
Or see the brown mice bob
Round and round the oatmeal-chest.
For he comes, the human child,
To the waters and the wild
With a faery, hand in hand,
From a world more full of weeping than he can
understand.

THE PRIEST OF COLOONY

Good Father John O'Hart
   In penal days rode out
To a *shoneen*[1] in his freelands,
   With his snipe marsh and his trout.

In trust took he John's lands,
   —*Sleiveens*[2] were all his race—
And he gave them as dowers to his daughters,
   And they married beyond their place.

But Father John went up,
   And Father John went down;
And he wore small holes in his shoes,
   And he wore large holes in his gown.

All loved him, only the *shoneen,*
   Whom the devils have by the hair,
From the wives and the cats and the children
   To the birds in the white of the air.

[1] Shoneen = upstart.
[2] Sleiveen = mean fellow, sneak.

The birds, for he opened their cages,
  As he went up and down;
And he said with a smile, "Have peace now,"
  And went his way with a frown.

But if when anyone died,
  Came keeners hoarser than rooks,
He bade them give over their keening,
  For he was a man of books.

And these were the works of John,
  When weeping score by score,
People came into Coloony,
  For he'd died at ninety-four.

There was no human keening;
  The birds from Knocknarea,
And the world round Knocknashee,
  Came keening in that day—

The young birds and old birds
  Came flying, heavy and sad;
Keening in from Tiraragh,
  Keening from Ballinafad;

Keening from Innismurry,
  Nor stayed for bit or sup;
This way were all reproved
  Who dig old customs up.

FAIRY SONG

from *The Land of Heart's Desire*

THE wind blows out of the gates of the day,
The wind blows over the lonely of heart
And the lonely of heart is withered away,
While the faeries dance in a place apart,

[597]

Shaking their milk-white feet in a ring,
Tossing their milk-white arms in the air;
For they hear the wind laugh, and murmur and
     sing
Of a land where even the old are fair,
And even the wise are merry of tongue;
But I heard a reed of Coolaney say,
"When the wind has laughed and murmured
     and sung,
The lonely of heart is withered away!"

DOWN BY THE SALLEY GARDENS

Down by the salley gardens my love and I did meet;
She passed the salley gardens with little snow-white feet.
She bid me take love easy, as the leaves grow on the tree;
But I, being young and foolish, with her would not agree.

In a field by the river my love and I did stand,
And on my leaning shoulder she laid her snow-white hand.
She bid me take life easy, as the grass grows on the weirs;
But I was young and foolish, and now am full of tears.

THE LAKE ISLE OF INNISFREE

Henry David Thoreau's *Walden* is said to have inspired Yeats to write
this poem.

I will arise and go now, and go to Innisfree,
And a small cabin build there, of clay and wattles made;
Nine bean rows will I have there, a hive for the honey bee,
And live alone in the bee-loud glade.

And I shall have some peace there, for peace comes dropping
     slow,

Dropping from the veils of the morning to where the cricket
    sings;
There midnight's all a glimmer, and noon a purple glow,
And evening full of the linnet's wings.

I will arise and go now, for always night and day
I hear lake water lapping with low sounds by the shore;
While I stand on the roadway, or on the pavements gray,
I hear it in the deep heart's core.

THE BALLAD OF FATHER GILLIGAN

THE old priest Peter Gilligan
Was weary night and day;
For half his flock were in their beds,
Or under green sods lay.

Once, while he nodded on a chair,
At the moth-hour of eve,
Another poor man sent for him,
And he began to grieve.

"I have no rest, nor joy, nor peace,
For people die and die";
And after cried he, "God forgive!
My body spake, not I!"

He knelt, and leaning on the chair
He prayed and fell asleep;
And the moth-hour went from the fields,
And stars began to peep.

They slowly into millions grew,
And leaves shook in the wind;
And God covered the world with shade,
And whispered to mankind.

[599]

Upon the time of sparrow-chirp
When moths came once more,
The old priest Peter Gilligan
Stood upright on the floor.

"Mavrone, mavrone! the man has died
While I slept on the chair";
He roused his horse out of its sleep,
And rode with little care.

He rode now as he never rode,
By rocky lane and fen;
The sick man's wife opened the door:
"Father! you come again!"

"And is the poor man dead?" he cried.
"He died an hour ago."
The old priest Peter Gilligan
In grief swayed to and fro.

"When you were gone, he turned and died
As merry as a bird."
The old priest Peter Gilligan
He knelt him at that word.

"He Who hath made the night of stars
For souls who tire and bleed,
Sent one of His great angels down
To help me in my need.

"He Who is wrapped in purple robes,
With planets in His care,
Had pity on the least of things
Asleep upon a chair."

THE HOST OF THE AIR

O'DRISCOLL drove with a song
The wild duck and the drake
From the tall and tufted reeds
Of the drear Hart Lake.

And he saw how the reeds grew dark
At the coming of night tide,
And dreamed of the long dim hair
Of Bridget his bride.

He heard while he sang and dreamed
A piper piping away,
And never was piping so sad,
And never was piping so gay.

And he saw young men and young girls
Who danced on a level place
And Bridget his bride among them,
With a sad and a gay face.

The dancers crowded about him,
And many a sweet thing said,
And a young man brought him red wine
And a young girl white bread.

But Bridget drew him by the sleeve,
Away from the merry bands,
To old men playing at cards
With a twinkling of ancient hands.

The bread and the wine had a doom,
For these were the host of the air;
He sat and played in a dream
Of her long dim hair.

[601]

He played with the merry old men
And thought not of evil chance,
Until one bore Bridget his bride
Away from the merry dance.

He bore her away in his arms,
The handsomest young man there,
And his neck and his breast and his arms
Were drowned in her long dim hair.

O'Driscoll scattered the cards
And out of his dream he awoke:
Old men and young men and young girls
Were gone like a drifting smoke.

But he heard high up in the air
A piper piping away,
And never was piping so sad,
And never was piping so gay.

RED HANRAHAN'S SONG ABOUT IRELAND

THE old brown thorn trees break in two high over Cummen
        Strand,
Under a bitter black wind that blows from the left hand;
Our courage breaks like a tree in a black wind and dies,
But, we have hidden in our hearts the flame out of the eyes
Of Cathleen, the daughter of Houlihan.

The wind has bundled up the clouds high over Knocknarea,
And thrown the thunder on the stones for all that Maeve can
        say.
Angers that are like noisy clouds have set our hearts abeat;
But we have all bent low and low kissed the quiet feet
Of Cathleen, the daughter of Houlihan.

The yellow pool has overflowed high up on Clooth-na-Bare,
For the wet winds are blowing out of the clinging air;
Like heavy flooded waters our bodies and our blood;
But purer than a candle before the Holy Rood
Is Cathleen, the daughter of Houlihan.

THE WILD SWANS AT COOLE

THE trees are in their autumn beauty,
The woodland paths are dry,
Under the October twilight the water
Mirrors a still sky;
Upon the brimming water among the stones
Are nine-and-fifty swans.

The nineteenth autumn has come upon me
Since I first made my count;
I saw, before I had well finished,
All suddenly mount
And scatter wheeling in great broken rings
Upon their clamorous wings.

I have looked upon those brilliant creatures,
And now my heart is sore.
All's changed since I, hearing at twilight,
The first time on this shore,
The bell-beat of their wings above my head,
Trod with a lighter tread.

Unwearied still, lover by lover,
They paddle in the cold
Companionable streams or climb the air;
Their hearts have not grown old;
Passion or conquest, wander where they will,
Attend upon them still.

But now they drift on the still water
Mysterious, beautiful;
Among what rushes will they build,
By what lake's edge or pool
Delight men's eyes when I awake some day
To find they have flown away?

BYZANTIUM

THE unpurged images of day recede;
The Emperor's drunken soldiery are abed;
Night resonance recedes, night-walkers' song
After the cathedral gong;
A starlit or a moonlit dome disdains
All that man is,
All mere complexities,
The fury and the mire of human veins.

Before me floats an image, man or shade,
Shade more than man, more image than a shade;
For Hades' bobbin bound in mummy-cloth
May unwind the winding path;
A mouth that has no moisture and no breath
Breathless mouths may summon;
I hail the superhuman;
I call it death-in-life and life-in-death.

Miracle, bird or golden handiwork,
More miracle than bird or handiwork,
Planted on the starlit golden bough,
Can like the cocks of Hades crow,
Or, by the moon embittered, scorn aloud
In glory of changeless metal
Common bird or petal
And all complexities of mire or blood.

At midnight on the Emperor's pavement flit
Flames that no faggot feeds, nor steel has lit,
Nor storm disturbs, flames begotten of flame,
Where blood-begotten spirits come
And all complexities of fury leave,
Dying into a dance,
An agony of trance,
An agony of flame that cannot singe a sleeve.

Astraddle on the dolphin's mire and blood,
Spirit after spirit! The smithies break the flood,
The golden smithies of the Emperor!
Marbles of the dancing floor
Break bitter furies of complexity,
Those images that yet
Fresh images beget,
That dolphin-torn, that gong-tormented sea.

'I AM OF IRELAND'

'I am of Ireland,
And the Holy Land of Ireland,
And time runs on,' cried she.
'Come out of charity,
Come dance with me in Ireland.'

One man, one man alone
In that outlandish gear,
One solitary man
Of all that rambled there
Had turned his stately head.
'That is a long way off,
And time runs on,' he said,
'And the night grows rough.'

'I am of Ireland,
And the Holy Land of Ireland,

[605]

And time runs on,' cried she.
'Come out of charity
And dance with me in Ireland.'

'The fiddlers are all thumbs,
Or the fiddle-string accursed,
The drums and the kettledrums
And the trumpets all are burst,
And the trombone,' cried he,
'The trumpet and trombone,'
And cocked a malicious eye,
'But time runs on, runs on.'

'I am of Ireland,
And the Holy Land of Ireland,
And time runs on,' cried she.
'Come out of charity
And dance with me in Ireland.'

TOM THE LUNATIC

SANG old Tom the lunatic
That sleeps under the canopy;
"What change has put my thoughts astray
And eyes that had so keen a sight?
What has turned to smoking wick
Nature's pure unchanging light?

"Huddon and Duddon and Daniel O'Leary,
Holy Joe, the beggar-man,
Wenching, drinking, still remain
Or sing a penance on the road;
Something made these eyeballs weary
That blinked and saw them in a shroud.

"Whatever stands in field or flood,
Bird, beast, fish or man,

Mare or stallion, cock or hen,
Stands in God's unchanging eye
In all the vigour of its blood;
In that faith I live or die."

ETHNA CARBERY
(1866-1902)

THE LOVE-TALKER

I MET the Love-Talker one eve in the glen,
He was handsomer than any of our handsome young men,
His eyes were blacker than the sloe, his voice sweeter far
Than the crooning of old Kevin's pipes beyond in Coolnagar.

I was bound for the milking with a heart fair and free—
My grief! my grief! that bitter hour drained the life from me;
I thought him human lover, though his lips on mine were cold,
And the breath of death blew keen on me within his hold.

I know not what way he came, no shadow fell behind,
But all the sighing rushes swayed' beneath a fairy wind;
The thrush ceased its singing, a mist crept about,
We two clung together—with the world shut out.

Beyond the ghostly mist I could hear my cattle low,
The little cow from Ballina, clean as driven snow,
The dun cow from Kerry, the roan from Inisheer,
Oh, pitiful their calling—and his whispers in my ear!

His eyes were a fire; his words were a snare;
I cried my mother's name, but no help was there;
I made the blessed Sign—then he gave a dreary moan,
A wisp of cloud went floating by, and I stood alone.

[607]

Running ever thro' my head is an old-time rune—
"Who meets the Love-Talker must weave her shroud soon."
My mother's face is furrowed with the salt tears that fall,
But the kind eyes of my father are the saddest sight of all.

I have spun the fleecy lint and now my wheel is still,
The linen length is woven for my shroud fine and chill,
I shall stretch me on the bed where a happy maid I lay—
Pray for the soul of Maire Og at dawning of the day!

DORA SIGERSON SHORTER
(1866-1917)

THE PIPER ON THE HILL

(A Child's Song)

THERE sits a piper on the hill
 Who pipes the livelong day,
And when he pipes both loud and shrill,
 The frightened people say:
"The wind, the wind is blowing up
 'Tis rising to a gale,"
The women hurry to the shore
 To watch some distant sail.
The wind, the wind, the wind, the wind
 Is blowing to a gale.

But when he pipes all sweet and low,
 The piper on the hill,
I hear the merry women go
 With laughter, loud and shrill:
"The wind, the wind is coming south
 'Twill blow a gentle day."
They gather on the meadow-land
 To toss the yellow hay.

[608]

The wind, the wind, the wind, the wind
Is blowing south to-day.

And in the morn, when winter comes,
   To keep the piper warm,
The little Angels shake their wings
   To make a feather storm:
"The snow, the snow has come at last!"
   The happy children call.
And "ring around" they dance in glee,
   And watch the snowflakes fall.
The wind, the wind, the wind, the wind
   Has spread a snowy pall.

But when at night the piper plays,
   I have not any fear,
Because God's windows open wide
   The pretty tune to hear;
And when each crowding spirit looks,
   From it's star window-pane,
A watching mother may behold
   Her little child again.
The wind, the wind, the wind, the wind
   May blow her home again.

SIXTEEN DEAD MEN

The sixteen dead men of 1916: Thomas Clarke, Sean MacDermot, Padraic Pearse, James Connolly, Thomas MacDonagh, Eamonn Ceannt, Joseph Plunkett (signers of the *Proclamation*); Edmund Daly, Michael O'Hanrahan, William Pearse, Cornelius Colbert, Michael Mallin, Sean Heuston, Thomas Ceannt, John MacBride and Roger Casement (who was hung later, in August).

HARK! in the still night. Who goes there?
   "Fifteen dead men." Why do they wait?
   "Hasten, comrade, death is so fair."
Now comes their Captain through the dim gate.

[609]

Sixteen dead men! What on their sword?
   "A nation's honour proud do they bear."
What on their bent heads? *God's holy word;*
   All of their nation's heart blended in prayer."

Sixteen dead men! What makes their shroud?
   "All of their nation's love wraps them around."
Where do their bodies lie, brave and so proud?
   "Under the gallows-tree in prison ground."

Sixteen dead men! Where do they go?
   "To join their regiment, where Sarsfield leads;
Wolfe Tone and Emmet, too, well do they know.
   There shall they bivouac, telling great deeds."

Sixteen dead men! Shall they return?
   "Yea, they shall come again, breath of our breath.
They on our nation's hearth made old fires burn.
   Guard her unconquered soul, strong in their death."

THE KINE OF MY FATHER

The kine of my father, they are straying from my keeping;
   The young goat's at mischief, but little can I do:
For all through the night did I hear the banshee keening;
   O youth of my loving, and is it well with you?

All through the night sat my mother with my sorrow;
   'Wisht, it is the storm, O one childeen of my heart!'
My hair with the wind, and my two hands clasped in anguish;
   Black head of my darling! too long are we apart.

Were your grave at my feet, I would think it half a blessing;
   I could herd then the cattle, and drive the goats away;
Many a Paternoster I would say for your safe keeping;
   I could sleep above your heart until the dawn of day.

I see you on the prairie, hot with thirst and faint with hunger;
  The head that I love lying low upon the sand.
The vultures shriek impatient, and the coyote dogs are howl-
    ing,
  Till the blood is pulsing cold within your clenching hand.

I see you on the waters, so white, so still, forsaken,
  Your dear eyes unclosing beneath a foreign rain:
A plaything of the winds, you turn and drift unceasing;
  No grave for your resting; Oh, mine the bitter pain!

All through the night did I hear the banshee keening:
  Somewhere you are dying, and nothing can I do:
My hair with the wind, and my two hands clasped in anguish;
  Bitter is your trouble—and I am far from you.

BALLAD OF THE LITTLE BLACK HOUND

Who knocks at the Geraldine's door to-night
  In the black storm and the rain?
With the thunder crash and the shrieking wind
  Comes the moan of a creature's pain.

And once they knocked, yet never a stir
  To show that the Geraldine knew;
And twice they knocked, yet never a bolt
  The listening Geraldine drew.

And thrice they knocked ere he moved his chair,
  And said, "Whoever it be,
I dare not open the door to-night
  For a fear has come to me."

Three times he rises from out his chair,
  And three times he sits him down.
"Now what has made faint this heart of mine?"
  He says with a growing frown.

[611]

"Now what has made me a coward to-night,
    Who never knew fear before?
But I swear that the hand of a little child
    Keeps pulling me from the door."

The Geraldine rose from his chair at last
    And opened the door full wide;
"Whoever is out in the storm," said he,
    "May in God's name come inside!"

He who was out in the storm and rain
    Drew back at the Geraldine's call.
"Now who comes not in the Holy Name
    Will never come in at all."

He looked to the right, he looked to the left,
    And never a one saw he;
But right in his path lay a coal black hound,
    A-moaning right piteously.

"Come in," he cried, "you little black hound,
    Come in, I will ease your pain;
My roof shall keep you to-night at least
    From the lash of wind and rain."

The Geraldine took up the little black hound,
    And put him down by the fire.
"So sleep you there, poor wandering one,
    As long as your heart desire."

The Geraldine tossed on his bed that night,
    And never asleep went he
For the crowing of his little red cock,
    That did crow most woefully.

For the howling of his own wolf-hound,
    That cried at the gate all night.

[612]

He rose and went to the banquet hall
  At the first of morning light.

He looked to the right, he looked to the left,
  At the rug where the dog lay on;
But the reindeer skin was burnt in two,
  And the little black hound was gone.

And, traced in the ashes, these words he read:
  "For the soul of your first-born son,
I will make you rich as you once were rich
  Ere the glass of your luck was run."

The Geraldine went to the west window,
  And then he went to the east,
And saw his desolate pasture fields,
  And the stables without a beast.

"So be it, as I love no woman,
  No son shall ever be mine;
I would that my stables were full of steeds,
  And my cellars were full of wine."

"I swear it, as I love no woman,
  And never a son have I,
I would that my sheep and their little lambs
  Should flourish and multiply.

So yours be the soul of my first-born son."
  Here the Geraldine slyly smiled,
But from the dark of the lonely room
  Came the cry of a little child.

The Geraldine went to the west window,
  He opened and out did lean,
And lo! the pastures were full of kine,
  All chewing the grass so green.

[613]

And quickly he went to the east window,
  And his face was pale to see,
For lo! he saw to the empty stalls
  Brave steeds go three by three.

The Geraldine went to the great hall door,
  In wonder at what had been,
And there he saw the prettiest maid,
  That ever his eyes had seen.

And long he looked at the pretty young maid,
  And swore there was none so fair;
And his heart went out of him like a hound,
  And hers like a timid hare.

Each day he followed her up and down,
  And each night he could not rest,
Until at last the pretty young maid
  Her love for him confessed.

They wooed and they wed, and the days went by
  As quick as such good days will,
And at last came the cry of his first-born son
  The cup of his joy to fill.

And the summer passed, and the winter came;
  Right fair was the child to see,
And he laughed at the shriek of a bitter storm
  As he sat on his father's knee.

Who rings so loud at the Geraldine's gate?
  Who knocks so loud at the door?
"Now rise you up, my pretty young wife,
  For twice they have knocked before."

Quickly she opened the great hall door,
  And "Welcome you in," she cried,

But there only entered a little black hound,
 And he would not be denied.

When the Geraldine saw the little black dog,
 He rose with a fearful cry,
"I sold my child to the Devil's hound
 In forgotten days gone by."

He drew his sword on the little black hound,
 But it would not pierce its skin,
He tried to pray, but his lips were dumb
 Because of his grievous sin.

Then the fair young wife took the black hound's throat
 Both her small white hands between.
And he thought he saw one of God's angels
 Where his sweet young wife had been.

Then he thought he saw from God's spirit
 The hound go sore oppressed,
But he woke to find his own dead wife
 With her dead child on her breast.

Quickly he went to the west window,
 Quickly he went to the east;
No help in the desolate pasture fields,
 Or the stables that held no beast.

He flung himself at his white wife's side,
 And the dead lips moved and smiled,
Then came somewhere from the lonely room
 The laugh of a little child.

[615]

GEORGE WILLIAM RUSSELL (A. E.)
(1867-1935)

THE LONELY

LONE and forgotten
Through a long sleeping,
In the heart of age
A child woke weeping.

No invisible mother
Was nigh him there
Laughing and nodding
From earth and air.

No elfin comrades
Came at his call,
And the earth and the air
Were blank as a wall.

The darkness thickened
Upon him creeping,
In the heart of age
A child lay weeping.

SALUTATION

Written for those who took part in the 1916 Rebellion.

YOUR dream had left me numb and cold
But yet my spirit rose in pride,
Re-fashioning in burnished gold
The images of those who died,
Or were shut in the penal cell—
Here's to you, Pearse, your dream, not mine,
But yet the thought—for this you fell—
Turns all life's water into wine.

[616]

I listened to high talk from you,
Thomas MacDonagh, and it seemed
The words were idle, but they grew
To nobleness, by death redeemed.
Life cannot utter things more great
Than life can meet with sacrifice,
High words were equalled by high fate,
You paid the price. You paid the price.

The hope lives on, age after age,
Earth with her beauty might be won
For labor as a heritage—
For this has Ireland lost a son,
This hope into a flame to fan
Men have put life by with a smile.
Here's to you, Connolly, my man,
Who cast the last torch on the pile.

Here's to the women of our race
Stood by them in the fiery hour,
Rapt, lest some weakness in their blood
Rob manhood of a single power—
You, brave as such a hope forlorn,
Who smiled through crack of shot and shell,
Though the world look on you with scorn,
Here's to you, Constance,[1] in your cell.

Here's to you, men I never met,
But hope to meet behind the veil,
Thronged on some starry parapet
That looks down upon Inisfail,
And see the confluence of dreams
That clashed together in our night,
One river born of many streams
Roll in one blaze of blinding light!

[1] Constance, Countess de Markievicz, one of the leaders of '16 and sister of Eva Gore-Booth.

REFUGE

Twilight, a timid fawn, went glimmering by,
   And Night, the dark-blue hunter, followed fast,
Ceaseless pursuit and flight were in the sky,
   But the long chase had ceased for us at last.

We watched together while the driven fawn
   Hid in the golden thicket of the day.
We, from whose hearts pursuit and flight were gone,
   Knew on the hunter's breast her refuge lay.

WHEN

When mine hour is come
Let no teardrop fall
And no darkness hover
Round me where I lie.
Let the vastness call
One who was its lover,
Let me breathe the sky.

Where the lordly light
Walks along the world,
And its silent tread
Leaves the grasses bright,
Leaves the flowers uncurled,
Let me to the dead
Breathe a gay goodnight.

CHARLES WEEKES
(1867-1946)

POPPIES

THE sudden night is here at once:
   The lost lamb cries and runs and stands,
   For all the poppy cups are hands
To seize and take him when he runs.

The dusky cups are blood colour;
   And like a cup of blood this one
   To drink, and be with Babylon,
And love and kiss the lips of her.—

Thy sins as snow!—just then it burned
   The dark—a flaming face and bust;
   And just beneath here in the dust
The Scarlet Woman laughed and turned.

THINK

THINK, the ragged turf-boy urges
   O'er the dusty road his asses;
Think, on the sea-shore far the lonely
   Heron wings along the sand;
Think, in woodland under oak-boughs
   Now the streaming sunbeam passes:
And bethink thee thou art servant
   To the same all-moving hand.

SOLSTICE

THE day is tired with idleness and awe.
The fishing-boats stand fixed along the sea.

[619]

Upon the heather hangs the drowsy bee
O'ercome with sweetness. Even within the claw
Of yonder bird the tettix fills his maw,
And burns with gold and crimson. Silently
A reaper passes dreamlike. Creatures free
Within the prisoning heat and this one law—
                                    The day is tired.

The sun stands still upon the livid sky;
And the great mountains go up to it there,
Fable on wondrous fable; and the air
Pulses with flame and darkness everywhere
—Or only in my brain, upon mine eye,
And still about my forehead and my hair.
                                    The day is tired.

IN BRITTANY

In Brittany I lost my way:
    Ah, happy girl-child of sixteen,
    Whatever my strange tongue might mean
You knew not, nor the thing to say,

Till a mad kiss fell on your lips,
    When, unconfused, you ceased to smile,
    And answered: "Up the hill a mile
Stands fair 'Our Lady of the Ships':

"We pray there for our folk at sea
    And then they are not wrecked nor tossed,
    But come back safe and are not lost—
And you may pray there, sir, for me."

[620]

THOMAS BOYD
(1867-1927)

TO THE LEANÁN SHEE

(The Fairy Mistress)

WHERE is thy lovely perilous abode?
  In what strange phantom-land
Glimmer the fairy turrets whereto rode
  The ill-starred poet band?

Say, in the Isle of Youth hast thou thy home,
  The sweetest singer there,
Stealing on wingéd steed across the foam
  Through the moonlit air?

And by the gloomy peaks of Erigal,
  Haunted by storm and cloud,
Wing past, and to thy lover there let fall
  His singing robe and shroud?

Or, where the mists of bluebell float beneath
  The red stems of the pine,
And sunbeams strike thro' shadow, dost thou breathe
  The word that makes him thine?

Or, is thy palace entered thro' some cliff
  When radiant tides are full,
And round thy lover's wandering starlit skiff
  Coil in luxurious lull?

And would he, entering on the brimming flood,
  See caverns vast in height,
And diamond columns, crowned with leaf and bud,
  Glow in long lanes of light.

[621]

And there the pearl of that great glittering shell
    Trembling, behold thee lone,
Now weaving in slow dance an awful spell,
    Now still upon thy throne?

Thy beauty! ah, the eyes that pierce him thro'
    Then melt as in a dream;
The voice that sings the mysteries of the blue
    And all that Be and Seem!

Thy lovely motions answering to the rhyme
    That ancient Nature sings,
That keeps the stars in cadence for all time,
    And echoes thro' all things!

Whether he sees thee thus, or in his dreams,
    Thy light makes all lights dim;
An aching solitude from henceforth seems
    The world of men to him.

Thy luring song, above the sensuous roar,
    He follows with delight,
Shutting behind him Life's last gloomy door,
    And fares into the Night.

THE HEATH

THROUGH the purple dusk on this pathless heath
Wanders a horse with its rider, Death.
The steed like its master is old and grim,
And the flame in his eye is burning dim.

The crown of the rider is red with gold,
For he is lord of the lea and the wold.
A-tween his ribs, against the sky
Glimmer the stars as he rideth by.

A hungry scythe o'er his shoulder bare
Glints afar through the darkening air,
And the sudden clank of his horse's hoof
Frightens the Wanderer aloof.

JOHN EGLINTON
(1868-   )

THE WINDS

"Who are the winds? Who are the winds?"
    —The storm was blowing wild—
"Who are the winds? Who are the winds?"
    —So question'd me the wild-eyed child.

"They are the souls, O child," I said,
    "Of men who long since ceased to hope;
And lastly, wishing to be dead,
    They lay down on the mountain-slope,
    And sigh'd their wills away;
And nature taking them hath made
    Round and about the world to stray.
Yet oft is waked the fitful pain,
    Which causes them to blow,
And still the passion stirs again
    Which vex'd them long ago;
And then no longer linger they,
But with a wild shriek sweep away,
And the green waves whiten to the moon,
And ships are wreck'd, and shores are strewn."

EVA GORE-BOOTH
(1870-1926)

THE LITTLE WAVES OF BREFFNY

THE grand road from the mountain goes shining to the sea,
  And there is traffic in it and many a horse and cart,
But the little roads of Cloonagh are dearer far to me,
  And the little roads of Cloonagh go rambling through my
    heart.

A great storm from the ocean goes shouting o'er the hill,
  And there is glory in it and terror on the wind,
But the haunted air of twilight is very strange and still,
  And the little winds of twilight are dearer to my mind.

The great waves of the Atlantic sweep storming on the way,
  Shining green and silver with the hidden herring shoal,
But the Little Waves of Breffny have drenched my heart in
    spray,
  And the Little Waves of Breffny go stumbling through my
    soul.

SEUMAS MacMANUS
(1870-   )

SHANE O'NEILL

The great Ulster chief and indomitable fighter Shane O'Neill, known in
Irish history as Shane the Proud, for long years defied Elizabeth's might in
Ireland, and throughout his life proved himself a whirlwind terror, not
only to the invader's army, but to the English and Scotch planters who
came after the English army.

ON THY wild and windy upland, Tornamona,
  High above the tossing Moyle,

[624]

Lies in slumber, deep and dreamless now, a warrior
  Weary-worn with battle-toil.
On his mighty breast the little canna blossoms,
  And the scented bog-bines trail;
While the winds from Lurigaiden whisper hush-songs
  Round the bed of Shane O'Neill.

Time was once, O haughty Warrior, when you slept not
  To the crooning of the wind;
There was once a Shane whom daisies could not smother,
  And whom bog-weeds could not bind—
Once a Shane with death-shafts from his fierce eye flashing,
  With dismay in fist of mail—
Shane, whose throbbing pulses sang with singing lightning—
  Shane, our Shane, proud Shane O'Neill!

Him the hungry Scot knew, and the thieving Saxon,
  Traitorous Eireannach as well;
For their mailed throats often gurgled in his grasping,
  As he hurled their souls to hell.
Sassenach now and flouting Scot and Irish traitor
  Breathe his name and turn not pale,
Set their heel upon the warrior's breast, not tremble—
  God! the breast of Shane O'Neill!

Will you never, O our Chieftain, snap the sleep-cords?
  Never rise in thunderous wrath—
Through the knaves and slaves that bring a blight on Uladh,
  Sweeping far a dread red swath?
O'er the surges shout, O you on Tornamona,
  Hark, the soul-shout of the Gael!
"Rise, O Chief, and lead us from our bitter bondage—
  Rise, in God's name, Shane O'Neill."

[625]

TOM MAGUIRE

(c. 1870-   )

BOLD ROBERT EMMET

THE struggle is over, the boys are defeated,
  Old Ireland's surrounded with sadness and gloom,
We were defeated and shamefully treated,
  And I, Robert Emmet, awaiting my doom.
Hung, drawn and quartered, sure that was my sentence,
  But soon I will show them no coward am I,
My crime is the love of the land I was born in—
  A hero I lived and a hero I'll die.

Chorus
  Bold Robert Emmet, the darling of Erin,
  Bold Robert Emmet will die with a smile,
  Farewell companions both loyal and daring,
  I'll lay down my life for the Emerald Isle.

The barque lay at anchor awaiting to bring me
  Over the billows to the land of the free;
But I must see my sweetheart for I know she will cheer me,
  And with her I will sail far over the sea.
But I was arrested and cast into prison,
  Tried as a traitor, a rebel, a spy;
But no one can call me a knave or a coward—
  A hero I lived and a hero I'll die.

  Bold Robert Emmet, *etc.*

Hark! the bell's tolling, I well know its meaning,
  My poor heart tells me it is my death knell;
In come the clergy, the warder is leading,
  I have no friends here to bid me farewell.
Goodbye, old Ireland, my parents and sweetheart,
  Companions in arms, to forget you must try;

[626]

I am proud of the honour, it was only my duty—
A hero I lived and a hero I'll die.

Bold Robert Emmet, *etc.*

JOHN MILLINGTON SYNGE
(1871-1909)

BEG-INNISH

BRING Kateen-beug and Maurya Jude
   To dance in Beg-Innish,
And when the lads (they're in Dunquin)
   Have sold their crabs and fish,
Wave fawny shawls and call them in,
And call the little girls who spin,
And seven weavers from Dunquin,
   To dance in Beg-Innish.

I'll play you jigs, and Maurice Kean,
   Where nets are laid to dry,
I've silken strings would draw a dance
   From girls are lame or shy;
Four strings I've brought from Spain and France
To make your long men skip and prance,
Till stars look out to see the dance
   Where nets are laid to dry.

We'll have no priest or peeler in
   To dance in Beg-Innish;
But we'll have drink from M'riarty Jim
   Rowed round while gannets fish,
A keg with porter to the brim,
That every lad may have his whim,
Till we up sails with M'riarty Jim
   And sail from Beg-Innish.

[627]

THE PASSING OF THE SHEE

ADIEU, sweet Angus, Maeve, and Fand,
Ye plumed yet skinny Shee,
That poets played with hand in hand
To learn their ecstasy.

We'll stretch in Red Dan Sally's ditch,
And drink in Tubber fair,
Or poach with Red Dan Philly's bitch
The badger and the hare.

QUEENS

SEVEN dog-days we let pass
Naming Queens in Glenmacnass,
All the rare and royal names
Wormy sheepskin yet retains;
Etain, Helen, Maeve, and Fand,
Golden Deirdre's tender hand;
Bert, the big-foot, sung by Villon,
Cassandra, Ronsard found in Lyon.
Queens of Sheba, Meath, and Connaught,
Coifed with crown, or gaudy bonnet;
Queens whose finger once did stir men,
Queens were eaten of fleas and vermin,
Queens men drew like Mona Lisa,
Or slew with drugs in Rome and Pisa.

We named Lucrezia Crivelli,
And Titian's lady with amber belly,
Queens acquainted in learned sin,
Jane of Jewry's slender shin;
Queens who cut the bogs of Glanna,
Judith of Scripture, and Glorianna,
Queens who wasted the East by proxy,
Or drove the ass-cart, a tinker's doxy.

Yet these are rotten—I ask their pardon—
And we've the sun on rock and garden;
These are rotten, so you're the Queen
Of all are living, or have been.

PATRICK MacDONOUGH
(1871-   )

BRING HOME THE POET

"If I die here, bury me up there on the mountain—the mountain ceme-
tery, Rocquebrune, France—and then after a year or so dig me up and
bring me privately to Sligo." William Butler Yeats.

BRING home the poet, laurel-crowned,
Lay him to rest in Irish ground;
Make him a grave near Sligo Bay,
At fair Drumcliffe or Knocknarea,
For near his mother's kindred dwelt,
And at Drumcliffe his fathers knelt,
And all about in beauty's haze,
The print of proud, heroic days,
With wind and wave in druid hymn
To chant for aye his requiem.
And he'll have mourners at his bier,
The fairy hosts who hold him dear,
And Father Gilligan, he'll be there,
The martial Maeve and Deirdre fair,
And lads he knew in town and glen,
The fisher folk and sailor men;
The Dooney fiddler and the throng
He made immortal with his song;
And proud in grief his rightful queen,
Ni Houlihan, the brave Kathleen.
Bring home the poet, let him rest
In the old land he loved the best.

[629]

LYNN DOYLE
(1873-   )

AN ULSTERMAN

I DO not like the other sort;
They're tricky an' they're sly,
An' couldn't look you in the face
Whenever they pass by.
Still I'll give in that here an' there,
You'll meet a decent man;
I would make an exception, now,
About wee Michael Dan.

But, then, he's from about the doors,
An' lived here all his days,
An', mixin' with us in an' out,
He's fell into our ways.
He pays his debts an' keeps his word
An' does the best he can.
If only all the Papishes
Were like wee Michael Dan!

A better neighbour couldn't be.
He borrows an' he lends;
An'—bar a while about the Twelfth
When him an' me's not friends—
He'll never wait until he's asked
To lend a helpin' han'.
There's quite a wheen of Protestants
I'd swop for Michael Dan.

Of course he'd burn me at the stake,
I know that very well;
An' told me one day to my face
I'm not too safe from hell.
But when I backed a bill for him

[630]

He met it like a man.
There's sparks of Christianity
About wee Michael Dan.

So, while I have my private doubts
About him reachin' heaven,
His feet keeps purty near the pad
On six days out of seven;
An' if it falls within the scope
Of God Almighty's plan
To save a single Papish sowl,
I hope it's Michael Dan.

JAMES H. COUSINS
(1873-   )

HIGH AND LOW

HE STUMBLED home from Clifden fair
With drunken song, and cheeks aglow.
Yet there was something in his air
That told of kingship long ago.
I sighed—and inly cried
With grief that one so high should fall so low.

He snatched a flower and sniffed its scent,
And waved it toward the sunset sky.
Some old sweet rapture through him went
And kindled in his bloodshot eye.
I turned—and inly burned
With joy that one so low should rise so high.

THE CORNCRAKE

I HEARD him faintly, far away,
(*Break! Break!—Break! Break!*)
Calling to the dawn of day,
  "Break! Break!"

I heard him in the yellow morn
(*Shake! Shake!—Shake! Shake!*)
Shouting thro' the rustling corn,
  "Shake! Shake!"

I heard him near where one lay dead
  (*Ache! Ache!*)
Crying among poppies red,
  "Ache! Ache!—Ache! Ache!"

And where a solemn yew-tree waves
  (*Wake! Wake!*)
All night he shouts among the graves,
  "Wake! Wake!—Wake! Wake!"

OMENS

WHEN the snail crawls over the bare flag-stone;
When the sun to the moon is nigh;
When the spear-grass on the white sea-sand
Draws its ring awry;
Hold thou thy breath,
For Death,
Death passeth by.

THOMAS MacDONAGH
(1878-1916)

JOHN-JOHN

I DREAMT last night of you, John-John,
    And thought you called to me;
And when I woke this morning, John,
    Yourself I hoped to see;
But I was all alone, John-John,
    Though still I heard your call:
I put my boots and bonnet on,
    And took my Sunday shawl,
And went, full sure to find you, John,
                To Nenagh fair.

The fair was just the same as then,
    Five years ago to-day,
When first you left the thimble men
    And came with me away;
For there again were thimble men
    And shooting galleries,
And card-trick men and Maggie men
    Of all sorts and degrees—
But not a sight of you, John-John,
                Was anywhere.

I turned my face to home again,
    And called myself a fool
To think you'd leave the thimble men
    And live again by rule,
And go to mass and keep the fast
    And till the little patch:
My wish to have you home was past
    Before I raised the latch
And pushed the door and saw you, John,
                Sitting down there.

[633]

How cool you came in here, begad,
  As if you owned the place!
But rest yourself there now, my lad,
  'Tis good to see your face;
My dream is out, and now by it
  I think I know my mind:
At six o'clock this house you'll quit,
  And leave no grief behind;—
But until six o'clock, John-John,
          My bit you'll share.

My neighbours' shame of me began
  When first I brought you in;
To wed and keep a tinker man
  They thought a kind of sin;
But now this three year since you're gone
  'Tis pity me they do,
And that I'd rather have John-John,
  Than that they'd pity you.
Pity for me and you, John-John,
          I could not bear.

Oh, you're my husband right enough,
  But what's the good of that?
You know you never were the stuff
  To be the cottage cat,
To watch the fire and hear me lock
  The door and put out Shep—
But there now, it is six o'clock
  And time for you to step.
God bless and keep you far, John-John!
          And that's my prayer.

OF A POET PATRIOT

His songs were a little phrase
  Of eternal song,

[634]

Drowned in the harping of lays
    More loud and long.

His deed was a single word,
    Called out alone
In a night when no echo stirred
    To laughter or moan.

But his songs new souls shall thrill,
    The loud harps dumb,
And his deed the echoes fill
    When the dawn is come.

IN PARIS

So HERE is my desert and here am I
    In the midst of it alone,
Silent and free as a hawk in the sky,
    Unnoticed and unknown.

I speak to no one from sun to sun,
    And do my single will,
Though round me loud voiced millions run
    And life is never still.

There goes the bell of the Sorbonne
    Just as in Villon's day—
He heard it here go sounding on,
    And stopped his work to pray—

Just in this place, in time of snow,
    Alone, at a table bent—
Four hundred and fifty years ago
    He wrote that Testament.

LORD DUNSANY
(1878-   )

A CALL TO THE WILD

JIMSON lives in a new
  Small house where the view is shrouded
With hideous hoardings, a view
  That is every year more crowded.

Every year he is vexed
  With some new noise as a neighbor;
The tram-lines are coming next
  And the street is noisy with labor.

But one thing he sees afar,
  From a window over his back-door,
Is a wood as wild as a star,
  On a hill untouched by contractor.

Thither at times, forlorn,
  From the clamor of things suburban
He turns, as the Arab at dawn
  To Mecca inclines his turban.

And this is the curious prayer
  That he prays when his heart sickens,
"Oh fox come down from your lair
  And steal our chickens."

A HETERODOXY

I DREAMED one night I came
  Somehow to Heaven, and there
Transfigured shapes like flame
  Moved effortless in air.

All silent were the Blest,
　　Calmly their haloes shone,
When through them all there pressed
　　One spirit whirling on.

He like a comet seemed,
　　But wild and glad and free,
And all through Heaven, I dreamed,
　　Rushed madly up to me.

Back from his haloed head
　　A flaming tail streamed far,
This way and that it sped
　　And waved from star to star,

And, as I saw it shot
　　Like searchlights through the sky,
I knew my dog had got
　　To Heaven as well as I.

OLIVER ST. JOHN GOGARTY
(1878-　　)

NON DOLET

OUR friends go with us as we go
Down the long path where Beauty wends,
Where all we love foregathers, so
Why should we fear to join our friends?

Who would survive them to outlast
His children; to outwear his fame—
Left when the Triumph has gone past—
To win from Age not Time a name?

Then do not shudder at the knife
That death's indifferent hand drives home;
But with the Strivers leave the Strife,
Nor, after Caesar, skulk in Rome.

LEDA AND THE SWAN

THOUGH her Mother told her
　Not to go a-bathing,
Leda loved the river
　And she could not keep away:
Wading in its freshets
　When the noon was heavy;
Walking by the water
　At the close of day.

Where between its waterfalls,
　Underneath the beeches,
Gently flows a broader
　Hardly moving stream,
And the balanced trout lie
　In the quiet reaches;
Taking all her clothes off,
　Leda went to swim.

There was not a flag-leaf
　By the river's margin
That might be a shelter
　From a passer-by;
And a sudden whiteness
　In the quiet darkness,
Let alone the splashing,
　Was enough to catch an eye.

But the place was lonely,
　And her clothes were hidden;

Even cattle walking
　　In the ford had gone away;
Every single farm-hand
　　Sleeping after dinner—
What's the use of talking?
　　There was no one in the way.

In, without a stitch on,
　　Peaty water yielded,
Till her head was lifted
　　With its ropes of hair;
It was more surprising
　　Than a lily gilded
Just to see how golden
　　Was her body there:

Lolling in the water,
　　Lazily uplifting
Limbs that on the surface
　　Whitened into snow;
Leaning on the water,
　　Indolently drifting,
Hardly any faster
　　Than the foamy bubbles go.

You would say to see her
　　Swimming in the lonely
Pool, or after, dryer,
　　Putting on her clothes:
"O but she is lovely,
　　Not a soul to see her,
And how lovely only
　　Leda's Mother knows!"

Under moving branches
　　Leisurely she dresses,
And the leafy sunlight
　　Made you wonder were

All its woven shadows
  But her golden tresses,
Or a smock of sunlight
  For her body bare.

When on earth great beauty
  Goes exempt from danger,
It will be endangered
  From a source on high;
When unearthly stillness
  Falls on leaves, the ranger,
In his wood-lore anxious,
  Gazes at the sky.

While her hair was drying,
  Came a gentle languor,
Whether from the bathing
  Or the breeze she didn't know.
Anyway she lay there,
  And her Mother's anger
(Worse if she had wet hair)
  Could not make her dress and go.

Whitest of all earthly
  Things, the white that's rarest,
Is the snow on mountains
  Standing in the sun;
Next the clouds above them,
  Then the down is fairest
On the breast and pinions
  Of a proudly sailing swan.

And she saw him sailing
  On the pool where lately
She had stretched unnoticed,
  As she thought, and swum;
And she never wondered
  Why, erect and stately,

[640]

Where no river weed was
  Such a bird had come.

What was it she called him:
  Goosey-goosey gander?
For she knew no better
  Way to call a swan;
And the bird responding
  Seemed to understand her,
For he left his sailing
  For the bank to waddle on.

Apple blossoms under
  Hills of Lacedaemon,
With the snow beyond them
  In the still blue air,
To the swan who hid them
  With his wings asunder,
Than the breasts of Leda,
  Were not lovelier!

Of the tales that daughters
  Tell their poor old mothers,
Which by all accounts are
  Often very odd;
Leda's was a story
  Stranger than all others.
What was there to say but,
  Glory be to God?

And she half-believed her,
  For she knew her daughter;
And she saw the swan-down
  Tangled in her hair.
Though she knew how deeply
  Runs the stillest water;
How could she protect her
  From the winged air?

[641]

Why is it effects are
  Greater than their causes?
Why should causes often
  Differ from effects?
Why should what is lovely
  Fill the world with harness?
And the most deceived be
  She who least suspects?

When the hyacinthine
  Eggs were in the basket,—
Blue as at the whiteness
  Where a cloud begins:
Who would dream there lay there
  All that Trojan brightness;
Agamemnon murdered;
  And the mighty Twins?

BETWEEN BRIELLE AND MANASQUAN

THE old sea captains, when their work
  Was done on the eternal sea,
Came each ashore and built a house
  And settled down reluctantly;
And in his front lawn each set up
A flagstaff and a telescope.

Each little house was painted white
  With shutters gay and pointed gables
From which the vines hung loose or tight
  Or twisted round like coiled-up cables;
And each green lawn was so well dressed
It seemed a little sea at rest.

And some were stocky men with beards
  And some were tawny blue-eyed men;

[642]

And when they talked you might have heard
  Surnames that end in '-ing' or '-sen';
All sensed, since they had left the scene,
A falling off in things marine.

You cannot find their houses now,
  The place is so much built upon;
They lived—they say who ought to know—
  Between Brielle and Manasquan;
But you can find in some old store
The curious things they brought ashore:

Old compasses, chronometers,
  And here a sextant ornamented,
A binnacle and carven wares;
  A captain's spyglass, rather dented;
A keg that raxed a pirate's throttle;
A schooner, full-rigged, in a bottle.

Weapons with silver work inlaid;
  Blue glass the dealer said was Bristol's;
Carved shells and bits of Chinese jade;
  Two old brass-barreled flintlock pistols;
And, if these failed to take your fancy,
A figurehead called "Spumy Nancy."

These old seafarers in their day,
  If asked about impressions wrought
By isles of Ind or far Cathay,
  Could give no record of their thought:
What wonder worker ever knows
The wonder of the things he does?

Aye; but the little children knew
  What deep lagoons they anchored in,
What reefs they took their vessels through,
  And of strange cargoes hard to win.

[643]

The Isles of Spice, typhoons and thunder,
The Yellow sea and all its wonder.

They came to think, as they grew old
   And found themselves with few compeers,
That things grow better when they're told,
   And they themselves improved with years;
They'd sail again, did it beseem
Experienced men to take to steam.

Meanwhile, the long-deserted sea
   Resented them as one neglected;
She swished her tides resentfully
   And tons and tons of sand collected
Which silted up the narrow way
That leads to Barnagat's still bay.

So that they lived as men marooned;
   They could not sail now if they hankered;
You'd think, to see their homes festooned,
   A fleet was in the Bay and anchored,
So gaily grew the creepers mounting,
So gaily flew the flagstaff's bunting.

TO A FRIEND IN THE COUNTRY

(Wyckoff, New Jersey)

You like the country better than the town
And very willingly would dwell therein
Afar from the intolerable din
That makes New York a barbarous Babylon;
But far more willingly would I be gone
From all this mad bombardment of the brain
To fields where still and comely thoughts may reign
Deep in your stately mansion old and brown
And colored like a Springtime copper beech:

[644]

My God, I would give anything to reach
Your old house standing in the misty rain,
And turn my thoughts to things that do not pass
While gazing through a window at the grass
And wet young oak leaves fingering the pane.

PADRAIC PEARSE
(1879-1916)

THE REBEL

I COME of the seed of the people, the people that sorrow,
That have no treasure but hope,
No riches laid up but a memory
Of an ancient glory.
My mother bore me in bondage, in bondage my mother was
        born,
I am the blood of serfs;
The children with whom I have played, the men and women
        with whom I have eaten,
Have had masters over them, they have been under the lash of
        masters,
And, though gentle, have served churls;
The hands that have touched mine, the dear hands whose touch
        is familiar to me,
Have worn shameful manacles, have been bitten at the wrist
        by manacles,
Have grown hard with the manacles and the task-work of
        strangers,
I am flesh of the flesh of these lowly, I am bone of their bone,
I have never submitted;
I that have a soul greater than the souls of my people's masters,
I have vision and prophecy and the gift of fiery speech,
I that have spoken with God on the top of His holy hill.

And because I am of the people, I understand the people,
I am sorrowful with their sorrow, I am hungry with their de-
    sire:
My heart has been heavy with the grief of mothers,
My eyes have been wet with the tears of children,
I have yearned with old wistful men,
And laughed or cursed with young men;
Their shame is my shame, and I have reddened for it,
Reddened for that they have gone in want, while others have
    been full,
Reddened for that they have walked in fear of lawyers and of
    their jailors
With their writs of summons and their handcuffs,
Men mean and cruel!
I could have borne stripes on my body rather than this shame
    of my people.
I say to my people that they are holy, that they are august, de-
    spite their chains,
That they are greater than those that hold them, and stronger
    and purer,
That they have put need of courage, and to call on the name of
    their God,
God the unforgetting, the dear God that loves the peoples For
    whom He died naked, suffering shame.
And I say to my people's masters: Beware,
Beware of the thing that is coming, beware of the risen people,
Who shall take what ye would not give. Did ye think to con-
    quer the people,
Or that Law is stronger than life and than men's desire to be
    free?
We will try it out with you, ye that have harried and held,
Ye that have bullied and bribed, tyrants, hypocrites, liars!

THE MOTHER

Written at his mother's request, just before he and his brother went out to fight in the Rising of 1916.

I DO not grudge them; Lord, I do not grudge
My two strong sons that I have seen go out
To break their strength and die, they and a few,
In bloody protest for a glorious thing.
They shall be spoken of among their people,
The generations shall remember them,
And call them blessed;
But I will speak their names to my own heart
In the long nights;
The little names that were familiar once
Round my dead hearth.
Lord, thou art hard on mothers:
We suffer in their coming and their going;
And tho' I grudge them not, I weary, weary
Of the long sorrow—And yet I have my joy:
My sons were faithful and they fought.

THE FOOL

SINCE the wise men have not spoken, I speak that am only a
    fool;
A fool that has loved his folly,
Yea, more than the wise men their books or their counting
    houses, or their quiet homes,
Or their fame in men's mouths;
A fool that in all his days hath done never a prudent thing,
Never hath counted the cost, nor recked if another reaped
The fruit of his mighty sowing, content to scatter the seed;
A fool that is unrepentant, and that soon at the end of all
Shall laugh in his lonely heart as the ripe ears fall to the reap-
    ing-hooks
And the poor are filled that were empty,
Tho' he go hungry.

[647]

I have squandered the splendid years that the Lord God gave
    to my youth
In attempting impossible things, deeming them alone worth
    the toil.
Was it folly or grace? Not men shall judge me, but God.
I have squandered the splendid years:
Lord, if I had the years I would squander them over again,
Aye, fling them from me!
For this I have heard in my heart, that a man shall scatter, not
    hoard,
Shall do the deed of to-day, nor take thought of to-morrow's
    teen,
Shall not bargain or huxter with God; or was it a jest of Christ's
And is this my sin before men, to have taken Him at His word?

The lawyers have sat in council, the men with the keen, long
    faces,
And said, "This man is a fool," and others have said, "He
    blasphemeth;"
And the wise have pitied the fool that hath striven to give a
    life
In the world of time and space among the bulks of actual
    things,
To a dream that was dreamed in the heart, and that only the
    heart could hold.

O wise men, riddle me this: what if the dream come true?
What if the dream come true? and if millions unborn shall
    dwell
In the house that I shaped in my heart, the noble house of my
    thought?
Lord, I have staked my soul, I have staked the lives of my kin
On the truth of Thy dreadful word. Do not remember my fail-
    ures,
But remember this my faith.

And so I speak.
Yea, ere my hot youth pass, I speak to my people and say:

Ye shall be foolish as I; ye shall scatter, not save;
Ye shall venture your all, lest ye lose what is more than all;
Ye shall call for a miracle, taking Christ at His word.
And for this I will answer, O people, answer here and hereafter,
O people that I have loved shall we not answer together?

JOSEPH CAMPBELL
(1879-1944)

THE POET LOOSED A WINGÈD SONG

THE poet loosed a wingèd song
Against the hulk of England's wrong.
Were poisoned words at his command,
'Twould not avail for Ireland.

The soldier lifted up a sword,
And on the hills in battle poured
His life-blood like an ebbing sea—
And still we pine for liberty.

The friar spoke his bitter hope,
And danced upon the gallows rope.
Were he to dance that dance again
A hundred times, 'twould be in vain.

Christ save us! Only thou canst save!
The nation staggers to the grave.
Can genius, valour, faith be given,
And win no recompense of heaven?

No, Christ! by Ireland's martyrs, no!
'Twas not for this we suffered so.
Die, die again on Calvary tree,
If needs be, Christ, to set us free!
To set us free!

[649]

THE HERB-LEECH

I HAVE gathered *luss*[1]
At the wane of the moon,
And supped its sap
With a yewen spoon.
I have set a spell
By the carn of Medb,
And smelt the mould
Of the red queen's grave.
I have dreamed a dearth
In the darkened sun,
And felt the hand
Of the Evil One.
I have fathomed war
In the comet's tail,
And heard the crying
Of Gall and Gael.
I have seen the spume
On the dead priest's lips,
And the 'holy fire'
On the spars of ships;
And the shooting stars
On Barthelmy's Night,
Blanching the dark
With ghostly light;
And the corpse-candle
Of the seer's dream,
Bigger in girth
Than a weaver's beam;
And the shy hearth-fairies
About the grate,
Blowing the turves
To a whiter heat.
All things on earth
To me are known,
For I have the gift
Of the Murrain Stone!

[1] Luss = foxglove.

THE OLD WOMAN

As A white candle
In a holy place,
So is the beauty
Of an aged face.

As the spent radiance
Of the winter sun,
So is a woman
With her travail done.

Her brood gone from her,
And her thoughts as still
As the waters
Under a ruined mill.

THE TINKERS

"ONE *ciarog* knows another *ciarog,*
And why shouldn't I know you, you rogue?"
"They say a stroller will never pair
Except with one of his kind and care . . ."
So talked two tinkers prone in the shough—
And then, as the fun got a trifle rough,
They flitted: he with his corn-straw bass,
She with her load of tin and brass:
As mad a match as you would see
In a twelvemonth's ride thro' Christendie.
He roared—they both were drunk as hell:
She danced, and danced it mighty well!
I could have eyed them longer, but
They staggered for the Quarry Cut:
That half perch seemed to trouble them more
Than all the leagues they'd tramped before.
Some'll drink at the fair the morrow,

[651]

And some'll sup with the spoon of sorrow;
But whether *they'll* get as far as Droichid
The night—well, who knows that but God?

A FIGHTING-MAN

A FIGHTING-MAN he was,
Guts and soul;
His blood was hot and red
As that on Cain's hand-towel.

A copper-skinned six-footer,
Hewn out of the rock.
Who would stand up against
His hammer-knock?

Not a sinner—
No, and not one dared!
Giants showed clean heels
When his arm was bared.

I've seen him swing an anvil
Fifty feet,
Break a bough in two,
And tear a twisted sheet.

And the music of his roar—
Like oaks in thunder cleaving;
Lips foaming red froth,
And flanks heaving.

God! a goodly man,
A Gael, the last
Of those that stood with Dan
On Mullach-Maist!

THE BESOM-MAN

DID you see Paidin,
Paidin, the besom-man,[1]
Last night as you came by
Over the mountain?

A barth of new heather
He bore on his shoulder,
And a bundle of whitlow-grass
Under his oxter.[2]

I spied him as he passed
Beyond the carn head,
But no eye saw him
At the hill foot after.

What has come over him?
The women are saying.
What can have crossed
Paidin, the besom-man?

The bogholes he knew
As the curlews know them,
And the rabbits' pads,
And the derelict quarries.

He was humming a tune—
The "Enchanted Valley"—
As he passed me westward
Beyond the carn.

I stood and I listened,
For his singing was strange:
It rang in my ears
The long night after.

[1] Besom = broom. [2] Oxter = arm.

What has come over
Paidin, the besom-man?
What can have crossed him?
The women keep saying.

They talk of the fairies—
And, God forgive me,
Paidin knew *them*
Like his prayers!

Will you fetch word
Up to the cross-roads
If you see track of him,
Living or dead?

The boys are loafing
Without game or caper;
And the dark piper
Is gone home with the birds.

THREE COLTS EXERCISING IN A SIX-ACRE

THREE colts exercising in a six-acre,
A hilly sweep of unfenced grass over the road.

What a picture they make against the skyline!
Necks stretched, hocks moving royally, tails flying;
Farm-lads up, and they crouching low on their withers.

I have a journey to go—
A lawyer to see, and a paper to sign in the Tontine—
But I slacken my pace to watch them.

[654]

THE UNFROCKED PRIEST

HE LEANT at the door
  In his priest's clothes—
Greasy black they were:
  And he bled at the nose.

He leant at the door,
  And the blood trickled down:
A man of the country,
  More than the town.

He was of God's anointed,
  A priest, no less:
But he had been unfrocked
  For drunkenness.

For that, or worse,
  And flesh is only human,
For some wrong-doing
  With a woman.

And in his father's house
  He lived at ease,
Reading his books,
  As quiet as the trees.

No one troubled him
  As he went in and out,
And he smoked his clay,
  And he grew stout.

And he tramped the parish
  In the summer days,
Thinking high thoughts
  And giving God praise.

[655]

None but blessed him
      As he walked the hills,
For he gave to the poor
      And he cured their ills.

There was no herb
      That grew in the grass,
But he saw its virtue
      As in a glass.

No rath, no Mass-bush
      No ogham stone,
But he knew its story
      As his own.

He had a scholar's knowledge
      Of Greek,
And dabbled in Hebrew
      And Arabic.

And in his time
      (He died in 'eighty-seven)
He wrote two epics
      And a "Dream of Heaven."

I saw him once only
      In his priest's clothes
At his father's door:
      And he bled at the nose.

O GLORIOUS CHILDBEARER

O GLORIOUS childbearer,
O secret womb,
O gilded bridechamber, from which hath come the sightly
      Bridegroom forth,

O amber veil,
Thou sittest in heaven, the white love of the Gael.
Thy head is crowned with stars, thy radiant hair
Shines like a river thro' the twilight air;
Thou walkest by trodden ways and trackless seas,
Immaculate of man's infirmities.

I WILL GO WITH MY FATHER A-PLOUGHING

I WILL go with my father a-ploughing
To the green field by the sea,
And the rooks and the crows and the seagulls
Will come flocking after me.
I will sing to the patient horses
With the lark in the white of the air,
And my father will sing the plough-song
That blesses the cleaving share.

I will go with my father a-sowing
To the red field by the sea,
And the rooks and the gulls and the starlings
Will come flocking after me.
I will sing to the striding sowers
With the finch on the flowering sloe,
And my father will sing the seed-song
That only the wise men know.

I will go with my father a-reaping
To the brown field by the sea,
And the geese and the crows and the children
Will come flocking after me.
I will sing to the weary reapers
With the wren in the heat of the sun,
And my father will sing the scythe-song
That joys for the harvest done.

[657]

I AM THE GILLY OF CHRIST

I AM the gilly of Christ,
The mate of Mary's Son;
I run the roads at seeding time,
And when the harvest's done.

I sleep among the hills,
The heather is my bed;
I dip the termon-well for drink,
And pull the sloe for bread.

No eye has ever seen me,
But shepherds hear me pass,
Singing at fall of even
Along the shadowed grass.

The beetle is my bellman,
The meadow-fire my guide,
The bee and bat my ambling nags
When I have need to ride.

All know me only the Stranger,
Who sits on the Saxons' height:
He burned the bacach's little house
On last St. Brigid's Night.

He sups off silver dishes,
And drinks in a golden horn,
But he will wake a wiser man
Upon the Judgment Morn!

I am the gilly of Christ,
The mate of Mary's Son;
I run the roads at seeding time,
And when the harvest's done.

The seed I sow is lucky,
The corn I reap is red,

And whoso sings the Gilly's Rann
Will never cry for bread.

SEUMAS O'SULLIVAN
(1879-

THE TWILIGHT PEOPLE

IT IS a whisper among the hazel bushes;
It is a long, low, whispering voice that fills
With a sad music the bending and swaying rushes;
It is a heart-beat deep in the quiet hills.

Twilight people, why will you still be crying,
Crying and calling to me out of the trees?
For under the quiet grass the wise are lying,
And all the strong ones are gone over the seas.

And I am old, and in my heart at your calling
Only the old dead dreams a-fluttering go;
As the wind, the forest wind, in its falling
Sets the withered leaves fluttering to and fro.

CREDO

I CANNOT pray, as Christians use to pray,
Before the holy Rood,
Nor on the sacred mysteries seven, as they,
Believing brood.

Nor can I say with those whom pride makes sure,
Our hearts emancipate
Have scorn of ancient symbols that endure
Out-lasting late.

[659]

For I have seen Lord Angus in the trees,
And bowing heard
When Spring a lover whispered in their leaves
The living word.

Have known the sun, the wind's sweet agency
And the soft rains that bless
And lead the year through coloured pageantry
To fruitfulness.

Yea, by the outstretched hands, the dimming sight,
The pierced side,
Known when in every bough that shrinks from light
The Lord of life has died.

RAIN

(Donegal)

ALL day long
The gray rain beating,
On the bare hills
Where the scant grass cannot cover,
The gray rocks peeping
Through the salt herbage.
All day long
The young lambs bleating
Stand for covering
Where the scant grass is
Under the gray wall,
Or seeking softer shelter
Under tattered fleeces
Nuzzle the warm udders.
All day long
The little waves leaping
Round the gray rocks
By the brown tide borders,

[660]

Round the black headlands
Streaming with rain.

LULLABY

HUSHEEN the herons are crying,
Away in the rain and the sleet,
Flying and flying and flying
With never a rest to their feet.

But warm in your coverlet nestle,
Wee bird, till the dawn of the day,
Nor dream of the wild wings that wrestle
In the night and the rain and the gray.

Come, sweetheart, the bright ones would bring you
By the magical meadows and streams,
With the light of your dreaming they build you
A house on the hill of your dreams.

But you stir in your sleep and you murmur,
As though the wild rain and the gray
Wet hills with the winds ever blowing
Had driven your dreams away.

And dearer the wind in its crying,
And the secrets the wet hills hold,
Than the goldenest place they could find you
In the heart of a country of gold.

MOIRA O'NEILL
(Dates not known)

SEA WRACK

THE wrack was dark an' shiny where it floated in the sea,
There was no one in the brown boat but only him an' me;
Him to cut the sea wrack, me to mind the boat,
An' not a word between us the hours we were afloat.
       The wet wrack,
       The sea wrack,
       The wrack was strong to cut.

We laid it on the grey rocks to wither in the sun,
An' what should call my lad then, to sail from Cushendun?
With a low moon, a full tide, a swell upon the deep,
Him to sail the old boat, me to fall asleep.
       The dry wrack,
       The sea wrack,
       The wrack was dead so soon.

There' a fire low upon the rocks to burn the wrack to kelp,
There' a boat gone down upon the Moyle, an' sorra one to
      help!
Him beneath the salt sea, me upon the shore,
By sunlight or moonlight we'll lift the wrack no more.
       The dark wrack,
       The sea wrack,
       The wrack may drift ashore.

THOMAS M. KETTLE
(1880-1916)

TO MY DAUGHTER BETTY, THE GIFT OF GOD

IN WISER days, my darling rosebud, blown
To beauty proud as was your mother's prime,
In that desired, delayed, incredible time,
You'll ask why I abandoned you, my own,
And the dear heart that was your baby throne,
To dice with death. And oh! they'll give you rhyme
And reason: some will call the thing sublime,
And some decry it in a knowing tone.
So here, while the mad guns curse overhead,
And tired men sigh with mud for couch and floor,
Know that we fools, now with the foolish dead,
Died not for flag, nor King, nor Emperor—
But for a dream, born in a herdman's shed,
And for the secret Scripture of the poor.

ALICE MILLIGAN
(1866-

WHEN I WAS A LITTLE GIRL

WHEN I was a little girl,
In a garden playing
A thing was often said
To chide us delaying:

When after sunny hours,
At twilight's falling,
Down through the garden walks
Came our old nurse calling

[663]

"Come in! for it's growing late,
And the grass will wet ye!
Come in! or when it's dark
The Fenians will get ye."

Then, at this dreadful news,
All helter-skelter,
The panic-struck little flock
Ran home for shelter.

And round the nursery fire
Sat still to listen,
Fifty bare toes on the hearth,
Ten eyes a-glisten.

To hear of a night in March,
And loyal folk waiting,
To see a great army of men
Come devastating.

An Army of Papists grim,
With a green flag o'er them,
Red-coats and black police
Flying before them.

But God (Who our nurse declared
Guards British dominions)
Sent down a fall of snow
And scattered the Fenians.

"But somewhere they're lurking yet,
Maybe they're near us,"
Four little hearts pit-a-pat
Thought "Can they hear us?"

Then the wind-shaken pane
Sounded like drumming;
"Oh!" they cried, "tuck us in,
The Fenians are coming!"

Four little pairs of hands
In the cots where she led those,
Over their frightened heads
Pulled up the bedclothes.

But one little rebel there,
Watching all with laughter,
Thought "When the Fenians come
I'll rise and go after."

Wished she had been a boy
And a good deal older—
Able to walk for miles
With a gun on her shoulder.

Able to lift aloft
The Green Flag o'er them
(Red-coats and black police
Flying before them).

And, as she dropped asleep,
Was wondering whether
God, if they prayed to Him,
Would give fine weather.

A SONG OF FREEDOM

In Cavan of little lakes,
As I was walking with the wind,
And no one seen beside me there,
There came a song into my mind:
It came as if the whispered voice
Of one, but none of human kind,
Who walked with me in Cavan then,
And he invisible as wind.

[665]

On Urris of Inish-Owen,
As I went up the mountain side,
The brook that came leaping down
Cried to me—for joy it cried;
And when from off the summit far
I looked o'er land and water wide,
I was more joyous than the brook
That met me on the mountain side.

To Ara of Connacht's isles,
As I went sailing o'er the sea,
The wind's word, the brook's word,
The wave's word, was plain to me—
"As we are, though she is not
As we are, shall Banba be—
There is no King can rule the wind,
There is no fetter for the sea."

DANIEL CORKERY
(1878-   )

THE CALL

HERE at the village crossing,
Beneath the hawthorn bushes,
The young men gathered nightly,
    From smithy, plough, and stall.

Some were silent, drowsy,
Their happy eyes moved slowly,
And the pipe that they were smoking
    They drew with every limb!

And some were silent, thoughtful,
In their young eyes a wonder,

[666]

The world was wide, and wider
  Than all their fathers' fields!

But others on their coming
Would break the dewy stillness
I heard their warm, rich laughter,
  I heard their wrestling feet.

Each night I gave them greeting,
They greeted from the darkness,
A pipe was moved to speak it,
  The wrestling feet were stilled.

So till that wondrous Easter,
But now their talk is Ireland,
"Ireland! Ireland! Ireland!"
  I catch as I go by.

Were I an Irish mother,
And a gossip came and told me:
"Your boy is at the crossing,
  He, and the others, too.

"And their talk, it is of Ireland,
I heard them and I passing."
My heart for sudden coldness
  Would cease awhile to beat;

So many an Irish mother
Has seen her boy grow silent;
Just as he reached to manhood
  Grow silent, proud, and straight;

So many an Irish mother
Has seen her boy go from her,
As if they had bewitched him,
  The fierce old Irish dead!

[667]

PADRAIC COLUM
(1881-   )

GARADH

FOR the poor body that I own
  I could weep many a tear:
The hours have stolen flesh and bone,
  And left a changeling here.

Four feeble bones are left to me,
  And the basket of my breast.
And I am mean and ugly now
  As the scald flung from the nest.

The briars drag me at the knee,
  The brambles go within,
And often do I feel him turn
  The old man in my skin.

The strength is carded from my bones,
  The swiftness drained from me.
And all the living thoughts I had
  Are like far ships at sea!

THE PLOUGHER

SUNSET and silence! A man: around him earth savage, earth
    broken;
Beside him two horses—a plough!

Earth savage, earth broken, the brutes, the dawn-man there in
    the sunset,
And the Plough that is twin to the Sword, that is founder of
    cities!

[668]

"Brute-tamer, plough-maker, earth-breaker! Canst hear? There
    are ages between us.
Is it praying you are as you stand there alone in the sunset?

"Surely our sky-born gods can be naught to you, earth child
    and earth master?
Surely your thoughts are of Pan, or of Wotan, or Dana?

"Yet, why give thought to the gods? Has Pan led your brutes
    where they stumble?
Has Dana numbed pain of the child-bed, or Wotan put hands
    to your plow?

"What matter your foolish reply! O man, standing lone and
    bowed earthward,
Your task is a day near its close. Give thanks to the night-
    giving God."

Slowly the darkness falls, the broken lands blend with the
    savage;
The brute-tamer stands by the brutes, a head's breadth only
    above them.

A head's breadth? Ay, but therein is hell's depth, and the
    height up to heaven,
And the thrones of the gods and their halls, their chariots,
    purples and splendours.

A CRADLE SONG

O, MEN from the fields!
Come gently within.
Tread softly, softly,
O! men coming in.

Mavourneen is going
From me and from you,

Where Mary will fold him
With mantle of blue!

From reek of the smoke
And cold of the floor,
And the peering of things
Across the half-door.

O, men from the fields!
Soft, softly come thro'.
Mary puts round him
Her mantle of blue.

BLANAID SALKELD
(1880-

PEGGY

WHITER there is not nor rosier,
Bluer there is not nor goldener—a flower:
Prim movements fettered by modesty,
Brave heart, unflinching eye:
Most gently, a girl of twenty
Who has loved no man, loves me.

Rich she is, in warm living silences—
And the firelight glow
At dusk thrown
On her hair, cheek, shoulder,
Strikes a magic tint
From her hid spirit.

I must turn gardener, holding this flower of price—
Till, and nourish well my Here of life;
Lest she be lonely, have of her kin
Spring flowers—fragrant flingers

[670]

After giddy wings!
She will not befriend them, if they love not me.
So, for her sake, their gracious glee
Will smile on me.

Spring flashes clear
From peak to peak,
And a white foam-leaf. . . .
Ah, there . . . Ah, here. . . .
About the blue sea
Unfurls gently,
And a girl of twenty
Who has loved no man, loves me.

THAT CORNER

MAN is most anxious not to stir
Out of the unblessed beat
Of sounds that recur
In house or on street.
Not only the birds' morning prayers,
But light steppings up stairs,
Rap on the bedroom door,
We have heart-beats for.
The postman's knock, though it spill
Rejection and vulgar bill—
At noon, the baker's basket creaks;
Hooves, hoots, factory-shrieks;
Hollow tattle of the trams;
Or a door slams;
Buzz of flies; chapel bells,
And a thousand sounds else.
The casual spirit poises,
Elegantly,
Tired of being free,
Between the usual noises.

[671]

Love's mood, however,
Is contrary to this hankering,
This holding on to the seat
Of life's speeding jolty car.
Love is in a fever
To escape the tinkering
Minutes that beat—
Familiar,
Only varied by fear—
On eye and ear.
Now I would leap clear.
What bait shall I procure to lure him out of time?
Not from the sea into the salty drought—
But cleanly out
Of days' and nights' faint metre and false rhyme,
To hold him safe
Round final angle,
Corner, where no jangle-tangle
Makes stir to chafe:
From this inadequate night and day,
I would steal him away.

MEDITATION

BLINDED and deafened by the seas,
The critics of a midget cluster,
Under the malt electric lustre,
Centered within a tavern's smother,
Drool goldenly on one another,
And let the passing poet freeze.
A hearth that flickers to child voices
Is cradled in the city noises;
The lit panes and the flags of town
He counts, and sees no step his own.
He is pierced by far images:
Astray among dim Autumn seas,
A dreaming swallow drops to peace.

[672]

We that would talk for trees and cows,
Eagle and cloud—for close and start
Of lifting joy behind lit brows,
Or pain at nucleus of the heart—
Are whispered out of shape and sense,
Each twisted from his proper stance,
And absorbed into wide innocence
Of Art's early bonfire dance.

The rebel flower in my vase,
Bolt upright, its back to the sun,
Reminds me of the thing I was
Before my thwart will was done.

Now I make muffled poetry,
With no aim, quite out of my course,
Like a muslin-trapped bumble bee
Buzzing away its life force.

DARRELL FIGGIS
(1882-1925)

INISGALLUN

THE winds are roaring out of the West
Where the clouds are in stormy saffron drest,
And the curlew and wild-geese are calling and crying
Over the straits in Inisgallun,
The heron and cormorant wailing and sighing,
Mingling a wild and an endless tune.

The winds are roaring out of the West
Over the waters of strife and unrest,
The shrieking rain in the low pools falling,
The strong waves beating a ceaseless rune,

[673]

And the heron and curlew and wild-geese calling,
Vainly lamenting in Inisgallun.

The froth and fume of the maddened sea
Spit thro' the torn air ceaselessly;
And the dark low bog in anguish crying,
And the heather wailing in bitter pain;
For the winds from out of the West are flying
And the Earth will never find peace again.

JAMES JOYCE
(1882-1941)

WHAT COUNSEL HAS THE HOODED MOON

WHAT counsel has the hooded moon
    Put in thy heart, my shyly sweet,
Of Love in ancient plenilune,
    Glory and stars beneath his feet—
A sage that is but kith and kin
With the comedian Capuchin?

Believe me rather that am wise
    In disregard of the divine,
A glory kindles in those eyes,
    Trembles to starlight. Mine, O Mine!
No more be tears in moon or mist
For thee, sweet sentimentalist.

BID ADIEU, ADIEU, ADIEU

BID adieu, adieu, adieu,
    Bid adieu to girlish days,
Happy Love is come to woo
    Thee and woo thy girlish ways—

The zone that doth become thee **fair**,
The snood upon thy yellow hair.

When thou hast heard his name **upon**
    The bugles of the cherubim
Begin thou softly to unzone
    Thy girlish bosom unto him
And softly to undo the snood
That is the sign of maidenhood.

STRINGS IN THE EARTH AND AIR

    STRINGS in the earth and air
      Make music sweet;
    Strings by the river where
      The willows meet.

    There's music along the river,
      For Love wanders there,
    Pale flowers on his mantle,
      Dark leaves on his hair.

    All softly playing,
      With head to the music bent,
    And fingers straying
      Upon an instrument.

ALL DAY I HEAR THE NOISE OF WATERS

ALL day I hear the noise of waters
      Making moan,
Sad as the sea-bird is, when going
      Forth alone,
He hears the winds cry to the **waters'**
      Monotone.

[675]

The gray winds, the cold winds are blowing
　　Where I go.
I hear the noise of many waters
　　Far below.
All day, all night, I hear them flowing
　　To and fro.

JAMES STEPHENS
(1882-　　)

CHILL OF THE EVE

A LONG, green swell
Slopes soft to the sea,
And a far-off bell
Swings sweet to me,
As the grey, chill day
　Slips away from the lea.

Spread cold and far,
Without one glow
From a mild, pale star,
Is the sky's steel bow,
And the grey, chill day
　Slips away below.

That green tree grieves
To the air around,
And the whispering leaves
Have a lonely sound,
As the grey, chill day
　Slips away from the ground.

The long grass bends
With a rippling rush
To the soft, white ends

[676]

Where the roots are lush,
And the grey, chill day
　Slips away in a hush.

Down by the shore
The slow waves twine
From the rock-strewn floor
To the shell-edged line,
And the grey, chill day
　Slips away with a whine.

And dark, more dark,
The shades settle down,
Far off is a spark
From the lamp-lit town,
And the grey, chill day
　Slips away with a frown.

FOSSILS

AND then she saw me creeping,
Saw and stood
Transfixed upon the fringes of the wood,
And straight went leaping.

Headlong down the pitch
Of the curved hill,
Over the ditch
And through the skirt of bushes by the rill
She pelted screaming,
Swerved from the water sideways with a twist
Just as I clutched and missed.

Flashed white beneath my hand and doubled back,
Swift as a twisting hare upon her track,
Hot for the hill again,
But all in vain.

[677]

Her hair swung far behind,
Straight as a stream balanced upon the wind,
O, it was black, dipped
In the dregs of midnight with a spark
Caught from a star that smouldered in the dark.

It I gripped,
Drew for a moment tight,
Jerked with a victor's cry
Down in the grasses high
Her to the hot, brown earth and threatened—daft
And then she laughed.

THE SATYR

THERE came a satyr creeping through the wood,
　His hair fell on his breast, his legs were slim:
His eyes were laughing wickedly, he stood
　And peeped about on every side of him.

He peeped about, he minced upon the ground,
　He put a thin hand up to hide a grin:
He doubled up and laughed without a sound;
　The very bodiment of happy sin.

The bodiment of sin: timid and wild
　And limber as a goat: his pointed feet
Were not at peace an instant: like a child
　He danced and glanced, and like a goat was fleet.

He danced, he peeped, but at a sound I made,
　A crackling twig, he turned and suddenly
In three great jumps he bounded to the shade,
　And disappeared among the greenery.

[678]

TANIST

REMEMBER the spider
Weaving a snare
—And that you did it
Everywhere:

Remember the cat
Tormenting a bird
—And that you did it
In deed and word:

Remember the fool
Frustrating the good
—And that you did it
Whenever you could:

Remember the devil
And treachery
—And that you did it
When you were he:

Remember all ill,
That man can know
—And that you did it
When you were so:

And then remember
Not to forget
—That you did it
And do it yet.

ON A LONELY SPRAY

UNDER a lonely sky a lonely tree
Is beautiful. All that is loneliness
Is beautiful. A feather lost at sea;

A staring owl; a moth; a yellow tress
Of seaweed on a rock, is beautiful.

The night-lit moon, wide-wandering in sky;
A blue-bright spark, where ne'er a cloud is up;
A wing, where no wing is, it is so high;
A bee in winter, or a buttercup,
Late-blown, are lonely, and are beautiful.

She, whom you saw but once, and saw no more;
That he, who startled you, and went away;
The eye that watched you from a cottage door;
The first leaf, and the last; the break of day;
The mouse, the cuckoo, and the cloud, are beautiful.

For all that is, is lonely; all that may
Will be as lonely as is that you see;
The lonely heart sings on a lonely spray,
The lonely soul swings lonely in the sea,
And all that loneliness is beautiful.

All, all alone, and all without a part
Is beautiful, for beauty is all where;
Where is an eye is beauty, where an heart
Is beauty, brooding out, on empty air,
All that is lonely and is beautiful.

WINIFRED M. LETTS
(1882-   )

THE SPIRES OF OXFORD

I saw the spires of Oxford
As I was passing by,
The gray spires of Oxford
Against a pearl-gray sky,

My heart was with the Oxford men
Who went abroad to die.

The years go fast in Oxford,
    The golden years and gay,
The hoary Colleges look down
    On careless boys at play.
But when the bugles sounded war
    They put their games away.

They left the peaceful river,
    The cricket-field, the quad,
The shaven lawns of Oxford
    To seek a bloody sod—
They gave their merry youth away
    For country and for God.

God rest you, happy gentlemen,
    Who laid your good lives down,
Who took the khaki and the gun
    Instead of cap and gown.
God bring you to a fairer place
    Than even Oxford town.

A SOFT DAY

    A soft day, thank God!
    A wind from the south
    With a honeyed mouth;
    A scent of drenching leaves,
    Briar and beech and lime,
        White elder-flower and thyme
And the soaking grass smells sweet,
Crushed by my two bare feet,
        While the rain drips,
Drips, drips, drips from the eaves.

[681]

A soft day, thank God!
The hills wear a shroud
Of silver cloud;
The web the spider weaves
Is a glittering net;
The woodland path is wet,
And the soaking earth smells sweet
Under my two bare feet,
And the rain drips,
Drips, drips, drips from the leaves.

WISHES FOR WILLIAM

THESE things I wish you for our friendship's sake—
A sunburnt thatch, a door to face the sun
At westering, the noise of homing rooks;
A kind, old lazy chair, a courtly cat
To rub against your knees;
Shelves of well-chosen books;
I wish you these.

I wish you friends whose wisdom makes them kind,
Well-leisured friends to share your evening's peace,
Friends who can season knowledge with a laugh;
A hedge of lavender, a patch of thyme,
With sage and marjoram and rosemary,
A damask rosebush and a hive of bees,
And cabbages that hold the morning dew,
A blackbird in the orchard boughs-all these,
And—God bless you.

Children, no matter whose, to watch for you
With flower faces at your garden gate,
And one to watch the clock with eager eyes,
Saying: "He's late—he's late."

LOLA RIDGE
(1883-1941)

THE EDGE

I THOUGHT to die that night in the solitude
    where they would never find me . . .
But there was time . . .
And I lay quietly on the drawn knees of the mountain
    staring into the abyss.

I do not know how long . . .
I could not count the hours, they ran so fast—
Like little bare-foot urchins—shaking my hands away.
But I remember
Somewhere water trickled like a thin severed vein . . .
And a wind came out of the grass,
Touching me gently, tentatively, like a paw.

As the night grew
The gray cloud that had covered the sky like sackcloth
Fell in ashen folds about the hills,
Like hooded virgins pulling their cloaks about them . . .
There must have been a spent moon,
For the Tall One's veil held a shimmer of silver. . . .

That too I remember,
And the tenderly rocking mountain,
Silence,
And beating stars. . . .

Dawn
Lay like a waxen hand upon the world,
And folded hills
Broke into a sudden wonder of peaks, stemming clear and cold
Till the Tall One bloomed like a lily,
Flecked with sun

[683]

Fine as a golden pollen.
It seemed a wind might blow it from the snow.

I smelled the raw sweet essences of things,
And heard spiders in the leaves,
And ticking of little feet
As tiny creatures came out of their doors
To see God pouring light into his star.

It seemed life held
No future and no past but this.

And I too got up stiffly from the earth
And held my heart up like a cup.

WIND IN THE ALLEYS

WIND, rising in the alleys,
My spirit lifts in you like a banner
    streaming free of hot walls.
You are full of unshaped dreams . . .
You are laden with beginnings . . .
There is hope in you . . . not sweet . . .
    acrid as blood in the mouth.
Come into my tossing dust
Scattering the peace of old deaths,
Wind rising out of the alleys
Carrying stuff of flame.

PEADAR KEARNEY
(1883-1942)

The three songs that follow became familiar to all Ireland after the
Rebellion of 1916. They were pronounced seditious by the British and the
Defense of the Realm Act authorized the arrest of any one heard singing
them.

THE SOLDIER'S SONG

WE'LL sing a song, a soldier's song,
With cheering rousing chorus,
As round our blazing fires we throng
The starry heavens o'er us:
Impatient for the coming fight,
And as we wait the morning's light,
Here in the silence of the night,
We'll chant a soldier's song.

Chorus

Soldiers are we, whose lives are pledged to Ireland
Some have come from a land beyond the wave;
Sworn to be free, no more our ancient sireland
Shall shelter the despot or the slave.
To-night we'll man the Bearna Boaghail.
In Erin's cause, come woe or weal,
'Mid cannon's roar and rifle's peal,
We'll chant a soldier's song.

In valleys green and towering crag
Our fathers fought before us,
And conquered 'neath the same old flag
That's proudly floating o'er us.
We're children of a fighting race,
That never yet has known disgrace.
And as we march the foe to face
We'll chant a soldier's song.

Soldiers are we, *etc.*

Sons of the Gael, men of the Pale,
The long-watched day is breaking;
The serried hosts of Innisfail
Shall set the tyrant quaking:
Our camp-fires now are burning low,
See, in the East a silvery glow,

Out yonder waits the Saxon foe,
So chant a soldier's song.

Soldiers are we, *etc.*

THE TRI-COLORED RIBBON

I HAD a true love, if ever a girl had one,
I had a true love, a brave lad was he;
One fine Easter Monday with his gallant comrades,
He started away for to make Ireland free;

Chorus

So close to my heart I wear the tri-colored ribbon, O,
Close to my heart, until death comes to me,
And if any one should ask me why I'm wearing that
    ribbon, O,
It's all for my true love I never more shall see.

He whispered, "Good-bye, Old Ireland is calling,
High over Dublin the tri-color flies,
In the streets of the city, the foeman is falling,
And wee birds are singing—Old Ireland, Arise."

So close to my heart, *etc.*

His bandolier around him, his bright bayonet shining,
His short service rifle—a beauty to see,
There was joy in his eyes, though he left me repining,
And started away for to make Ireland free.

So close to my heart, *etc.*

WHACK FOL THE DIDDLE

I'll sing you a song of Peace and Love,
Whack fol the diddle lol the dido day.

[686]

To the land that reigns all lands above,
Whack fol the diddle lol the dido day.
May peace and plenty be her share,
Who kept our homes from want and care,
Oh, "God bless England" is our prayer,
Whack fol the diddle lol the dido day.

Chorus

Whack fol the diddle lol the dido day,
So we say, Hip Hurray!
Come and listen while we pray
Whack fol the diddle lol the dido day.

When we were savage, fierce and wild,
Whack etc.
She came as a mother to her child,
Whack etc.
She gently raised us from the slime,
Kept our hands from hellish crime,
And sent us to Heaven in her own good time,
Whack etc.

Chorus

Our fathers oft were naughty boys,
Whack etc.
Pikes and guns are dangerous toys,
Whack etc.
From Beal-'n-ath Buidhe to Peter's Hill
They made poor England weep her fill,
But old Britannia loves us still,
Whack etc.

Chorus

Oh, Irishmen forget the past,
Whack etc.
And think of the day that is coming fast,
Whack etc.
When we shall all be civilized,

[687]

Neat and clean, and well advised,
Oh, won't Mother England be surprised,
Whack etc.

Chorus

SHANE LESLIE
(1885-   )

THE FOUR WINDS

Every wind in Ireland has its colour. The ashes of her exiles are sup-
posed to float back on the winds, and to blight the fields at home.

THE white wind whispers of the woes
And exiled bitterness
Of those to whom the southern floes
Bring no forgetfulness.

The western winds wing palely thro'
The tiding creeks, and cry
The unsleeping grief of sleepers who
Outcast of Ireland lie.

The eastern comes, with purple stain,
To tell the bitter fate
Of men in lilied harness slain
Before a stranger's gate.

And from the north the sad grey wind
Hath lovers' ashes borne
To their beloved, but to find
A bed of blighted corn.

FLEET STREET

I never see the newsboys run
  Amid the whirling street,
  With swift untiring feet,
To cry the latest venture done,
But I expect one day to hear
  Them cry the crack of doom
  And risings from the tomb,
With great Archangel Michael near;
And see them running from the Fleet
  As messengers of God,
  With Heaven's tidings shod
About their brave, unwearied feet.

MONAGHAN

Monaghan, mother of a thousand
Little moulded hills,
Set about with little rivers
Chained to little mills.

Rich and many-pastured Monaghan,
Mild thy meadows lie,
Melting to the distant mountains
On the mirrored sky.

Lovely, lowly-lying Monaghan,
On thy little lakes
Float and tremble lordly lilies
Hoed by fairies' rakes.

Silvered o'er with sunshine, or by
Night with shimmering fog,
Where thy sloping cornland meets
Beauteous fields of bog.

[689]

Humbly hid with heath and lichen
Waits thy turf of old,
While the hasty bees come hiding
Honey thro' thy mould.

Thro' and thro' thy restless rushes
Run a thousand rills,
Lisping long-forgotten little
Songs of Ireland's ills.

For thy mingled chaplet, oak and
Beechwood thou dost bind
Green in summer, and in winter
Musical with wind.

PADRIC GREGORY
(1886-   )

THE DREAM-TELLER

I was a dreamer: I dreamed
A dream at the dark of dawn,
When the stars hung over the mountains
    And morn was wan.

I dreamed my dream at morn,
At noon, at the even-light,
But I told it to you, dark woman,
    One soft glad night.

And the sharing of my dream
Has brought me only this:
The gnawing pain of loss, the ache
    For your mouth to kiss.

[690]

I walked the high hills last night,
And low, where the pale stars gleam,
God's cold Voice spake: "If you dream again,
Tell none your dream;
Tell none your dream!"

JOSEPH MARY PLUNKETT
(1887-1916)

OUR HERITAGE

THIS heritage to the race of Kings:
Their children and their children's seed
Have wrought their prophecies in deed
Of terrible and splendid things.

The hands that fought, the hearts that broke
In old immortal tragedies,
These have not failed beneath the skies,
Their children's heads refuse the yoke.

And still their hands shall guard the sod
That holds their father's funeral urn,
Still shall their hearts volcanic burn
With anger of the Sons of God.

No alien sword shall earn as wage
The entail of their blood and tears,
No shameful price for peaceful years
Shall ever part this heritage.

SEE THE CROCUS' GOLDEN CUP

See the crocus' golden cup
Like a warrior leaping up
At the summons of the spring,
"Guard turn out!" for welcoming
Of the new elected year.
The blackbird now with psalter clear
Sings the ritual of the day
And the lark with bugle gay
Blows reveillé to the morn,
Earth and heaven's latest born.

TO G. K. CHESTERTON

(Air: "The Night Before Larry Was Stretched")

Now, Gilbert, you know you're our man,
The only one equal to seven—
Tho' you stand on the earth yet you span
With your hands the four quarters of Heaven.
Yes, your head stretches up thro' the sky
And you puzzle the angels with riddles,
But they answer you back by-and-by
With the music of millions of fiddles,
While the Universe dances a jig.

So, champion of all that's sublime,
Our madly magnificent mountain,
Now take up the cudgels for Time,
Tap the Truth, let it flow as a fountain;
And when we have drunk to the dregs
And topple round tipsy as topers,
Then set us up straight on our legs—
We'll be merry (there's none of us mopers)—
Then see us safe home to the boss.

I SEE HIS BLOOD UPON THE ROSE

I SEE his blood upon the rose
And in the stars the glory of his eyes,
His body gleams amid eternal snows,
His tears fall from the skies.

I see his face in every flower;
The thunder and the singing of the birds
Are but his voice—and carven by his power
Rocks are his written words.

All pathways by his feet are worn,
His strong heart stirs the ever-beating sea,
His crown of thorns is twined with every thorn,
His cross is every tree.

AN PILIBÍN
(1887-   )

RETROSPECT

TODAY when I heard
    A curlew cry
    By the salt flood,
    Pitiful memory
    Awoke, and stirred
    Along my blood
    In reverie.

Like a bird's cry
    Above the bright sea,
    In keen clean air,
    Passionate ecstasy
    Came once to me:

[693]

Sweet and fair
The years should be.

But the wind lifted
A dream as vain
As a bird's cry
At dusk, in pain:
And vapour drifted,
Darkening the sky
With driven rain.

PATRICK MacGILL
(1890-   )

THE CONGER EEL

THE waters dance on the ocean crest, or swirl in the cyclone's
   breath,
But down below where the divers go, they sullenly sleep in
   death,
Where the slime is holding the cutter's stays, where the sailors'
   bones are white,
Where the phantoms sweep through the eerie deep in realms of
   endless night,
'T is there it holds its sway supine, and plaits its every reel,
The silent, sibilant, sombre, sinous, stealthy Conger eel,
The silky Conger eel, the solemn-eyed Conger eel—
It circles by where the dead men lie, the spectral Conger eel.

The devil fish, grim in its cavern dim, a sinister siren lies,
And the shark will seize on its frightened prey where the spu-
   mous surges rise,
The dolphin may play in its riotous way where the waters are
   calm and slow,
The whale may spout like a geyser out by the ice of an Arctic
   floe,

[694]

But down a hundred fathoms or more below the lance-edged
    keel,
It slily slides, 'neath the shifty tides, the sensuous Conger eel,
The lily-soft Conger eel, the green-eyed Conger eel,
It grovels in grime and the stagnant slime, the hideous Conger
    eel.

And there in its sluggish realms of woe it has reigned for un-
    numbered years.
It feasted of old on the Vikings bold, and the Spanish bucca-
    neers,
And kings and the sons of kings have gone to lie on its ban-
    quet board,
And many a lady young and fair from the arms of her drown-
    ing lord—
But down below no blush of shame comes to the lips that steal
The kisses soft from the lady fair; the passionless Conger eel
The cynical Conger eel, carnivorous Conger eel,
May lie on the breast of the maiden chaste and never a tremor
    feel—
That vampire Conger eel.

DEDICATION

I SPEAK with a proud tongue of the people who were
And the people who are,
The worthy of Ardara, the Rosses and Inishkeel,
My kindred—
The people of the hills and the dark-haired passes
My neighbours on the lift of the brae,
In the lap of the valley.

To them Slainthé!

I speak of the old men,
The wrinkle-rutted,

Who dodder about foot-weary—
For their day is as the day that has been and is no more—
Who warm their feet by the fire,
And recall memories of the times that are gone;
Who kneel in the lamplight and pray
For the peace that has been theirs—
And who beat one dry-veined hand against another
Even in the sun—
For the coldness of death is on them.

I speak of the old women
Who danced to yesterday's fiddle
And dance no longer.
They sit in a quiet place and dream
And see visions
Of what is to come,
Of their issue,
Which has blossomed to manhood and womanhood—
And seeing thus
They are happy
For the day that was leaves no regrets,
And peace is theirs,
And perfection.

I speak of the strong men
Who shoulder their burdens in the hot day,
Who stand on the market-place
And bargain in loud voices,
Showing their stock to the world.
Straight the glance of their eyes—
Broad-shouldered,
Supple.
Under their feet the holms blossom,
The harvest yields.
And their path is of prosperity.

I speak of the women,
Strong-hipped, full-bosomed,

[696]

Who drive the cattle to graze at dawn,
Who milk the cows at dusk.
Grace in their homes,
And in the crowded ways
Modest and seemly—
Mother of children!

I speak of the children
Of the many townlands,
Blossoms of the Bogland,
Flowers of the Valley,
Who know not yesterday, nor to-morrow,
And are happy,
The pride of those who have begot them.

And thus it is,
Ever and always,
In Ardara, the Rosses and Inishkeel—
Here, as elsewhere,
The Weak, the Strong, and the Blossoming—
And thus my kindred.

To them Slainthé.

H. L. DOAK
(1890-   )

THE SCARECROW

ONE shoulder up, the other down,
His hat upon a broomstick crown,
I saw a ragged scarecrow stand,
Guarding the sown and sunlit land.

Awhile I stood, and not a crow
Near the rich furrows dared to go.

But when I turned away, why then
They fell to work like husbandmen.

FRANCIS LEDWIDGE
(1891-1917)

THE HERONS

As I was climbing Ardan Mór
From the shore of Sheelin lake,
I met the herons coming down
Before the water's wake.

And they were talking in their flight
Of dreamy ways the herons go
When all the hills are withered up
Nor any waters flow.

A LITTLE BOY IN THE MORNING

HE WILL not come, and still I wait.
He whistles at another gate
Where angels listen. Ah, I know
He will not come, yet if I go
How shall I know he did not pass
Barefooted in the flowery grass?

The moon leans on one silver horn
Above the silhouettes of morn,
And from their nest sills finches whistle
Or stooping pluck the downy thistle.
How is the morn so gay and fair
Without his whistling in its air?

The world is calling, I must go.
How shall I know he did not pass
Barefooted in the shining grass?

TO A LINNET IN A CAGE

WHEN Spring is in the fields that stained your wing,
  And the blue distance is alive with song,
And finny quiets of the gabbing spring
  Rock lilies red and long.
At dewy daybreak, I will set you free
  In ferny turnings of the woodbine lane,
Where faint-voiced echoes leave and cross in glee
  The hilly swollen plain.

In draughty houses you forget your tune,
  The modulator of the changing hours,
You want the wide air of the moody noon,
  And the slanting evening showers.
So I will loose you, and your song shall fall
  When morn is white upon the dewy pane,
Across my eyelids, and my soul recall
  From worlds of sleeping pain.

A TWILIGHT IN MIDDLE MARCH

WITHIN the oak a throb of pigeon wings
Fell silent, and grey twilight hushed the fold,
And spiders' hammocks swung on half-oped things
That shook like foreigners upon our cold.
A gipsy lit a fire and made a sound
Of moving tins, and from an oblong moon
The river seemed to gush across the ground
To the cracked metre of a marching tune.

[699]

And then three syllables of melody
Dropped from a blackbird's flute, and died apart
Far in the dewy dark. No more but three,
Yet sweeter music never touched a heart
'Neath the blue domes of London. Flute and reed,
Suggesting feelings of the solitude
When will was all the Delphi I would heed,
Lost like a wind within a summer wood
From little knowledge where great sorrows brood.

JUNE

BROOM out the floor now, lay the fender by,
And plant this bee-sucked bough of woodbine there,
And let the window down. The butterfly
Floats in upon the sunbeam, and the fair
Tanned face of June, the nomad gipsy, laughs
Above her widespread wares, the while she tells
The farmers' fortunes in the fields, and quaffs
The water from the spider-peopled wells.

The hedges are all drowned in green grass seas,
And bobbing poppies flare like Elmo's light,
While siren-like the pollen-stained bees
Drone in the clover depths. And up the height
The cuckoo's voice is hoarse and broke with joy.
And on the lowland crops the crows make raid,
Nor fear the clappers of the farmer's boy,
Who sleeps, like drunken Noah, in the shade.

And loop this red rose in that hazel ring
That snares your little ear, for June is short
And we must joy in it and dance and sing,
And from her bounty draw her rosy worth.
Ay! soon the swallows will be flying south,
The wind wheel north to gather in the snow,

Even the roses spilt on youth's red mouth
Will soon blow down the road all roses go.

THOMAS MacDONAGH

HE SHALL not hear the bittern cry
In the wild sky, where he is lain,
Nor voices of the sweeter birds
Above the wailing of the rain.

Nor shall he know when loud March blows
Thro' slanting snows her fanfare shrill,
Blowing to flame the golden cup
Of many an upset daffodil.

But when the Dark Cow leaves the moor,
And pastures poor with greedy weeds,
Perhaps he'll hear her low at morn
Lifting her horn in pleasant meads.

THE DEATH OF AILILL

WHEN there was heard no more the war's loud sound,
And only the rough corn-crake filled the hours,
And hill winds in the furze and drowsy flowers,
Maeve in her chamber with her white head bowed
On Ailill's heart was sobbing: "I have found
The way to love you now," she said, and he
Winked an old tear away and said: "The proud
Unyielding heart loves never." And then she:
"I love you now, tho' once when we were young
We walked apart like two who were estranged
Because I loved you not, now all is changed."
And he who loved her always called her name
And said: "You do not love me; 'tis your tongue

[701]

Talks in the dusk; you love the blazing gold
Won in the battles, and the soldier's fame.
You love the stories that are often told
By poets in the hall." Then Maeve arose
And sought her daughter Findebar: "Oh, child,
Go tell your father that my love went wild
With all my wars in youth, and say that now
I love him stronger than I hate my foes. . . ."
And Findebar unto her father sped
And touched him gently on the rugged brow,
And knew by the cold touch that he was dead.

LAMENT FOR THE POETS: 1916

I HEARD the Poor Old Woman say:
"At break of day the fowler came,
And took my blackbirds from their songs
Who loved me well thro' shame and blame.

"No more from lovely distances
Their songs shall bless me mile by mile,
Nor to white Ashbourne call me down
To wear my crown another while.

"With bended flowers the angels mark
For the skylark the place they lie,
From there its little family
Shall dip their wings first in the sky.

"And when the first surprise of flight
Sweet songs excite, from the far dawn
Shall there come blackbirds loud with love,
Sweet echoes of the singers gone.

"But in the lonely hush of eve
Weeping I grieve the silent bills."

[702]

I heard the Poor Old Woman say
In Derry of the little hills.

THOMAS McGREEVY
(1893-   )

RED HUGH

"Red Hugh" O'Donnell, Prince of Tirconaill, went to Spain to consult with King Philip III after the defeat of the Irish and Spanish at Kinsale in 1601. He was lodged in the castle of Simancas during the negotiations but, poisoned by a certain James Blake, a Norman-Irish creature of Queen Elizabeth Tudor, he died there. As a member of the Third Order of Saint Francis, he was buried in the church of San Francisco at Valladolid. This church was destroyed during the nineteenth century and none of the tombs that were in it seems to have been preserved. *Author's Note*

JUAN DE JUNI the priest said,
Each J becoming H;

Berruguete, he said,
And the G was aspirate;

Ximenez, he said then
And aspirated first and last.

But he never said
And—it seemed odd—he
Never had heard
The aspirated name
Of the centuries-dead
Bright-haired young man
Whose grave I sought.

All day I passed
In greatly built gloom
From dusty gilt tomb
Marvellously wrought

To tomb
Rubbing
At mouldy inscriptions
With fingers wetted with spit
And asking
Where I might find it
And failing.

Yet when
Unhurried—
   Not as at home
   Where heroes, hanged, are buried
   With non-commissioned officers' bored maledictions
   Quickly in the gaol yard—

They brought
His blackening body
Here
To rest
Princes came
Walking
Behind it

And all Valladolid knew
And out to Simancas all knew
Where they buried Red Hugh.

HOMAGE TO HIERONYMUS BOSCH

A WOMAN with no face walked into the light;
A boy, in a brown-tree norfolk suit,
Holding on
Without hands
To her seeming skirt.

[704]

She stopped,
And he stopped,
And I, in terror, stopped, staring.

Then I saw a group of shadowy figures behind her.

It was a wild wet morning
But the little world was spinning on.

Liplessly, somehow, she addressed it:
The book must be opened
And the park too.

I might have tittered
But my teeth chattered
And I saw that the words, as they fell,
Lay, wriggling, on the ground.

There was a stir of wet wind
And the shadowy figures began to stir
When one I had thought dead
Filmed slowly out of his great effigy on a tomb near by
And they all shuddered

He bent as if to speak to the woman
But the nursery governor flew up out of the well of Saint Pat-
        rick,
Confiscated by his mistress,
And, his head bent,
Staring out over his spectacles,
And scratching the gravel furiously,
Hissed—
    The words went *pingg!* like bullets,
    Upwards, past his spectacles—
Say nothing, I say, say nothing, say nothing!
And he who had seemed to be coming to life
Gasped,

[705]

Began hysterically, to laugh and cry,
And, with a gesture of impotent and half-petulant despair,
Filmed back into his effigy again.

High above the Bank of Ireland
Unearthly music sounded,
Passing westwards.

Then, from the drains,
Small sewage rats slid out.
They numbered hundreds of hundreds, tens, thousands.
Each bowed obsequiously to the shadowy figures
Then turned and joined in a stomach dance with his brothers
        and sisters.
Being a multitude, they danced irregularly.
There was rat laughter,
Deeper here and there,
And occasionally she-rat cries grew hysterical.
The shadowy figures looked on, agonized.
The woman with no face gave a cry and collapsed.
The rats danced on her
And on the wriggling words
Smirking.
The nursery governor flew back into the well
With the little figure without hands in the brown-tree clothes.

GIOCONDA

(To Jean Lurcat)

THE hillsides were of rushing, silvered water,
Down,
And around,
And all across,
And about the white, gleaming tree-trunks,
Far as sensitive eyesight could see,
On both sides of the valley,

[706]

And beyond,
Everywhere,
The silvered swirling water!

The clouds,
Blue-gray
Lined with pink
And edged with silver,
Meditated.

The sun did not rise or set
Not being interested in the activities of politicians.

White manes tossed like spray.
Bluish snakes slid
Into the dissolution of a smile.

F. R. HIGGINS
(1896-1941)

THE GALLOWS TREE

THE thin wind seemed uneasy,
The white owl couldn't see,
As high in the light together
They sat on the gallows tree;
So still in that chill of evening,
Only the owl was grieving:
"Hell blind the light, I need the dark,
And where on earth can it be?"
"It's late to-night," the wind whispered,
High in the hangman's tree—
Whispered, whispered,
High in the hangman's tree.

From dusk the dark moved towards them,
Through hill and moor and whin
Until it hawed on a window,
Looked through and then stole in
To crouch on a sleeping old fellow,
His eyes wide open and yellow—
Wide open in sleep! And peeping through them
The limp dark whined:
"Why do those eyes lie open in sleep,
What's hid in the black of his mind?"
And then it slyly slid in
To the eyes of his mind.

And afterwards, while the owl dozed on
The wind sniffed company,
Found the limp dark leaning
Against the gallows tree—
Faint and befouled by creeping
Into that old man's dreaming—
"You've been in a pit again," said the wind;
"You've got the smell of the dead."
At that the owl leapt out of its sleep
And off in a blink it fled—
Blinking, blinking
Blue lightning as it fled.

That man slept fearing the gallows,
His mind a murderous scum,
Yet none but the dark could tell it,
And now the dark lay dumb;
Even the wind wasn't speaking,
Only the tree was creaking,
The wind was hid in a patch of dark,
And together they seemed to be
A lonely thing of rags and bones
High in the hangman's tree—
Creaking, creaking,
High in the hangman's tree.

PADRAIC O'CONAIRE GAELIC STORYTELLER

They've paid the last respects in sad tobacco
And silent is this wakehouse in its haze;
They've paid the last respects; and now their whiskey
Flings laughing words on mouths of prayer and praise;
And so young couples huddle by the gables,
O let them grope home through the hedgy night—
Alone I'll mourn my old friend, while the cold dawn
Thins out the holy candlelight.

Respects are paid to one loved by the people;
Ah, was he not—among our mighty poor—
The sudden wealth cast on those pools of darkness,
Those bearing, just, a star's faint signature;
And so he was to me, close friend, near brother,
Dear Padraic of the wide and sea-cold eyes—
So lovable, so courteous and noble,
The very West was in his soft replies.

They'll miss his heavy stick and stride in Wicklow—
His story-talking down Winetavern Street,
Where old men sitting in the wizen daylight
Have kept an edge upon his gentle wit;
While women on the grassy streets of Galway,
Who hearken for his passing—but in vain,
Shall hardly tell his step as shadows vanish
Through archways of forgotten Spain.

Ah, they'll say: Padraic's gone again exploring;
But now down glens of brightness, O he'll find
An alehouse overflowing with wise Gaelic
That's braced in vigour by the bardic mind,
And there his thoughts shall find their own forefathers—
In minds to whom our heights of race belong,
In crafty men, who ribbed a ship or turned
The secret joinery of song.

[709]

Alas, death mars the parchment of his forehead;
And yet for him, I know, the earth is mild—
The windy fidgets of September grasses
Can never tease a mind that loved the wild;
So drink his peace—this grey juice of the barley
Runs with a light that ever pleased his eye—
While old flames nod and gossip on the hearthstone
And only the young winds cry.

SONG FOR THE CLATTER-BONES

God rest that Jewy woman,
Queen Jezebel, the bitch
Who peeled the clothes from her shoulder-bones
Down to her spent teats
As she stretched out of the window
Among the geraniums, where
She chaffed and laughed like one half daft
Titivating her painted hair—

King Jehu he drove to her,
She tipped him a fancy beck;
But he from his knacky side-car spoke,
"Who'll break that dewlapped neck?"
And so she was thrown from the window;
Like Lucifer she fell
Beneath the feet of the horses and they beat
The light out of Jezebel.

That corpse wasn't planted in clover;
Ah, nothing of her was found
Save those grey bones that Hare-foot Mike
Gave me for their lovely sound;
And as once her dancing body
Made star-lit princes sweat,
So I'll just clack: though her ghost lacks a back
There's music in the old bones yet.

[710]

SUSAN L. MITCHELL
(1868-1930)

IMMORTALITY

Age cannot reach me where the veils of God have shut me in,
For me the myriad births of stars and suns do but begin,
And here how fragrantly there blows to me the holy **breath**,
Sweet from the flowers and stars and hearts of men,
   From life and death.

We are not old, O heart, we are not old,
  The breath that blows
The soul aflame is still a wandering wind
  That comes and goes;
And the stirred heart with sudden raptured life a moment
    glows.

A moment here—a bulrush's brown head in the grey rain,
A moment there—a child drowned and a heart quickened with
    pain;
The name of Death, the blue deep heaven, the scent of the salt
    sea,
The spicy grass, the honey robbed from the wild bee.

Awhile we walk the world on its wide roads and narrow ways,
And they pass by, the countless shadowy troops of nights and
    days;
We know them not, O happy heart, for you and I
Watch where within a slow dawn lightens up another sky.

AUSTIN CLARKE
(1896-   )

THE FAIR AT WINDGAP

THERE was airy music and sport at the fair
And showers were tenting on the bare field,
Laughter had knotted a crowd where the horses
And mares were backing, when carts from the wheelwright

Were shafted: bargains on sale everywhere and the barmen
Glassing neat whiskey or pulling black porter
On draught—and O the red brandy, the oatmeal
And the whiteness of flour in the weighing scale!

Calico petticoats, cashmere and blouses,
Blankets of buttermilk, flannel on stalls there,
Caps of bright tweed and corduroy trousers
And green or yellow ribbon with a stripe;
The tanner was hiding, the saddler plied the bradawl;
Barrows had chinaware, knives and blue razors,
Black twisted tobacco to pare in the claypipe
And ·the ha'penny harp that is played on a finger.

Soft as rain slipping through rushes, the cattle
Came: dealers were brawling at seven-pound-ten,
On heifers in calf a bargain was clapped
When ewes, that are nearer the grass, had taken
Two guineas; the blacksmith was filing the horn in his lap
For the fillies called up more hands than their height,
Black goats were cheap; for a sow in the stock
O'Flaherty got but the half of her farrow.

Balladmen, beggarmen, trick o' the loop men
And cardmen, hiding Queen Maeve up their sleeve,
Were picking red pennies and soon a prizefighter
Enticed the young fellows and left them all grieving:
While the marriageable girls were walking up and down
And the folk were saying that the Frenchmen
Had taken the herring from the brown tide
And sailed at daybreak, they were saying.

Twenty-five tinkers that came from Glentartan,
Not counting the jennets and barefooted women,
Had a white crop of metal upon every cart;
The neighbours were buying, but a red-headed man
Of them, swearing no stranger could bottom a kettle,
Leaped over the droves going down to the ocean,

Glibbed with the sunlight: blows were around him
And so the commotion arose at the fair.

(from the Irish)

MONK GIBBON
(1896-   )

THE BEES

T<small>HEN</small> to the bees one said,
"Knowledge from us is fled;
The stream is grown impure,
Nought that we say is sure;
The cloud of doubt clouds all,
Rain has begun to fall.

Come you, unto our aid,
Come, sages, honey-fed;
You who roam far and wide,
Many-winged, many-eyed.
Who, out of all your sort,
Show the most anxious thought,
Building the sixfold cell
Wondrously, very well;
You, who in honeyed dark
Brood on the mystery stark
Of birth and death and pain
And of re-birth again,
See summer follow spring
And autumn winter bring,
For whom were these things done?
For whom still shines the sun?
For whom does dew descend?
For whom the winter end?
It is not all for men?
Make our minds proud again.

[713]

Are we not last of things?
Have we not also wings,
And do we not one day
Spread them and pass away?"

His little friends replied,
"Wisdom with you has died.
Only the bees have souls.
Even in trees and holes
Of wood the wild bees know
More than your words now show.
Is not the world a field
Spread in the sun to yield
Honey and scent and dew,
Its share of labour too?
Is not night sent to cool
The too-warm liquid pool
Of golden sweetness, day
Only to show the way
To lonely flowers which
Hide in a far-off ditch?

"And is not heaven indeed
Rather another mead,
Untouched by time, unseen,
A hedge for ever green,
Seasonless, always spring
And early summer, a thing
Hid in the future, yet
Surer than autumns wet?
This is our hope, and we
Hold it in certainty
Though the hive leak and though
Winter and rain and snow
Break through the vaulting high
And send us out to die
Wingless upon the hill,
That field awaits us still,

And from the yellow sod
The bees return to God."

THE DISCOVERY

ADAM, who thought himself immortal still,
Though cast from Eden, not knowing yet of death,
Nor guessing that what has beginning ends,
Nor that the life goes also with the breath,

Wandering in empty fields one day,
Pushing the grass aside, finds Abel slain,
His arms thrown out, his head with briars twined,
And on the ground beside a dull red stain.

"Abel, it is not time for sleeping now;
Have you forgot the curse upon us put?"
So, standing by his side, he gazes down.
Thinking he jests, he stirs him with his foot.

Silence, no sound at all, a breathless calm;
The warm day sighs; its sighing does not last.
The grass-tops quiver slightly; through the grass
A small field-mouse, disturbed, goes hurrying past.

Then, seized with sudden fear, he flings himself
Beside the corpse, cries, "For your mother's sake
Give me an answer." Still no answer comes,
Only the cry, "Abel, awake, awake!"

DISPOSSESSED POET

I AM from Ireland,
The sad country,
Born, as can be proved,

[715]

In her chief city.
When I was a child,
I heard much slander
Touching her, from goose
And hissing gander.
When I was a youth,
A war sent me
Two seas off from her,
In longing twenty.
It was there I found
A taste for roaming,
As in summers hot
Bees do for swarming.
No land sees me now
Five moons or longer,
Even she who reared
Proves little stronger.
I have lost her speech;
Her men would count me
Stranger if I spoke,
Not of their country.
I have lost her ways,
Her thought, her murmur;
I have lost all
But my love for her.

EILEEN SHANAHAN
(1901-   )

THREE CHILDREN NEAR CLONMEL

I MET three children on the road—
The hawthorn trees were sweet with rain
The hills had drawn their white blinds down—
Three children on the road from town.

Their wealthy eyes in splendour mocked
Their faded rags and bare wet feet,
The King had sent his daughters out
To play at peasants in the street.

I could not see the palace walls;
The avenues were dumb with mist;
Perhaps a queen would watch and weep
For lips that she had borne and kissed—

And lost about the lonely world,
With treasury of hair and eye
The tigers of the world will spring,
The merchants of the world will buy.

And one will sell her eyes for gold,
And one will barter them for bread,
And one will watch their glory fade
Beside the looking-glass, unwed.

A hundred years will softly pass,
Yet on the Tipperary hills
The shadows of a king and queen
Will darken on the daffodils.

JIM CONNELL
(contemporary)

NEW WORDS TO THE TUNE OF "O'DONNEL ABU"

Workers of Ireland, why crouch ye like cravens
To clutch at existence of insult and want?
Why stand to be plucked by an army of ravens
Or hoodwinked for ever by twaddle and cant?
    Think on the wrongs you bear;
    Think on the rags you wear;

[717]

Think on the insults endured from your birth;
Toiling in snow and rain,
Piling up heaps of gain,
All for the tyrants that grind ye to earth.

Your brains are as keen as the brains of your masters,
In swiftness and strength you surpass them, by far.
Your brave hearts have taught you to laugh at disasters,
You vastly outnumber your tyrants in war.
    Why, then, like cowards stand,
    Using not brain nor hand,
    Thankful like dogs
    When they throw you a bone?
    What right have they to take
    Things that we toil to make?
    Know ye not, comrades, that all is our own?

Despise all the talk of these fat agitators
Who rave about *Ireland* or *Freedom* or worse.
Expect not your rights from political praters,
But manfully trust in your courage and force.
    Waste not your ready blows,
    Seek not for foreign foes,
    Your bitterest enemy treads your own soil.
    The sweaters that grind you,
    The ranters that blind you,
    The gluttons that revel while you are at toil.

Arise in our might, brothers, bear it no longer,
Assemble our masses throughout all the land,
We'll show these blood suckers who are the stronger
When workers and robbers confronted shall stand.
    Through castle, court, and hall,
    Over their acres all
    Onwards we'll sweep
    Like the waves of the sea,
    Claiming the wealth we've made,
    Ending the tyrants trade,
    Till Labour has triumphed and Ireland is Free!

PATRICK MacDONOGH
(1902-   )

SHE WALKED UNAWARE

O, SHE walked unaware of her own increasing beauty
That was holding men's thoughts from market or plough,
As she passed by, intent on her womanly duties
And she without leisure to be wayward or proud;
Or if she had pride then it was not in her thinking
But thoughtless in her body like a flower of good breeding.
The first time I saw her spreading coloured linen
Beyond the green willow she gave me gentle greeting
With no more intention than the leaning willow tree.

Though she smiled without intention yet from that day for-
        ward
Her beauty filled like water the four corners of my being,
And she rested in my heart like a hare in the form
That is shaped to herself. And I that would be singing
Or whistling at all times went silently then;
Till I drew her aside among straight stems of beeches
When the blackbird was sleeping and she promised that never
The fields would be ripe but I'd gather all sweetness,
A red moon of August would rise on our wedding.

October is spreading bright flame along stripped willows,
Low fires of the dogwood burn down to grey water—
God pity me now and all desolate sinners
Demented with beauty! I have blackened my thought
In drouths of bad longing, and all brightness goes shrouded
Since he came with his rapture of wild words that mirrored
Her beauty and made her ungentle and proud.
To-night she will spread her brown hair on his pillow,
But I shall be hearing the harsh cries of wild fowl.

SONG FOR A PROUD RELATION

MOCKING your slow sepulchral horns
Chuckles the twitter of plucked strings,
In pastures of proud unicorns
A dunghill cock has clapped his wings,
    Hey *cock-a-doo, a-doodle-doo!*
Sing wanton I to reverend you.

Though you parade a peasant name
Sedate through mock-ancestral shade,
Beware my flickering tongues of flame,
My gay and garrulous gasconade!
    For *cock-a-doo, a-doodle-doo!*
Is all my reverence for you.

When, lifeless as the mind you bore,
Your pompous flesh to burial goes
A tattered scarecrow'll dance before,
A poor relation, thumb to nose!
    And *cock-a-doo, a-doodle-doo!*
Will be his epitaph for you.

THE WIDOW OF DRYNAM

I STAND in my door and look over the low fields of Drynam.
No man but the one man has known me, no child but the one
Grew big at my breast, and what are my sorrows beside
That pride and that glory? I come from devotions on Sunday
And leave them to pity or spite; and though I who had music
    have none
But crying of seagulls at morning and calling of curlews at
    night,
I wake and remember my beauty and think of my son
Who would stare the loud fools into silence
And rip the dull parish asunder.

[720]

Small wonder indeed he was wild with breeding and beauty
And why would my proud lad not straighten his back from the
    plough?
My son was not got and I bound in a cold bed of duty
Nor led to the side of the road by some clay-clabbered lout!
No, but rapt by a passionate poet away from the dancers
To curtains and silver and firelight,—
O wisely and gently he drew down the pale shell of satin
And all the bright evening's adornment and clad me
Again in the garment of glory, the joy of his eyes.

I stand in my door and look over the low fields of Drynam
When skies move westward, the way he will come from the
    war;
Maybe on a morning of March when a thin sun is shining
And starlings have blackened the thorn,
He will come, my bright limb of glory, my mettlesome wild
    one,
With coin in his pocket and tales on the tip of his tongue,
And the proud ones that slight me will bring back forgotten
    politeness
To see me abroad on the roads with my son,
The two of us laughing together or stepping in silence.

LYLE DONAGHY
(1902-1949)

A LEITRIM WOMAN

PEOPLE of Ireland—I am an old woman; I am near my end;
I have lived, now, for seventy-five years in your midst;
I have grown up among you, toiled among you, suffered with
    you and enjoyed with you;
I have given and received in faith and honour;
what was to be endured I have endured, what was to be fought

[721]

against I have fought against, what was to be done I
    have done;
I have married in my country; I have borne two men-children
    and three women-children,
  two sons and three daughters of a Fenian father;
I have brought them up to love and serve Ireland,
  to fight for her to death,
  to work for her at home and abroad,
  to cherish the old glory of Ireland and to strive manfully
    to bring in new light—
  to go forward;
I have brought them up in faith, to know freedom, and love
    justice,
  to take sides with the poor against their spoilers, against the
    leaders who say to a strong class "Hold all thou hast,
    take all thou canst,"
  to unbind heavy burdens and grievous to be borne from
    men's shoulders,
  to render unto the people what is the people's;

I have brought them up to believe in our Lord's prayer,
  to believe in the coming of His Kingdom upon earth and
    to labour that it come indeed;
The strength of my body has gone into the soil of this land, and
    the strength of my children's bodies;
the strength of my soul and the strength of my children's soul
    has been given in the cause of the people of this land;
I have suffered, I have endured, when they were in exile and
    in danger of death—
now my husband and one son are dead,
  my last son deported without trial, uncharged—
the spoilers and their friends
the strong and their helpers
  have taken him from me;

I am old, now, and near to death;
those who would have supported me and eased my going have
    been taken from me—

I looked for a little peace before the hour of my departure,
    my last son in the house with me, to see me into the grave—
they have driven him forth—
may the curse of heaven, if there be a heaven, light on them;
    the curse of the widow and childless light on them;
    the curse of the poor without advocates,
    the curse of the old without protection,
    the curse of a mother light on them.

LINOTA RUFESCENS

So, HERE we meet—after long seeking—
a gorse wild over wooded hill-slope fitted us well
for we were both distinctly of the wilderness—
you, linnet of mountain marsh and wild and the seed-bearing
        conifers that clothe the hill-slope,
and I, seeker of every beautiful wild glory that the wreckful
        aeons have spawned in desert mountain
    or wherever in waste places, of the dust that's whirled
    in the stark daedal wind—
we met in a fit place—
I sought you long and now I have you, all to myself, and take
        you up in my hands
    having found you, here, dead—
The Lesser Redpoll—that is your pretty name—is it quaint a
        little?
    it is not less becoming—
I look well at every feather—bloodred forehead and crown
lightly carmine breast and pink in some darker feather—
I will remember this also among beautiful things—
let me note the spread of wing stretched out fan-wise which
        bore you, alive, on the air—
So, I lay you back again, here, where I found you, sepulchred
    in silver, in the fork of the birch—

[723]

FRANK O'CONNOR
(1903-   )

THREE OLD BROTHERS

WHILE some go dancing reels and some
  Go stuttering love in ditches
The three old brothers rise from bed,
  And moan, and pin their breeches;
And one says, "I can sleep no more,
  I'd liefer far go weeping,
For how should honest men lie still
  When brats can spoil their sleeping?"
And blind Tom says, that's eighty years,
  "If I was ten years younger
I'd take a stick and welt their rumps
  And gall their gamest runner!"
But James the youngest cries, "Praise God,
  We have outlived our passion!"
And by their fire of roots all three
  Praise God after a fashion.

Says James, "I loved when I was young
  A lass of one and twenty
That had the grace of all the queens
  And broke men's hearts in plenty,
But now the girl's a gammy crone
  With no soft sides or boosom,
And all the lads she kist's abed
  Where the fat worm chews 'em;
And though she had no kiss for me,
  And though myself is older,
And though my thighs are cold to-night,
  Their thighs I think are colder!"

And Blind Tom says, "I knew a man
  A girl refused for lover

[724]

Worked in America forty years
And heaped copper on copper,
And came back all across the foam,
Dressed in his silks and satins,
And watched for her from dawn to dark
And from Compline to Matins,
And when she passed him in her shawl
He cracked his sides for laughing,
And went back happy to the west
And heeded no man's scoffing,
And Christ!" moans Tom, "if I'd his luck
I'd not mind cold nor coughing!"

Says Patcheen then, "My lot's a lot
All men on earth might envy,
That saw the girl I could not get
Nurse an untimely baby!"
And all three say, "Dear heart! Dear heart!"
And James the youngest mutters,
"Praise God we have outlived our griefs
And not fell foul like others,
Like Paris and the Grecian chiefs
And the three Ulster brothers!"

EWART MILNE
(1903-   )

TINKER'S MOON

FOUR children on a rumbling cart,
A woman trudging beside that load,
A lank man leaving the horse to guide
A wet road: a dry road:
A gravelly road that a woman shall walk
And a lank man leave the horse to guide;
The tinker's children take their chance, and bide.

[725]

A lane leads on to one more lane,
An uphill to one more hill;
A potato patch to thin on the way, a hen to kill,
And hunger again: and sleep again:
And a moonlight flit while the salmon leaps
From a smouldering spot by the riverside;
The tinker's children take their chance, and bide.
When Wicklow woods first seemed to wait,
As still they wait tonight;
I heard that creaking, rumbling cart,
And stars the same were out.
When you gave pennies to the youngest child,
A silent child: a tawny child:
The tinker's children meekly are, and mild.
And still I hear strange woods among
Whenever a creaking cart goes down;
The singsong twang of that bawneen man:
"Thank you my lady, thank you my lady,"
As when you gave the child a penny.
I heard it in an Irish voice to-day,
And saw again though long gone by
Four children on a rumbling cart,
A woman trudging beside that load,
A lank man leaving the horse to guide
A wet road: a dry road:
A gravelly road for a moonlight flit
From a smouldering spot by the riverside;
I saw the stony, rocky road where the tinker's children bide.

RHODA COGHILL

(1903-   )

THE PLOUGH-HORSE

ON A wide-open, windless Autumn morning
When shadows are all on the other side of the hedge or the tree,

A slim young rook slides away like a knife-blade
From the branch-stump, notched and broken as an old tooth,
Where his eager bright brothers noisily
Push each other down—I'm King of the Castle!—
With wings rising like tattered heraldry;
With torn wings flapping they regain their balance.

From behind a sturdy tree in the quiet, sunny distance,
Solemnly comes the stolid brown plough-horse, Tony:
No harness about him now, no harrow behind him,
While the furrows are idle and himself at leisure,
Shoulder-bare he plods forward in the resting field,
His gait not changing, his muscles anticipating
The solid jolting weight again of the ghostly gear
That he wears as surely buckled on him now
As a sleepwalking monk would carry his girdle and habit.

DEAD

I was the moon.
A shadow hid me
and I knew what it meant
not to be at all.
The moon in eclipse is sad
and sinless.
There is no passion in her plight.
Cold, unlighted,
moving in trance,
she comes to her station
or passes again to her place;
uncovers her loneliness:
eyeless behind no eyelids
has neither sleeping nor waking,
no body, parts, nor passions,
no loving, perceiving,
having, nor being;

[727]

moves only in a wayless night;
and drifting, as a ship without direction,
sinks to a forgotten depth,
among weeds,
among stones.

PATRICK KAVANAGH
(1905-   )

A GLUT ON THE MARKET

MY SOUL was an old horse
Offered for sale in twenty fairs:
I offered him to the Church—the buyers
Were little men who feared his unusual airs.
One said, let him remain unbid
In the wind and rain and hunger
Of sin and we will get him—
With the winkers thrown in—for nothing.

Then the men of State looked at
What I'd brought for sale,
One minister wondering if
Another horse-body would fit the tail
That he'd kept for sentiment—
The relic of his own soul—
Said, I will graze him in lieu of his labour.
I lent him for a week or more
And he came back a hurdle of bones,
Starved, overworked, in despair.
I nursed him on the roadside grass
To shape him for another fair.

I lowered my price. I stood him where
The broken-winded, spavined stand

[728]

And crooked shopkeepers said that he
Might do a season on the land
But not for high-paid work in towns—
He'd do a tinker, possibly.
I begged, O make some offer now,
A soul is a poor man's tragedy.
—He'll draw your dungiest cart, I said,
Show you short-cuts to Mass,
Teach weather-lore, at night collect
Bad debts from poor men's grass.
                    And they would not.

Where the
Tinkers quarrel I went down
With my horse, my soul.
I cried, who will bid me half-a-crown?
From their rowdy bargaining
Not one turned. Soul, I prayed,
I have hawked you through the world
Of Church and State and meanest trade;
But this evening halter off,
Never again will it go on.
On the south side of ditches
There is grazing of the sun;
No more haggling with the world . . .
As I said these words he grew
Wings upon his back. Now I may ride him
Every land my imagination knew.

MEMORY OF BROTHER MICHAEL

IT WOULD never be morning, always evening,
Golden sunset, golden age—
When Shakespeare, Marlowe and Jonson were writing
The future of England page by page
A nettle-wild grave was Ireland's stage.

[729]

It would never be spring, always autumn
After a harvest always lost—
When Drake was winning seas for England
We sailed in puddles of the past
Chasing the ghost of Brendan's mast.

The seeds among the dust were less than dust,
Dust we sought, decay,
The young sprout rising smothered in it
Cursed for being in the way—
And the same is true to-day.

Culture is always something that was,
Something pedants can measure:
Skull of bard, thigh of chief,
Depth of dried-up river.
Shall we be thus forever?
Shall we be thus forever?

PADRAIC FALLON
(1906-   )

WISDOM

WHO'D love again on this old rambling star
Where love, cast out of God's harem,
Grows coarse in the weather over a gypsy fire
Of sticks and cowdung? Who, having come to sense,
Tenting with her but comes to know
As mere illusions
Those dark eyes heavy with dream
Of lost kingdoms,
The Sound of strings and drums
She carries about her soft in the air as echo?
Having won at length to wisdom, who'd wish to know
Once more an empty fallen queen of Pharaoh?

[730]

Bear with me then I, that was hunter once,
Guess rightly that you have as many dewy
Turnings as a hare; but having come to sense
I know the glittering ancient self in you
Is not for dog and horn. So you may stay
As a sitting hare in the dew
Quietly assembling the moon in each cold eye,
Unless in folly I find
Like Solomon a second wind
And on this falling star seek more than a dog's day,
Running with that old stager who lived and died in the faith
That the crown of love is . . . to be in at the death.

VIRGIN

I

THE lady who intervenes
In the Trinity assumes
Her rights on a side altar,
A great wick that no flame lames
In a quiet arch of candle flames.

And over the dim paving
Where drowned lights are stepping stones,
In the cave of the nave,
Soled with silences that stir like water
Or whispers of prayer the women falter.

Slowly, glimmering
One after one for a moment in that still arch,
Each puts her penny in the money box,
Each lights a candle and burns there
As if she'd set it to her hair.

Then one after one each woman grows
Anonymous;

They pass, and are the past:
O sighing history
Shuffling by that knee!

Candles die in their small
Concepts of virginity but she,
Older than the vine, sits always in the sun
Turning on all the one face
Full of grace.

Moon to what sun?
Mother of one son,
Shall I turn my back upon you and walk out
Lest I with the women find you inside me—
A tree, a growing reverie?

A great tree
Drinking a thousand roots in me
Growing till it pushes through my skull—for who
To gather up
As I flower at the top?

II

Her hands are not tangible;
Her face drifts; and over all
Her body is the quality of distance
And the shine of water.

If guesses were gods,
How they would stride out towards her, seven leagues in each
    boot!
If gods are guesses, still I am moderate
In thinking they'd touch heaven through her thought.

How the heavens depend on her!
Did her weather alter it would mean
Angels and their wide glories melting in the air
To fall in a bright shower round her like rain.

O how be intimate with this
Translucent Atlas? Yet sometimes I awake
Softly as if I had been kissed
And blessed—to feel the whole earth quake.

D. J. O'SULLIVAN
(1906-   )

DAWN IN INISHTRAHULL

THE moon shines on the Isle of Inishtrahull,
Bejewelling nuptial tinted herring-gull,
May-fly dancing in the balmy air,
And moth returning to its daylight lair.

A shoal of herring breaking out at sea
Sparkle like hoar-frost on an aspen tree,
Spindrift in the shaded rocky cleft,
And raised-beach quartz that the ice-ages left.

The droning beetles seek the crevassed walls
To dive into when hungry lapwing calls;
Earwigs, likewise into earthed homes,
And red-ants under scarred lichened stones.

An otter seeking rest on rock remote
Glistens with phosphorescence on his coat
The snail Arborum, with his watery glue,
And bunch of pearlwort in a crystal dew.

The flaming sun ascends o'er Cantyre's Mull,
Flings out its arms, day breaks on Inishtrahull!

DRINKING TIME

Two black heifers and a red
Standing on the river-bed,
Filling up their belly-tanks,
Water swirling 'round their flanks.

In the stirred-up river mud
Elvers wriggle, flat-fish scud;
Where the torrent's slow and deep
Sea-bound smolt lie half-asleep.

Buzzing flies bite bovine flesh,
Twitching tails make rainbow-splash,
One black sucks a tadpole in,
Sniffs and snorts create a din.

Now the farmer's voice is heard
Above the cymbal-tinkling ford,
'Bramble, Bluebell, Buttercup;
Hi, come out, come cow—up!'

In answer to the urging call
They leave for shelter'd byre stall,
Oaten mash and hay-strewn bed,
Two black heifers and a red.

LIAM MacGOWAN
(contemporary)

CONNOLLY

James Connolly was executed May 1916 by a British firing squad. Too sick to stand he faced the firing party in a bath chair. In the poem a Welsh "Tommy" speaks.

THE man was all shot through that came to-day
Into the barrack square;

[734]

A soldier I—I am not proud to say
We killed him there;
They brought him from the prison hospital.
To see him in that chair
I thought his smile would far more quickly call
A man to prayer.

Maybe we cannot understand this thing
That makes these rebels die;
And yet all things love freedom and the Spring
Clear in the sky!
I think I would not do this deed again
For all that I hold by;
Gaze down my rifle at his breast—but then
A soldier I.

They say that he was kindly—different, too
Apart from all the rest;
A lover of the poor; and all shot through
His wounds ill drest,
He came before us, faced us like a man,
Who knew a deeper pain
Than blows or bullets—ere the world began;
Died he in vain?

Ready present! And he just smiling—God!
I felt my rifle shake.
His wounds were opened out and round that chair
Was one red lake;
I swear his lips said 'Fire'! when all was still
Before my rifle spat
That cursed lead—And I was picked to kill
A man like that.

EILEEN BRENNAN
(1913-   )

THOUGHTS AT THE MUSEUM

ONE would not hope to meet
the concentrated poignancy of
'Sixteen'
but it's there in a grey-green coat
of Casement's
a pierced soiled hat,
in the gilt of a solitary button
and the photograph of many a young head held high.
And the soul of it's wove
in the letters there
"We do not fear to die":
"I do not fear to die":
"I shall watch the fight from above" . . .
Then a little boy says
hushedly
"Kevin Barry—see";
and reads aloud the proclamation.
Words, words, words.
So many relics of those dead.
Did they fight for symbols unseen?
And will others again fight for words,
for a veiled Kathleen—
or united for an undivided free land
for soil that the people will care and share
for a land with a home and a life
for the like of the wan little fellow there?

BRYAN MacMAHON
(contemporary)

CORNER BOYS

DAY in, day out,
The line of corner boys,
Ex-soldiers most,
Expectorate, expatiate,
On subtleties of scandal,
On ways of catching fish
In distant lands.
On housing schemes and strikes,
On handy ways of killing men,
On bawds.
On charms and spells
On mysteries of birth and death,
And ways of welding steel,
On inside alterations
Wrought by fever,
On constipation and on ailments
On pigeons and pagodas,
On rhombuses and razors . . .
God's truth! Who'd patronize the halls of Art
And schools of great renown,
When here,
A step beyond your door,
The gleanings of the globe
Are thrown into your lap?
Few finger-posts have trod the way they point,
Embittered, lonely, cynical,
What if they tell of maids
With awful malevolence
In their downfall?
These who have seen
The sun behind a minaret,
The strands of France,

The cobalt seas. . . .
While here,
Here the lonesome Kerry winds
Shriek up along the draughty streets,
And howl around the corner
Where the corner boys are growing grey,
Dreaming of sunny skies.

JOHN HEWITT
(1907-   )

LOAD

TODAY we carted home the last brown sheaf
and hookt the scythe agenst the dry barn wall:
the yellow border's on the chestnut leaf,
the beech leaf's yellow all.

Tomorrow we must bring the apples in,
they are as big as they shall ever be:
already starlings eager to begin
have tasted many a tree.

And in the garden, all the roses done,
the light lies gently, faint and almost cold,
on wither'd goldenrod and snapdragon
and tarnisht marigold.

STANISLAUS LYNCH
(1907-   )

BLUE PETER

DOES your heart go back to Galway, to The Blazers and stone
walls,

[738]

As you stand so lonely, listening, while an English blackbird
    calls?
You were lovely when you left me! Perfect mover, sound and
    game,
Now, you've chronic laminitis! Useless, cast-off, stiff and lame.
Heated hooves! They once rang challenge where the walls
    were high and wide,
Changing feet with rhythmed rattle, on-and-off them in your
    stride.
How I hoped to see you famous! Hear some glowing story told
Of a Point-to-Point achievement by my dashing six-year-old.
Now, poor monument to man's neglect, I'd rather see you dead
Than the sight of shifting fore-legs propping-up your gallant
    head.
Oh, I know the cause . . . Hard gallop, lazy groom, then
    founder, chill.
Groom or owner's fault . . . what matter? Peter boy, you
    paid the bill.

Yes, I know. They're all so kind to you. They say you'll soon
    be sound.
But you and I know better . . . 'Tis good-bye to Horn and
    Hound.

LOUIS MacNEICE
(1907-   )

BAGPIPE MUSIC

It's no go the merry-go-round, it's no go the rickshaw,
All we want is a limousine and a ticket for the peepshow.
Their knickers are made of crepe-de-chine, their shoes are
    made of python,
Their halls are lined with tiger rugs and their walls with heads
    of bison.

[739]

John MacDonald found a corpse, put it under the sofa,
Waited till it came to life and hit it with a poker,
Sold its eyes for souvenirs, sold its blood for whiskey,
Kept its bones for dumb-bells to use when he was fifty.

It's no go the Yogi-Man, it's no go Blavatsky,
All we want is a bank balance and a bit of skirt in a taxi.

Annie MacDougall went to milk, caught her foot in the
     heather,
Woke to hear a dance record playing of Old Vienna.
It's no go your maidenheads, it's no go your culture,
All we want is a Dunlop tyre and the devil mend the puncture.

The Laird o' Phelps spent Hogmannay declaring he was sober;
Counted his feet to prove the fact and found he had one foot
     over.
Mrs. Carmichael had her fifth, looked at the job with repulsion,
Said to the midwife 'Take it away; I'm through with over-
     production.'

It's no go the gossip column, it's no go the Ceilidh,
All we want is a mother's help and a sugar-stick for the baby.

Willie Murray cut his thumb, couldn't count the damage,
Took the hide of an Ayrshire cow and used it for a bandage.
His brother caught three hundred cran when the seas were
     lavish,
Threw the bleeders back in the sea and went upon the parish.

It's no go the Herring Board, it's no go the Bible,
All we want is a packet of fags when our hands are idle.

It's no go the picture palace, it's no go the stadium,
It's no go the country cot with a pot of pink geraniums.
It's no go the Government grants, it's no go the elections,
Sit on your arse for fifty years and hang your hat on a pension.

[740]

It's no go my honey love, it's no go my poppet;
Work your hands from day to day, the winds will blow the
    profit.
The glass is falling hour by hour, the glass will fall for ever,
But if you break the bloody glass you won't hold up the
    weather.

NOSTALGIA

IN COCK-WATTLE sunset or grey
Dawn when the dagger
Points again of longing
For what was never home
We needs must turn away
From the voices that cry "Come—"
That under-sea ding-donging.

Dingle-dongle, bells and bluebells,
Snapdragon solstice, lunar lull,
The wasp circling the honey
Or the lamp soft on the snow—
These are the time at which
The will is vunerable,
The trigger-finger slow,
The spirit lonely.

These are the times at which
Aloneness is too ripe
When homesick for the hollow
Heart of the Milky Way
The soundless clapper calls
And we would follow
But earth and will are stronger
And nearer—and we stay.

CARRICKFERGUS

I was born in Belfast between the mountain and the gantries
  To the hooting of lost sirens and the clang of trams:
Thence to Smoky Carrick in County Antrim
  Where the bottle-neck harbour collects the mud which jams

The little boats beneath the Norman castle,
  The pier shining with lumps of crystal salt;
The Scotch Quarter was a line of residential houses
  But the Irish Quarter was a slum for the blind and halt.

The brook ran yellow from the factory stinking of chlorine,
  The yarn-mill called its funeral cry at noon;
Or lights looked over the lough to the lights of Bangor
  Under the peacock aura of a drowning moon.

The Norman walled this town against the country
  To stop his ears to the yelping of his slave
And built a church in the form of a cross but denoting
  The list of Christ on the cross, in the angle of the nave.

I was the rector's son, born to the anglican order,
  Banned for ever from the candles of the Irish poor;
The Chichesters knelt in marble at the end of a transept
  With ruffs about their necks, their portion sure.

The war came and a huge camp of soldiers
  Grew from the ground in sight of our house with long
Dummies hanging from gibbets for bayonet practice
  And the sentry's challenge echoing all day long;

A Yorkshire terrier ran in and out by the gate-lodge
  Barred to civilians, yapping as if taking affront:
Marching at ease and singing 'Who Killed Cock Robin?'
  The troops went out by the lodge and off to the Front.

[742]

The steamer was camouflaged that took me to England—
    Sweat and khaki in the Carlisle train;
I thought that the war would last for ever and sugar
    Be always rationed and that never again

Would the weekly papers not have photos of sandbags
    And my governess not make bandages from moss
And people not have maps above the fireplace
    With flags on pins moving across and across—

Across the hawthorn hedge the noise of bugles,
    Flares across the night,
Somewhere on the lough was a prison ship for Germans,
    A cage across their sight.

I went to school in Dorset, the world of parents
    Contracted into a puppet world of sons
Far from the mill girls, the smell of porter, the salt-mines
    And the soldiers with their guns.

COUNTY SLIGO

In Sligo the country was soft; there were turkeys
    Gobbling under sycamore trees
And the shadows of clouds on the mountains moving
    Like browsing cattle at ease.

And little distant fields were sprigged with haycocks
    And splashed against a white
Roadside cottage a welter of nasturtium
    Deluging the sight,

And pullets pecking the flies from around the eyes of heifers
    Sitting in farmyard mud
Among hydrangeas and the falling ear-rings
    Of fuchsias red as blood.

[743]

But in Mayo the tumbledown walls went leap-frog
  Over the moors,
The sugar and salt in the pubs were damp in the casters
  And the water was brown as beer upon the shores

Of desolate loughs, and stumps of hoary bog-oak
  Stuck up here and there
And as the twilight filtered on the heather
  Water-music filled the air,

And when the night came down upon the bogland
  With all-enveloping wings
The coal-black turf-stacks rose against the darkness
  Like the tombs of nameless kings.

ROBERT FARREN
(1909-   )

THE MASON

NOTHING older than stone but the soil and the sea and the sky.
Nothing stronger than stone but water and air and fire.
Nothing worthier than stone but the harp-string, the word and
      the tree.
Nothing humbler or stubborner than stone—whatever it be!

Stone is the bone of the world, under moor, under loam,
Under ocean and churchyard-corruption of buried bone;
Floor of the mountain, pound of the ocean, the world's cord.
God's creature, stone, that once was the vault of its Lord.

God gave me stone to know for a womb with child,
The time of delivery come but waiting the knife:
I free the stone-born glory into the air,
Rounded and grooved and edged and grained and rare.

[744]

I have mastered the grain, the make, the temper of stone,
Fingering it and considering, touching with hand and with
     soul,
Quarrying it out of the course, piercing and severing it,
With a chirp of meeting metals like a bird's chirp.

Basalt I know—bottle-green, still pools of stone
Harder than hawk's beak, shark's tooth or tusk of the boar;
Basalt—the glass-stone, stone without pore or wart;
Couseway-stone stepped across Moyle-fjord in the north.

Granite I know—dust-pearl with silver eyes—
That moulds domed hills, with snow, rain, wind and time.
Marble—the multiple-tinted—the satin-fleshed
Daughter of the King of white Greece in the lands of the west.

Dark flint I know with the feel of a fox's tongue,
The unconsumed cold carrier of fire, its young:
Stone of hair-edges and thorn-points, the dagger stone,
Spear-stone, swordstone, hatchet-stone, hearth-gilly stone.

O Christ, the stone which the builders rejected
And which is become the head of the corner,
Part me from them the stone shall grind when it fall;
Leave me not a stone in thine enemies' hand!

TO THE BELL-RINGER

HAUL on the rope. Make the high bell lean
backward like rowers' shoulders; forward again,
rowing the air. Make bronze clash upon bronze,
clang, and go thinning on the wind like streaming hair.
Haul on the rope. Smite the metals. Make huge, long sound.

[745]

IMMOLATION

On TAUT air—bells; lifted, adoring eyes;
and, sinner, seraph, GOD, look upon GOD.

Honour to Thee and praise!
Love unto Thee and praise!
Honour and love to Thee, O Lord, and praise.

Christ, star-told in the east,
Christ, lover of "these least,"
Christ of the marriage-feast
in this White Host.

Christ by the kings adored,
Christ come to bring the sword
Christ the Incarnate Word
in this White Host.

Christ of the uncast stone,
Christ in the Garden prone,
Christ agonized, alone
in this White Host.

Christ with ensanguined cheek,
Christ from the scourging weak,
Christ with his mockers meek
in this White Host.

Christ of the supper room,
Christ of the empty tomb,
Christ of the Day of Doom
in this White Host.

Who was, before the Sun,
Who lived, ere Life begun,
Who shall, when Time be done,
in this White Host.

Who dreamed this realm of earth
Who called the seas to birth,
Who made the stars for mirth,
in this White Host.

Who Glory is and Light
Who Majesty and Might
Who fullness of Delight
in this White Host.

Who dread Divinity
Who One in Trinity,
Who is Infinity,
in this White Host.

Jesu, with Magdalen I join my plea,
with him who craved remembrance
from the tree,
with drowning Peter: "Lord deliver me"
by this White Host.

W. R. RODGERS
(1909-   )

BEAGLES

OVER rock and wrinkled ground
Ran the lingering nose of hound,
The little and elastic hare
Stretched herself nor stayed to stare.

Stretched herself, and far away
Darted through the chinks of day,
Behind her, shouting out her name,
The whole blind world galloping came.

[747]

Over hills a running line
Curled like a whip-lash, fast and fine,
Past me sailed the sudden pack
Along the taut and tingling track.

From the far flat scene each shout
Like jig-saw piece came tumbling out,
I took and put them all together,
And then they turned into a tether.

A tether that held me to the hare
Here, there, and everywhere.

SPRING

RACK upon rack of leaves all elbowing
From end to end of every bony wood,
And frill upon frill of water hanging
From hill to hill, and over all, in tiers,
The tiny shrapnel-bursts of song that hood
And hem the climbing lark tunnelling clear.

All the bells and hullabalooes of joy
Ring in the tingling flesh of bull and boy,
Everywhere in our loud and lighted land
The lewdest notions now make holiday,
Now on the least mouse-blink of nakedness
Pounces the lion, lust. Limbs and lambs play.

Old lonely men lean back in limousines,
Miser-fingers locked on their bellies' purse,
Looking fixedly ahead as they slide
Silently on like shadows across screens
Past the Easter crowds banked up on pavements,
Waiting for a wedding, mobbing a bride.

W. B. STANFORD
(1910-   )

UNDERTONE

WHEN the landfolk of Galway converse with a stranger,
softly the men speak, more softly the women,
light words on their lips, and an accent that sings
in traditional cadences (once plucked by harpists
to cheer melancholic carousals of kings),
when the landfolk of Galway converse with a stranger.

But under the cadences, under the light lips,
under the lilt of the harp-plucking bard,
threaded deep in its socket of anger and loneliness
a passion, with piercing and tightening screw, grips
their minds' inner engine and presses it hard.

When the landfolk of Galway converse with a stranger,
softly the men speak, more softly the women;
yet older than harp-playing, older than welcomes,
an undertone threatens Fomorian danger,
when the landfolk of Galway converse with a stranger.

SEAN JENNETT
(1910-   )

I WAS A LABOURER

From CYCLE: Seven War Poems

I WAS a labourer in the smoky valley,
within the high walls, the tall dark walls of the mills,
where the hills go up to the wild moor.
I am a dog of the dales, broad is my speech,

[749]

and my ways are not the smooth ways of the south,
but hard, and used to keener weather.
All week I worked among the looms
while the cloth slacked out and the shuttles clacked
swiftly, as the woof was shot through the warp
and through my brain dim with the webs of years.
All week I was the servant of the loom,
chained to the steel for the promise of meagre coin,
six days a week, but Sunday comes
soon, and I am my master for the waking day
that found me with my whippet on the moor.
O my faithful lass! Soft was her fell;
her eyes were like deep pools stained with peat,
shafted with light; and intelligent.
She was long in the body, but strong of limb and rib,
and her muscles moved under the skin
like currents in a bay of the river.
She was swift as the wind or as the summer swallow,
and I would pit her with the local dogs,
backing her swiftness with my sweaty coin
and many a shilling have I won with her
to spend on some wet evening in a pub
or buy the tickets at the picture palace
when I took out the girl I meant to marry—
but that is all forgotten with the flesh.
I was a labourer in the smoky valley:
I am a brittle bone projecting from the sand.

CECIL FFRENCH SALKELD

(1910-   )

WATER-FRONT

Down by the bridge
They sit and wait
Packed bub to bub

[750]

In the back of the pub:
Queens in their parlour
Surrounded by ardour
Secret, elate.

On the wet table
Half-filled glasses:
Nelly was able
To put up a Stout
Before we set out

Nelly was dear
To her sailor brother,
Now there's nobody here
To stand us another.
On the wet table
Half-filled glasses
That Nelly was able—
But everything passes . . .

TERENCE WARD
(1910-   )

KEVIN BARRY

On November 20th, 1920, Kevin Barry, aged eighteen, was hanged in reprisal by the British Authorities. He had been captured during an attack on an armoured force in Dublin. (He was hanged in Mountjoy Jail.) Because of his youth and of rumours of his ill-treatment in prison and because of his refusal to betray his friends, his name has been kept in memory throughout Ireland.

I CANNOT forget
The sight of that straight young neck
In the clasp of the hempen rope
That day in November.

And I see always
The minions of the Saxon foe,
And hear the wailing of the women
That day in November.

I think of his youth
And the years that beckoned him on,
And he dying in the grey shadows
That day in November.

Where was our manhood,
O sons of the sorrowful Queen,
To let the brutal foeman triumph undisturbed
That day in November?

Have you sworn deeply
That the day of reckoning is near,
For the evil crew who murdered Kevin Barry
That day in November?

DENIS WRAFTER
(1910-   )

BRAGGART!

THEY say you're in love with that keck-eyed lad
The priest is making your own to-day,
But if that's your tutor in love I vow
An hour with me would improve your play!
O were I not bound to a dark-haired woman,
Whose green eyes follow me day and night,
I'd teach you a trick of the art or two
Would burn you up like a moth in the light.

You passed me haughtily down the street,
With your town-bred boy in fop's attire,

But I caught you turning your golden head—
And ever was smoke the child of fire!
O were I not tied to an ardent woman,
Whose eyes are my warders night and day,
To free your heart from that manikin's wiles
Would be all my labour and all my pay.

I've watched you go towards the grove at eve,
His snow-white hand in your yellow glove,
Till the blood runs black in my veins to see
Such beauty matched with so mean a love.
Ah, had I not roved with a Spanish woman—
Would slit my throat in another's bed,
My arms around you to-night would banish
That stripling out of your delicate head.

DONAGH MacDONAGH
(1912-   )

THE INVITATION

THE horse of poetry nibbles
The summer-riddled grass,
Lifting his heavy head
To the young girls as they pass;

Riderless he may drowse
Till the year turn over.
Leap girl upon his back
And he will race for ever.

THE VETERANS

STRICT hairshirt of circumstance tears the flesh
Off most delicate bones;

[753]

Years of counter and office, the warped mesh
Of social living, dropping on stones,
Wear down all that was rough and worthy
To a common denominator of dull tones.

So these, who in the sixteenth year of the century
Saw their city, a Phoenix upturned,
Settle under her ashes and bury
Hearts and brains that more frantically burned
Than the town they destroyed, have with the corrosion of time
Spent more than they earned;

And with their youth has shrunk their singular mystery
Which for one week set them in the pulse of the age,
Their spring adventure petrified in history,
A line on a page,
Betrayed into the hands of students who question
Oppressed and oppressor's rage.

Only the dead beneath their granite signatures
Are untroubled by the touch of day and day,
Only in them the first rich vision endures;
Those over clay
Retouch in memory, with sentiment relive,
April and May.

NIALL SHERIDAN
(1912-   )

POEM

As ROCK to sun or storm
My heart lies bare,
Untutored to beware
The keen bright shock of lovely face and form—

Or that more subtle snare,
Her thoughtless grace of gesture,
The eternal careless vesture
Of beauty that enmeshes eager eye.

All words of praise I chose
Blundered from my heart—
No stratagem of art
Could fix that light enchantment in a pose,
No studied phrase impart
The breath-arresting charm,
The dire and sweet alarm
Of beauty that outruns the eager eye.

DENIS DEVLIN
(1908-   )

ENCOUNTER

"OUR saints are poets, Milton and Blake,
Who would rib men with pride against the spite
Of God," the Englishman said, and in the silence
Hatred sparkled along our bones. He said:
"Celt, your saints adorn the poor with roses
And praise God for standing still."

Between the two of us, François from Touraine,
Where women and the wheat ripen and fall due
Suavely at evening, smiled, teasing the breadcrumbs.
He whispered: "Patience; listen to the world's
Growth, rustling in fire and childlike water!"

And I: "Milton and Marvell, like the toady, Horace,
Praised the men of power for the good
They happened on, with bible and sword; the wretched
Hold out their begging-bowls at the wooden gates,
Too poor to weep, too poor to weep with tears."

[755]

Boxflower scent. Fumes of burgundy.
Nagging children at the tables
A dream's remove from their fathers smoking
Along the boulevard laid with yellow evening.

THE STATUE AND THE PERTURBED BURGHERS

EMPTIED and pearly skulls
Lie humbly among the roots of the grass.
The inhabitants know it only too well
Walking delicately
Under the trees.
They have stayed this fluttering boy in tight marble
For a fresh similitude
Of their rare immersion in stillness,
Planted foaming trees
For coolness.

People of worth and wealth
Glancing with care at their modes of life,
Walls, cradles, windows, amber orchards.

My watch ticks as loud as a sledgehammer in an empty street.
Muffle the panting hours my fountain, disdain them
Boy with the beaked chin.

The tendrils of fountain water thread that silk music
From the hollow of scented shutters
Crimson and blind
Crimson and blind
As though it were my sister,
Fireflies on the rosewood
Spinet playing,
With barely escaping voice
With arched fastidious wrists to be so gentle.

LESLIE DAIKEN
(1912-   )

SPRING, ST. STEPHEN'S GREEN

WHITEWINGED circus
of kittiewaking
parabolas of bodies
swooping roundabout.

Strong drakewings
cleaned with preening
are crashing down
upon the lucid coolpond
with steely stiff featherflashes.

Plashed is the pondface
quivered with buff quill
with lively leg and bill
with webfeet tangerine—
a tammany grace.

Headbobbling drakesheen
from greenshot velveteen
and a wineplush breastlapping
and prestdown ducktapping
from flat bills nippling.

Swift crystal beads
oily globular
spring from bright backs:
and a male claptrapping
into mating tactics
murmuringly merges.

Quaggling!
and mallard dabbling

[757]

are coy: paddling
fussy and featherflustered.

Pleasantplash!

BOHERNABREENA

SLEEPS tranquilly the lake—a slender throat
furred by a bearskin coil of shaggy trees.
A restless trout stirs bosom-deep; the lake
heaves ripple-sighs amid its reveries.
Now flocks of long-tailed tits, bark-scouring, make
wheezy discordances like jangled keys.—
Else all is moody-quiet as a moat.

But on the hills no midge nor fly can thrive
in furry warmth, for steel-trapped is the clay.
Crunching rimed shreds, cold sheep and heifers strive
to keep themselves alive; (their hoof-tracks stray
close to the hedgerow-corners, filmed with sheets
of ice too light to bend a grassy blade,
gelatinoid and snailshell-thin). Yet poisoned sweets,
those orange fungi, moss-pillowed in the shade,
are left untrodden.
                          Tinkling like swung glass,
a farm-fed robin's crystal-fluid notes
drip down the valley, clearer than spring-water:

   "Feeding is foul and cattle are cold;
   the year is sickening, wizened, old.
   The larches are losing their saffron hair,
   and O how the maidenly birch is bare!
   If you look at the beech you'd see blood-stains there.
   Three scentless blooms hold fast to a whin.
   See a dewdrop bearding a berry's chin:
   know, then, that verdure is going to die,

but a last wildrose tells a beautiful lie
to the frost-bitten earth and funereal sky."

LINES WRITTEN IN A COUNTRY PARSON'S
ORCHARD

THE stock whom Cromwell planted here,
Tough seedlings of efficiency,
Has walled its acres in, from fear,
Founded a generous dynasty.

His plea with God, his door ajar
The Rector listens to the rooks;
Puzzling the scourge of total war
Clings to his fishing-rods and books

And so, the Mistress of the House,
Her servants mortgaged to the times,
Now weeds and plants, her haughty grouse
Hushed by the apple-trees and limes.

And if the Mistress' back is bent,
Her heart is broken from the knowledge
That all her psalms and thrift have meant
Sweet nothing to her son at College.

In raffia gardening-hat, and gloves,
Godly as one of Millet's GLEANERS,
Stooping, she sighs because she loves
The youth despite his misdemeanours.

Each week her pleas oppress the lad:
'Oh, make Dean Swift your inspiration . . .'
She disremembers Swift went mad
Before his genius shocked the nation.

[759]

Unanswered every one. The boy,
Pursuing an evasive Venus,
Is amorous, matricidal, coy—
A nineteen-year-old blond Adonis.

Impatient of the rustic Church,
His bibles all are secular:
Should Mary leave him in the lurch
He'll follow his integral star,

And, poet of the mouldering home,
He still will live to sing and see
How little reaped where they had sown—
The generous Ascendancy.

LARCH HILL

Now trees are weedy mazes, upright, still,
Like meager bristles on the mountains' backs.
Bleak, birdless, lonely as a ruined mill
Where only water slithers down, Larch Hill
Might be modelled out of plastic wax.

Moving water, moss-girth, smothers all,
Persistent monody that seems to ape
The far off thunder of a waterfall.

In ditches umber runnels, scurrying to swell
The brook, lick leaf-clogged driftwood to a foam
Like beaten whites of eggs. Down in the dell
A puffed out redbreast mopes beneath a dome
Of tangled hawthorn twigs, peevish, unwell.

Horses, fetlock-deep in muddy tide,
Hug the shelter of the scraggy hedges,
Lower lips hanging loosely down, heavy-eyed.

[760]

Here in the wicker cradle of the heights
No heat can penetrate. The morning's frost
Is powdery on the blades and spites
Diurnally the battling sun. A rigid crust
Of icy crystals coats the ground, for nights.

GEORGE M. BRADY
(1916-   )

THE AUTUMN HOUSE

FROM my window, facing South,
I watch the leaf-light birds
That lately shared my roof
Set off without farewells
Journeying to the sun.

The branch hangs from a sky
That soon will shelter none
The widowed light puts on
Its threadbare shroud
I wait alone

In a house where none
Prepare for what may come
Across the water's hill
Where all the clocks are still
Nobody heeds my talk
And down the draughty
Passage-way nobody walks.

THE GENERATIONS

Now, in the evenings, when the light
Goes suddenly, and the houses are
Hushed in a dusk of uneasy birds,
We within doors draw close to the breathing fire,
Circle of lamplight, voices, outside the night
Of darkened air threatening a storm,
A night of possible loss. Warmed by words
We sometimes forget the life we end
Here by the water, near the windy quays,
Life stretched from minute to staring minute,
Dragging its heels along the cobbled streets,
Watching, waiting, listening to the seas
Rising, but for the moment only comforted

For dawn brings the birds of stone,
The stifled cry lost when the shutter bangs
And the black wind ruffles the Northern cock,
Dawn brings the empty bay, the stranded boats,
And white as ghost-light the lighthouse on the rock
Derelict, where our women go each morning,
Where Time is the water washing each day ashore,
The faded message in a drifting bottle.

And we rise with the light to our partial death,
To a day of habit, to a sky
That answers no-one. And sometimes
We pray. But always Time brings in the sea
To eat our fields, beat down the makeshift walls,
And take from us again our living sons.

MUREDACH J. DOOHER
(1916-

RENASCENCE

By BANKS where burned awhile the rose
And roved the goldenrod
I lay through wheeling ages,
Gossiping with God.

When centuries of lichens
Concealed my name and stone,
A quickening of the sinews,
A bustling of the bone,

Came over me, usurping,
One wing-filled afternoon,
Prerogative of chrysalis.
Renouncing my cocoon,

I poised my reeling pinions
Upon a neighboring spray.
Then, bowing gravely left and right,
I wandered soft away.

FREDA LAUGHTON
(1907-   )

RAIN ON A COTTAGE ROOF

From within
Slight rain seems to purr;
A heavier shower murmur,
As bees hum.

[763]

Huge hands pummel and knead
The roof under
Thunder's indigo stampede.

Rain hoofs thrum.
Now hear the house become
A drum.

THE WOMAN WITH CHILD

How I am held within a tranquil shell,
As if I too were close within a womb,
I too enfolded as I fold the child.

As the tight bud enwraps the pleated leaf,
The blossom furled like an enfolded fan,
So life enfold me as I fold my flower.

As water lies within a lovely bowl,
I lie within my life, and life again
Lies folded fast within my living cell.

The apple waxes at the blossom's root,
And like the moon I mellow to the round
Full circle of my being, till I too

Am ripe with living and my fruit is grown.
Then break the shell of life. We shall be born,
My child and I, together, to the sun.

[764]

MAURICE CRAIG
(1919-   )

WINTER

Love's equinoctial gales are past, the path
Along the long lanes leads again through night.
    The trees are bare, the air
    A halo round each lamp.

Gentlest imaginable groundswell heaving
Hardly disturbs the wrack. The wave that broke
    Over us both, has passed,
    And now the calm succeeds.

And now the fire's the focus of the room
By winter made so. Like a gay salute
    There crackles in the hearth
    The holly's fusillade.

ROBERT GREACEN
(1920-   )

CYCLING TO DUBLIN

Pulling the dead sun's weight through County Meath,
We cycled through the knotted glass of afternoon,
Aware of the bright fog in the narrow slot of breath,
And the cycles' rhyming, coughing croon.

"O hurry to Dublin, to Dublin's fair city,
Where colleens, fair colleens are ever so pretty,
O linger no longer in lumbering languor,
Gallop the miles, the straight-backed miles without number.'

[765]

We were the Northmen, hard with hoarded words on tongue,
Driven down by home disgust to the broad lands and rich talk,
To the country of poets and pubs and cow-dung
Spouting and sprouting from every stalk. . . .

"O hurry to Dublin, to Dublin's fair city,
Where colleens, fair colleens are ever so pretty,
O linger no longer in lumbering languor,
Gallop the miles, the straight-backed miles without number."

TO A FAITHLESS LOVER

To you, holding in spent hands all seasons' memories,
Bush and briar, thorn and thistle and tree,
I send my love all wrapped and sealed
With the tense, white paper of my sentiment.
Crying in the various nights of muffled rain
(O live lead lash on the window-sill)
For you are frozen and alien from my side,
I send my freshness and my ardour.
To you, folding on hard palms all seasons' memories,
Gorse and foxglove, berry and subtle, humming bee,
I post my love all crumbled and sealed
With the gum of lips you stealing stormed to starve.

ROY McFADDEN
(1921-   )

THE ORATOR

"Remember Pearse," he said; "if we
Lose Irish we lose Ireland." They
looked and listened stupidly
Like country folk on holiday.

[766]

If Yeats were still alive maybe
He could breathe vigour into clay,
Conjure an aristocracy,
And add grandeur to decay.

But he too was responsible
For this dull ash of men, for he
Was often as contemptible
In bartering all for poetry.

Yes, I have heard some people tell
Of petty spite and tyranny,
For psychic sight and psychic smell
Both failed to teach him charity.

If Yeats were still alive maybe
Ireland would cut a dash again.
But men can starve on poetry
And bullets break the poet's pen.

We need another death. Who knows—
Before the resurrection—
Instead of arrogance and pose
We'll need a Sheehy Skeffington.

VALENTIN IREMONGER
(1918-

SPRING STOPS ME SUDDENLY

SPRING stops me suddenly like ground
Glass under a door, squeaking and gibbering,
I put my hand to my cheek and the tips
Of my fingers feel blood pulsing and quivering.

[767]

A bud on a branch brushes the back
Of my hand and I look, without moving, down.
Summer is there, screwed and fused, compressed,
Neat as a bomb, its casing a dull brown.

From the window of a farther tree I hear
A chirp and a twitter; I blink.
A tow-headed vamp of a finch on a branch
Cocks a roving eye, tips me the wink

And, instantly, the whole great hot-lipped ensemble
Of buds and birds, of clay and glass doors,
Reels in with its ragtime chorus, staggering
The theme of the time, a jam-session's rattle and roar

With drums of summer jittering in the background
Dully, and deeper down and more human, the sobbing
Oboes of autumn falling across the track of the tune,
Winter's furtive bassoon like a sea-lion snorting and bobbing.

There is something here I do not get,
Some menace that I do not comprehend,
Yet, so intoxicating is the song,
I cannot follow its thought right to the end.

So up the garden path I go with Spring
Promising sacks and robes to rig my years
And a young girl to gladden my heart in a tartan
Scarf and freedom from my facile fears.

INDEX OF POETS

A. E. *see* RUSSELL, GEORGE
ALEXANDER, CECIL F. 494
ALLINGHAM, WILLIAM 509
AMERGIN 3
AN PILIBIN 693
ANSTER, JOHN 386

BANIM, JOHN 414
BARD OF THOMOND, *see* HOGAN, MICHAEL
BARRETT, EATON STANNARD 385
BERKELEY, GEORGE 333
BICKERSTAFF, ISAAC 347
BOUCICAULT, DION 301
BOYD, THOMAS 621
BRADY, GEORGE M. 761
BRENNAN, EILEEN 736
BROOKE, STOPFORD A. 530

CALLANAN, J. J. 393
CAMPBELL, JOSEPH 649
CARBERY, ETHNA 607
CAROLAN, TURLOUGH 177
CASEY, JOHN KEEGAN 550
CLARKE, AUSTIN 711
CLARKE, J. I. C. 552
COGHILL, RHODA 726
COLMAN, SAINT 15
COLUM, PADRAIC 668
COLUMCILLE 51, 101
CONNELL, JIM 717
CORKERY, DANIEL 666
CORMAC 21
COUSINS, J. H. 631
CRAIG, MAURICE 765
CRAWFORD, ISABELLA V. 556

DAIKEN, LESLIE 757
DARLEY, GEORGE 396
DAVIS, THOMAS 467
DERMODY, THOMAS 367
DEVERE, AUBREY 486
DEVLIN, DENIS 755
DOAK, H. L. 697
DONAGHY, LYLE 721
DOOHER, MUREDACH J. 763
DOWDEN, EDWARD 537
DOWLING, BARTHOLOMEW 500
DOYLE, LYNN 630

DRENNAN, WILLIAM 359
DUNSANY, LORD 636

EGLINTON, JOHN 623
ENGLISH, WILLIAM 197

FALLON, PADRAIC 730
FARREN, ROBERT 744
FERGUSON, SAMUEL 444
FERRITER, PIERCE 152
FIGGIS, DARRELL 673
FLAVELL, THOMAS 180
FFRENCH SALKELD, CECIL *see* SALKELD
FRIAR MICHAEL OF KILDARE 307

GEOGHEGAN, ARTHUR G. 464
GIBBON, MONK 713
GOGARTY, OLIVER ST. J. 274, 637
GOLDSMITH, OLIVER 334
GORE-BOOTH, EVA 624
GRAVES, ALFRED P. 555
GREACEN, ROBERT 765
GREGORY, LADY 560
GREGORY, PADRIC 690
GRIFFIN, GERALD 415

HEALY, PATRICK 199
HEWITT, JOHN 738
HICKEY, EMILY H. 549
HIGGINS, F. R. 707
HINKSON, KATHERINE TYNAN 588
HOGAN, MICHAEL 529

INGRAM, JOHN KELLS 505
IREMONGER, VALENTIN 767
IRWIN, THOMAS CAULFIELD 502
ITA, SAINT 19

JENNETT, SEAN 749
JOYCE, JAMES 674
JOYCE, ROBERT DWYER 527

KAVANAGH, PATRICK 728
KEARNEY, PEADAR 685
KEATING, GEOFFREY 154
KENNY, JAMES 384
KETTLE, THOMAS 663
KICKHAM, CHARLES JOSEPH 525

LARMINIE, WILLIAM 559
LAUGHTON, FREDA 763
LAWLESS, EMILY 547
LECKY, WILLIAM E. H. 534
LEDWIDGE, FRANCIS 698
LE FANU, SHERIDAN 483
LEO, see CASEY, JOHN KEEGAN
LESLIE, SHANE 688
LETTS, WINIFRED 680
LEVER, CHARLES 440
LOVER, SAMUEL 407
LYNCH, STANISLAUS 738

McBURNEY, WILLIAM 540
McCANN, MICHAEL JOSEPH 507
McCARTHY, DENIS A. 587
MacCARTHY, DENIS FLORENCE 489
MacCATHMHAOIL, see CAMPBELL, JOSEPH
MacCOLMAIN, RUMAN 52
MacCONGLINNE 93
MacDERMOTT, MARTIN 503
MacDONAGH, DONAGH 753
MacDONAGH, THOMAS 633
MacDONOGH, PATRICK 719
MacDONOUGH, PATRICK 629
MacELGUN, CATHAL BUIDHE 235
McFADDEN, ROY 766
MacGABHANN, LIAM, see MAC-GOWAN
MacGAWRAN, HUGH 165
McGEE, THOMAS D'ARCY 518
MacGILL, PATRICK 694
MacGOWAN, LIAM 734
McGREEVY, THOMAS 703
MacLIAG 55
MacMAHON, BRYAN 737
MacMANUS, SEUMAS 624
MacMORE, DALLAN 32
MacNEICE, LOUIS 739
MAGEE, WM. KIRKPATRICK, see EGLINTON, JOHN
MAGRATH, ANDREW 187
MAGUIRE, TOM 626
MAHONY, FRANCIS S. 365, 431
MALONE, CARROLL, see McBURNEY, WM.
MANGAN, JAMES CLARENCE 423
MERRIMAN, BRIAN 204
MICHAEL, FRIAR, see FRIAR MICHAEL
MILLIGAN, ALICE 663
MILLIKIN, RICHARD 362
MILNE, EWART 725
MITCHELL, SUSAN 299, 711

MOLLOY, JAMES LYMAN 532
MOORE, THOMAS 374
MOORE, TOM JR. 292
MULCHINOCK, WILLIAM PEMBROKE 493

NININE 17
NUGENT, GERALD 148

O'BRIEN, FITZ-JAMES 523
O'CAROLAN, see CAROLAN
O'CEARNAIGH, PEADAR, see KEARNEY, PEADAR
O'CONNOR, FRANK 724
O'CURNAIN, DIARMAD 200
O'DALA, DONNCHADH MOR, 116
O'DALY, CARROL 117
O'DUGAN, MAURICE 151
O'FARACHAIN, ROIBEARD, see FARREN, ROBERT
O'FLAHERTY, CHARLES 390
O'GILLAN, ANGUS 115
O'GNIVE, FEARFLATHA 140
O'HUSSEY, EOCHADH 160
O'KEEFFE, JOHN 348
O'KELLY, PATRICK 354
O'LEARY, JOSEPH 386
O'NEILL, MOIRA 662
O'RAHILLY, EGAN 172
O'REILLY, JOHN BOYLE 541
O'RYAN, EDMOND 171
O'SHAUGHNESSY, ARTHUR 538
O'SULLIVAN, D. J. 733
O'SULLIVAN, OWEN ROE 349
O'SULLIVAN, SEUMAS 659
O'TUOMY, JOHN 186

PARNELL, FANNY 563
PARNELL, THOMAS 331
PATRICK, SAINT 12, 24
PEARSE, PADRAIC 240, 645
PILIBIN, AN, see AN PILIBIN
PLUNKETT, JOSEPH MARY 691
POLLOCK, J. H., see AN PILIBIN
PROUT, FATHER, see MAHONY, FRANCIS

RAFTERY, ANTHONY 230
REYNOLDS, GEORGE NUGENT 366
RIDGE, LOLA 683
RODGERS, W. R. 747
ROLLESTON, T. W. H. 586
RUSSELL, GEORGE WM. (AE) 616

SALKELD, BLANAID 670
SALKELD, CECIL FFRENCH 750
SEDULIUS, CAELIUS 8
SHANAHAN, EILEEN 716
SHANLY, CHARLES DAWSON 464
SHERIDAN, NIALL 754
SHERIDAN, RICHARD B. 352
SHORTER, DORA SIGERSON 608
SIGERSON, GEORGE 531
SPERANZA, see WILDE, LADY
STANFORD, W. B. 749
STARKEY, JAMES, see O'SULLIVAN,
    SEUMAS
STEPHENS, JAMES 676
STOKES, WHITLEY 528
SULLIVAN, T. D. 522
SWIFT, JONATHAN 323
SYNGE, JOHN M. 627

TATE, NAHUM 322
TODHUNTER, JOHN 535
TORNA 6
TYNAN, KATHERINE, see HINKSON,
    KATHERINE T.
TYRRELL, ROBERT Y. 274

WALSH, EDWARD 439
WARD, TERENCE 751
WEEKES, CHARLES 619
WILDE, LADY 494
WILDE, OSCAR 564
WILLIAMS, RICHARD D'ALTON 499
WOLFE, CHARLES 388
WRAFTER, DENIS 752

YEATS, WILLIAM BUTLER 594

INDEX OF TRANSLATORS

ALSPACH, R. K. 307
AN CRAOBHIN, *see* HYDE, DOUGLAS

BROOKE, CHARLOTTE 171

CALLANAN, J. J. 181, 183, 193, 196
COSTELLO, MRS. 228
CROKER, THOMAS CROFTON 158

D'ALTON, JOHN 177, 199
DINNEEN, P. S. 172-174
DUNN, JOSEPH 82

FERGUSON, SAMUEL 6, 61, 76, 78, 140, 151, 177, 182, 189, 197, 202
FLOWER, ROBIN 20, 27
FOX, GEORGE 180

GREGORY, LADY 238
GWYNN, EDWARD 63-67

HULL, ELEANOR 18, 145, 229
HYDE, DOUGLAS 3, 231-234, 237

JONES, HOWARD MUMFORD 104, 105

LEAHY, A. H. 74
LONGFORD, EARL OF 149, 150, 152

MACALISTER, R. A. S. 4
MACDONAGH, THOMAS 235, 240
MACNEILL, EOIN 4, 133-137

MANGAN, JAMES CLARENCE 55-57, 87, 142, 161-163, 168, 175, 186, 187
MEYER, KUNO 12, 22, 24-26, 30-46, 49-54, 71-73, 93-95, 104, 122, 127-131

O'CURRY, EUGENE 47, 111-114, 179
O'DONOGHUE, T. 172-174
O'DONOVAN, JOHN 121
O'FAOLAIN, SEAN 48, 116
O'GRADY, STANDISH HAYES 108-111, 114, 126-131
O'KEEFE, J. G. 96

PEARSE, PADRAIC 146-148, 154-156, 237
PETRIE, GEORGE 195

REEVES, WILLIAM 101
ROBINSON, F. N. 18, 30
ROLLESTON, T. W. H. 105, 115

SEYMOUR, ST. JOHN 317
SIGERSON, GEORGE 5, 8, 19, 21, 117-119, 184, 200
STEPHENS, JAMES 230
STOKES, WHITLEY 12, 15, 17, 24-26, 77, 81
STRACHAN, JOHN 12, 15, 17, 43
SWIFT, JONATHAN 165

USSHER, ARLAND 204

WALSH, EDWARD 191, 194

INDEX OF POEMS

Abbey Asaroe 510
Aeolian Harp 512
After Aughrim 464
After Death 563
Agricultural Irish Girl 244
Ah, What Woes Are Mine 171
Aileen Aroon 415
Aldfrid's Itinerary 57
All Day I Hear the Noise of Waters 675
An Evil World 114
Angel's Whisper 408
Apples 323
Arran of the Many Stags 128
As Rock to Sun or Storm 754
Autumn House, The 761
Autumn Song 537
Aux Carmélites 592

Bad Luck to This Marching 440
Bagpipe Music 739
Ballad of Father Gilligan 599
Ballad of Reading Gaol 565-585
Ballad of the Little Black Hound 611-615
Banshee, The 535
Bantry Bay 533
Barney O'Hea 413
Battle Eve of the Brigade 478
Beagles 747
Beagle's Cry 136
Bees, The 713
Beg-Innish 627
Believe Me If All Those Endearing Young Charms 378
Beloved, It Is Morn 549
Besom Man, The 653
Between Brielle and Manasquan 642
Bid Adieu, Adieu, Adieu 674
Bishop Butler of Kilcash 244
Blackbird, The 104
Blackbird, The 246
Blessed Be the Holy Will of God 237
Blessings on Doneraile 357
Blue Peter 738
Boatman's Hymn 189
Bohernabreena 758
Bold Phelim Brady, the Bard of Armagh 248

Bold Robert Emmet 626
Boyne Water 249
Braggart 752
Brennan on the Moor 250
Brian O'Linn 252
Bring Home the Poet 629
Bubble, The 515
Burial of King Cormac 459
Burial of Sir John Moore 388
By Coelia's Arbor 352
Byzantium 604

Call, The 666
Call of the Morning 399
Call to the Wild 636
Canoe, The 556
Careful Husband, The 150
Carrickfergus 742
Cashel of Munster 197
Castlehyde 254
Cean-Salla 426
Celtic Cross 520
Celts, The 518
Chill of the Eve 676
Chorus of Spirits 400
Church Bell at Night 105
Clare's Dragoons 479
Cockles and Mussels 256
Colleen Oge Asthore 257
Colleen Rue 258
Colloquy of the Ancients, four poems 125
Columcille's Greeting to Ireland 101
Columcille the Scribe 52
Combat of Ferdiad and Cuchulain 82
Conger Eel, The 694
Connolly 734
Constancy 544
Convict of Clonmel 193
Coolun, The 151
Corn Crake, The 632
Corner Boys 737
County of Mayo, The 180
County Sligo 743
Cradle Song 669
Credhe's Lament 129
Credo 659
Cromwell, More Power to 173
Croppy Boy, The 540

Crucifixion, The 104
Cruiskeen Lawn 259
Cry of the Dreamer 542
Cuchulain (see Red Branch Cycle)
Cuckoo Song 588
Cup of O'Hara 177
Curse of Doneraile 355
Cycling to Dublin 765

Dark Rosaleen 142
Dawning of the Day 194
Dawn in Inishtrahull 733
Dead 727
Dead at Clonmacnois, The 115
Dear, Dark Head 203
Dear Was He 111
Death Deposed 515
Death of Ailill 701
Decayed Monastery, A 367
Dedication 695
Deer's Cry (or Patrick's Breast-
    plate) 12
Deirdre's Farewell to Alba 76
Deirdre's Farewell to Scotland 77
Deirdre's Lament 81
Deirdre's Lament for the Sons of
    Usnagh 78
Dermot, Death of King (see An Evil
    World)
Description of a City Shower, 329
Description of an Irish Feast 164
Deserted Village, The 334-346
Dinnshenchas, three poems 61-70
Dirge of the Munster Forest 547
Disappointment 544
Discovery, The 715
Dispossessed Poet 715
Donall Oge: Grief of a Girl's Heart
    238
Doran's Ass 260
Down by the Salley Gardens 598
Downfall of the Gael 140
Do You Remember That Night 179
Dreams 494
Dream-Teller, The 690
Drinking Time 734
Drunkard to His Bottle 484
Dry Be That Tear 354
Duanaire Finn, three poems 133
Duke Is the Lad, The 384
Dumb, Dumb, Dumb 262
Dying Girl 497

Early Thoughts 534

Earth and Man 530
Easter Song, four passages 8-12
Easter Week 263
Edge, The 683
Eileen Aroon 117
Eire 361
Elegy on the Glory of Her Sex 346
Emma 346
Enchanted Fawn 63
Encounter 755
Epistle of Condolence 381
Errors of Ecstasie 396
Eve's Lament 42
Extermination 499

Faerie's Child 502
Fair at Windgap, The 711
Fair-Haired Girl, The 202
Fair Hills of Ireland 182
Fairies In New Ross 407
Fairies, The 509
Fairy Nurse 439
Fairy Song 597
Fairy Thorn 457
Famine Year, The 494
Farewell, O Patrick Sarsfield 168
Farewell to Fál 148
Fate of King Dathi 467
Father O'Flynn 555
Feast of Saint Brigid of Kildare 47
Fenian Cycle (see Ossianic)
Fighting Man, A 652
Fighting Race, The 552
Finn's Advice to MacLugach 126
Finn's Great Wolfdog Bran 132
Fleet Street 689
Fontenoy 476
Fool, The 647
Foray of Con O'Donnell 489
Forever 541
Fossils 677
Four Winds, The 688
Friar of Orders Gray 348

Gallows Tree, The 707
Garadh 668
Garryowen 264
Generations, The 762
Gentle Echo on Woman 324
Geraldine's Daughter, The 175
Gioconda 706
Girl I Left Behind Me, The 471
Girl I Love, The 196
Girl of the Red Mouth 503

Girl's Song, A 593
Glut on the Market, A 728
God Save Ireland 522
God's Blessing on Munster 24
Gone! Gone! Forever Gone 420
Gone in the Wind 425
Grave of Rury, The 586
Groves of Blarney 362

Hail, Fair Morning 109
Happy Beggarman 265
Harp That Once Through Tara's
  Halls 381
Heath, The 622
Heavenly Banquet 48
Heavenly Pilot 22
He Charges Her to Lay Aside Her
  Weapons 152
Herb-Leech, The 650
Hermit's Song 28
Herons, The 698
Herrings 324
He Said That He Was Not Our
  Brother 414
Heterodoxy, A 636
He Who Forsakes the Clerkly Life
  108
High and Low 631
Holy Man, The 17
Homage to Hieronymus Bosch 704
Hospitality in Ancient Ireland 49
Host of the Air, The 601
Hosts of Faery 73
How Happy the Little Birds 237
Human Life 486
Humours of Donnybrook Fair 265
Humours of Donnybrook Fair 390
Hunt of Sliabh Truim, The, two
  poems 131
Hymn Against Pestilence 15
Hymn from Beatrice 483

I Am of Ireland 605
I Am Raftery 231
I Am the Gilly of Christ 658
I Hear the Wave 114
I Know Where I'm Going 267
I Love My Love in the Morning
  417
I See His Blood Upon the Rose 693
I Want to Be Married and Cannot
  Tell How 268
I Was a Labourer 749
I Will Go with My Father 657

I'll Never Get Drunk Any More 268
Icarus 769
Icham of Irlaunde 306
Ideal 240
If I might Choose 386
Irish Hurrah, The 475
Immolation 746
Immortality 711
In Brittany 620
In Paris 635
Incantation 5
Infinite, The 546
Inisgallun 673
Invitation, The 753
Invocation to Ireland 4
Irish Council Bill 299
Irishman's Christening, An 270
It's Little for Glory I Care 442

Jesukin 19
John Baynham's Epitaph 369
John-John 633
Johnny, I Hardly Knew Ye 271
June 700

Keen Thyself, Poor Wight 155
Kerry Dance 532
Kevin Barry 751
Killyburn Brae 274
Kincora 55
Kine of My Father, The 610
Kiss, The 149
Kitty of Coleraine 467
Know Ye Not That Lovely River
  422

Lake Isle of Innisfree 598
Lament for Corc and Niall 6
Lament for the Death of Owen Roe
  O'Neill 474
Lament for the Death of Thomas
  Davis 444
Lament for the Poets: 1916 702
Lament of Maev Leith Dherg 105
Lament of the Mangaire Sugach 191
Land of Cokaygne 311-317
Larch Hill 760
Larks 593
Larry M'Hale 443
Last Night 404
Last Rose of Summer 378
Lay of the Famine 275
Lay of the Forlorn 399
Leda and the Swan 638-642

Leitrim Woman, A 721
Leprehaun, The 527
Let the Toast Pass 353
Liadin and Curither 31
Life of St. Cellach of Killala, three
   poems 108-111
Line of Beauty 539
Lines to The Blessed Sacrament
   393
Lines Written in a Country Par-
   son's Orchard 759
Linota Rufescens 723
Little Black Rose 488
Little Boy in the Morning, A 698
Little Dark Rose, The 146
Little Waves of Breffny, The 624
Little White Cat 228
Load 738
Lonely, The 616
Longford Legend 277
Love Is a Hunter Boy 380
Lover and Echo 119
Love's Despair 200
Love-Talker, The 607
Lullaby 661
Lullaby of the Woman of the
   Mountain 241
Lupracaun, The 513

Macha, Story of 61
Mackenna's Dream 279
Magh Lena, Battle of (see I Hear
   the Wave)
Magrath's Reply to O'Tuomy 187
Maid of the Sweet Brown Knowe
   282
Maid That Sold Her Barley 281
Maids of Elfin-Mere 517
Maire, My Girl 551
Man for Galway 441
Man of the North Countrie 520
Mary le More 366
Mary the Cook Maid's Letter 325
Mason, The 744
Meditation 672
Memory of Brother Michael 729
Memory of the Dead 505
Message of Peace 544
Midnight Court, The 204-227
Miller of the Dee 347
Minot's Ledge 523
Minstrel Boy, The 375
Molly Bawn and Brian Oge 284
Monaghan 689

Mona Lisa 538
Monk and His Pet Cat, The 26
Mother, The 647
Mothers' Lament, The 50
Mrs. McGrath 285
My Grave 470
My Grief on Fal's Proud Plain 156
My Grief on the Sea 233
My Little Lodge 18
Mystery of Amergin 3
Mythological Cycle, three poems 71-
   75

Nameless One, The 423
Nameless Ruin, The 559
National Presage 507
Native Irishman, The 287
Nell Flaherty's Drake 289
Nepenthe 404
New Words to O'Donnell Abu 717
Night Before Larry Was Stretched,
   The 289
Night Piece on Death 332
Non Dolet 637
Nostalgia 741

Ode 538
Ode to Myself 372
O'Donnell Aboo 507
O'Duffy's Ironsides 292
Of a Poet Patriot 634
Oh Blame Not the Bard 375
O'Hussey's Ode to the Maguire 160
Oh Yield, Fair Lids 352
Old Story Over Again, The 384
Old Woman, The 651
Old Woman of Beare, The 39
Old Woman Remembers, The 560
Omens 632
O, Glorious Childbearer 656
O Mighty Melancholy Wind 537
On a Cock Which Was Stolen from
   a Good Priest 174
On a Lonely Spray 679
On a Pair of Shoes Presented to
   Him 172
On the Death of Dr. Swift 327
On the Defeat of Ragnall 93
On the Flightiness of Thought 44
On the Prospect of Planting Arts in
   America 333
O'Neill's War Song 529
Onions 323
Orator, The 766

O Say, My Brown Drimin 183
Ossianic (or Fenian) Cycle, eleven poems 121-133
O'Tuomy's Drinking Song 186
Our Heritage 691
Outlaw of Loch Lene 196
O Woman Full of Wile 154

Paddy's Metamorphosis 382
Padraic O'Conaire, Gaelic Story-teller 709
Panegyric on Geese 431
Pangur Ban 27
Passing of the Shee, The 627
Patrick Healy's Wishes 199
Patrick's Breastplate (*see* Deer's Cry)
Peace to the Slumberers 380
Pearl of the White Breast 195
Peggy 670
Piper on the Hill, The 608
Plougher, The 668
Plough Horse, The 726
Poet Loosed a Wingéd Song, The 649
Poppies 619
Prayer 18
Prayers, Four 229
Prayer to St. Patrick 17
Prayer to the Virgin 43
Priest of Colooney 596
Progress of Poetry 328

Quaker's Meeting 411
Queens 628

Rain 660
Rain on a Cottage Roof 763
Rakes of Mallow 294
Rebel, The 645
Recollection in Autumn 768
Red Branch (or Cuchulain) Cycle, three poems 75-86
Red Breast of Aquitania 432
Red Hanrahan's Song About Ireland 602
Red Hugh 703
Red Man's Wife, The 232
Refuge 618
Renascence 763
Requiescat 564
Retrospect 693
Revel, The 500
Reynard the Fox 295

Riddle 324
Ringleted Youth of My Love 234
Rising of the Moon, The 550
Robin's Cross 403
Rodney's Glory 349
Roisin Dubh 145
Rory of the Hill 525
Rose of Tralee 493
Ruined Nest 54
Runilda's Chant 401

Saint Brendan's Prophecy 158
Saint Ita's Fosterling 20
Saint Kevin 409
Saint Patrick's Purgatory 116
Salutation 616
Satire on the People of Kildare 317-321
Satyr, The 678
Scarecrow, The 697
Scene in a Madhouse 487
Scribe, The 25
Sea God's Address to Bran 71
Seagull, To a 419
Sea-Ritual 402
Sea Wrack 662
See the Crocus' Golden Cup 692
Serenade 394
Serenade of a Loyal Martyr 401
Shandon Bells 437
Shane O'Neill 624
Shan Van Vocht, The 297
Shapes and Signs 427
Sheep and Lambs 591
Shepherd's Despair 373
She Walked Unaware 719
Sixteen Dead Men 609
Sleep Song of Diarmaid and Grainne 133
Sleep That Like the Couchéd Dove 418
Small Silver-Coloured Bookworm 331
Smith's Song 531
Social Future 506
Soft Day, A 681
Soldier's Song, The 685
Solstice 619
Song of Carroll's Sword 32
Song of Crede 35
Song of Finn 121
Song of Fionnuala 379
Song of Freedom 665
Song of the Fairies 74

Song of the Forest Trees 111
Song of O'Ruark 376
Song of the Sea 52
Song of the Spirits 486
Song of Winter 37
Song for a Proud Relation 720
Song for the Clatter-Bones 710
Spires of Oxford, The 680
Spring 748
Spring, St. Stephen's Green 757
Spring Stops Me Suddenly 767
Stanzas on Woman 346
Statue and Perturbed Burghers 756
Stolen Child, The 594
Storm, The 173
Stranger's Grave, The 547
Strings in the Earth and Air 675
Summer Has Come 36
Summer Is Gone 24
Sweeney the Mad 96
Sweet Jesus 307-311
Sword of Tethra, The 559

Tailor That Came from Mayo 587
Tanist 679
Tara 67
Testament of Cathaeir Mor 87
That Corner 671
Think 619
Thomas MacDonagh 701
Thoughts at the Museum 736
Three Children Near Clonmel 716
Three Colts Exercising 654
Three Old Brothers 724
Time I've Lost in Wooing, The 374
Tinkers, The 651
Tinker's Moon 725
Tipperary Recruiting Song 299
To a Faithless Lover 766
To a Friend in the Country 642
To a Linnet in a Cage 699
To Crinog 46
To G. K. Chesterton 692
To My Daughter, Betty 663
To the Bellringer 745
To the Blessed Virgin Mary 421
To the Ingleezee Khafir 428
To the Leanán Shee 621
To-day 545
Tom the Lunatic 606
Tone's Grave 481
Triads of Ireland 22
Tri-Colored Ribbon, The 686
Tryst After Death 122

Twenty Golden Years Ago 429
Twilight in Middle March 699
Twilight People, The 659

Ulsterman, An 630
Undertone 749
Unfrocked Priest, The 655

Veterans, The 753
Viking, The 528
Viking Terror 30
Virgin 731
Vision That Appeared to Me 93

Wake of William Orr 359
Walker of the Snow 464
War Song of O'Driscol 420
Water-Front 750
Wearin' of the Green, The 300
Welshmen of Tirawley, The 446-457
West's Asleep, The 472
Whack Fol the Diddle 686
What Are Outward Forms 348
What Counsel Has the Hooded Moon 674
What Will You Do, Love 407
Wheatlet Son of Milklet 95
When 618
When I Was a Little Girl 663
While Shepherds Watched 322
Whisky, Drink Divine 386
White Cockade 181
White Rose, A 543
Why, Liquor of Life 177
Widow of Drynam 720
Wild Swans at Coole 603
Willy Reilly 302
Wind in the Alleys 684
Winds, The 623
Winter 765
Winter Is Cold 127
Wisdom 730
Wishes for William 682
Witch, The 590
Woman 385
Woman of Three Cows 163
Woman with Child 764
Wry Rowan 137

Yellow Bittern, The 235
Youghall Harbor 198
Young Molly Bawn 304